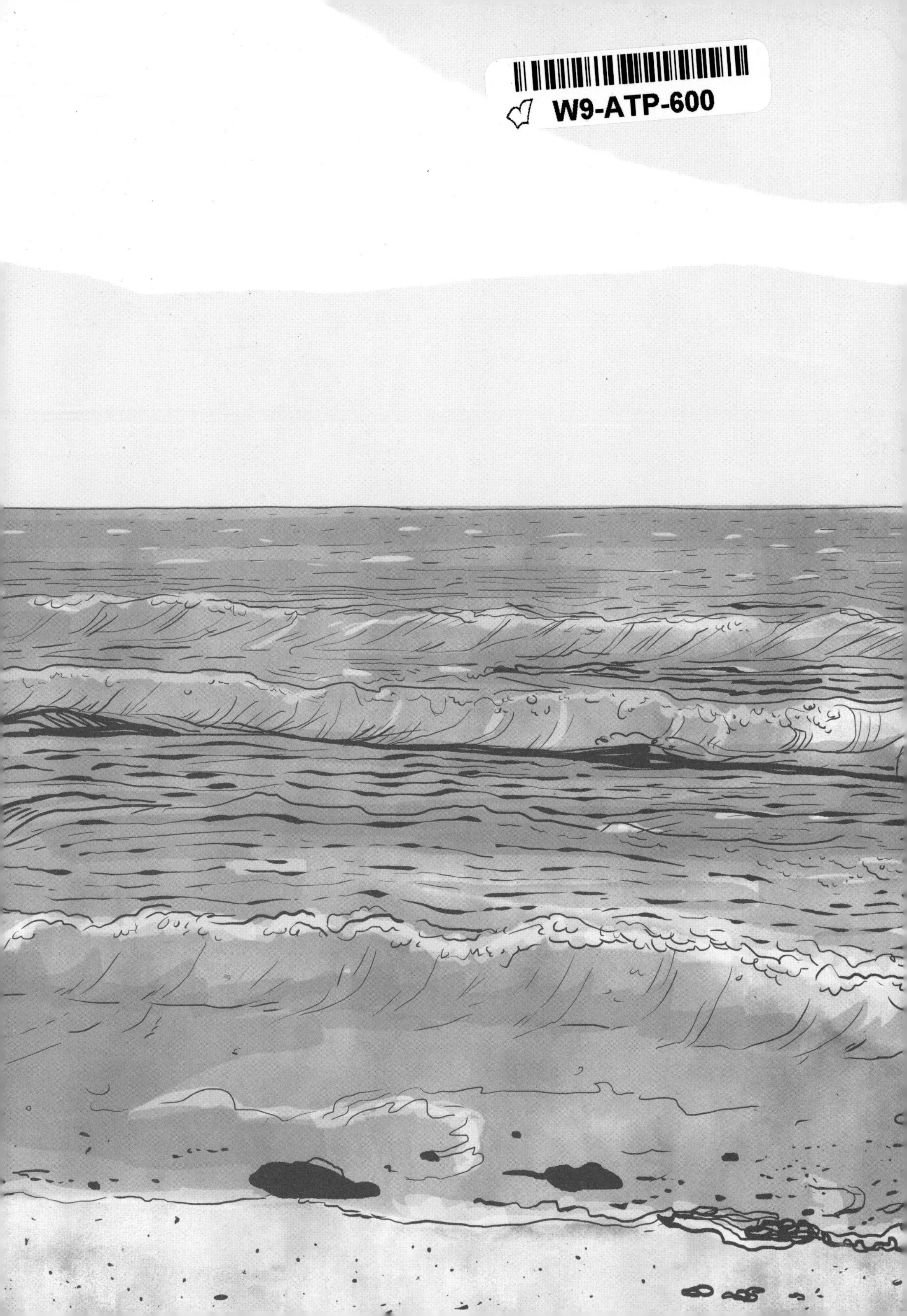

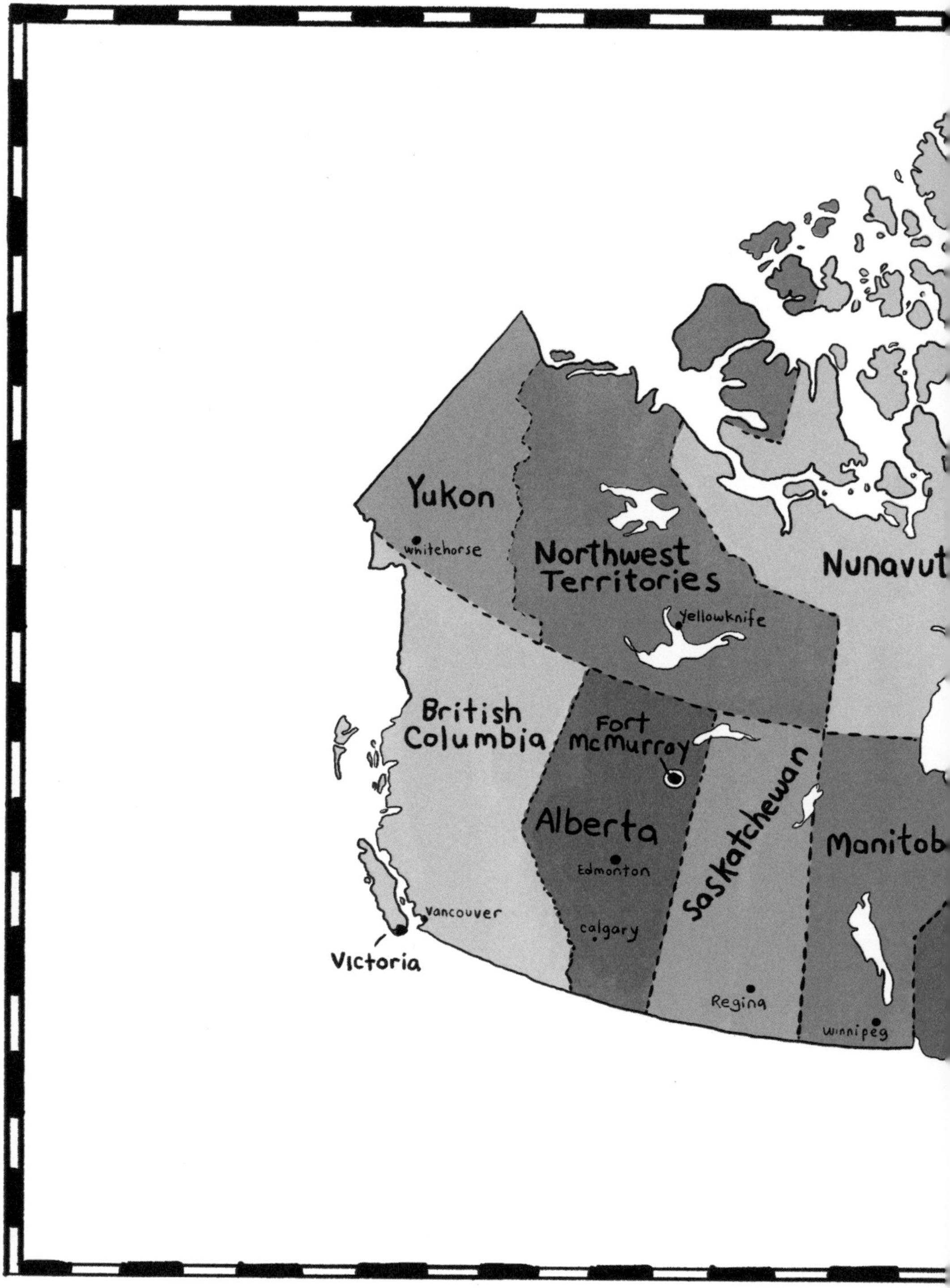
Yukon
Whitehorse
Northwest Territories
Yellowknife
Nunavut
British Columbia
Fort McMurray
Alberta
Edmonton
Calgary
Saskatchewan
Regina
Manitob
Winnipeg
Vancouver
Victoria

CANADA

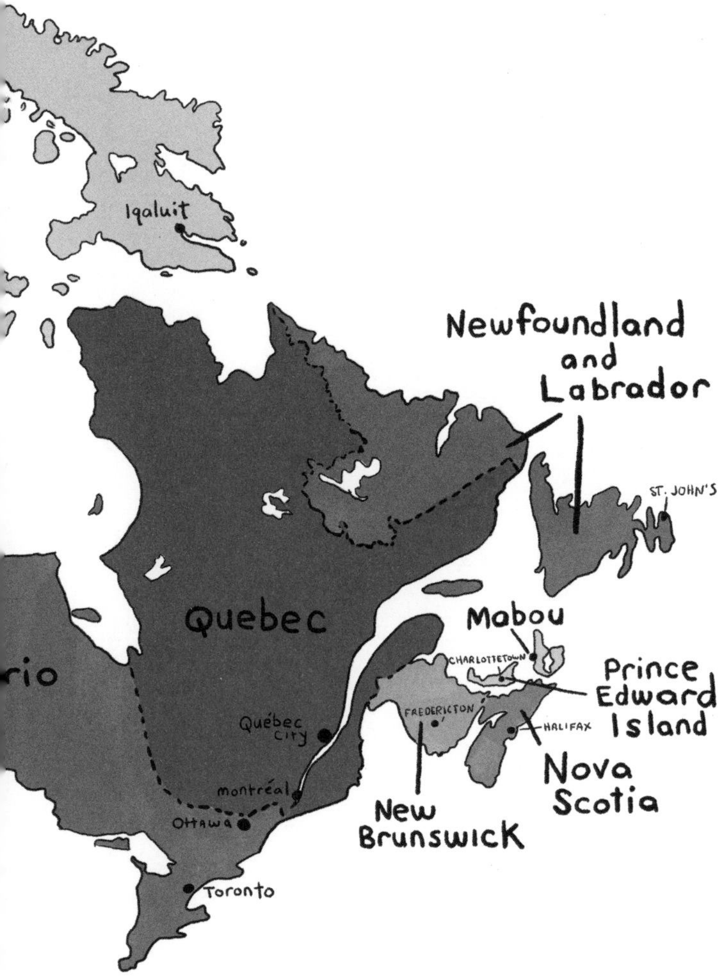
Iqaluit
Newfoundland and Labrador
ST. JOHN'S
Quebec
rio
Mabou
CHARLOTTETOWN
Prince Edward Island
FREDERICTON
HALIFAX
Québec City
Nova Scotia
montréal
OTTAWA
New Brunswick
Toronto

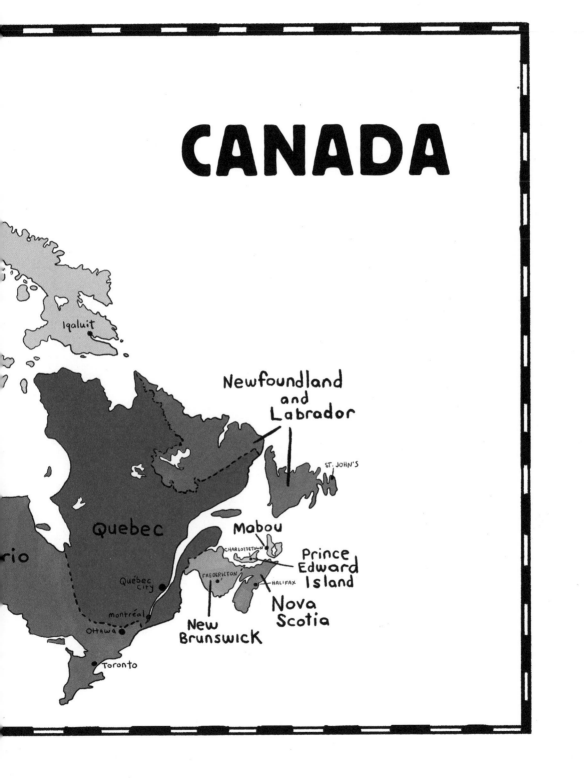

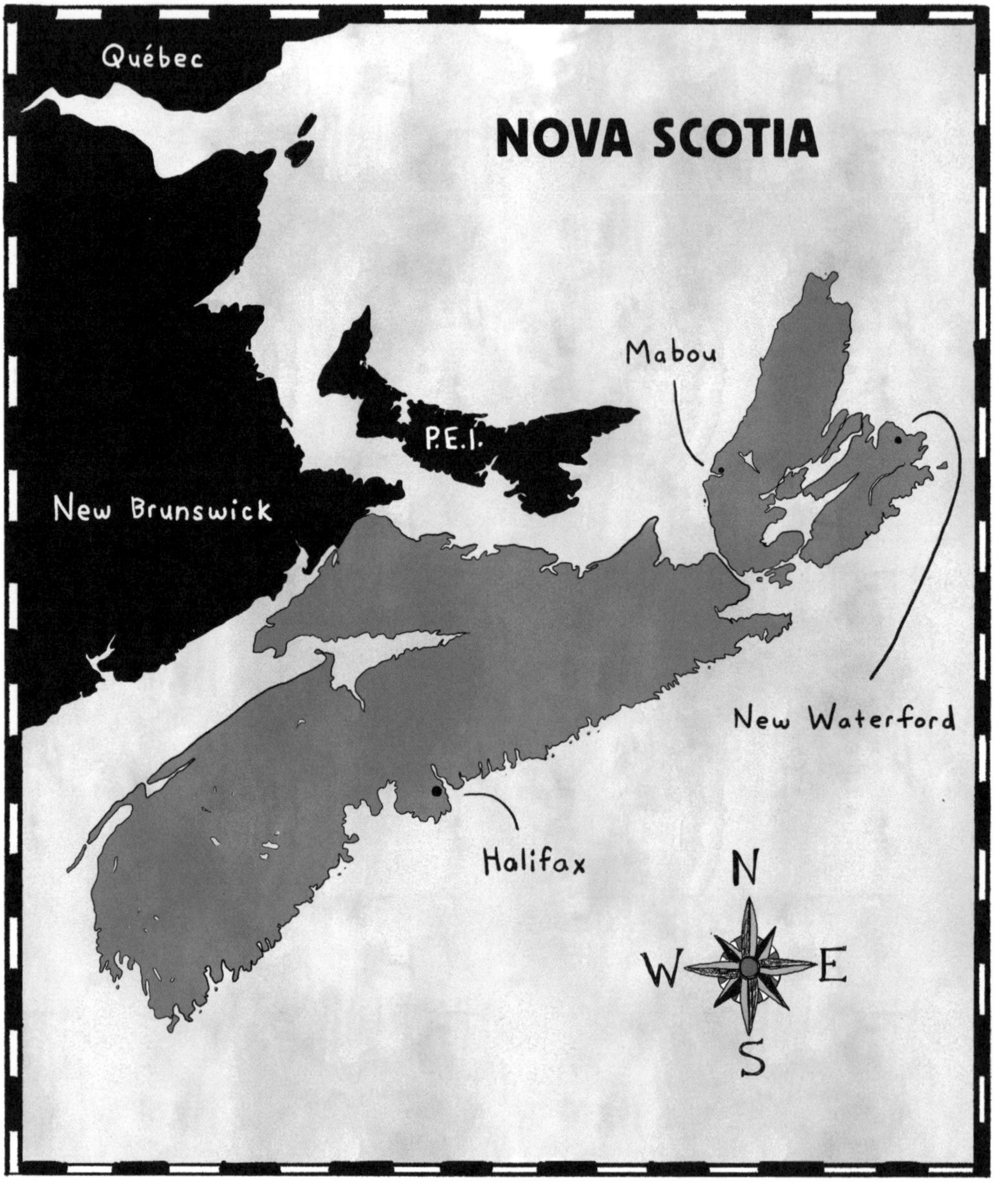
Québec
NOVA SCOTIA
Mabou
P.E.I.
New Brunswick
New Waterford
Halifax
N
W
E
S

ALBERTA'S OIL SANDS
LAKE ATHABASCA
FORT CHIPEWYAN
WOOD BUFFALO NATIONAL PARK
FORT CHIPEWYAN WINTER RD
ALBERTA
SASKATCHEWAN
ATHABASCA RIVER
TRUE NORTH RD
SYNCRUDE AURORA
ALBIAN SANDS
SHELL
END OF HIGHWAY 63
FORT MCKAY
SYNCRUDE
MILDRED LAKE
(BASE MINE)
SUNCOR
HIGHWAY 63
FORT MC MURRAY
CLEARWATER RIVER
ATHABASCA RIVER
GREGOIRE LAKE
ANZAC
LONG LAKE
OPTI - NEXEN
HIGHWAY 881
TO EDMONTON
HIGHWAY 63

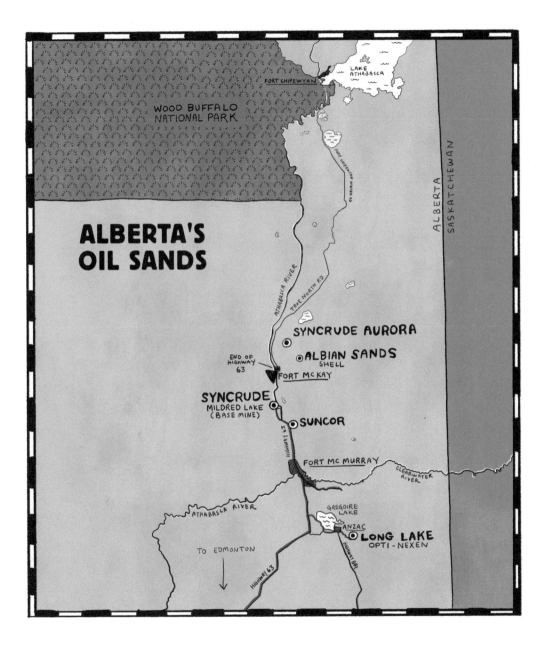

"The Island" lyrics on page 11 by Kenzie MacNeil. "I'll Be There Christmas Eve" lyrics on page 94 by Ron Hynes. "Crazy Bitch" lyrics on page 166 by Keith Nelson, Josh Todd & Buckcherry. "Ridin'" lyrics on page 236 by Oscar Salinas, Juan Salinas, Krayzie Bone & Chamillionaire. "Peter's Dream" lyrics on pages 244–255 by Lennie Gallant. "An Innis Aigh" lyrics on page 254 by Angus Y. MacLellan. "Coal Town Road" lyrics on page 292 by Allister MacGillivray.

"Effects of the Tar Sands: Fort Mackay, Alberta" Interview on pages 358–360 copyright © 2007, 2022 Celina Harpe, used with permission and edited for space.

ISBN 978-1-77046-289-2 | First edition: September 2022 | Second printing: November 2022
Printed in China | 10 9 8 7 6 5 4 3 2
Cataloguing data available from Library and Archives Canada
Published in the USA by Drawn & Quarterly, a client publisher of Farrar, Straus and Giroux
Published in Canada by Drawn & Quarterly, a client publisher of Raincoast Books

Drawn & Quarterly and the author acknowledge the support of the Government of Canada and the Canada Council for the Arts.

The environmental footprint of this edition was neutralized through carbon offsetting programs to support reforestation in Canada.

DUCKS

Two Years in the Oil Sands

KATE BEATON

Drawn & Quarterly

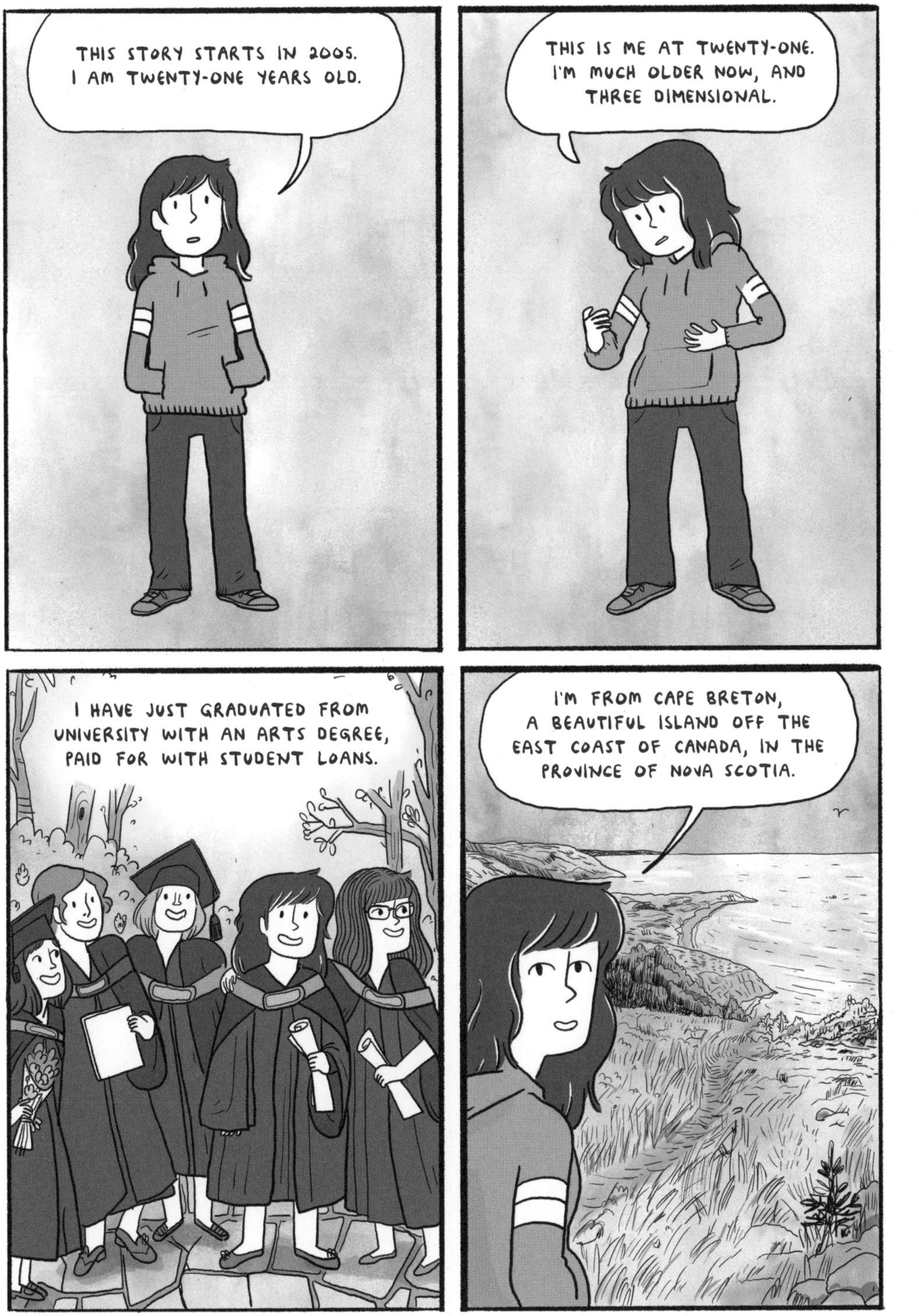
THIS STORY STARTS IN 2005.
I AM TWENTY-ONE YEARS OLD.
THIS IS ME AT TWENTY-ONE.
I'M MUCH OLDER NOW, AND
THREE DIMENSIONAL.
I HAVE JUST GRADUATED FROM
UNIVERSITY WITH AN ARTS DEGREE,
PAID FOR WITH STUDENT LOANS.
I'M FROM CAPE BRETON,
A BEAUTIFUL ISLAND OFF THE
EAST COAST OF CANADA, IN THE
PROVINCE OF NOVA SCOTIA.

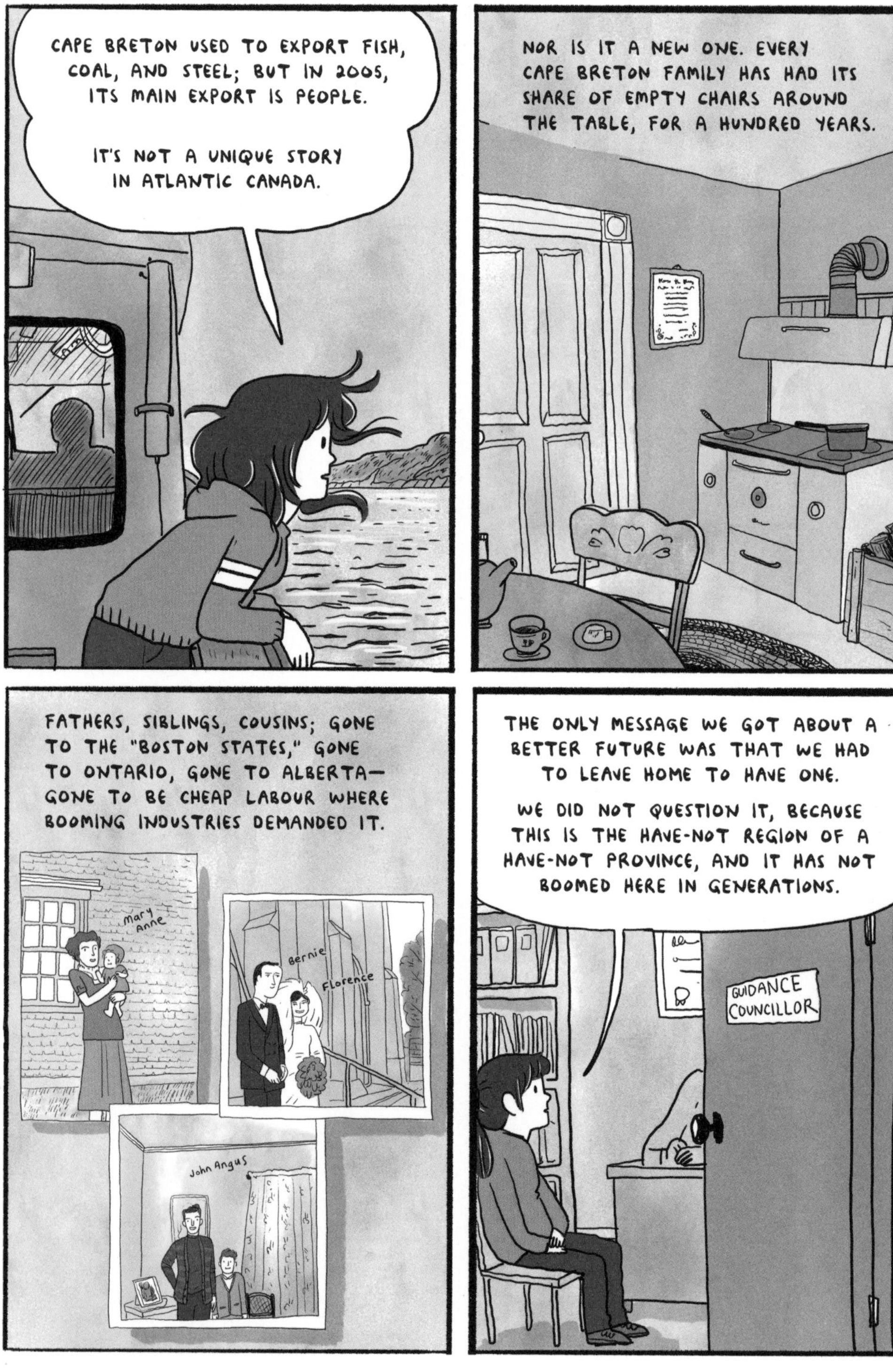
CAPE BRETON USED TO EXPORT FISH, COAL, AND STEEL; BUT IN 2005, ITS MAIN EXPORT IS PEOPLE.
IT'S NOT A UNIQUE STORY IN ATLANTIC CANADA.
NOR IS IT A NEW ONE. EVERY CAPE BRETON FAMILY HAS HAD ITS SHARE OF EMPTY CHAIRS AROUND THE TABLE, FOR A HUNDRED YEARS.
FATHERS, SIBLINGS, COUSINS; GONE TO THE "BOSTON STATES," GONE TO ONTARIO, GONE TO ALBERTA— GONE TO BE CHEAP LABOUR WHERE BOOMING INDUSTRIES DEMANDED IT.
Mary Anne
Bernie
Florence
John Angus
THE ONLY MESSAGE WE GOT ABOUT A BETTER FUTURE WAS THAT WE HAD TO LEAVE HOME TO HAVE ONE.
WE DID NOT QUESTION IT, BECAUSE THIS IS THE HAVE-NOT REGION OF A HAVE-NOT PROVINCE, AND IT HAS NOT BOOMED HERE IN GENERATIONS.
GUIDANCE COUNCILLOR

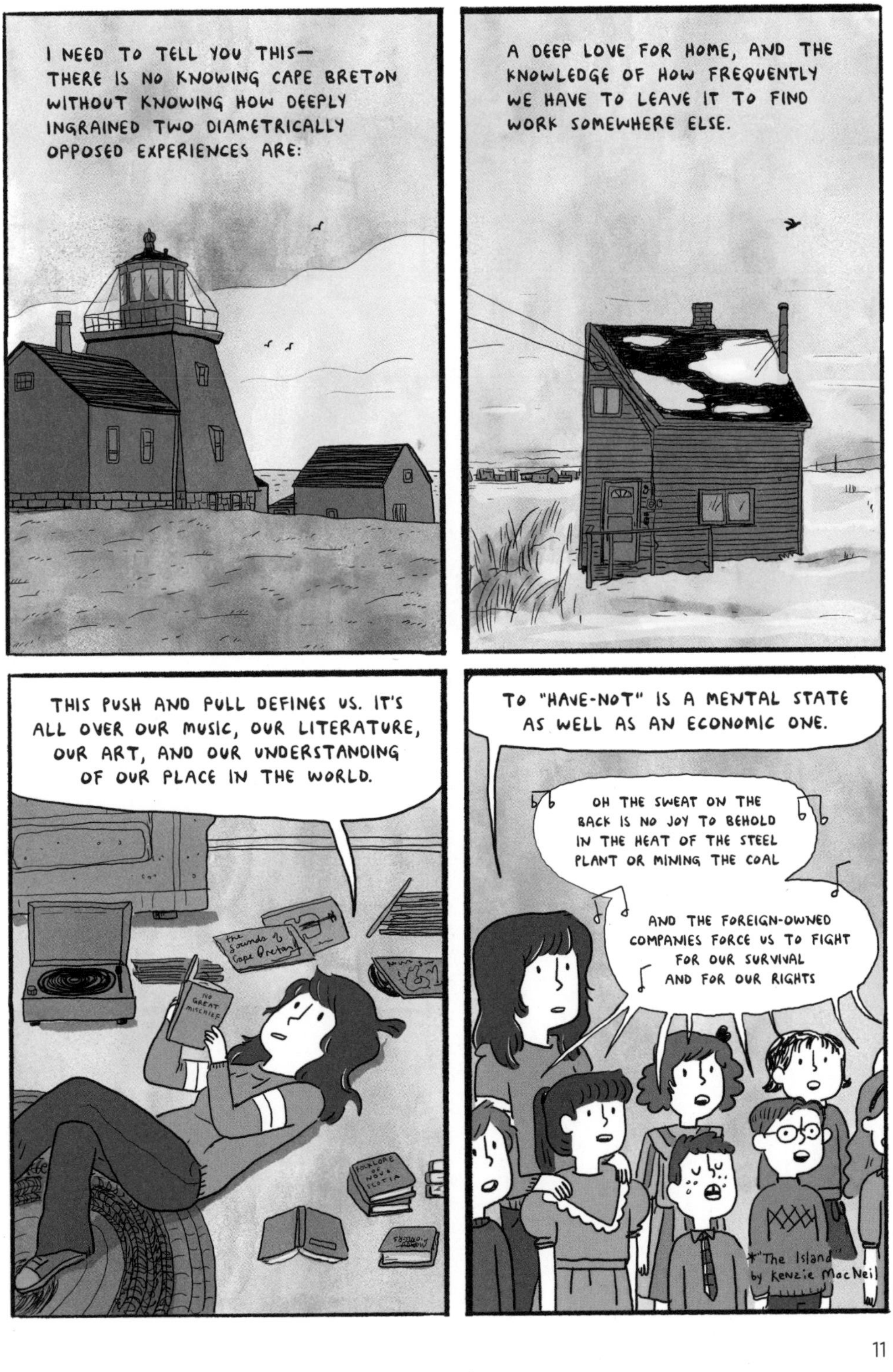
I NEED TO TELL YOU THIS— THERE IS NO KNOWING CAPE BRETON WITHOUT KNOWING HOW DEEPLY INGRAINED TWO DIAMETRICALLY OPPOSED EXPERIENCES ARE:
A DEEP LOVE FOR HOME, AND THE KNOWLEDGE OF HOW FREQUENTLY WE HAVE TO LEAVE IT TO FIND WORK SOMEWHERE ELSE.
THIS PUSH AND PULL DEFINES US. IT'S ALL OVER OUR MUSIC, OUR LITERATURE, OUR ART, AND OUR UNDERSTANDING OF OUR PLACE IN THE WORLD.
the sounds of Cape Breton
NO GREAT MISCHIEF
FOLKLORE OF NOVA SCOTIA
TO "HAVE-NOT" IS A MENTAL STATE AS WELL AS AN ECONOMIC ONE.
OH THE SWEAT ON THE BACK IS NO JOY TO BEHOLD IN THE HEAT OF THE STEEL PLANT OR MINING THE COAL
AND THE FOREIGN-OWNED COMPANIES FORCE US TO FIGHT FOR OUR SURVIVAL AND FOR OUR RIGHTS
*"The Island" by Kenzie MacNeil

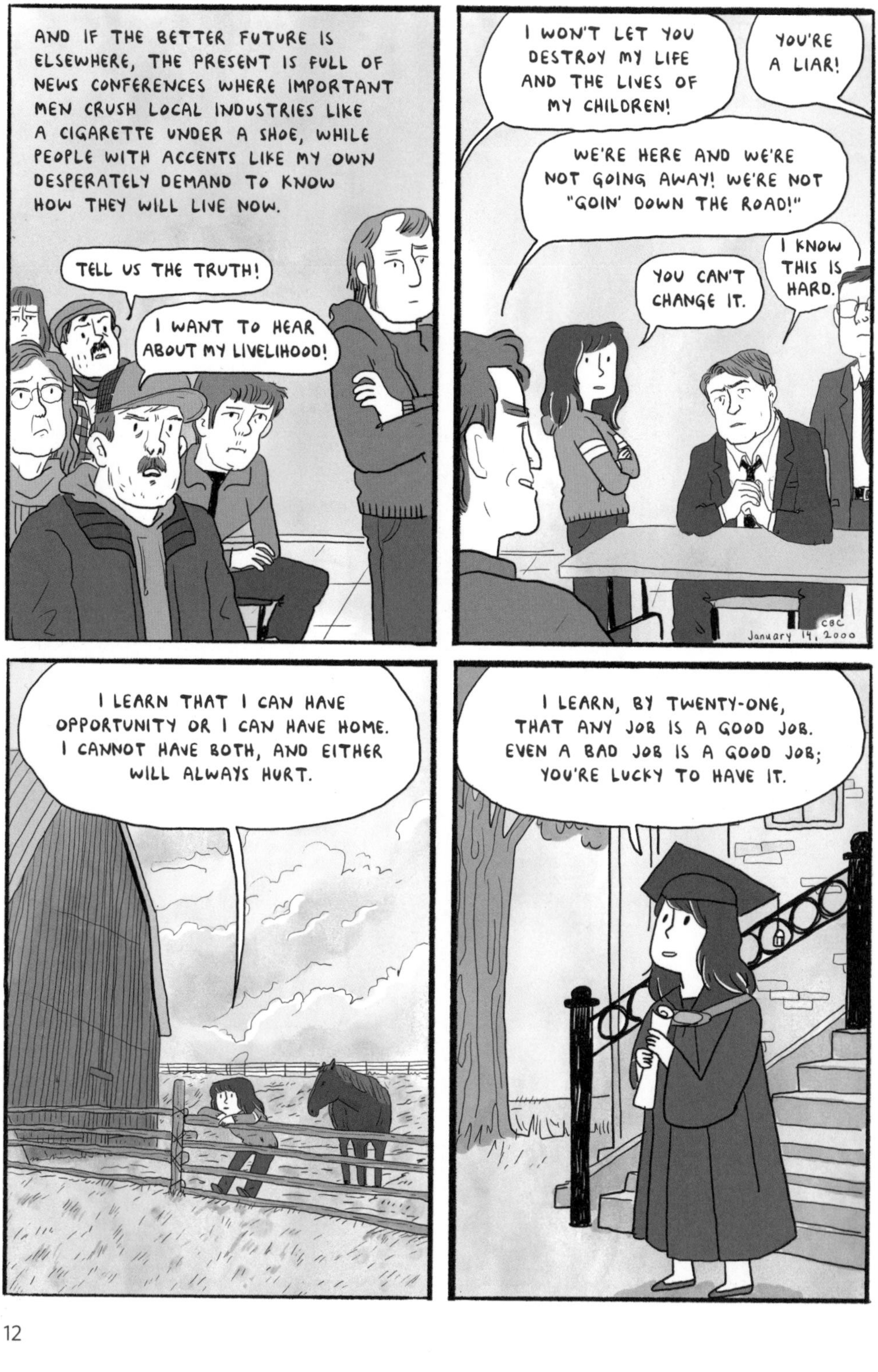
AND IF THE BETTER FUTURE IS ELSEWHERE, THE PRESENT IS FULL OF NEWS CONFERENCES WHERE IMPORTANT MEN CRUSH LOCAL INDUSTRIES LIKE A CIGARETTE UNDER A SHOE, WHILE PEOPLE WITH ACCENTS LIKE MY OWN DESPERATELY DEMAND TO KNOW HOW THEY WILL LIVE NOW.
TELL US THE TRUTH!
I WANT TO HEAR ABOUT MY LIVELIHOOD!
I WON'T LET YOU DESTROY MY LIFE AND THE LIVES OF MY CHILDREN!
YOU'RE A LIAR!
WE'RE HERE AND WE'RE NOT GOING AWAY! WE'RE NOT "GOIN' DOWN THE ROAD!"
YOU CAN'T CHANGE IT.
I KNOW THIS IS HARD.
CBC January 14, 2000
I LEARN THAT I CAN HAVE OPPORTUNITY OR I CAN HAVE HOME. I CANNOT HAVE BOTH, AND EITHER WILL ALWAYS HURT.
I LEARN, BY TWENTY-ONE, THAT ANY JOB IS A GOOD JOB. EVEN A BAD JOB IS A GOOD JOB; YOU'RE LUCKY TO HAVE IT.

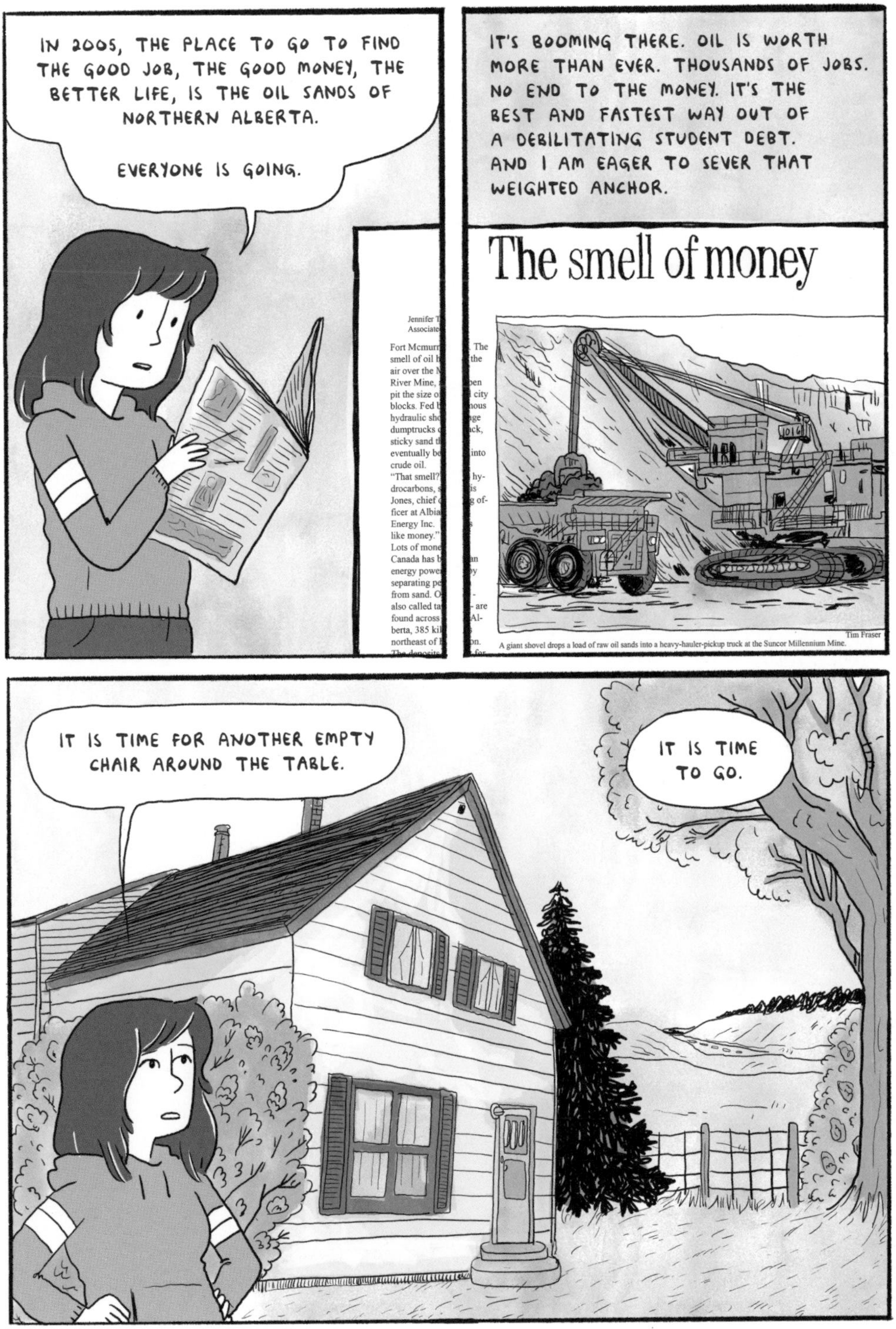
IN 2005, THE PLACE TO GO TO FIND THE GOOD JOB, THE GOOD MONEY, THE BETTER LIFE, IS THE OIL SANDS OF NORTHERN ALBERTA.
EVERYONE IS GOING.
IT'S BOOMING THERE. OIL IS WORTH MORE THAN EVER. THOUSANDS OF JOBS. NO END TO THE MONEY. IT'S THE BEST AND FASTEST WAY OUT OF A DEBILITATING STUDENT DEBT. AND I AM EAGER TO SEVER THAT WEIGHTED ANCHOR.
The smell of money
Tim Fraser
A giant shovel drops a load of raw oil sands into a heavy-hauler-pickup truck at the Suncor Millennium Mine.
IT IS TIME FOR ANOTHER EMPTY CHAIR AROUND THE TABLE.
IT IS TIME TO GO.

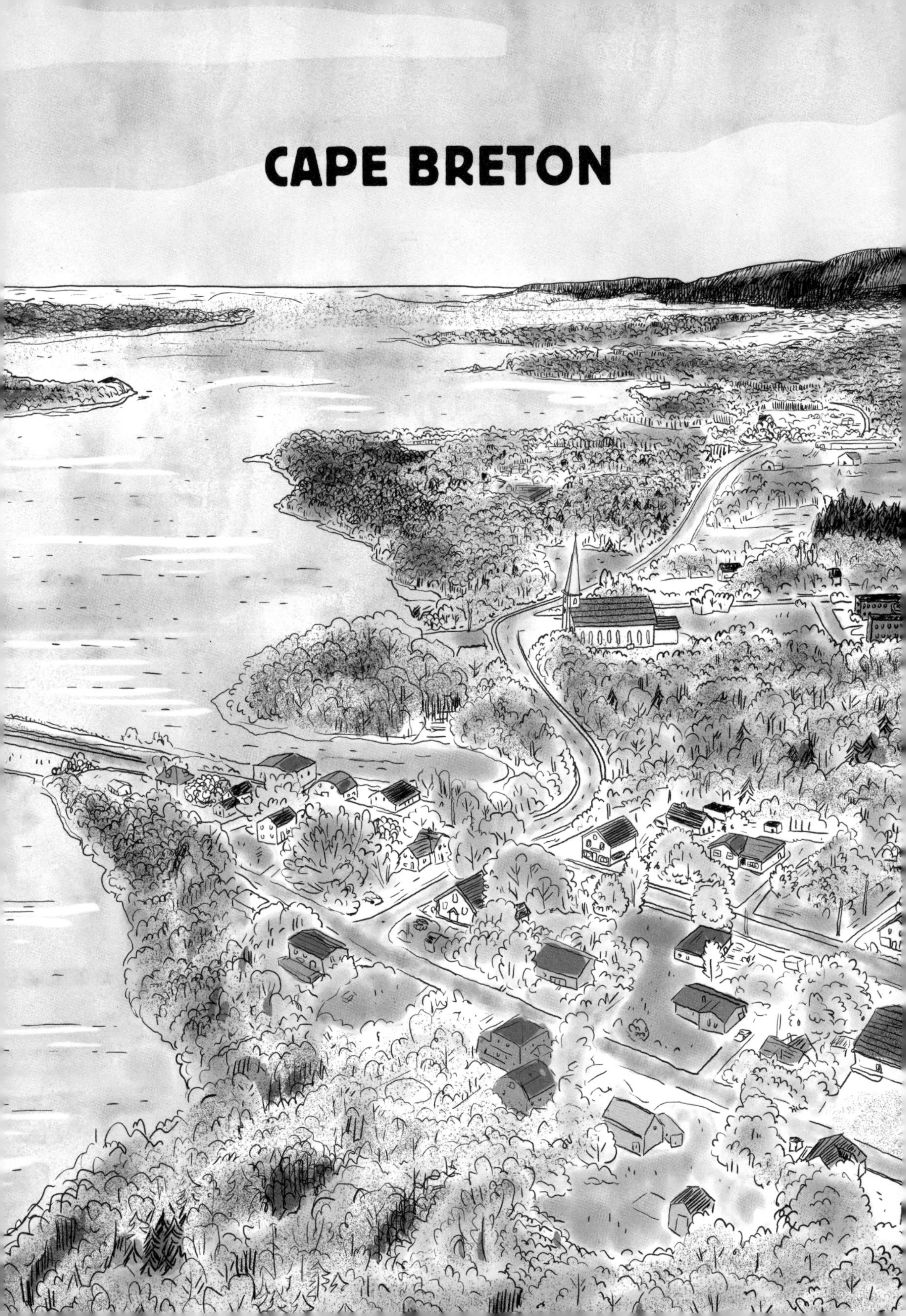
CAPE BRETON

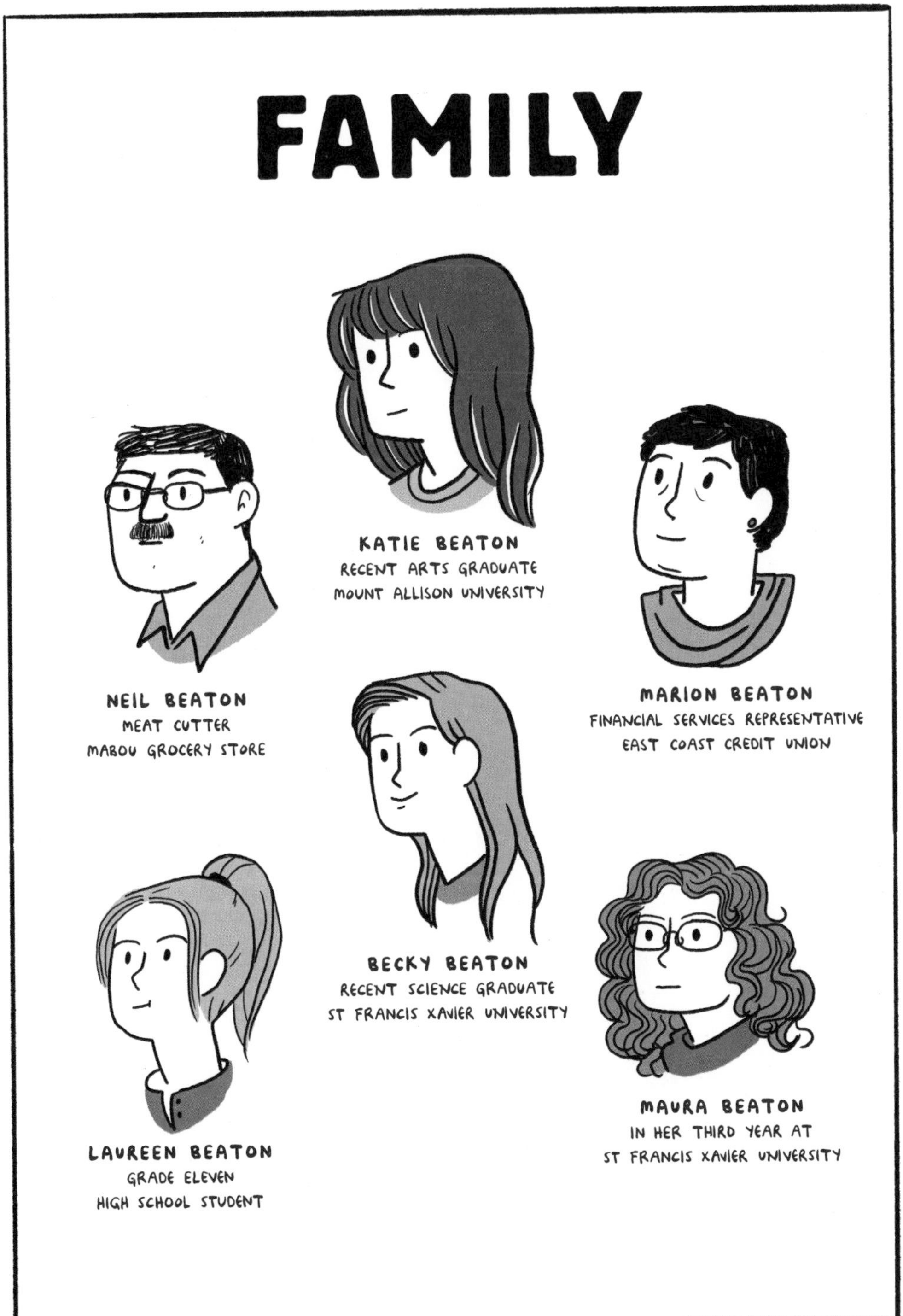
FAMILY
KATIE BEATON
RECENT ARTS GRADUATE
MOUNT ALLISON UNIVERSITY
NEIL BEATON
MEAT CUTTER
MABOU GROCERY STORE
MARION BEATON
FINANCIAL SERVICES REPRESENTATIVE
EAST COAST CREDIT UNION
BECKY BEATON
RECENT SCIENCE GRADUATE
ST FRANCIS XAVIER UNIVERSITY
MAURA BEATON
IN HER THIRD YEAR AT
ST FRANCIS XAVIER UNIVERSITY
LAUREEN BEATON
GRADE ELEVEN
HIGH SCHOOL STUDENT

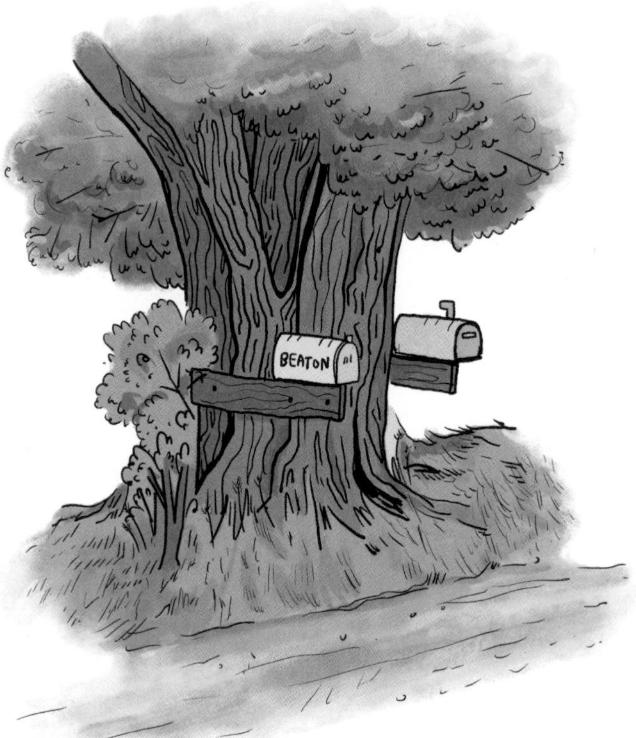
BEATON

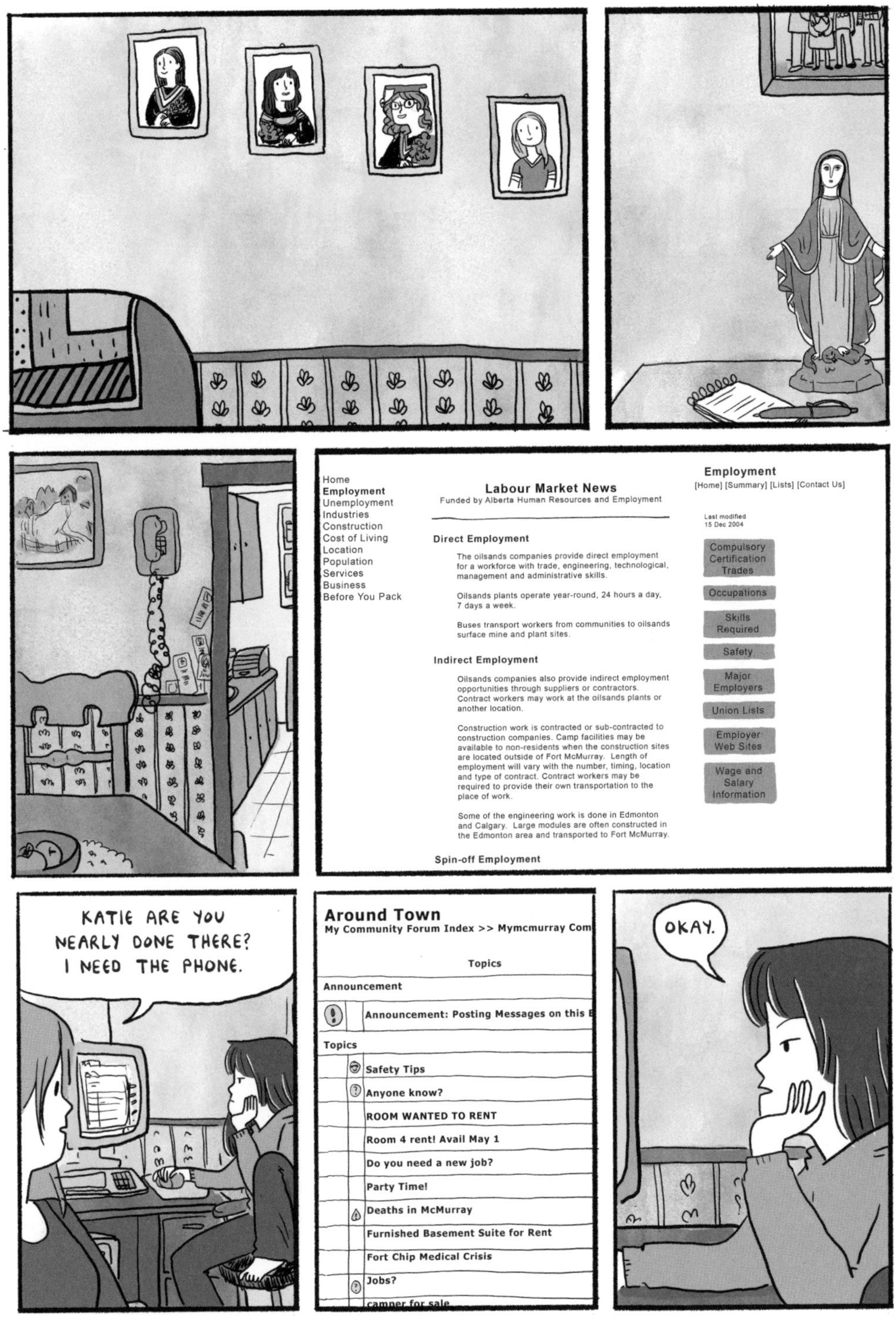
Home
Employment
Unemployment
Industries
Construction
Cost of Living
Location
Population
Services
Business
Before You Pack
Labour Market News
Funded by Alberta Human Resources and Employment
Direct Employment
The oilsands companies provide direct employment for a workforce with trade, engineering, technological, management and administrative skills.
Oilsands plants operate year-round, 24 hours a day, 7 days a week.
Buses transport workers from communities to oilsands surface mine and plant sites.
Indirect Employment
Oilsands companies also provide indirect employment opportunities through suppliers or contractors. Contract workers may work at the oilsands plants or another location.
Construction work is contracted or sub-contracted to construction companies. Camp facilities may be available to non-residents when the construction sites are located outside of Fort McMurray. Length of employment will vary with the number, timing, location and type of contract. Contract workers may be required to provide their own transportation to the place of work.
Some of the engineering work is done in Edmonton and Calgary. Large modules are often constructed in the Edmonton area and transported to Fort McMurray.
Spin-off Employment
Employment
[Home] [Summary] [Lists] [Contact Us]
Last modified
15 Dec 2004
Compulsory Certification Trades
Occupations
Skills Required
Safety
Major Employers
Union Lists
Employer Web Sites
Wage and Salary Information
KATIE ARE YOU NEARLY DONE THERE? I NEED THE PHONE.
Around Town
My Community Forum Index >> Mymcmurray Com
Topics
Announcement
Announcement: Posting Messages on this
Topics
Safety Tips
Anyone know?
ROOM WANTED TO RENT
Room 4 rent! Avail May 1
Do you need a new job?
Party Time!
Deaths in McMurray
Furnished Basement Suite for Rent
Fort Chip Medical Crisis
Jobs?
OKAY.

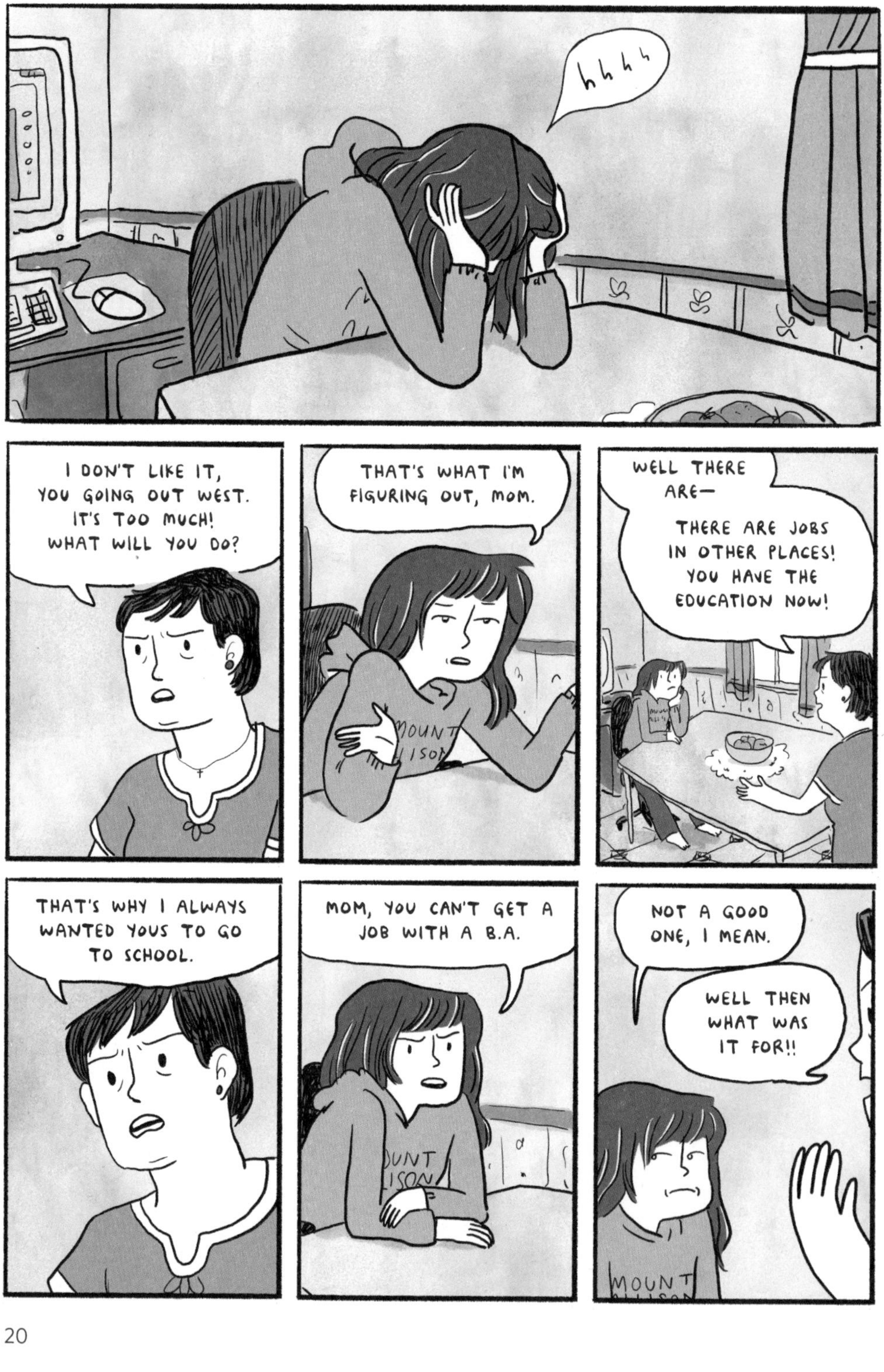
hhhh
I DON'T LIKE IT, YOU GOING OUT WEST. IT'S TOO MUCH! WHAT WILL YOU DO?
THAT'S WHAT I'M FIGURING OUT, MOM.
WELL THERE ARE—
THERE ARE JOBS IN OTHER PLACES! YOU HAVE THE EDUCATION NOW!
THAT'S WHY I ALWAYS WANTED YOUS TO GO TO SCHOOL.
MOM, YOU CAN'T GET A JOB WITH A B.A.
NOT A GOOD ONE, I MEAN.
WELL THEN WHAT WAS IT FOR!!

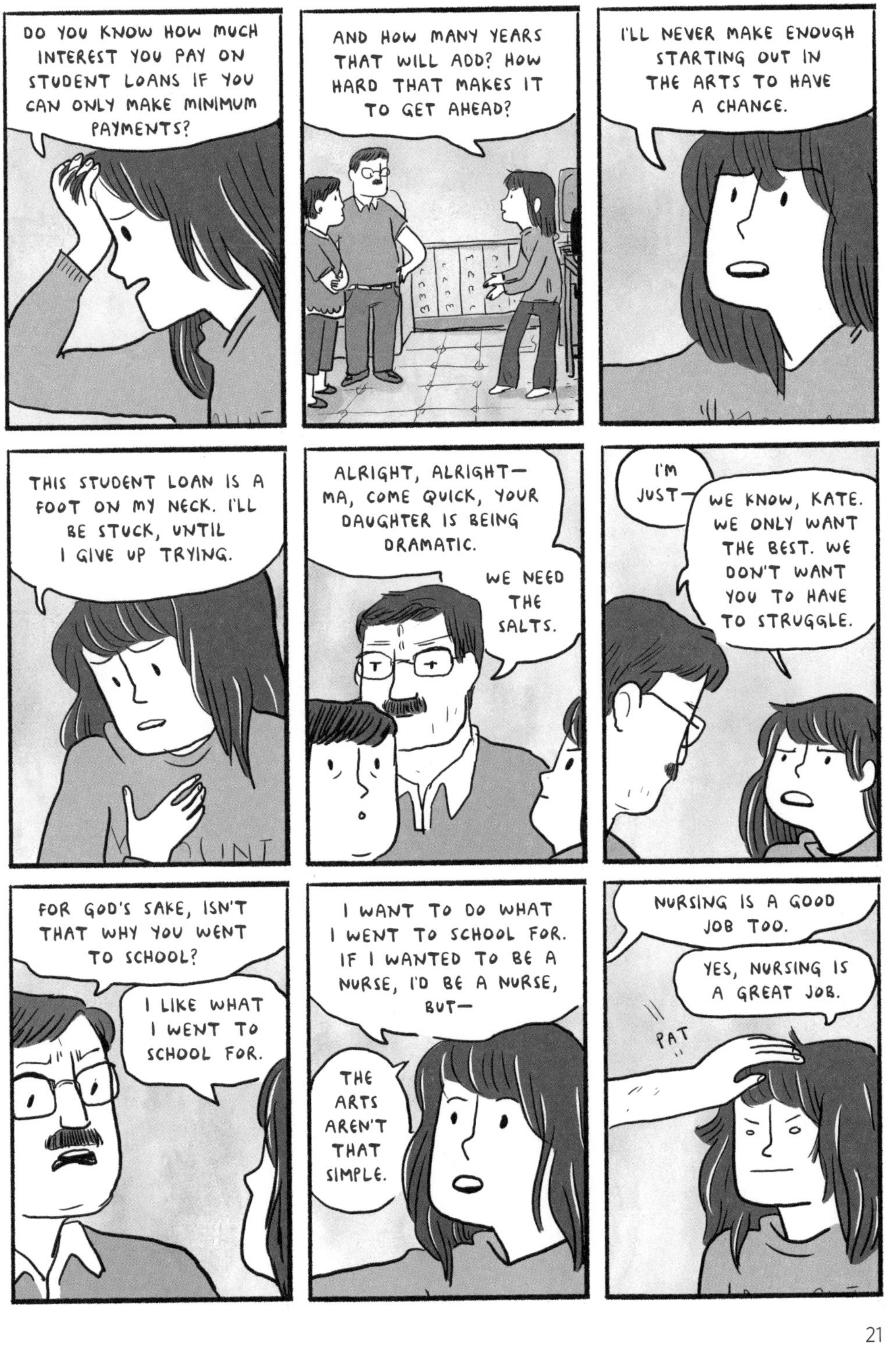
DO YOU KNOW HOW MUCH INTEREST YOU PAY ON STUDENT LOANS IF YOU CAN ONLY MAKE MINIMUM PAYMENTS?
AND HOW MANY YEARS THAT WILL ADD? HOW HARD THAT MAKES IT TO GET AHEAD?
I'LL NEVER MAKE ENOUGH STARTING OUT IN THE ARTS TO HAVE A CHANCE.
THIS STUDENT LOAN IS A FOOT ON MY NECK. I'LL BE STUCK, UNTIL I GIVE UP TRYING.
ALRIGHT, ALRIGHT— MA, COME QUICK, YOUR DAUGHTER IS BEING DRAMATIC.
WE NEED THE SALTS.
I'M JUST—
WE KNOW, KATE. WE ONLY WANT THE BEST. WE DON'T WANT YOU TO HAVE TO STRUGGLE.
FOR GOD'S SAKE, ISN'T THAT WHY YOU WENT TO SCHOOL?
I LIKE WHAT I WENT TO SCHOOL FOR.
I WANT TO DO WHAT I WENT TO SCHOOL FOR. IF I WANTED TO BE A NURSE, I'D BE A NURSE, BUT—
THE ARTS AREN'T THAT SIMPLE.
NURSING IS A GOOD JOB TOO.
YES, NURSING IS A GREAT JOB.
PAT

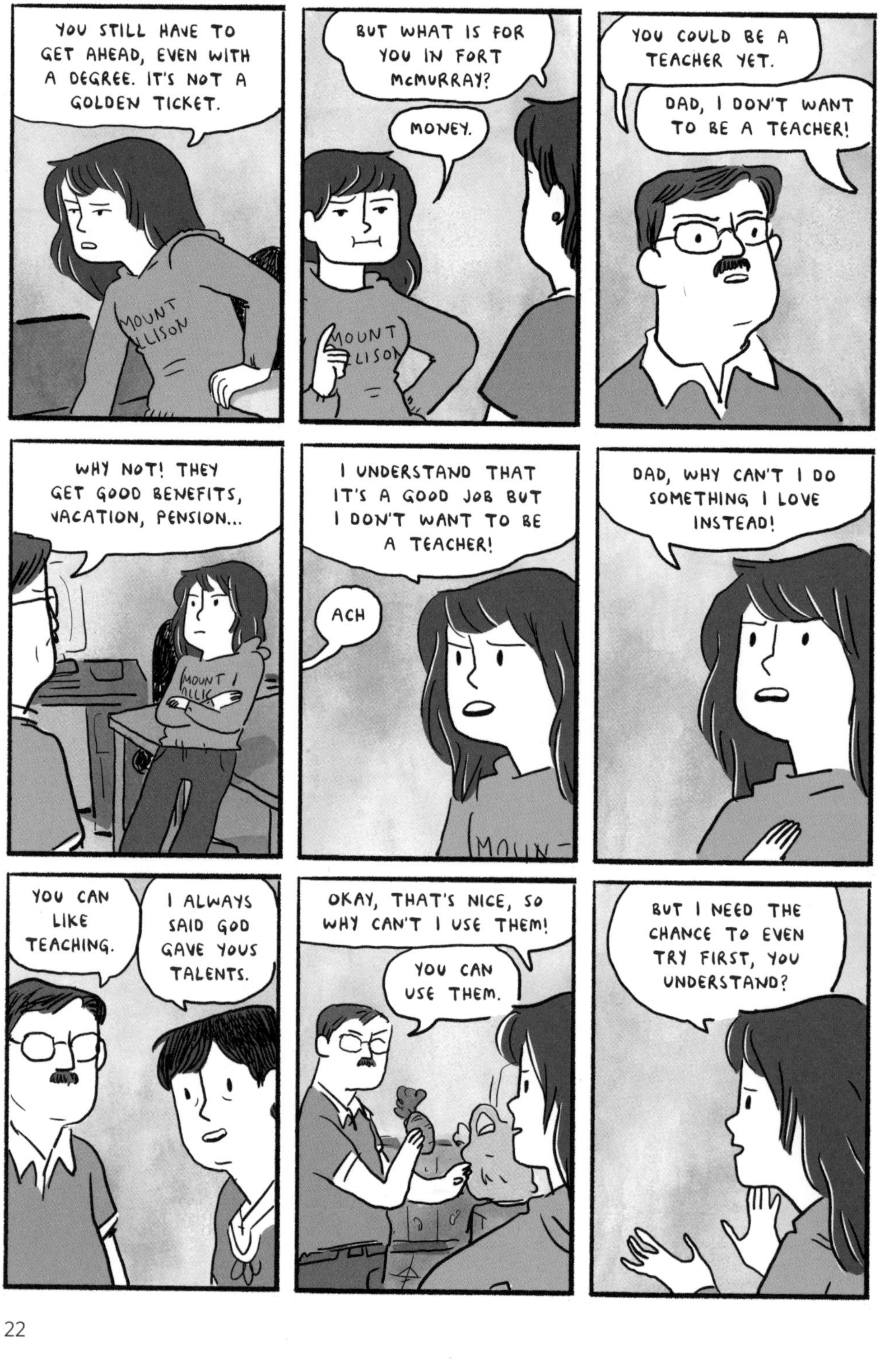
YOU STILL HAVE TO GET AHEAD, EVEN WITH A DEGREE. IT'S NOT A GOLDEN TICKET.
MOUNT ALLISON
BUT WHAT IS FOR YOU IN FORT McMURRAY?
MONEY.
YOU COULD BE A TEACHER YET.
DAD, I DON'T WANT TO BE A TEACHER!
WHY NOT! THEY GET GOOD BENEFITS, VACATION, PENSION...
I UNDERSTAND THAT IT'S A GOOD JOB BUT I DON'T WANT TO BE A TEACHER!
ACH
DAD, WHY CAN'T I DO SOMETHING I LOVE INSTEAD!
YOU CAN LIKE TEACHING.
I ALWAYS SAID GOD GAVE YOUS TALENTS.
OKAY, THAT'S NICE, SO WHY CAN'T I USE THEM!
YOU CAN USE THEM.
BUT I NEED THE CHANCE TO EVEN TRY FIRST, YOU UNDERSTAND?

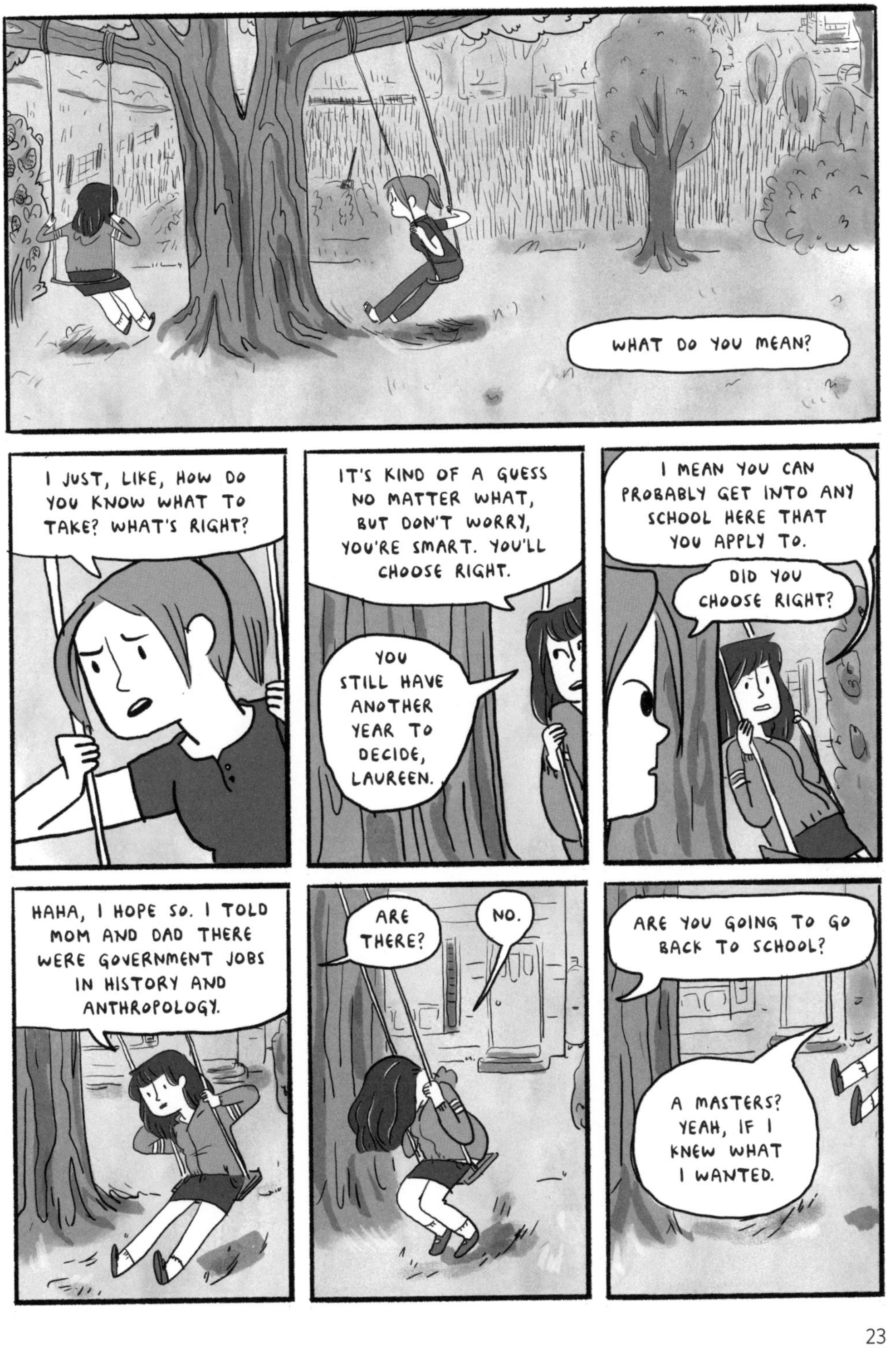
WHAT DO YOU MEAN?
I JUST, LIKE, HOW DO YOU KNOW WHAT TO TAKE? WHAT'S RIGHT?
IT'S KIND OF A GUESS NO MATTER WHAT, BUT DON'T WORRY, YOU'RE SMART. YOU'LL CHOOSE RIGHT.
YOU STILL HAVE ANOTHER YEAR TO DECIDE, LAUREEN.
I MEAN YOU CAN PROBABLY GET INTO ANY SCHOOL HERE THAT YOU APPLY TO.
DID YOU CHOOSE RIGHT?
HAHA, I HOPE SO. I TOLD MOM AND DAD THERE WERE GOVERNMENT JOBS IN HISTORY AND ANTHROPOLOGY.
ARE THERE?
NO.
ARE YOU GOING TO GO BACK TO SCHOOL?
A MASTERS? YEAH, IF I KNEW WHAT I WANTED.

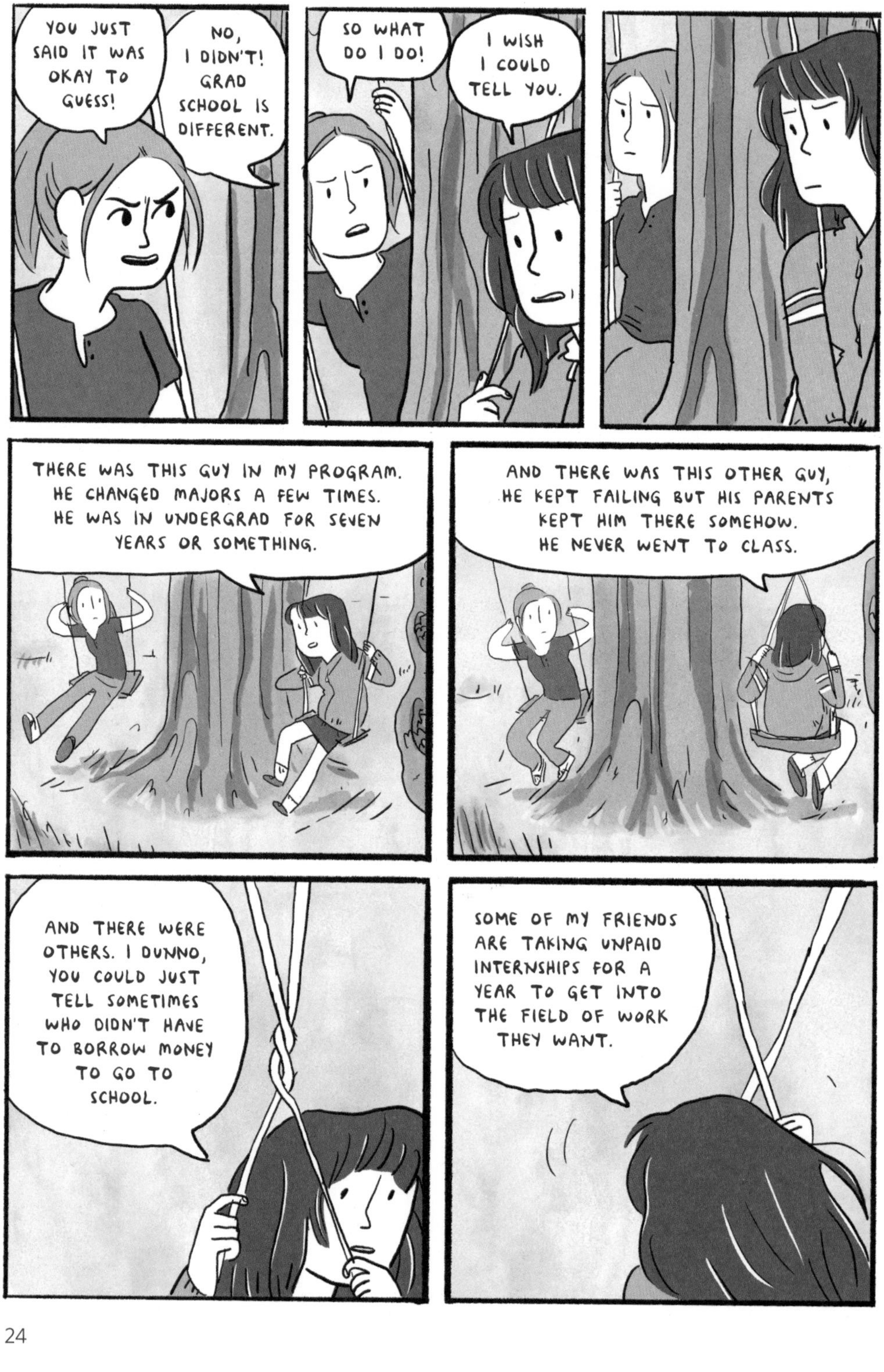
YOU JUST SAID IT WAS OKAY TO GUESS!
NO, I DIDN'T! GRAD SCHOOL IS DIFFERENT.
SO WHAT DO I DO!
I WISH I COULD TELL YOU.
THERE WAS THIS GUY IN MY PROGRAM. HE CHANGED MAJORS A FEW TIMES. HE WAS IN UNDERGRAD FOR SEVEN YEARS OR SOMETHING.
AND THERE WAS THIS OTHER GUY, HE KEPT FAILING BUT HIS PARENTS KEPT HIM THERE SOMEHOW. HE NEVER WENT TO CLASS.
AND THERE WERE OTHERS. I DUNNO, YOU COULD JUST TELL SOMETIMES WHO DIDN'T HAVE TO BORROW MONEY TO GO TO SCHOOL.
SOME OF MY FRIENDS ARE TAKING UNPAID INTERNSHIPS FOR A YEAR TO GET INTO THE FIELD OF WORK THEY WANT.

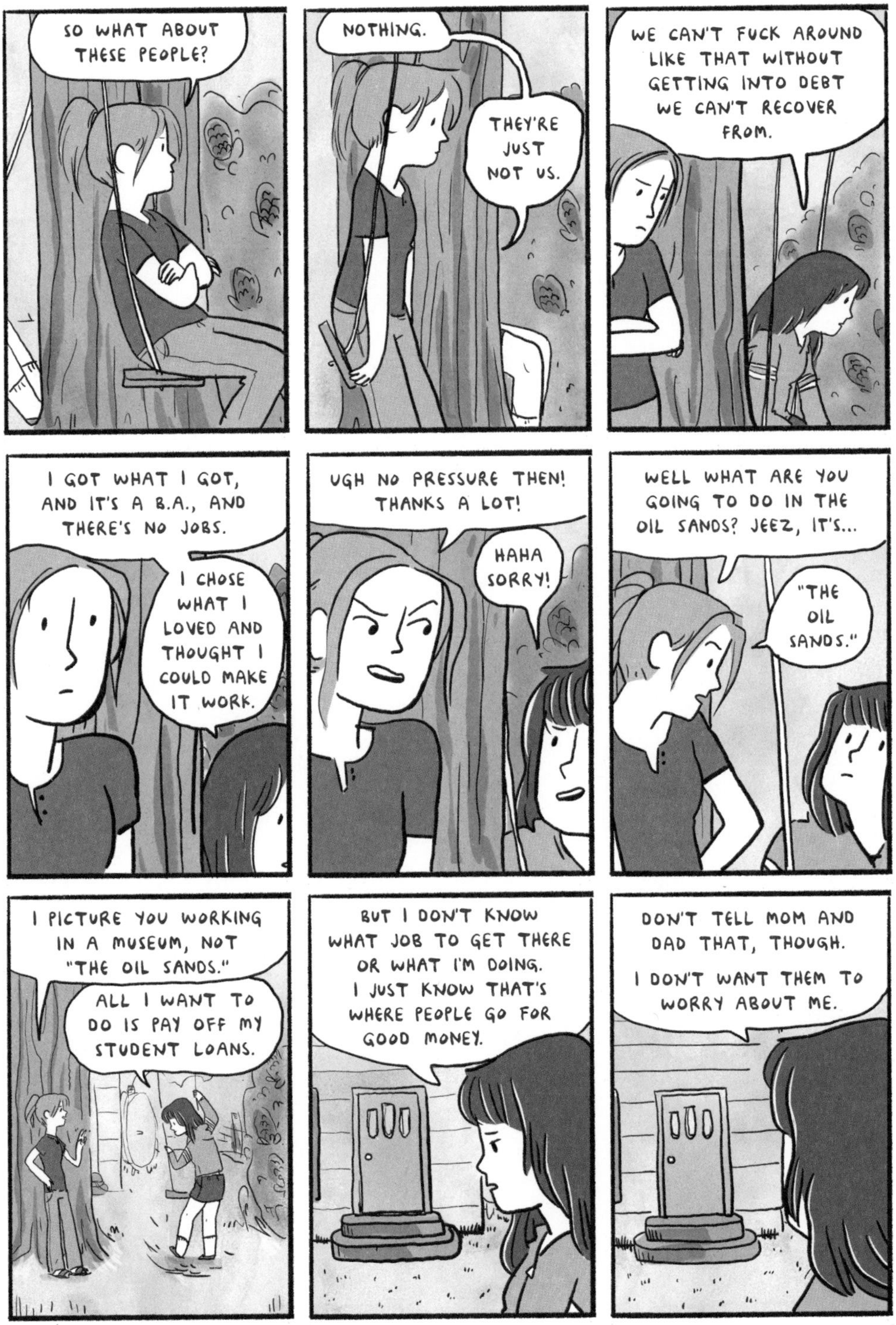
SO WHAT ABOUT THESE PEOPLE?
NOTHING.
THEY'RE JUST NOT US.
WE CAN'T FUCK AROUND LIKE THAT WITHOUT GETTING INTO DEBT WE CAN'T RECOVER FROM.
I GOT WHAT I GOT, AND IT'S A B.A., AND THERE'S NO JOBS.
I CHOSE WHAT I LOVED AND THOUGHT I COULD MAKE IT WORK.
UGH NO PRESSURE THEN! THANKS A LOT!
HAHA SORRY!
WELL WHAT ARE YOU GOING TO DO IN THE OIL SANDS? JEEZ, IT'S...
"THE OIL SANDS."
I PICTURE YOU WORKING IN A MUSEUM, NOT "THE OIL SANDS."
ALL I WANT TO DO IS PAY OFF MY STUDENT LOANS.
BUT I DON'T KNOW WHAT JOB TO GET THERE OR WHAT I'M DOING. I JUST KNOW THAT'S WHERE PEOPLE GO FOR GOOD MONEY.
DON'T TELL MOM AND DAD THAT, THOUGH.
I DON'T WANT THEM TO WORRY ABOUT ME.

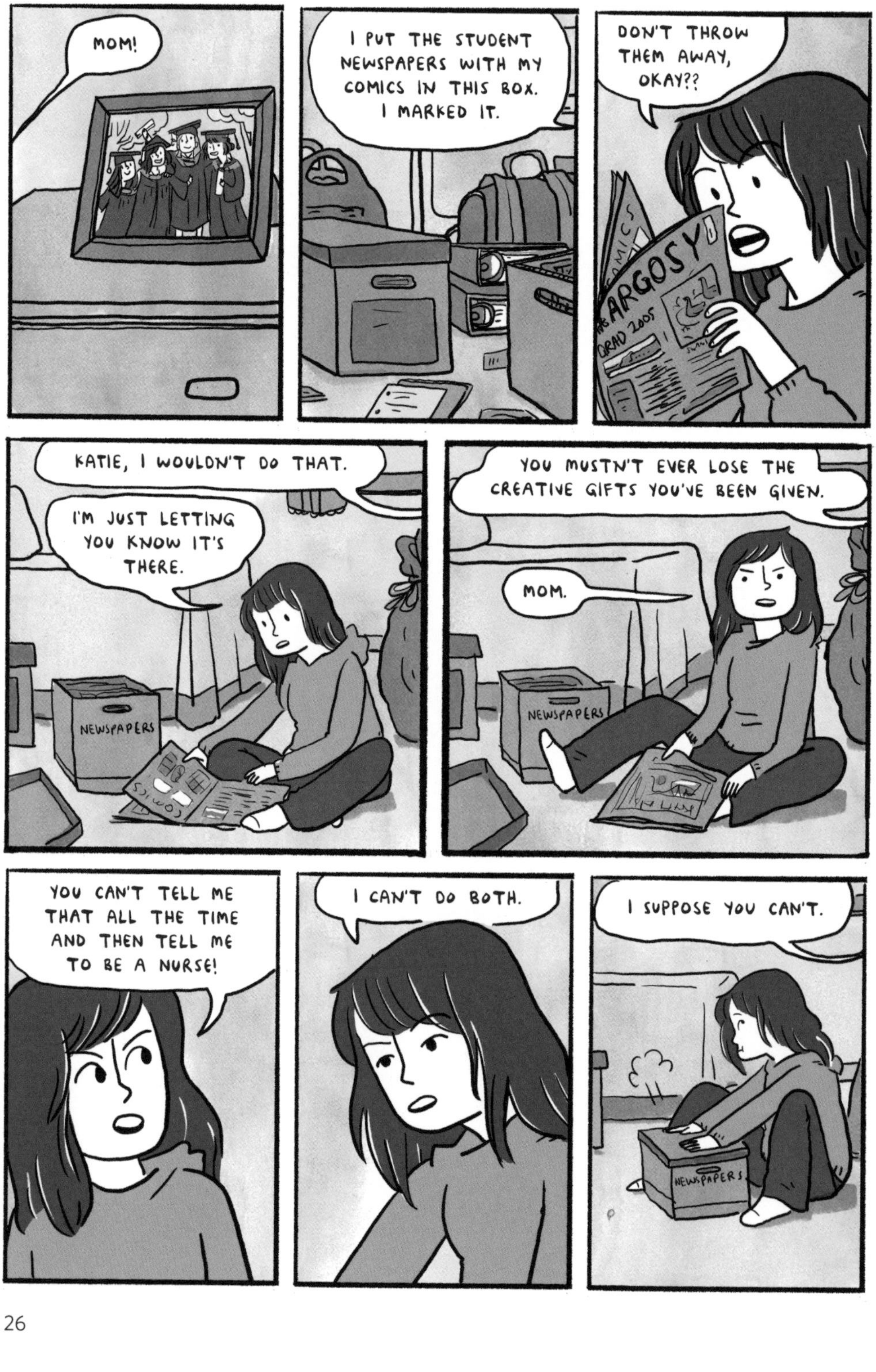
MOM!
I PUT THE STUDENT NEWSPAPERS WITH MY COMICS IN THIS BOX. I MARKED IT.
DON'T THROW THEM AWAY, OKAY??
ARGOSY
GRAD 2005
KATIE, I WOULDN'T DO THAT.
I'M JUST LETTING YOU KNOW IT'S THERE.
NEWSPAPERS
YOU MUSTN'T EVER LOSE THE CREATIVE GIFTS YOU'VE BEEN GIVEN.
MOM.
NEWSPAPERS
YOU CAN'T TELL ME THAT ALL THE TIME AND THEN TELL ME TO BE A NURSE!
I CAN'T DO BOTH.
I SUPPOSE YOU CAN'T.
NEWSPAPERS

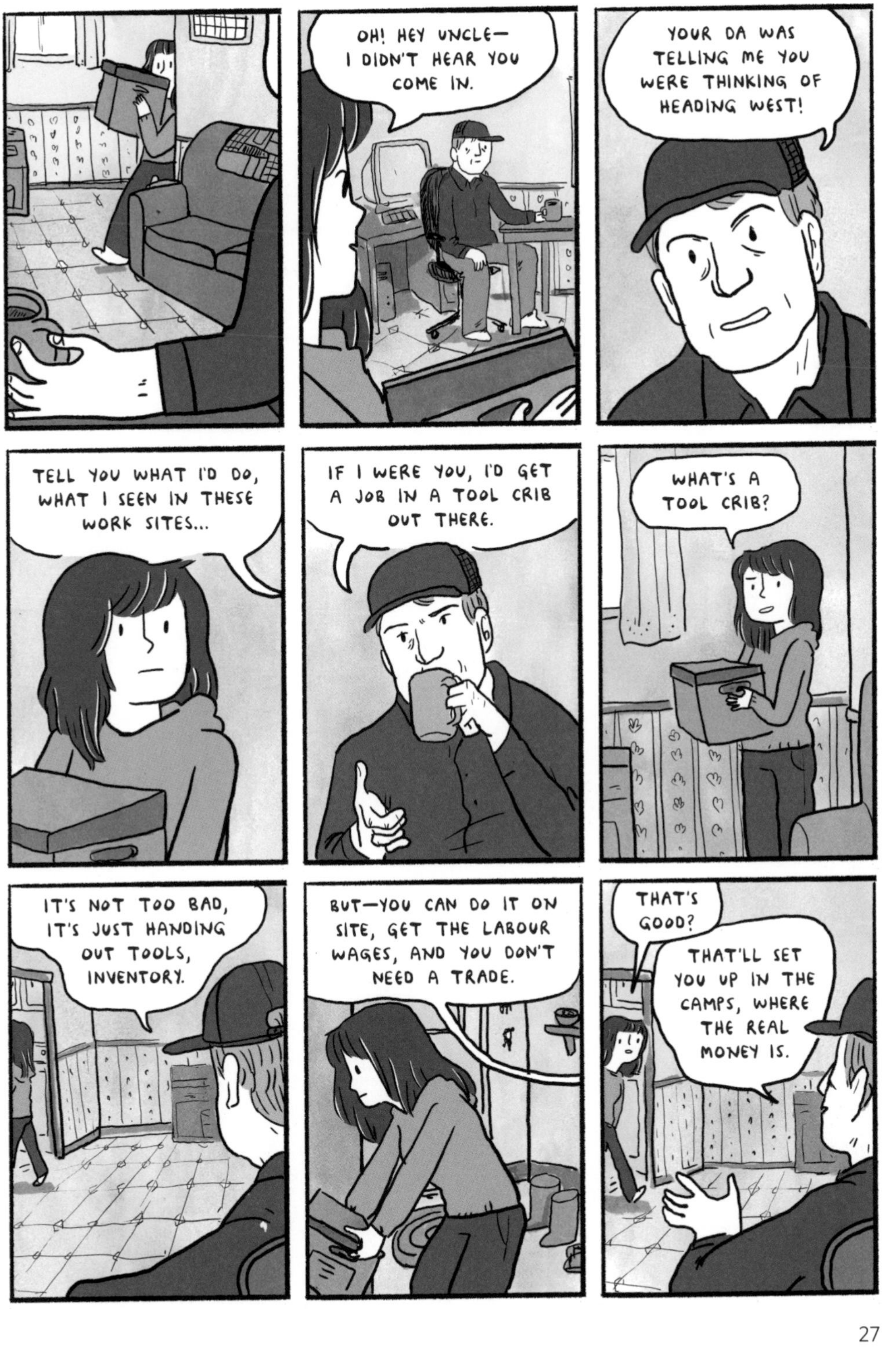
OH! HEY UNCLE—
I DIDN'T HEAR YOU COME IN.
YOUR DA WAS TELLING ME YOU WERE THINKING OF HEADING WEST!
TELL YOU WHAT I'D DO, WHAT I SEEN IN THESE WORK SITES...
IF I WERE YOU, I'D GET A JOB IN A TOOL CRIB OUT THERE.
WHAT'S A TOOL CRIB?
IT'S NOT TOO BAD, IT'S JUST HANDING OUT TOOLS, INVENTORY.
BUT—YOU CAN DO IT ON SITE, GET THE LABOUR WAGES, AND YOU DON'T NEED A TRADE.
THAT'S GOOD?
THAT'LL SET YOU UP IN THE CAMPS, WHERE THE REAL MONEY IS.

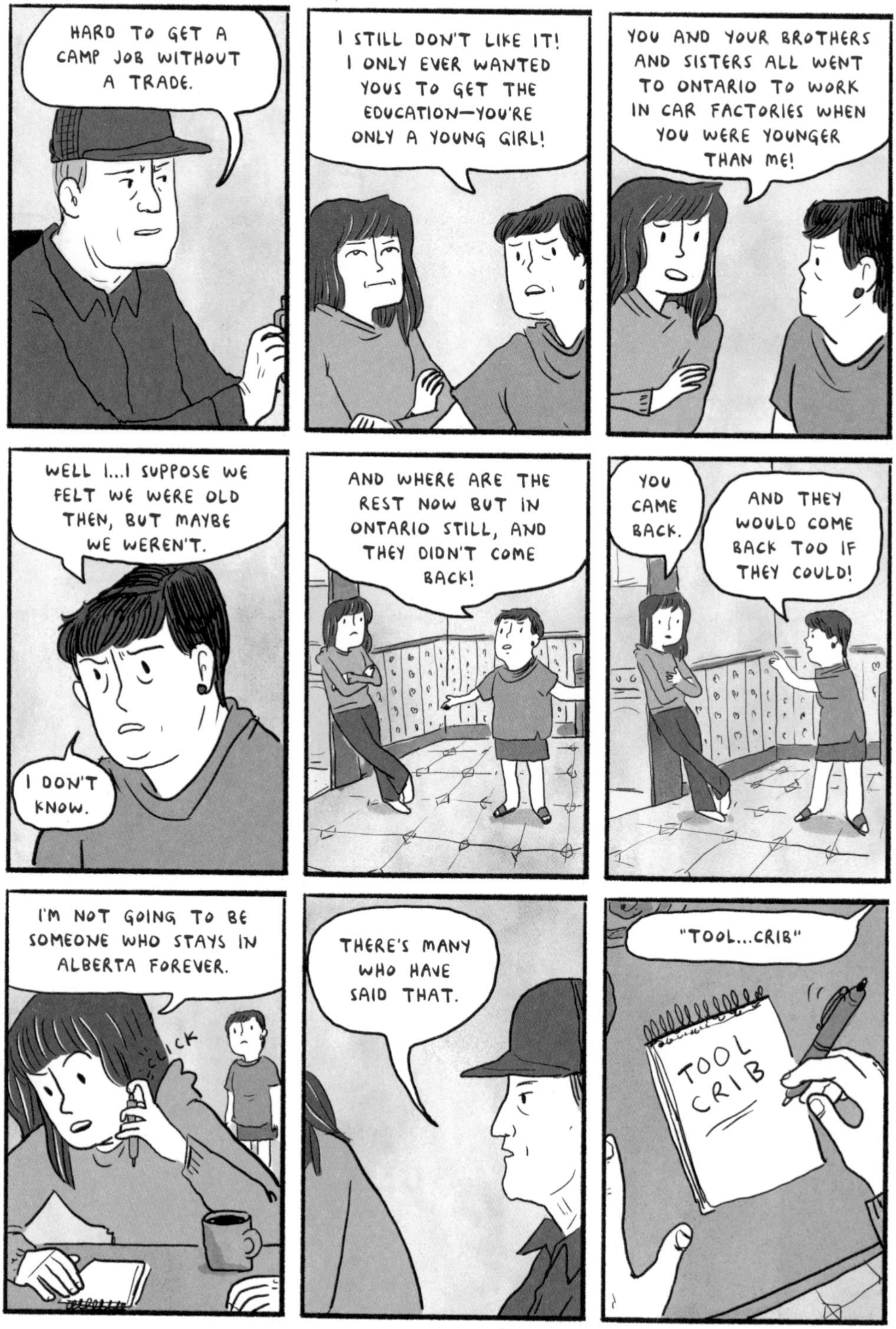
HARD TO GET A CAMP JOB WITHOUT A TRADE.
I STILL DON'T LIKE IT! I ONLY EVER WANTED YOUS TO GET THE EDUCATION—YOU'RE ONLY A YOUNG GIRL!
YOU AND YOUR BROTHERS AND SISTERS ALL WENT TO ONTARIO TO WORK IN CAR FACTORIES WHEN YOU WERE YOUNGER THAN ME!
WELL I...I SUPPOSE WE FELT WE WERE OLD THEN, BUT MAYBE WE WEREN'T.
I DON'T KNOW.
AND WHERE ARE THE REST NOW BUT IN ONTARIO STILL, AND THEY DIDN'T COME BACK!
YOU CAME BACK.
AND THEY WOULD COME BACK TOO IF THEY COULD!
I'M NOT GOING TO BE SOMEONE WHO STAYS IN ALBERTA FOREVER.
CLICK
THERE'S MANY WHO HAVE SAID THAT.
"TOOL...CRIB"
TOOL CRIB

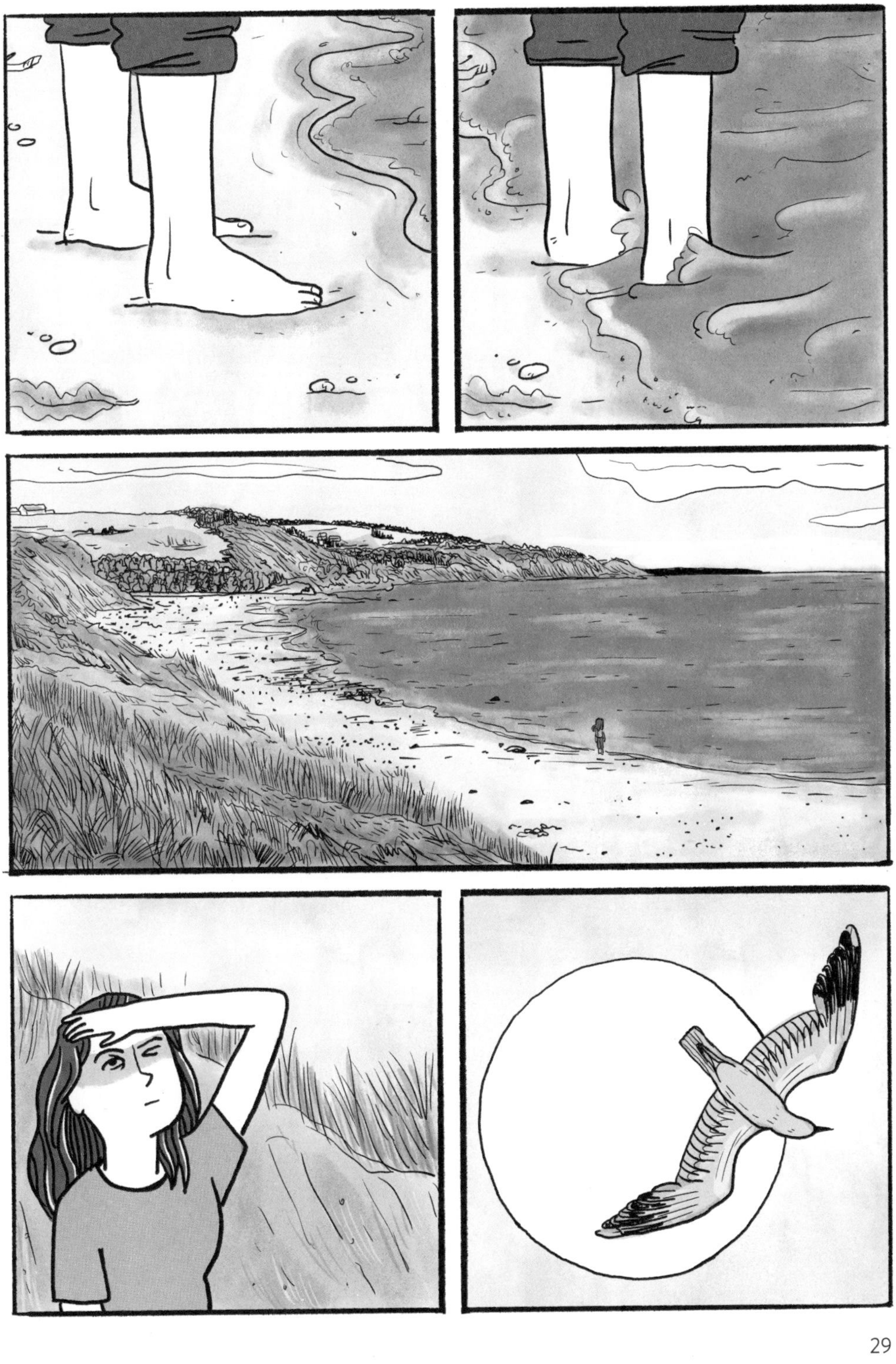

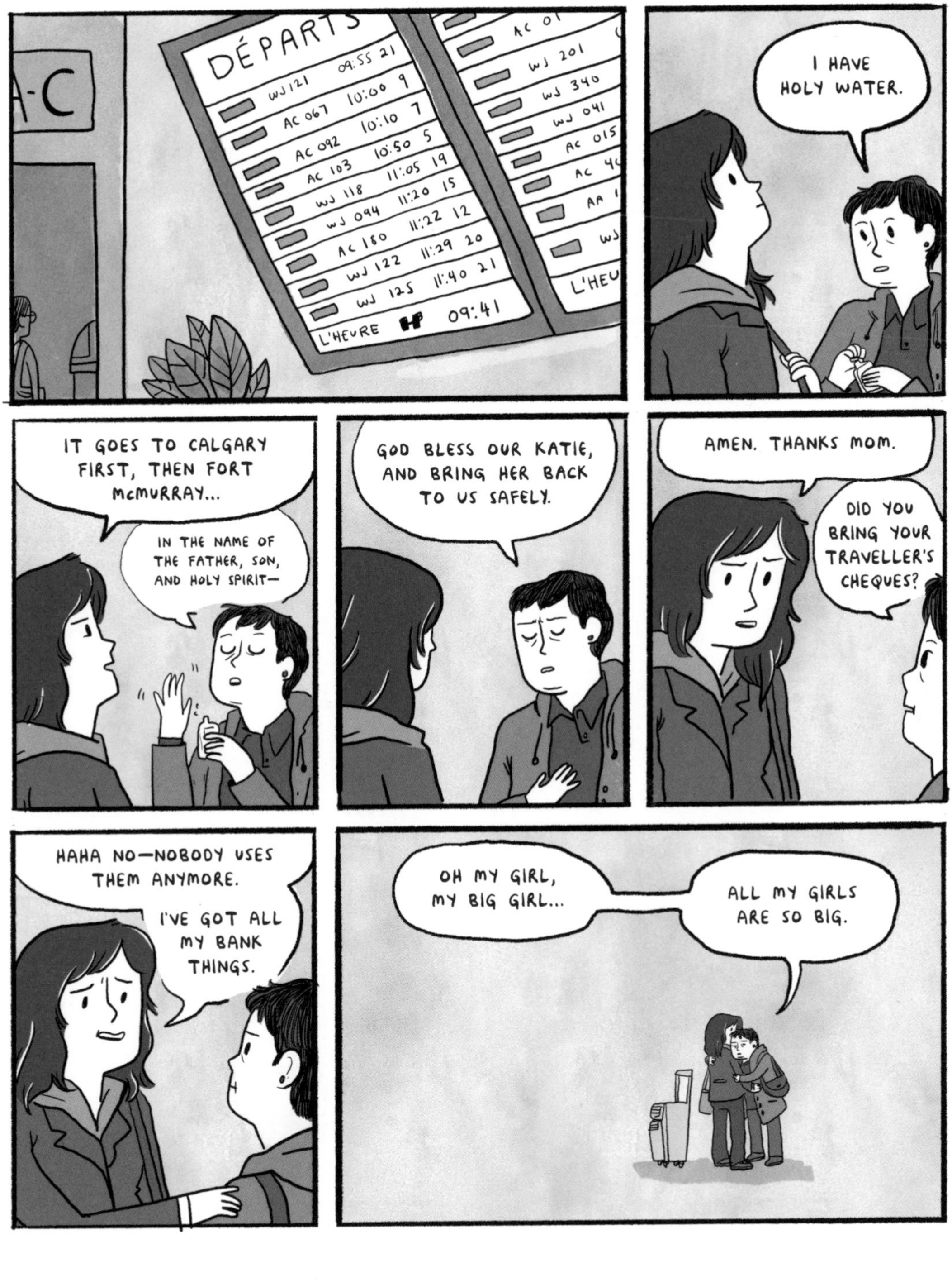
A-C
DÉPARTS
WJ 121 09:55 21
AC 067 10:00 9
AC 092 10:10 7
AC 103 10:50 5
WJ 118 11:05 19
WJ 094 11:20 15
AC 180 11:22 12
WJ 122 11:29 20
WJ 125 11:40 21
L'HEURE 09:41
I HAVE HOLY WATER.
IT GOES TO CALGARY FIRST, THEN FORT McMURRAY...
IN THE NAME OF THE FATHER, SON, AND HOLY SPIRIT—
GOD BLESS OUR KATIE, AND BRING HER BACK TO US SAFELY.
AMEN. THANKS MOM.
DID YOU BRING YOUR TRAVELLER'S CHEQUES?
HAHA NO—NOBODY USES THEM ANYMORE.
I'VE GOT ALL MY BANK THINGS.
OH MY GIRL, MY BIG GIRL...
ALL MY GIRLS ARE SO BIG.

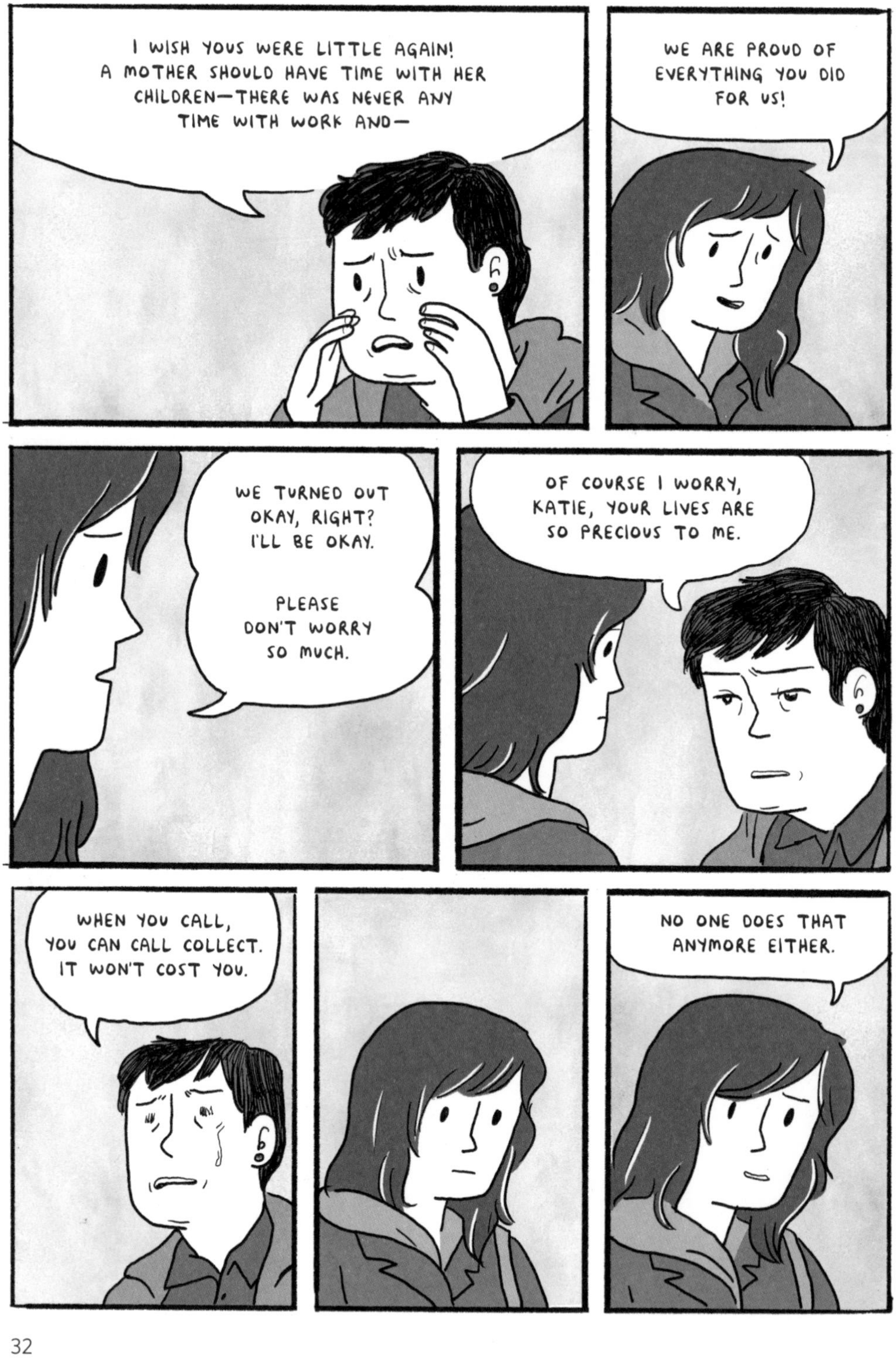
I WISH YOUS WERE LITTLE AGAIN! A MOTHER SHOULD HAVE TIME WITH HER CHILDREN—THERE WAS NEVER ANY TIME WITH WORK AND—
WE ARE PROUD OF EVERYTHING YOU DID FOR US!
WE TURNED OUT OKAY, RIGHT? I'LL BE OKAY.
PLEASE DON'T WORRY SO MUCH.
OF COURSE I WORRY, KATIE, YOUR LIVES ARE SO PRECIOUS TO ME.
WHEN YOU CALL, YOU CAN CALL COLLECT. IT WON'T COST YOU.
NO ONE DOES THAT ANYMORE EITHER.

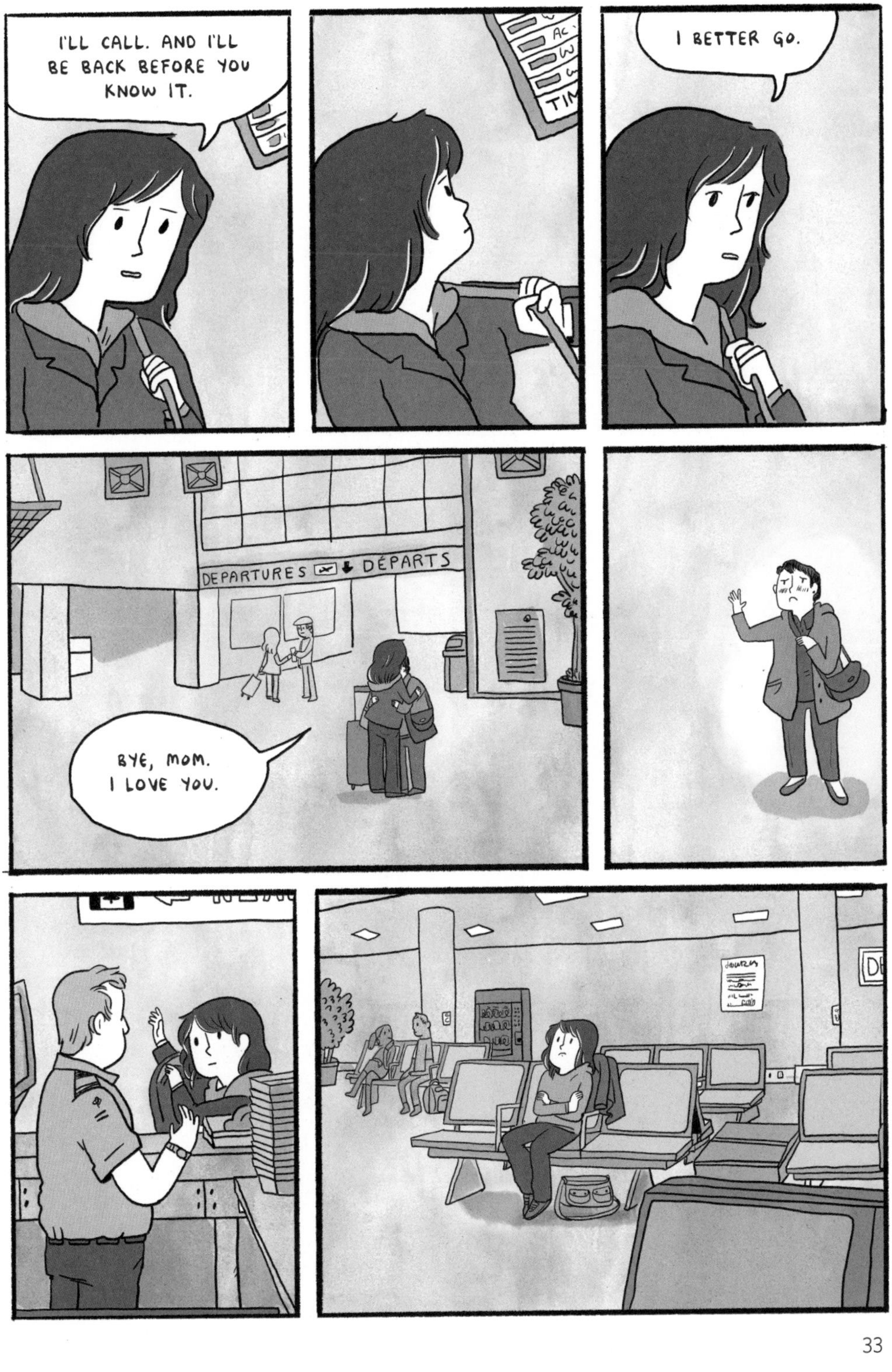
I'LL CALL. AND I'LL BE BACK BEFORE YOU KNOW IT.
I BETTER GO.
DEPARTURES DÉPARTS
BYE, MOM. I LOVE YOU.

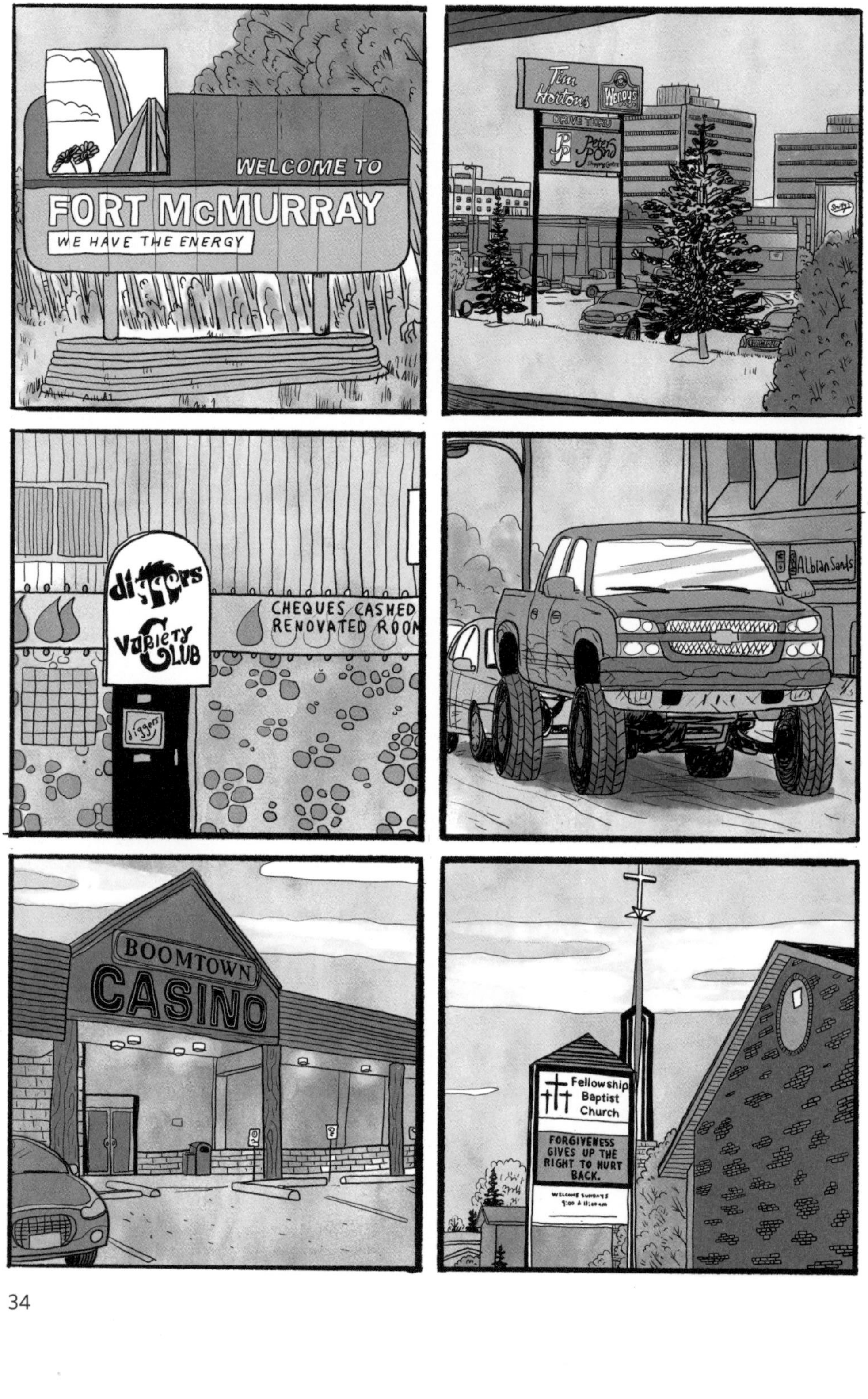
WELCOME TO
FORT McMURRAY
WE HAVE THE ENERGY
Tim Hortons
Wendy's
DRIVE THRU
Peter Pond
Shopping Centre
diggers
Variety Club
CHEQUES CASHED
RENOVATED ROOM
diggers
Albian Sands
BOOMTOWN
CASINO
Fellowship Baptist Church
FORGIVENESS GIVES UP THE RIGHT TO HURT BACK.
WELCOME SUNDAYS
9:00 & 11:00am

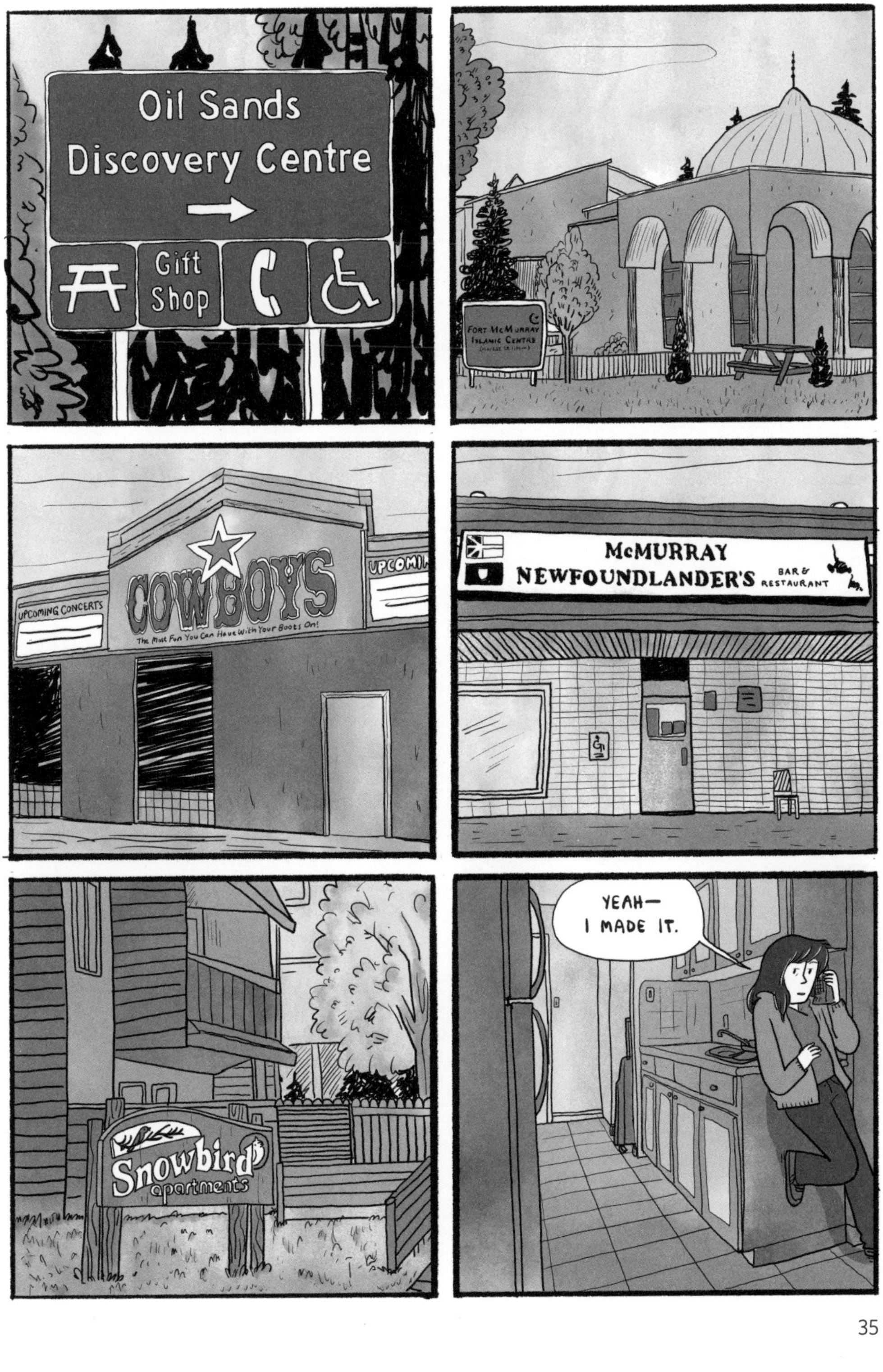
Oil Sands
Discovery Centre
Gift Shop
FORT McMURRAY ISLAMIC CENTRE
UPCOMING CONCERTS
COWBOYS
The Most Fun You Can Have With Your Boots On!
McMURRAY
NEWFOUNDLANDER'S
BAR & RESTAURANT
Snowbird
apartments
YEAH—
I MADE IT.

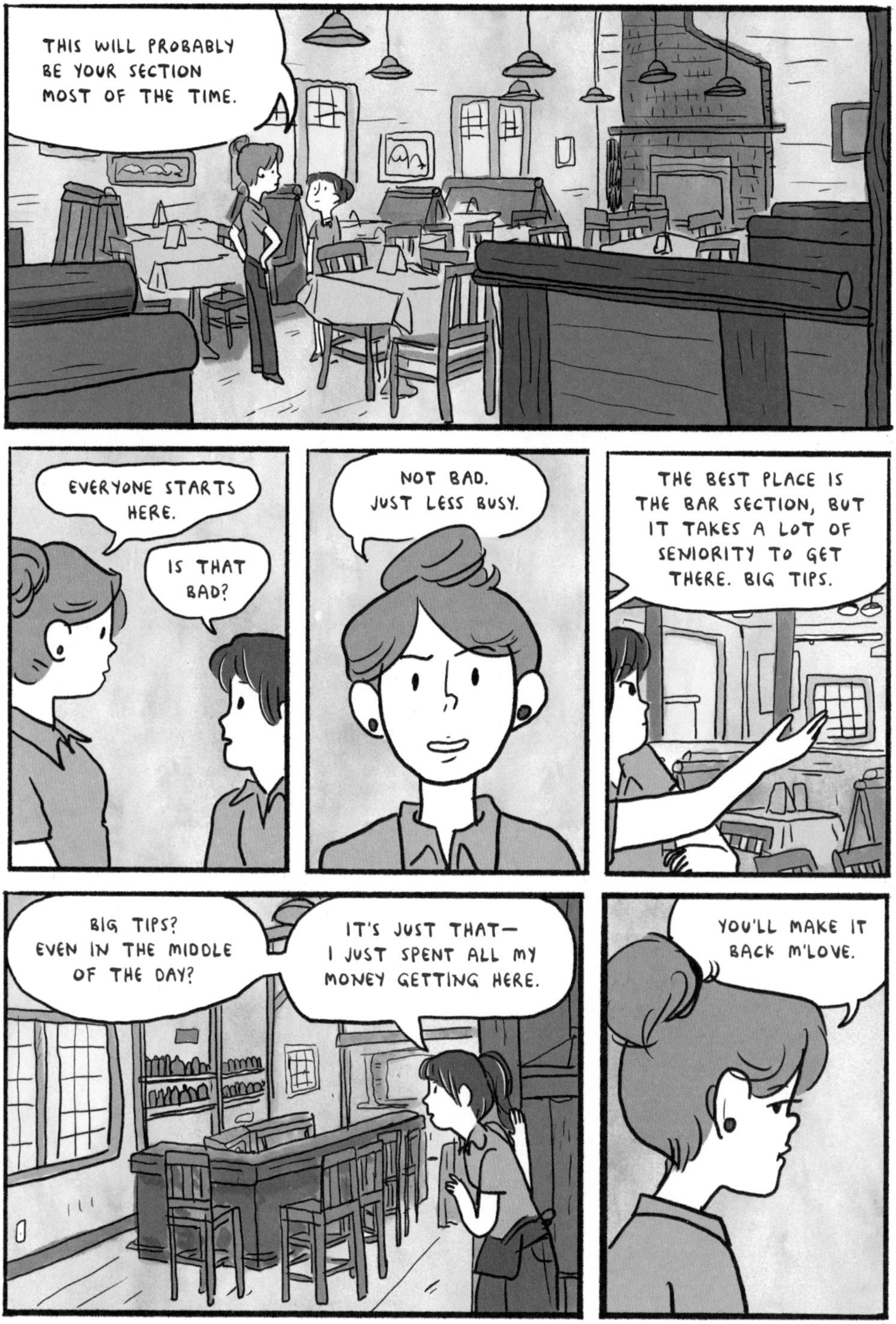
THIS WILL PROBABLY BE YOUR SECTION MOST OF THE TIME.
EVERYONE STARTS HERE.
IS THAT BAD?
NOT BAD. JUST LESS BUSY.
THE BEST PLACE IS THE BAR SECTION, BUT IT TAKES A LOT OF SENIORITY TO GET THERE. BIG TIPS.
BIG TIPS? EVEN IN THE MIDDLE OF THE DAY?
IT'S JUST THAT— I JUST SPENT ALL MY MONEY GETTING HERE.
YOU'LL MAKE IT BACK M'LOVE.

TAP
TAP
CLA
BLP
BLP
BLP
BLP
BLP
BLP
CLA
HELLO? I'M CALLING ABOUT THE AD IN THE PAPER—THE TOOL CRIB POSITION?

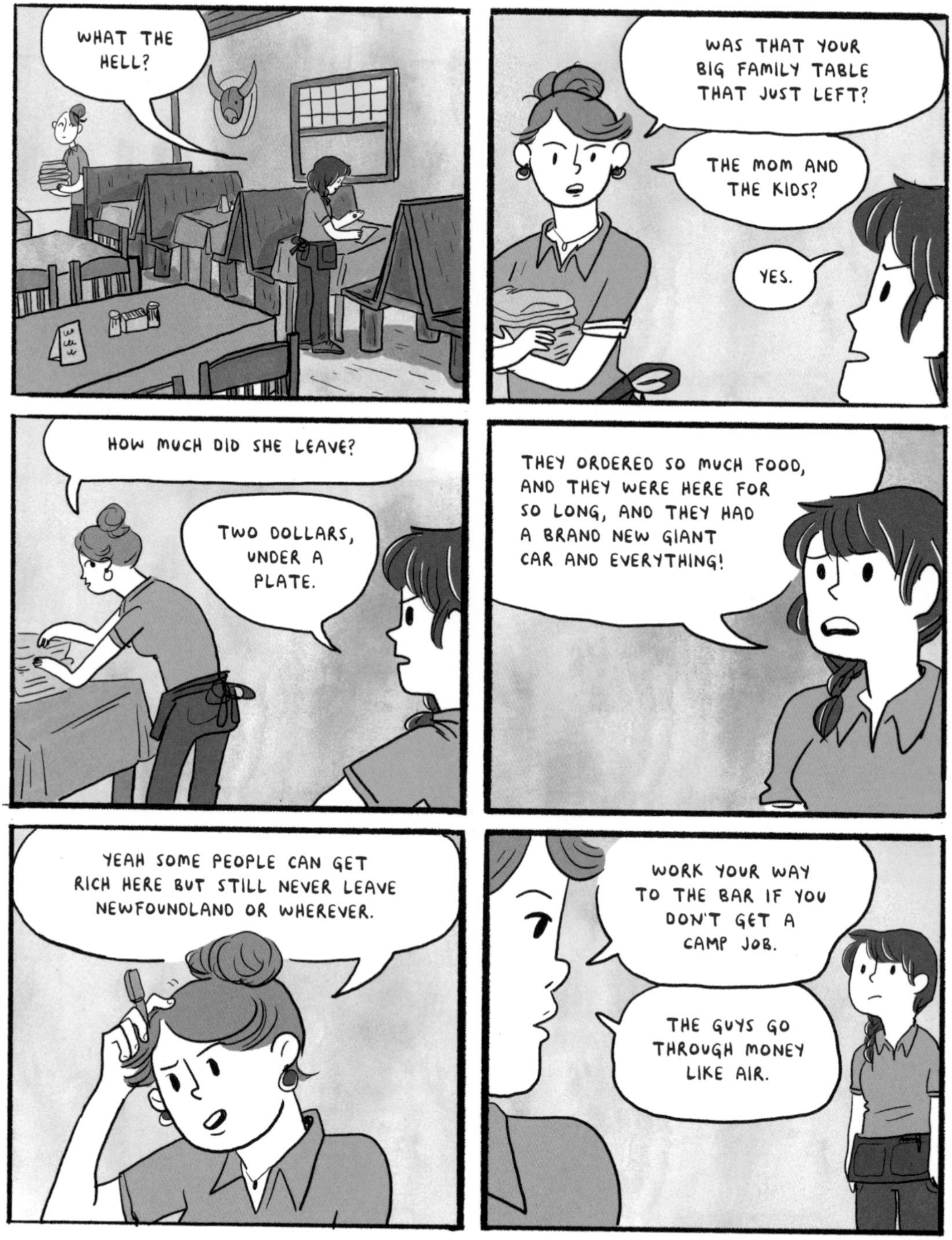
WHAT THE HELL?
WAS THAT YOUR BIG FAMILY TABLE THAT JUST LEFT?
THE MOM AND THE KIDS?
YES.
HOW MUCH DID SHE LEAVE?
TWO DOLLARS, UNDER A PLATE.
THEY ORDERED SO MUCH FOOD, AND THEY WERE HERE FOR SO LONG, AND THEY HAD A BRAND NEW GIANT CAR AND EVERYTHING!
YEAH SOME PEOPLE CAN GET RICH HERE BUT STILL NEVER LEAVE NEWFOUNDLAND OR WHEREVER.
WORK YOUR WAY TO THE BAR IF YOU DON'T GET A CAMP JOB.
THE GUYS GO THROUGH MONEY LIKE AIR.

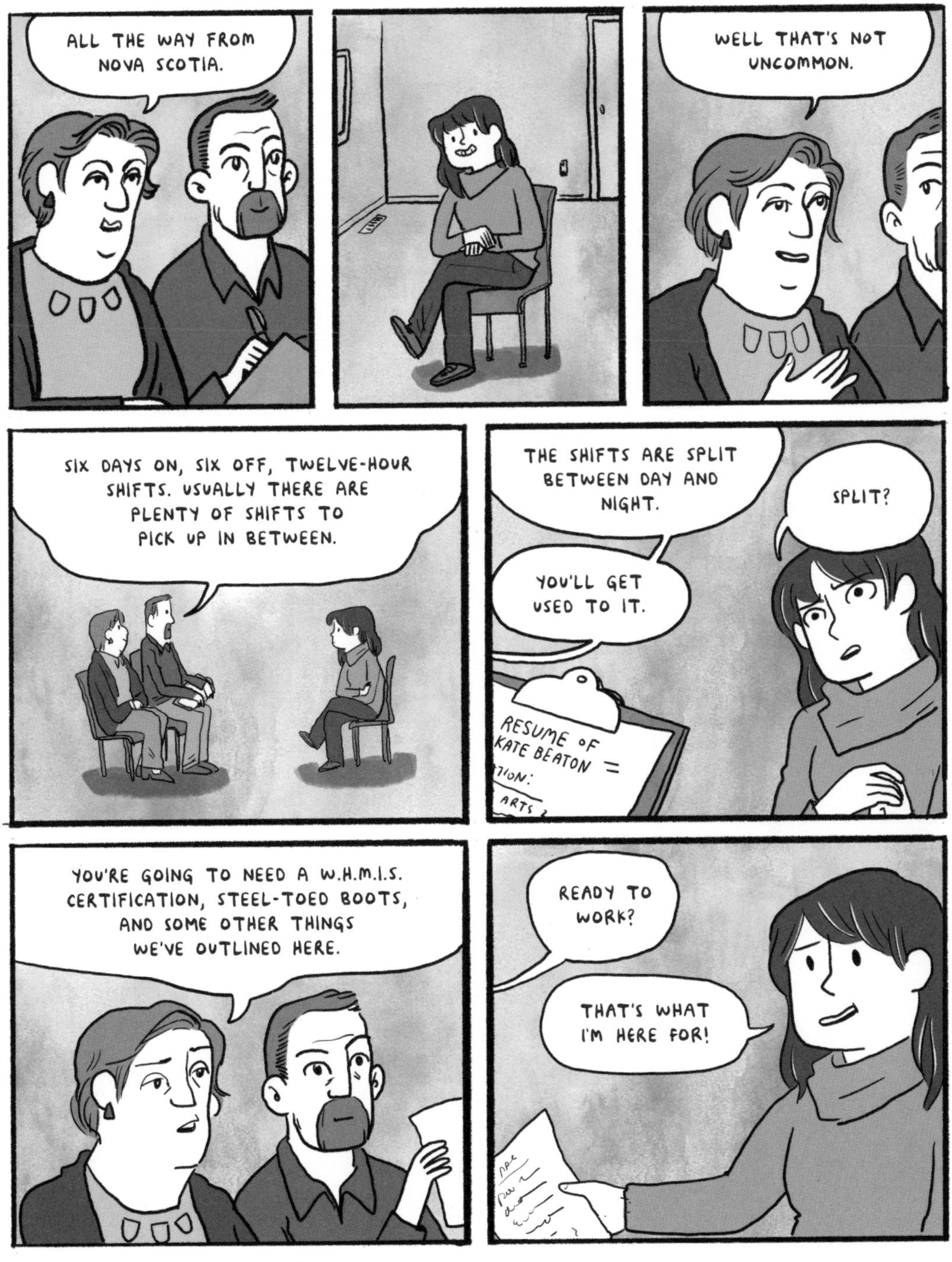
ALL THE WAY FROM NOVA SCOTIA.
WELL THAT'S NOT UNCOMMON.
SIX DAYS ON, SIX OFF, TWELVE-HOUR SHIFTS. USUALLY THERE ARE PLENTY OF SHIFTS TO PICK UP IN BETWEEN.
THE SHIFTS ARE SPLIT BETWEEN DAY AND NIGHT.
SPLIT?
YOU'LL GET USED TO IT.
RESUME OF KATE BEATON
YOU'RE GOING TO NEED A W.H.M.I.S. CERTIFICATION, STEEL-TOED BOOTS, AND SOME OTHER THINGS WE'VE OUTLINED HERE.
READY TO WORK?
THAT'S WHAT I'M HERE FOR!

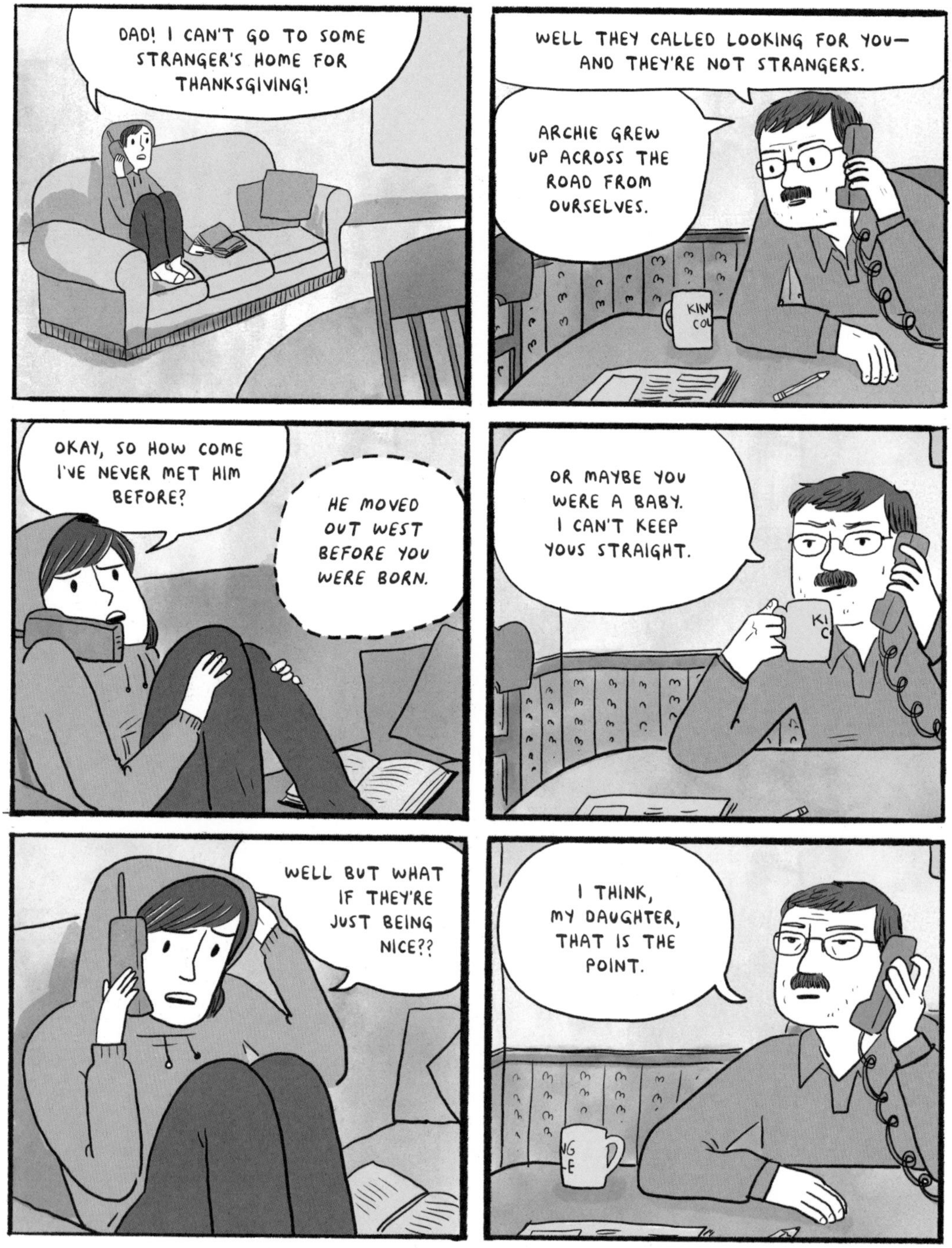
DAD! I CAN'T GO TO SOME STRANGER'S HOME FOR THANKSGIVING!
WELL THEY CALLED LOOKING FOR YOU— AND THEY'RE NOT STRANGERS.
ARCHIE GREW UP ACROSS THE ROAD FROM OURSELVES.
OKAY, SO HOW COME I'VE NEVER MET HIM BEFORE?
HE MOVED OUT WEST BEFORE YOU WERE BORN.
OR MAYBE YOU WERE A BABY. I CAN'T KEEP YOUS STRAIGHT.
WELL BUT WHAT IF THEY'RE JUST BEING NICE??
I THINK, MY DAUGHTER, THAT IS THE POINT.

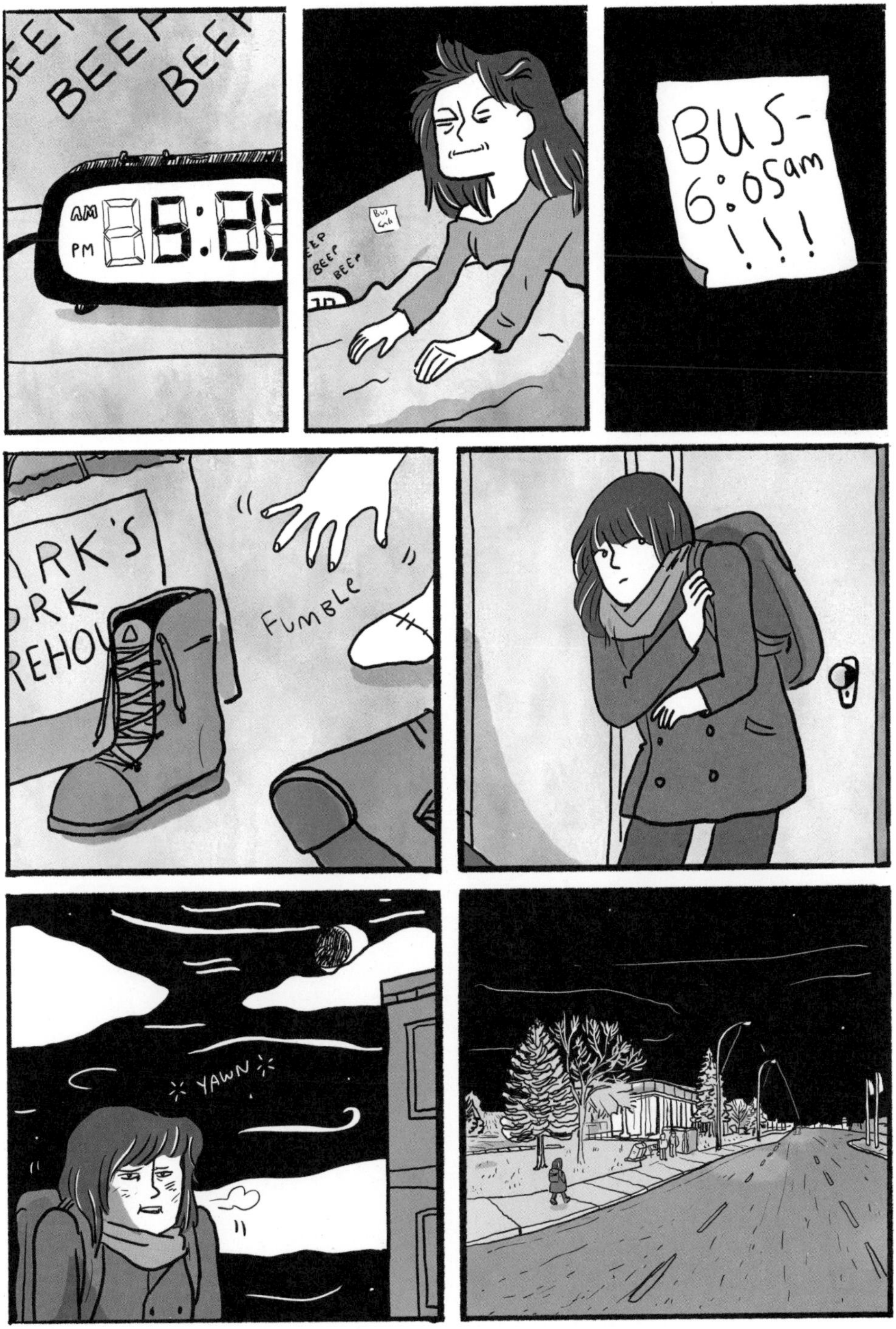
BEEP
BEEP
BEEP
AM
PM
BUS-
6:05am
!!!!
FUMBLE
YAWN

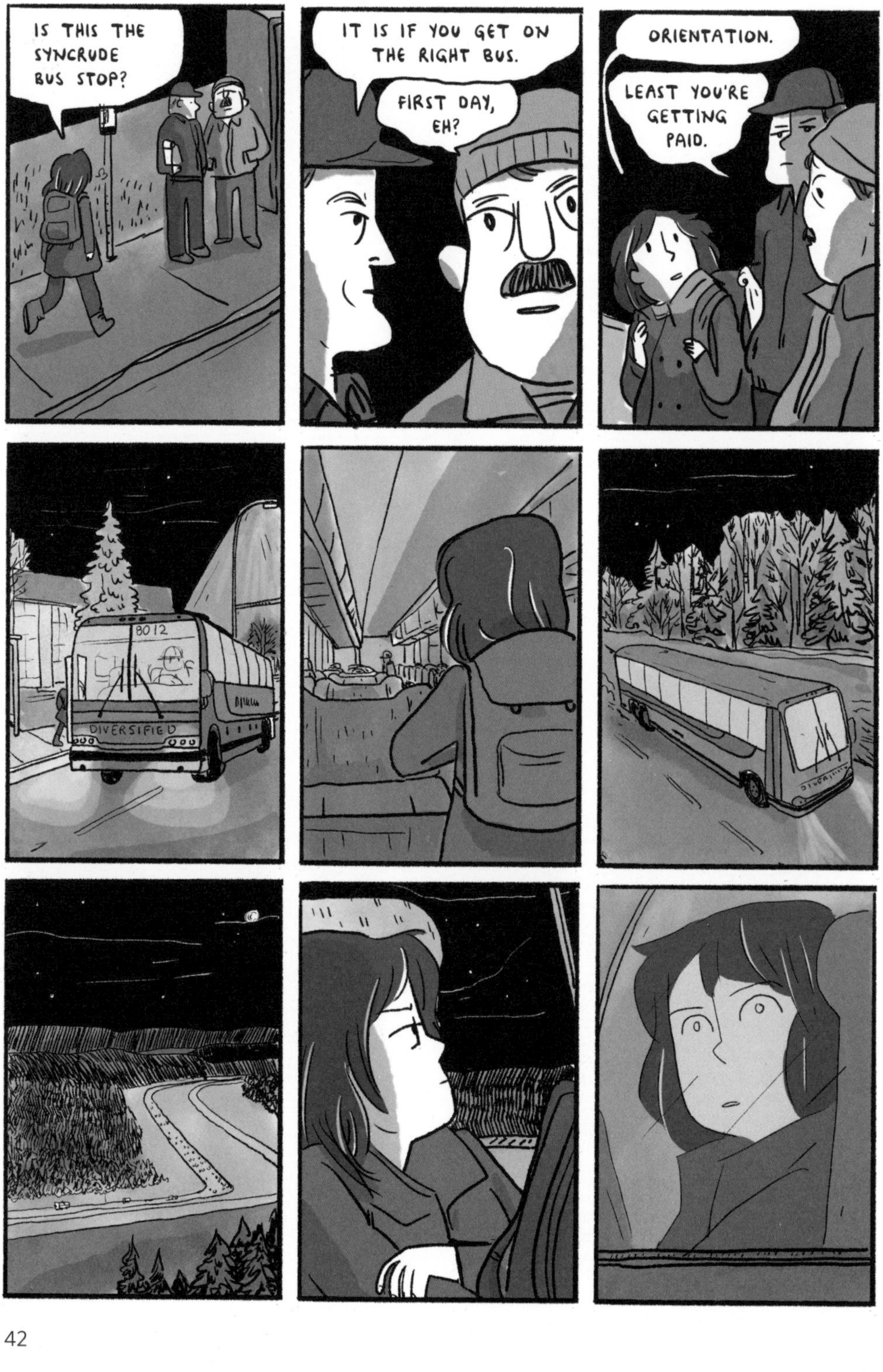
IS THIS THE SYNCRUDE BUS STOP?
IT IS IF YOU GET ON THE RIGHT BUS.
FIRST DAY, EH?
ORIENTATION.
LEAST YOU'RE GETTING PAID.
8012
DIVERSIFIED

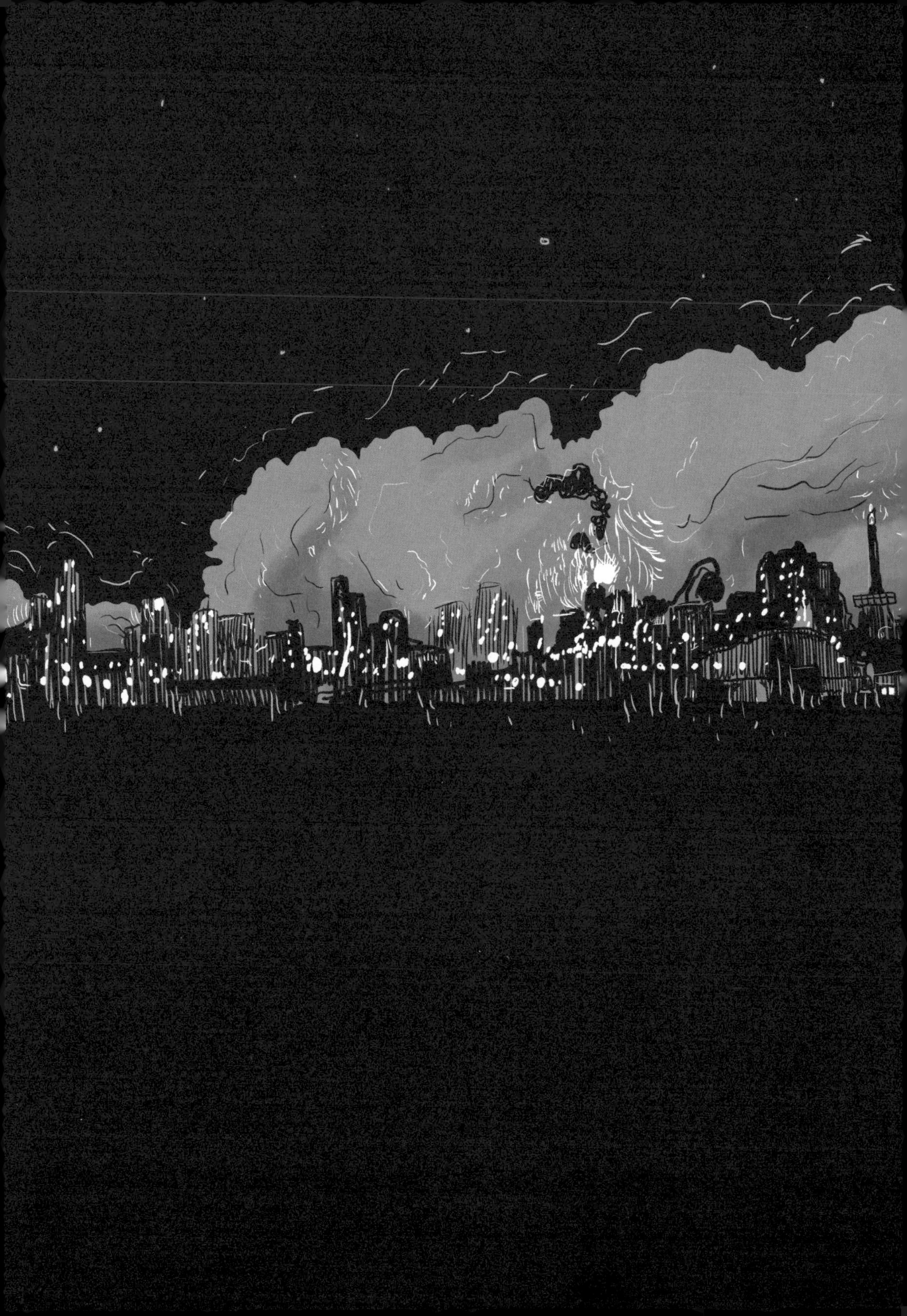

SYNCRUDE
MILDRED LAKE

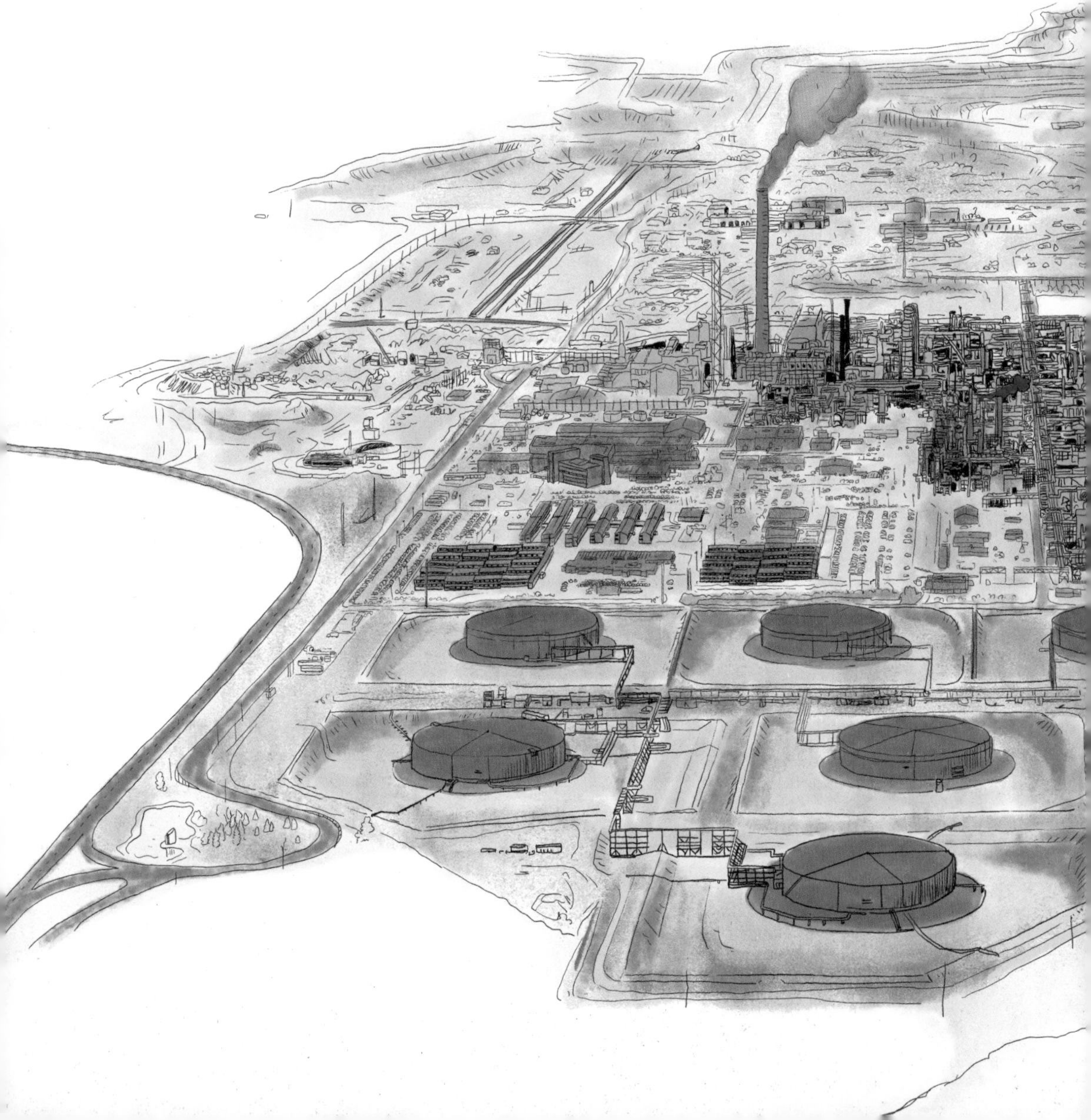

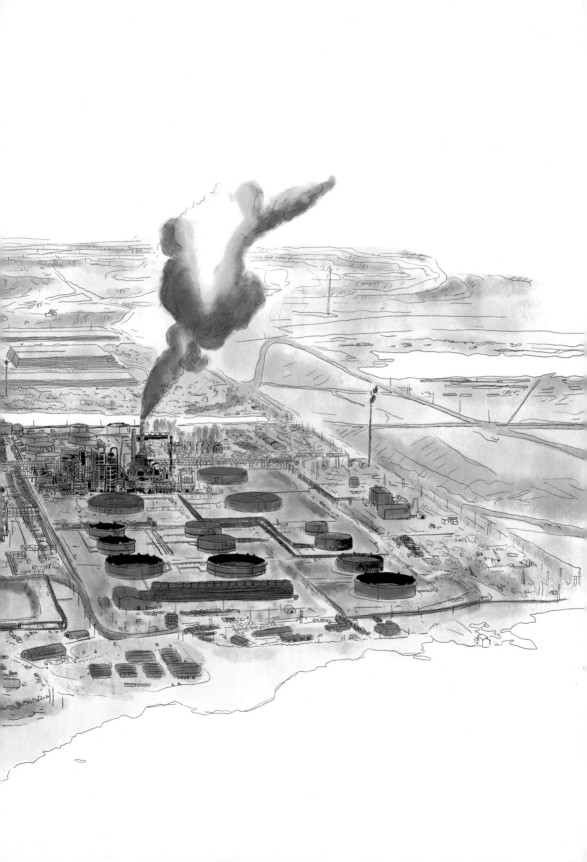

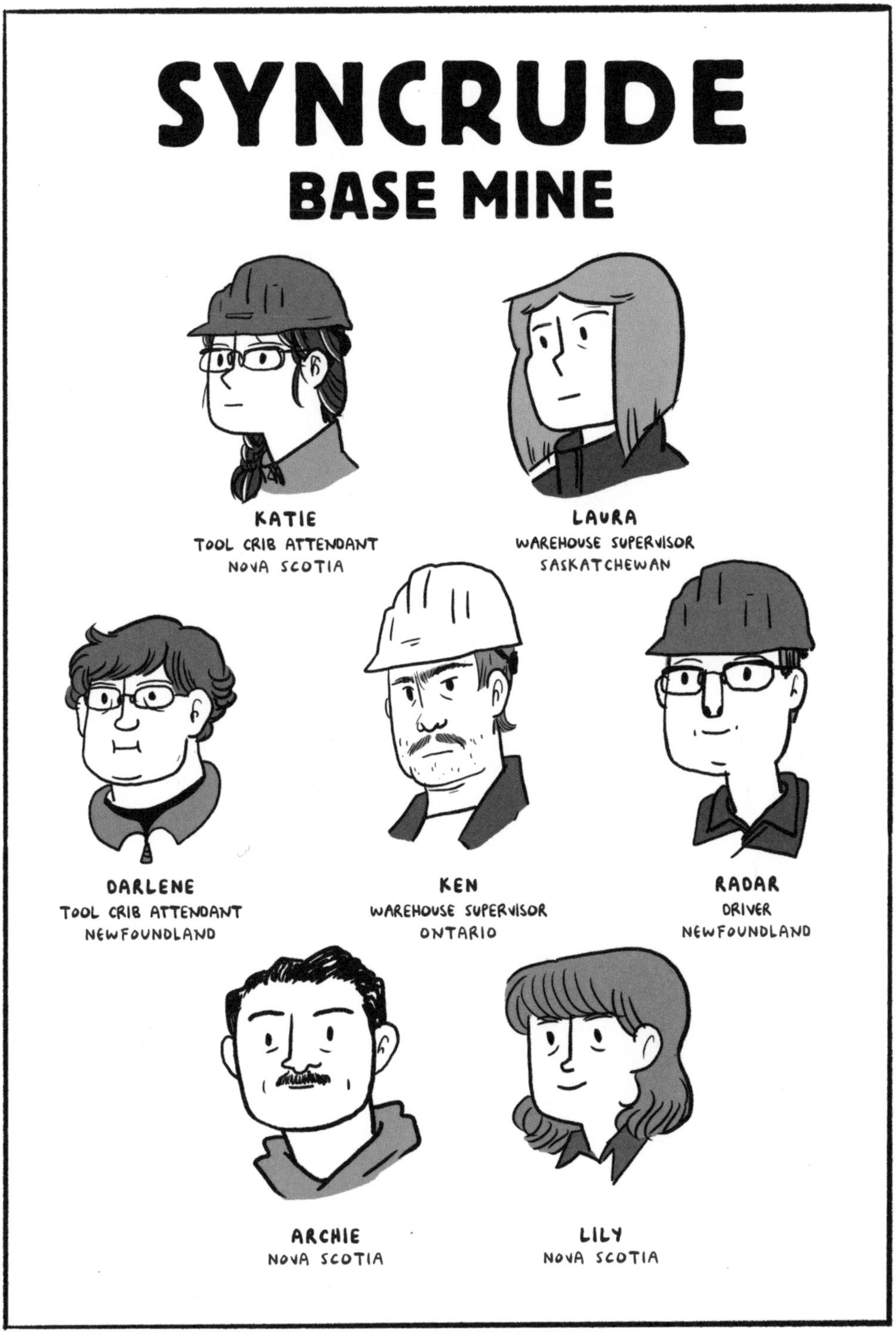
SYNCRUDE
BASE MINE
KATIE
TOOL CRIB ATTENDANT
NOVA SCOTIA
LAURA
WAREHOUSE SUPERVISOR
SASKATCHEWAN
DARLENE
TOOL CRIB ATTENDANT
NEWFOUNDLAND
KEN
WAREHOUSE SUPERVISOR
ONTARIO
RADAR
DRIVER
NEWFOUNDLAND
ARCHIE
NOVA SCOTIA
LILY
NOVA SCOTIA

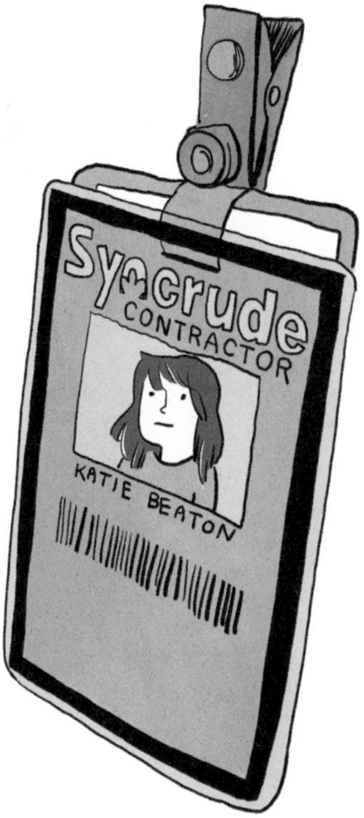

Syncrude
CONTRACTOR
KATIE BEATON

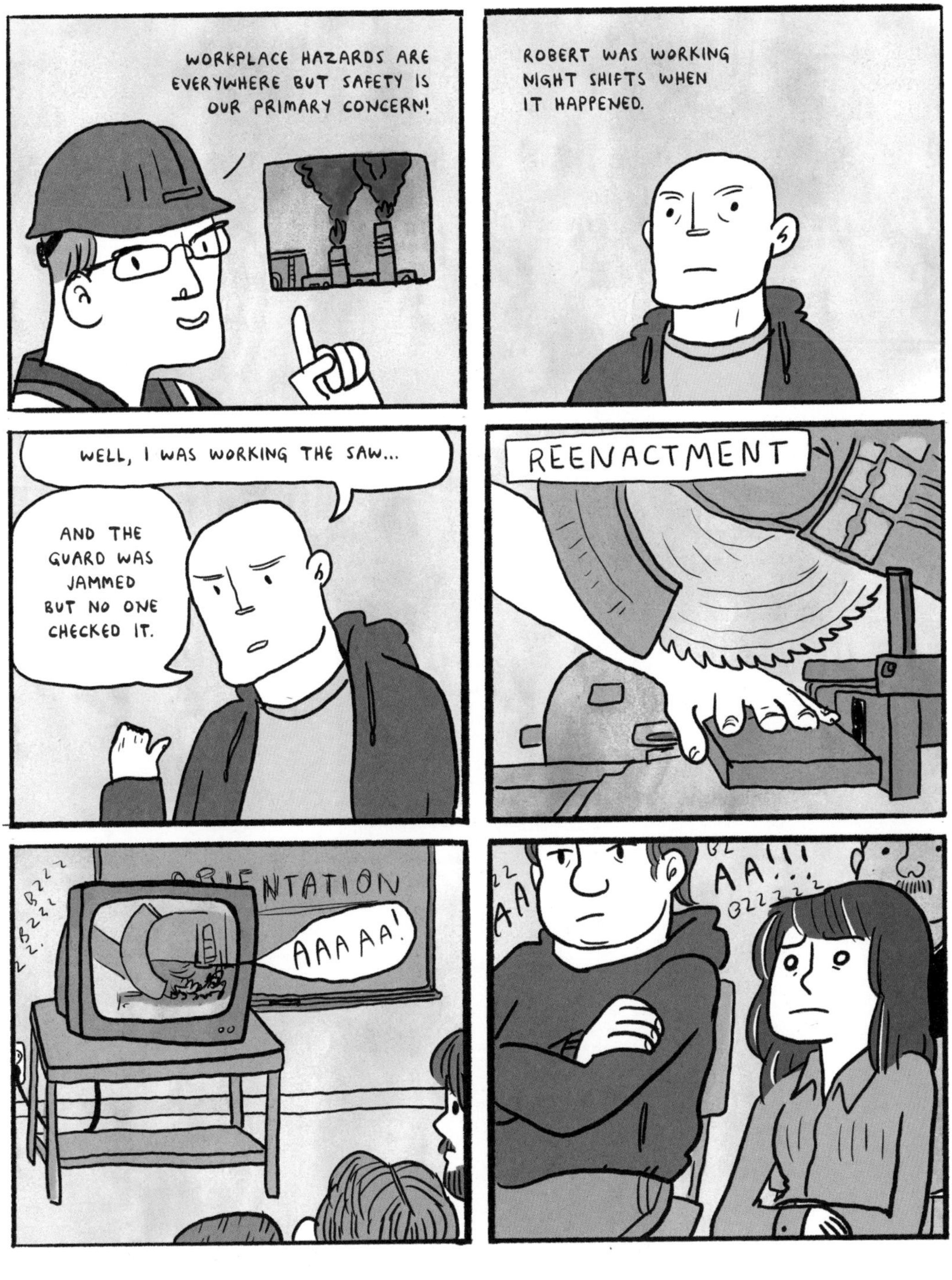

WORKPLACE HAZARDS ARE EVERYWHERE BUT SAFETY IS OUR PRIMARY CONCERN!
ROBERT WAS WORKING NIGHT SHIFTS WHEN IT HAPPENED.
WELL, I WAS WORKING THE SAW...
AND THE GUARD WAS JAMMED BUT NO ONE CHECKED IT.
REENACTMENT
ORIENTATION
AAAAA!
AA!!!

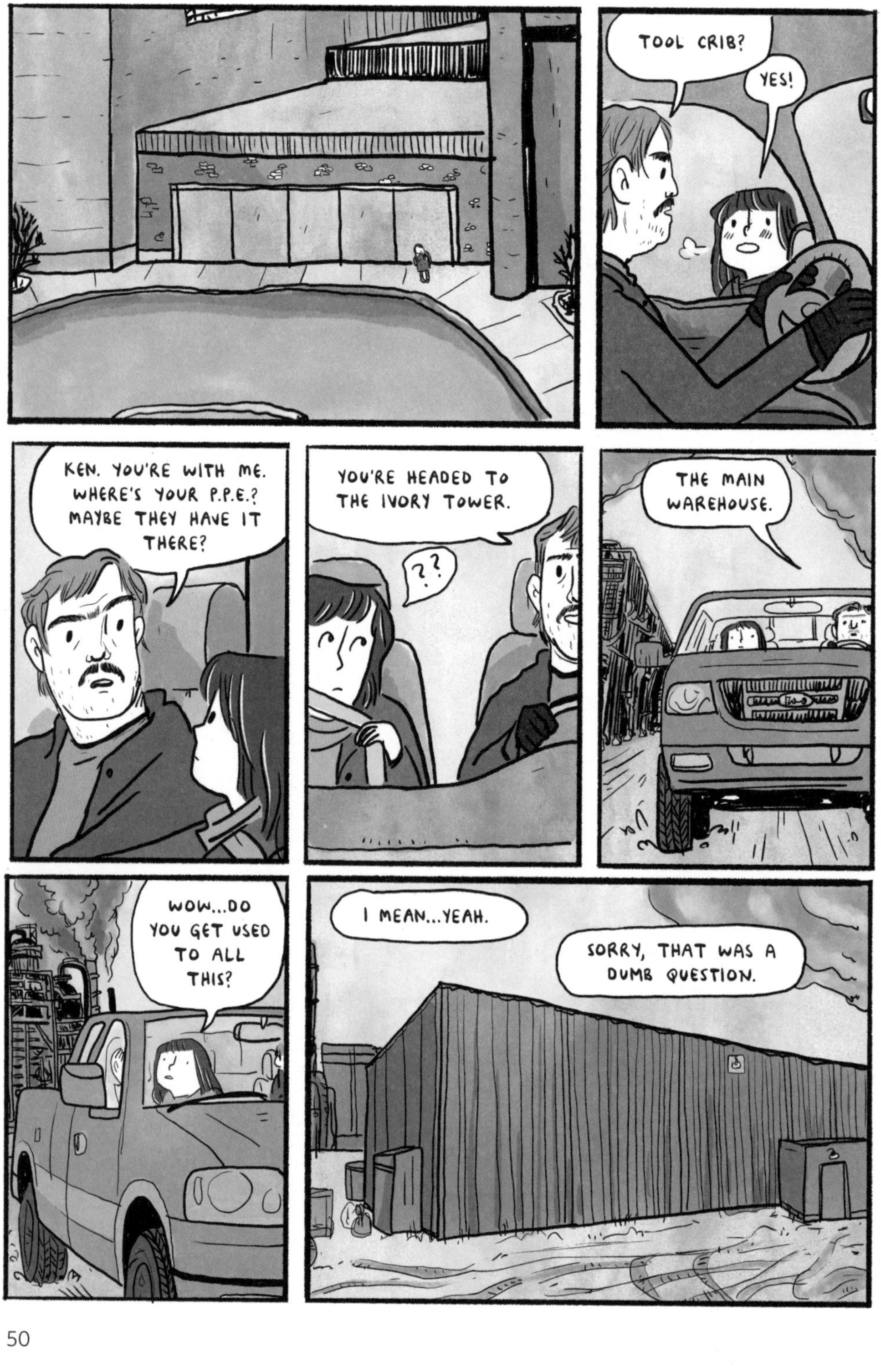
TOOL CRIB?
YES!
KEN. YOU'RE WITH ME. WHERE'S YOUR P.P.E.? MAYBE THEY HAVE IT THERE?
YOU'RE HEADED TO THE IVORY TOWER.
??
THE MAIN WAREHOUSE.
WOW...DO YOU GET USED TO ALL THIS?
I MEAN...YEAH.
SORRY, THAT WAS A DUMB QUESTION.

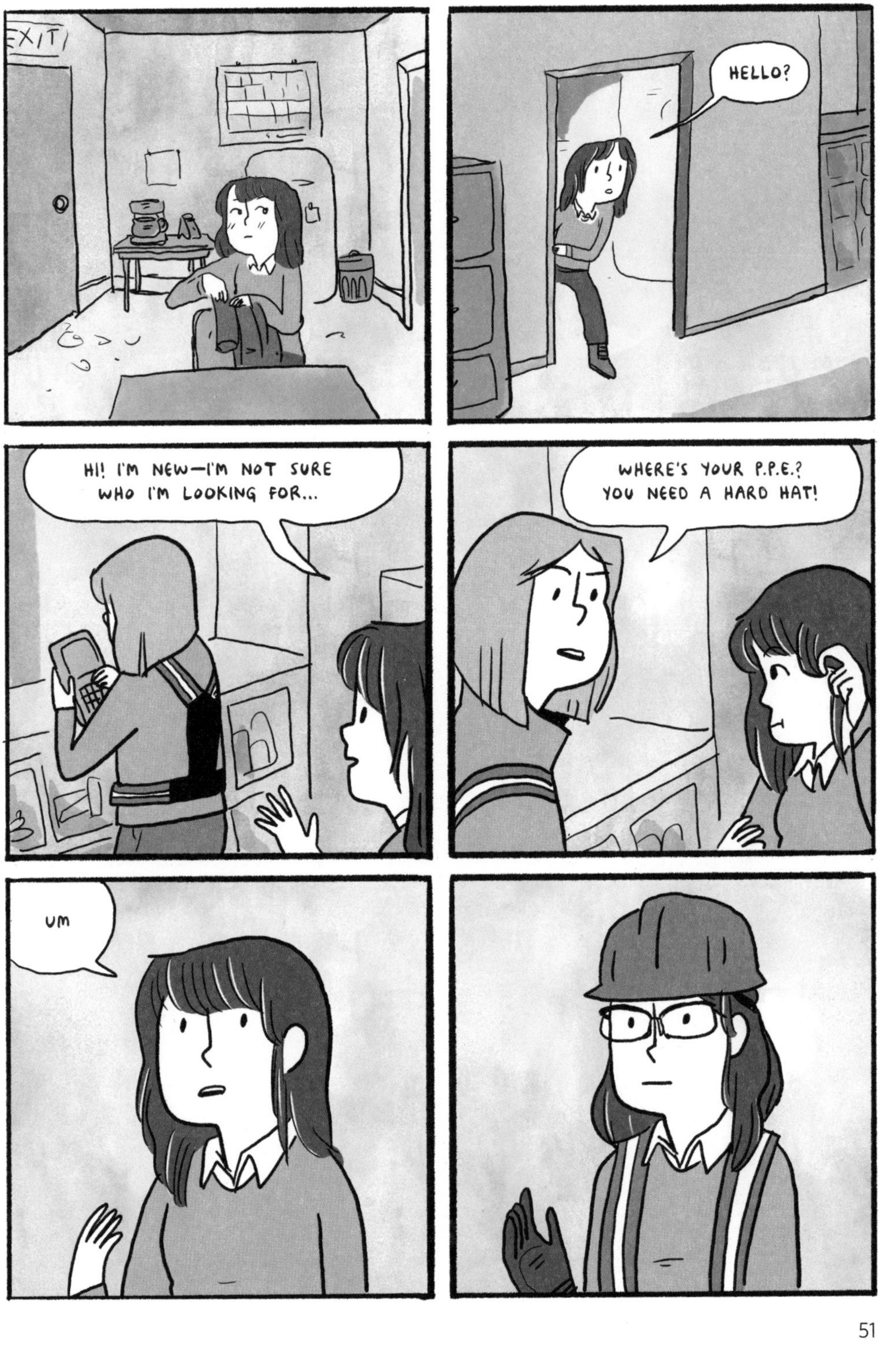
EXIT
HELLO?
HI! I'M NEW—I'M NOT SURE WHO I'M LOOKING FOR...
WHERE'S YOUR P.P.E.? YOU NEED A HARD HAT!
UM

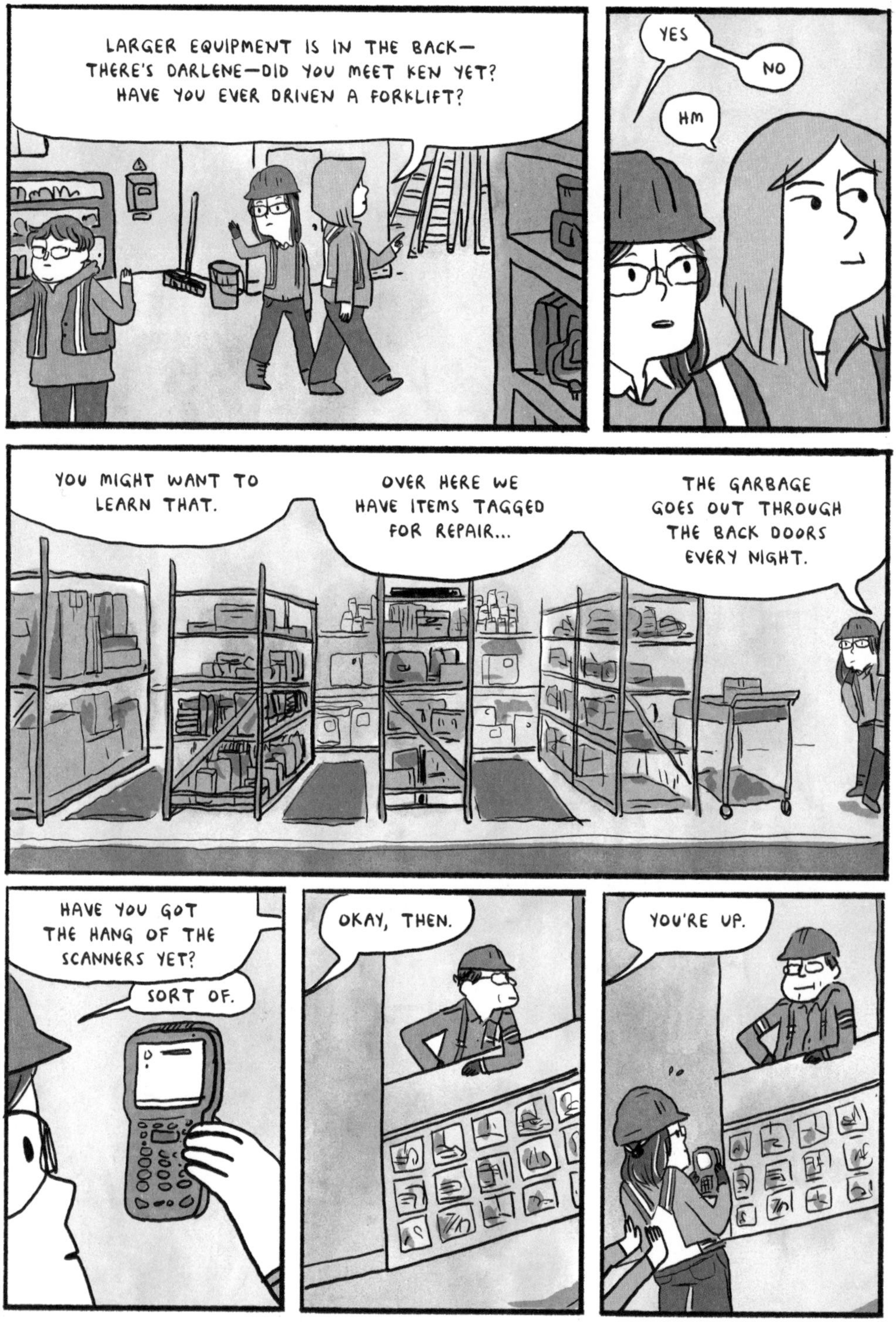
LARGER EQUIPMENT IS IN THE BACK— THERE'S DARLENE—DID YOU MEET KEN YET? HAVE YOU EVER DRIVEN A FORKLIFT?
YES
NO
HM
YOU MIGHT WANT TO LEARN THAT.
OVER HERE WE HAVE ITEMS TAGGED FOR REPAIR...
THE GARBAGE GOES OUT THROUGH THE BACK DOORS EVERY NIGHT.
HAVE YOU GOT THE HANG OF THE SCANNERS YET?
SORT OF.
OKAY, THEN.
YOU'RE UP.

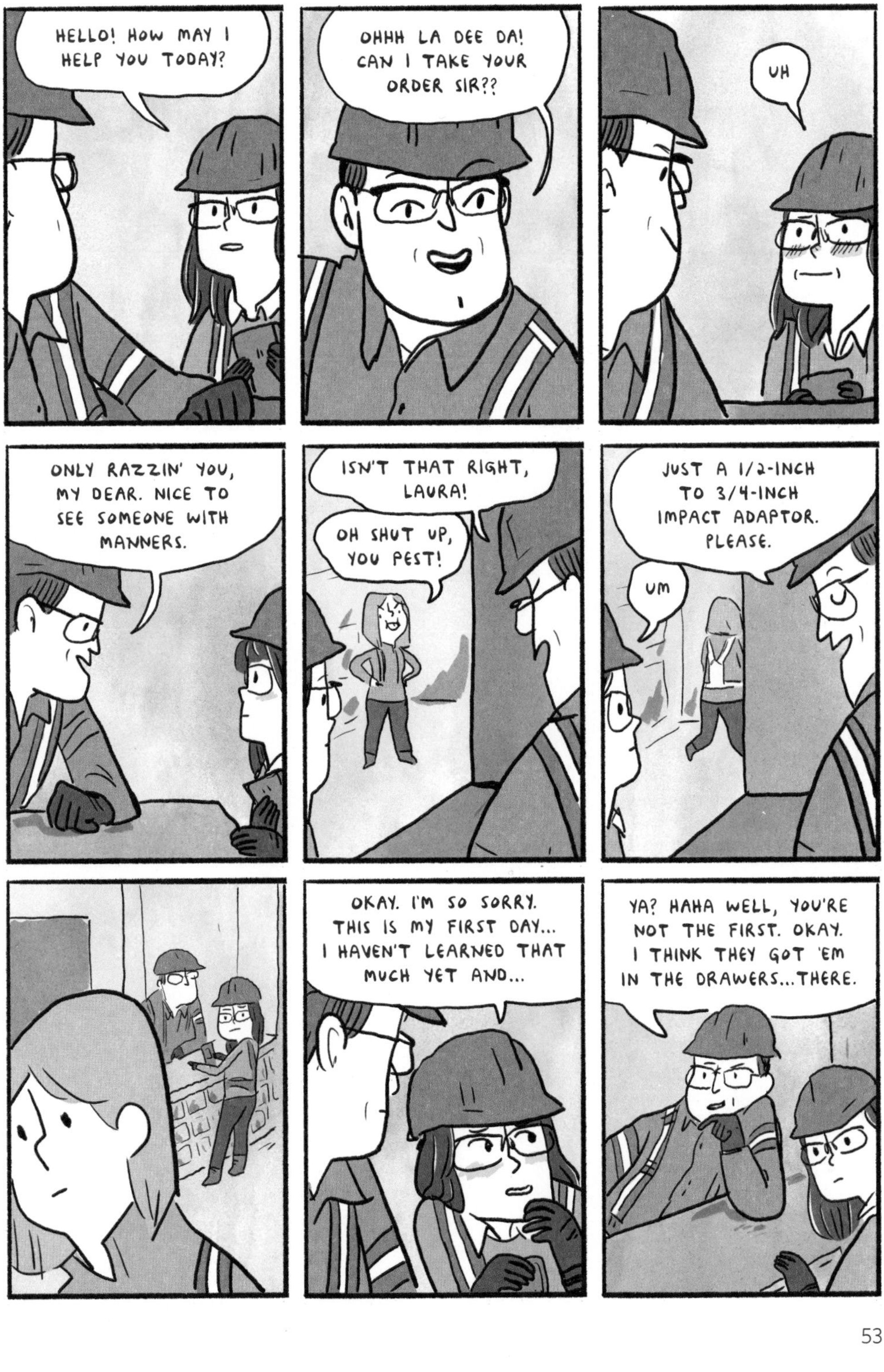

HELLO! HOW MAY I HELP YOU TODAY?
OHHH LA DEE DA! CAN I TAKE YOUR ORDER SIR??
UH
ONLY RAZZIN' YOU, MY DEAR. NICE TO SEE SOMEONE WITH MANNERS.
ISN'T THAT RIGHT, LAURA!
OH SHUT UP, YOU PEST!
JUST A 1/2-INCH TO 3/4-INCH IMPACT ADAPTOR. PLEASE.
UM
OKAY. I'M SO SORRY. THIS IS MY FIRST DAY... I HAVEN'T LEARNED THAT MUCH YET AND...
YA? HAHA WELL, YOU'RE NOT THE FIRST. OKAY. I THINK THEY GOT 'EM IN THE DRAWERS...THERE.

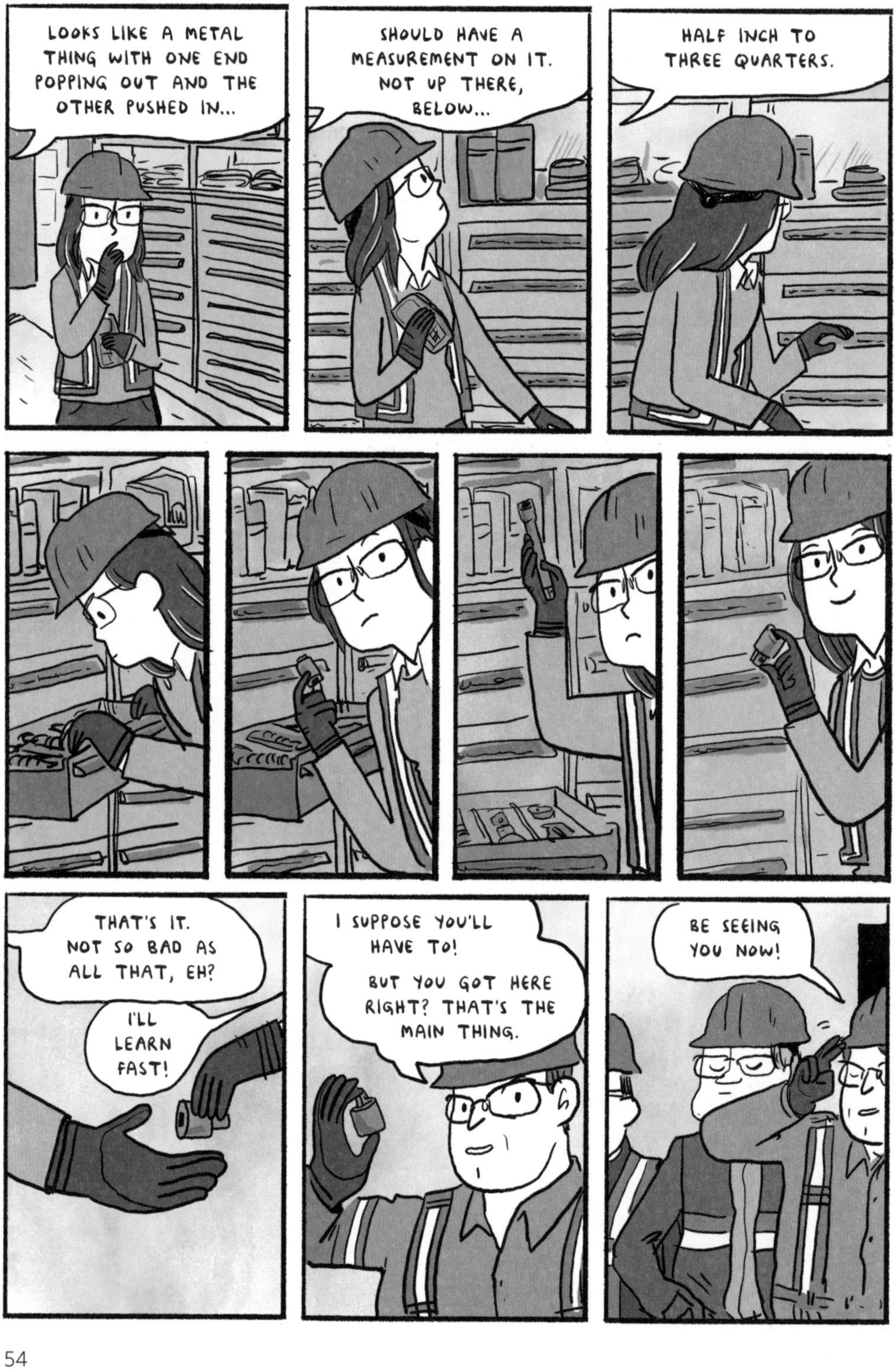
LOOKS LIKE A METAL THING WITH ONE END POPPING OUT AND THE OTHER PUSHED IN...
SHOULD HAVE A MEASUREMENT ON IT. NOT UP THERE, BELOW...
HALF INCH TO THREE QUARTERS.
THAT'S IT. NOT SO BAD AS ALL THAT, EH?
I'LL LEARN FAST!
I SUPPOSE YOU'LL HAVE TO!
BUT YOU GOT HERE RIGHT? THAT'S THE MAIN THING.
BE SEEING YOU NOW!

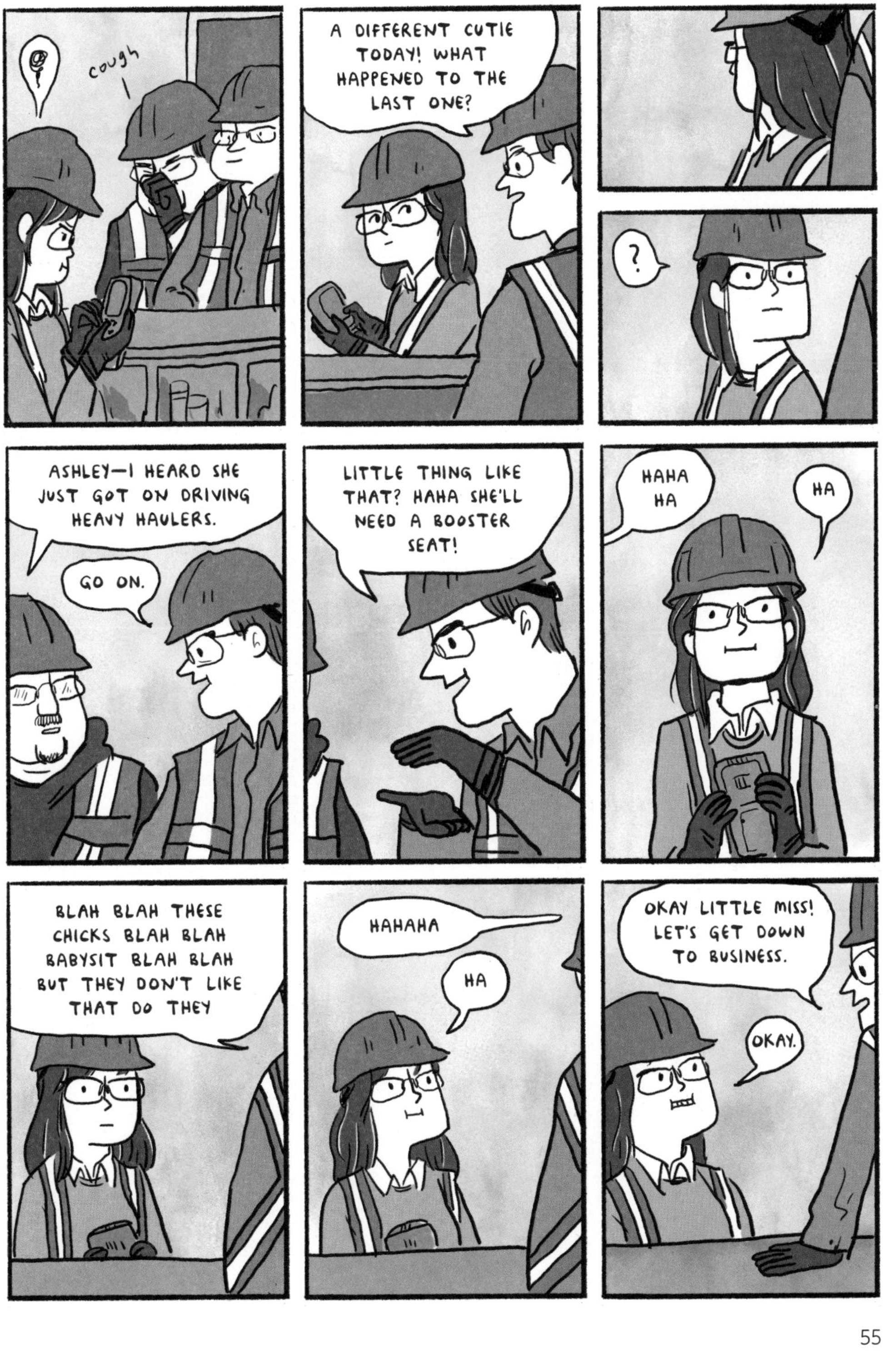
cough
A DIFFERENT CUTIE TODAY! WHAT HAPPENED TO THE LAST ONE?
?
ASHLEY—I HEARD SHE JUST GOT ON DRIVING HEAVY HAULERS.
GO ON.
LITTLE THING LIKE THAT? HAHA SHE'LL NEED A BOOSTER SEAT!
HAHA HA
HA
BLAH BLAH THESE CHICKS BLAH BLAH BABYSIT BLAH BLAH BUT THEY DON'T LIKE THAT DO THEY
HAHAHA
HA
OKAY LITTLE MISS! LET'S GET DOWN TO BUSINESS.
OKAY.

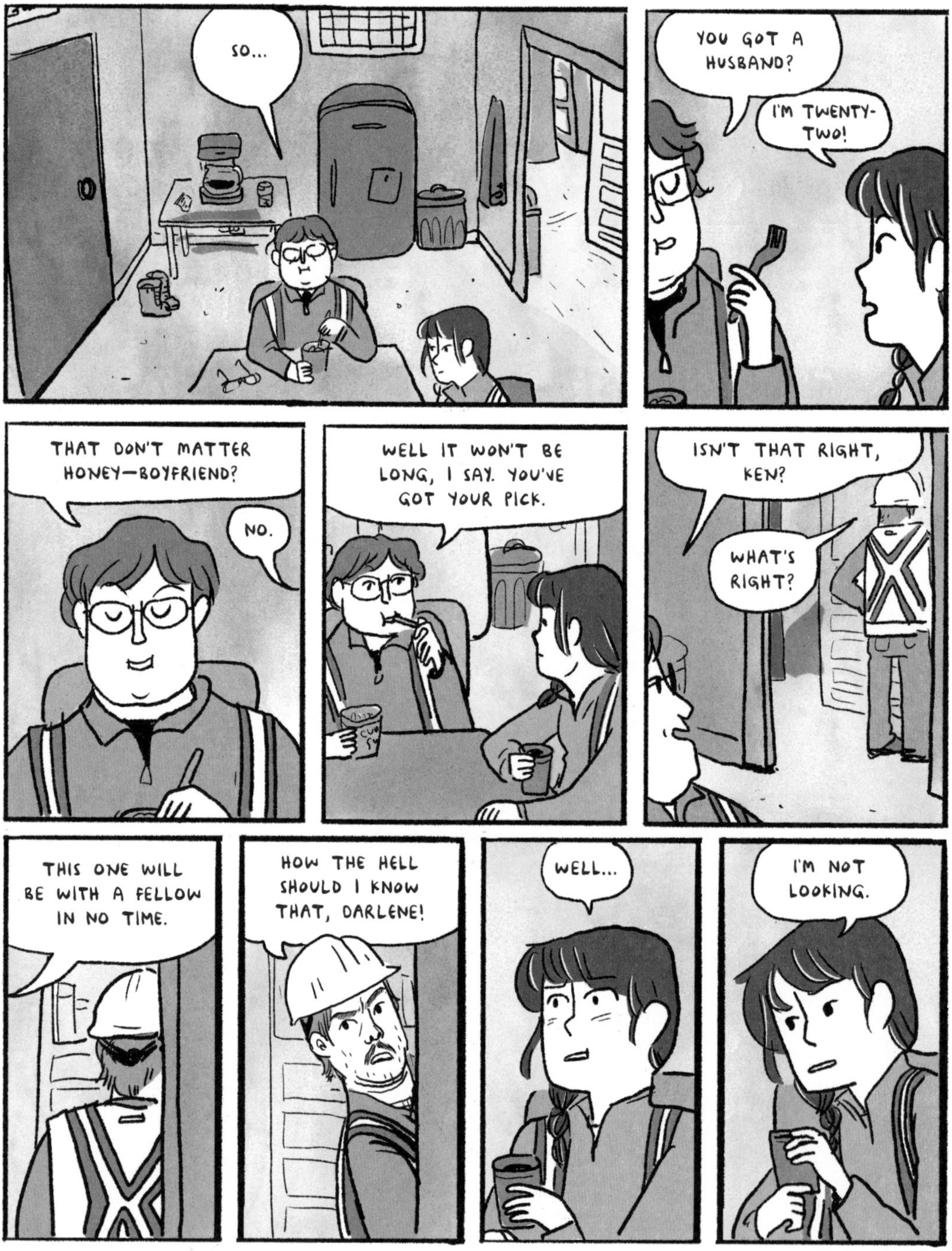
SO...
YOU GOT A HUSBAND?
I'M TWENTY-TWO!
THAT DON'T MATTER HONEY—BOYFRIEND?
NO.
WELL IT WON'T BE LONG, I SAY. YOU'VE GOT YOUR PICK.
ISN'T THAT RIGHT, KEN?
WHAT'S RIGHT?
THIS ONE WILL BE WITH A FELLOW IN NO TIME.
HOW THE HELL SHOULD I KNOW THAT, DARLENE!
WELL...
I'M NOT LOOKING.

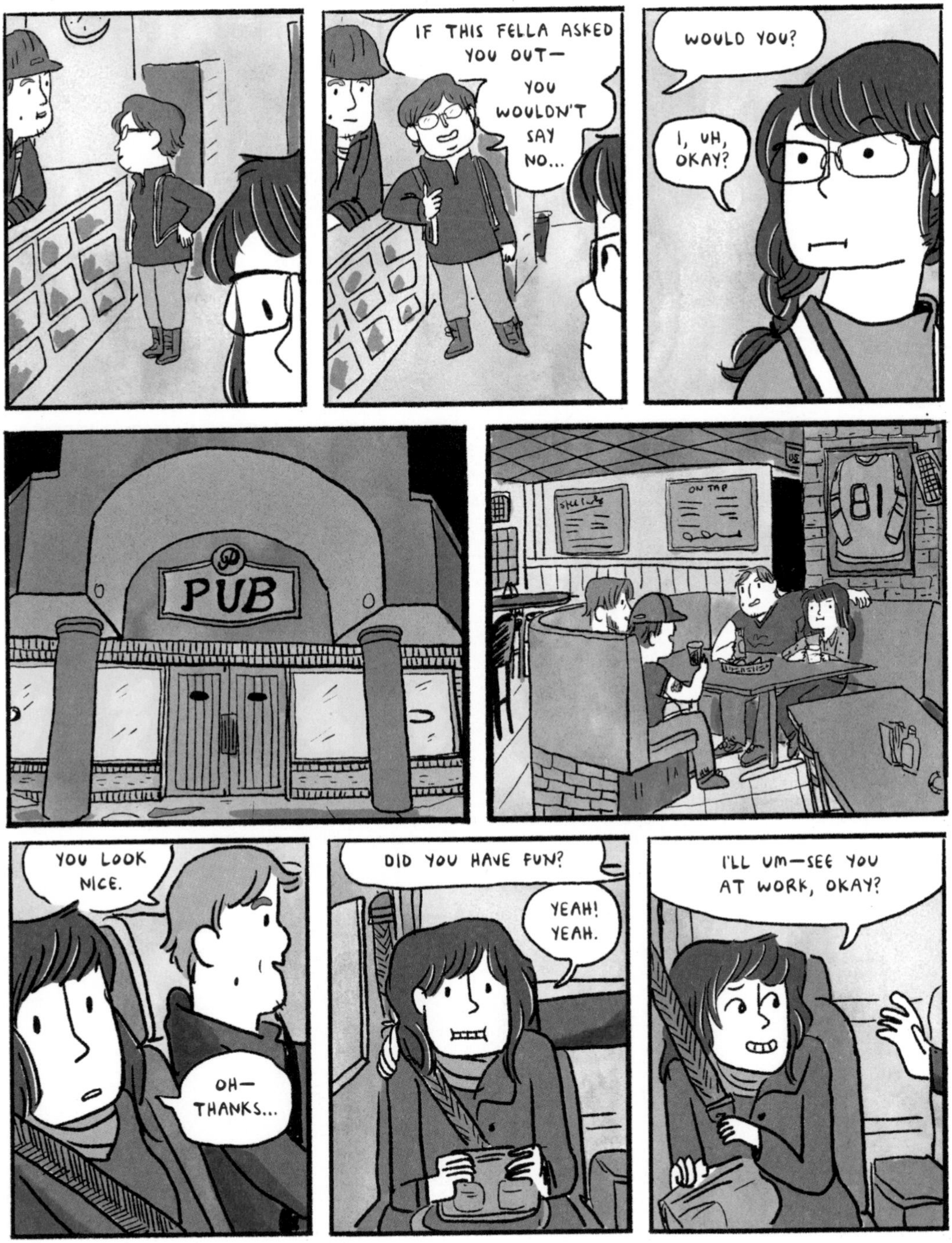
IF THIS FELLA ASKED YOU OUT—
YOU WOULDN'T SAY NO...
WOULD YOU?
I, UH, OKAY?
PUB
ON TAP
81
YOU LOOK NICE.
OH—THANKS...
DID YOU HAVE FUN?
YEAH! YEAH.
I'LL UM—SEE YOU AT WORK, OKAY?

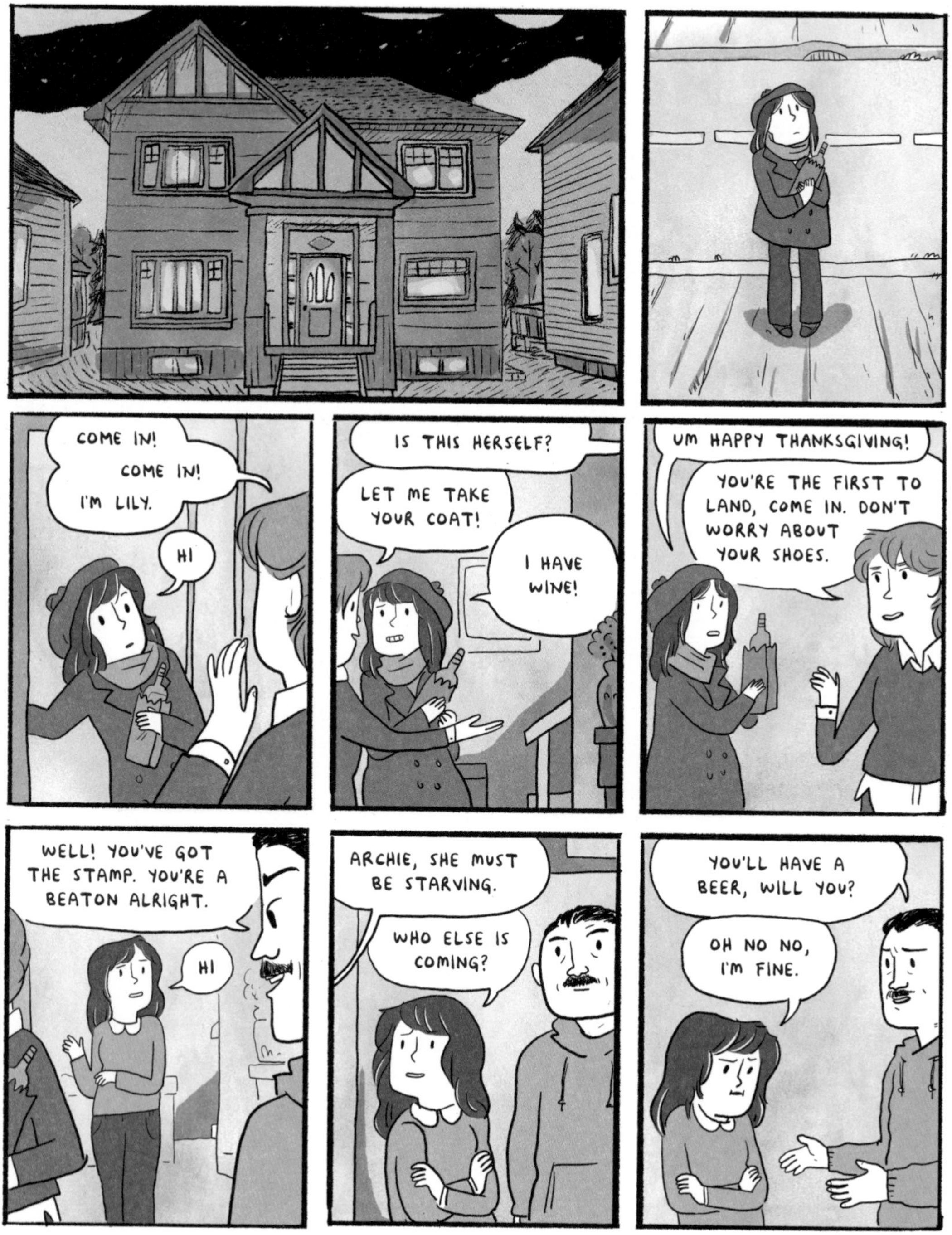
COME IN! COME IN! I'M LILY.
HI
IS THIS HERSELF?
LET ME TAKE YOUR COAT!
I HAVE WINE!
UM HAPPY THANKSGIVING!
YOU'RE THE FIRST TO LAND, COME IN. DON'T WORRY ABOUT YOUR SHOES.
WELL! YOU'VE GOT THE STAMP. YOU'RE A BEATON ALRIGHT.
HI
ARCHIE, SHE MUST BE STARVING.
WHO ELSE IS COMING?
YOU'LL HAVE A BEER, WILL YOU?
OH NO NO, I'M FINE.

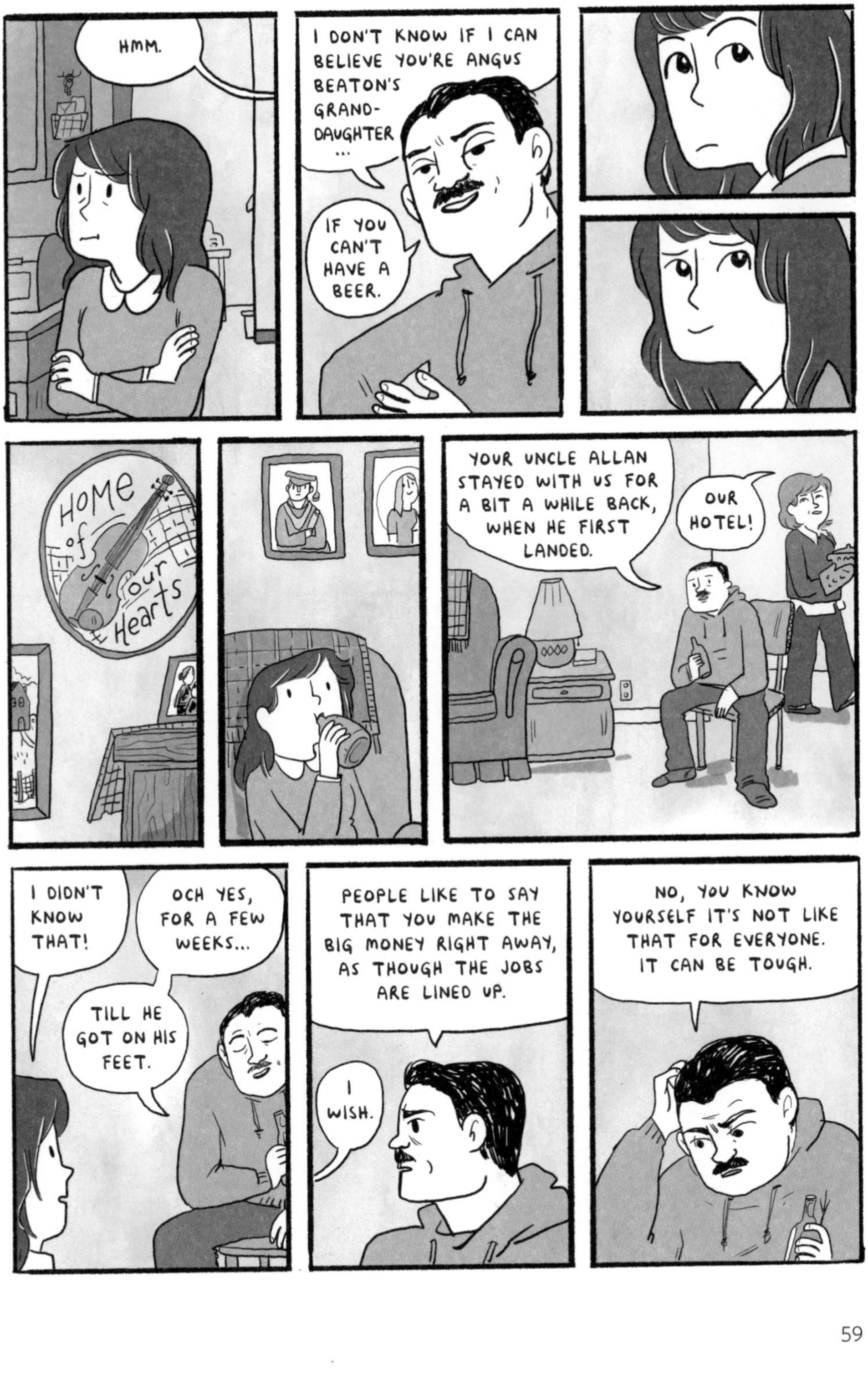
HMM.
I DON'T KNOW IF I CAN BELIEVE YOU'RE ANGUS BEATON'S GRAND-DAUGHTER ...
IF YOU CAN'T HAVE A BEER.
HOME of our Hearts
YOUR UNCLE ALLAN STAYED WITH US FOR A BIT A WHILE BACK, WHEN HE FIRST LANDED.
OUR HOTEL!
I DIDN'T KNOW THAT!
OCH YES, FOR A FEW WEEKS...
TILL HE GOT ON HIS FEET.
PEOPLE LIKE TO SAY THAT YOU MAKE THE BIG MONEY RIGHT AWAY, AS THOUGH THE JOBS ARE LINED UP.
I WISH.
NO, YOU KNOW YOURSELF IT'S NOT LIKE THAT FOR EVERYONE. IT CAN BE TOUGH.

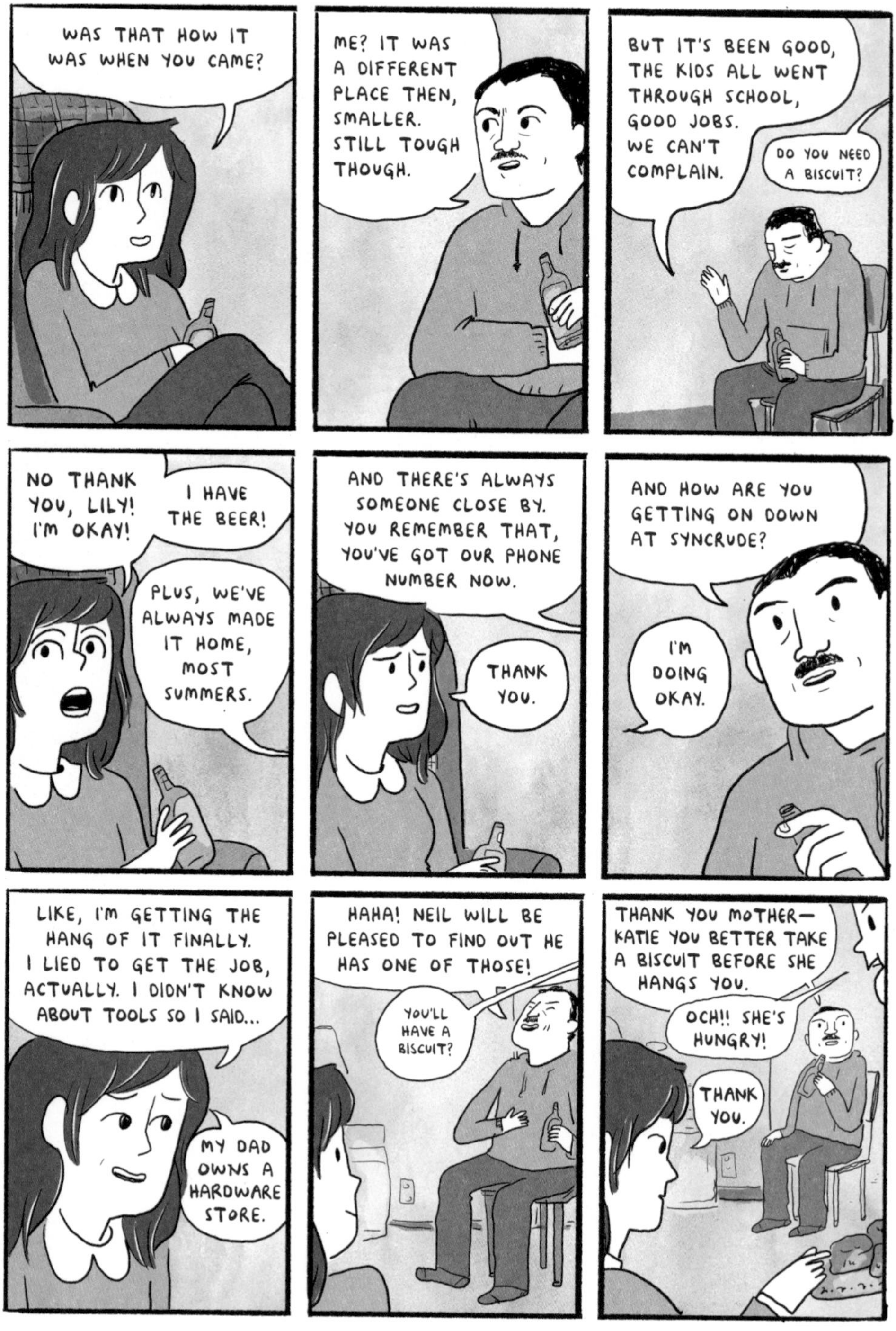
WAS THAT HOW IT WAS WHEN YOU CAME?
ME? IT WAS A DIFFERENT PLACE THEN, SMALLER. STILL TOUGH THOUGH.
BUT IT'S BEEN GOOD, THE KIDS ALL WENT THROUGH SCHOOL, GOOD JOBS. WE CAN'T COMPLAIN.
DO YOU NEED A BISCUIT?
NO THANK YOU, LILY! I'M OKAY!
I HAVE THE BEER!
PLUS, WE'VE ALWAYS MADE IT HOME, MOST SUMMERS.
AND THERE'S ALWAYS SOMEONE CLOSE BY. YOU REMEMBER THAT, YOU'VE GOT OUR PHONE NUMBER NOW.
THANK YOU.
AND HOW ARE YOU GETTING ON DOWN AT SYNCRUDE?
I'M DOING OKAY.
LIKE, I'M GETTING THE HANG OF IT FINALLY. I LIED TO GET THE JOB, ACTUALLY. I DIDN'T KNOW ABOUT TOOLS SO I SAID...
MY DAD OWNS A HARDWARE STORE.
HAHA! NEIL WILL BE PLEASED TO FIND OUT HE HAS ONE OF THOSE!
YOU'LL HAVE A BISCUIT?
THANK YOU MOTHER—KATIE YOU BETTER TAKE A BISCUIT BEFORE SHE HANGS YOU.
OCH!! SHE'S HUNGRY!
THANK YOU.

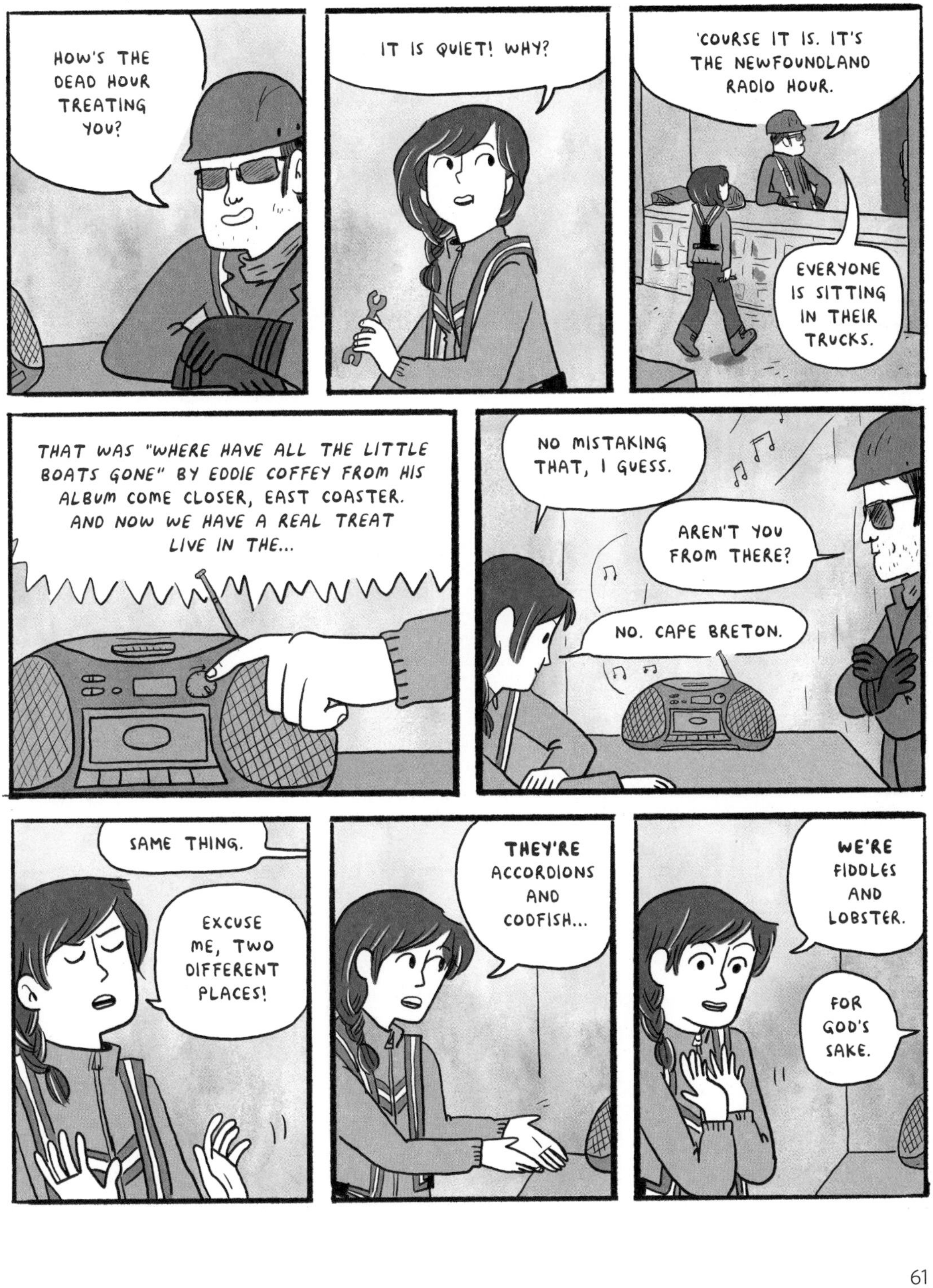
HOW'S THE DEAD HOUR TREATING YOU?
IT IS QUIET! WHY?
'COURSE IT IS. IT'S THE NEWFOUNDLAND RADIO HOUR.
EVERYONE IS SITTING IN THEIR TRUCKS.
THAT WAS "WHERE HAVE ALL THE LITTLE BOATS GONE" BY EDDIE COFFEY FROM HIS ALBUM COME CLOSER, EAST COASTER. AND NOW WE HAVE A REAL TREAT LIVE IN THE...
NO MISTAKING THAT, I GUESS.
AREN'T YOU FROM THERE?
NO. CAPE BRETON.
SAME THING.
EXCUSE ME, TWO DIFFERENT PLACES!
THEY'RE ACCORDIONS AND CODFISH...
WE'RE FIDDLES AND LOBSTER.
FOR GOD'S SAKE.

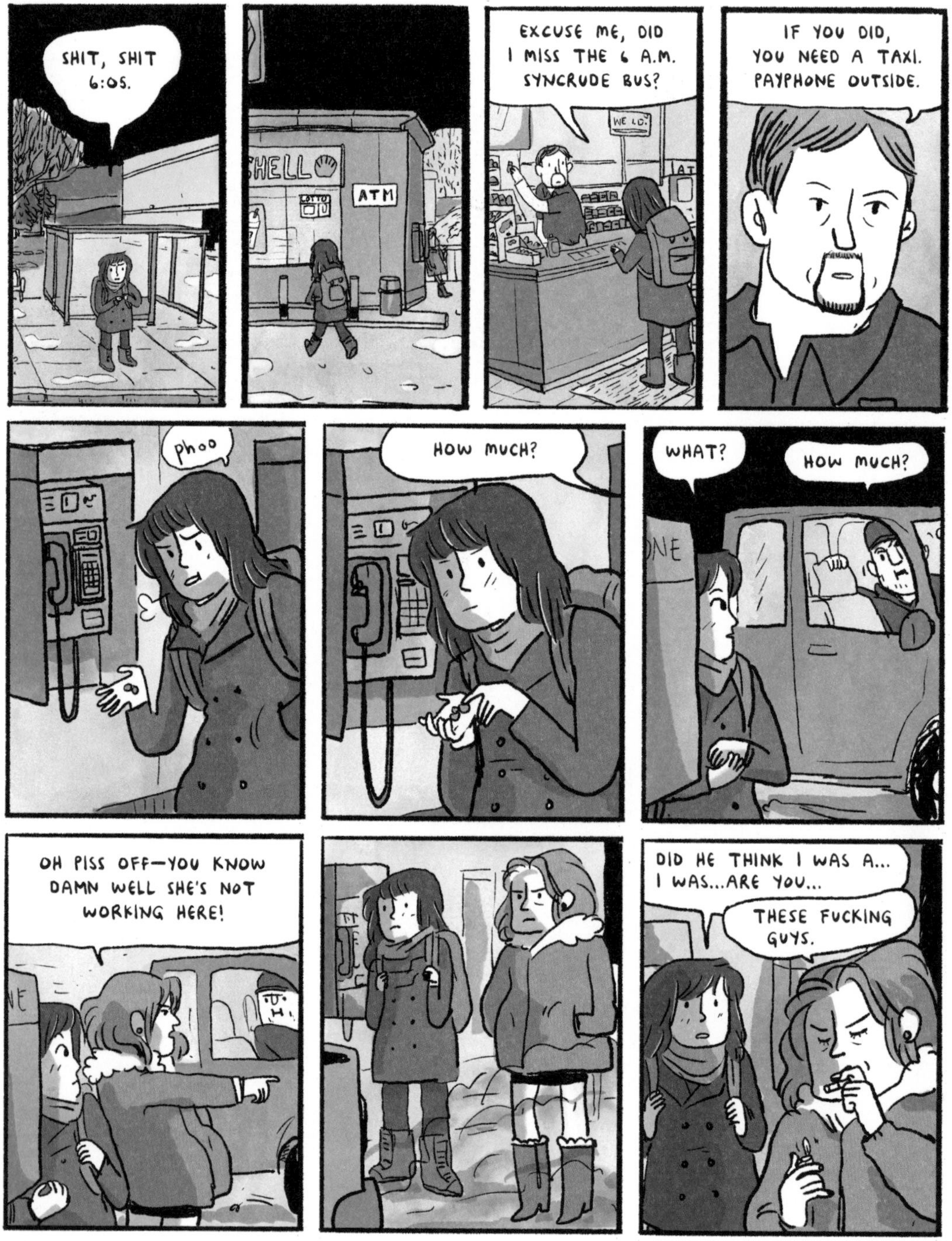
SHIT, SHIT 6:05.
SHELL
LOTTO
ATM
EXCUSE ME, DID I MISS THE 6 A.M. SYNCRUDE BUS?
IF YOU DID, YOU NEED A TAXI. PAYPHONE OUTSIDE.
phoo
HOW MUCH?
WHAT?
HOW MUCH?
OH PISS OFF—YOU KNOW DAMN WELL SHE'S NOT WORKING HERE!
DID HE THINK I WAS A... I WAS...ARE YOU...
THESE FUCKING GUYS.

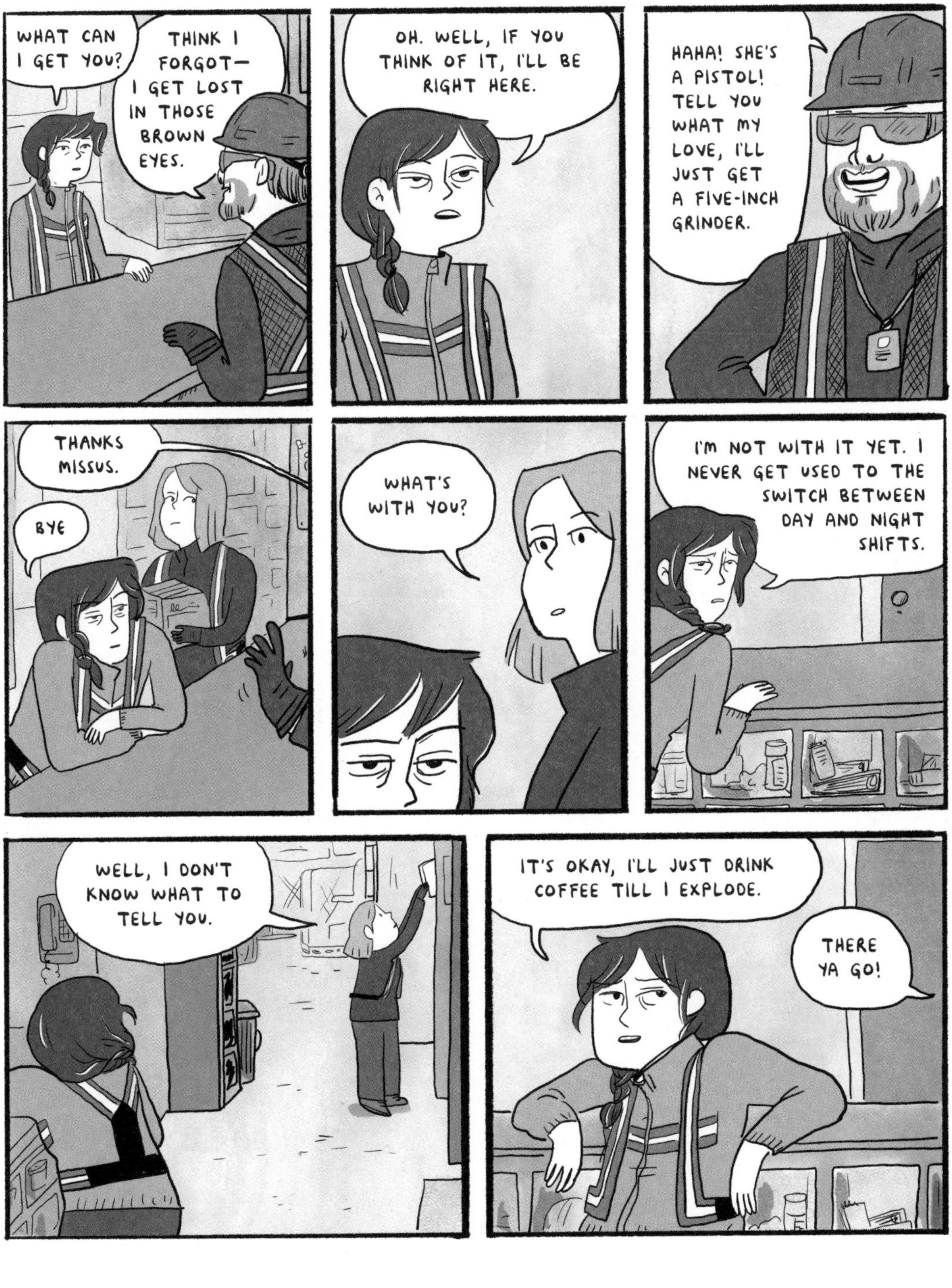
WHAT CAN I GET YOU?
THINK I FORGOT— I GET LOST IN THOSE BROWN EYES.
OH. WELL, IF YOU THINK OF IT, I'LL BE RIGHT HERE.
HAHA! SHE'S A PISTOL! TELL YOU WHAT MY LOVE, I'LL JUST GET A FIVE-INCH GRINDER.
THANKS MISSUS.
BYE
WHAT'S WITH YOU?
I'M NOT WITH IT YET. I NEVER GET USED TO THE SWITCH BETWEEN DAY AND NIGHT SHIFTS.
WELL, I DON'T KNOW WHAT TO TELL YOU.
IT'S OKAY, I'LL JUST DRINK COFFEE TILL I EXPLODE.
THERE YA GO!

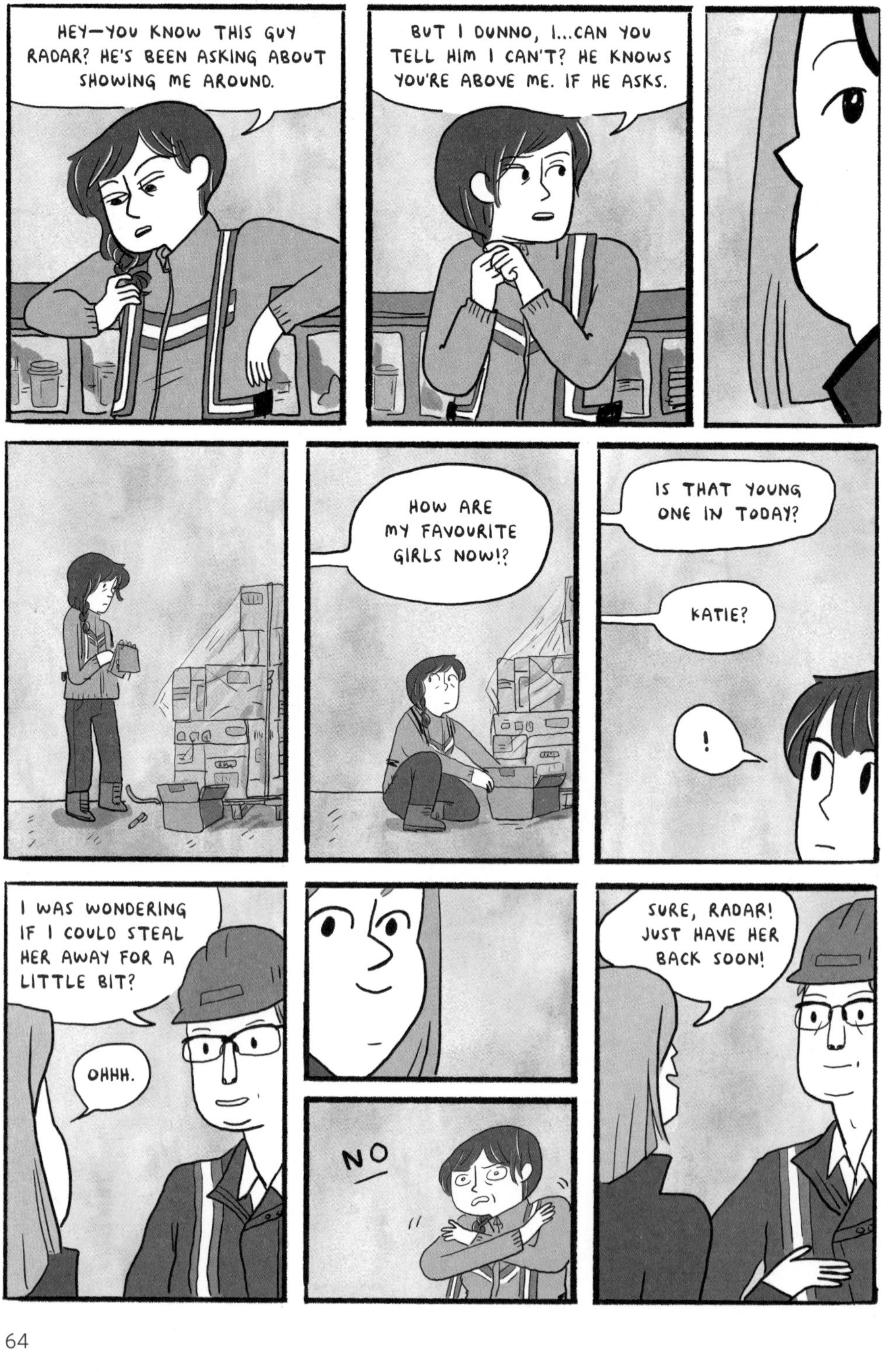
HEY—YOU KNOW THIS GUY RADAR? HE'S BEEN ASKING ABOUT SHOWING ME AROUND.
BUT I DUNNO, I...CAN YOU TELL HIM I CAN'T? HE KNOWS YOU'RE ABOVE ME. IF HE ASKS.
HOW ARE MY FAVOURITE GIRLS NOW!?
IS THAT YOUNG ONE IN TODAY?
KATIE?
!
I WAS WONDERING IF I COULD STEAL HER AWAY FOR A LITTLE BIT?
OHHH.
NO
SURE, RADAR! JUST HAVE HER BACK SOON!

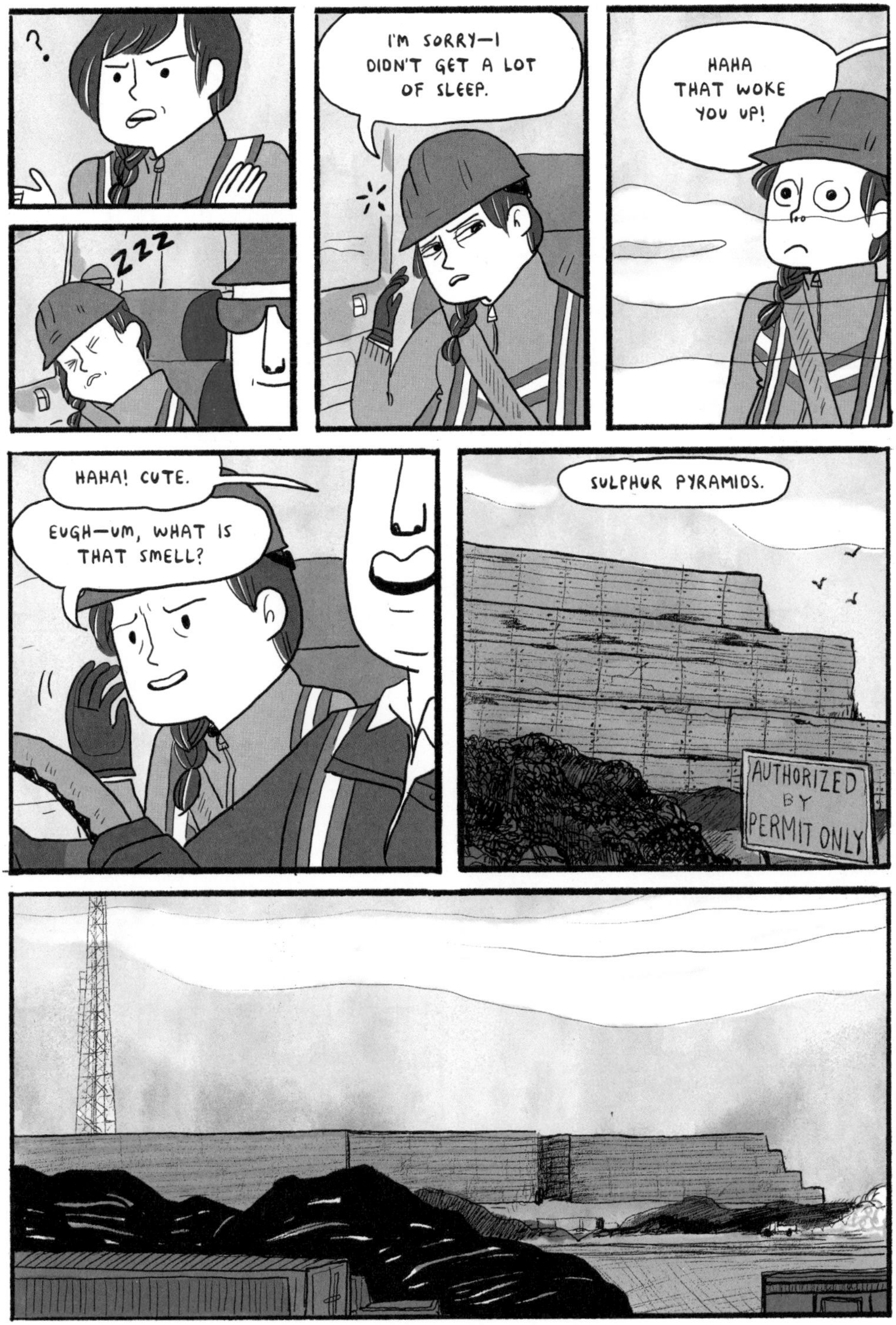
?
ZZZ
I'M SORRY—I DIDN'T GET A LOT OF SLEEP.
HAHA THAT WOKE YOU UP!
HAHA! CUTE.
EUGH—UM, WHAT IS THAT SMELL?
SULPHUR PYRAMIDS.
AUTHORIZED BY PERMIT ONLY

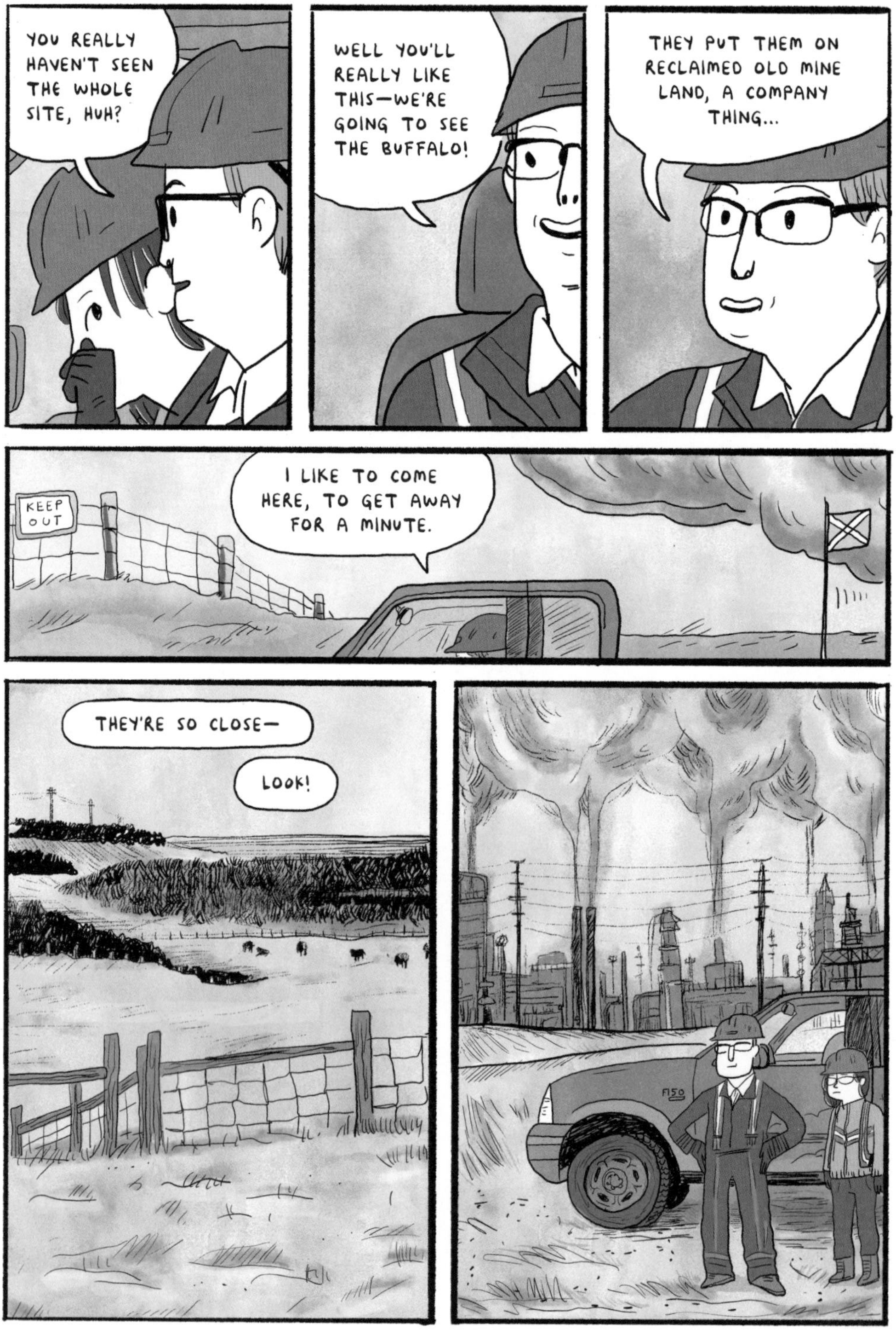
YOU REALLY HAVEN'T SEEN THE WHOLE SITE, HUH?
WELL YOU'LL REALLY LIKE THIS—WE'RE GOING TO SEE THE BUFFALO!
THEY PUT THEM ON RECLAIMED OLD MINE LAND, A COMPANY THING...
KEEP OUT
I LIKE TO COME HERE, TO GET AWAY FOR A MINUTE.
THEY'RE SO CLOSE—
LOOK!
F150

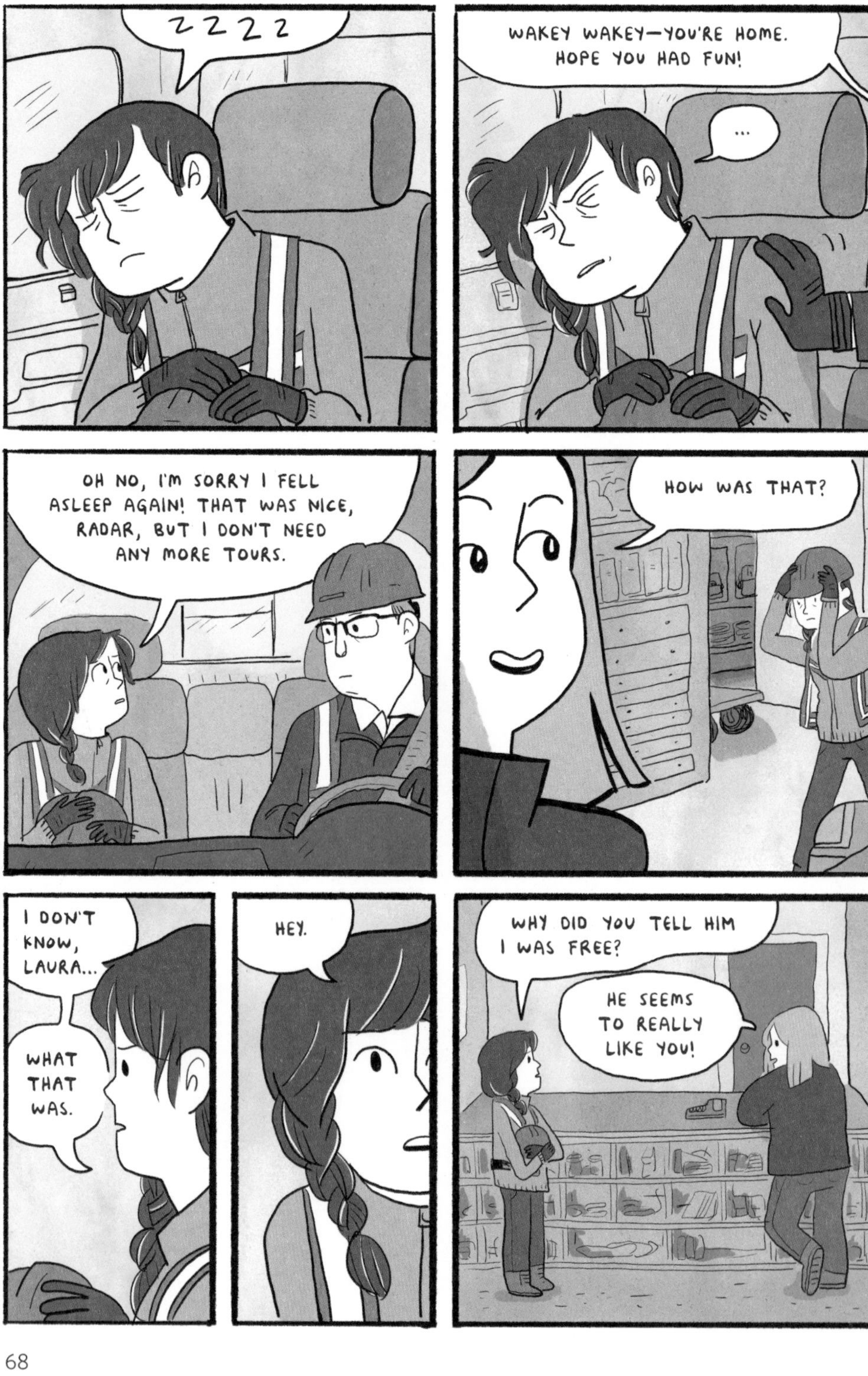
ZZZZ
WAKEY WAKEY—YOU'RE HOME. HOPE YOU HAD FUN!
...
OH NO, I'M SORRY I FELL ASLEEP AGAIN! THAT WAS NICE, RADAR, BUT I DON'T NEED ANY MORE TOURS.
HOW WAS THAT?
I DON'T KNOW, LAURA...
WHAT THAT WAS.
HEY.
WHY DID YOU TELL HIM I WAS FREE?
HE SEEMS TO REALLY LIKE YOU!

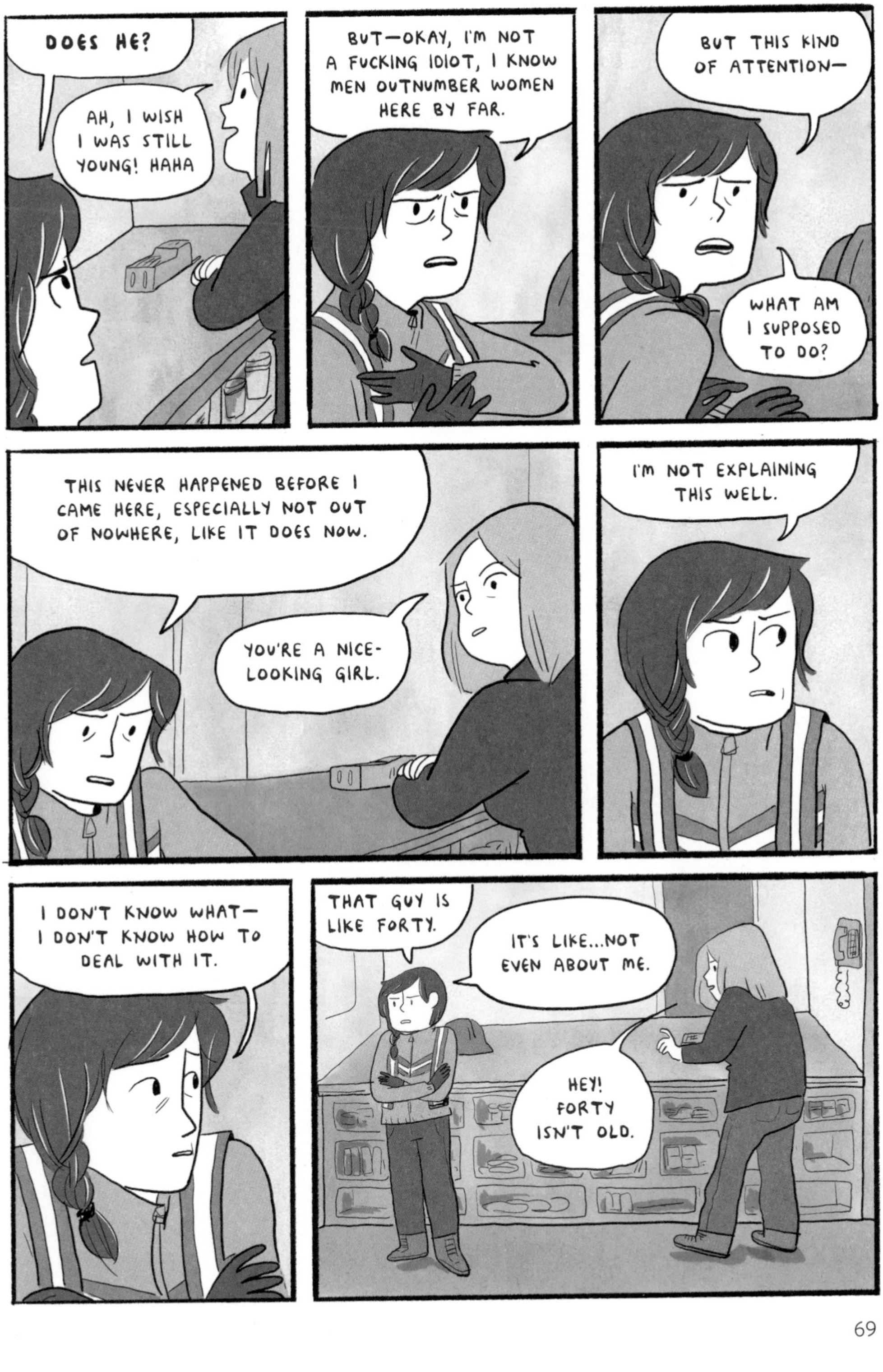
DOES HE?
AH, I WISH I WAS STILL YOUNG! HAHA
BUT—OKAY, I'M NOT A FUCKING IDIOT, I KNOW MEN OUTNUMBER WOMEN HERE BY FAR.
BUT THIS KIND OF ATTENTION—
WHAT AM I SUPPOSED TO DO?
THIS NEVER HAPPENED BEFORE I CAME HERE, ESPECIALLY NOT OUT OF NOWHERE, LIKE IT DOES NOW.
YOU'RE A NICE-LOOKING GIRL.
I'M NOT EXPLAINING THIS WELL.
I DON'T KNOW WHAT—I DON'T KNOW HOW TO DEAL WITH IT.
THAT GUY IS LIKE FORTY.
IT'S LIKE...NOT EVEN ABOUT ME.
HEY! FORTY ISN'T OLD.

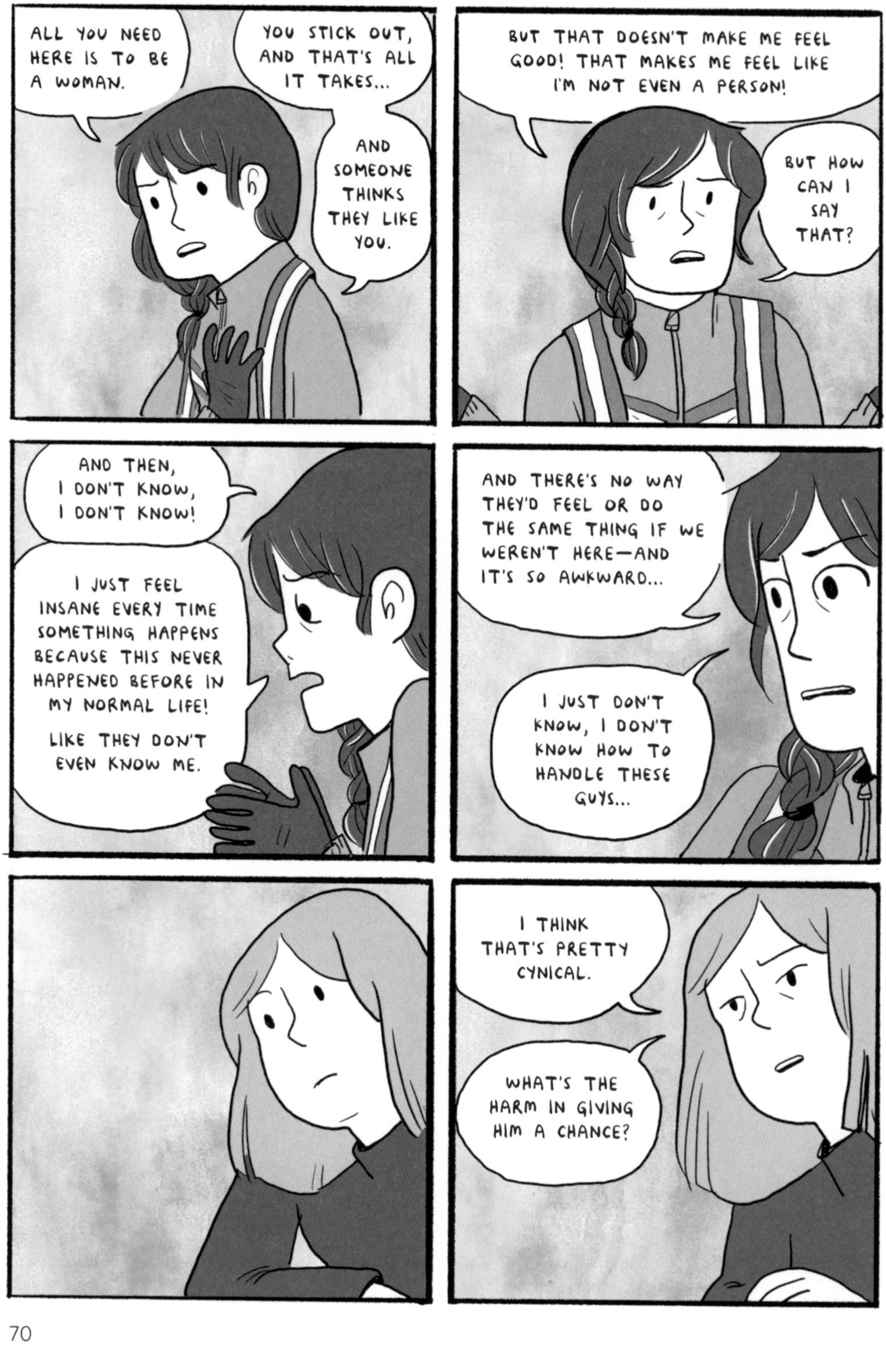
ALL YOU NEED HERE IS TO BE A WOMAN.
YOU STICK OUT, AND THAT'S ALL IT TAKES...
AND SOMEONE THINKS THEY LIKE YOU.
BUT THAT DOESN'T MAKE ME FEEL GOOD! THAT MAKES ME FEEL LIKE I'M NOT EVEN A PERSON!
BUT HOW CAN I SAY THAT?
AND THEN, I DON'T KNOW, I DON'T KNOW!
I JUST FEEL INSANE EVERY TIME SOMETHING HAPPENS BECAUSE THIS NEVER HAPPENED BEFORE IN MY NORMAL LIFE!
LIKE THEY DON'T EVEN KNOW ME.
AND THERE'S NO WAY THEY'D FEEL OR DO THE SAME THING IF WE WEREN'T HERE—AND IT'S SO AWKWARD...
I JUST DON'T KNOW, I DON'T KNOW HOW TO HANDLE THESE GUYS...
I THINK THAT'S PRETTY CYNICAL.
WHAT'S THE HARM IN GIVING HIM A CHANCE?

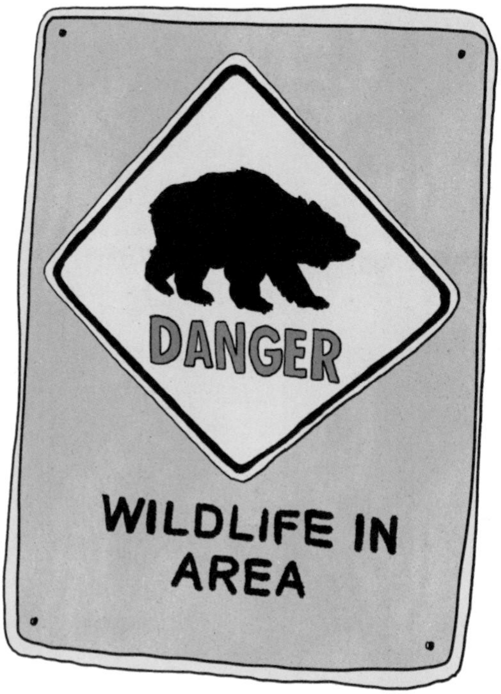
DANGER
WILDLIFE IN AREA

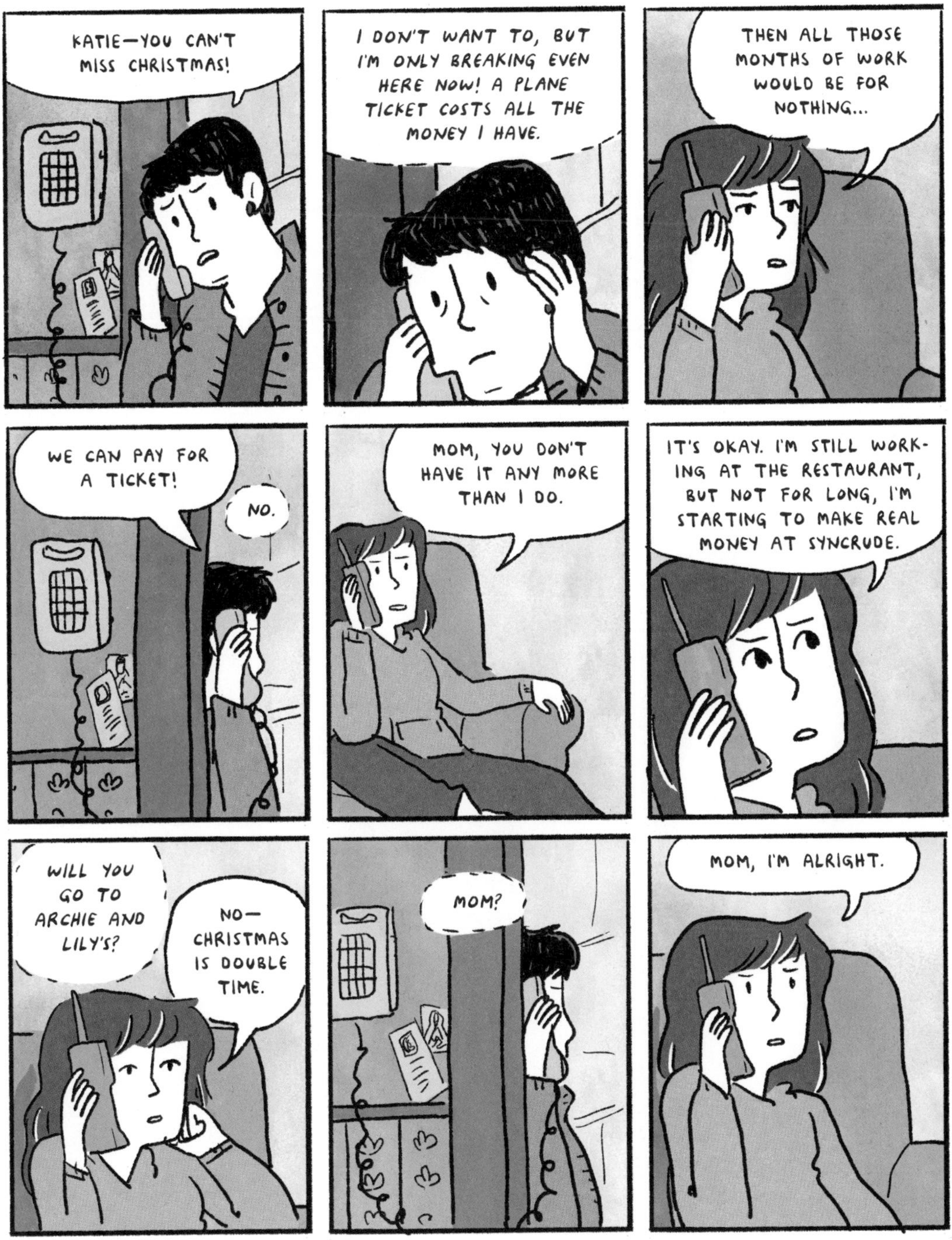
KATIE—YOU CAN'T MISS CHRISTMAS!
I DON'T WANT TO, BUT I'M ONLY BREAKING EVEN HERE NOW! A PLANE TICKET COSTS ALL THE MONEY I HAVE.
THEN ALL THOSE MONTHS OF WORK WOULD BE FOR NOTHING...
WE CAN PAY FOR A TICKET!
NO.
MOM, YOU DON'T HAVE IT ANY MORE THAN I DO.
IT'S OKAY. I'M STILL WORKING AT THE RESTAURANT, BUT NOT FOR LONG, I'M STARTING TO MAKE REAL MONEY AT SYNCRUDE.
WILL YOU GO TO ARCHIE AND LILY'S?
NO—CHRISTMAS IS DOUBLE TIME.
MOM?
MOM, I'M ALRIGHT.

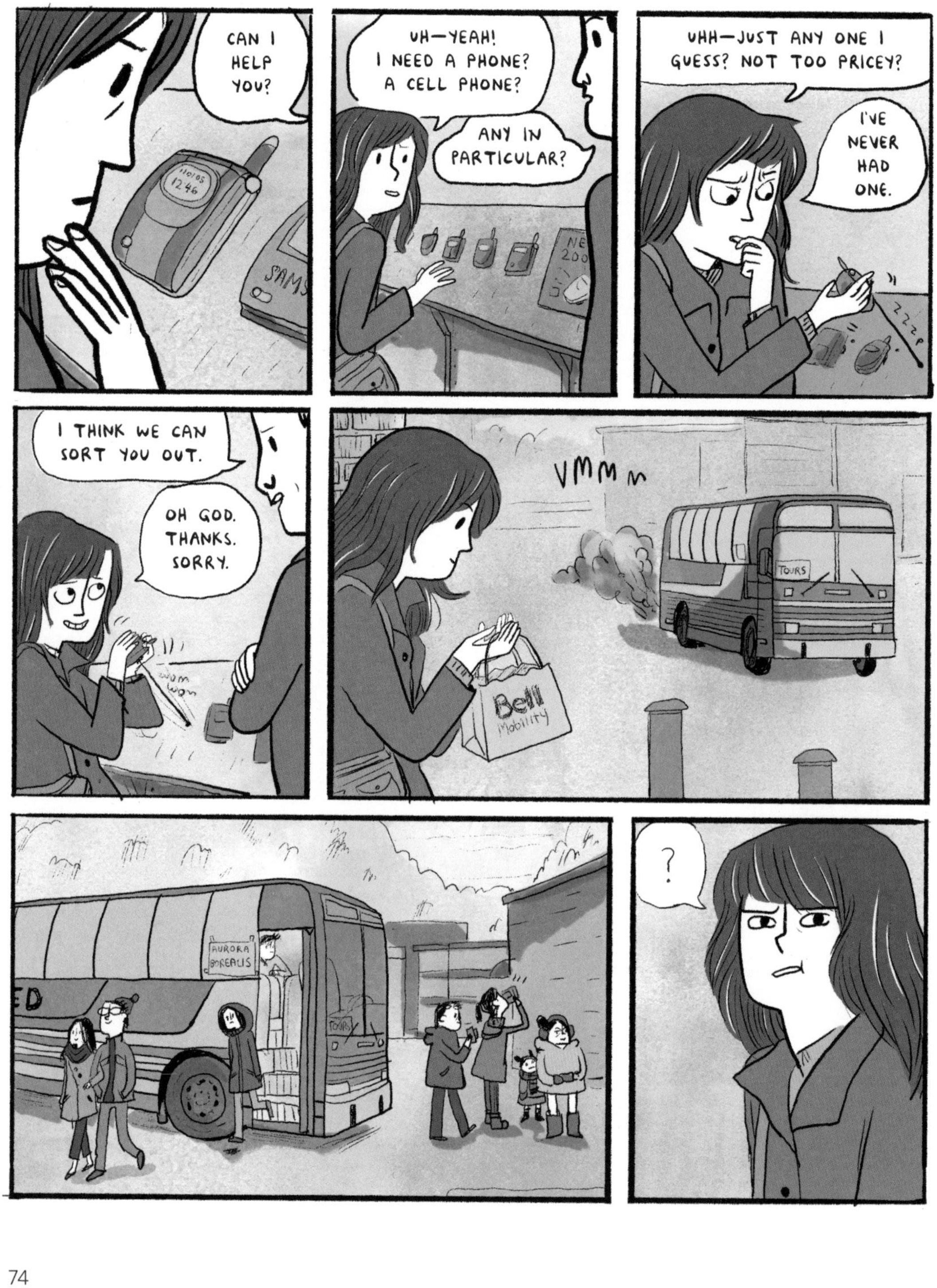
CAN I HELP YOU?
UH—YEAH! I NEED A PHONE? A CELL PHONE?
ANY IN PARTICULAR?
UHH—JUST ANY ONE I GUESS? NOT TOO PRICEY?
I'VE NEVER HAD ONE.
I THINK WE CAN SORT YOU OUT.
OH GOD. THANKS. SORRY.
VMMM
TOURS
Bell Mobility
AURORA BOREALIS
TOURS
?

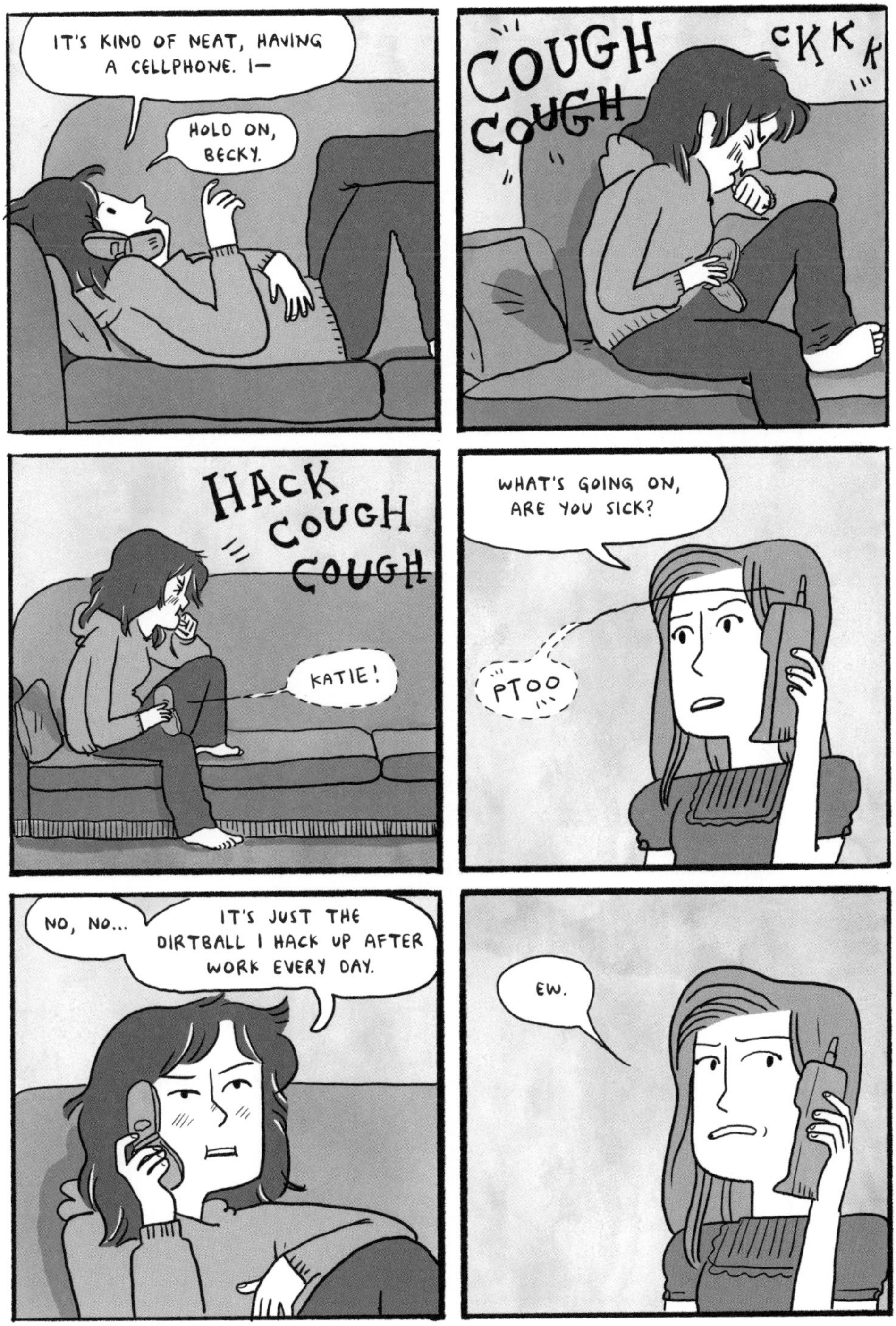
IT'S KIND OF NEAT, HAVING A CELLPHONE. I—
HOLD ON, BECKY.
COUGH COUGH
CKKK
HACK COUGH COUGH
KATIE!
WHAT'S GOING ON, ARE YOU SICK?
PTOO
NO, NO...
IT'S JUST THE DIRTBALL I HACK UP AFTER WORK EVERY DAY.
EW.

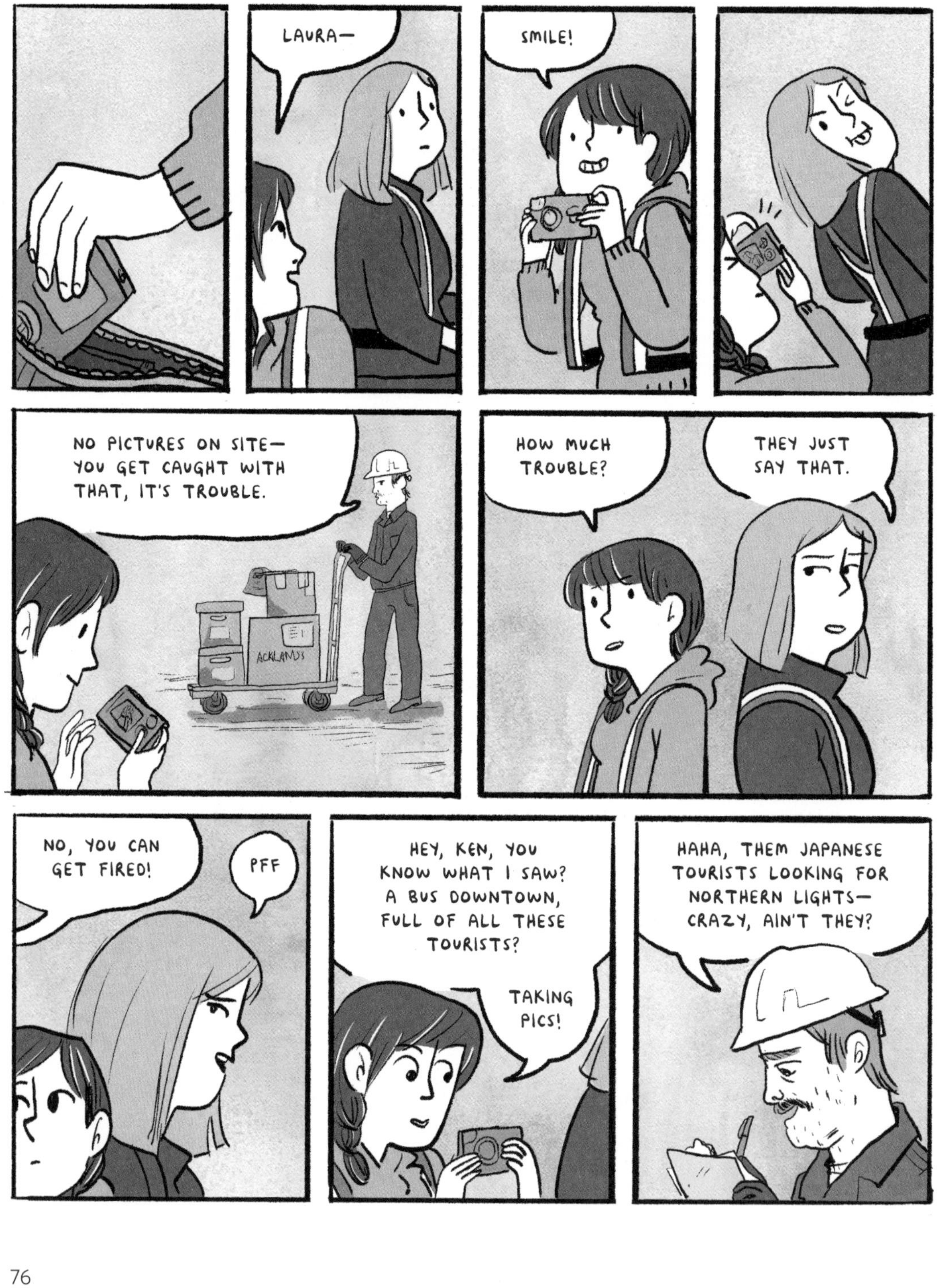
LAURA—
SMILE!
NO PICTURES ON SITE—
YOU GET CAUGHT WITH
THAT, IT'S TROUBLE.
HOW MUCH
TROUBLE?
THEY JUST
SAY THAT.
NO, YOU CAN
GET FIRED!
PFF
HEY, KEN, YOU
KNOW WHAT I SAW?
A BUS DOWNTOWN,
FULL OF ALL THESE
TOURISTS?
TAKING
PICS!
HAHA, THEM JAPANESE
TOURISTS LOOKING FOR
NORTHERN LIGHTS—
CRAZY, AIN'T THEY?

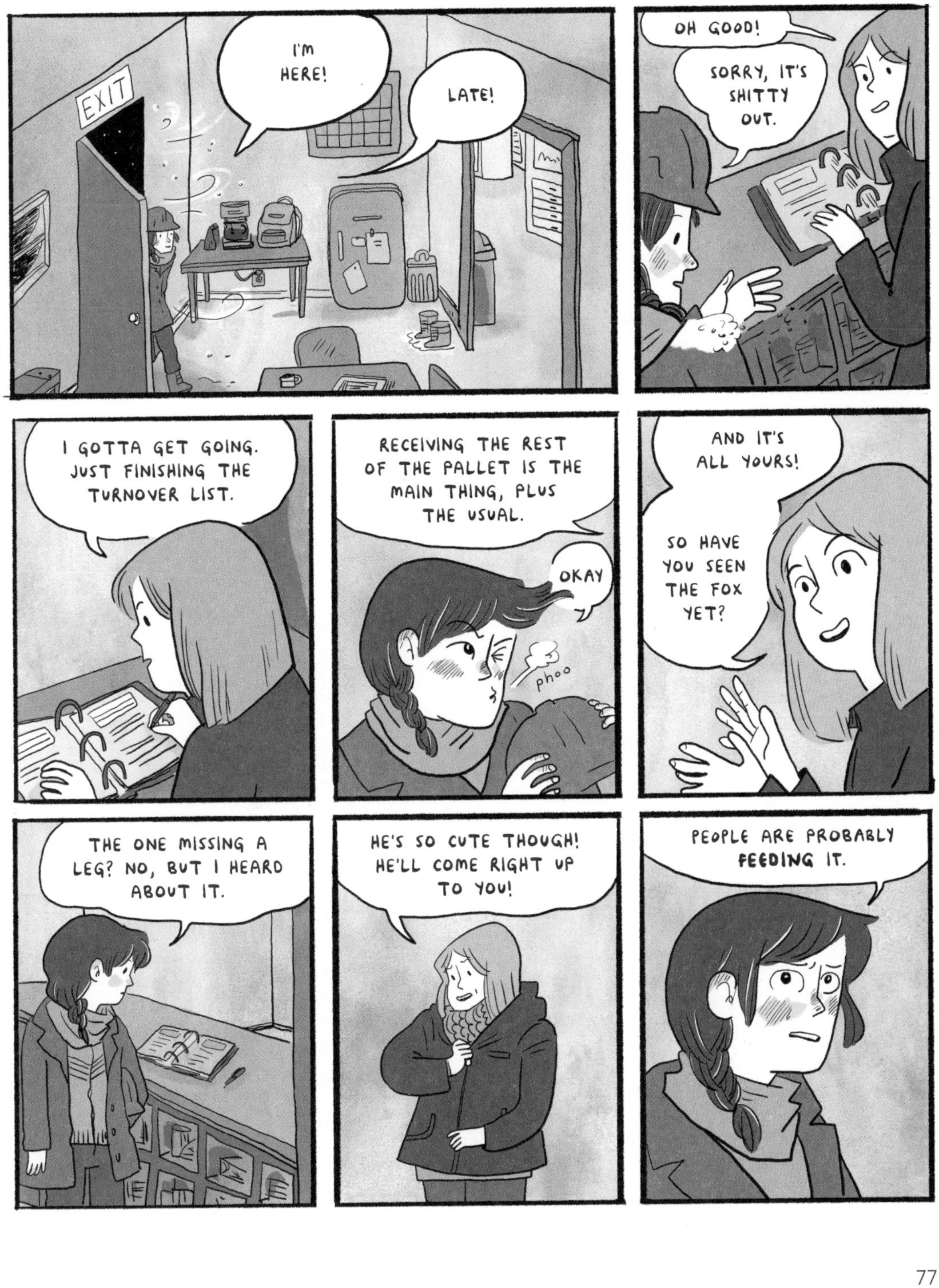
I'M HERE!
LATE!
OH GOOD!
SORRY, IT'S SHITTY OUT.
I GOTTA GET GOING. JUST FINISHING THE TURNOVER LIST.
RECEIVING THE REST OF THE PALLET IS THE MAIN THING, PLUS THE USUAL.
OKAY
phoo
AND IT'S ALL YOURS!
SO HAVE YOU SEEN THE FOX YET?
THE ONE MISSING A LEG? NO, BUT I HEARD ABOUT IT.
HE'S SO CUTE THOUGH! HE'LL COME RIGHT UP TO YOU!
PEOPLE ARE PROBABLY FEEDING IT.

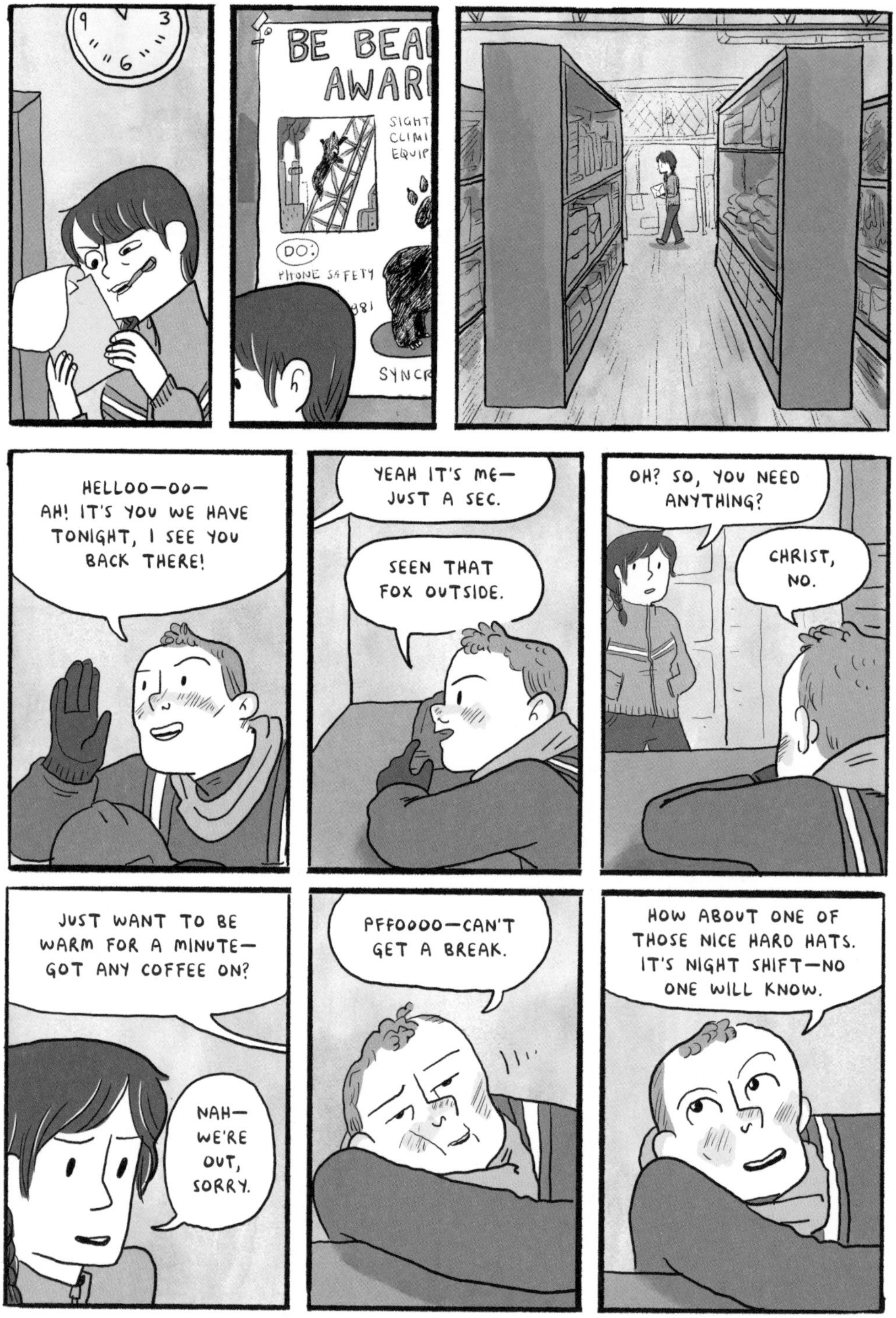
BE BEA
AWAR
SIGHT
CLIMI
EQUIP
DO:
PHONE SAFETY
SYNCR
HELLOO—OO—
AH! IT'S YOU WE HAVE TONIGHT, I SEE YOU BACK THERE!
YEAH IT'S ME— JUST A SEC.
SEEN THAT FOX OUTSIDE.
OH? SO, YOU NEED ANYTHING?
CHRIST, NO.
JUST WANT TO BE WARM FOR A MINUTE— GOT ANY COFFEE ON?
NAH— WE'RE OUT, SORRY.
PFFOOOO—CAN'T GET A BREAK.
HOW ABOUT ONE OF THOSE NICE HARD HATS. IT'S NIGHT SHIFT—NO ONE WILL KNOW.

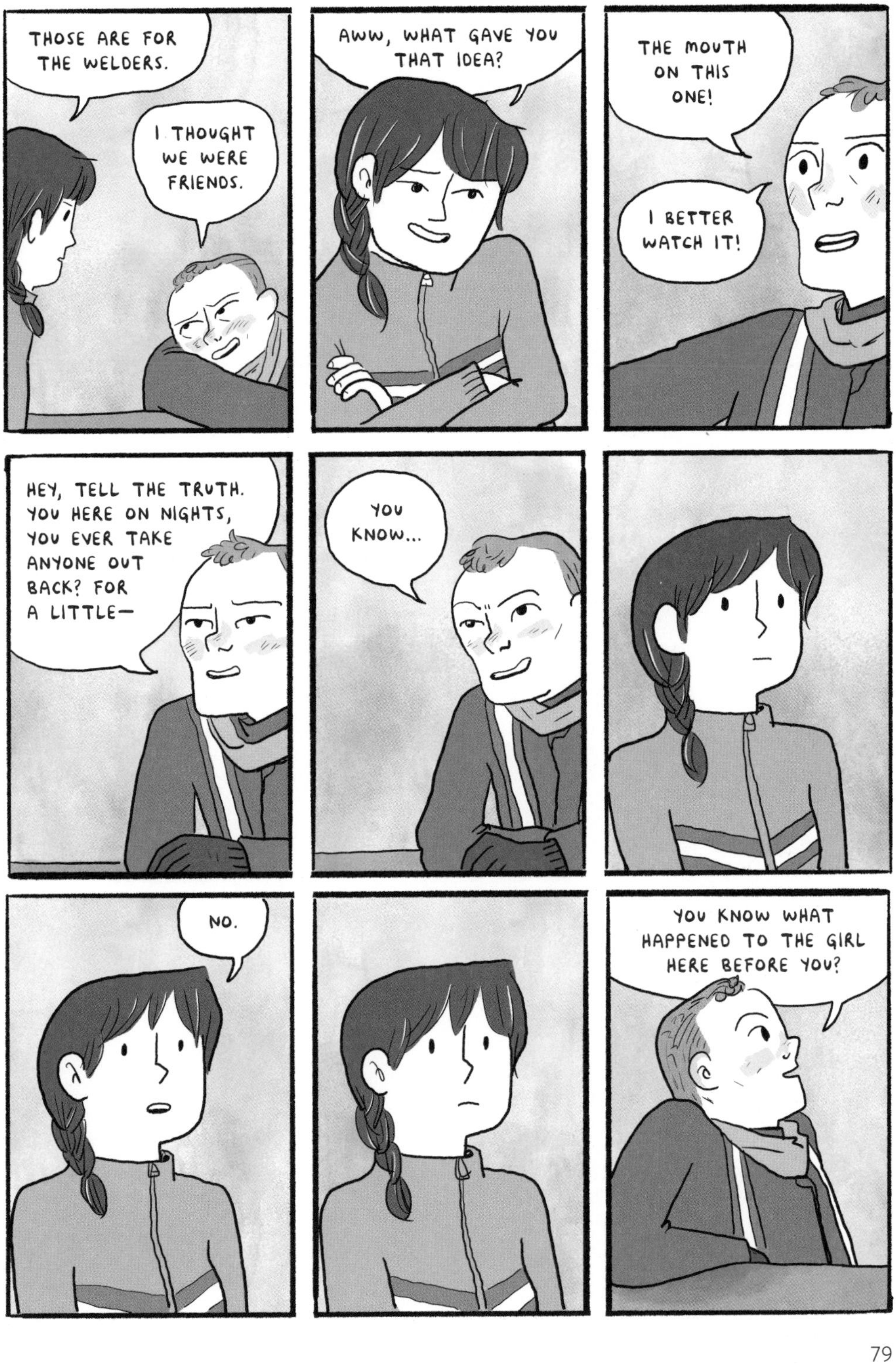
THOSE ARE FOR THE WELDERS.
I THOUGHT WE WERE FRIENDS.
AWW, WHAT GAVE YOU THAT IDEA?
THE MOUTH ON THIS ONE!
I BETTER WATCH IT!
HEY, TELL THE TRUTH. YOU HERE ON NIGHTS, YOU EVER TAKE ANYONE OUT BACK? FOR A LITTLE—
YOU KNOW...
NO.
YOU KNOW WHAT HAPPENED TO THE GIRL HERE BEFORE YOU?

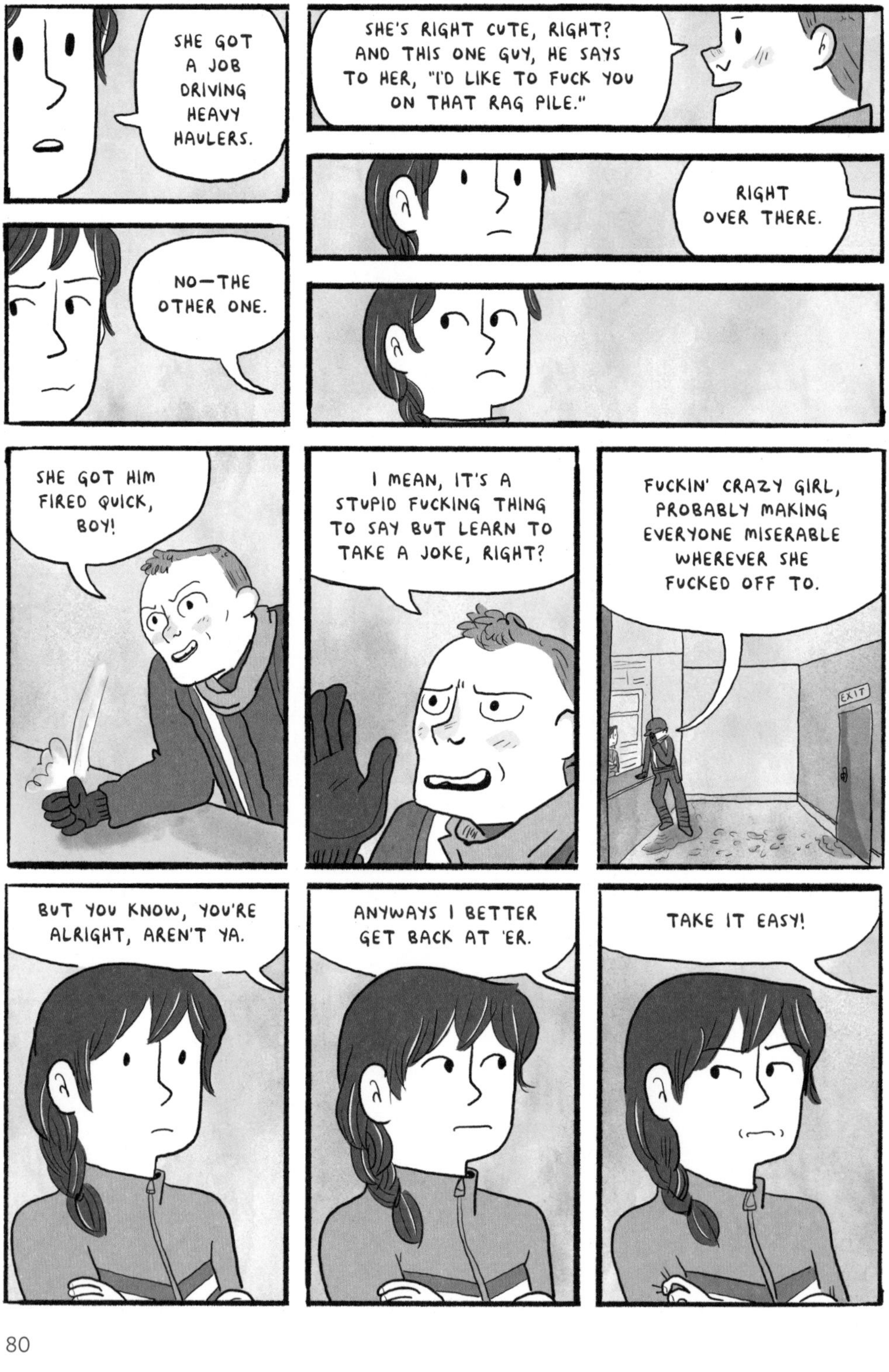
SHE GOT A JOB DRIVING HEAVY HAULERS.
SHE'S RIGHT CUTE, RIGHT? AND THIS ONE GUY, HE SAYS TO HER, "I'D LIKE TO FUCK YOU ON THAT RAG PILE."
RIGHT OVER THERE.
NO—THE OTHER ONE.
SHE GOT HIM FIRED QUICK, BOY!
I MEAN, IT'S A STUPID FUCKING THING TO SAY BUT LEARN TO TAKE A JOKE, RIGHT?
FUCKIN' CRAZY GIRL, PROBABLY MAKING EVERYONE MISERABLE WHEREVER SHE FUCKED OFF TO.
EXIT
BUT YOU KNOW, YOU'RE ALRIGHT, AREN'T YA.
ANYWAYS I BETTER GET BACK AT 'ER.
TAKE IT EASY!

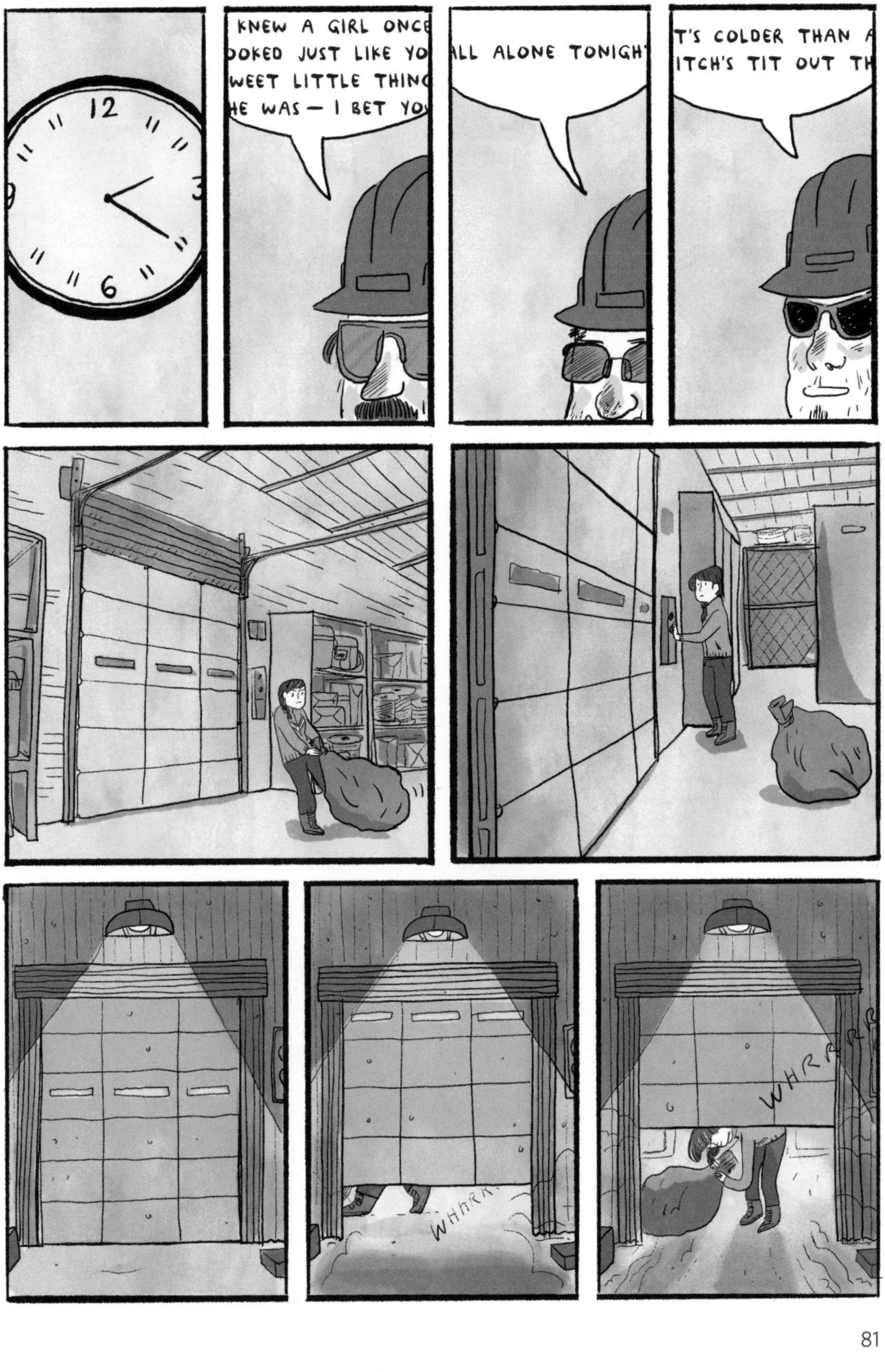

KNEW A GIRL ONCE
OOKED JUST LIKE YO
WEET LITTLE THING
HE WAS — I BET YO
ALL ALONE TONIGHT
T'S COLDER THAN A
ITCH'S TIT OUT TH
WHRRR
WHRRRR

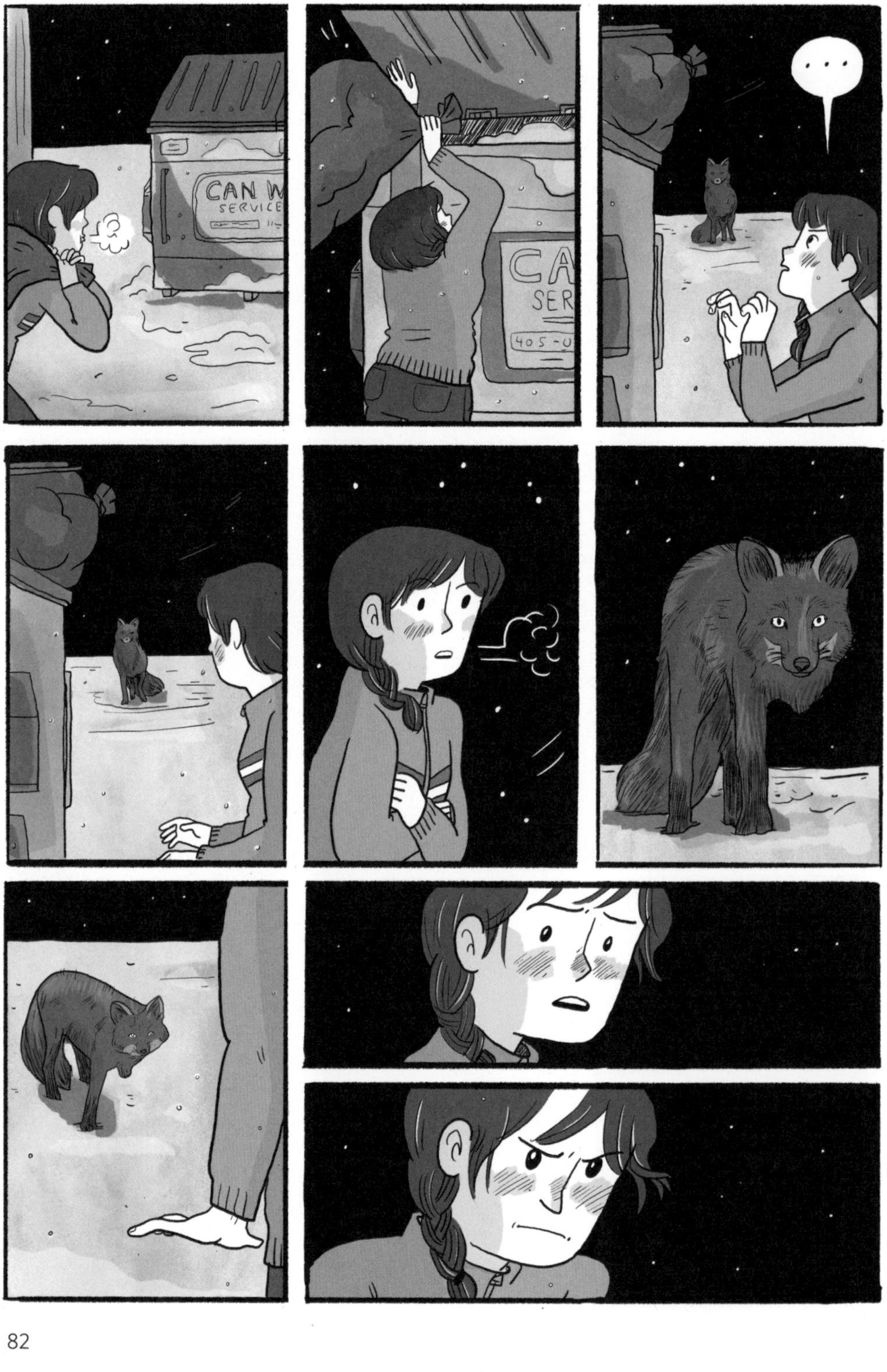
CAN W
SERVICE
...

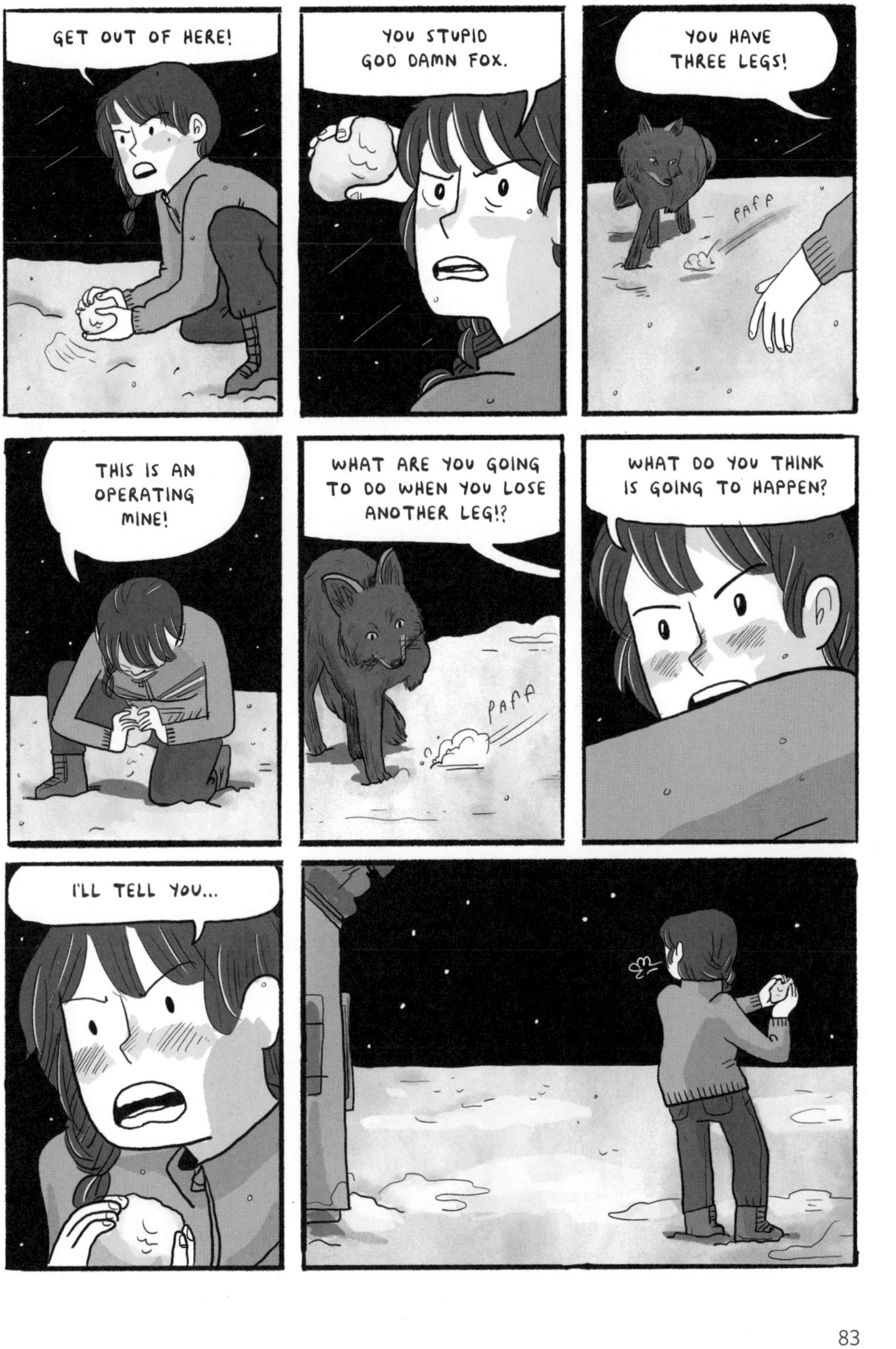
GET OUT OF HERE!
YOU STUPID GOD DAMN FOX.
YOU HAVE THREE LEGS!
PAFF
THIS IS AN OPERATING MINE!
WHAT ARE YOU GOING TO DO WHEN YOU LOSE ANOTHER LEG!?
PAFF
WHAT DO YOU THINK IS GOING TO HAPPEN?
I'LL TELL YOU...

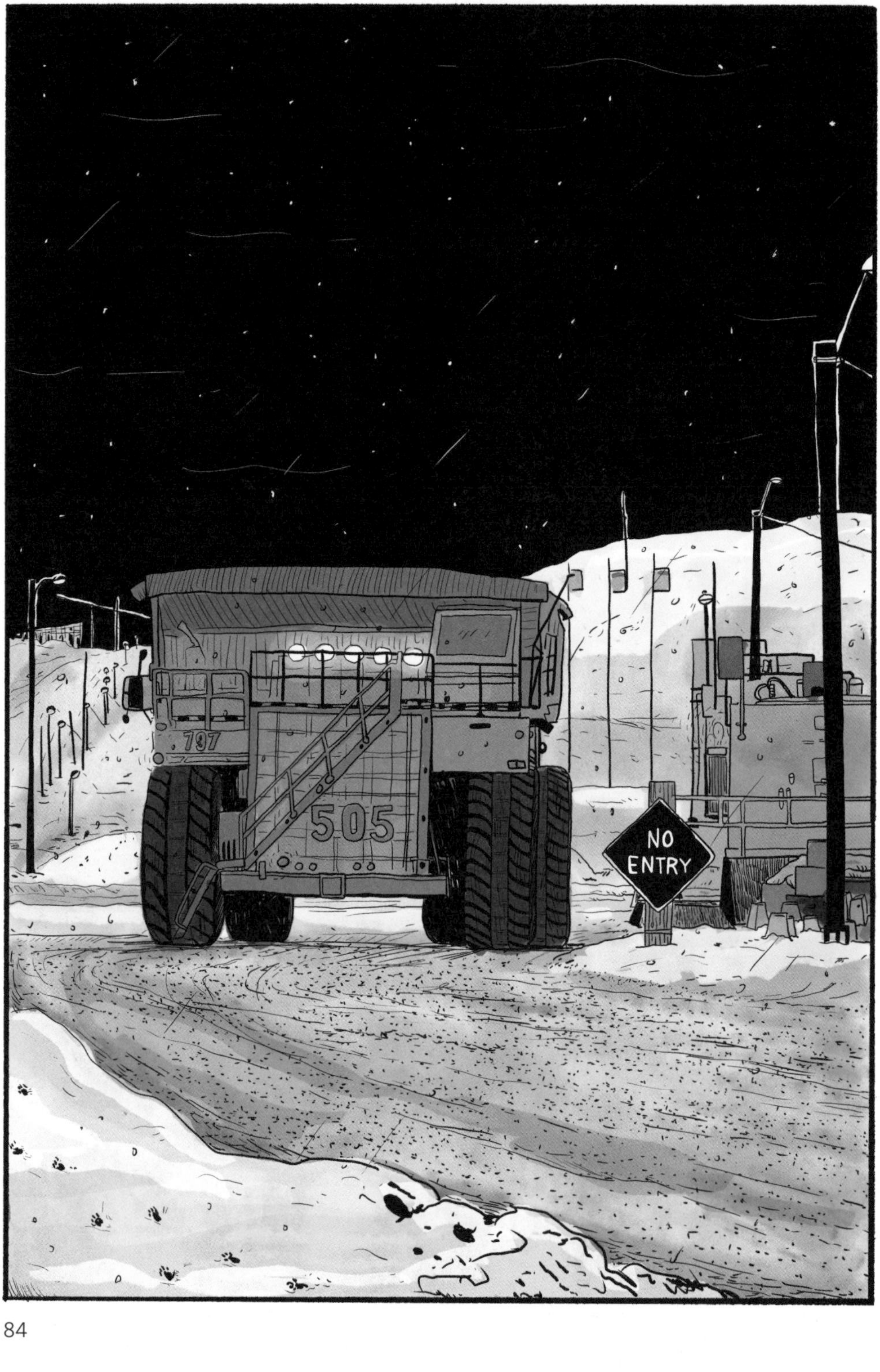
797
505
NO ENTRY

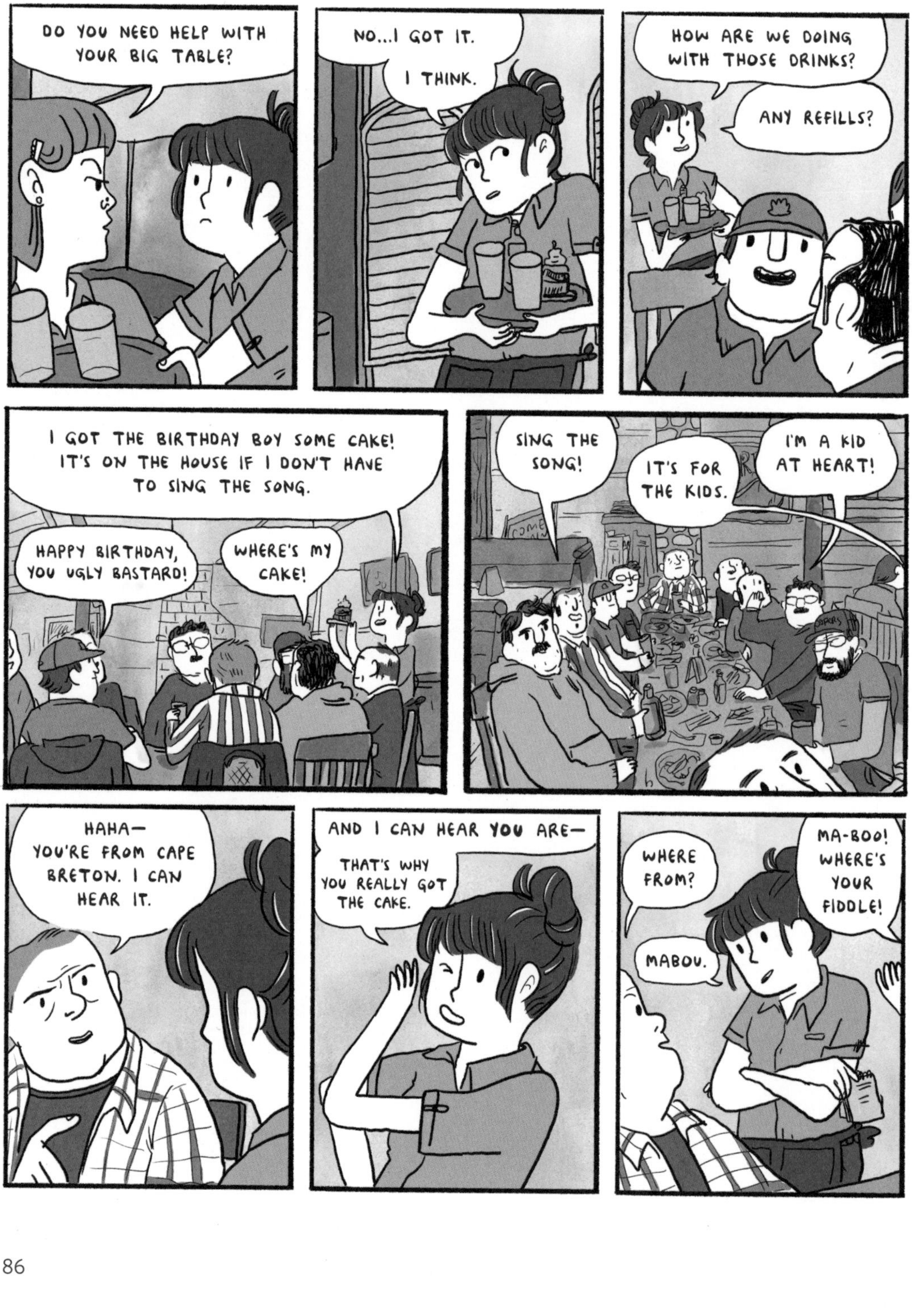
DO YOU NEED HELP WITH YOUR BIG TABLE?
NO...I GOT IT.
I THINK.
HOW ARE WE DOING WITH THOSE DRINKS?
ANY REFILLS?
I GOT THE BIRTHDAY BOY SOME CAKE! IT'S ON THE HOUSE IF I DON'T HAVE TO SING THE SONG.
HAPPY BIRTHDAY, YOU UGLY BASTARD!
WHERE'S MY CAKE!
SING THE SONG!
IT'S FOR THE KIDS.
I'M A KID AT HEART!
HAHA— YOU'RE FROM CAPE BRETON. I CAN HEAR IT.
AND I CAN HEAR **YOU** ARE—
THAT'S WHY YOU REALLY GOT THE CAKE.
WHERE FROM?
MABOU.
MA-BOO! WHERE'S YOUR FIDDLE!

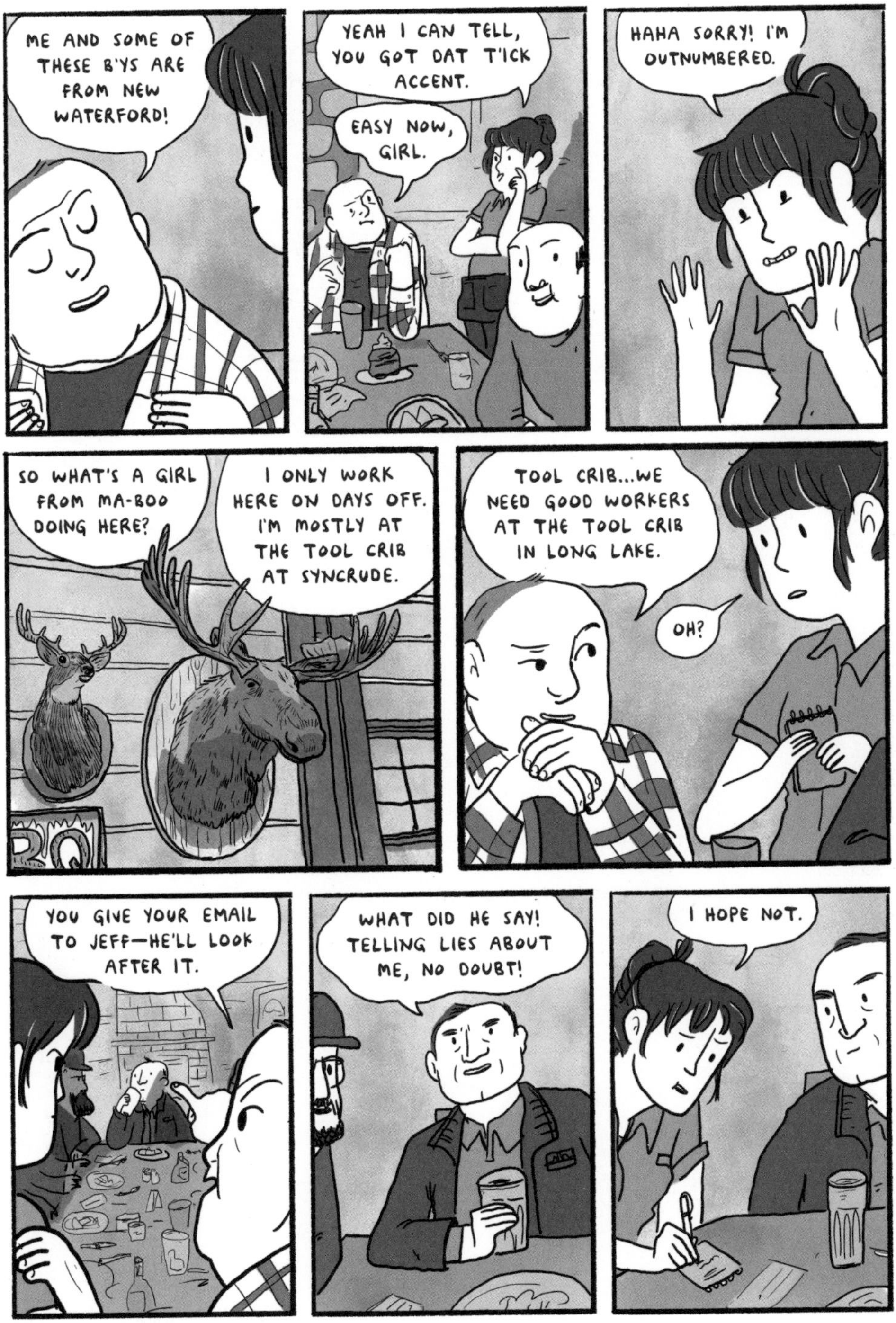
ME AND SOME OF THESE B'YS ARE FROM NEW WATERFORD!
YEAH I CAN TELL, YOU GOT DAT T'ICK ACCENT.
EASY NOW, GIRL.
HAHA SORRY! I'M OUTNUMBERED.
SO WHAT'S A GIRL FROM MA-BOO DOING HERE?
I ONLY WORK HERE ON DAYS OFF. I'M MOSTLY AT THE TOOL CRIB AT SYNCRUDE.
TOOL CRIB...WE NEED GOOD WORKERS AT THE TOOL CRIB IN LONG LAKE.
OH?
YOU GIVE YOUR EMAIL TO JEFF—HE'LL LOOK AFTER IT.
WHAT DID HE SAY! TELLING LIES ABOUT ME, NO DOUBT!
I HOPE NOT.

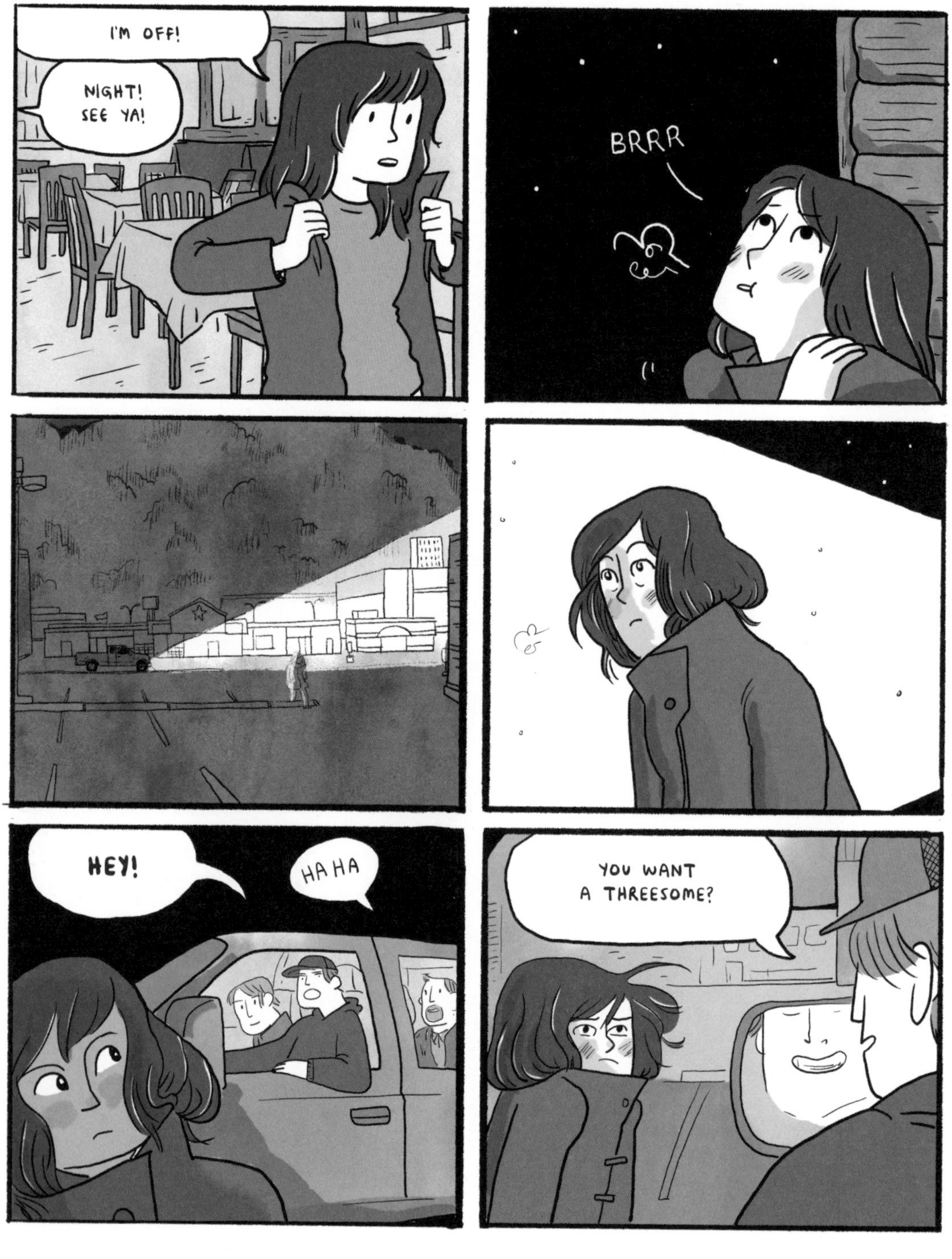
I'M OFF!
NIGHT! SEE YA!
BRRR
HEY!
HA HA
YOU WANT A THREESOME?

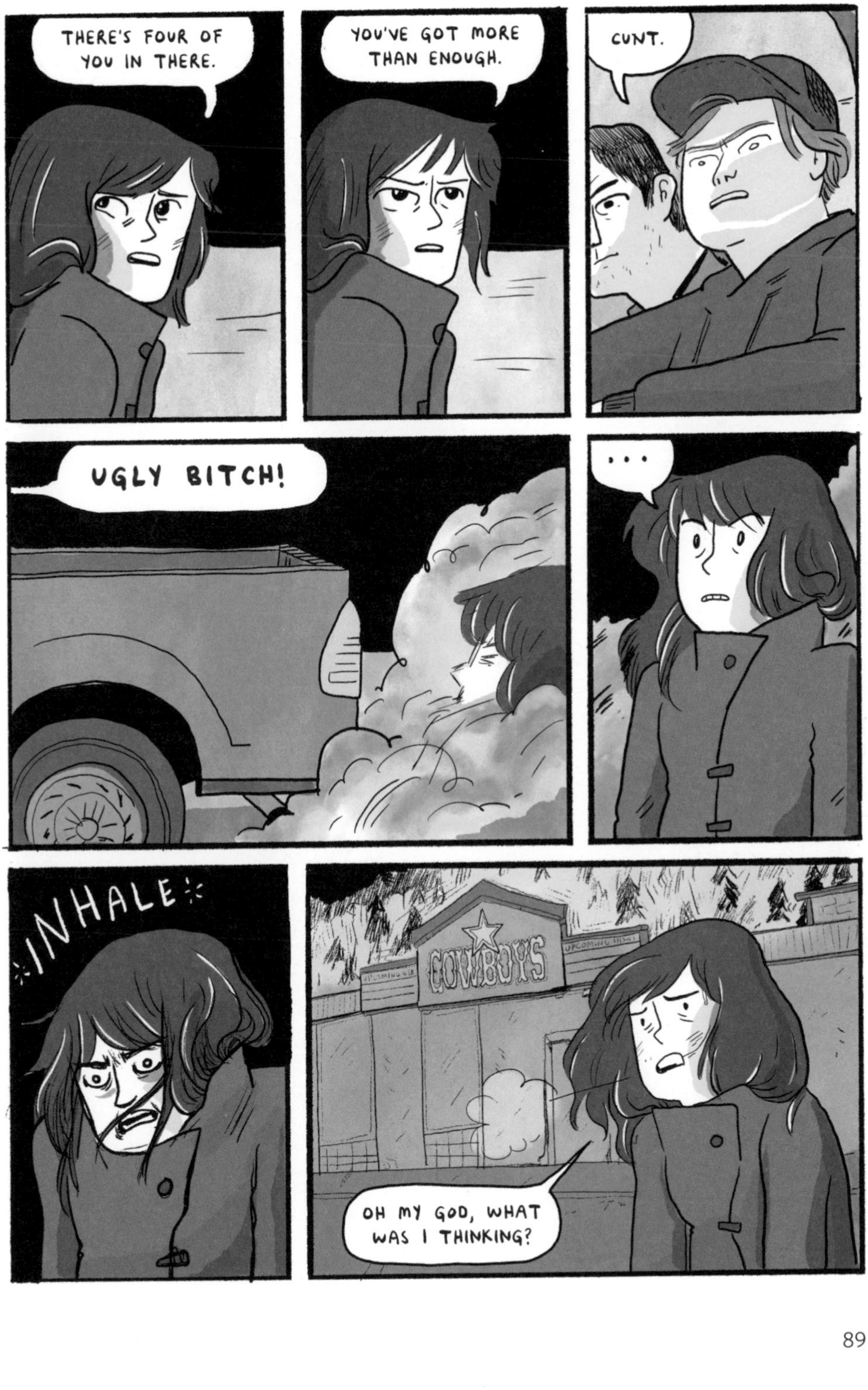
THERE'S FOUR OF YOU IN THERE.
YOU'VE GOT MORE THAN ENOUGH.
CUNT.
UGLY BITCH!
...
INHALE
COWBOYS
OH MY GOD, WHAT WAS I THINKING?

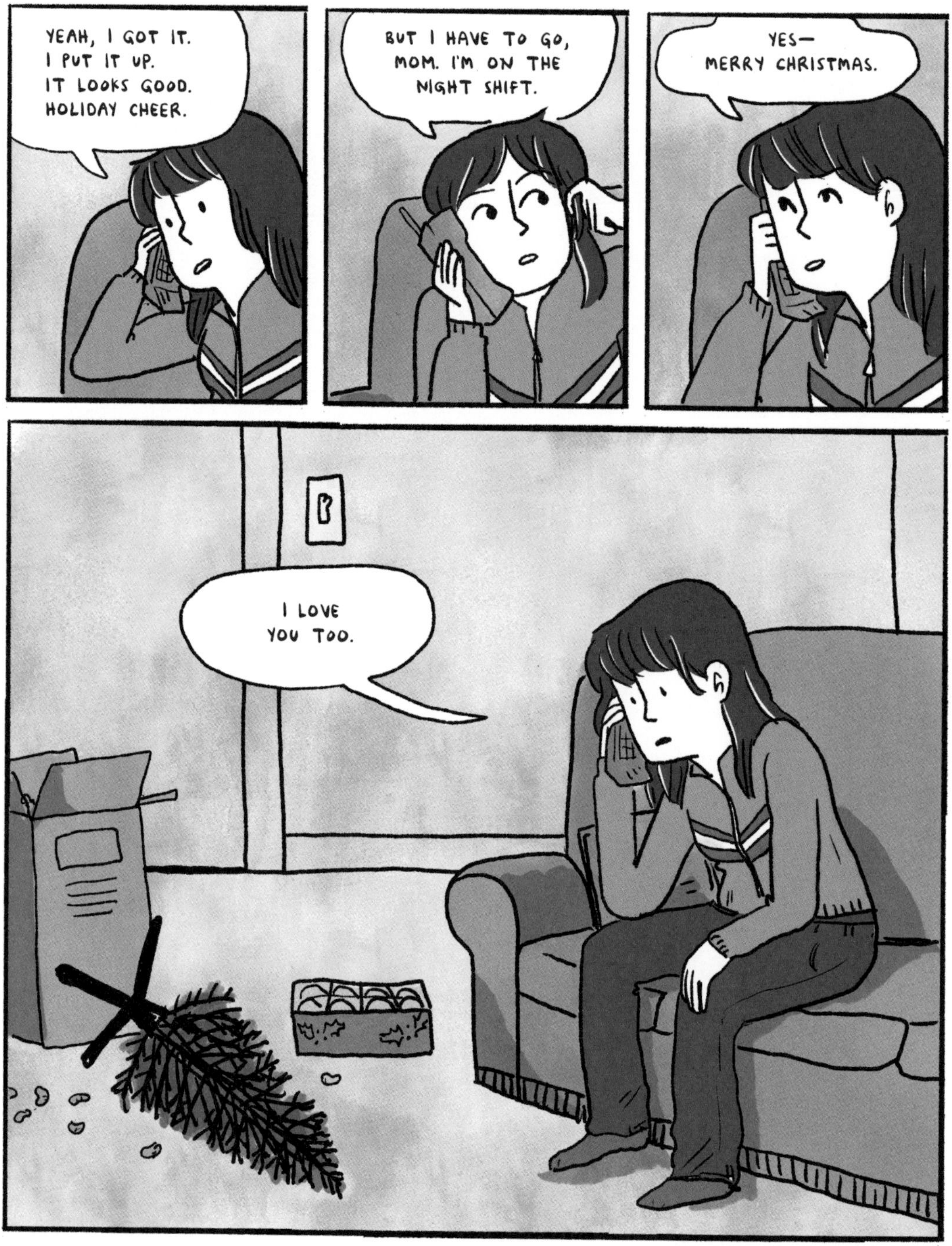
YEAH, I GOT IT. I PUT IT UP. IT LOOKS GOOD. HOLIDAY CHEER.
BUT I HAVE TO GO, MOM. I'M ON THE NIGHT SHIFT.
YES— MERRY CHRISTMAS.
I LOVE YOU TOO.

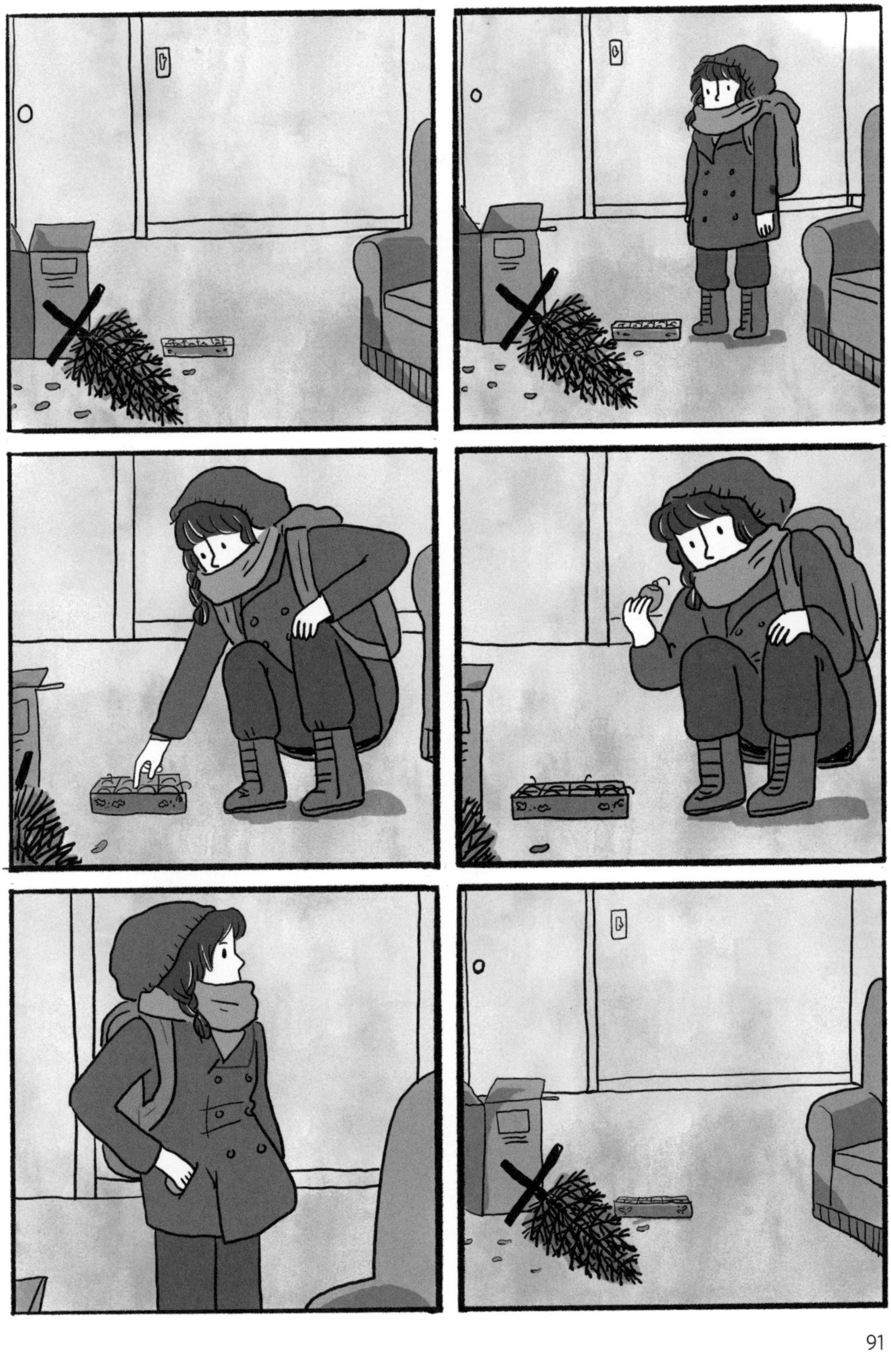

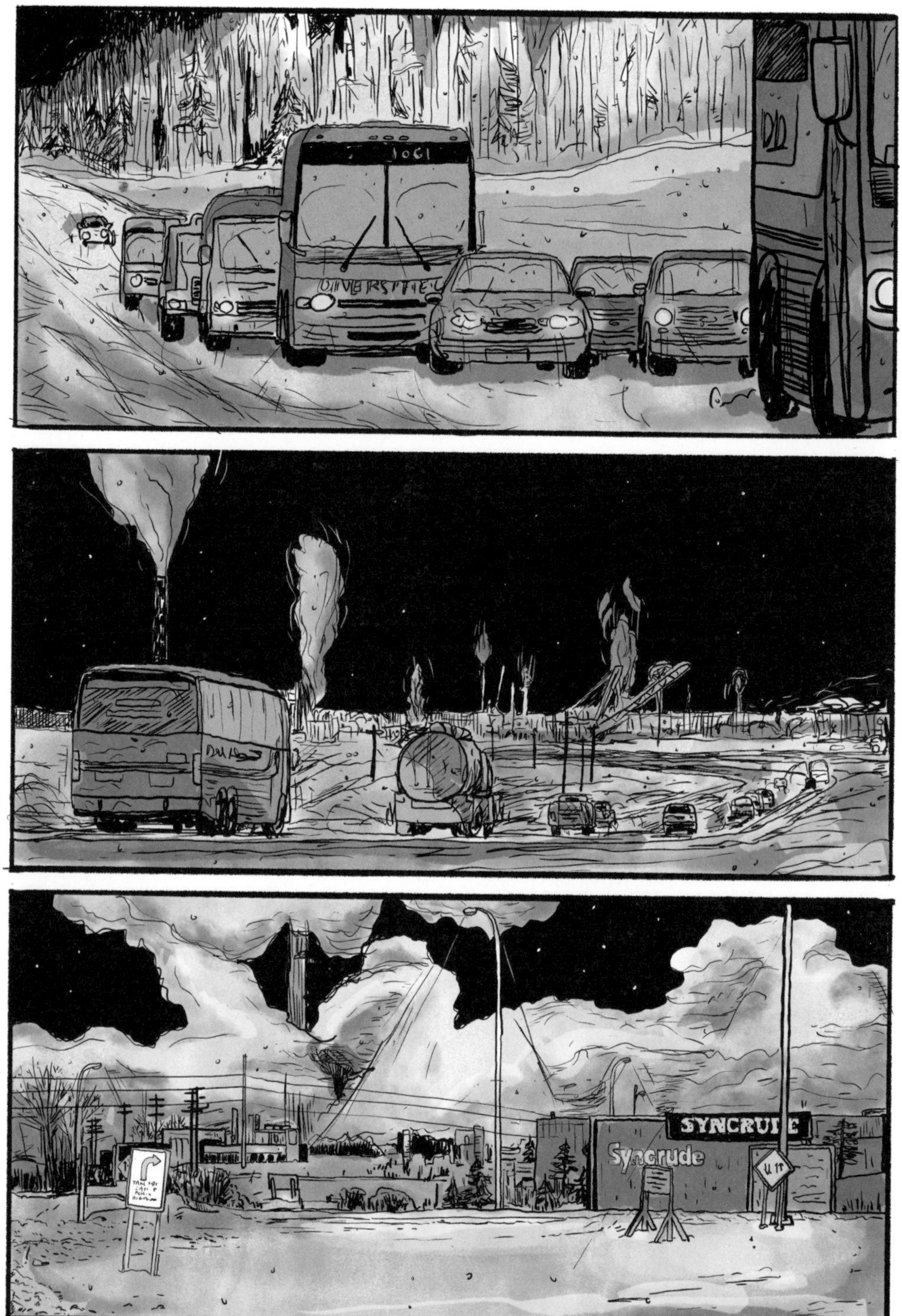
SYNCRUDE
Syncrude

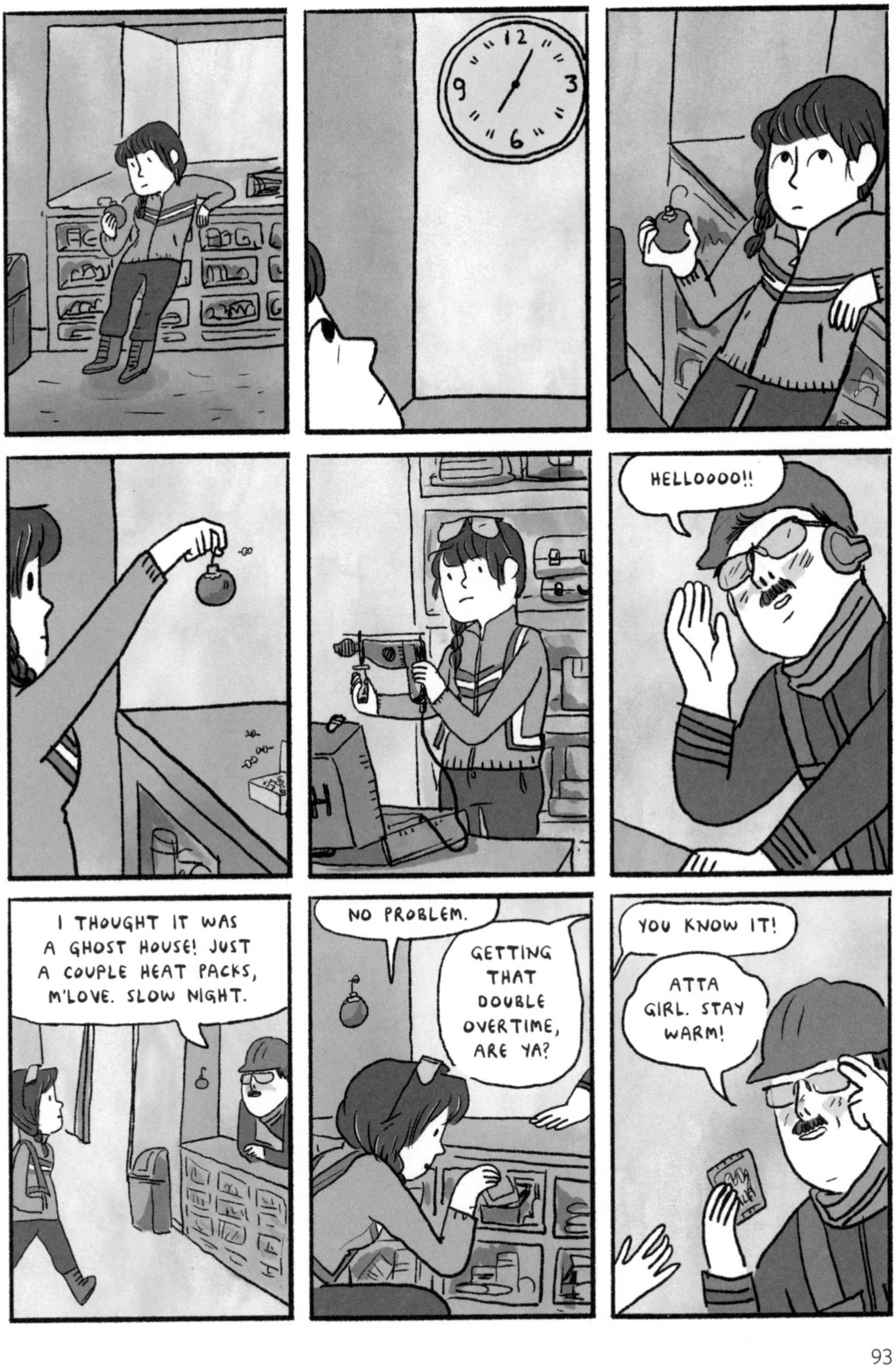
HELLOOOO!!
I THOUGHT IT WAS A GHOST HOUSE! JUST A COUPLE HEAT PACKS, M'LOVE. SLOW NIGHT.
NO PROBLEM.
GETTING THAT DOUBLE OVERTIME, ARE YA?
YOU KNOW IT!
ATTA GIRL. STAY WARM!

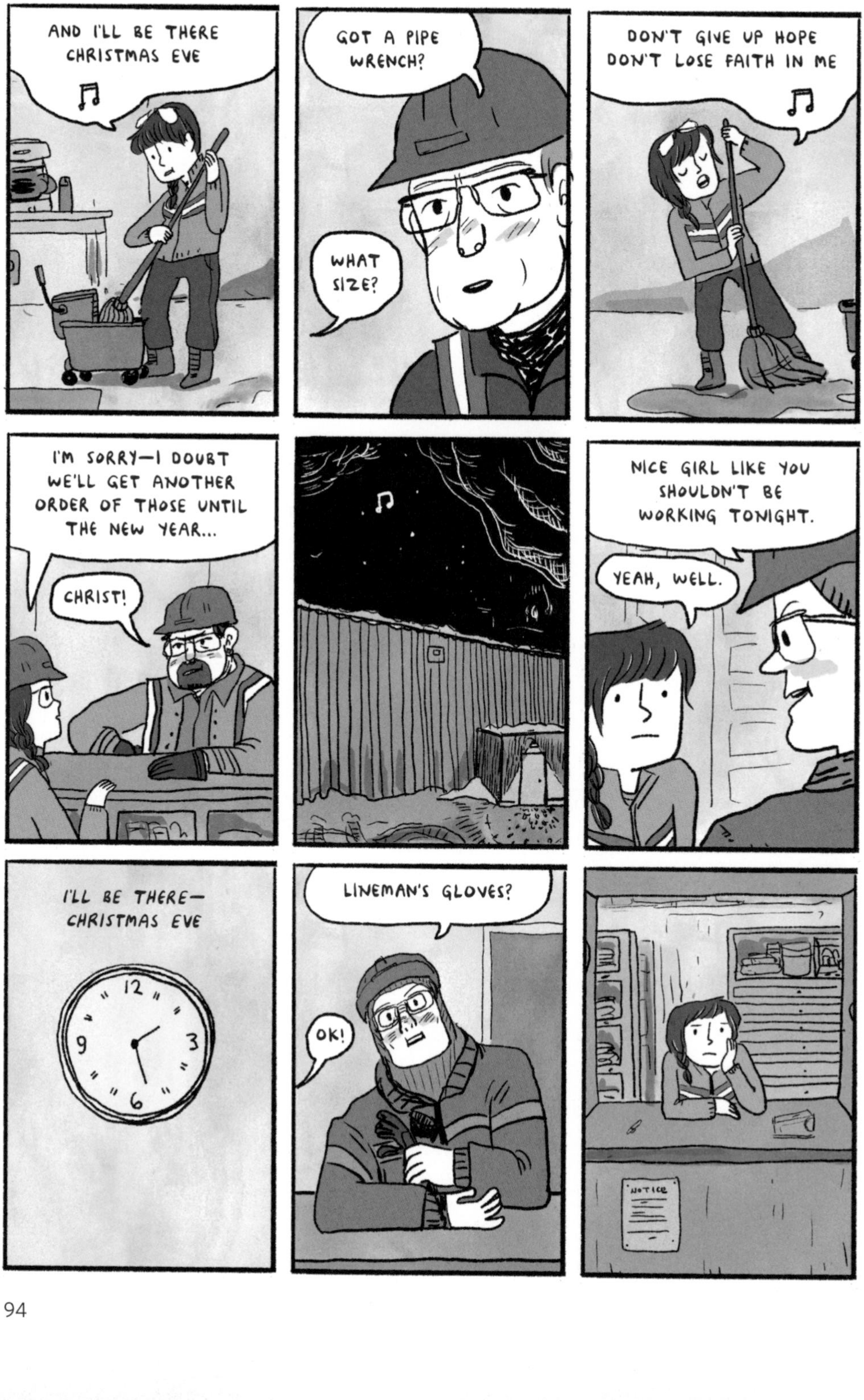
AND I'LL BE THERE CHRISTMAS EVE
GOT A PIPE WRENCH?
WHAT SIZE?
DON'T GIVE UP HOPE DON'T LOSE FAITH IN ME
I'M SORRY—I DOUBT WE'LL GET ANOTHER ORDER OF THOSE UNTIL THE NEW YEAR...
CHRIST!
NICE GIRL LIKE YOU SHOULDN'T BE WORKING TONIGHT.
YEAH, WELL.
I'LL BE THERE—CHRISTMAS EVE
12
3
6
9
LINEMAN'S GLOVES?
OK!
NOTICE

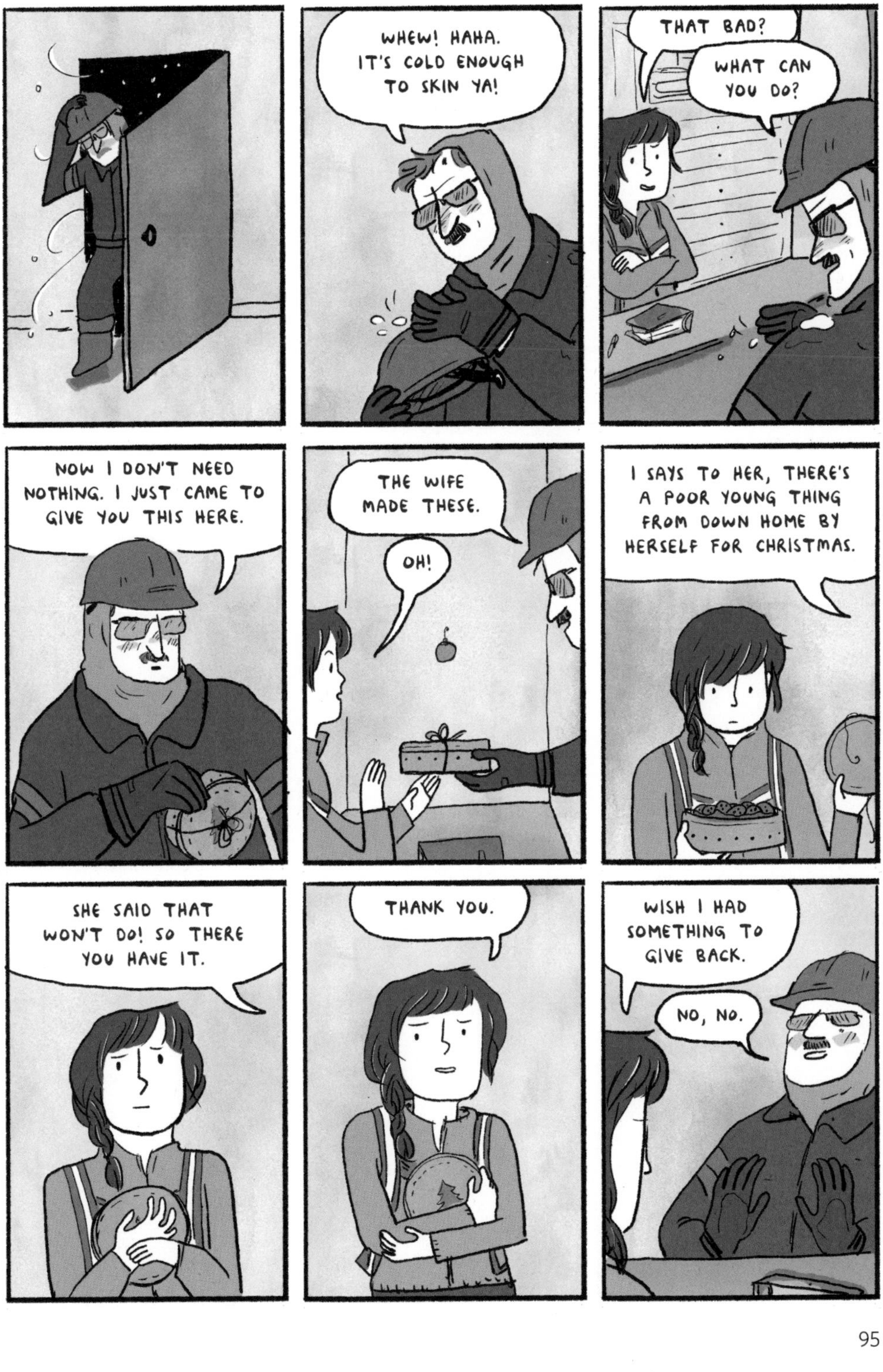
WHEW! HAHA. IT'S COLD ENOUGH TO SKIN YA!
THAT BAD?
WHAT CAN YOU DO?
NOW I DON'T NEED NOTHING. I JUST CAME TO GIVE YOU THIS HERE.
THE WIFE MADE THESE.
OH!
I SAYS TO HER, THERE'S A POOR YOUNG THING FROM DOWN HOME BY HERSELF FOR CHRISTMAS.
SHE SAID THAT WON'T DO! SO THERE YOU HAVE IT.
THANK YOU.
WISH I HAD SOMETHING TO GIVE BACK.
NO, NO.

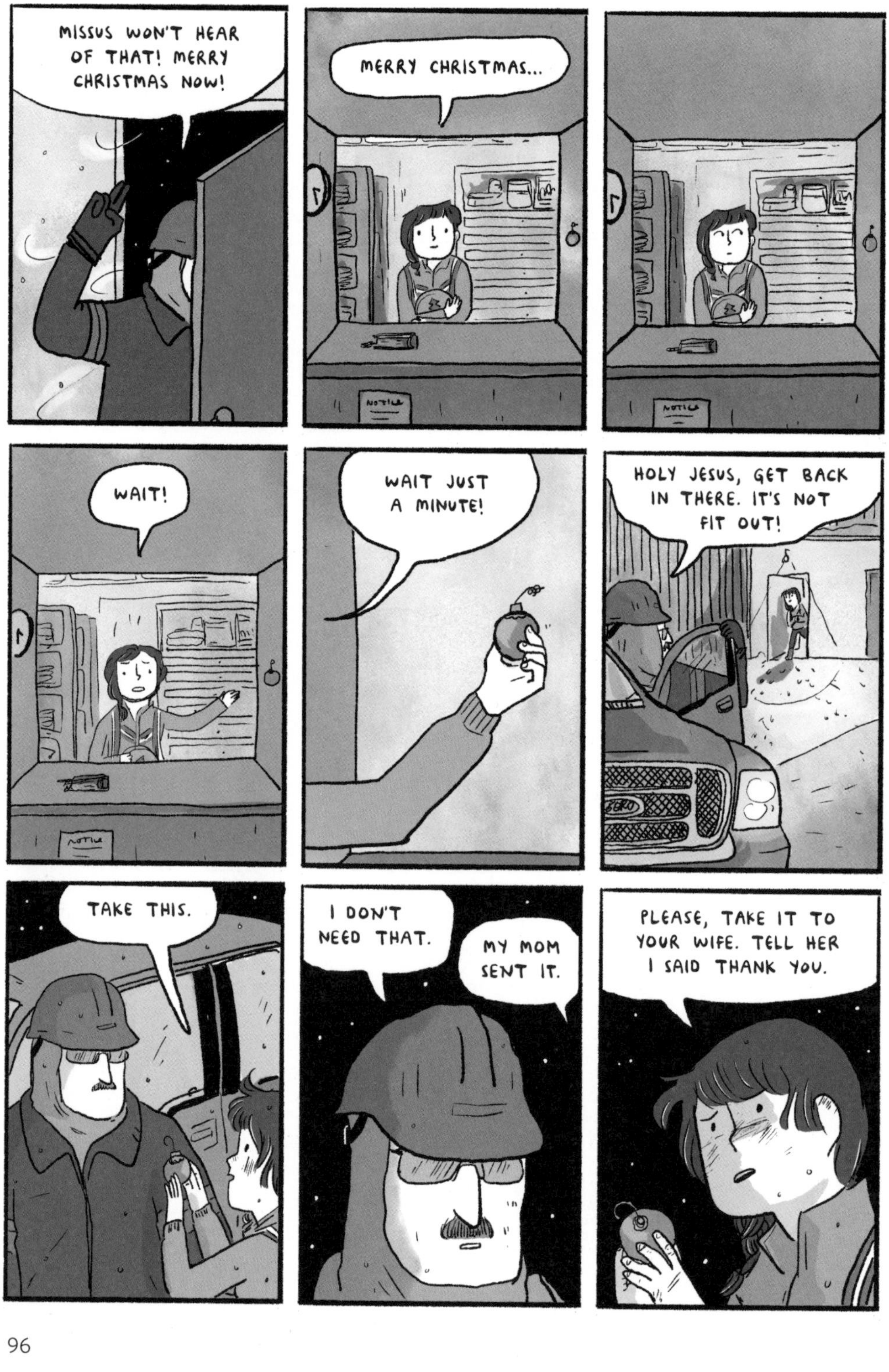
MISSUS WON'T HEAR OF THAT! MERRY CHRISTMAS NOW!
MERRY CHRISTMAS...
WAIT!
WAIT JUST A MINUTE!
HOLY JESUS, GET BACK IN THERE. IT'S NOT FIT OUT!
TAKE THIS.
I DON'T NEED THAT.
MY MOM SENT IT.
PLEASE, TAKE IT TO YOUR WIFE. TELL HER I SAID THANK YOU.

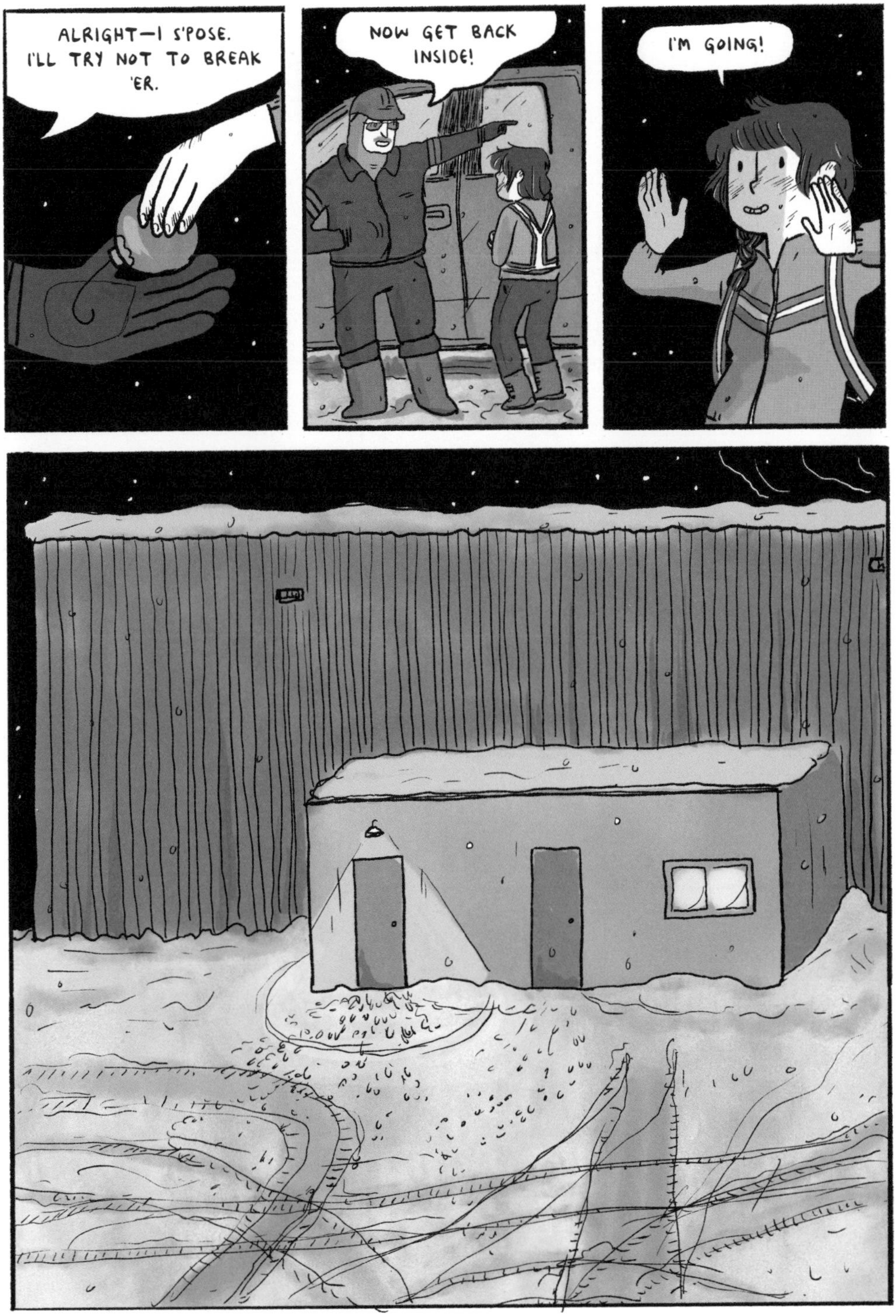
ALRIGHT—I S'POSE. I'LL TRY NOT TO BREAK 'ER.
NOW GET BACK INSIDE!
I'M GOING!

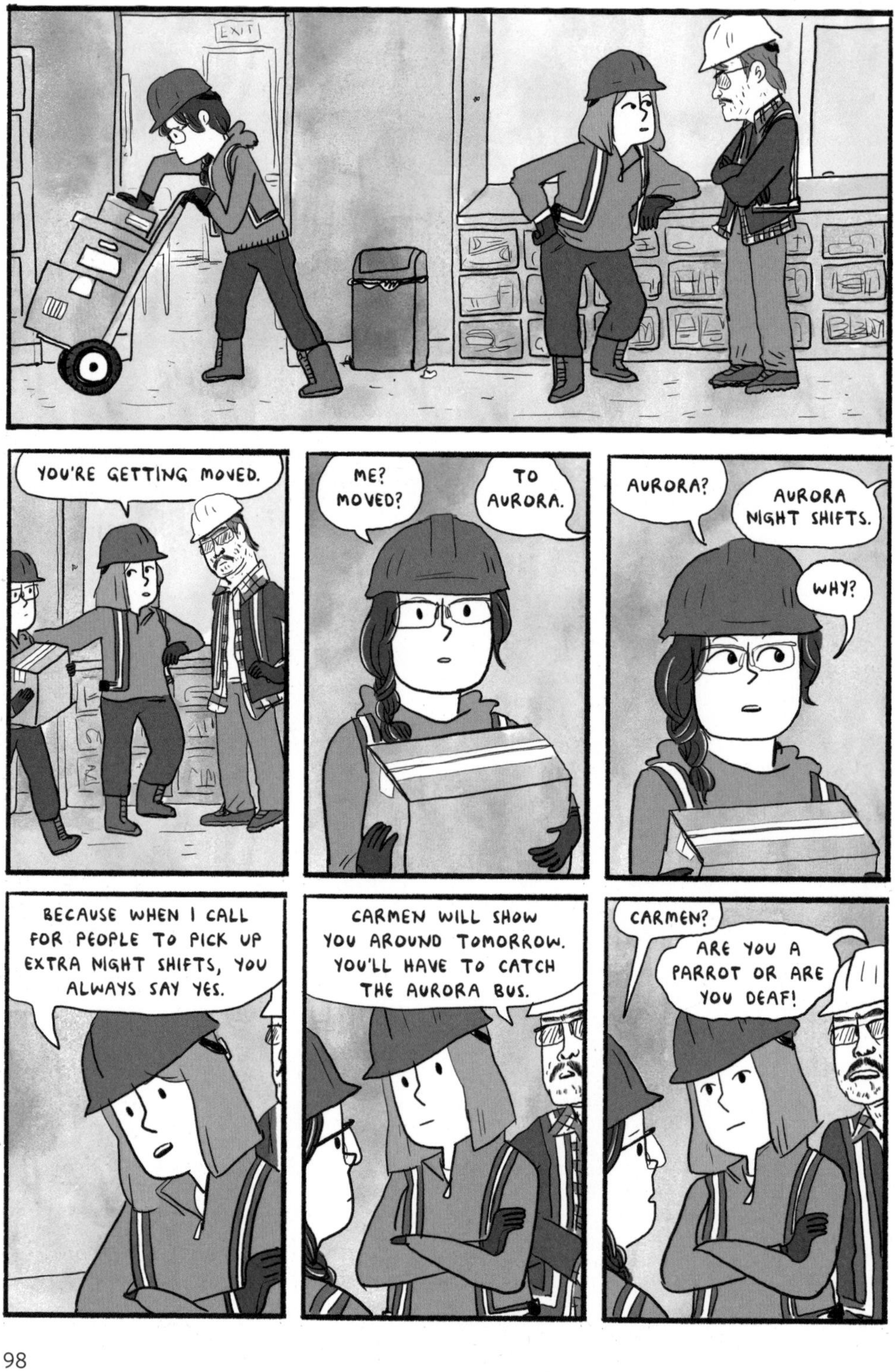
EXIT
YOU'RE GETTING MOVED.
ME? MOVED?
TO AURORA.
AURORA?
AURORA NIGHT SHIFTS.
WHY?
BECAUSE WHEN I CALL FOR PEOPLE TO PICK UP EXTRA NIGHT SHIFTS, YOU ALWAYS SAY YES.
CARMEN WILL SHOW YOU AROUND TOMORROW. YOU'LL HAVE TO CATCH THE AURORA BUS.
CARMEN?
ARE YOU A PARROT OR ARE YOU DEAF!

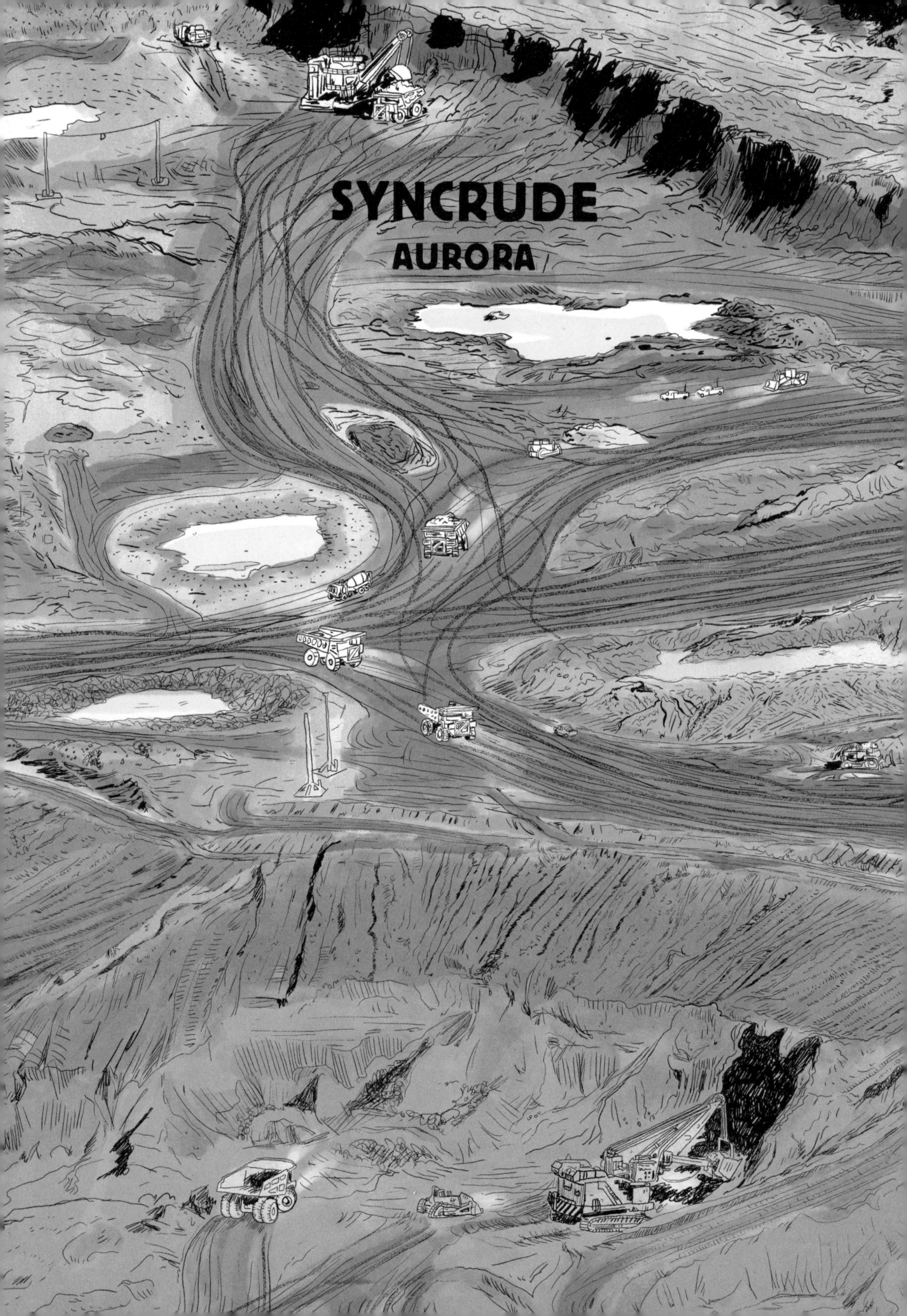
SYNCRUDE
AURORA

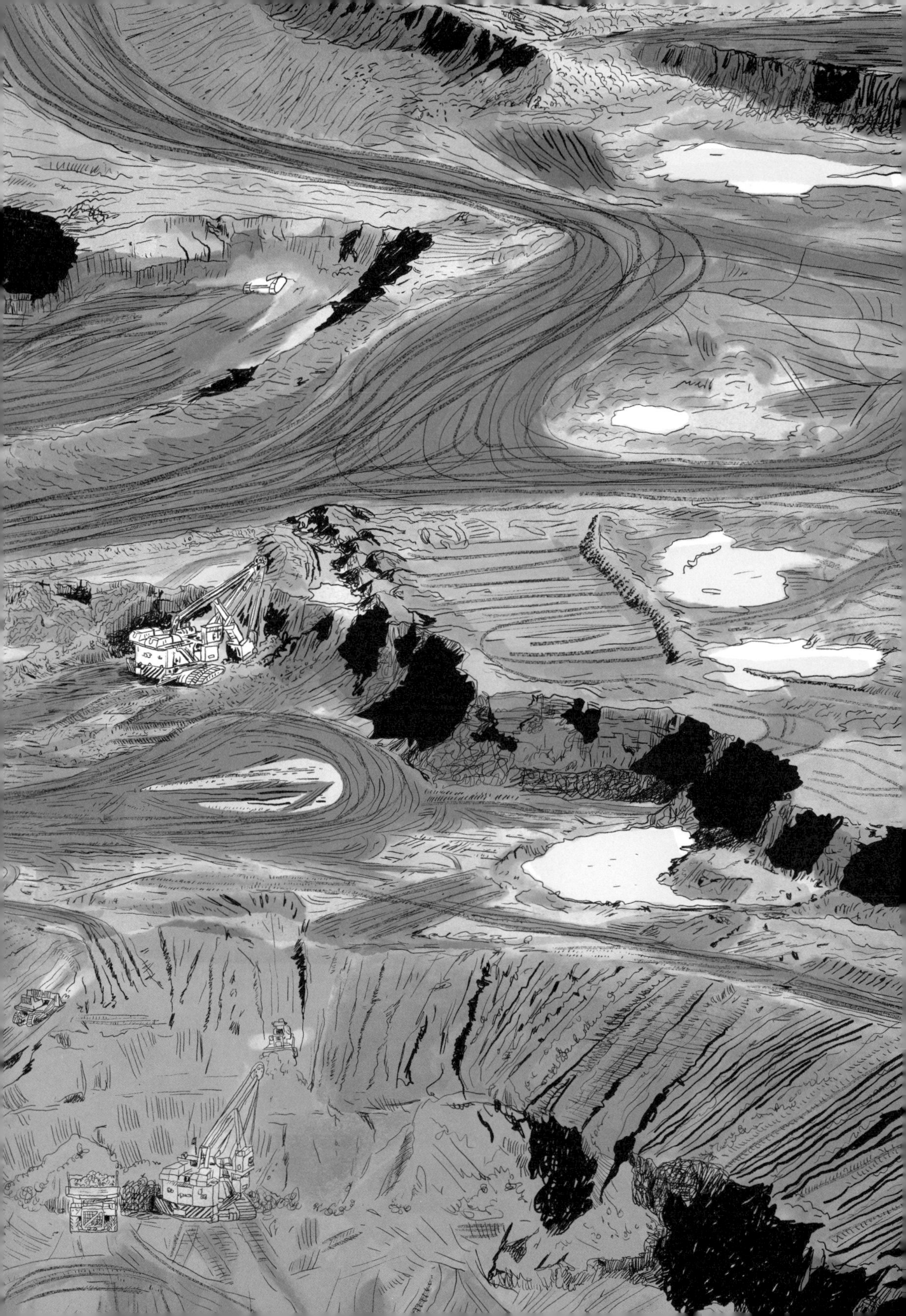

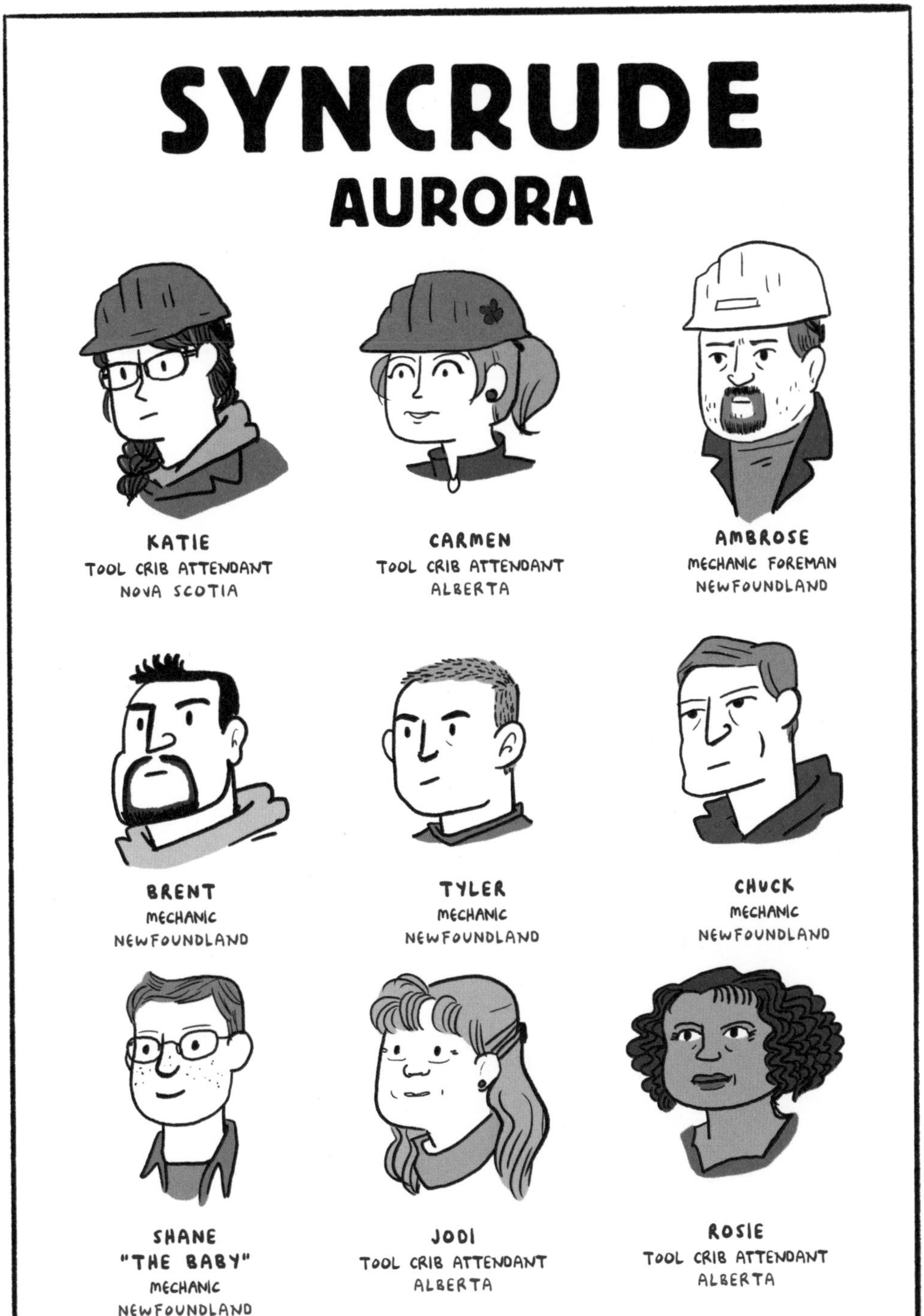
SYNCRUDE
AURORA
KATIE
TOOL CRIB ATTENDANT
NOVA SCOTIA
CARMEN
TOOL CRIB ATTENDANT
ALBERTA
AMBROSE
MECHANIC FOREMAN
NEWFOUNDLAND
BRENT
MECHANIC
NEWFOUNDLAND
TYLER
MECHANIC
NEWFOUNDLAND
CHUCK
MECHANIC
NEWFOUNDLAND
SHANE
"THE BABY"
MECHANIC
NEWFOUNDLAND
JODI
TOOL CRIB ATTENDANT
ALBERTA
ROSIE
TOOL CRIB ATTENDANT
ALBERTA

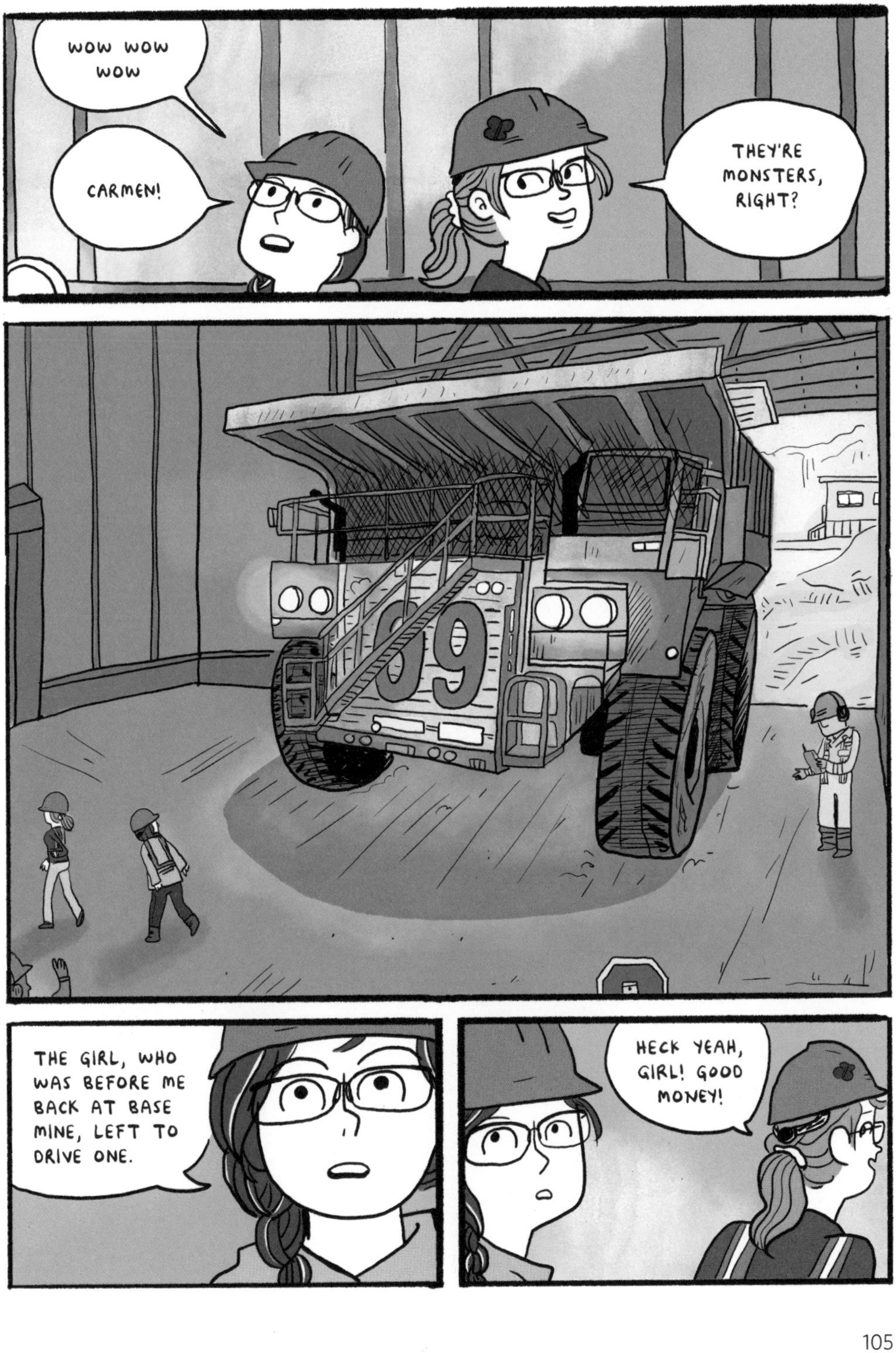
WOW WOW WOW
CARMEN!
THEY'RE MONSTERS, RIGHT?
THE GIRL, WHO WAS BEFORE ME BACK AT BASE MINE, LEFT TO DRIVE ONE.
HECK YEAH, GIRL! GOOD MONEY!

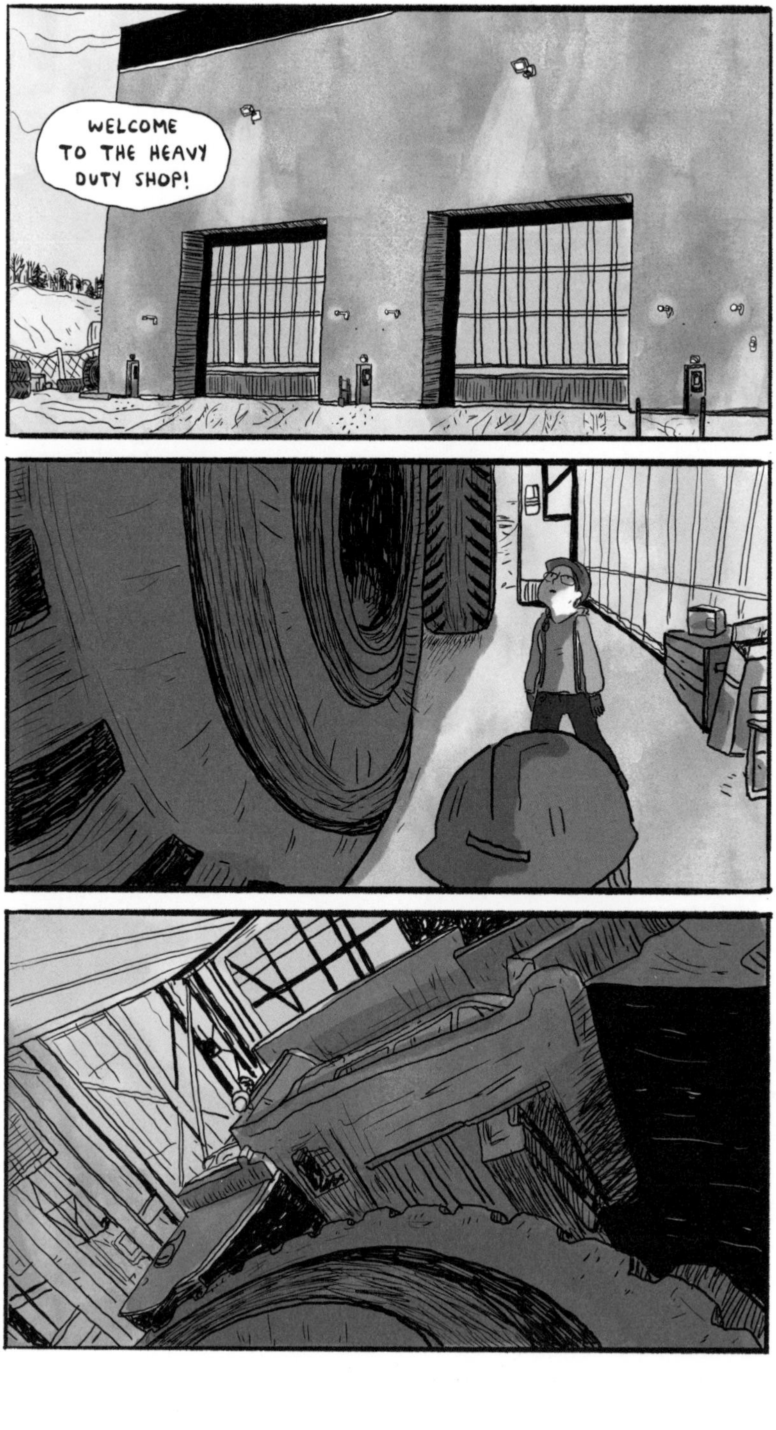
WELCOME TO THE HEAVY DUTY SHOP!

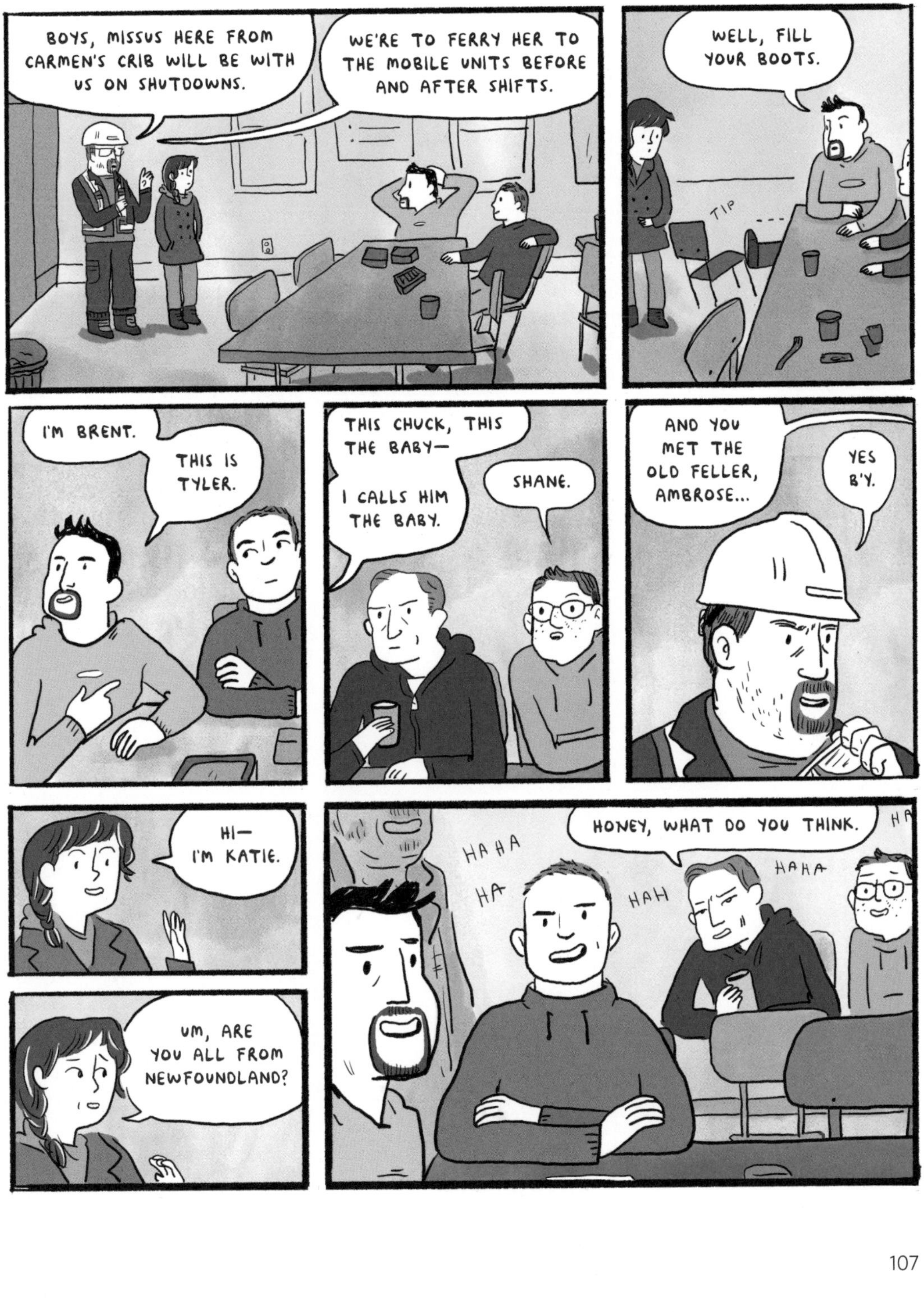

BOYS, MISSUS HERE FROM CARMEN'S CRIB WILL BE WITH US ON SHUTDOWNS.
WE'RE TO FERRY HER TO THE MOBILE UNITS BEFORE AND AFTER SHIFTS.
WELL, FILL YOUR BOOTS.
TIP
I'M BRENT.
THIS IS TYLER.
THIS CHUCK, THIS THE BABY—
I CALLS HIM THE BABY.
SHANE.
AND YOU MET THE OLD FELLER, AMBROSE...
YES B'Y.
HI— I'M KATIE.
UM, ARE YOU ALL FROM NEWFOUNDLAND?
HONEY, WHAT DO YOU THINK.
HA HA
HA
HAH
HAHA

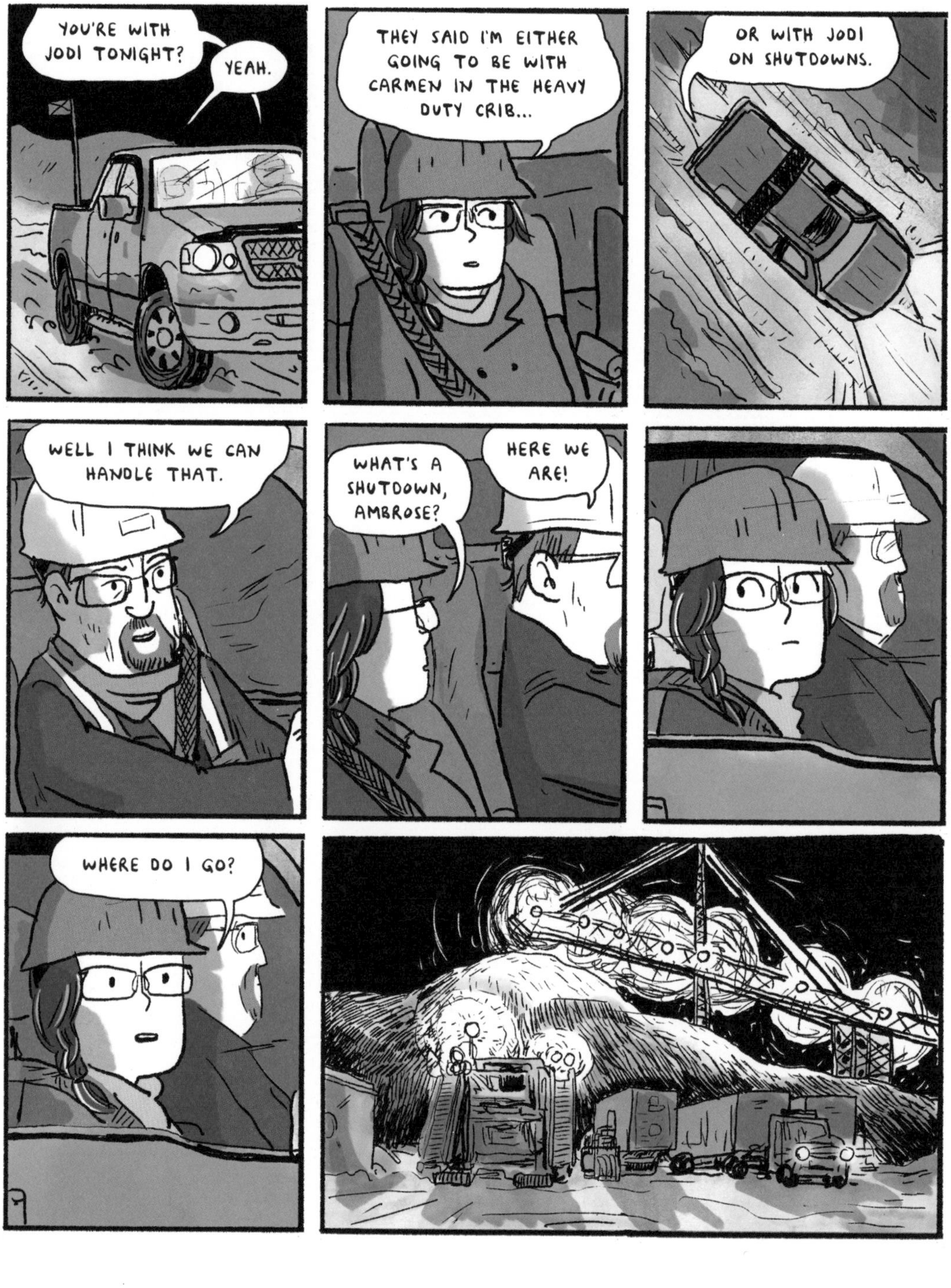
YOU'RE WITH JODI TONIGHT?
YEAH.
THEY SAID I'M EITHER GOING TO BE WITH CARMEN IN THE HEAVY DUTY CRIB...
OR WITH JODI ON SHUTDOWNS.
WELL I THINK WE CAN HANDLE THAT.
WHAT'S A SHUTDOWN, AMBROSE?
HERE WE ARE!
WHERE DO I GO?

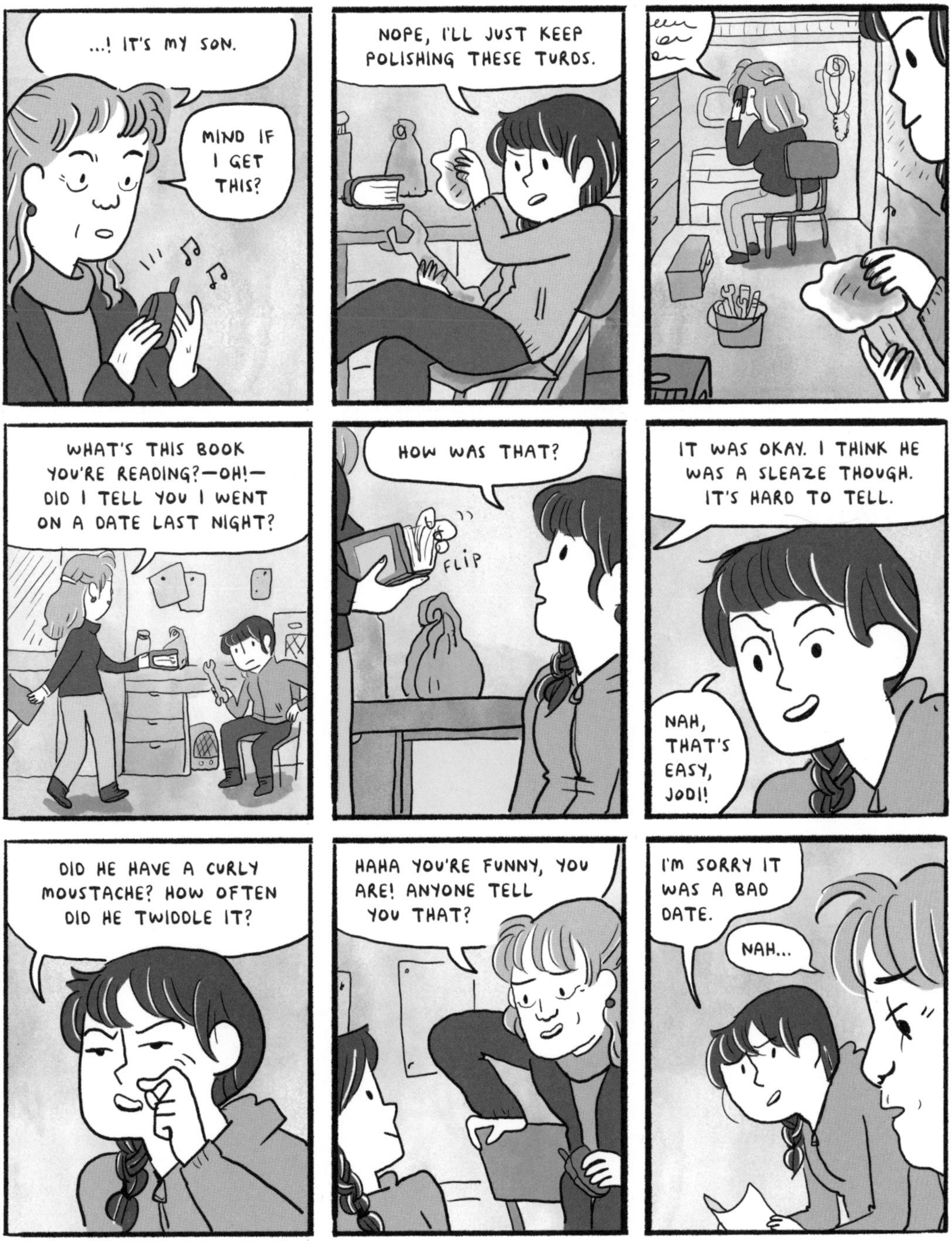
...! IT'S MY SON.
MIND IF I GET THIS?
NOPE, I'LL JUST KEEP POLISHING THESE TURDS.
WHAT'S THIS BOOK YOU'RE READING?—OH!—DID I TELL YOU I WENT ON A DATE LAST NIGHT?
HOW WAS THAT?
FLIP
IT WAS OKAY. I THINK HE WAS A SLEAZE THOUGH. IT'S HARD TO TELL.
NAH, THAT'S EASY, JODI!
DID HE HAVE A CURLY MOUSTACHE? HOW OFTEN DID HE TWIDDLE IT?
HAHA YOU'RE FUNNY, YOU ARE! ANYONE TELL YOU THAT?
I'M SORRY IT WAS A BAD DATE.
NAH...

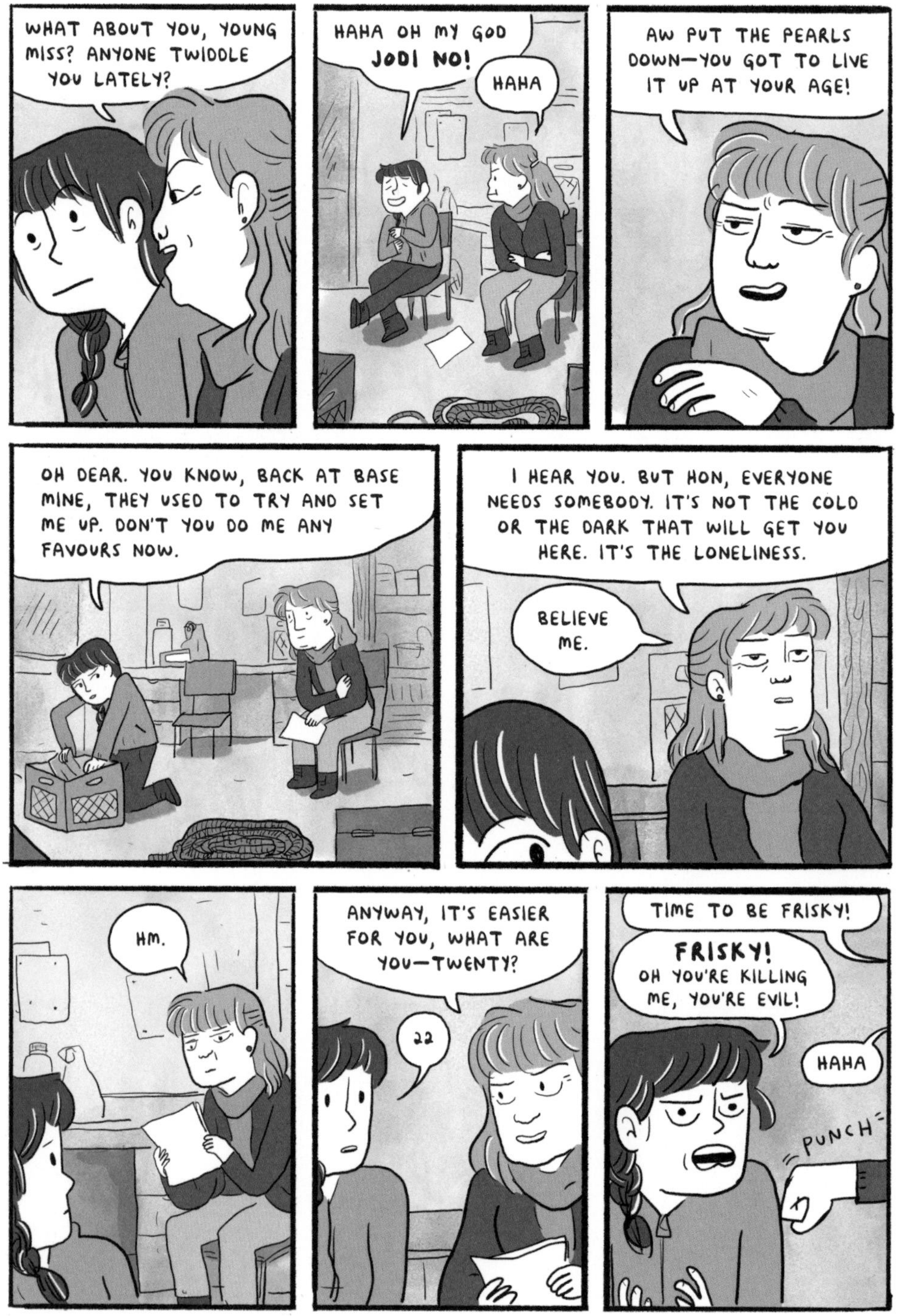
WHAT ABOUT YOU, YOUNG MISS? ANYONE TWIDDLE YOU LATELY?
HAHA OH MY GOD **JODI NO!**
HAHA
AW PUT THE PEARLS DOWN—YOU GOT TO LIVE IT UP AT YOUR AGE!
OH DEAR. YOU KNOW, BACK AT BASE MINE, THEY USED TO TRY AND SET ME UP. DON'T YOU DO ME ANY FAVOURS NOW.
I HEAR YOU. BUT HON, EVERYONE NEEDS SOMEBODY. IT'S NOT THE COLD OR THE DARK THAT WILL GET YOU HERE. IT'S THE LONELINESS.
BELIEVE ME.
HM.
ANYWAY, IT'S EASIER FOR YOU, WHAT ARE YOU—TWENTY?
22
TIME TO BE FRISKY!
FRISKY! OH YOU'RE KILLING ME, YOU'RE EVIL!
HAHA
PUNCH

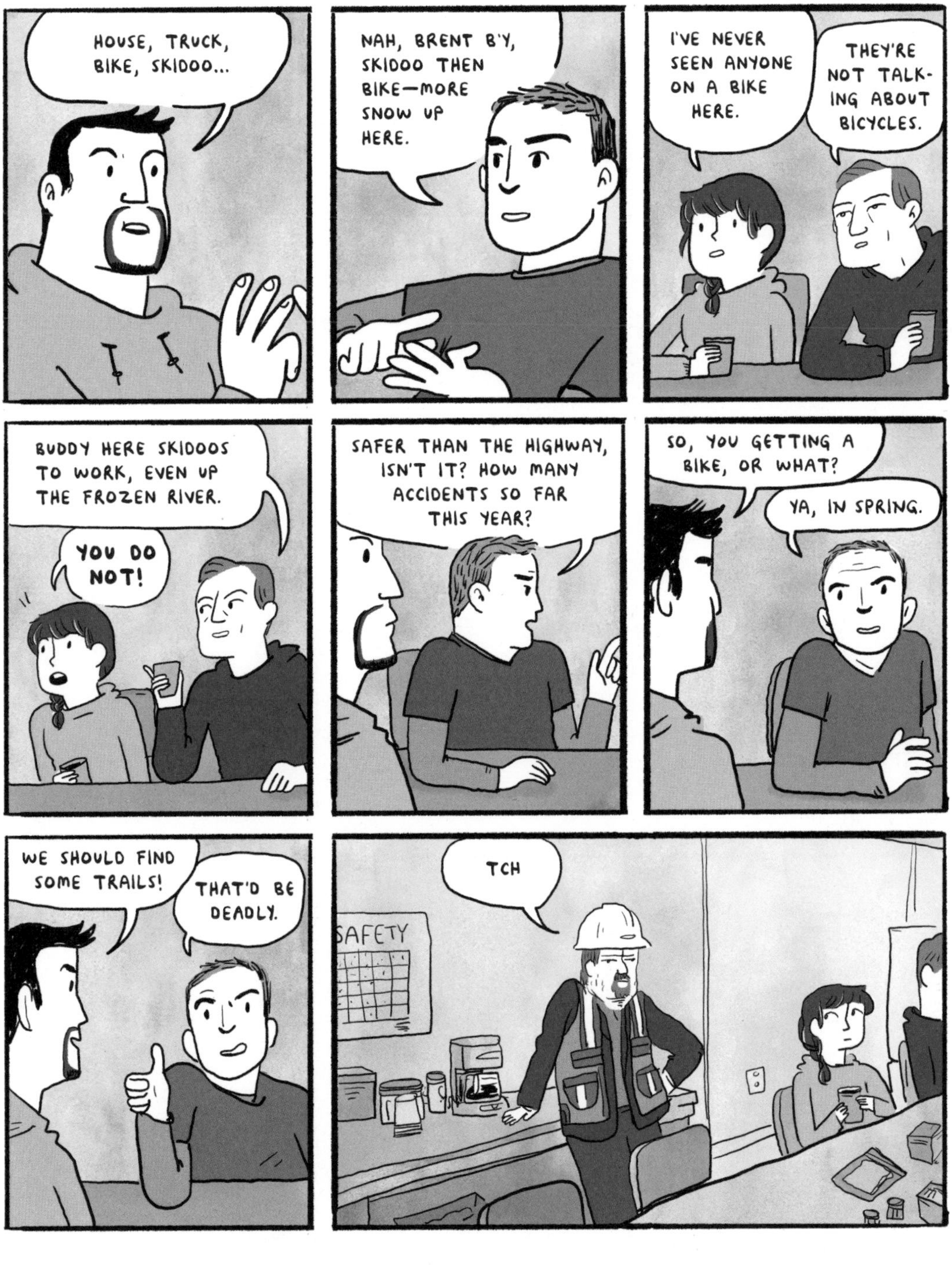
HOUSE, TRUCK, BIKE, SKIDOO...
NAH, BRENT B'Y, SKIDOO THEN BIKE—MORE SNOW UP HERE.
I'VE NEVER SEEN ANYONE ON A BIKE HERE.
THEY'RE NOT TALK-ING ABOUT BICYCLES.
BUDDY HERE SKIDOOS TO WORK, EVEN UP THE FROZEN RIVER.
YOU DO NOT!
SAFER THAN THE HIGHWAY, ISN'T IT? HOW MANY ACCIDENTS SO FAR THIS YEAR?
SO, YOU GETTING A BIKE, OR WHAT?
YA, IN SPRING.
WE SHOULD FIND SOME TRAILS!
THAT'D BE DEADLY.
TCH
SAFETY

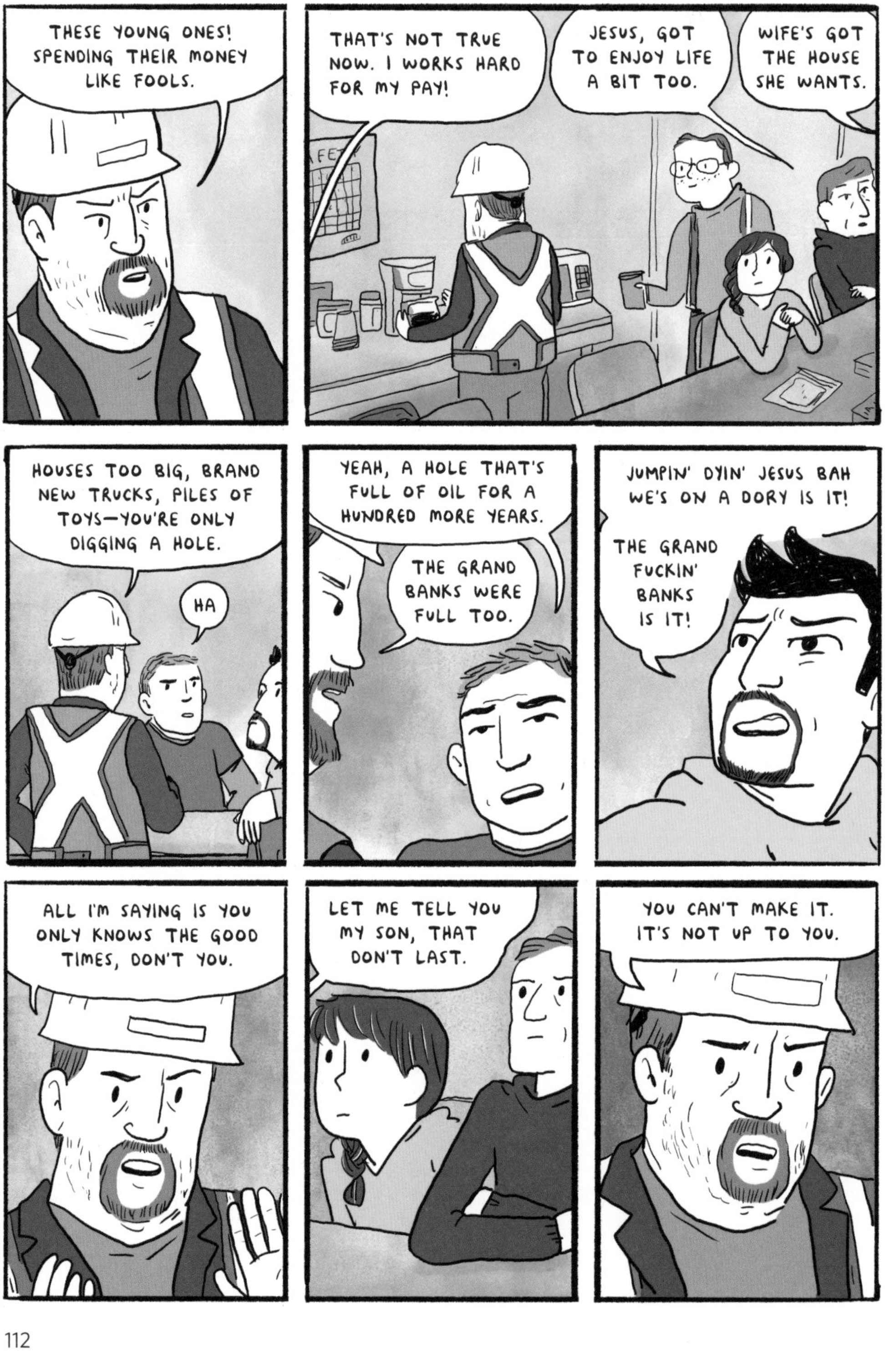

THESE YOUNG ONES! SPENDING THEIR MONEY LIKE FOOLS.
THAT'S NOT TRUE NOW. I WORKS HARD FOR MY PAY!
JESUS, GOT TO ENJOY LIFE A BIT TOO.
WIFE'S GOT THE HOUSE SHE WANTS.
HOUSES TOO BIG, BRAND NEW TRUCKS, PILES OF TOYS—YOU'RE ONLY DIGGING A HOLE.
HA
YEAH, A HOLE THAT'S FULL OF OIL FOR A HUNDRED MORE YEARS.
THE GRAND BANKS WERE FULL TOO.
JUMPIN' DYIN' JESUS BAH WE'S ON A DORY IS IT!
THE GRAND FUCKIN' BANKS IS IT!
ALL I'M SAYING IS YOU ONLY KNOWS THE GOOD TIMES, DON'T YOU.
LET ME TELL YOU MY SON, THAT DON'T LAST.
YOU CAN'T MAKE IT. IT'S NOT UP TO YOU.

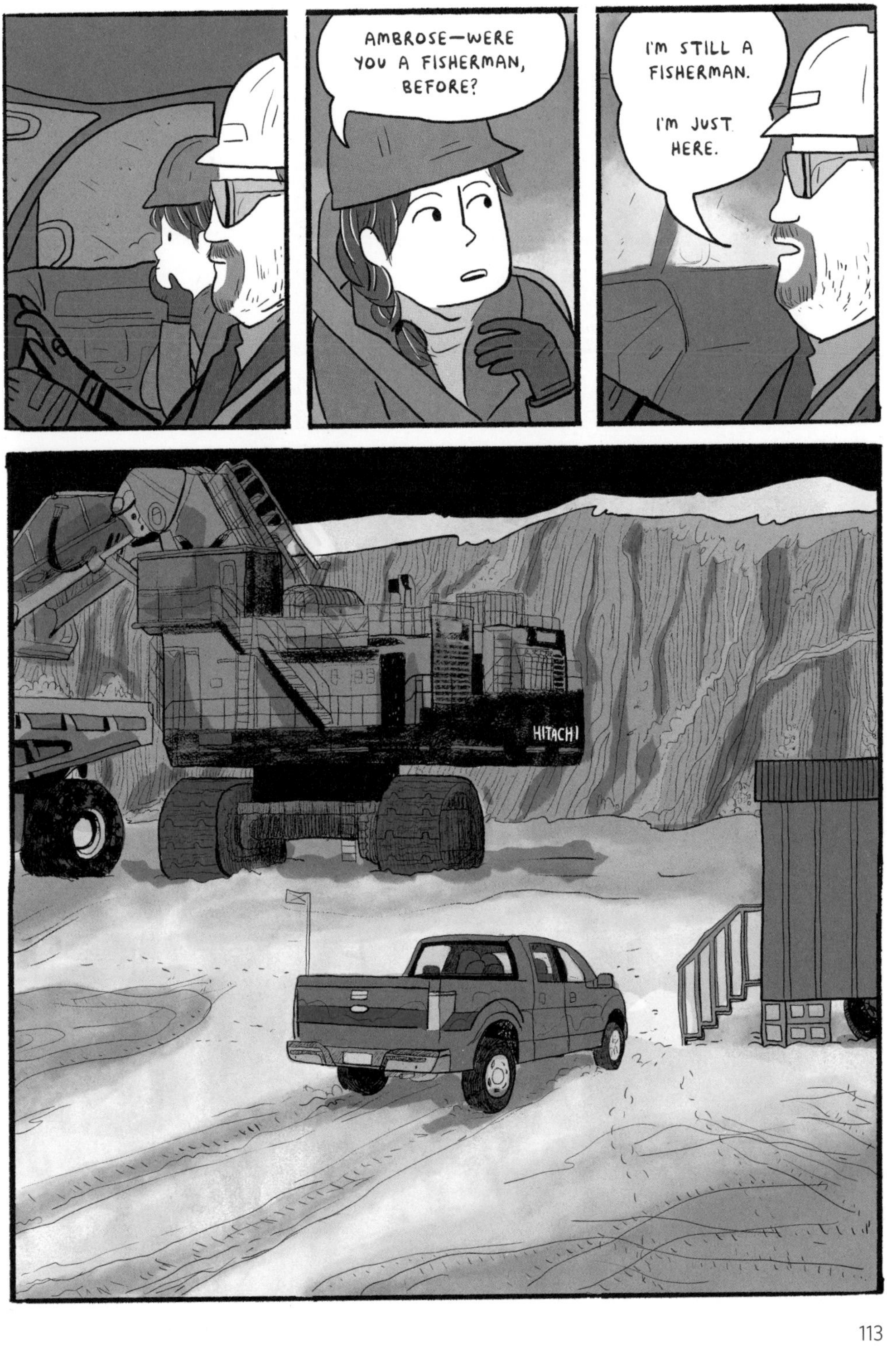
AMBROSE—WERE YOU A FISHERMAN, BEFORE?
I'M STILL A FISHERMAN.
I'M JUST HERE.
HITACHI

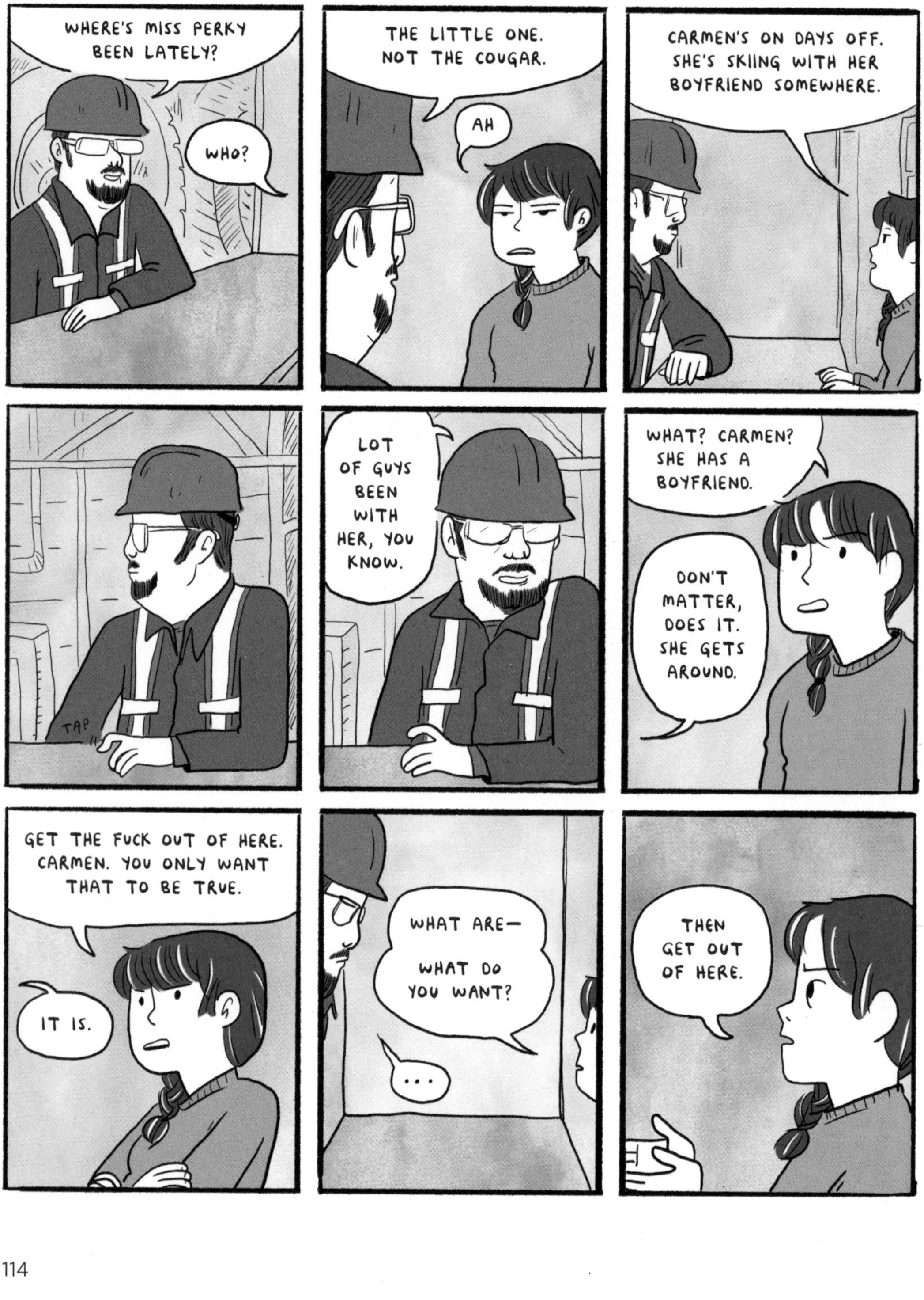
WHERE'S MISS PERKY BEEN LATELY?
WHO?
THE LITTLE ONE. NOT THE COUGAR.
AH
CARMEN'S ON DAYS OFF. SHE'S SKIING WITH HER BOYFRIEND SOMEWHERE.
TAP
LOT OF GUYS BEEN WITH HER, YOU KNOW.
WHAT? CARMEN? SHE HAS A BOYFRIEND.
DON'T MATTER, DOES IT. SHE GETS AROUND.
GET THE FUCK OUT OF HERE. CARMEN. YOU ONLY WANT THAT TO BE TRUE.
IT IS.
WHAT ARE—
WHAT DO YOU WANT?
...
THEN GET OUT OF HERE.

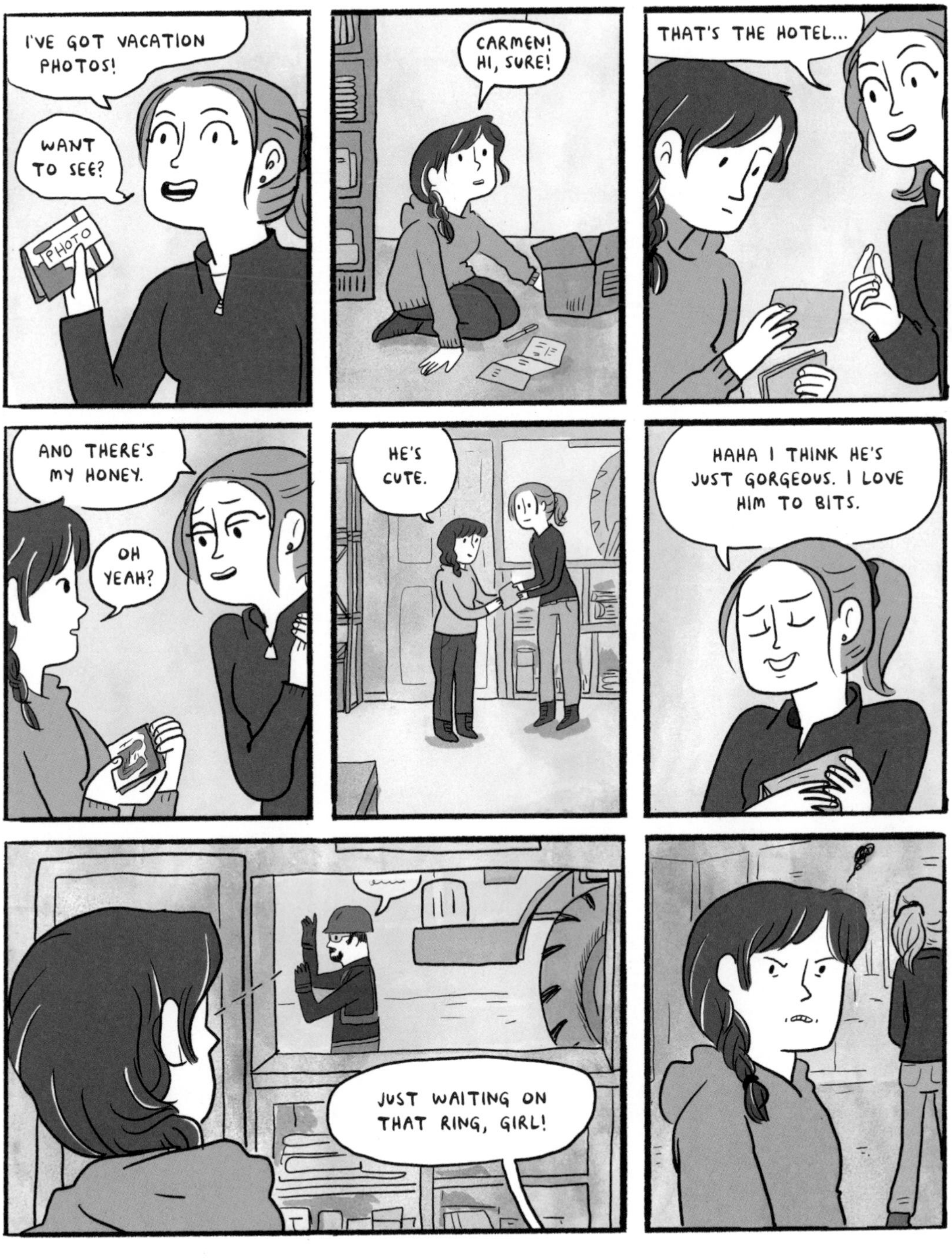
I'VE GOT VACATION PHOTOS!
WANT TO SEE?
PHOTO
CARMEN! HI, SURE!
THAT'S THE HOTEL...
AND THERE'S MY HONEY.
OH YEAH?
HE'S CUTE.
HAHA I THINK HE'S JUST GORGEOUS. I LOVE HIM TO BITS.
JUST WAITING ON THAT RING, GIRL!

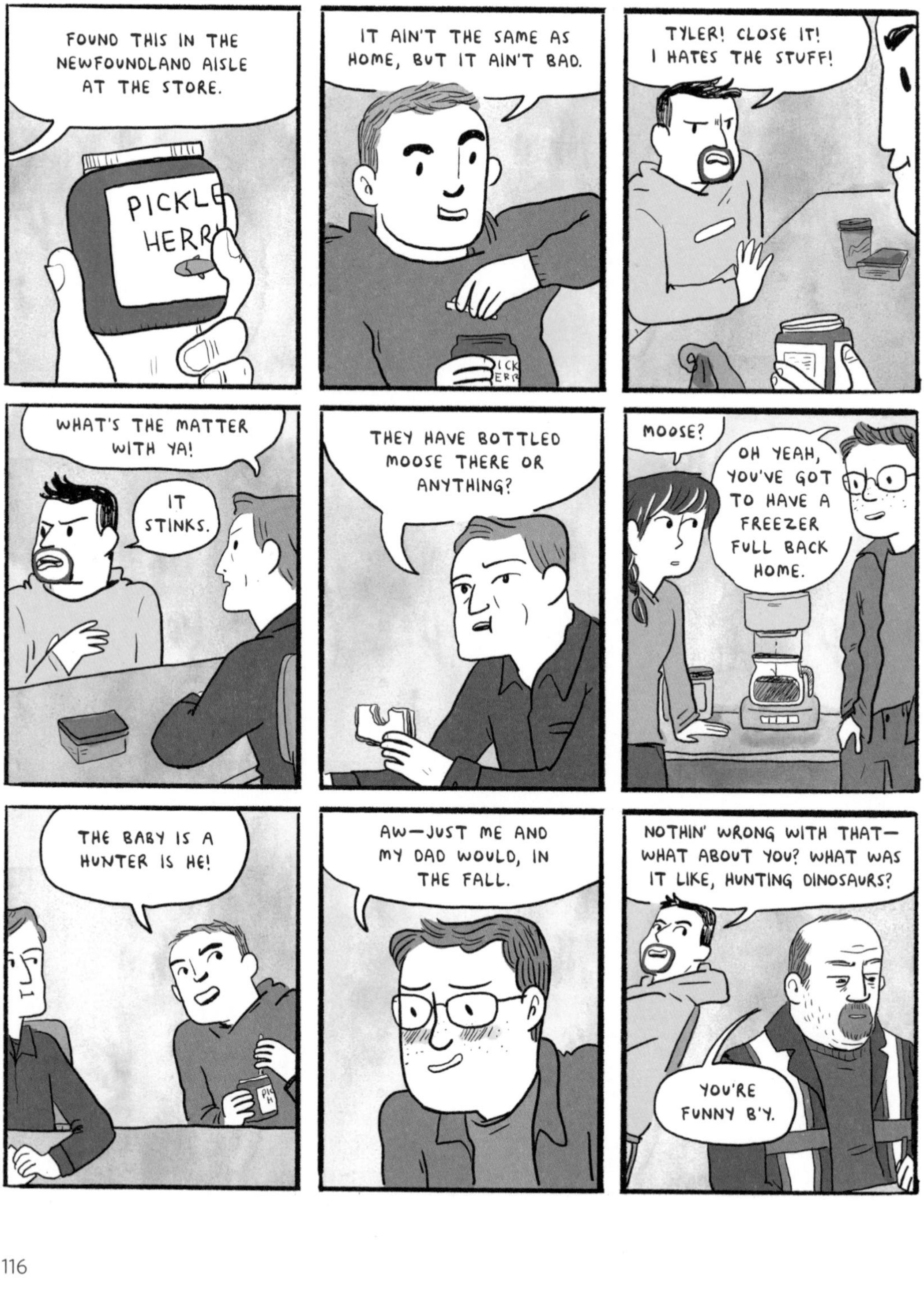
FOUND THIS IN THE NEWFOUNDLAND AISLE AT THE STORE.
PICKLE HERR
IT AIN'T THE SAME AS HOME, BUT IT AIN'T BAD.
TYLER! CLOSE IT! I HATES THE STUFF!
WHAT'S THE MATTER WITH YA!
IT STINKS.
THEY HAVE BOTTLED MOOSE THERE OR ANYTHING?
MOOSE?
OH YEAH, YOU'VE GOT TO HAVE A FREEZER FULL BACK HOME.
THE BABY IS A HUNTER IS HE!
AW—JUST ME AND MY DAD WOULD, IN THE FALL.
NOTHIN' WRONG WITH THAT—WHAT ABOUT YOU? WHAT WAS IT LIKE, HUNTING DINOSAURS?
YOU'RE FUNNY B'Y.

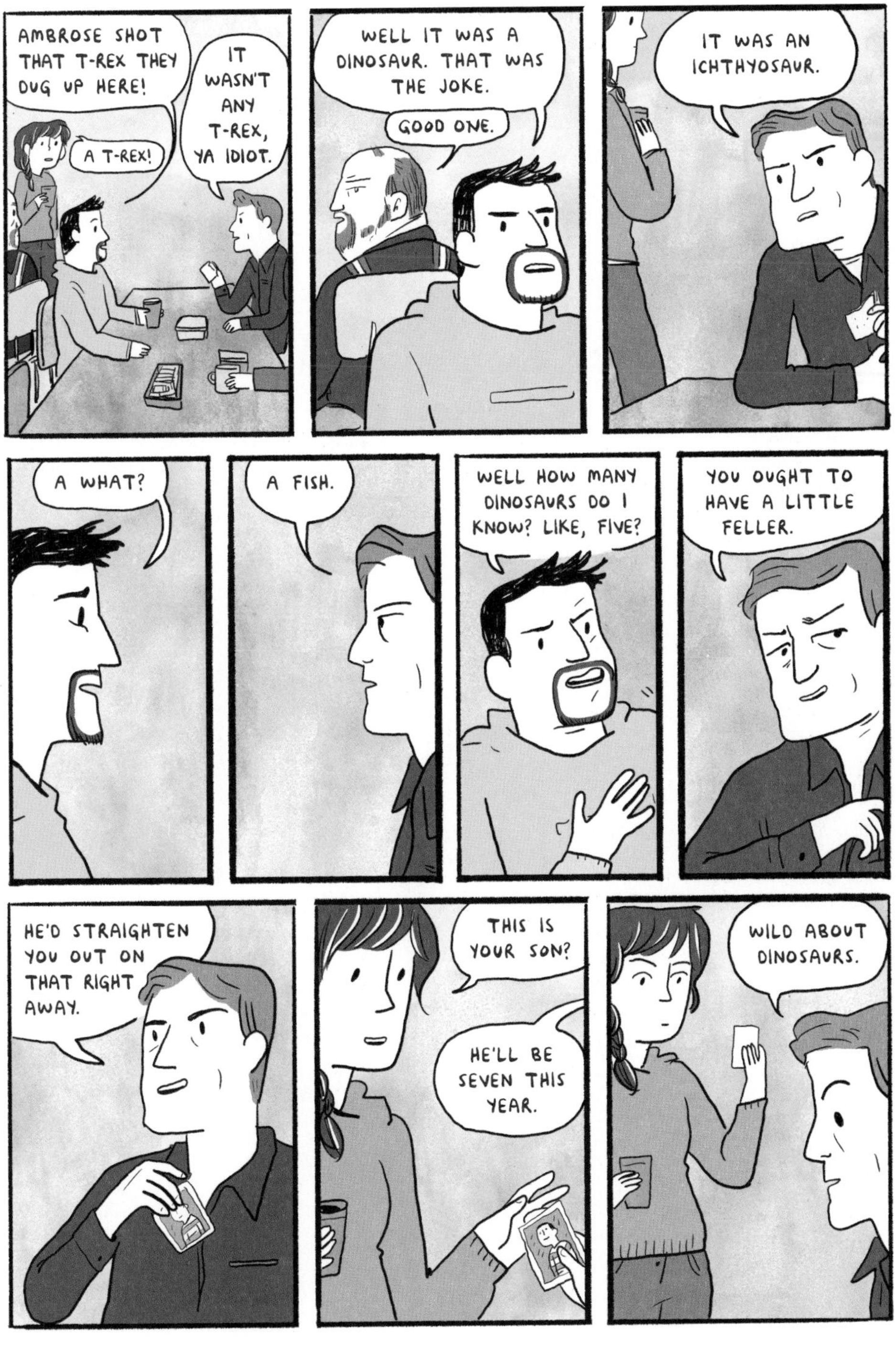

AMBROSE SHOT THAT T-REX THEY DUG UP HERE!
A T-REX!
IT WASN'T ANY T-REX, YA IDIOT.
WELL IT WAS A DINOSAUR. THAT WAS THE JOKE.
GOOD ONE.
IT WAS AN ICHTHYOSAUR.
A WHAT?
A FISH.
WELL HOW MANY DINOSAURS DO I KNOW? LIKE, FIVE?
YOU OUGHT TO HAVE A LITTLE FELLER.
HE'D STRAIGHTEN YOU OUT ON THAT RIGHT AWAY.
THIS IS YOUR SON?
HE'LL BE SEVEN THIS YEAR.
WILD ABOUT DINOSAURS.

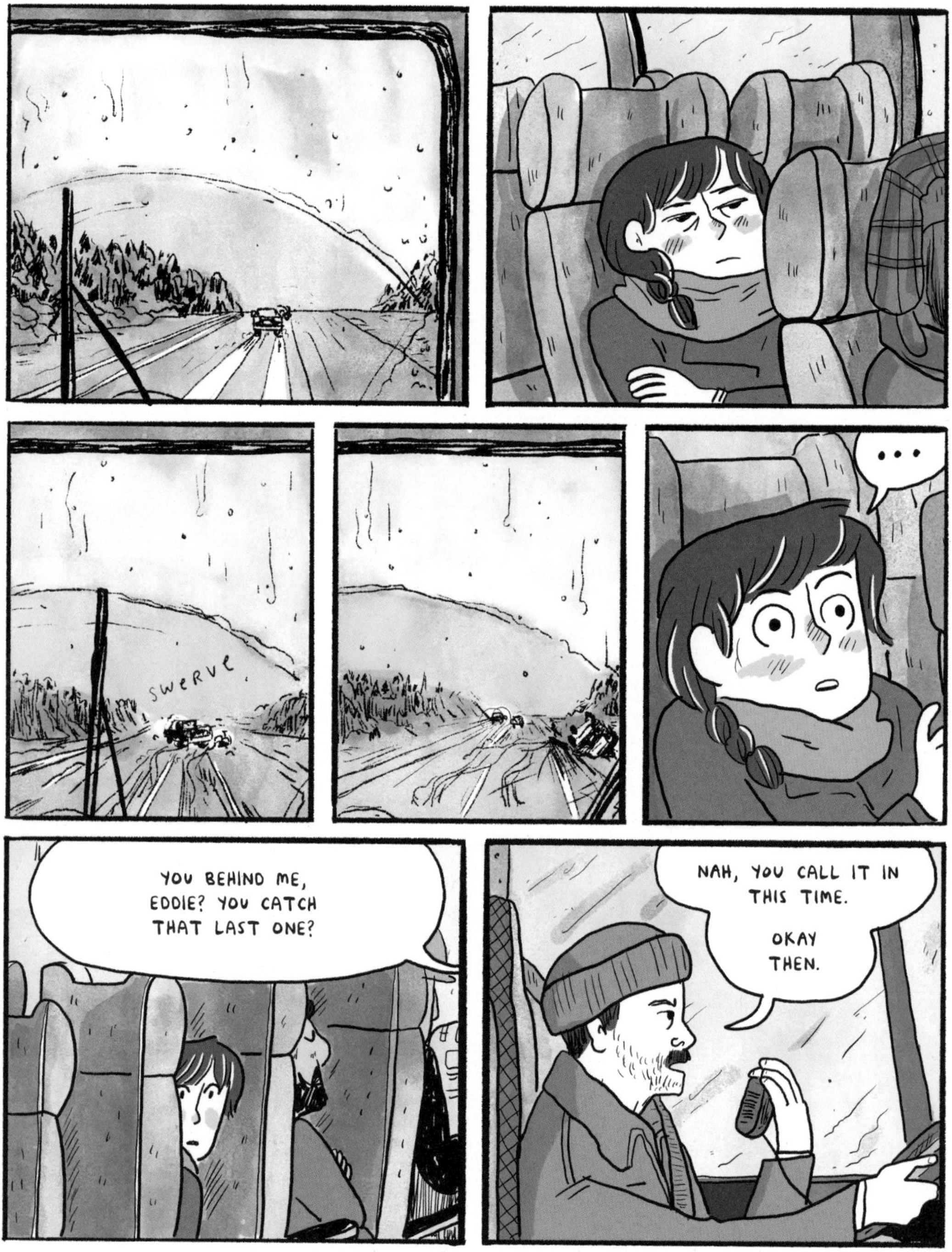
SWERVE
...
YOU BEHIND ME, EDDIE? YOU CATCH THAT LAST ONE?
NAH, YOU CALL IT IN THIS TIME.
OKAY THEN.

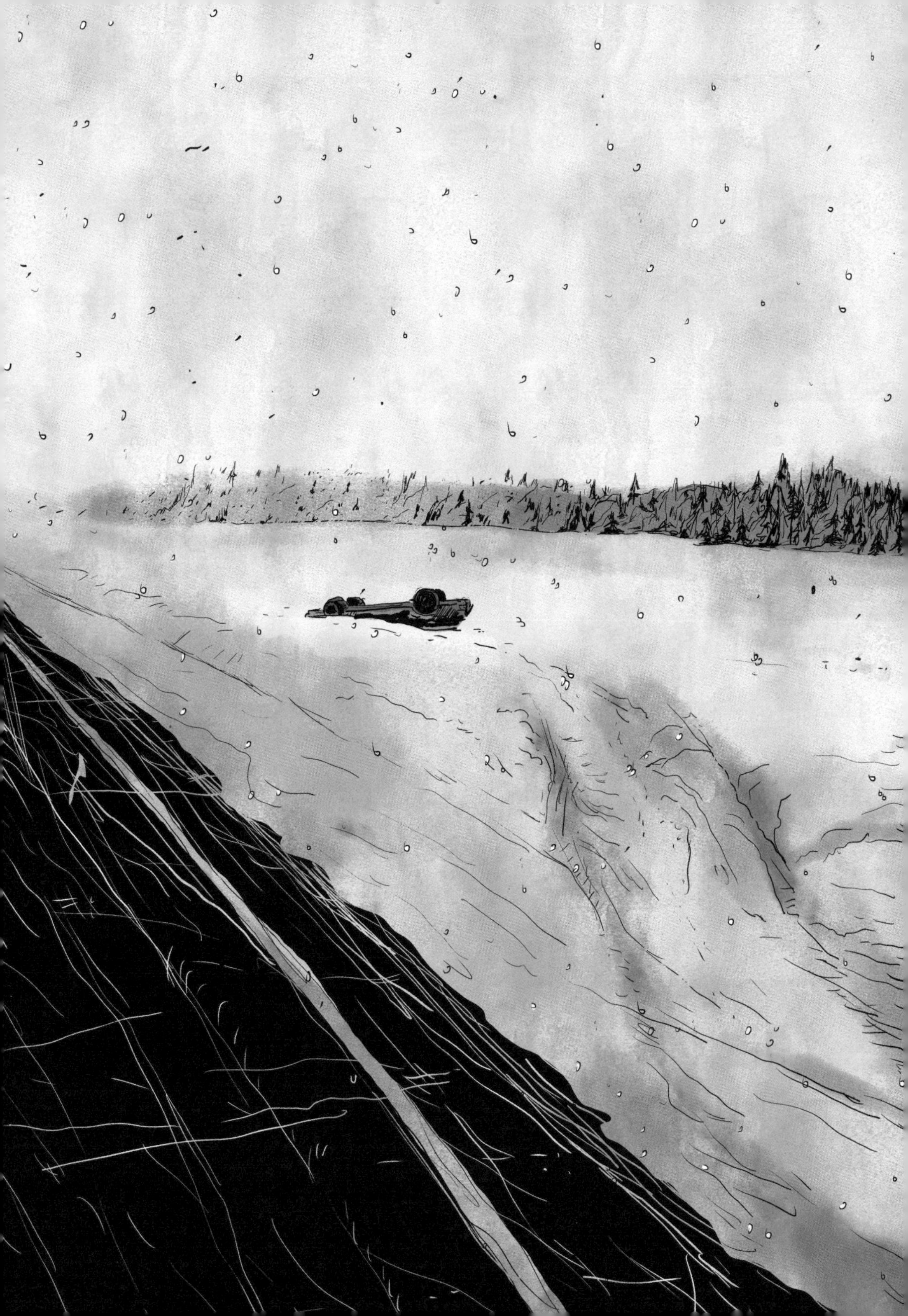

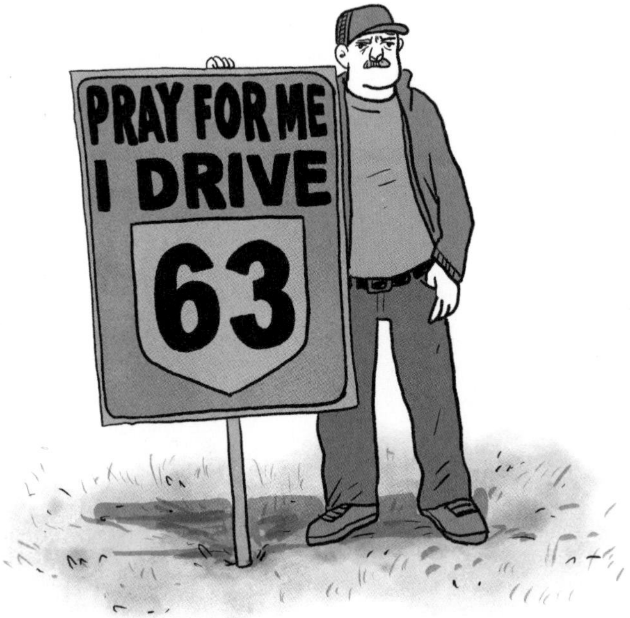
PRAY FOR ME
I DRIVE
63

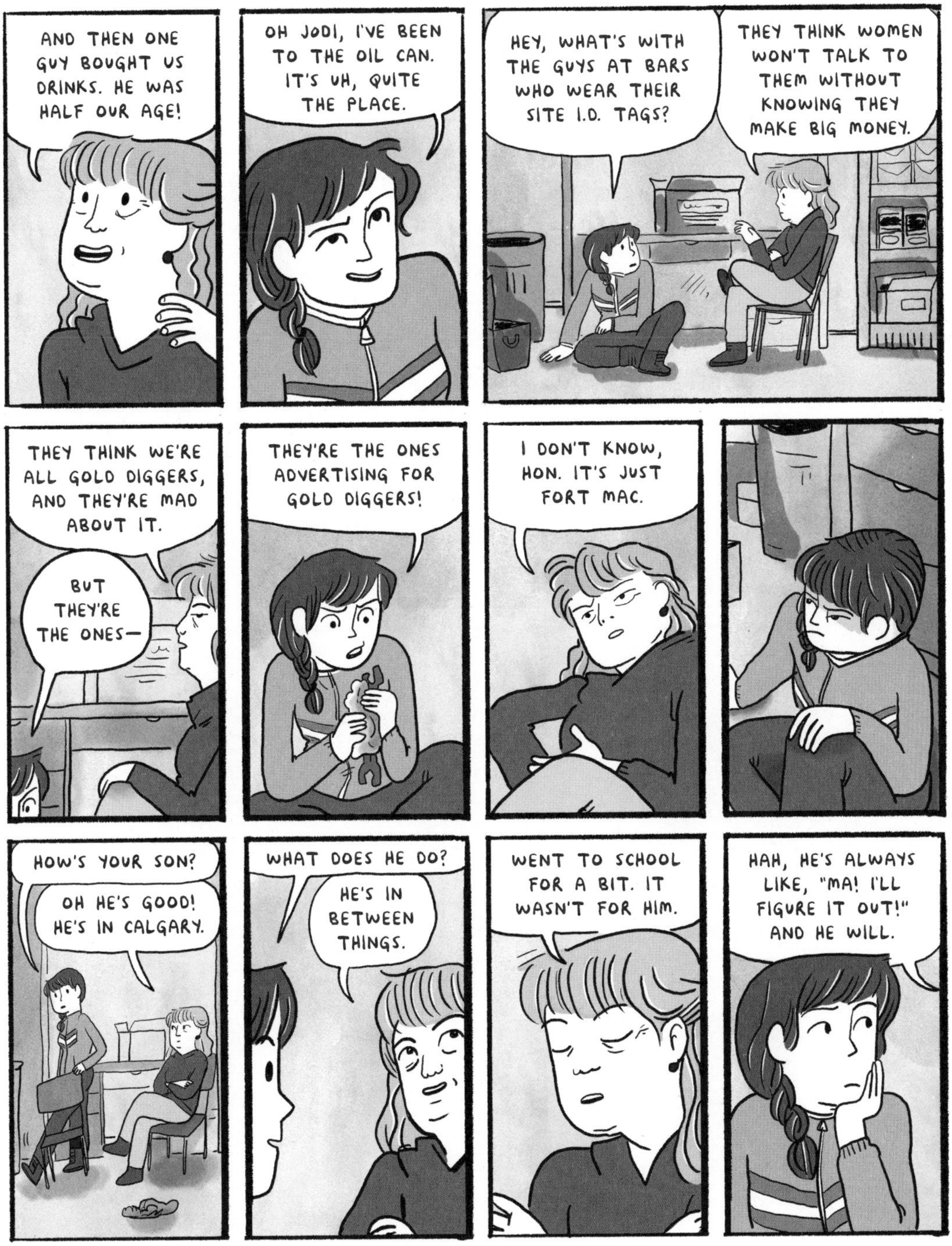
AND THEN ONE GUY BOUGHT US DRINKS. HE WAS HALF OUR AGE!
OH JODI, I'VE BEEN TO THE OIL CAN. IT'S UH, QUITE THE PLACE.
HEY, WHAT'S WITH THE GUYS AT BARS WHO WEAR THEIR SITE I.D. TAGS?
THEY THINK WOMEN WON'T TALK TO THEM WITHOUT KNOWING THEY MAKE BIG MONEY.
THEY THINK WE'RE ALL GOLD DIGGERS, AND THEY'RE MAD ABOUT IT.
BUT THEY'RE THE ONES—
THEY'RE THE ONES ADVERTISING FOR GOLD DIGGERS!
I DON'T KNOW, HON. IT'S JUST FORT MAC.
HOW'S YOUR SON?
OH HE'S GOOD! HE'S IN CALGARY.
WHAT DOES HE DO?
HE'S IN BETWEEN THINGS.
WENT TO SCHOOL FOR A BIT. IT WASN'T FOR HIM.
HAH, HE'S ALWAYS LIKE, "MA! I'LL FIGURE IT OUT!" AND HE WILL.

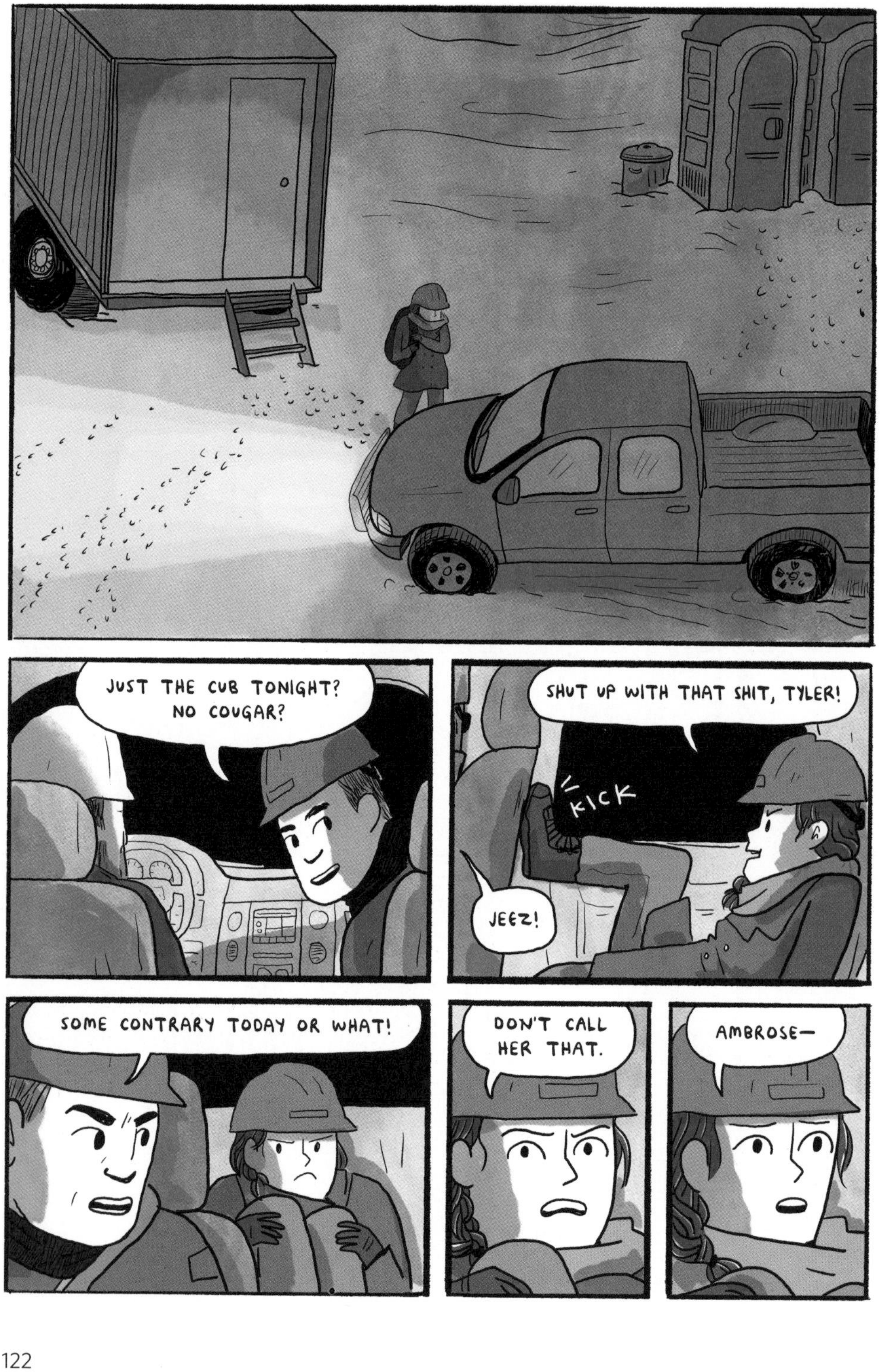

JUST THE CUB TONIGHT? NO COUGAR?
SHUT UP WITH THAT SHIT, TYLER!
KICK
JEEZ!
SOME CONTRARY TODAY OR WHAT!
DON'T CALL HER THAT.
AMBROSE—

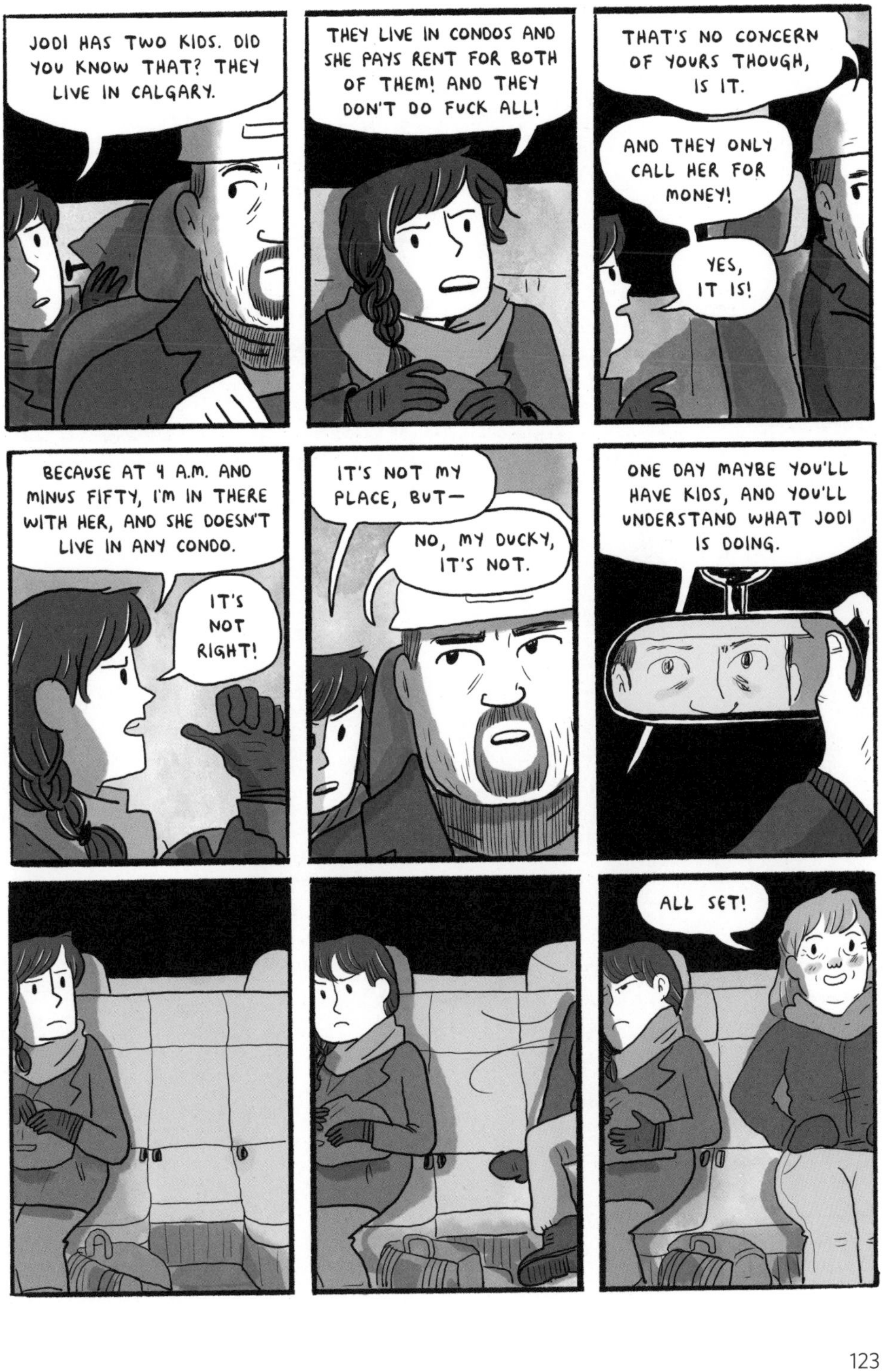
JODI HAS TWO KIDS. DID YOU KNOW THAT? THEY LIVE IN CALGARY.
THEY LIVE IN CONDOS AND SHE PAYS RENT FOR BOTH OF THEM! AND THEY DON'T DO FUCK ALL!
THAT'S NO CONCERN OF YOURS THOUGH, IS IT.
AND THEY ONLY CALL HER FOR MONEY!
YES, IT IS!
BECAUSE AT 4 A.M. AND MINUS FIFTY, I'M IN THERE WITH HER, AND SHE DOESN'T LIVE IN ANY CONDO.
IT'S NOT RIGHT!
IT'S NOT MY PLACE, BUT—
NO, MY DUCKY, IT'S NOT.
ONE DAY MAYBE YOU'LL HAVE KIDS, AND YOU'LL UNDERSTAND WHAT JODI IS DOING.
ALL SET!

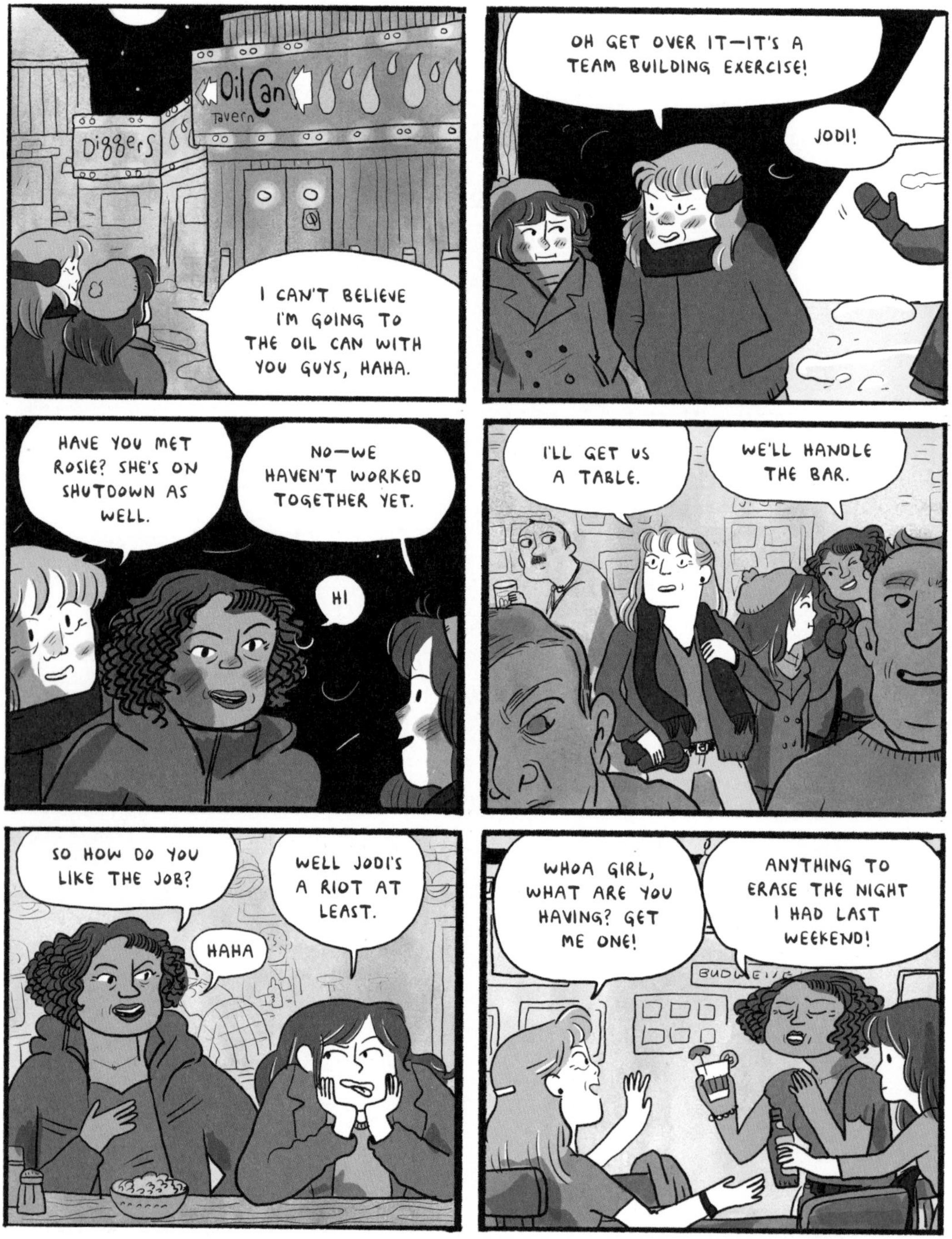
Diggers
Oil Can
Tavern
I CAN'T BELIEVE I'M GOING TO THE OIL CAN WITH YOU GUYS, HAHA.
OH GET OVER IT—IT'S A TEAM BUILDING EXERCISE!
JODI!
HAVE YOU MET ROSIE? SHE'S ON SHUTDOWN AS WELL.
NO—WE HAVEN'T WORKED TOGETHER YET.
HI
I'LL GET US A TABLE.
WE'LL HANDLE THE BAR.
SO HOW DO YOU LIKE THE JOB?
HAHA
WELL JODI'S A RIOT AT LEAST.
WHOA GIRL, WHAT ARE YOU HAVING? GET ME ONE!
ANYTHING TO ERASE THE NIGHT I HAD LAST WEEKEND!

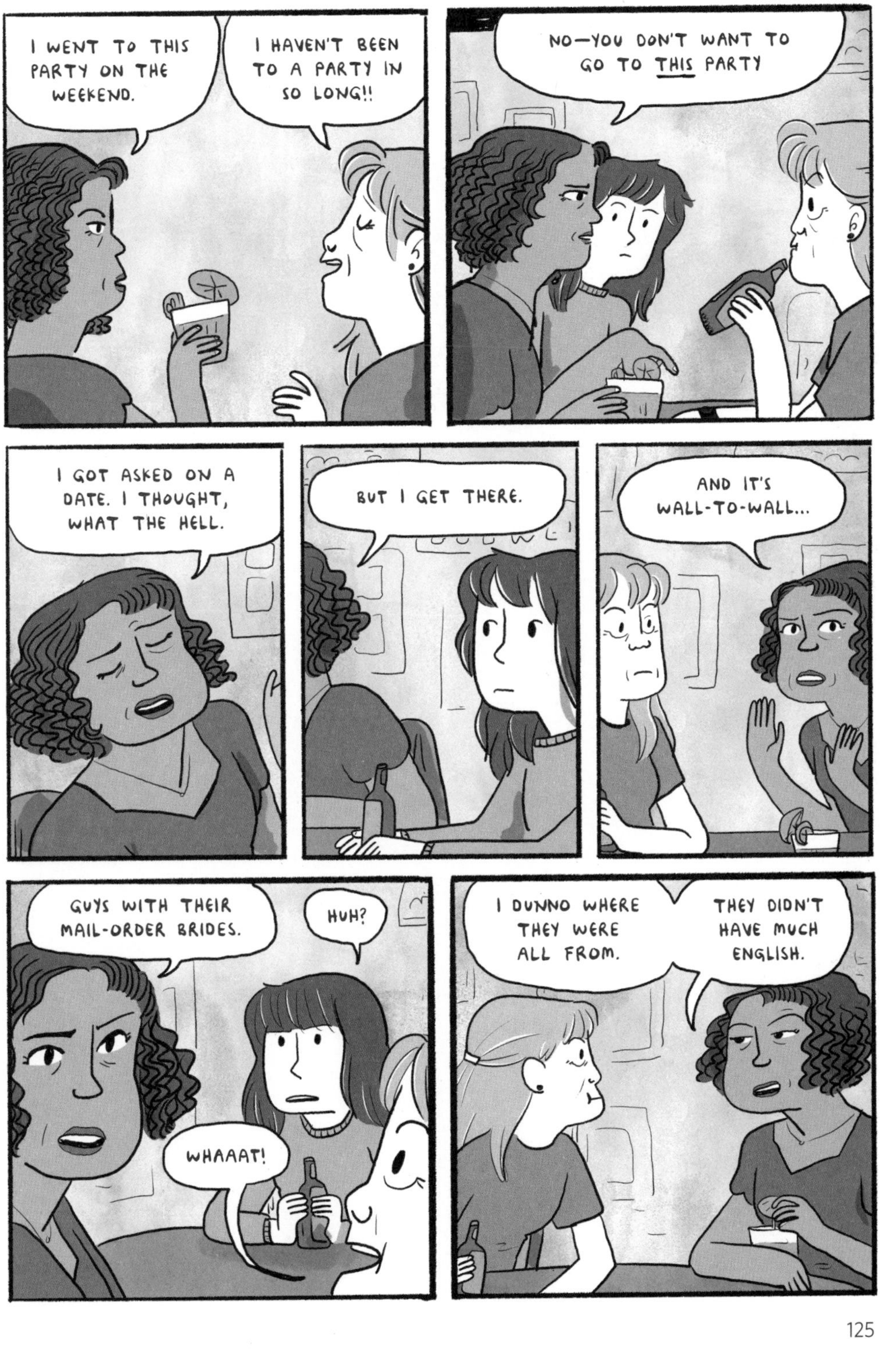
I WENT TO THIS PARTY ON THE WEEKEND.
I HAVEN'T BEEN TO A PARTY IN SO LONG!!
NO—YOU DON'T WANT TO GO TO THIS PARTY
I GOT ASKED ON A DATE. I THOUGHT, WHAT THE HELL.
BUT I GET THERE.
AND IT'S WALL-TO-WALL...
GUYS WITH THEIR MAIL-ORDER BRIDES.
HUH?
WHAAAT!
I DUNNO WHERE THEY WERE ALL FROM.
THEY DIDN'T HAVE MUCH ENGLISH.

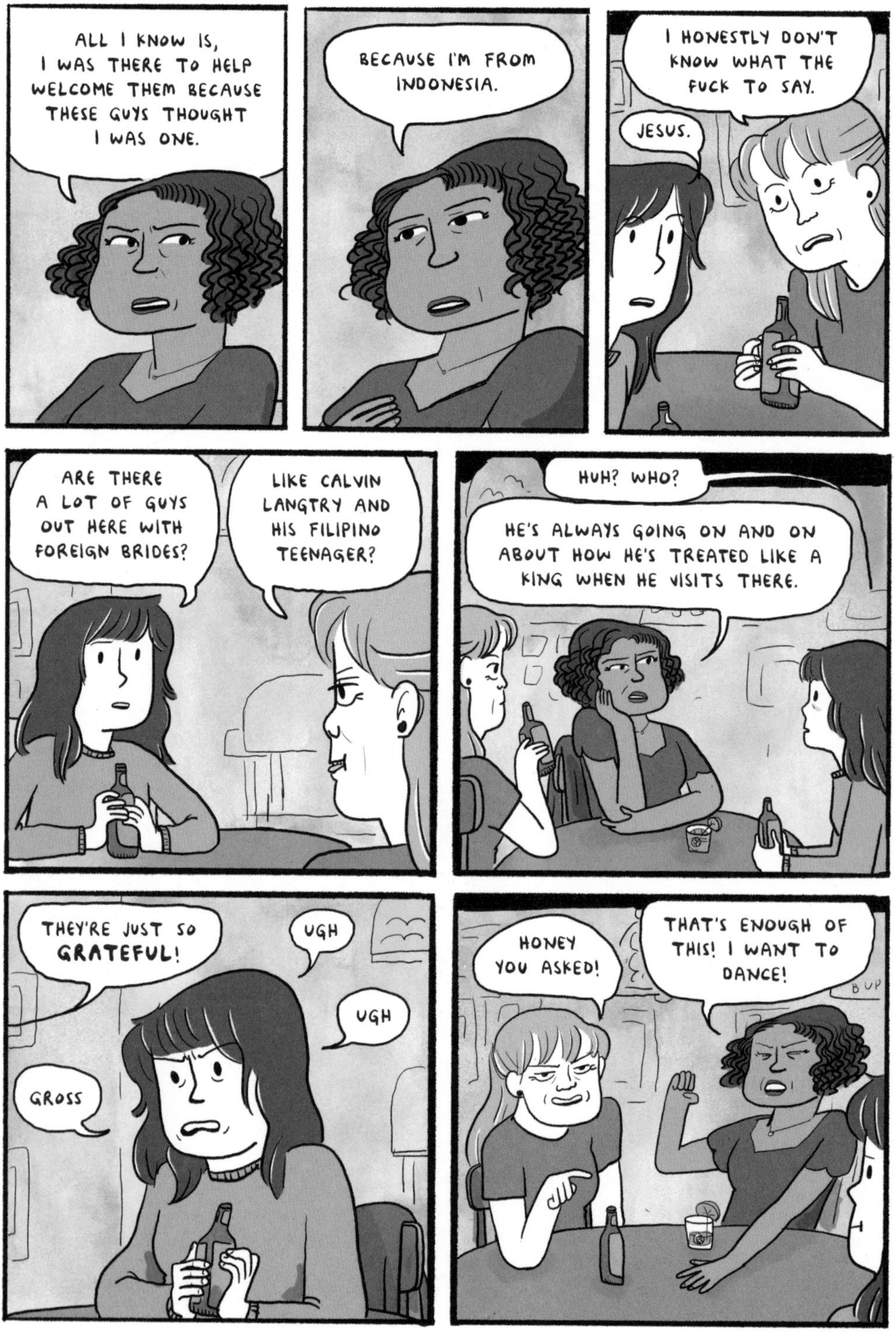
ALL I KNOW IS, I WAS THERE TO HELP WELCOME THEM BECAUSE THESE GUYS THOUGHT I WAS ONE.
BECAUSE I'M FROM INDONESIA.
I HONESTLY DON'T KNOW WHAT THE FUCK TO SAY.
JESUS.
ARE THERE A LOT OF GUYS OUT HERE WITH FOREIGN BRIDES?
LIKE CALVIN LANGTRY AND HIS FILIPINO TEENAGER?
HUH? WHO?
HE'S ALWAYS GOING ON AND ON ABOUT HOW HE'S TREATED LIKE A KING WHEN HE VISITS THERE.
THEY'RE JUST SO **GRATEFUL**!
UGH
UGH
GROSS
HONEY YOU ASKED!
THAT'S ENOUGH OF THIS! I WANT TO DANCE!
BUP

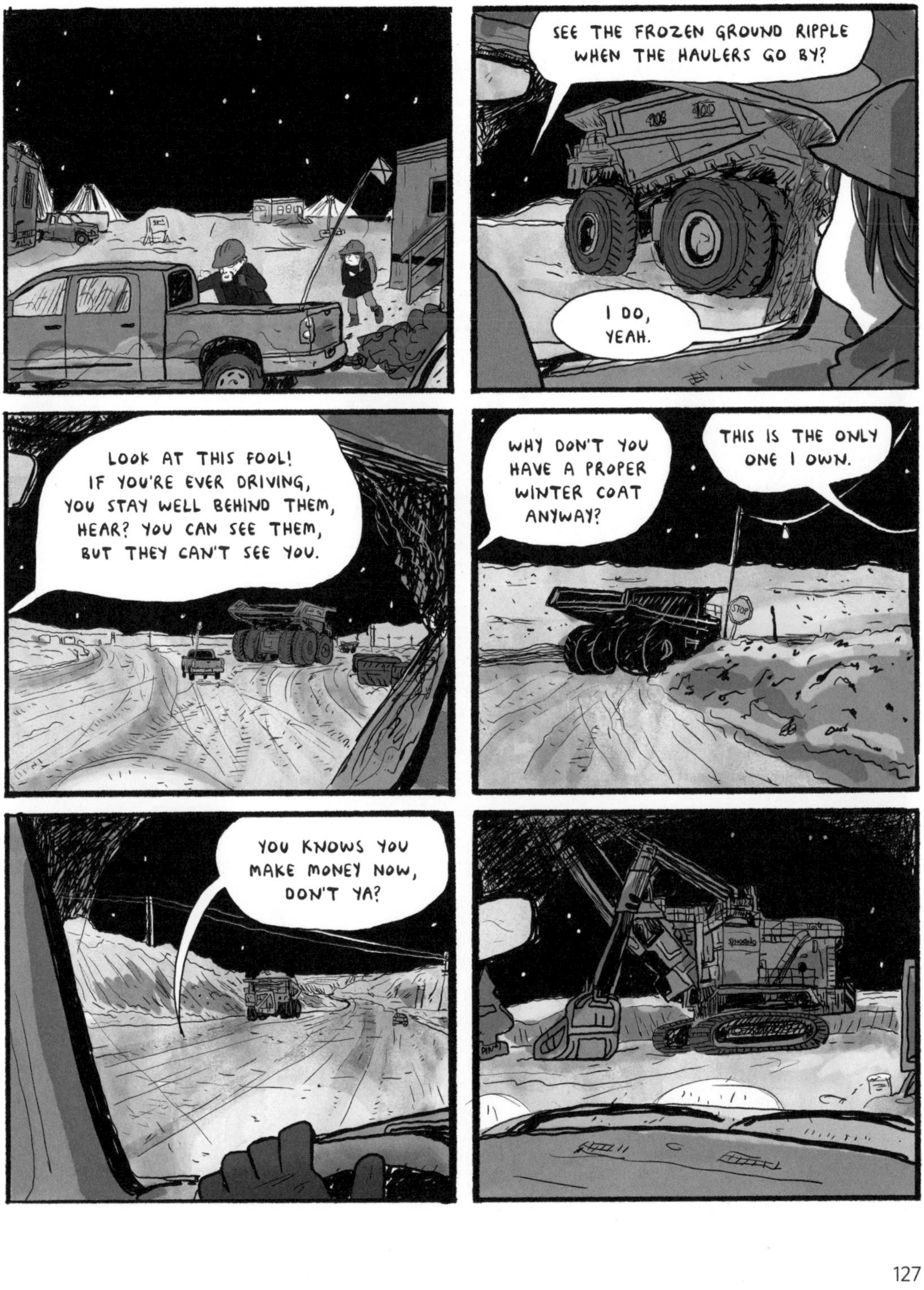
SEE THE FROZEN GROUND RIPPLE WHEN THE HAULERS GO BY?
I DO, YEAH.
LOOK AT THIS FOOL! IF YOU'RE EVER DRIVING, YOU STAY WELL BEHIND THEM, HEAR? YOU CAN SEE THEM, BUT THEY CAN'T SEE YOU.
WHY DON'T YOU HAVE A PROPER WINTER COAT ANYWAY?
THIS IS THE ONLY ONE I OWN.
YOU KNOWS YOU MAKE MONEY NOW, DON'T YA?
STOP

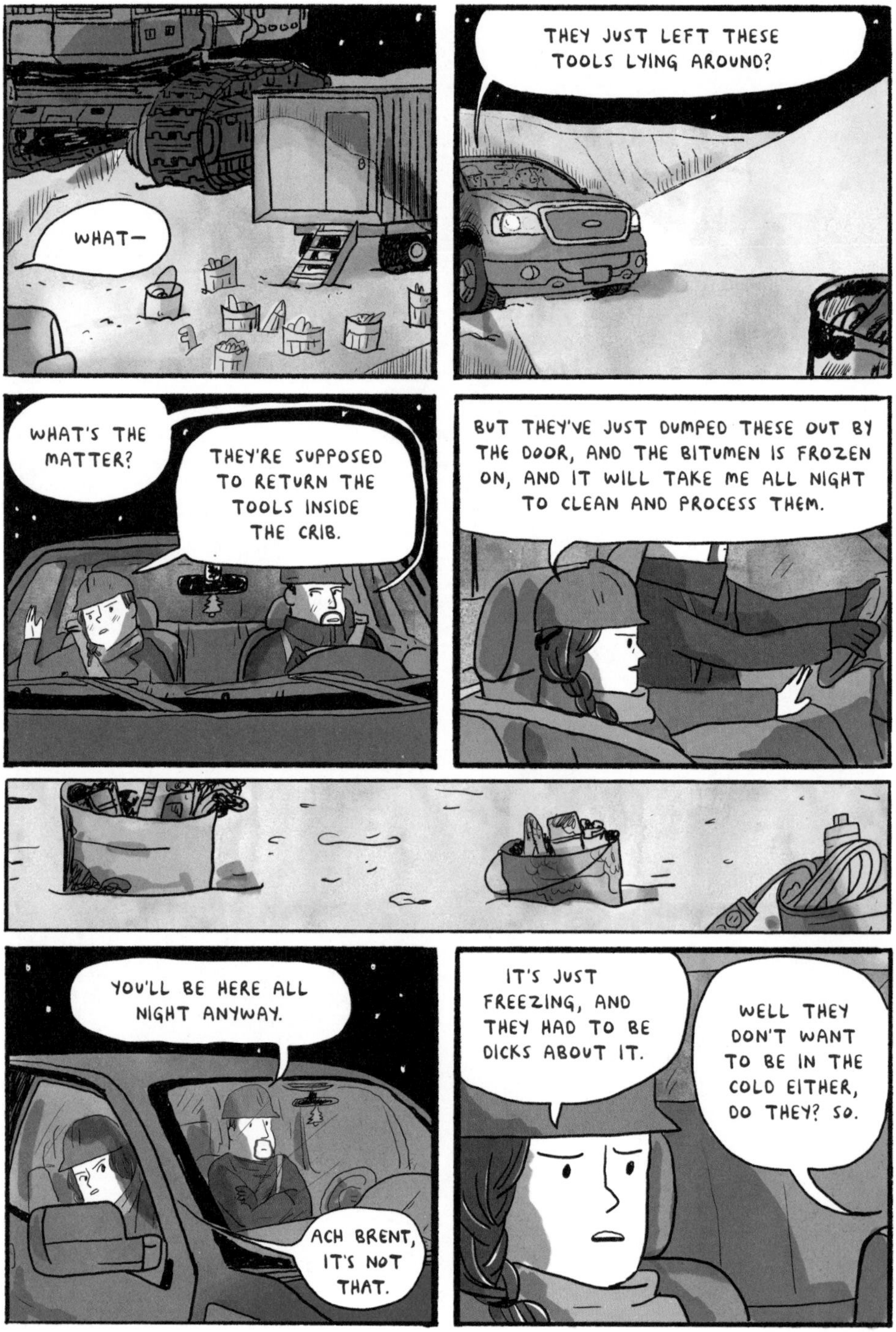
WHAT—
THEY JUST LEFT THESE TOOLS LYING AROUND?
WHAT'S THE MATTER?
THEY'RE SUPPOSED TO RETURN THE TOOLS INSIDE THE CRIB.
BUT THEY'VE JUST DUMPED THESE OUT BY THE DOOR, AND THE BITUMEN IS FROZEN ON, AND IT WILL TAKE ME ALL NIGHT TO CLEAN AND PROCESS THEM.
YOU'LL BE HERE ALL NIGHT ANYWAY.
ACH BRENT, IT'S NOT THAT.
IT'S JUST FREEZING, AND THEY HAD TO BE DICKS ABOUT IT.
WELL THEY DON'T WANT TO BE IN THE COLD EITHER, DO THEY? SO.

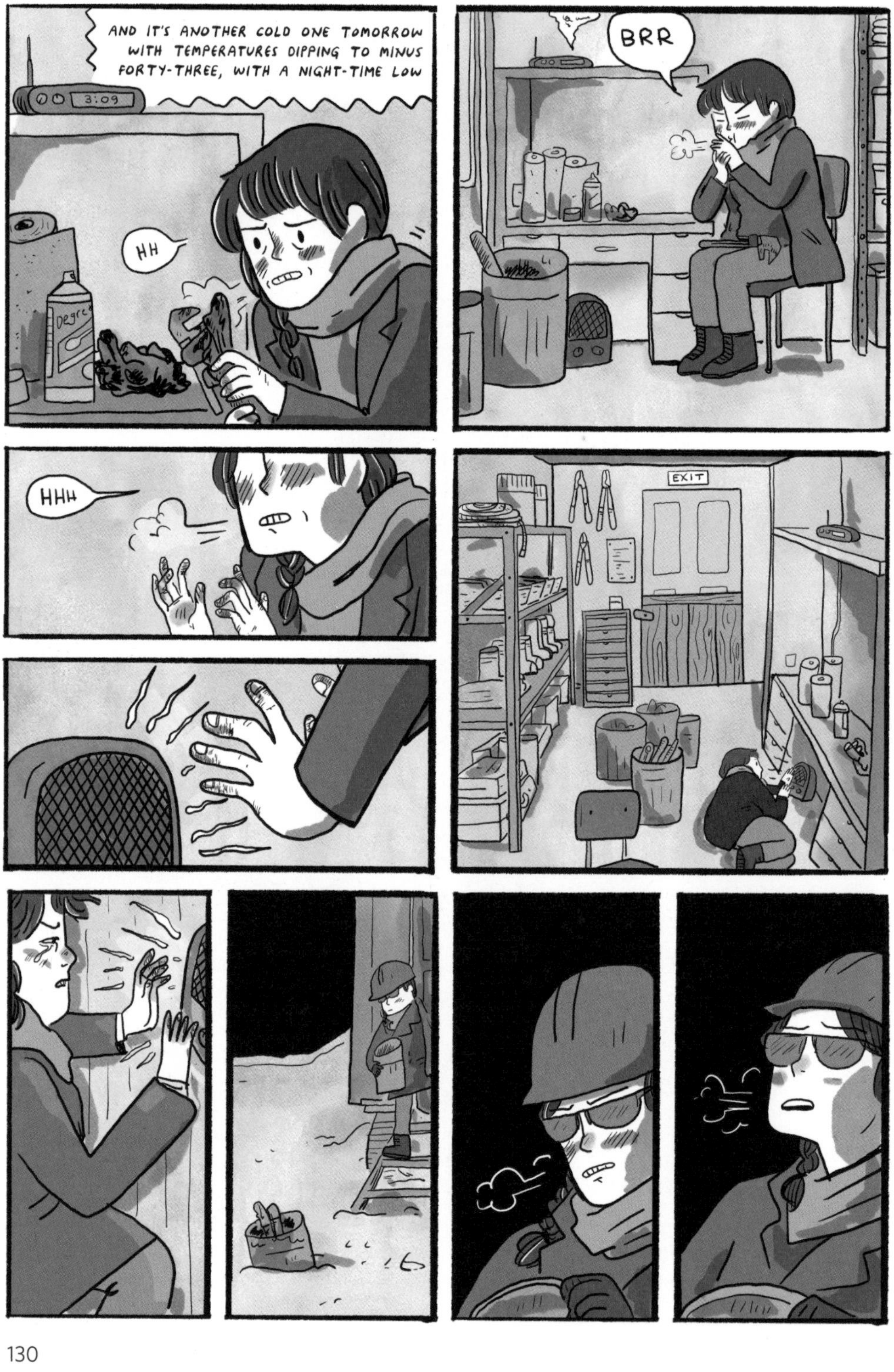
AND IT'S ANOTHER COLD ONE TOMORROW WITH TEMPERATURES DIPPING TO MINUS FORTY-THREE, WITH A NIGHT-TIME LOW
3:09
HH
BRR
HHH
EXIT

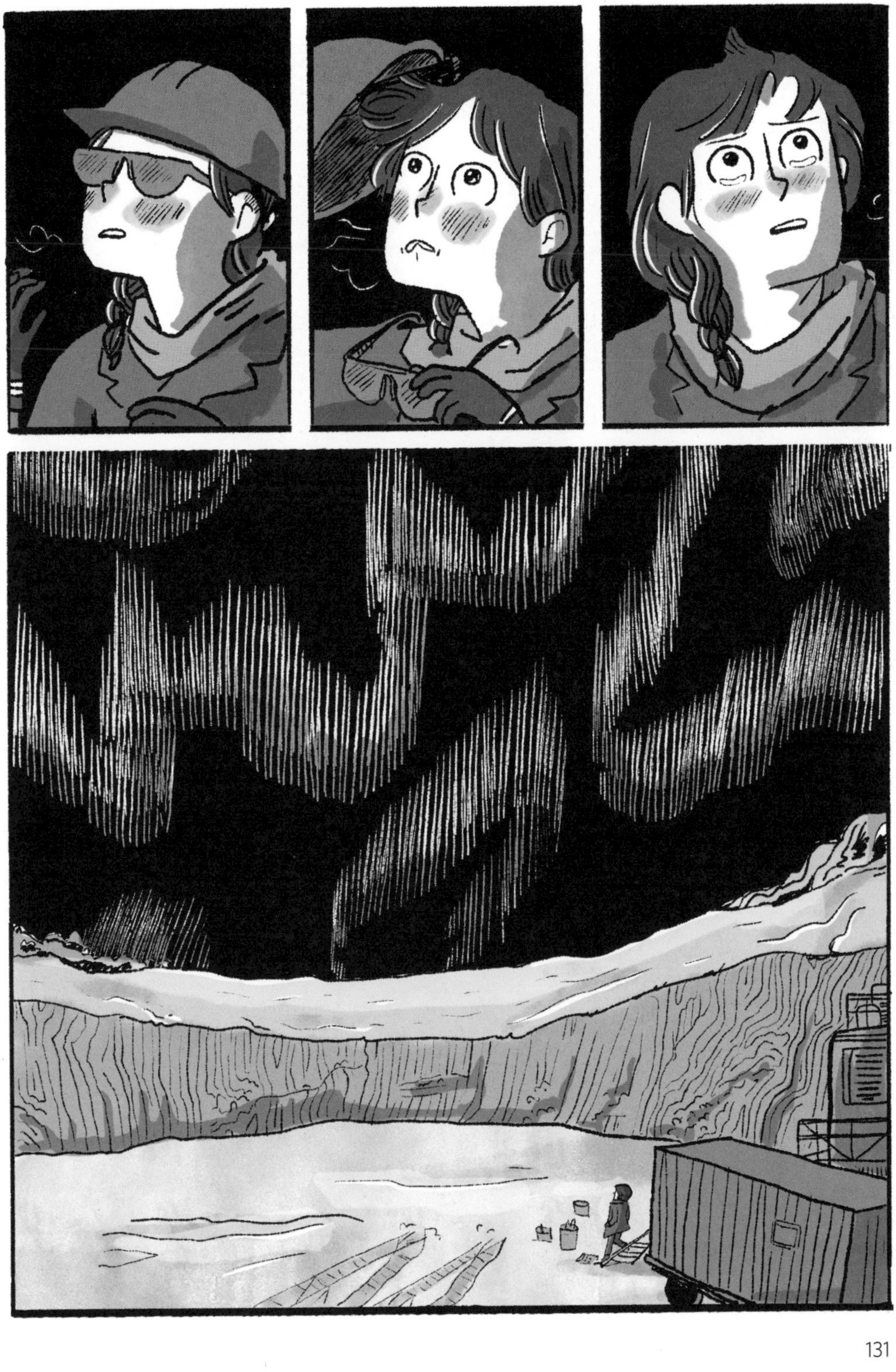

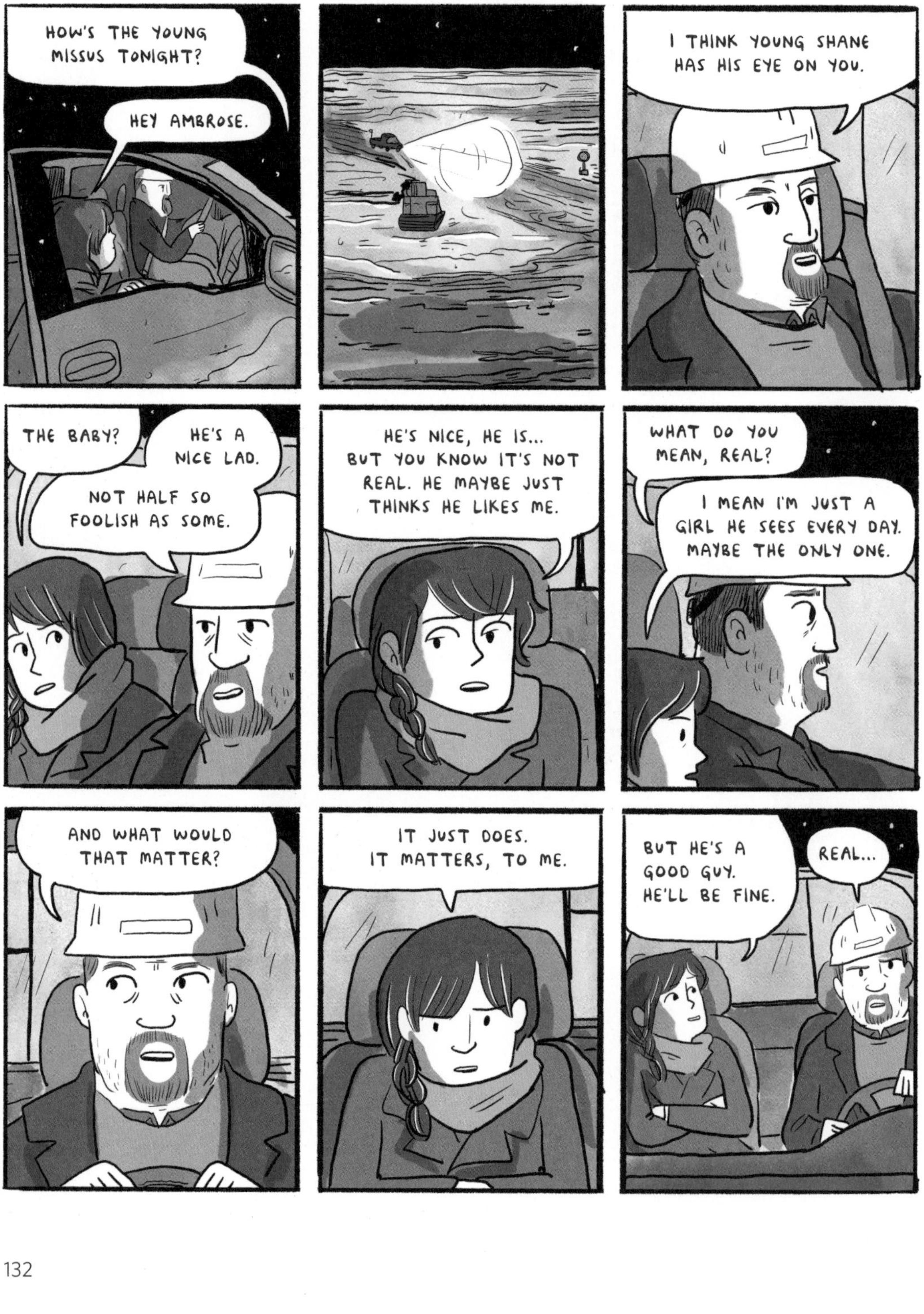
HOW'S THE YOUNG MISSUS TONIGHT?
HEY AMBROSE.
I THINK YOUNG SHANE HAS HIS EYE ON YOU.
THE BABY?
HE'S A NICE LAD.
NOT HALF SO FOOLISH AS SOME.
HE'S NICE, HE IS... BUT YOU KNOW IT'S NOT REAL. HE MAYBE JUST THINKS HE LIKES ME.
WHAT DO YOU MEAN, REAL?
I MEAN I'M JUST A GIRL HE SEES EVERY DAY. MAYBE THE ONLY ONE.
AND WHAT WOULD THAT MATTER?
IT JUST DOES. IT MATTERS, TO ME.
BUT HE'S A GOOD GUY. HE'LL BE FINE.
REAL...

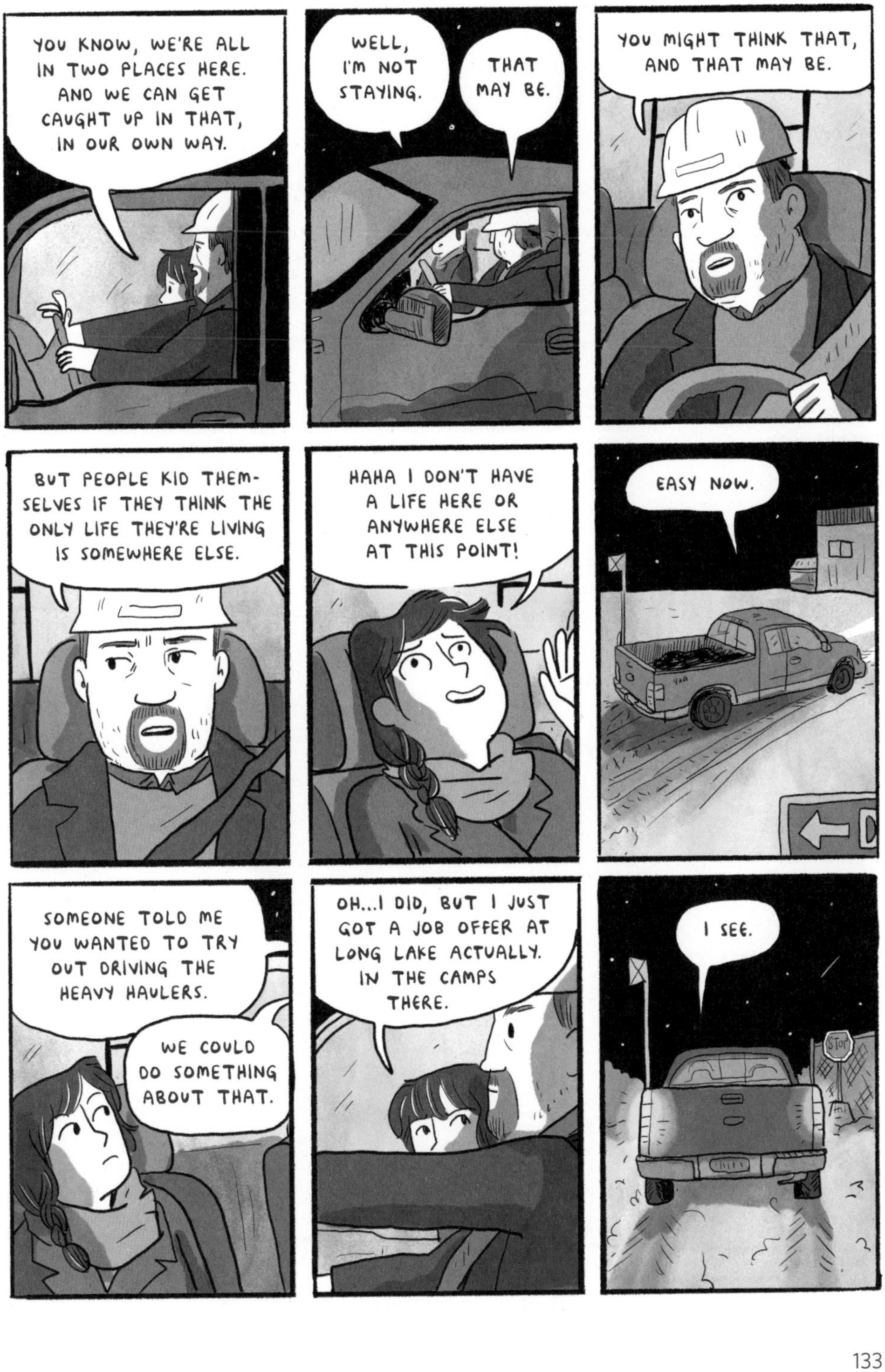
YOU KNOW, WE'RE ALL IN TWO PLACES HERE. AND WE CAN GET CAUGHT UP IN THAT, IN OUR OWN WAY.
WELL, I'M NOT STAYING.
THAT MAY BE.
YOU MIGHT THINK THAT, AND THAT MAY BE.
BUT PEOPLE KID THEMSELVES IF THEY THINK THE ONLY LIFE THEY'RE LIVING IS SOMEWHERE ELSE.
HAHA I DON'T HAVE A LIFE HERE OR ANYWHERE ELSE AT THIS POINT!
EASY NOW.
SOMEONE TOLD ME YOU WANTED TO TRY OUT DRIVING THE HEAVY HAULERS.
WE COULD DO SOMETHING ABOUT THAT.
OH...I DID, BUT I JUST GOT A JOB OFFER AT LONG LAKE ACTUALLY. IN THE CAMPS THERE.
I SEE.
STOP

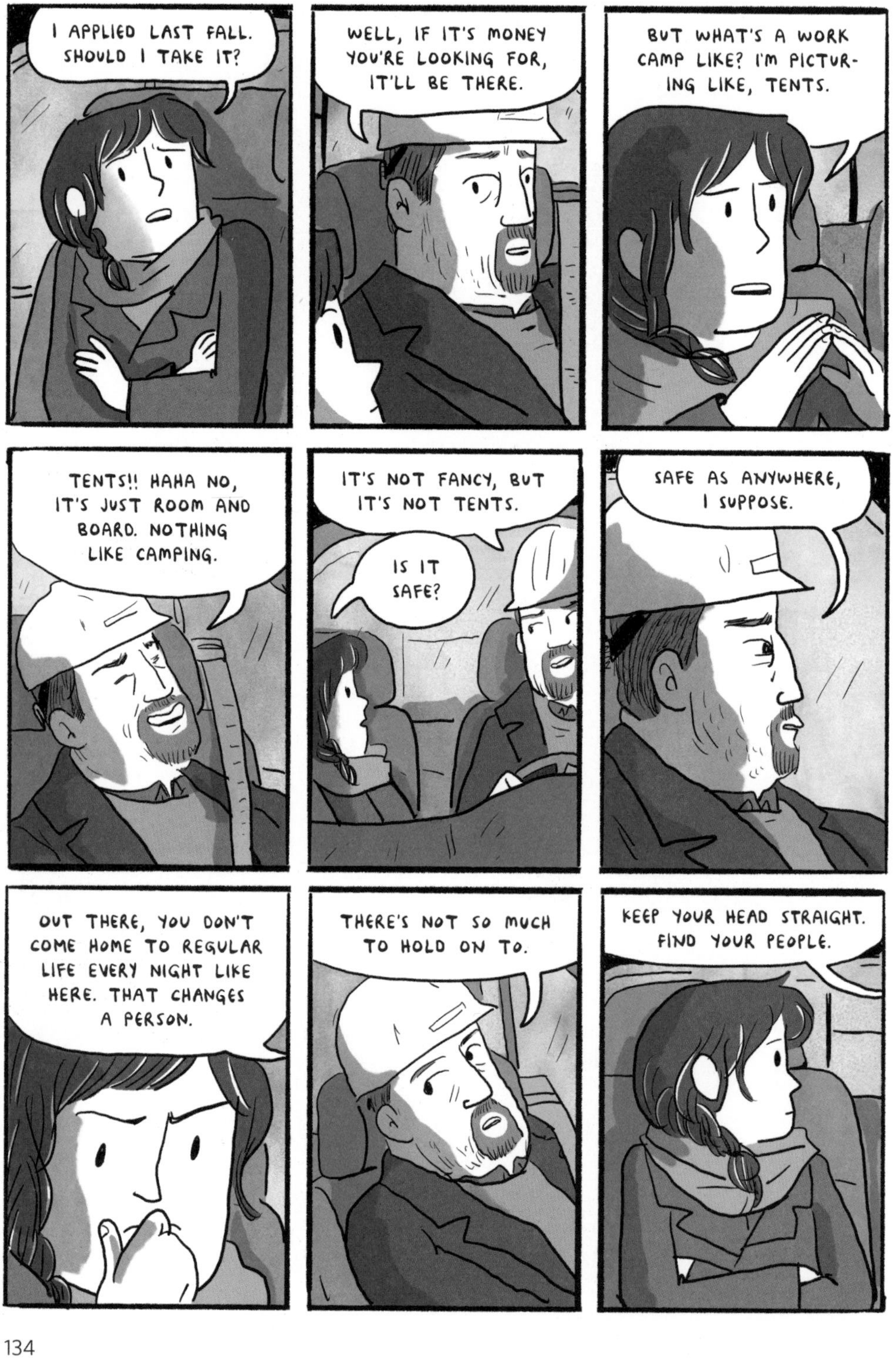
I APPLIED LAST FALL. SHOULD I TAKE IT?
WELL, IF IT'S MONEY YOU'RE LOOKING FOR, IT'LL BE THERE.
BUT WHAT'S A WORK CAMP LIKE? I'M PICTURING LIKE, TENTS.
TENTS!! HAHA NO, IT'S JUST ROOM AND BOARD. NOTHING LIKE CAMPING.
IT'S NOT FANCY, BUT IT'S NOT TENTS.
IS IT SAFE?
SAFE AS ANYWHERE, I SUPPOSE.
OUT THERE, YOU DON'T COME HOME TO REGULAR LIFE EVERY NIGHT LIKE HERE. THAT CHANGES A PERSON.
THERE'S NOT SO MUCH TO HOLD ON TO.
KEEP YOUR HEAD STRAIGHT. FIND YOUR PEOPLE.

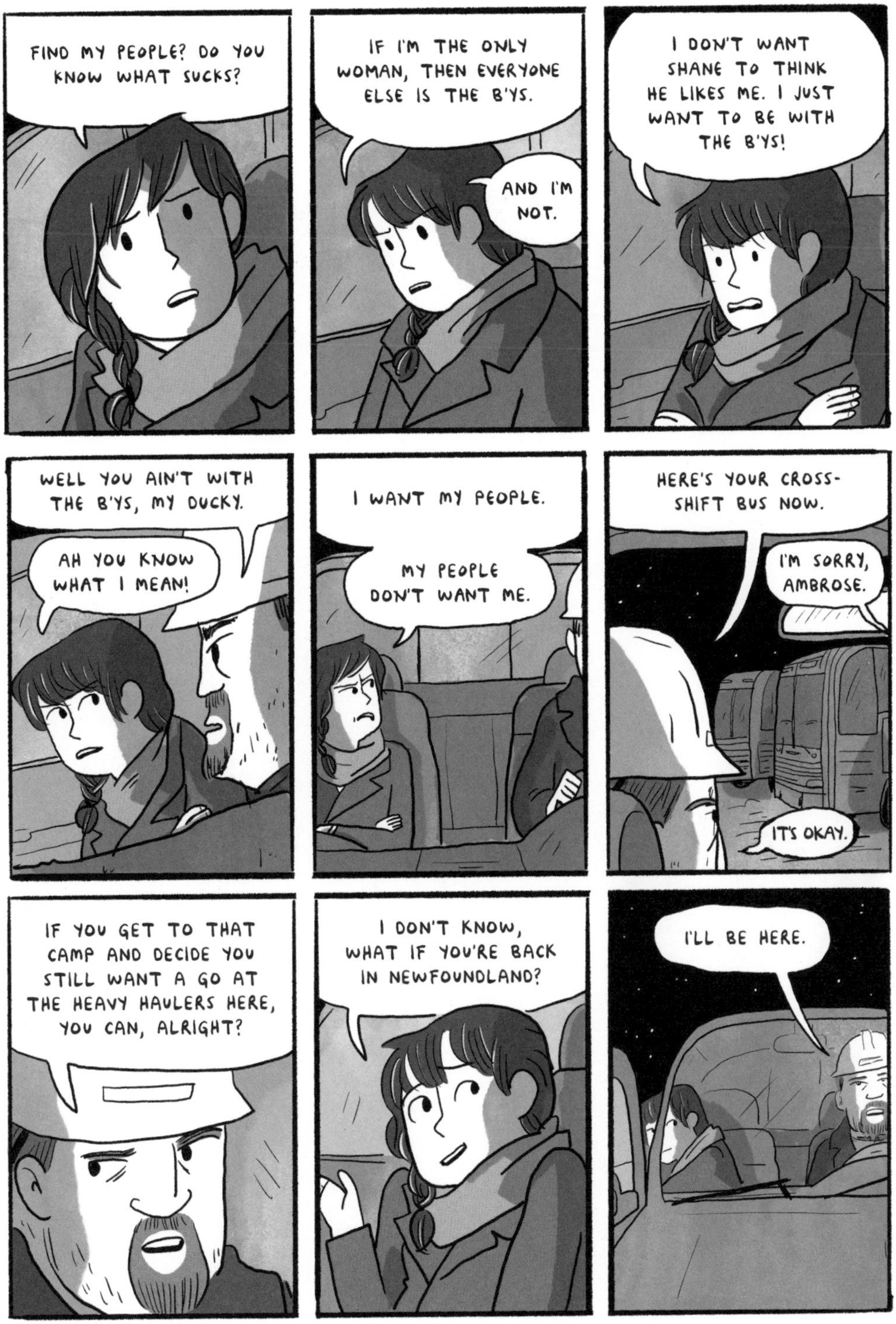
FIND MY PEOPLE? DO YOU KNOW WHAT SUCKS?
IF I'M THE ONLY WOMAN, THEN EVERYONE ELSE IS THE B'YS.
AND I'M NOT.
I DON'T WANT SHANE TO THINK HE LIKES ME. I JUST WANT TO BE WITH THE B'YS!
WELL YOU AIN'T WITH THE B'YS, MY DUCKY.
AH YOU KNOW WHAT I MEAN!
I WANT MY PEOPLE.
MY PEOPLE DON'T WANT ME.
HERE'S YOUR CROSS-SHIFT BUS NOW.
I'M SORRY, AMBROSE.
IT'S OKAY.
IF YOU GET TO THAT CAMP AND DECIDE YOU STILL WANT A GO AT THE HEAVY HAULERS HERE, YOU CAN, ALRIGHT?
I DON'T KNOW, WHAT IF YOU'RE BACK IN NEWFOUNDLAND?
I'LL BE HERE.

LONG LAKE
OPTI-NEXEN

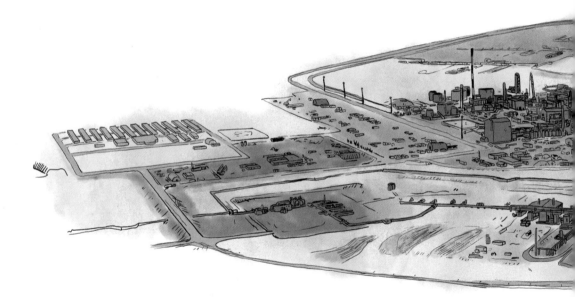

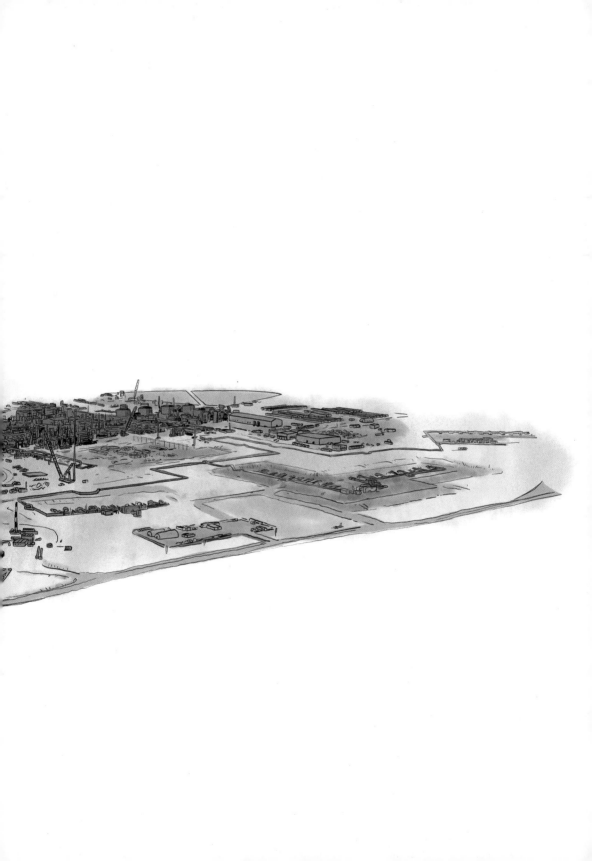

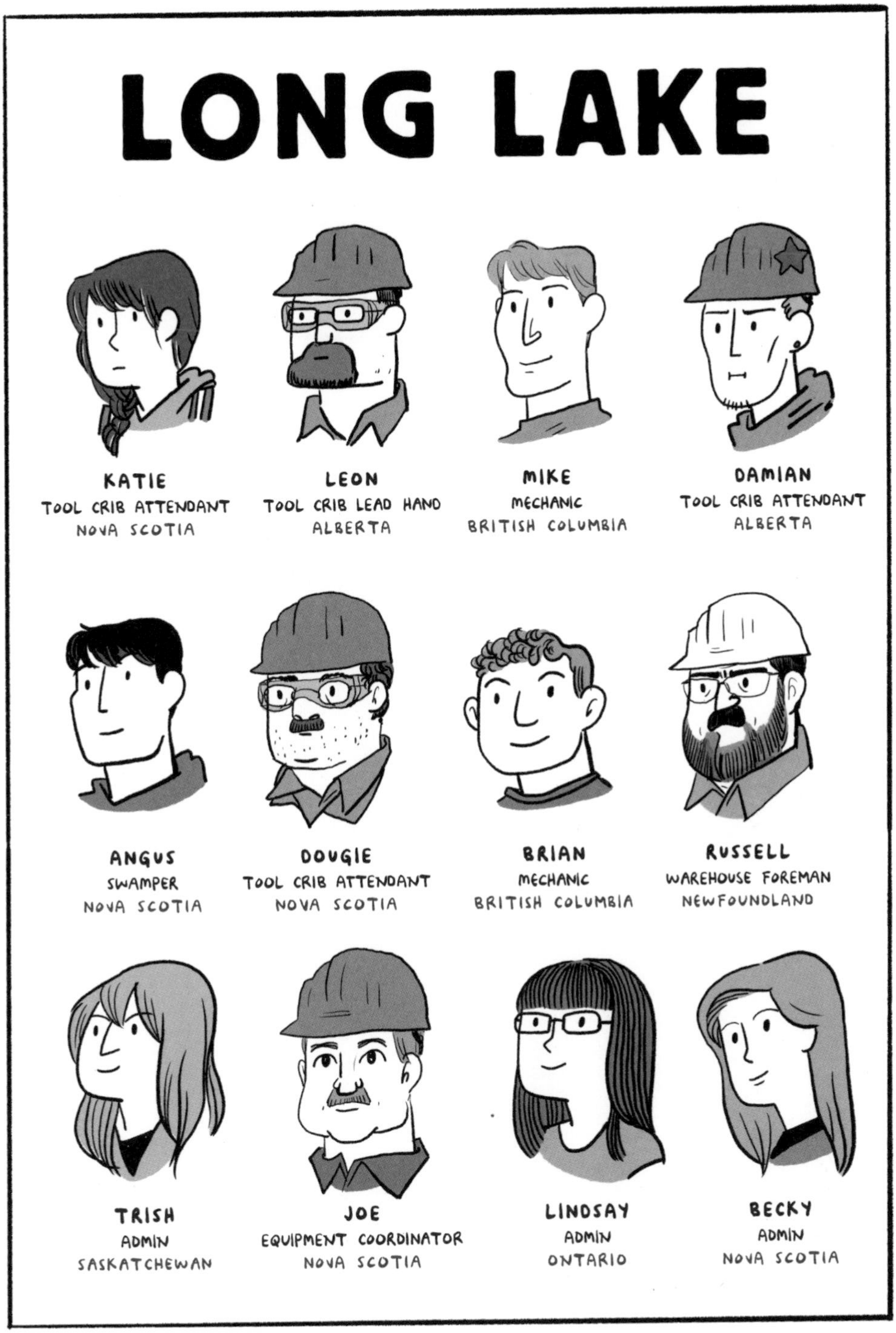

LONG LAKE
KATIE
TOOL CRIB ATTENDANT
NOVA SCOTIA
LEON
TOOL CRIB LEAD HAND
ALBERTA
MIKE
MECHANIC
BRITISH COLUMBIA
DAMIAN
TOOL CRIB ATTENDANT
ALBERTA
ANGUS
SWAMPER
NOVA SCOTIA
DOUGIE
TOOL CRIB ATTENDANT
NOVA SCOTIA
BRIAN
MECHANIC
BRITISH COLUMBIA
RUSSELL
WAREHOUSE FOREMAN
NEWFOUNDLAND
TRISH
ADMIN
SASKATCHEWAN
JOE
EQUIPMENT COORDINATOR
NOVA SCOTIA
LINDSAY
ADMIN
ONTARIO
BECKY
ADMIN
NOVA SCOTIA

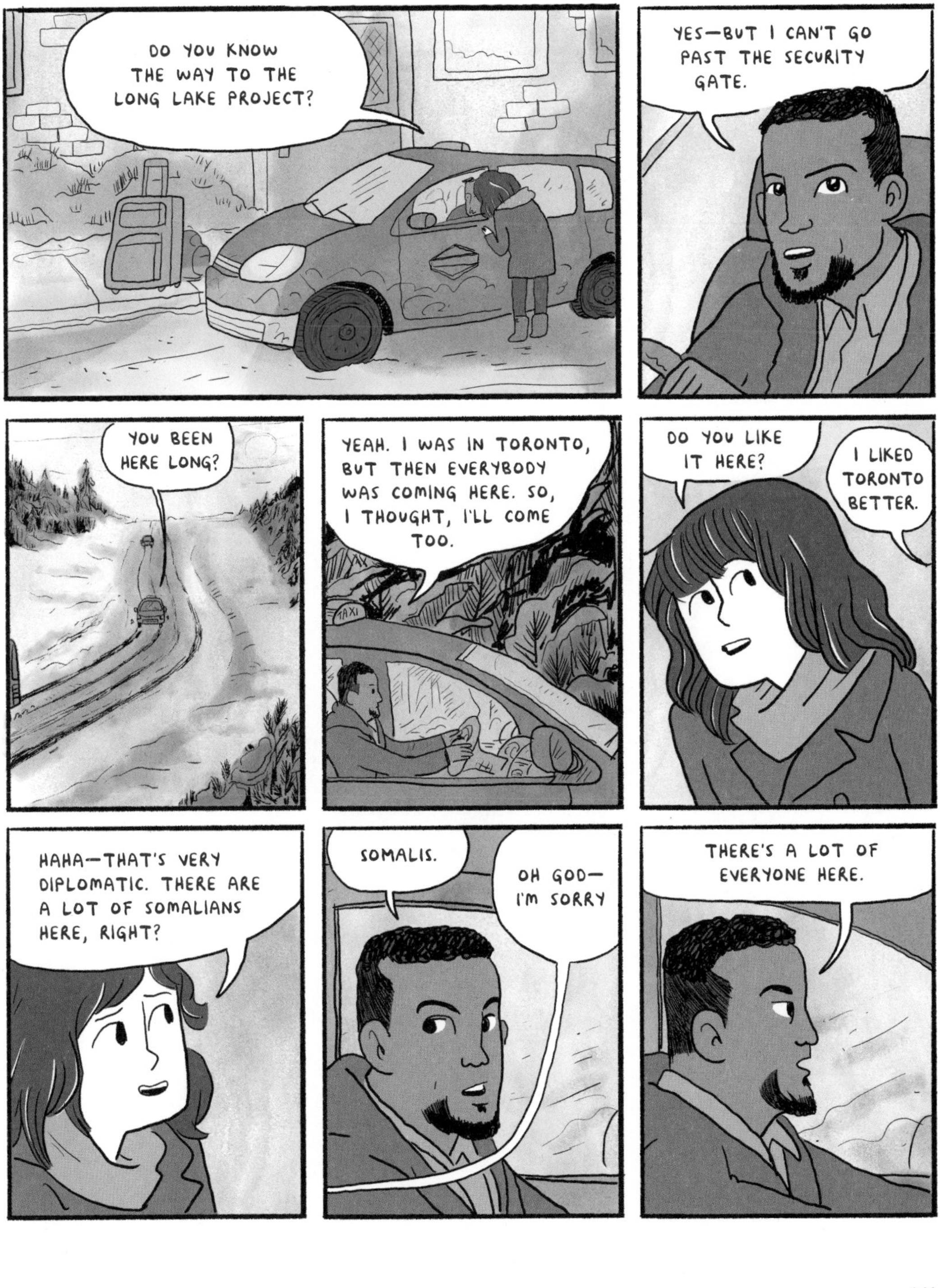
DO YOU KNOW THE WAY TO THE LONG LAKE PROJECT?
YES—BUT I CAN'T GO PAST THE SECURITY GATE.
YOU BEEN HERE LONG?
YEAH. I WAS IN TORONTO, BUT THEN EVERYBODY WAS COMING HERE. SO, I THOUGHT, I'LL COME TOO.
TAXI
DO YOU LIKE IT HERE?
I LIKED TORONTO BETTER.
HAHA—THAT'S VERY DIPLOMATIC. THERE ARE A LOT OF SOMALIANS HERE, RIGHT?
SOMALIS.
OH GOD— I'M SORRY
THERE'S A LOT OF EVERYONE HERE.

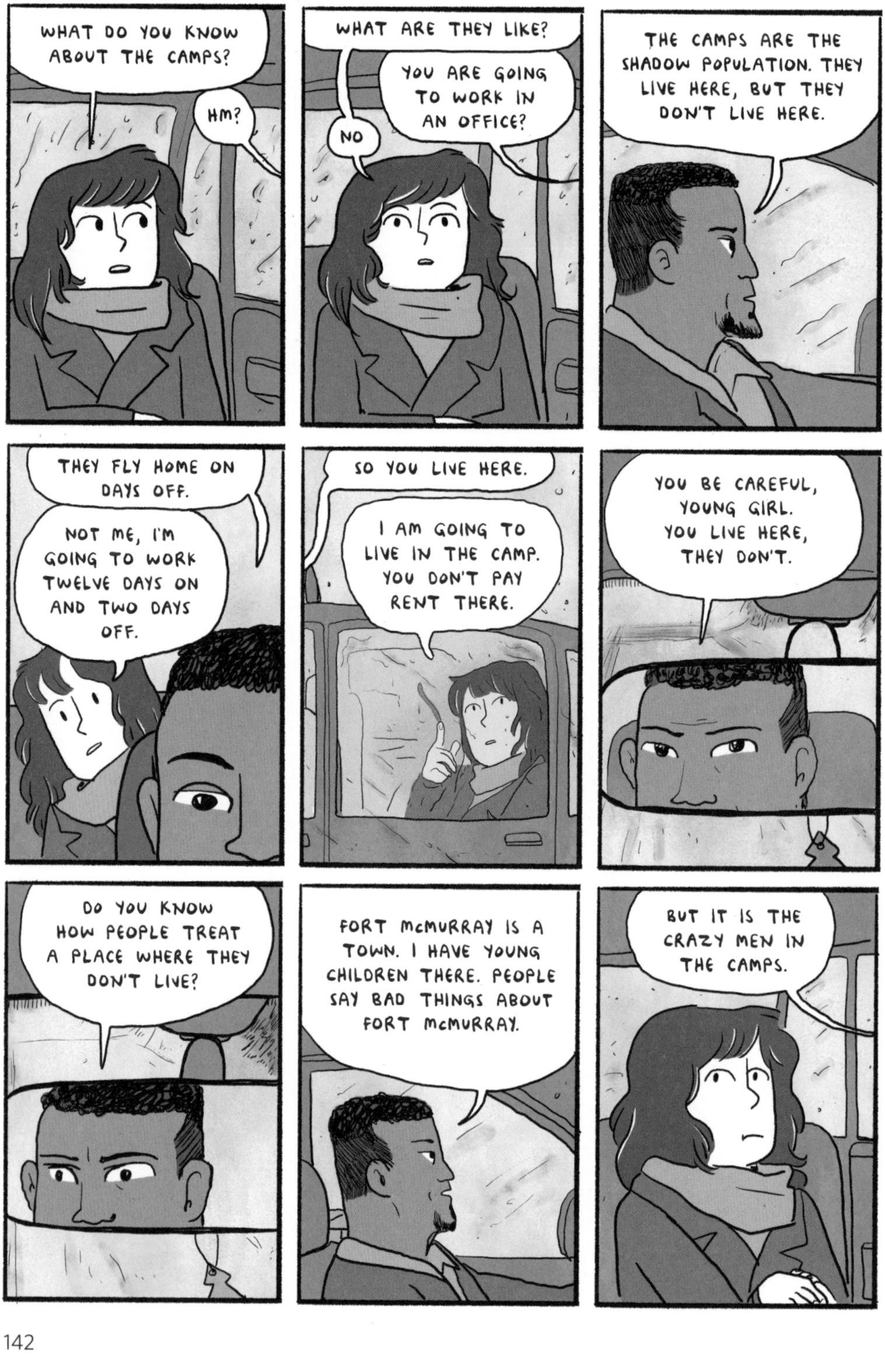
WHAT DO YOU KNOW ABOUT THE CAMPS?
HM?
WHAT ARE THEY LIKE?
NO
YOU ARE GOING TO WORK IN AN OFFICE?
THE CAMPS ARE THE SHADOW POPULATION. THEY LIVE HERE, BUT THEY DON'T LIVE HERE.
THEY FLY HOME ON DAYS OFF.
NOT ME, I'M GOING TO WORK TWELVE DAYS ON AND TWO DAYS OFF.
SO YOU LIVE HERE.
I AM GOING TO LIVE IN THE CAMP. YOU DON'T PAY RENT THERE.
YOU BE CAREFUL, YOUNG GIRL. YOU LIVE HERE, THEY DON'T.
DO YOU KNOW HOW PEOPLE TREAT A PLACE WHERE THEY DON'T LIVE?
FORT McMURRAY IS A TOWN. I HAVE YOUNG CHILDREN THERE. PEOPLE SAY BAD THINGS ABOUT FORT McMURRAY.
BUT IT IS THE CRAZY MEN IN THE CAMPS.

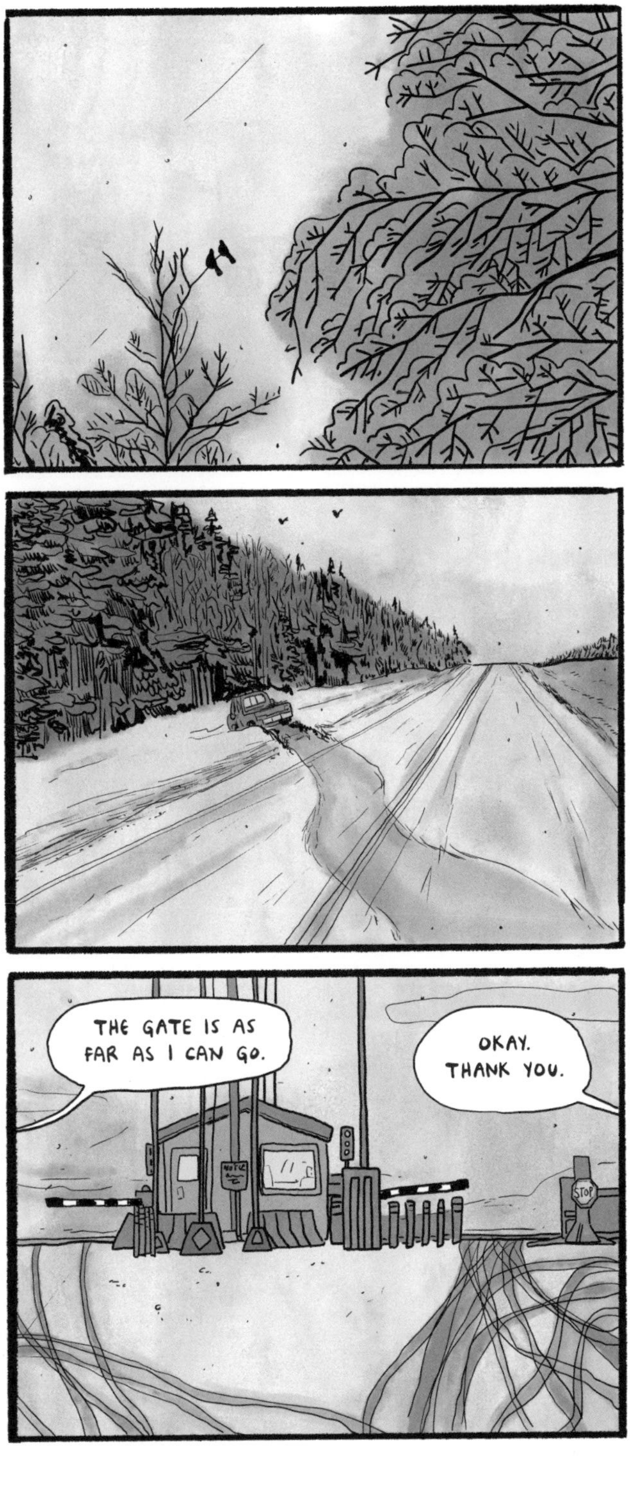
THE GATE IS AS FAR AS I CAN GO.
OKAY. THANK YOU.
STOP

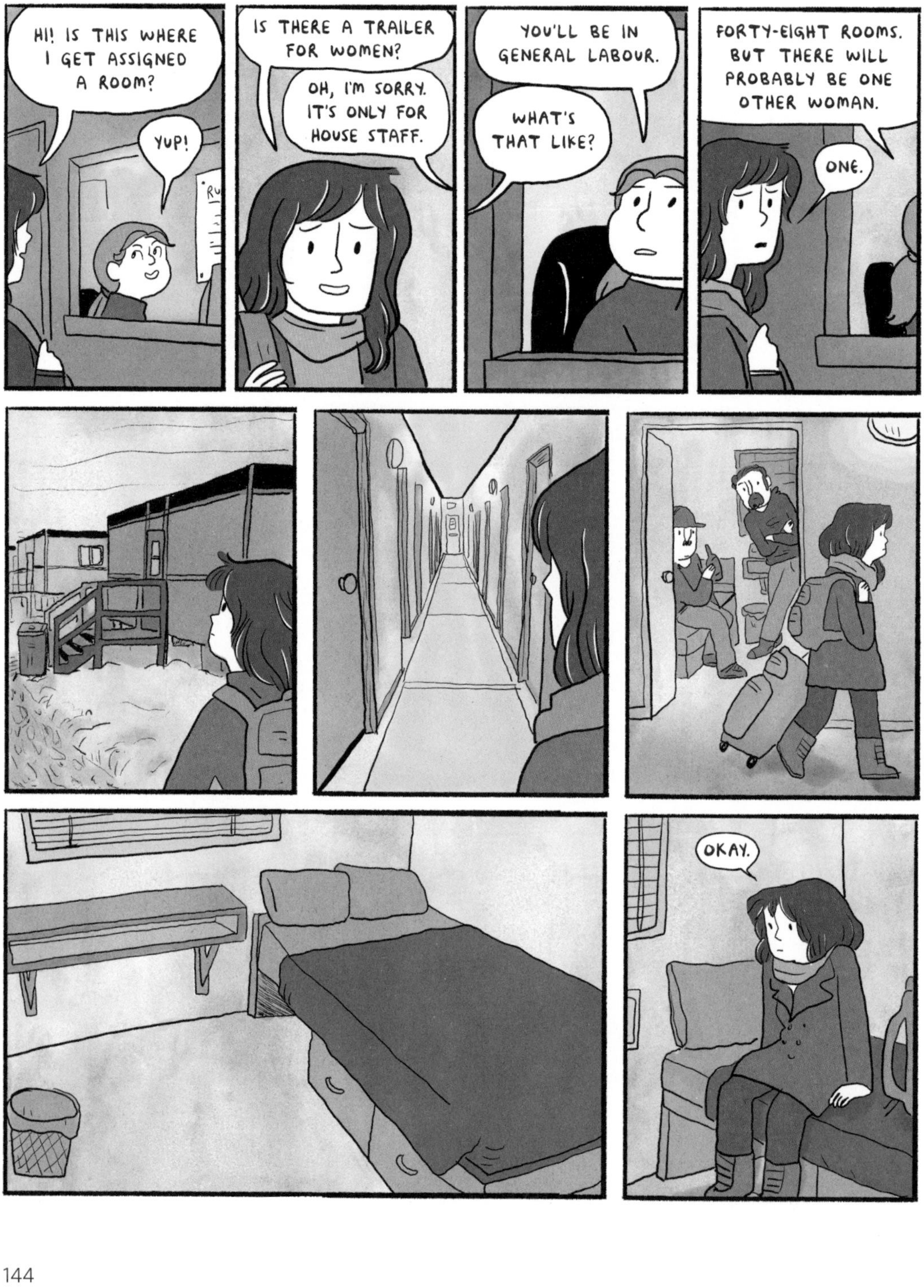
HI! IS THIS WHERE I GET ASSIGNED A ROOM?
YUP!
IS THERE A TRAILER FOR WOMEN?
OH, I'M SORRY. IT'S ONLY FOR HOUSE STAFF.
YOU'LL BE IN GENERAL LABOUR.
WHAT'S THAT LIKE?
FORTY-EIGHT ROOMS. BUT THERE WILL PROBABLY BE ONE OTHER WOMAN.
ONE.
OKAY.

UM, WHERE ARE THE BATHROOMS?

FAR END.

HEY CAPE BRETON! COME HAVE A DRINK WITH US!

HEY!

CAPE BRETON GIRL! WE KNOW WHERE YOU'RE FROM!

SOME PEOPLE FIND THE REENACTMENTS GRAPHIC.

SAFET
ON TH
JOB

I LOST MY HAND IN A GRINDING ACCIDENT.

ROBERT

OH NO

YEEAAAAUGHH

ZZZZ

HAHA

HAHA

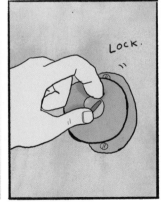

LOCK.

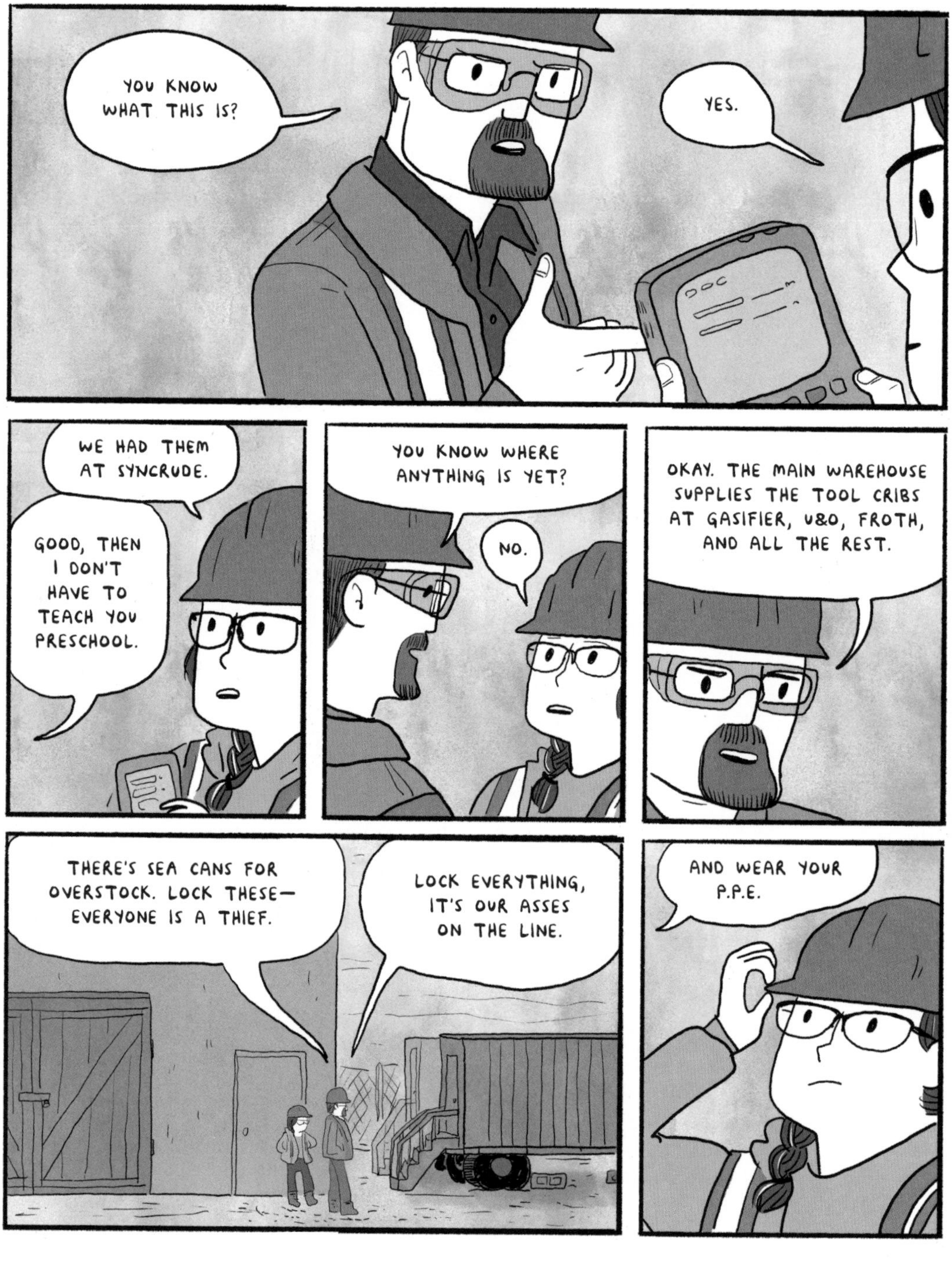
YOU KNOW WHAT THIS IS?
YES.
WE HAD THEM AT SYNCRUDE.
GOOD, THEN I DON'T HAVE TO TEACH YOU PRESCHOOL.
YOU KNOW WHERE ANYTHING IS YET?
NO.
OKAY. THE MAIN WAREHOUSE SUPPLIES THE TOOL CRIBS AT GASIFIER, U&O, FROTH, AND ALL THE REST.
THERE'S SEA CANS FOR OVERSTOCK. LOCK THESE— EVERYONE IS A THIEF.
LOCK EVERYTHING, IT'S OUR ASSES ON THE LINE.
AND WEAR YOUR P.P.E.

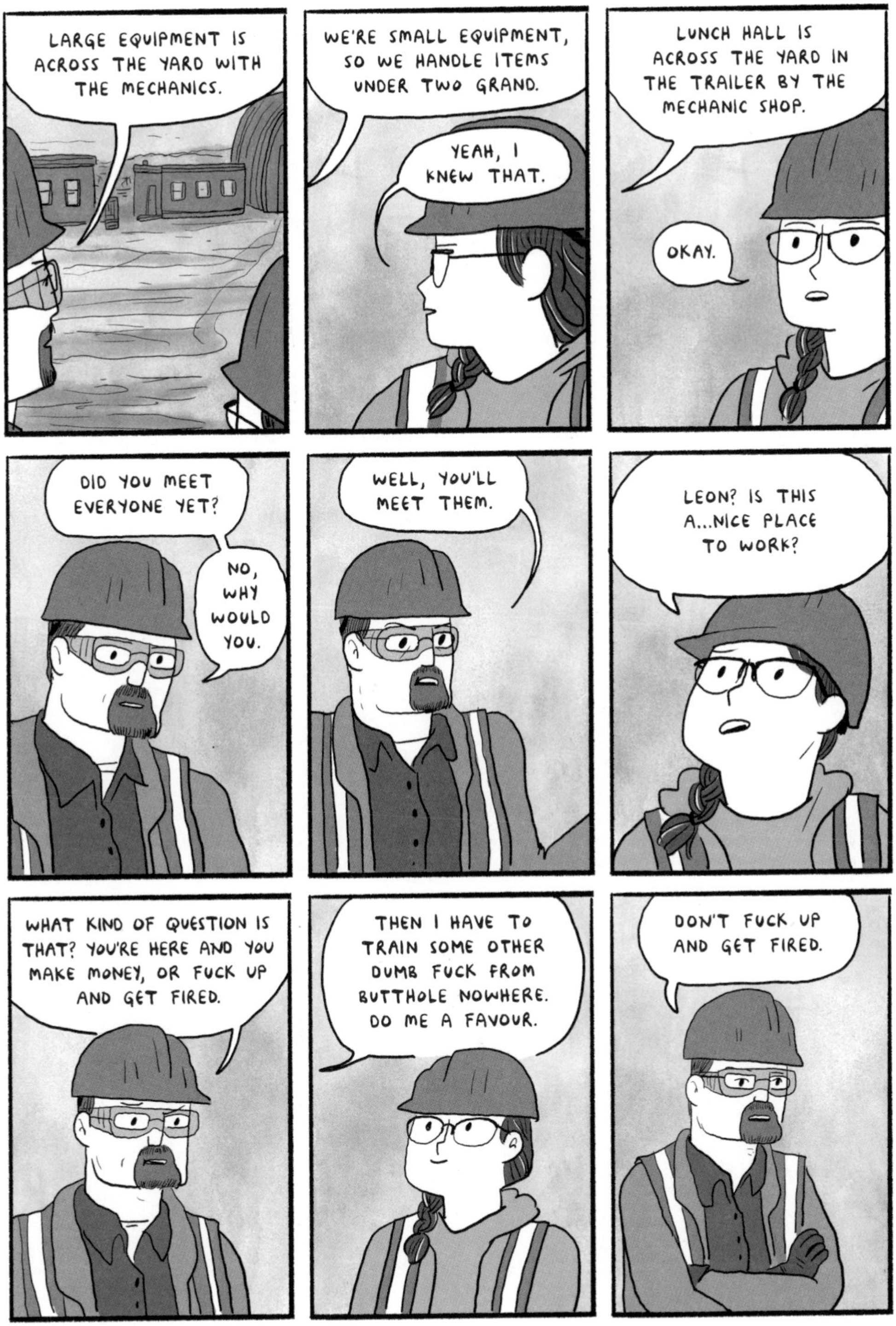
LARGE EQUIPMENT IS ACROSS THE YARD WITH THE MECHANICS.
WE'RE SMALL EQUIPMENT, SO WE HANDLE ITEMS UNDER TWO GRAND.
YEAH, I KNEW THAT.
LUNCH HALL IS ACROSS THE YARD IN THE TRAILER BY THE MECHANIC SHOP.
OKAY.
DID YOU MEET EVERYONE YET?
NO, WHY WOULD YOU.
WELL, YOU'LL MEET THEM.
LEON? IS THIS A...NICE PLACE TO WORK?
WHAT KIND OF QUESTION IS THAT? YOU'RE HERE AND YOU MAKE MONEY, OR FUCK UP AND GET FIRED.
THEN I HAVE TO TRAIN SOME OTHER DUMB FUCK FROM BUTTHOLE NOWHERE. DO ME A FAVOUR.
DON'T FUCK UP AND GET FIRED.

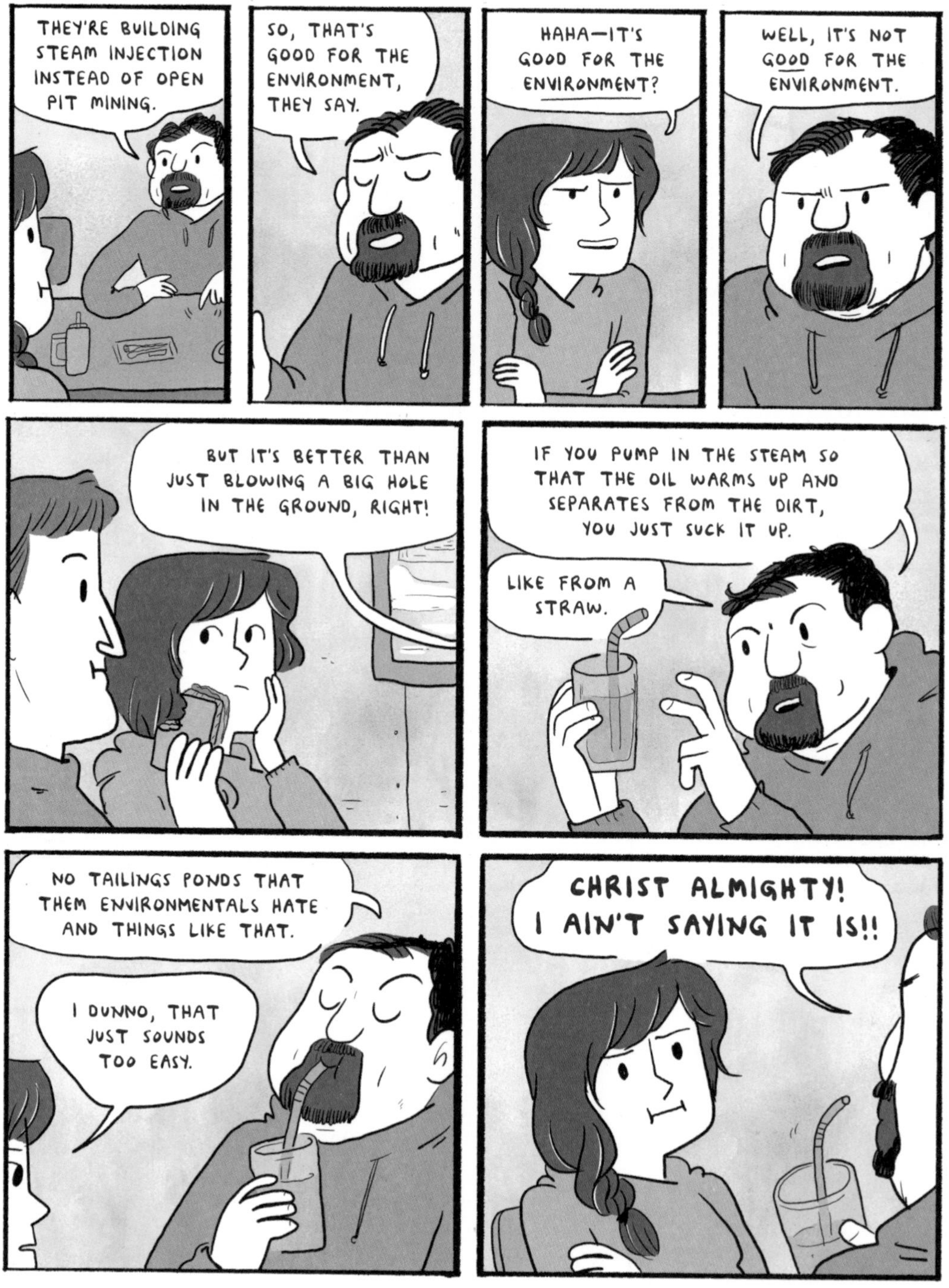
THEY'RE BUILDING STEAM INJECTION INSTEAD OF OPEN PIT MINING.
SO, THAT'S GOOD FOR THE ENVIRONMENT, THEY SAY.
HAHA—IT'S GOOD FOR THE ENVIRONMENT?
WELL, IT'S NOT GOOD FOR THE ENVIRONMENT.
BUT IT'S BETTER THAN JUST BLOWING A BIG HOLE IN THE GROUND, RIGHT!
IF YOU PUMP IN THE STEAM SO THAT THE OIL WARMS UP AND SEPARATES FROM THE DIRT, YOU JUST SUCK IT UP.
LIKE FROM A STRAW.
NO TAILINGS PONDS THAT THEM ENVIRONMENTALS HATE AND THINGS LIKE THAT.
I DUNNO, THAT JUST SOUNDS TOO EASY.
CHRIST ALMIGHTY! I AIN'T SAYING IT IS!!

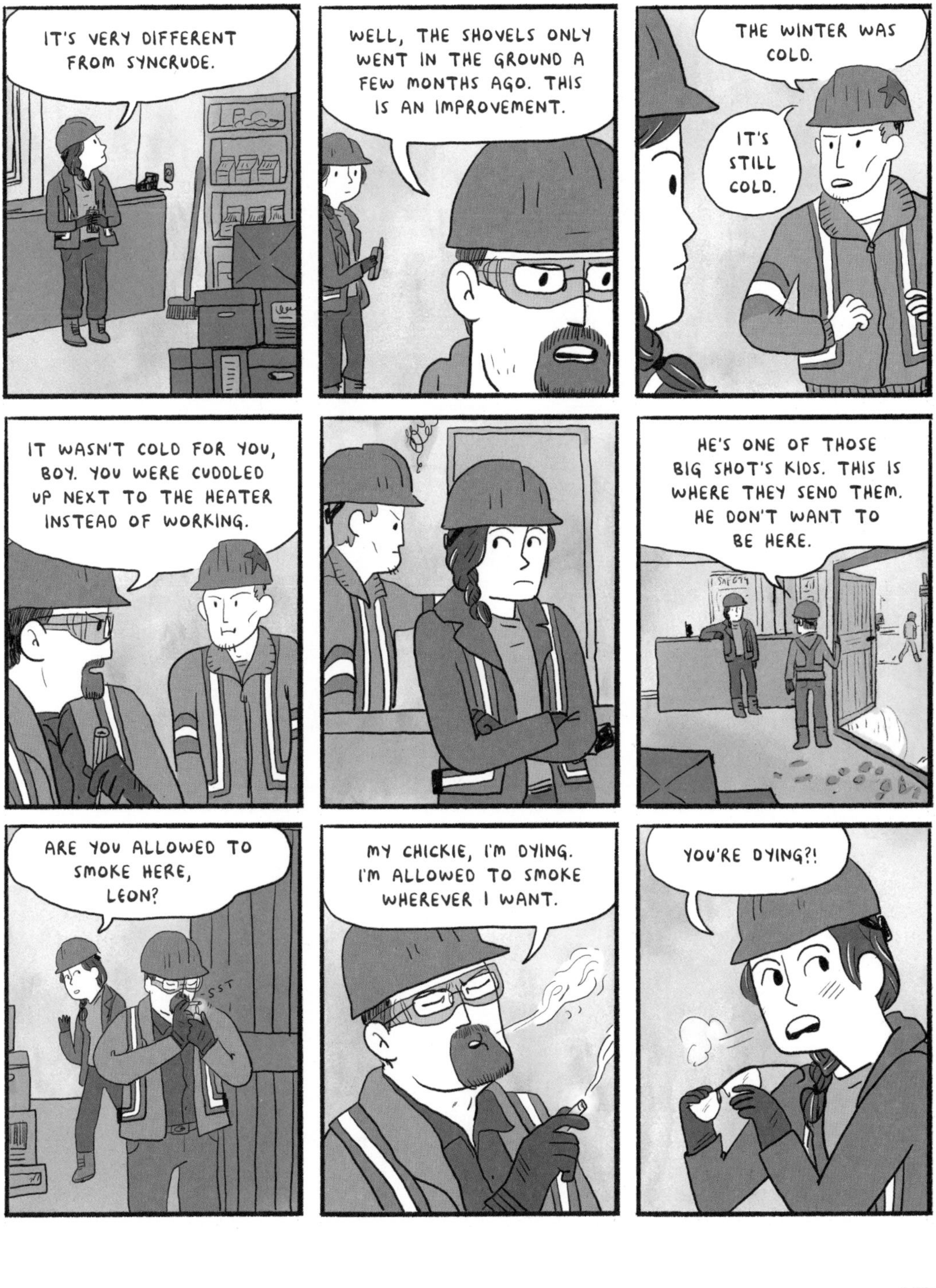
IT'S VERY DIFFERENT FROM SYNCRUDE.
WELL, THE SHOVELS ONLY WENT IN THE GROUND A FEW MONTHS AGO. THIS IS AN IMPROVEMENT.
THE WINTER WAS COLD.
IT'S STILL COLD.
IT WASN'T COLD FOR YOU, BOY. YOU WERE CUDDLED UP NEXT TO THE HEATER INSTEAD OF WORKING.
HE'S ONE OF THOSE BIG SHOT'S KIDS. THIS IS WHERE THEY SEND THEM. HE DON'T WANT TO BE HERE.
ARE YOU ALLOWED TO SMOKE HERE, LEON?
SST
MY CHICKIE, I'M DYING. I'M ALLOWED TO SMOKE WHEREVER I WANT.
YOU'RE DYING?!

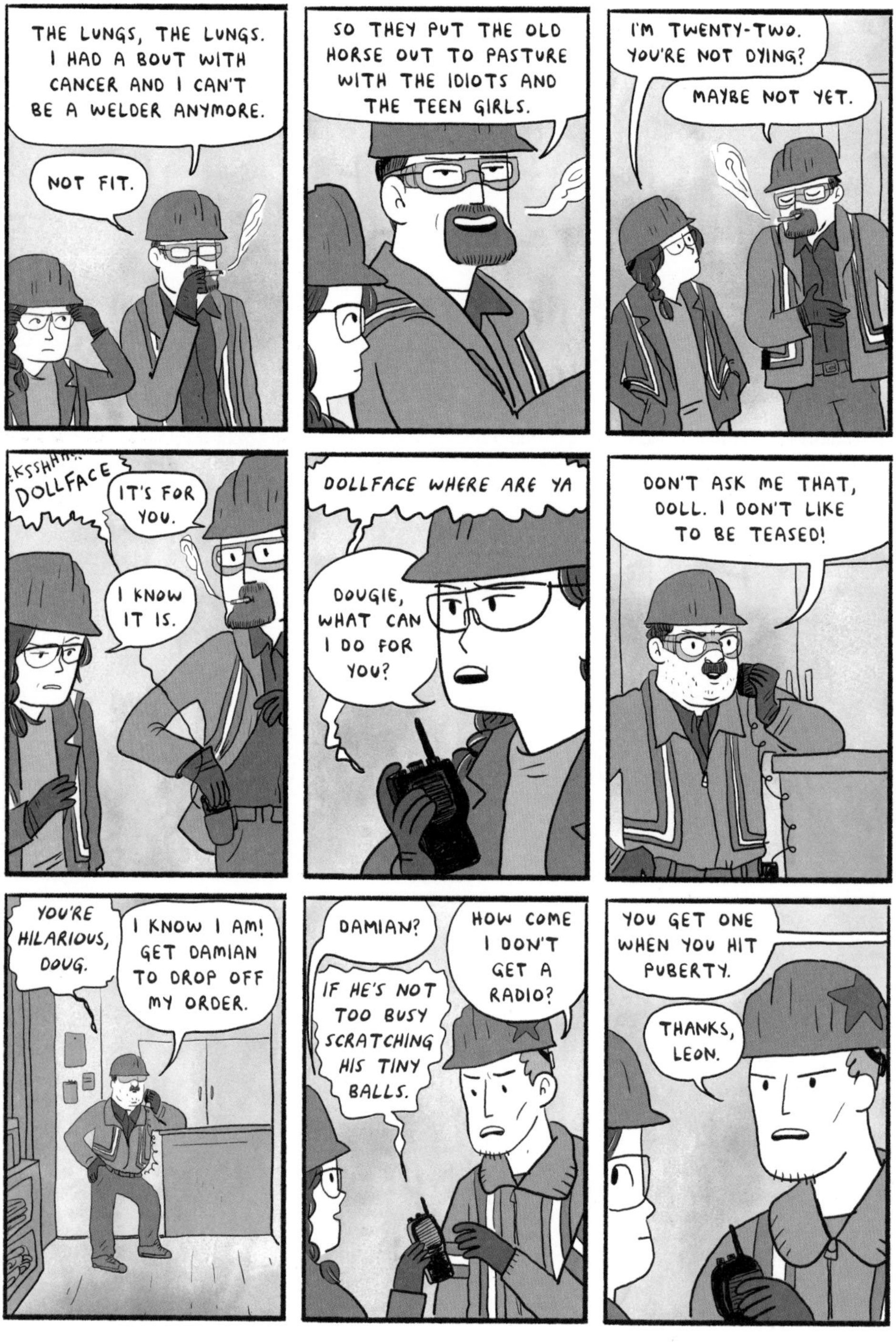
THE LUNGS, THE LUNGS. I HAD A BOUT WITH CANCER AND I CAN'T BE A WELDER ANYMORE.
NOT FIT.
SO THEY PUT THE OLD HORSE OUT TO PASTURE WITH THE IDIOTS AND THE TEEN GIRLS.
I'M TWENTY-TWO. YOU'RE NOT DYING?
MAYBE NOT YET.
DOLLFACE
IT'S FOR YOU.
I KNOW IT IS.
DOLLFACE WHERE ARE YA
DOUGIE, WHAT CAN I DO FOR YOU?
DON'T ASK ME THAT, DOLL. I DON'T LIKE TO BE TEASED!
YOU'RE HILARIOUS, DOUG.
I KNOW I AM! GET DAMIAN TO DROP OFF MY ORDER.
DAMIAN?
IF HE'S NOT TOO BUSY SCRATCHING HIS TINY BALLS.
HOW COME I DON'T GET A RADIO?
YOU GET ONE WHEN YOU HIT PUBERTY.
THANKS, LEON.

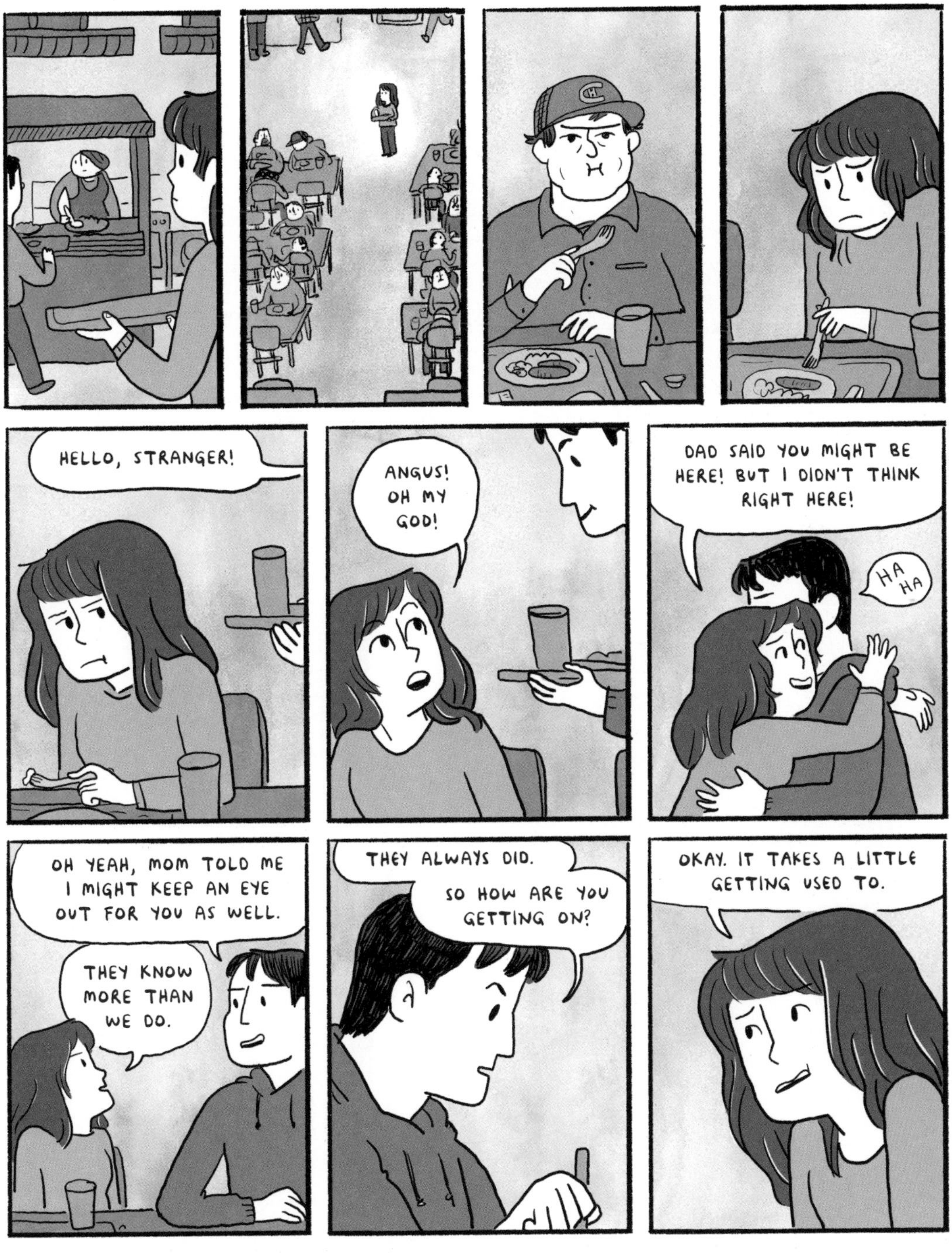
HELLO, STRANGER!
ANGUS! OH MY GOD!
DAD SAID YOU MIGHT BE HERE! BUT I DIDN'T THINK RIGHT HERE!
HA HA
OH YEAH, MOM TOLD ME I MIGHT KEEP AN EYE OUT FOR YOU AS WELL.
THEY KNOW MORE THAN WE DO.
THEY ALWAYS DID.
SO HOW ARE YOU GETTING ON?
OKAY. IT TAKES A LITTLE GETTING USED TO.

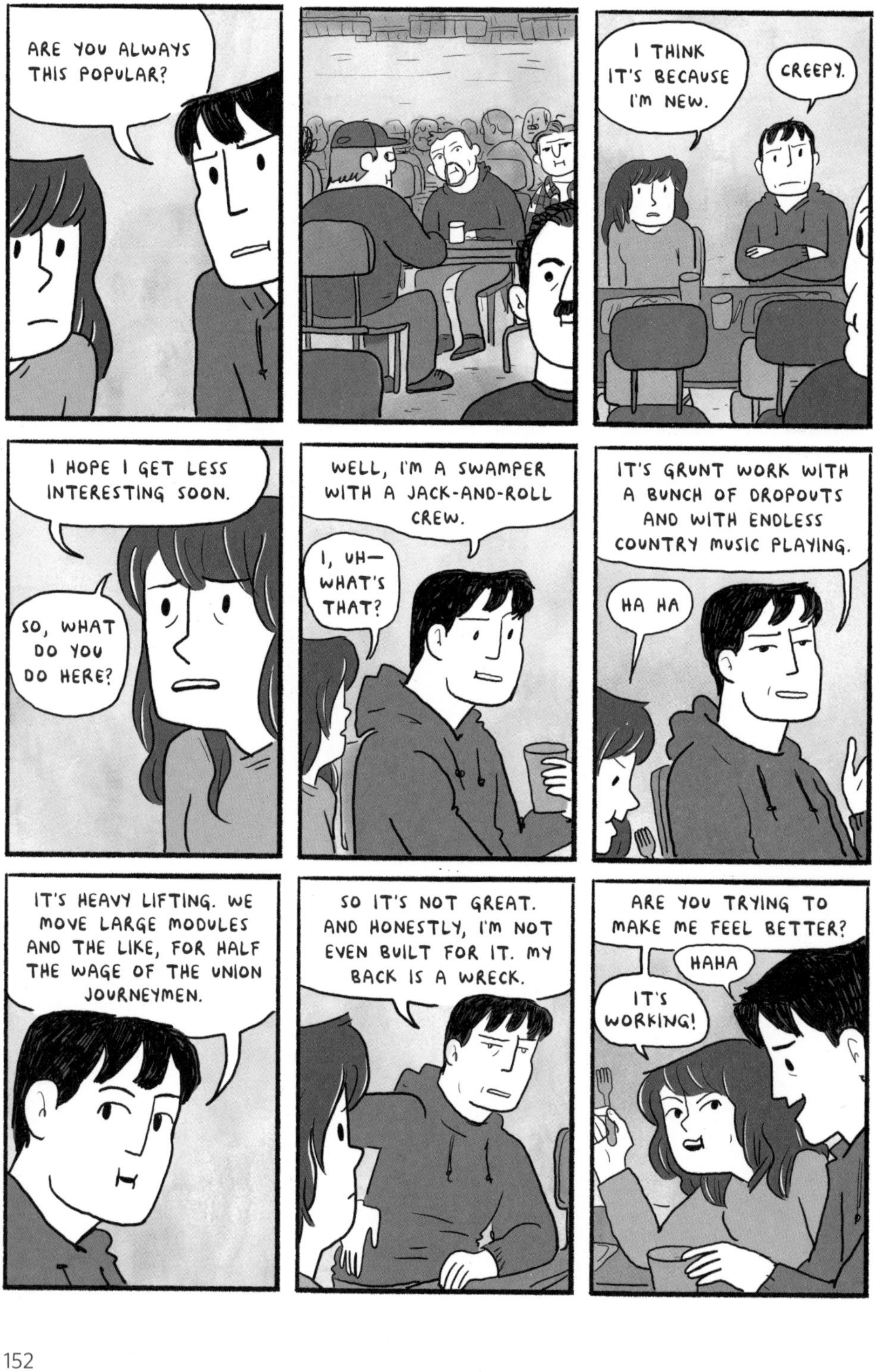
ARE YOU ALWAYS THIS POPULAR?
I THINK IT'S BECAUSE I'M NEW.
CREEPY.
I HOPE I GET LESS INTERESTING SOON.
SO, WHAT DO YOU DO HERE?
WELL, I'M A SWAMPER WITH A JACK-AND-ROLL CREW.
I, UH— WHAT'S THAT?
IT'S GRUNT WORK WITH A BUNCH OF DROPOUTS AND WITH ENDLESS COUNTRY MUSIC PLAYING.
HA HA
IT'S HEAVY LIFTING. WE MOVE LARGE MODULES AND THE LIKE, FOR HALF THE WAGE OF THE UNION JOURNEYMEN.
SO IT'S NOT GREAT. AND HONESTLY, I'M NOT EVEN BUILT FOR IT. MY BACK IS A WRECK.
ARE YOU TRYING TO MAKE ME FEEL BETTER?
HAHA
IT'S WORKING!

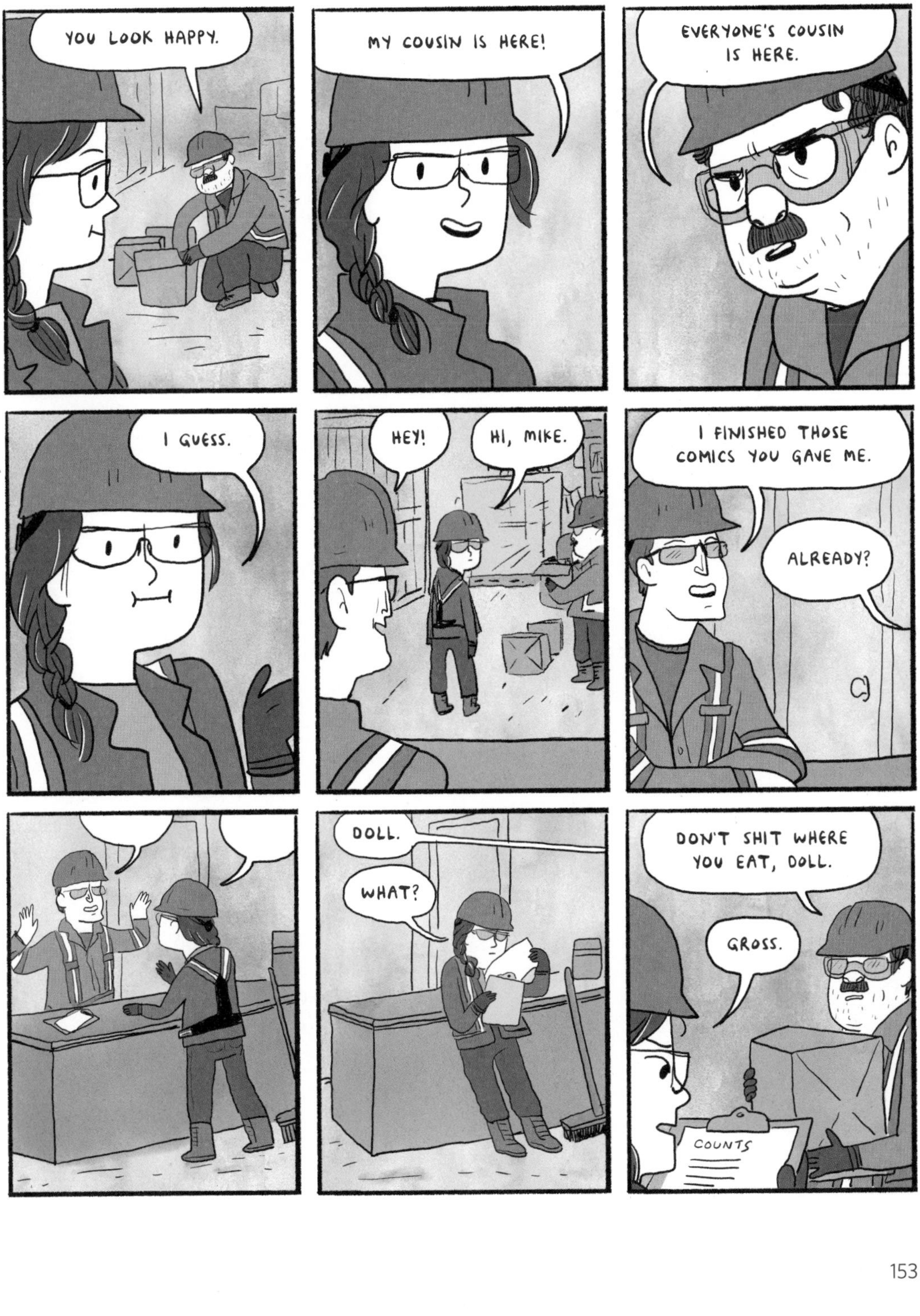
YOU LOOK HAPPY.
MY COUSIN IS HERE!
EVERYONE'S COUSIN IS HERE.
I GUESS.
HEY!
HI, MIKE.
I FINISHED THOSE COMICS YOU GAVE ME.
ALREADY?
DOLL.
WHAT?
DON'T SHIT WHERE YOU EAT, DOLL.
GROSS.
COUNTS

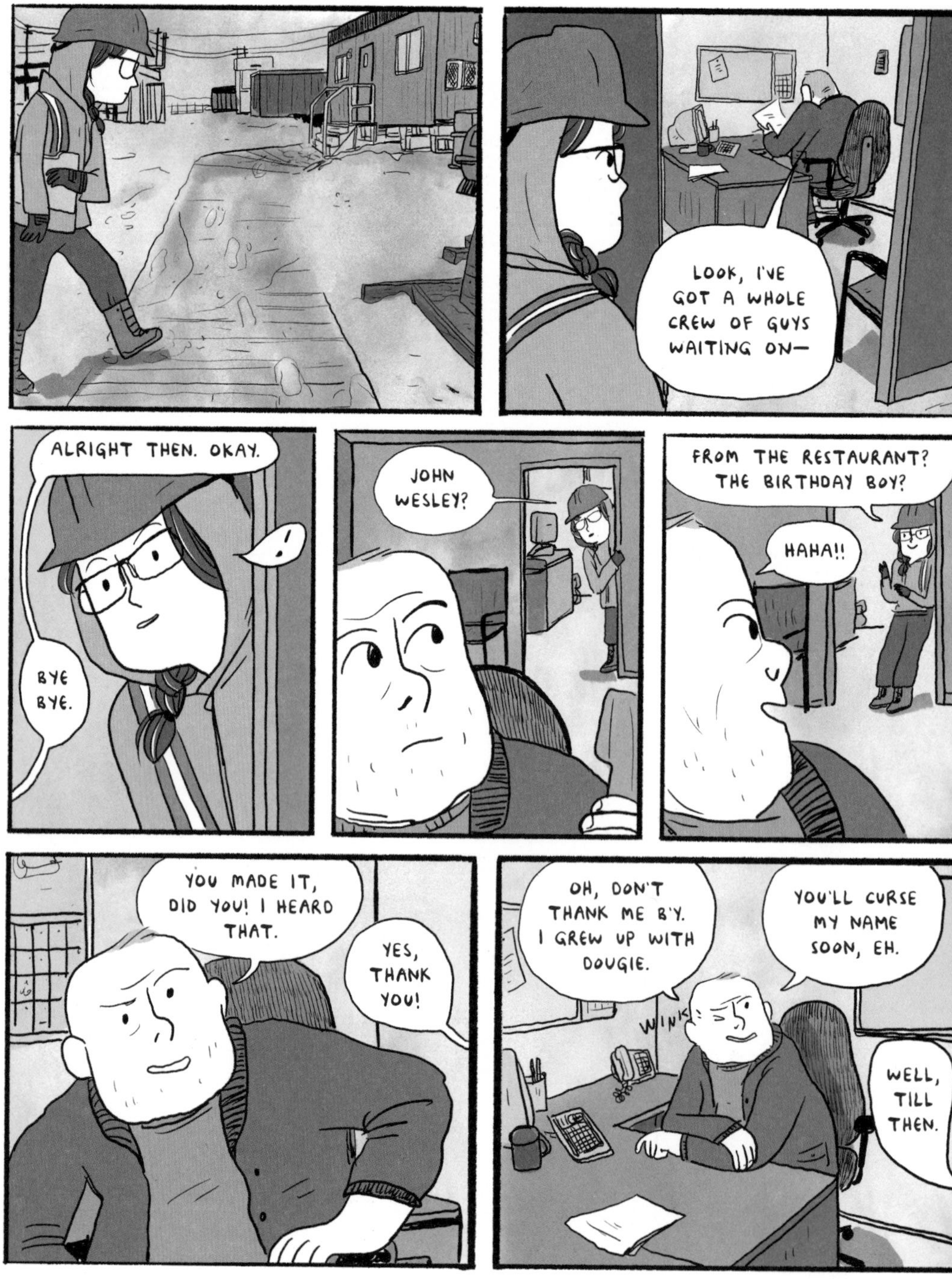
LOOK, I'VE GOT A WHOLE CREW OF GUYS WAITING ON—
ALRIGHT THEN. OKAY.
BYE BYE.
JOHN WESLEY?
FROM THE RESTAURANT? THE BIRTHDAY BOY?
HAHA!!
YOU MADE IT, DID YOU! I HEARD THAT.
YES, THANK YOU!
OH, DON'T THANK ME B'Y. I GREW UP WITH DOUGIE.
WINK
YOU'LL CURSE MY NAME SOON, EH.
WELL, TILL THEN.

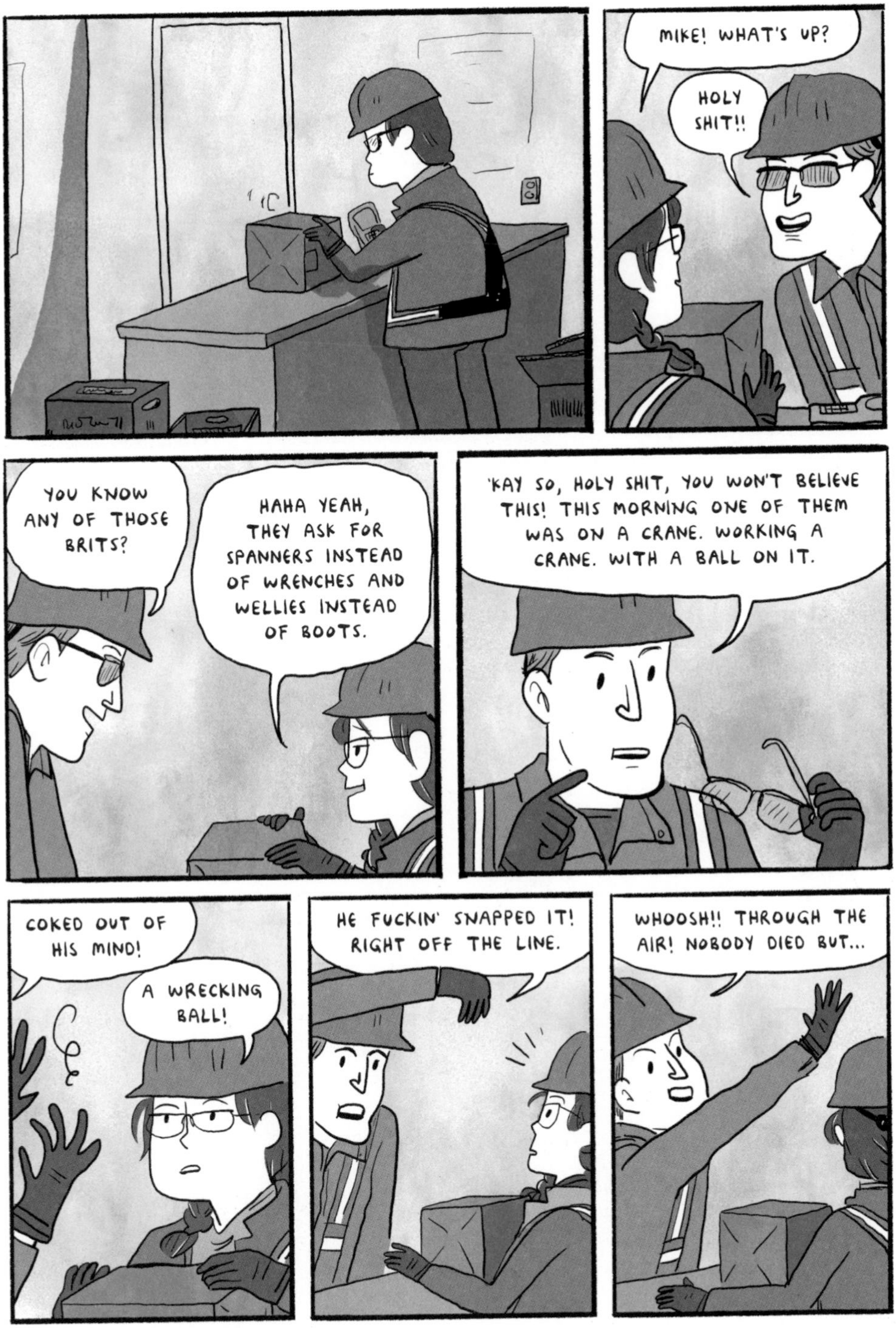
MIKE! WHAT'S UP?
HOLY SHIT!!
YOU KNOW ANY OF THOSE BRITS?
HAHA YEAH, THEY ASK FOR SPANNERS INSTEAD OF WRENCHES AND WELLIES INSTEAD OF BOOTS.
'KAY SO, HOLY SHIT, YOU WON'T BELIEVE THIS! THIS MORNING ONE OF THEM WAS ON A CRANE. WORKING A CRANE. WITH A BALL ON IT.
COKED OUT OF HIS MIND!
A WRECKING BALL!
HE FUCKIN' SNAPPED IT! RIGHT OFF THE LINE.
WHOOSH!! THROUGH THE AIR! NOBODY DIED BUT...

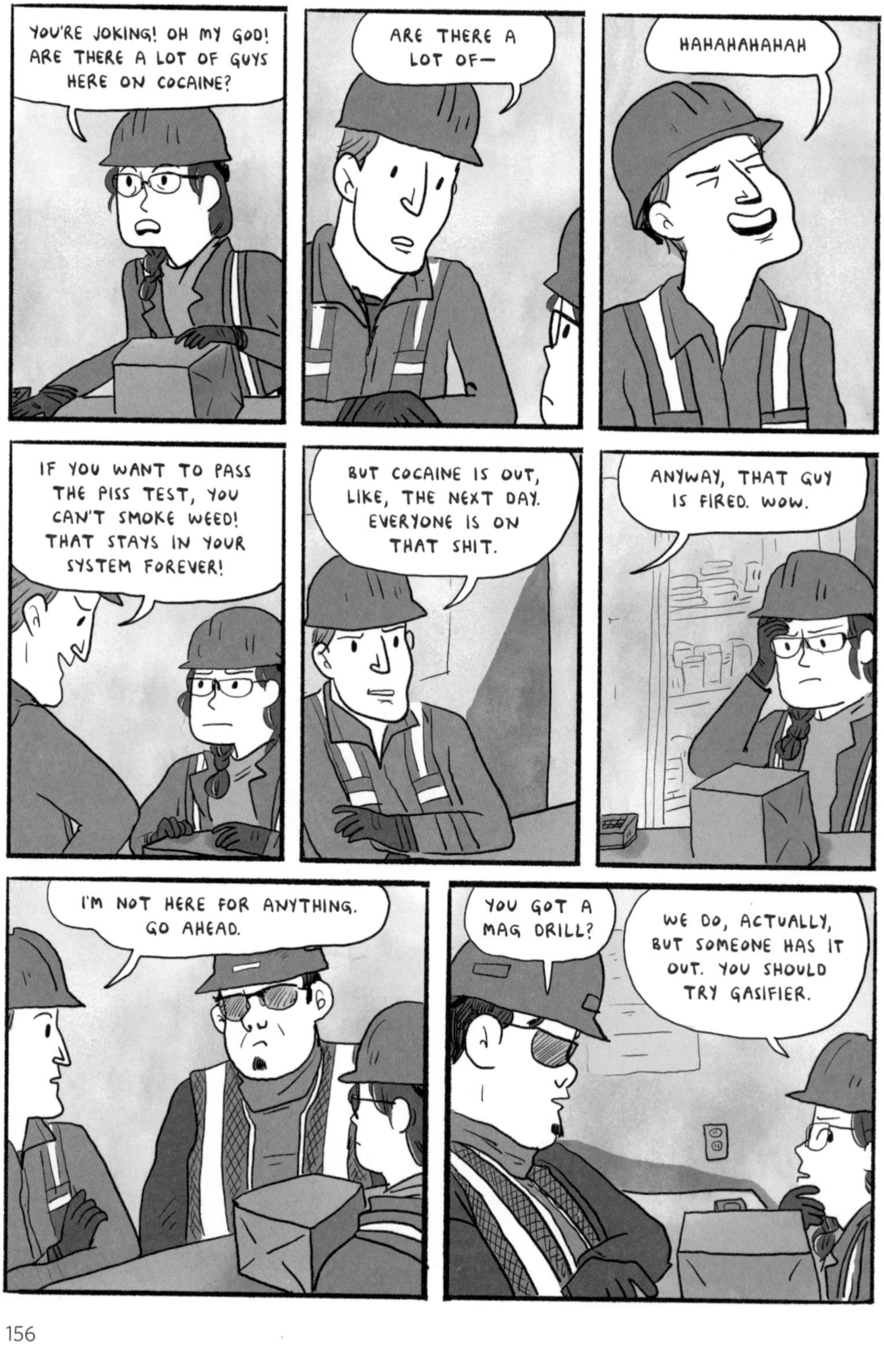
YOU'RE JOKING! OH MY GOD! ARE THERE A LOT OF GUYS HERE ON COCAINE?
ARE THERE A LOT OF—
HAHAHAHAHAH
IF YOU WANT TO PASS THE PISS TEST, YOU CAN'T SMOKE WEED! THAT STAYS IN YOUR SYSTEM FOREVER!
BUT COCAINE IS OUT, LIKE, THE NEXT DAY. EVERYONE IS ON THAT SHIT.
ANYWAY, THAT GUY IS FIRED. WOW.
I'M NOT HERE FOR ANYTHING. GO AHEAD.
YOU GOT A MAG DRILL?
WE DO, ACTUALLY, BUT SOMEONE HAS IT OUT. YOU SHOULD TRY GASIFIER.

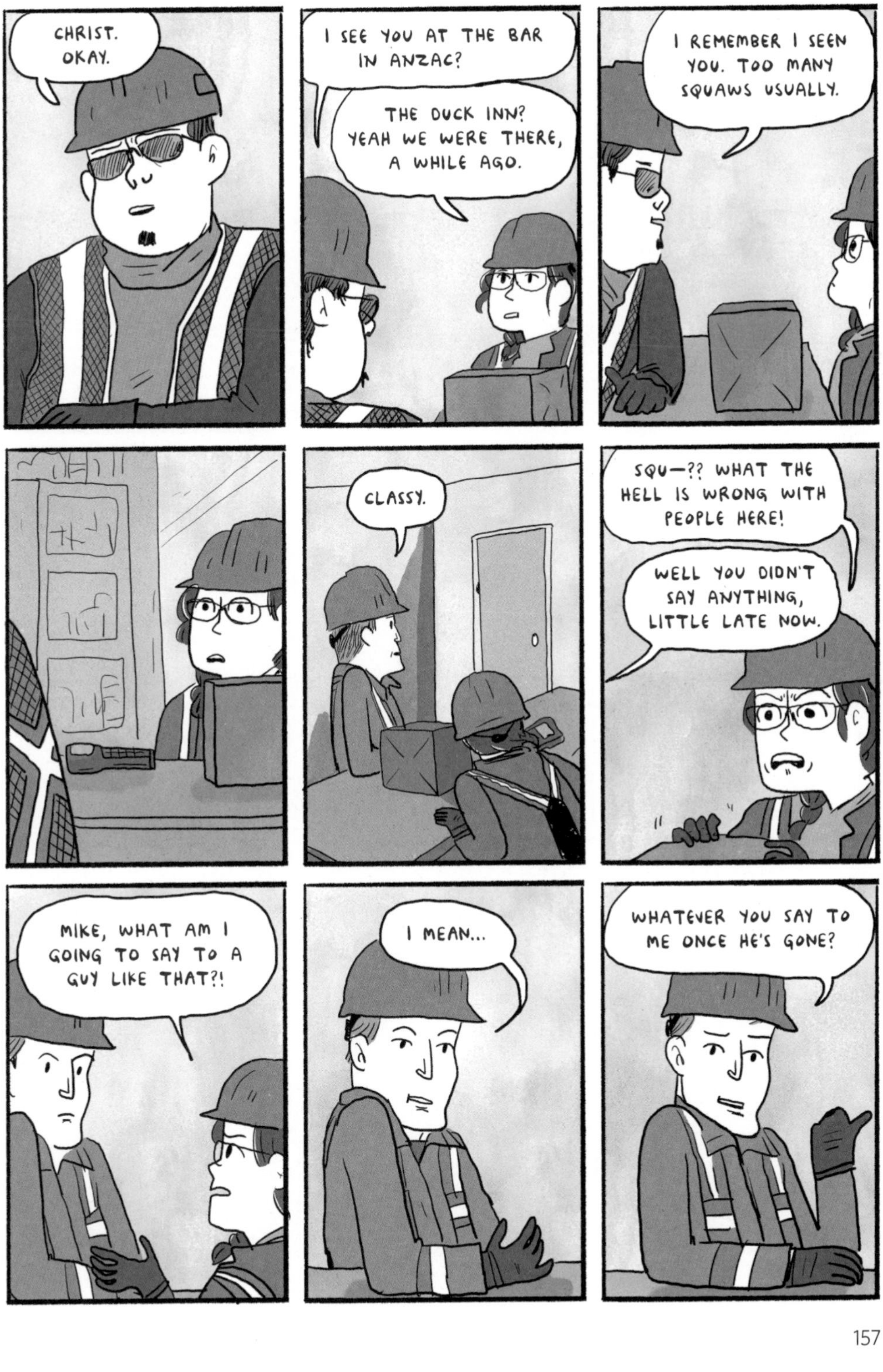
CHRIST. OKAY.
I SEE YOU AT THE BAR IN ANZAC?
THE DUCK INN? YEAH WE WERE THERE, A WHILE AGO.
I REMEMBER I SEEN YOU. TOO MANY SQUAWS USUALLY.
CLASSY.
SQU—?? WHAT THE HELL IS WRONG WITH PEOPLE HERE!
WELL YOU DIDN'T SAY ANYTHING, LITTLE LATE NOW.
MIKE, WHAT AM I GOING TO SAY TO A GUY LIKE THAT?!
I MEAN...
WHATEVER YOU SAY TO ME ONCE HE'S GONE?

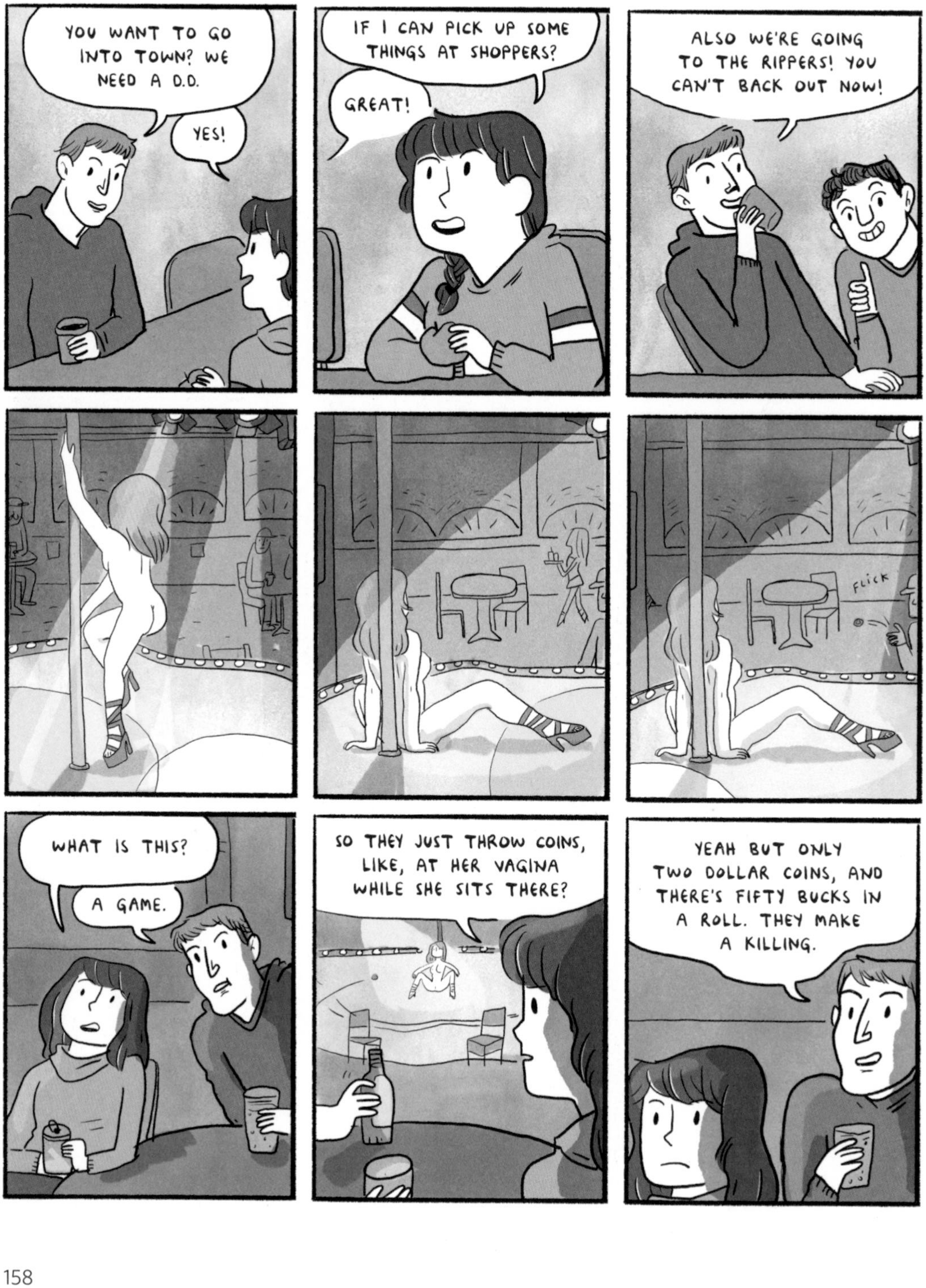
YOU WANT TO GO INTO TOWN? WE NEED A D.D.
YES!
IF I CAN PICK UP SOME THINGS AT SHOPPERS?
GREAT!
ALSO WE'RE GOING TO THE RIPPERS! YOU CAN'T BACK OUT NOW!
FLICK
WHAT IS THIS?
A GAME.
SO THEY JUST THROW COINS, LIKE, AT HER VAGINA WHILE SHE SITS THERE?
YEAH BUT ONLY TWO DOLLAR COINS, AND THERE'S FIFTY BUCKS IN A ROLL. THEY MAKE A KILLING.

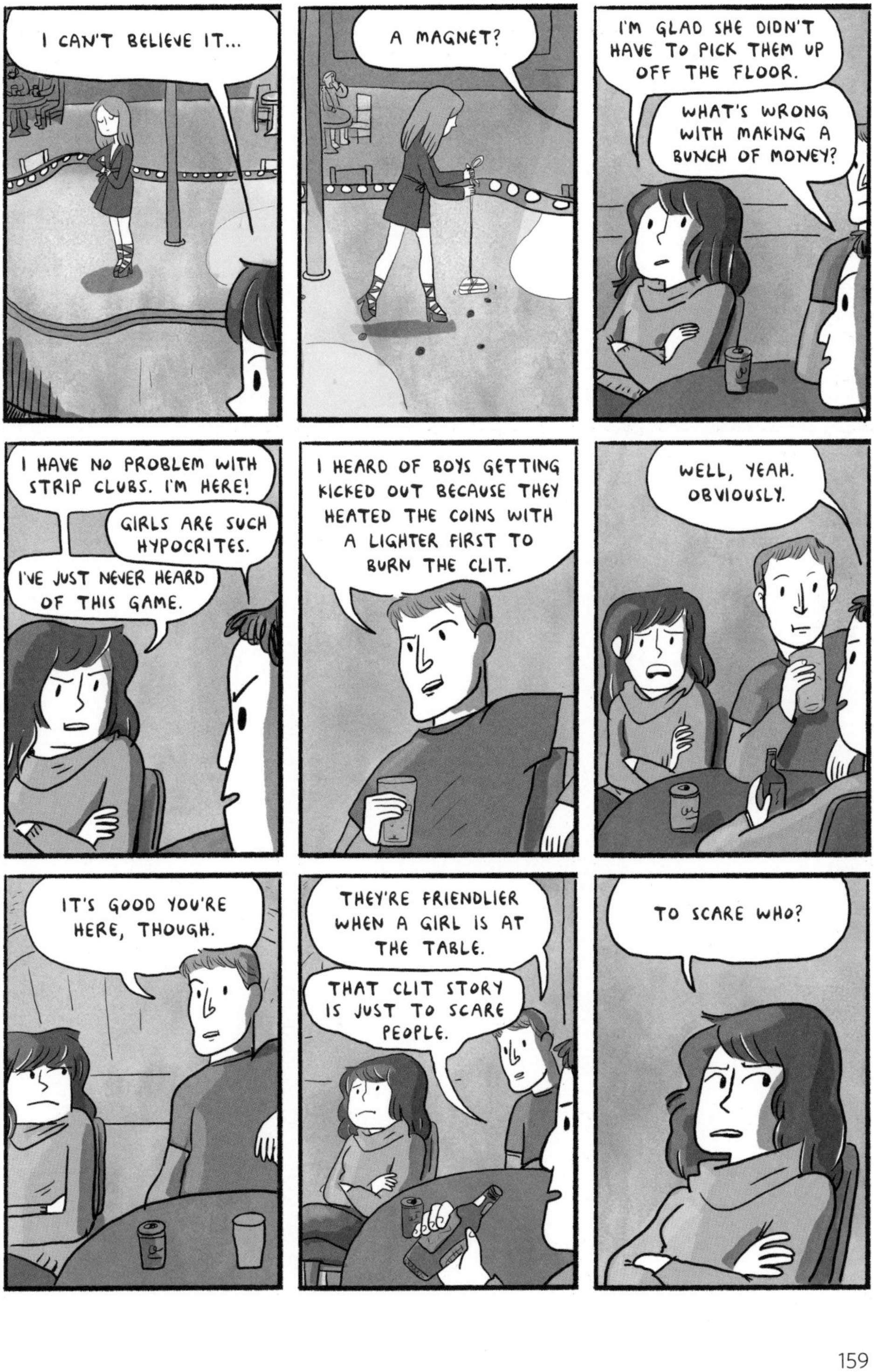
I CAN'T BELIEVE IT...
A MAGNET?
I'M GLAD SHE DIDN'T HAVE TO PICK THEM UP OFF THE FLOOR.
WHAT'S WRONG WITH MAKING A BUNCH OF MONEY?
I HAVE NO PROBLEM WITH STRIP CLUBS. I'M HERE!
GIRLS ARE SUCH HYPOCRITES.
I'VE JUST NEVER HEARD OF THIS GAME.
I HEARD OF BOYS GETTING KICKED OUT BECAUSE THEY HEATED THE COINS WITH A LIGHTER FIRST TO BURN THE CLIT.
WELL, YEAH. OBVIOUSLY.
IT'S GOOD YOU'RE HERE, THOUGH.
THEY'RE FRIENDLIER WHEN A GIRL IS AT THE TABLE.
THAT CLIT STORY IS JUST TO SCARE PEOPLE.
TO SCARE WHO?

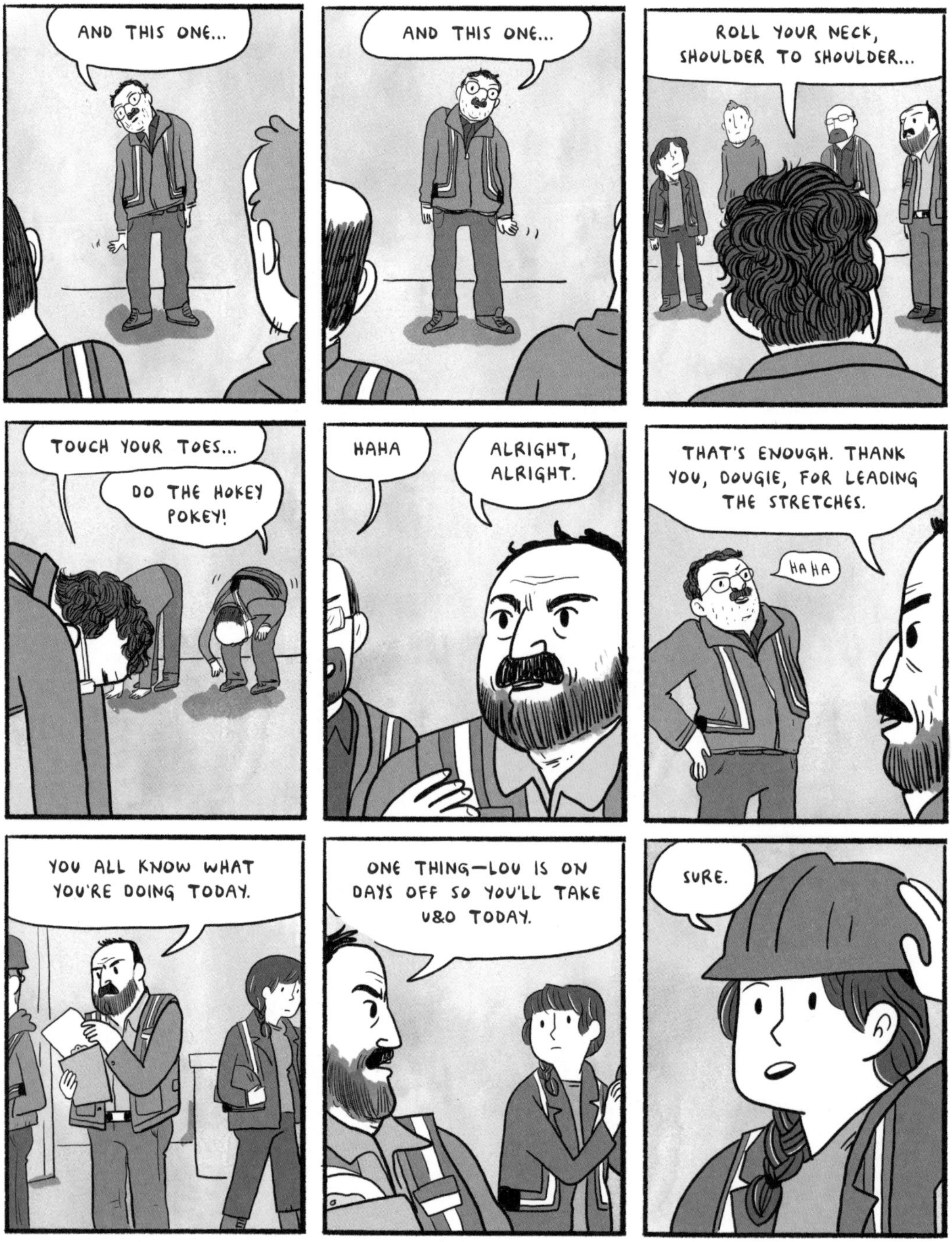
AND THIS ONE...
AND THIS ONE...
ROLL YOUR NECK, SHOULDER TO SHOULDER...
TOUCH YOUR TOES...
DO THE HOKEY POKEY!
HAHA
ALRIGHT, ALRIGHT.
THAT'S ENOUGH. THANK YOU, DOUGIE, FOR LEADING THE STRETCHES.
HA HA
YOU ALL KNOW WHAT YOU'RE DOING TODAY.
ONE THING—LOU IS ON DAYS OFF SO YOU'LL TAKE U&O TODAY.
SURE.

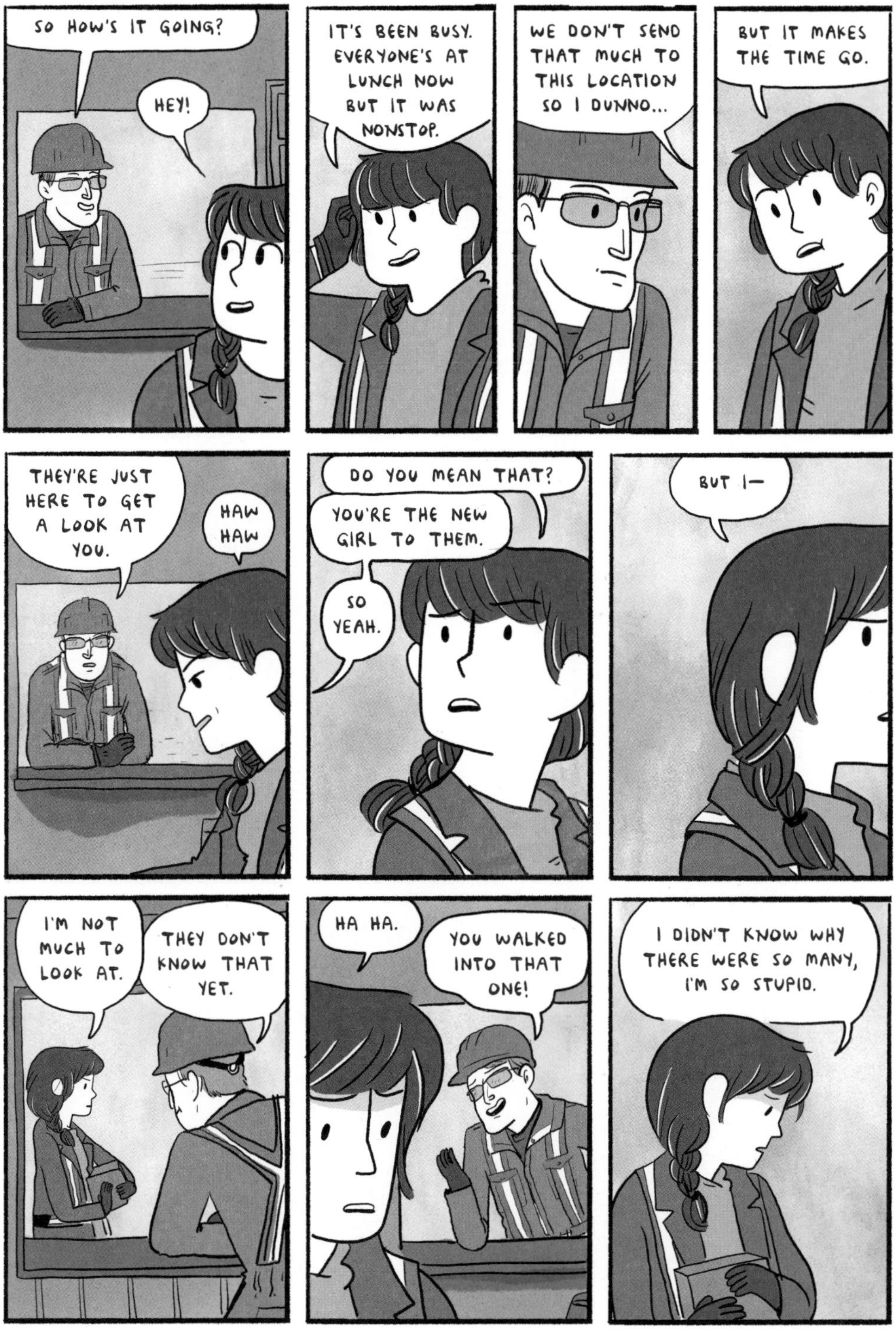
SO HOW'S IT GOING?
HEY!
IT'S BEEN BUSY. EVERYONE'S AT LUNCH NOW BUT IT WAS NONSTOP.
WE DON'T SEND THAT MUCH TO THIS LOCATION SO I DUNNO...
BUT IT MAKES THE TIME GO.
THEY'RE JUST HERE TO GET A LOOK AT YOU.
HAW HAW
DO YOU MEAN THAT?
YOU'RE THE NEW GIRL TO THEM.
SO YEAH.
BUT I—
I'M NOT MUCH TO LOOK AT.
THEY DON'T KNOW THAT YET.
HA HA.
YOU WALKED INTO THAT ONE!
I DIDN'T KNOW WHY THERE WERE SO MANY, I'M SO STUPID.

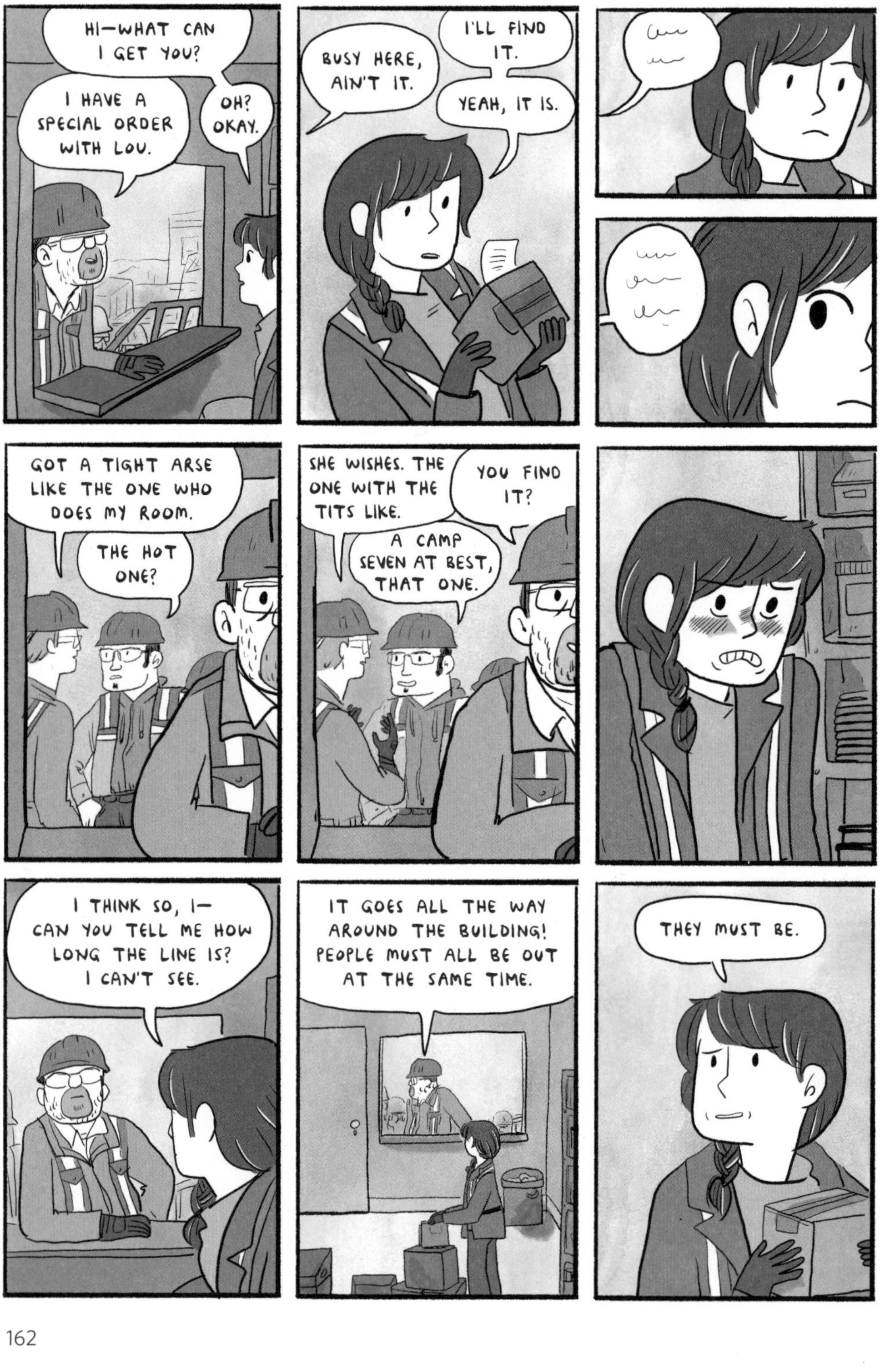
HI—WHAT CAN I GET YOU?
I HAVE A SPECIAL ORDER WITH LOU.
OH? OKAY.
BUSY HERE, AIN'T IT.
I'LL FIND IT.
YEAH, IT IS.
GOT A TIGHT ARSE LIKE THE ONE WHO DOES MY ROOM.
THE HOT ONE?
SHE WISHES. THE ONE WITH THE TITS LIKE.
A CAMP SEVEN AT BEST, THAT ONE.
YOU FIND IT?
I THINK SO, I— CAN YOU TELL ME HOW LONG THE LINE IS? I CAN'T SEE.
IT GOES ALL THE WAY AROUND THE BUILDING! PEOPLE MUST ALL BE OUT AT THE SAME TIME.
THEY MUST BE.

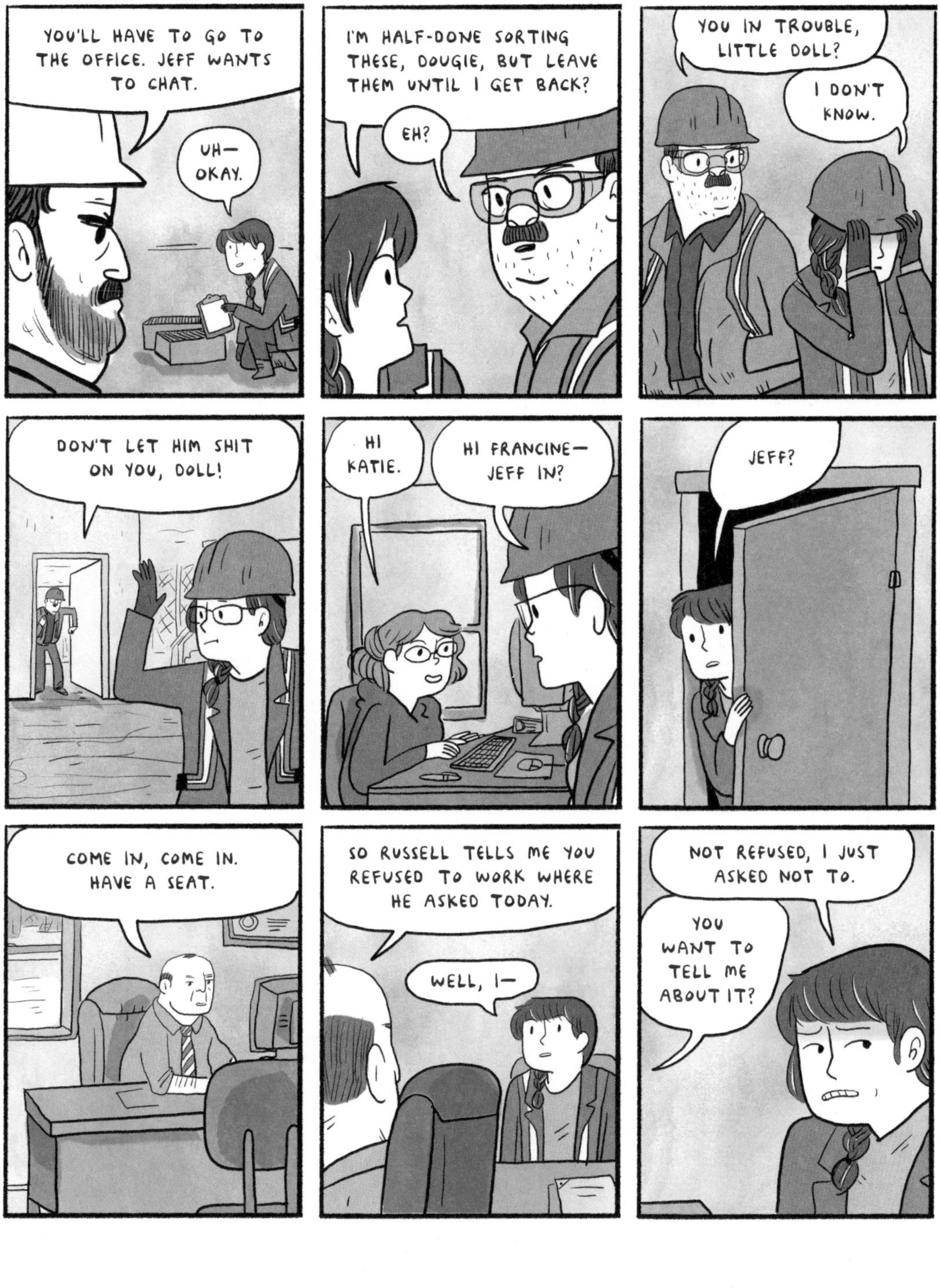
YOU'LL HAVE TO GO TO THE OFFICE. JEFF WANTS TO CHAT.
UH— OKAY.
I'M HALF-DONE SORTING THESE, DOUGIE, BUT LEAVE THEM UNTIL I GET BACK?
EH?
YOU IN TROUBLE, LITTLE DOLL?
I DON'T KNOW.
DON'T LET HIM SHIT ON YOU, DOLL!
HI KATIE.
HI FRANCINE— JEFF IN?
JEFF?
COME IN, COME IN. HAVE A SEAT.
SO RUSSELL TELLS ME YOU REFUSED TO WORK WHERE HE ASKED TODAY.
WELL, I—
NOT REFUSED, I JUST ASKED NOT TO.
YOU WANT TO TELL ME ABOUT IT?

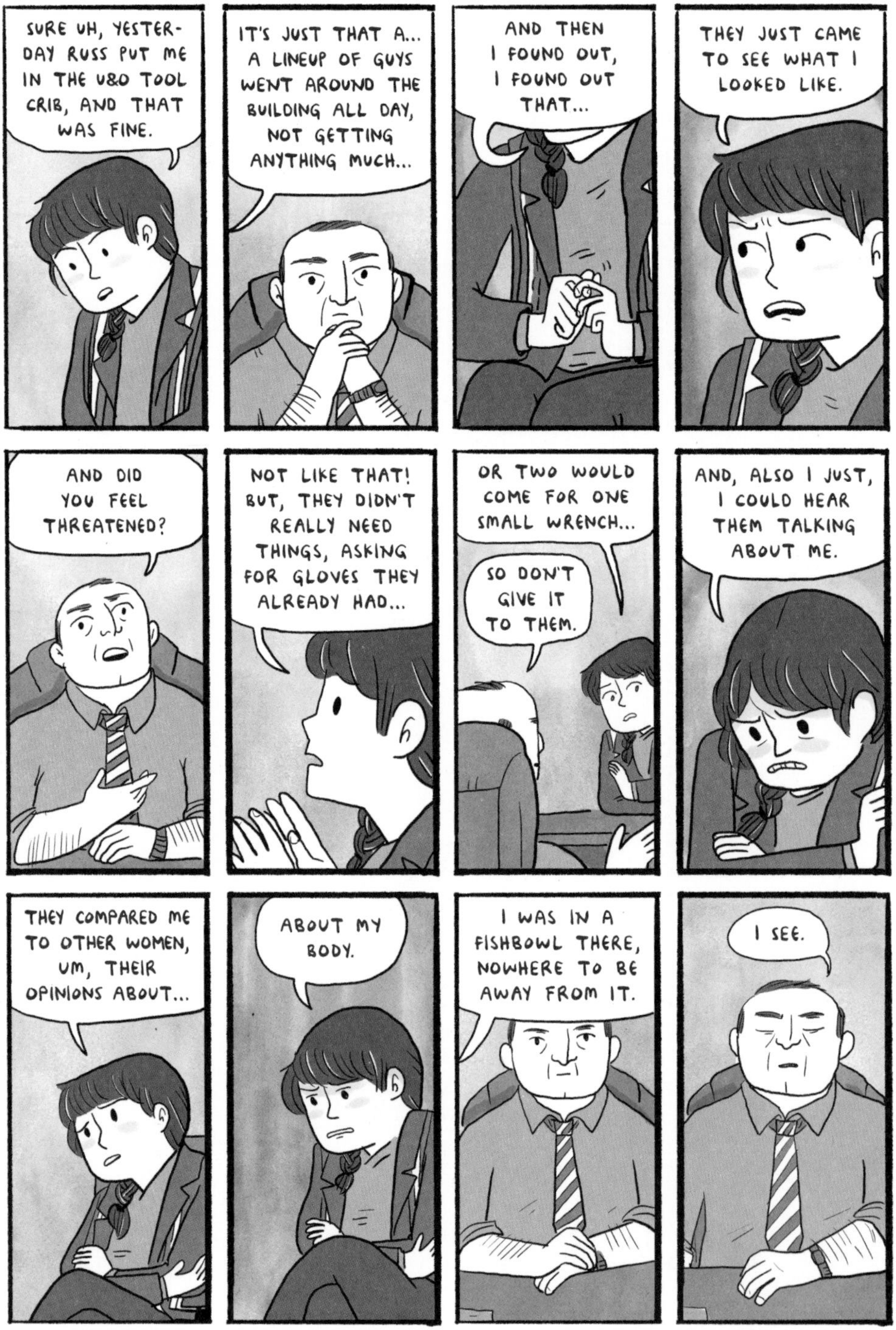
SURE UH, YESTERDAY RUSS PUT ME IN THE U&O TOOL CRIB, AND THAT WAS FINE.
IT'S JUST THAT A... A LINEUP OF GUYS WENT AROUND THE BUILDING ALL DAY, NOT GETTING ANYTHING MUCH...
AND THEN I FOUND OUT, I FOUND OUT THAT...
THEY JUST CAME TO SEE WHAT I LOOKED LIKE.
AND DID YOU FEEL THREATENED?
NOT LIKE THAT! BUT, THEY DIDN'T REALLY NEED THINGS, ASKING FOR GLOVES THEY ALREADY HAD...
OR TWO WOULD COME FOR ONE SMALL WRENCH...
SO DON'T GIVE IT TO THEM.
AND, ALSO I JUST, I COULD HEAR THEM TALKING ABOUT ME.
THEY COMPARED ME TO OTHER WOMEN, UM, THEIR OPINIONS ABOUT...
ABOUT MY BODY.
I WAS IN A FISHBOWL THERE, NOWHERE TO BE AWAY FROM IT.
I SEE.

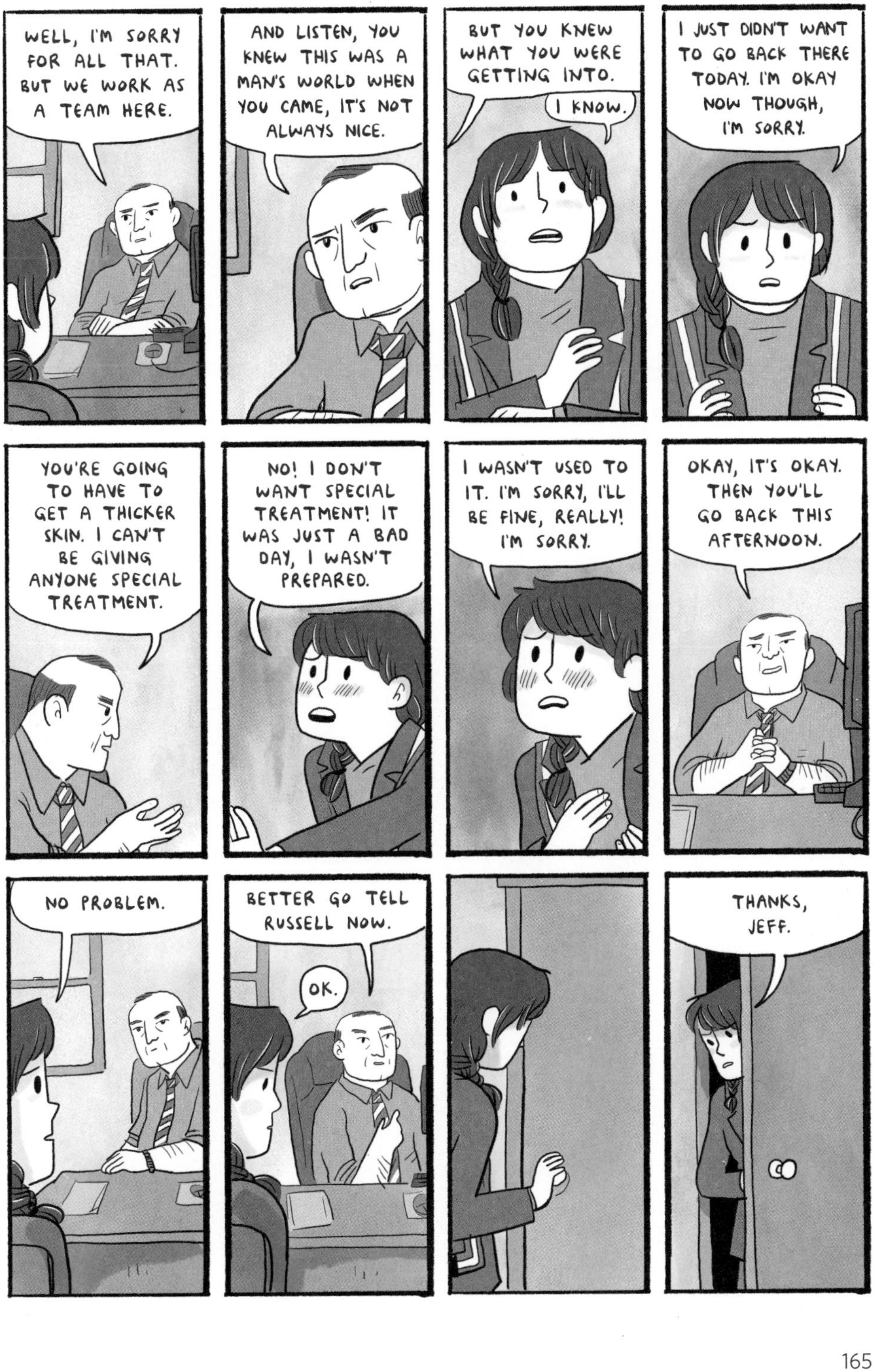
WELL, I'M SORRY FOR ALL THAT. BUT WE WORK AS A TEAM HERE.
AND LISTEN, YOU KNEW THIS WAS A MAN'S WORLD WHEN YOU CAME, IT'S NOT ALWAYS NICE.
BUT YOU KNEW WHAT YOU WERE GETTING INTO.
I KNOW.
I JUST DIDN'T WANT TO GO BACK THERE TODAY. I'M OKAY NOW THOUGH, I'M SORRY.
YOU'RE GOING TO HAVE TO GET A THICKER SKIN. I CAN'T BE GIVING ANYONE SPECIAL TREATMENT.
NO! I DON'T WANT SPECIAL TREATMENT! IT WAS JUST A BAD DAY, I WASN'T PREPARED.
I WASN'T USED TO IT. I'M SORRY, I'LL BE FINE, REALLY! I'M SORRY.
OKAY, IT'S OKAY. THEN YOU'LL GO BACK THIS AFTERNOON.
NO PROBLEM.
BETTER GO TELL RUSSELL NOW.
OK.
THANKS, JEFF.

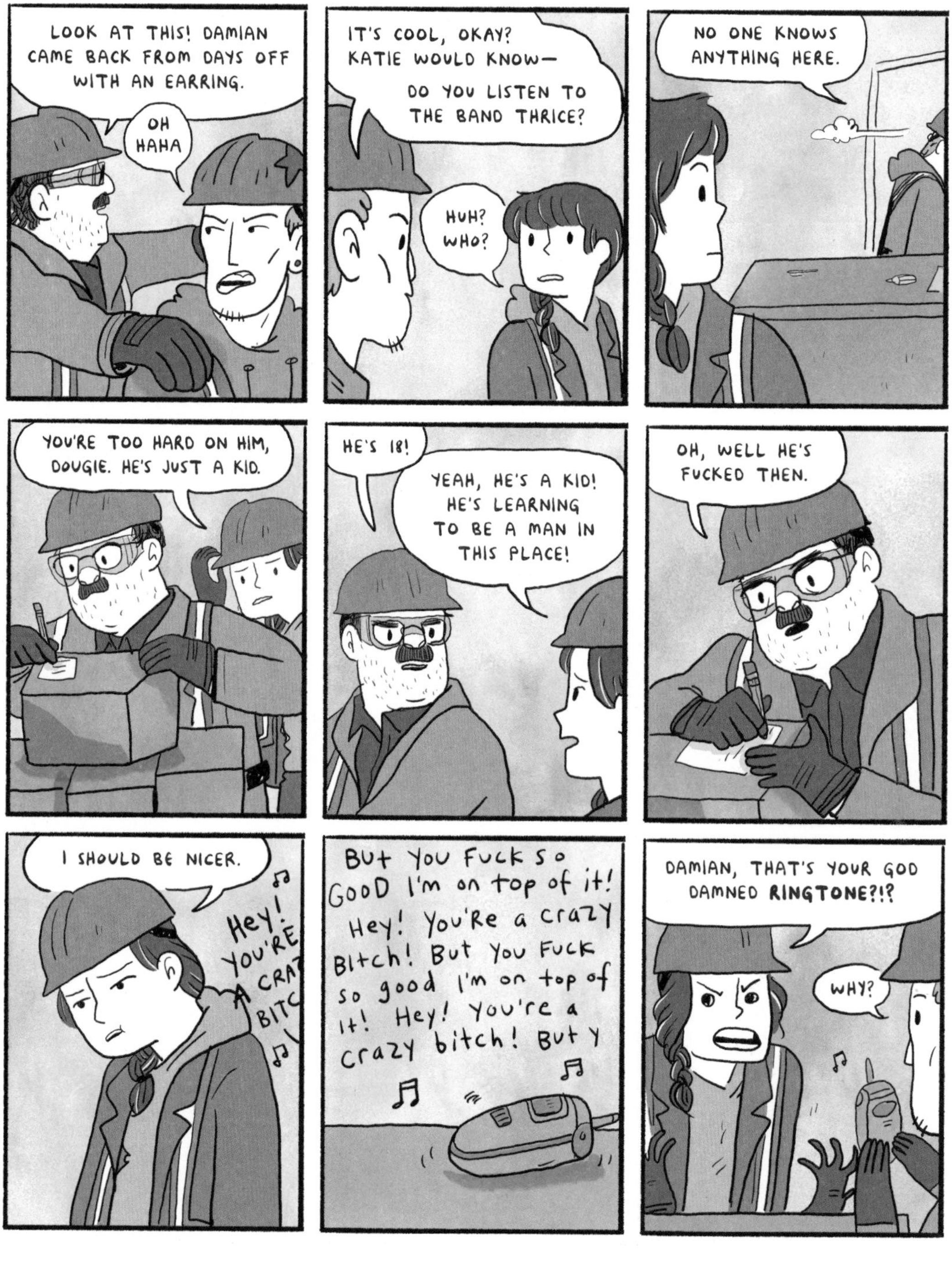
LOOK AT THIS! DAMIAN CAME BACK FROM DAYS OFF WITH AN EARRING.
OH HAHA
IT'S COOL, OKAY? KATIE WOULD KNOW—
DO YOU LISTEN TO THE BAND THRICE?
HUH? WHO?
NO ONE KNOWS ANYTHING HERE.
YOU'RE TOO HARD ON HIM, DOUGIE. HE'S JUST A KID.
HE'S 18!
YEAH, HE'S A KID! HE'S LEARNING TO BE A MAN IN THIS PLACE!
OH, WELL HE'S FUCKED THEN.
I SHOULD BE NICER.
Hey! YOU'RE A CRA BITC
But You Fuck so GooD I'm on top of it! Hey! You're a crazy Bitch! But You Fuck so good I'm on top of it! Hey! You're a crazy bitch! But y
DAMIAN, THAT'S YOUR GOD DAMNED **RINGTONE?!?**
WHY?

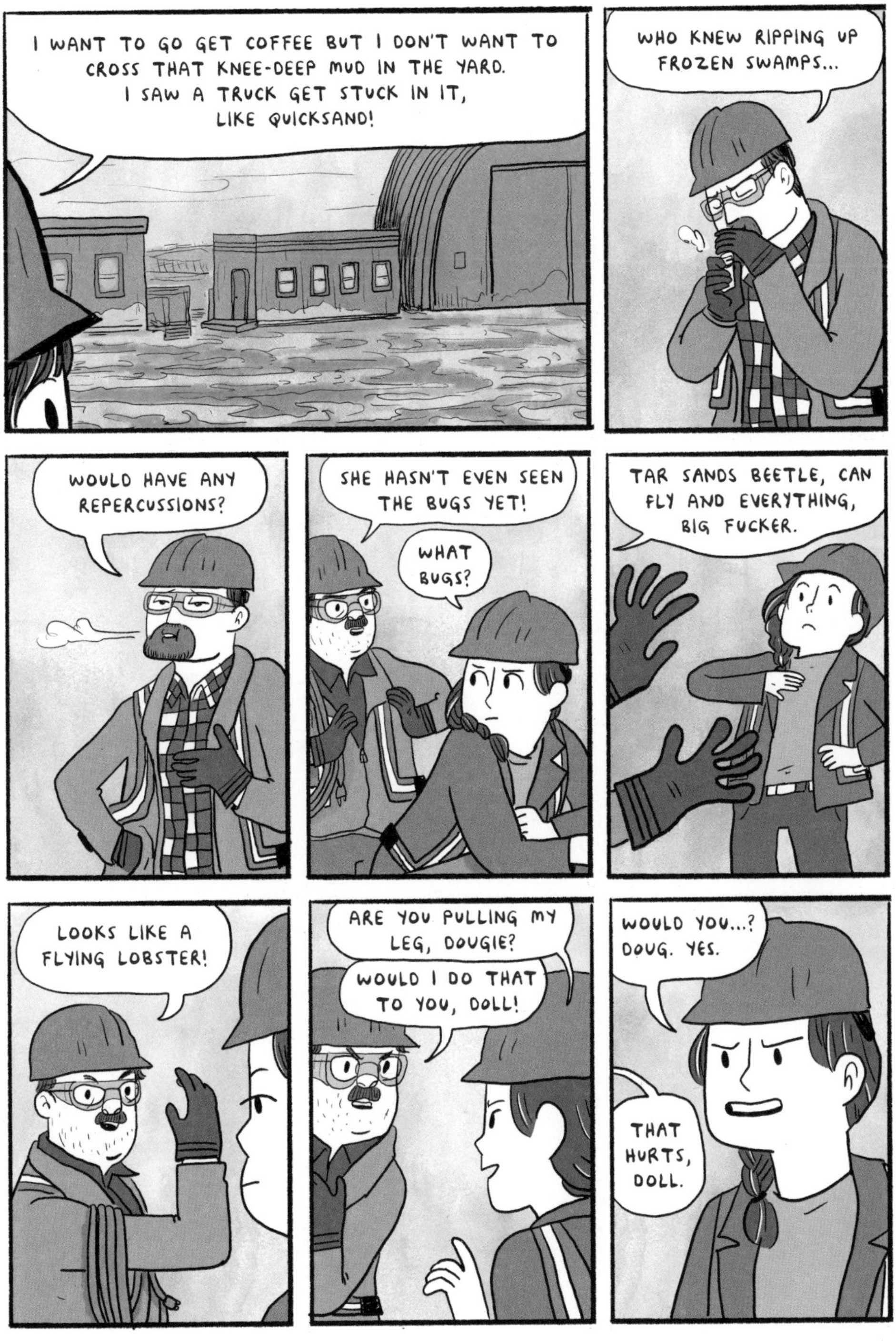

I WANT TO GO GET COFFEE BUT I DON'T WANT TO CROSS THAT KNEE-DEEP MUD IN THE YARD. I SAW A TRUCK GET STUCK IN IT, LIKE QUICKSAND!
WHO KNEW RIPPING UP FROZEN SWAMPS...
WOULD HAVE ANY REPERCUSSIONS?
SHE HASN'T EVEN SEEN THE BUGS YET!
WHAT BUGS?
TAR SANDS BEETLE, CAN FLY AND EVERYTHING, BIG FUCKER.
LOOKS LIKE A FLYING LOBSTER!
ARE YOU PULLING MY LEG, DOUGIE?
WOULD I DO THAT TO YOU, DOLL!
WOULD YOU...? DOUG. YES.
THAT HURTS, DOLL.

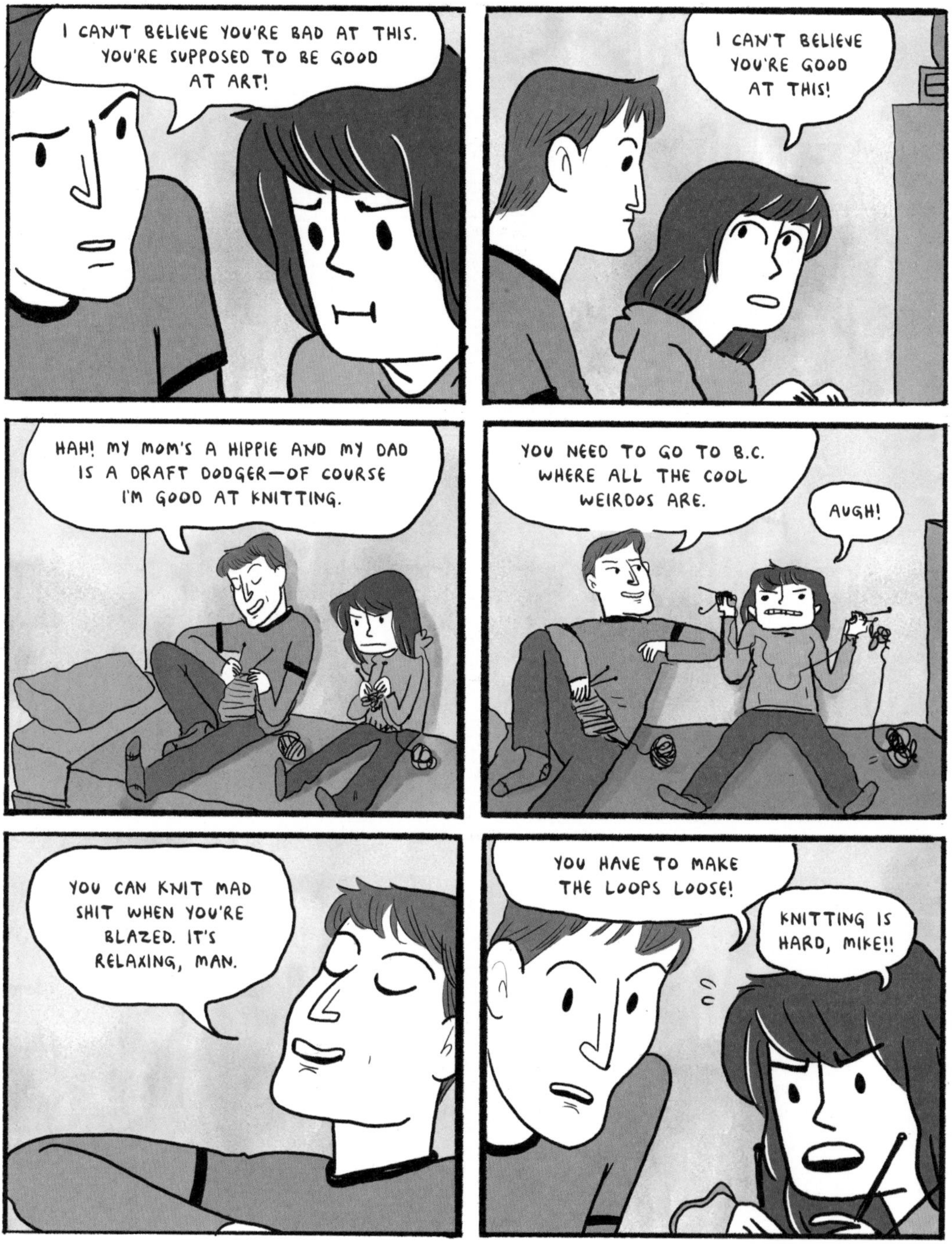
I CAN'T BELIEVE YOU'RE BAD AT THIS. YOU'RE SUPPOSED TO BE GOOD AT ART!
I CAN'T BELIEVE YOU'RE GOOD AT THIS!
HAH! MY MOM'S A HIPPIE AND MY DAD IS A DRAFT DODGER—OF COURSE I'M GOOD AT KNITTING.
YOU NEED TO GO TO B.C. WHERE ALL THE COOL WEIRDOS ARE.
AUGH!
YOU CAN KNIT MAD SHIT WHEN YOU'RE BLAZED. IT'S RELAXING, MAN.
YOU HAVE TO MAKE THE LOOPS LOOSE!
KNITTING IS HARD, MIKE!!

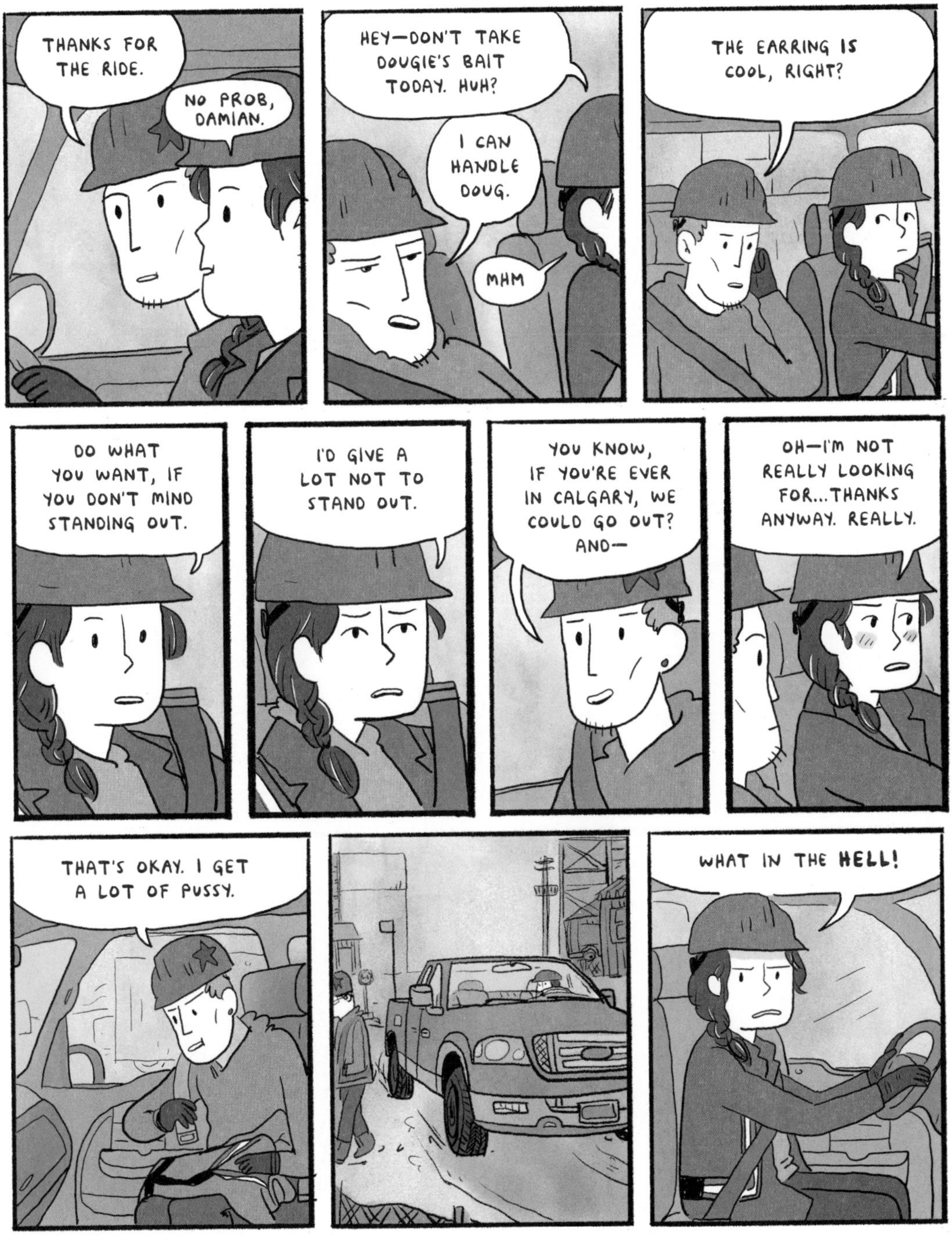
THANKS FOR THE RIDE.
NO PROB, DAMIAN.
HEY—DON'T TAKE DOUGIE'S BAIT TODAY. HUH?
I CAN HANDLE DOUG.
MHM
THE EARRING IS COOL, RIGHT?
DO WHAT YOU WANT, IF YOU DON'T MIND STANDING OUT.
I'D GIVE A LOT NOT TO STAND OUT.
YOU KNOW, IF YOU'RE EVER IN CALGARY, WE COULD GO OUT? AND—
OH—I'M NOT REALLY LOOKING FOR...THANKS ANYWAY. REALLY.
THAT'S OKAY. I GET A LOT OF PUSSY.
WHAT IN THE HELL!

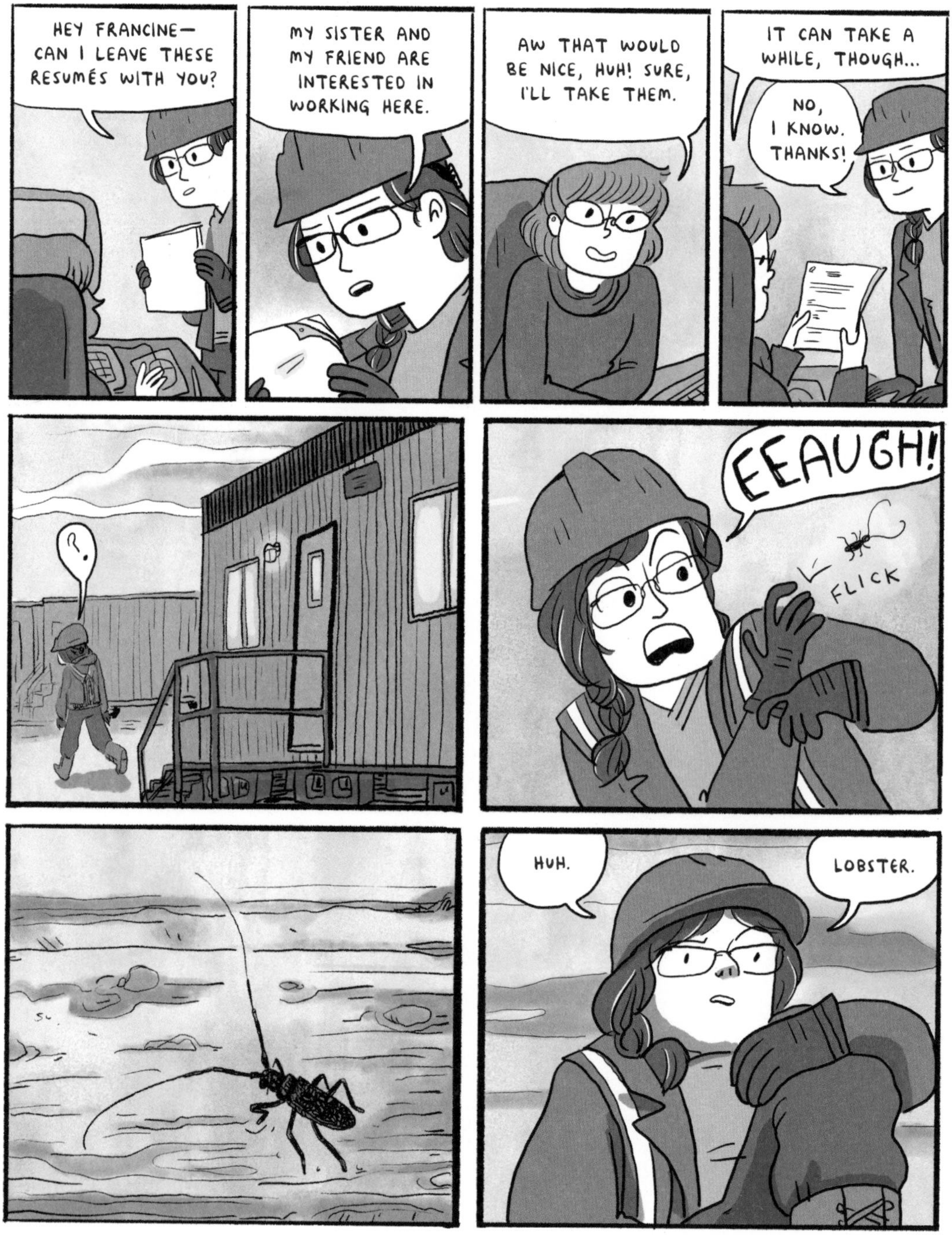
HEY FRANCINE— CAN I LEAVE THESE RESUMÉS WITH YOU?
MY SISTER AND MY FRIEND ARE INTERESTED IN WORKING HERE.
AW THAT WOULD BE NICE, HUH! SURE, I'LL TAKE THEM.
IT CAN TAKE A WHILE, THOUGH...
NO, I KNOW. THANKS!
?
EEAUGH!
FLICK
HUH.
LOBSTER.

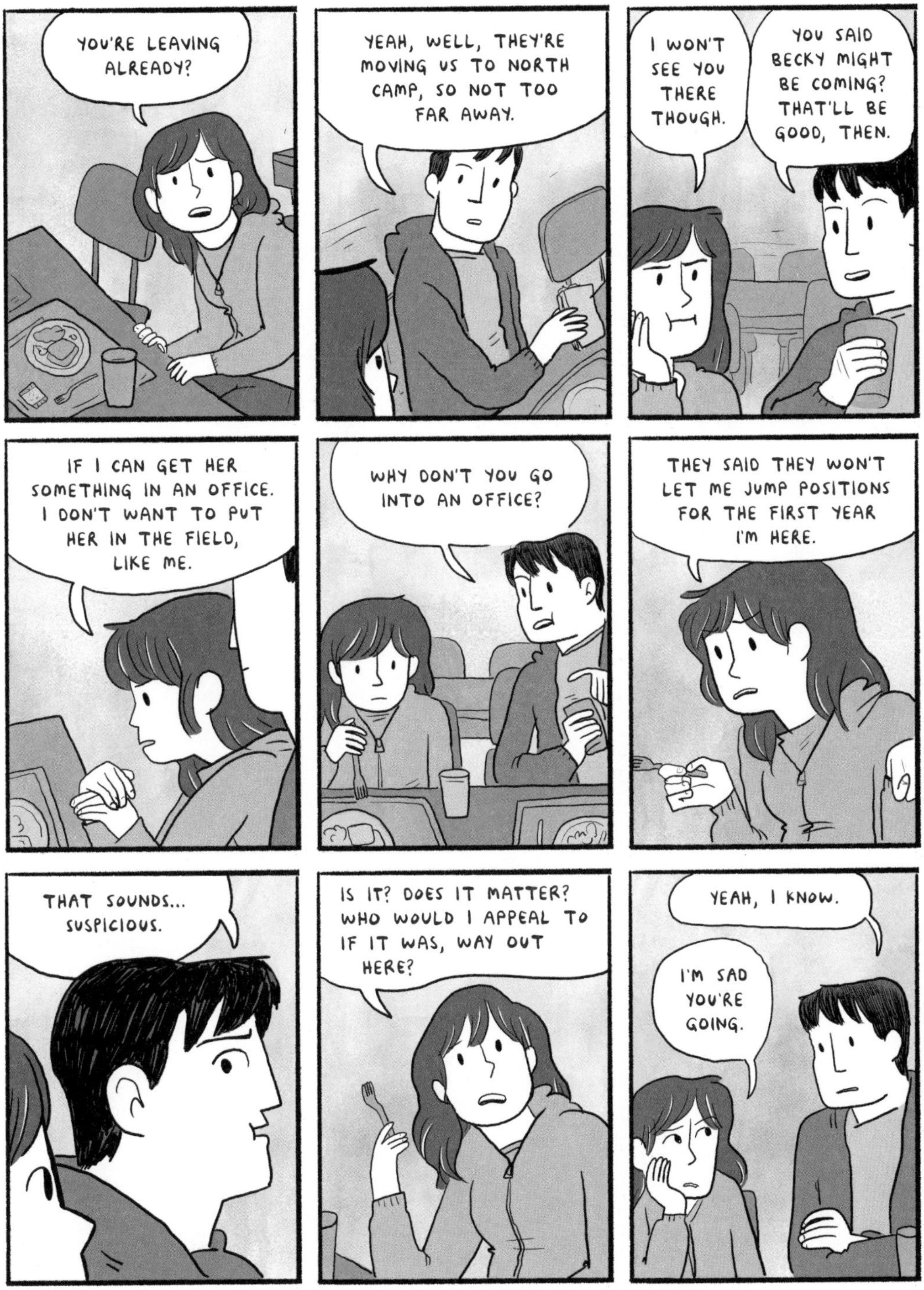
YOU'RE LEAVING ALREADY?
YEAH, WELL, THEY'RE MOVING US TO NORTH CAMP, SO NOT TOO FAR AWAY.
I WON'T SEE YOU THERE THOUGH.
YOU SAID BECKY MIGHT BE COMING? THAT'LL BE GOOD, THEN.
IF I CAN GET HER SOMETHING IN AN OFFICE. I DON'T WANT TO PUT HER IN THE FIELD, LIKE ME.
WHY DON'T YOU GO INTO AN OFFICE?
THEY SAID THEY WON'T LET ME JUMP POSITIONS FOR THE FIRST YEAR I'M HERE.
THAT SOUNDS... SUSPICIOUS.
IS IT? DOES IT MATTER? WHO WOULD I APPEAL TO IF IT WAS, WAY OUT HERE?
YEAH, I KNOW.
I'M SAD YOU'RE GOING.

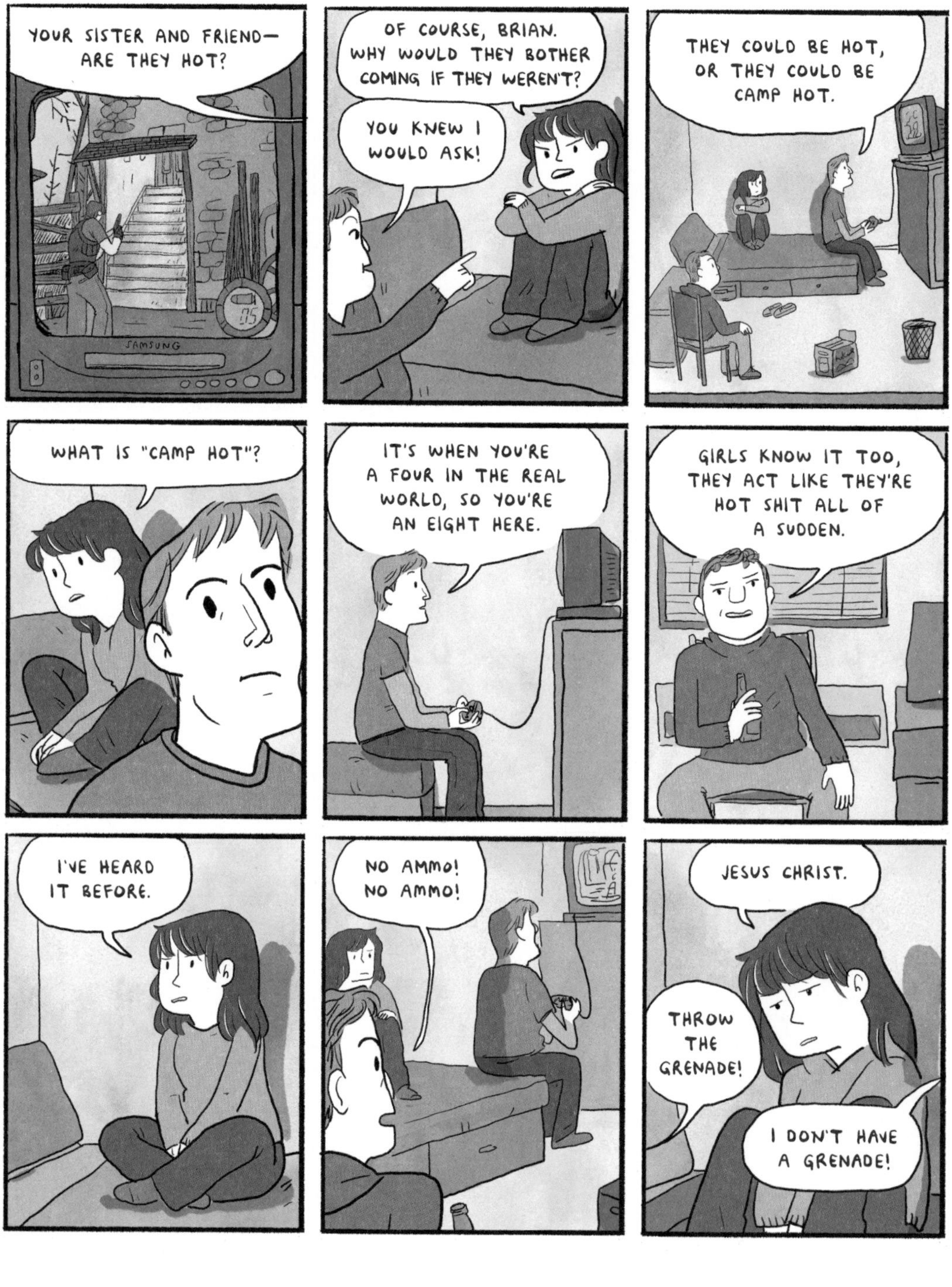
YOUR SISTER AND FRIEND—ARE THEY HOT?
SAMSUNG
OF COURSE, BRIAN. WHY WOULD THEY BOTHER COMING IF THEY WEREN'T?
YOU KNEW I WOULD ASK!
THEY COULD BE HOT, OR THEY COULD BE CAMP HOT.
WHAT IS "CAMP HOT"?
IT'S WHEN YOU'RE A FOUR IN THE REAL WORLD, SO YOU'RE AN EIGHT HERE.
GIRLS KNOW IT TOO, THEY ACT LIKE THEY'RE HOT SHIT ALL OF A SUDDEN.
I'VE HEARD IT BEFORE.
NO AMMO! NO AMMO!
JESUS CHRIST.
THROW THE GRENADE!
I DON'T HAVE A GRENADE!

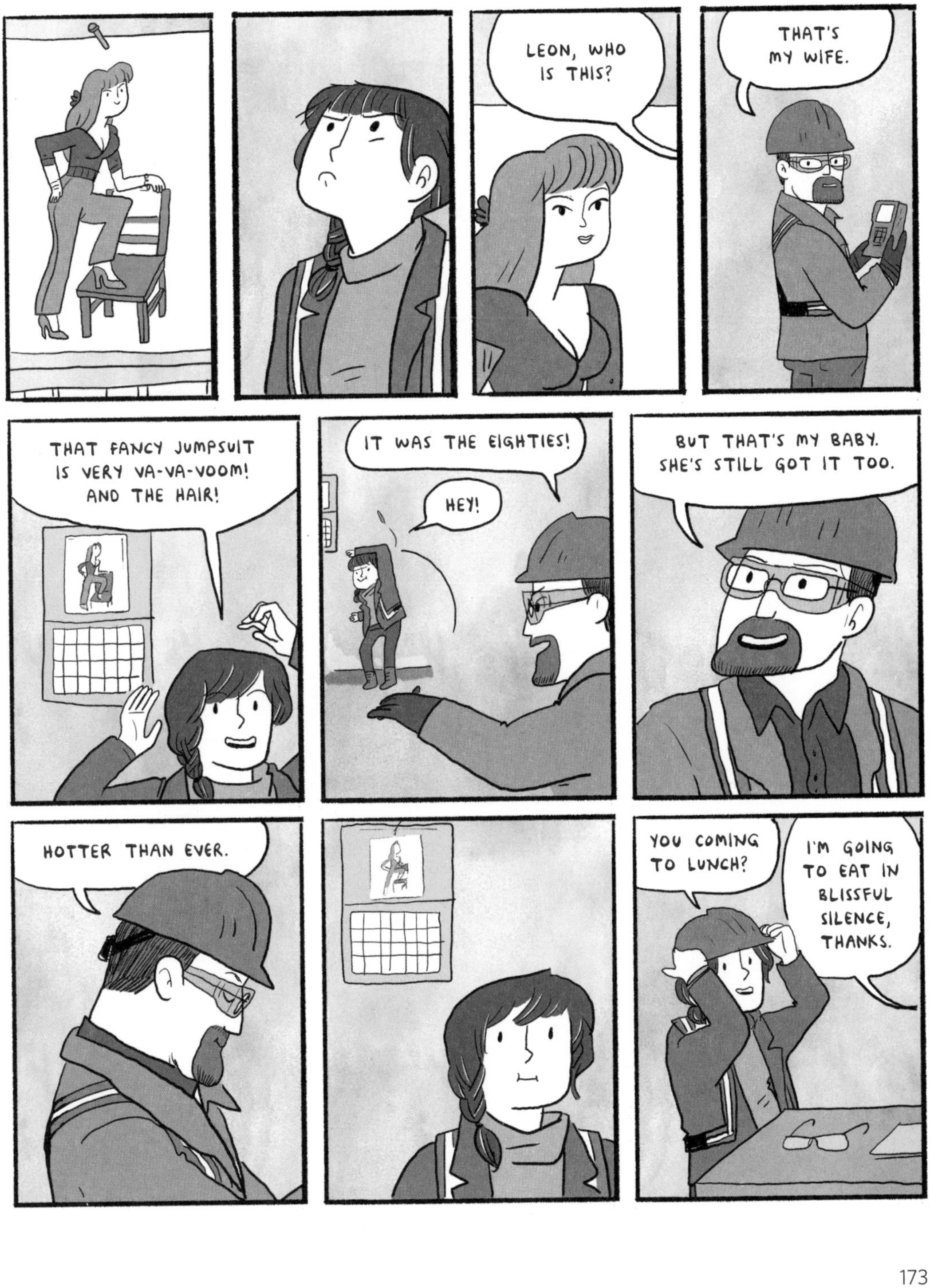
LEON, WHO IS THIS?
THAT'S MY WIFE.
THAT FANCY JUMPSUIT IS VERY VA-VA-VOOM! AND THE HAIR!
IT WAS THE EIGHTIES!
HEY!
BUT THAT'S MY BABY. SHE'S STILL GOT IT TOO.
HOTTER THAN EVER.
YOU COMING TO LUNCH?
I'M GOING TO EAT IN BLISSFUL SILENCE, THANKS.

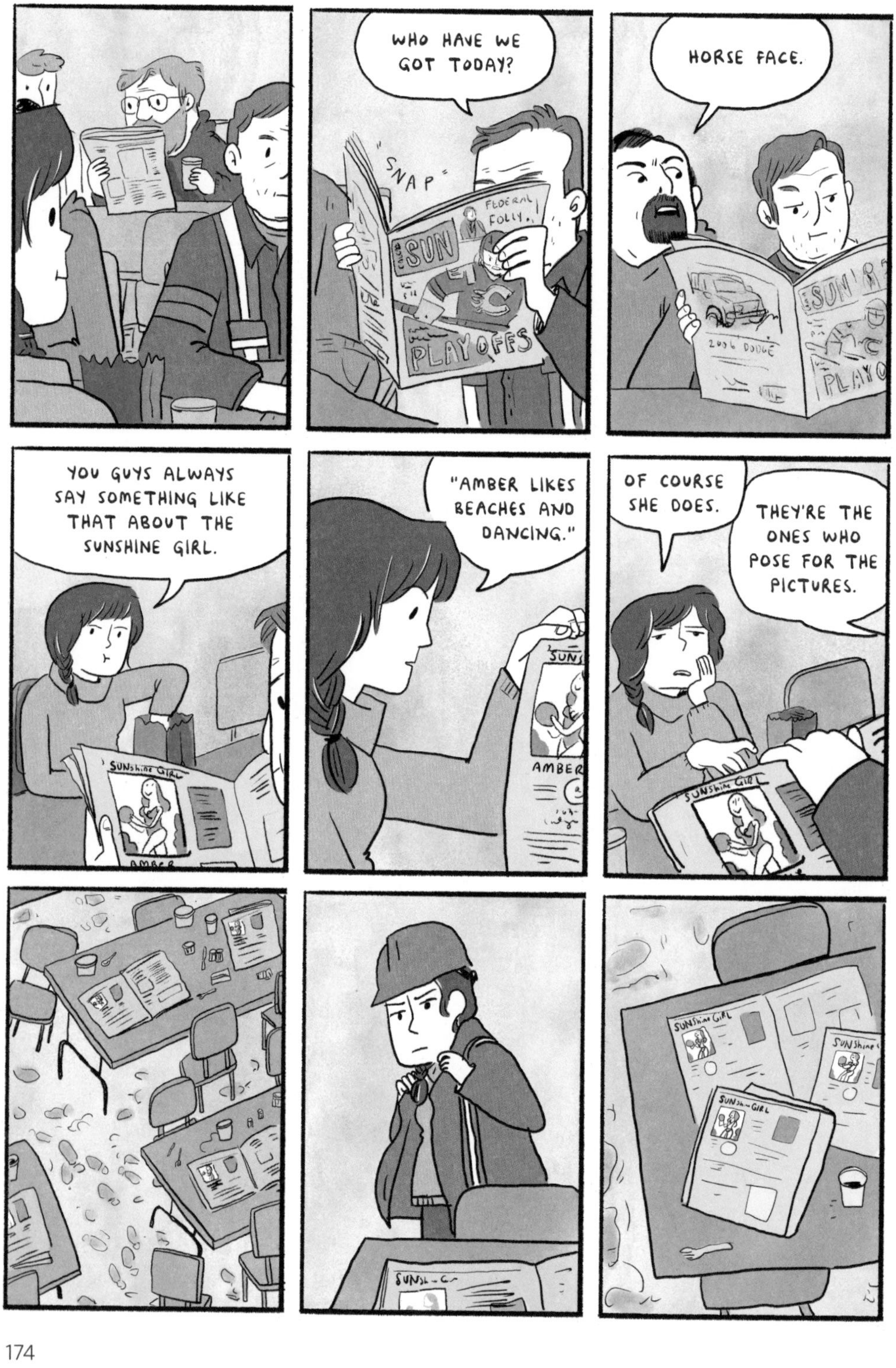
WHO HAVE WE GOT TODAY?
"SNAP"
FEDERAL FOLLY
SUN
PLAYOFFS
HORSE FACE.
SUN
2006 DODGE
YOU GUYS ALWAYS SAY SOMETHING LIKE THAT ABOUT THE SUNSHINE GIRL.
SUNshine GIRL
"AMBER LIKES BEACHES AND DANCING."
AMBER
OF COURSE SHE DOES.
THEY'RE THE ONES WHO POSE FOR THE PICTURES.
SUNshine GIRL
SUNshine GIRL

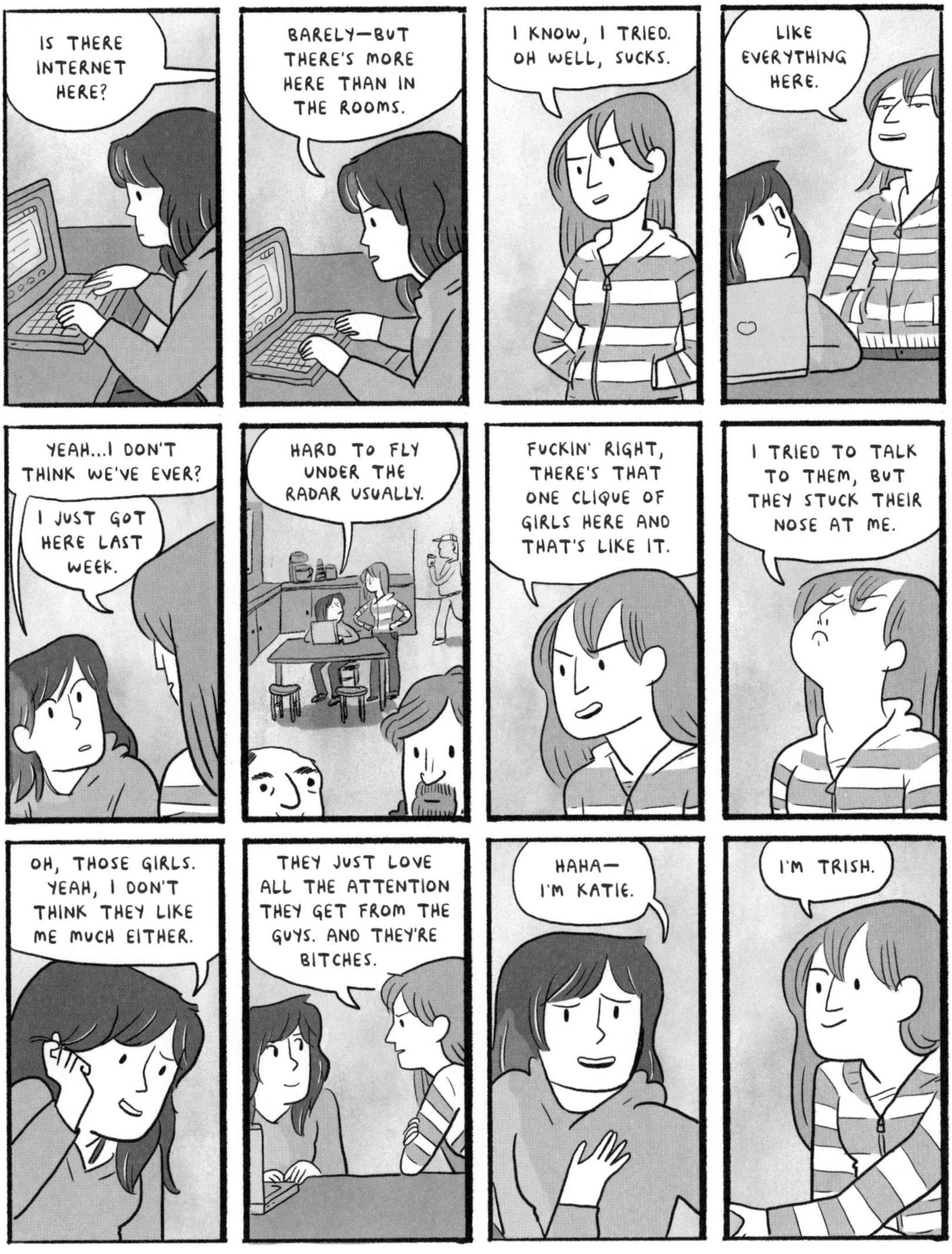
IS THERE INTERNET HERE?
BARELY—BUT THERE'S MORE HERE THAN IN THE ROOMS.
I KNOW, I TRIED. OH WELL, SUCKS.
LIKE EVERYTHING HERE.
YEAH...I DON'T THINK WE'VE EVER?
I JUST GOT HERE LAST WEEK.
HARD TO FLY UNDER THE RADAR USUALLY.
FUCKIN' RIGHT, THERE'S THAT ONE CLIQUE OF GIRLS HERE AND THAT'S LIKE IT.
I TRIED TO TALK TO THEM, BUT THEY STUCK THEIR NOSE AT ME.
OH, THOSE GIRLS. YEAH, I DON'T THINK THEY LIKE ME MUCH EITHER.
THEY JUST LOVE ALL THE ATTENTION THEY GET FROM THE GUYS. AND THEY'RE BITCHES.
HAHA— I'M KATIE.
I'M TRISH.

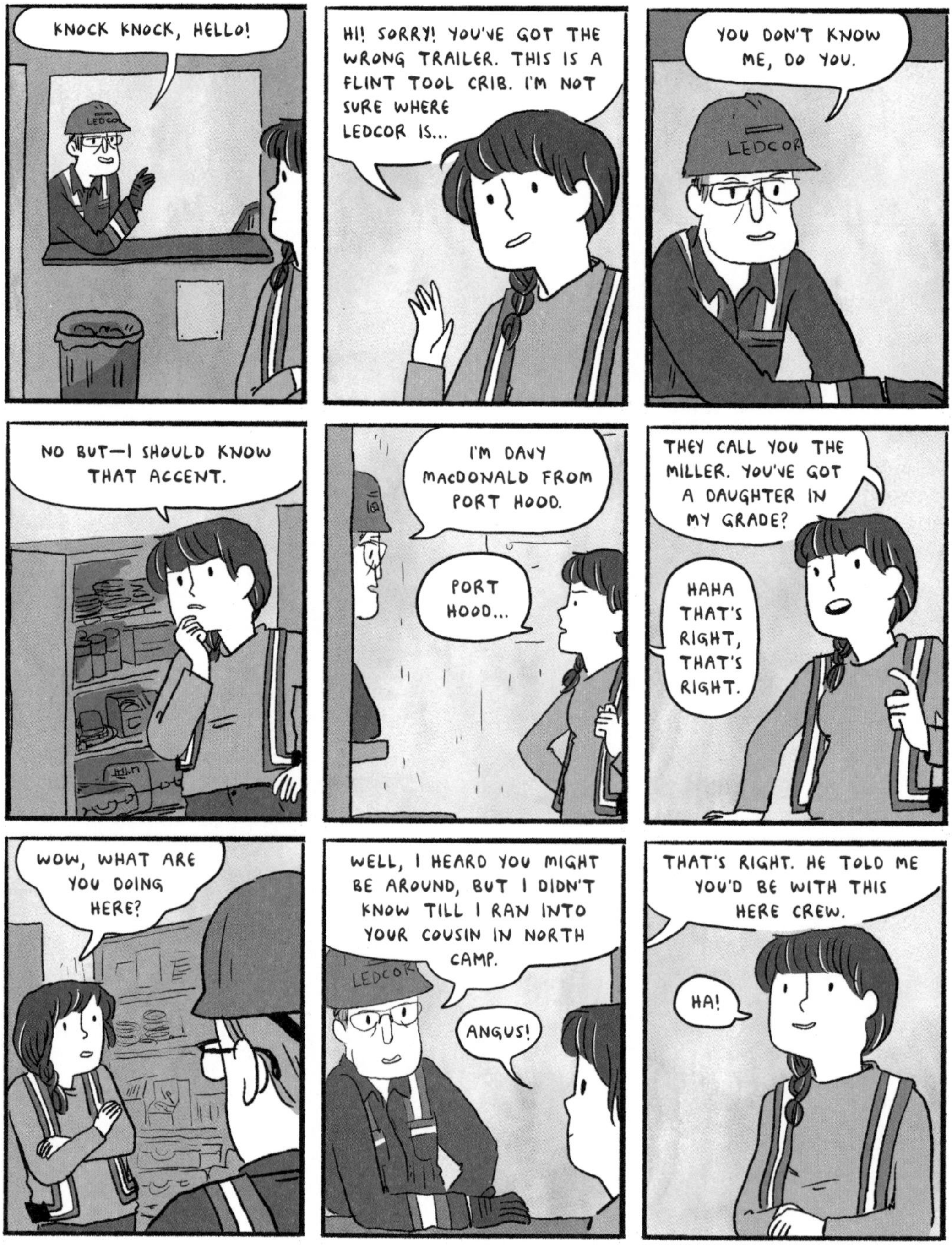
KNOCK KNOCK, HELLO!
HI! SORRY! YOU'VE GOT THE WRONG TRAILER. THIS IS A FLINT TOOL CRIB. I'M NOT SURE WHERE LEDCOR IS...
YOU DON'T KNOW ME, DO YOU.
NO BUT—I SHOULD KNOW THAT ACCENT.
I'M DAVY MACDONALD FROM PORT HOOD.
PORT HOOD...
THEY CALL YOU THE MILLER. YOU'VE GOT A DAUGHTER IN MY GRADE?
HAHA THAT'S RIGHT, THAT'S RIGHT.
WOW, WHAT ARE YOU DOING HERE?
WELL, I HEARD YOU MIGHT BE AROUND, BUT I DIDN'T KNOW TILL I RAN INTO YOUR COUSIN IN NORTH CAMP.
ANGUS!
THAT'S RIGHT. HE TOLD ME YOU'D BE WITH THIS HERE CREW.
HA!

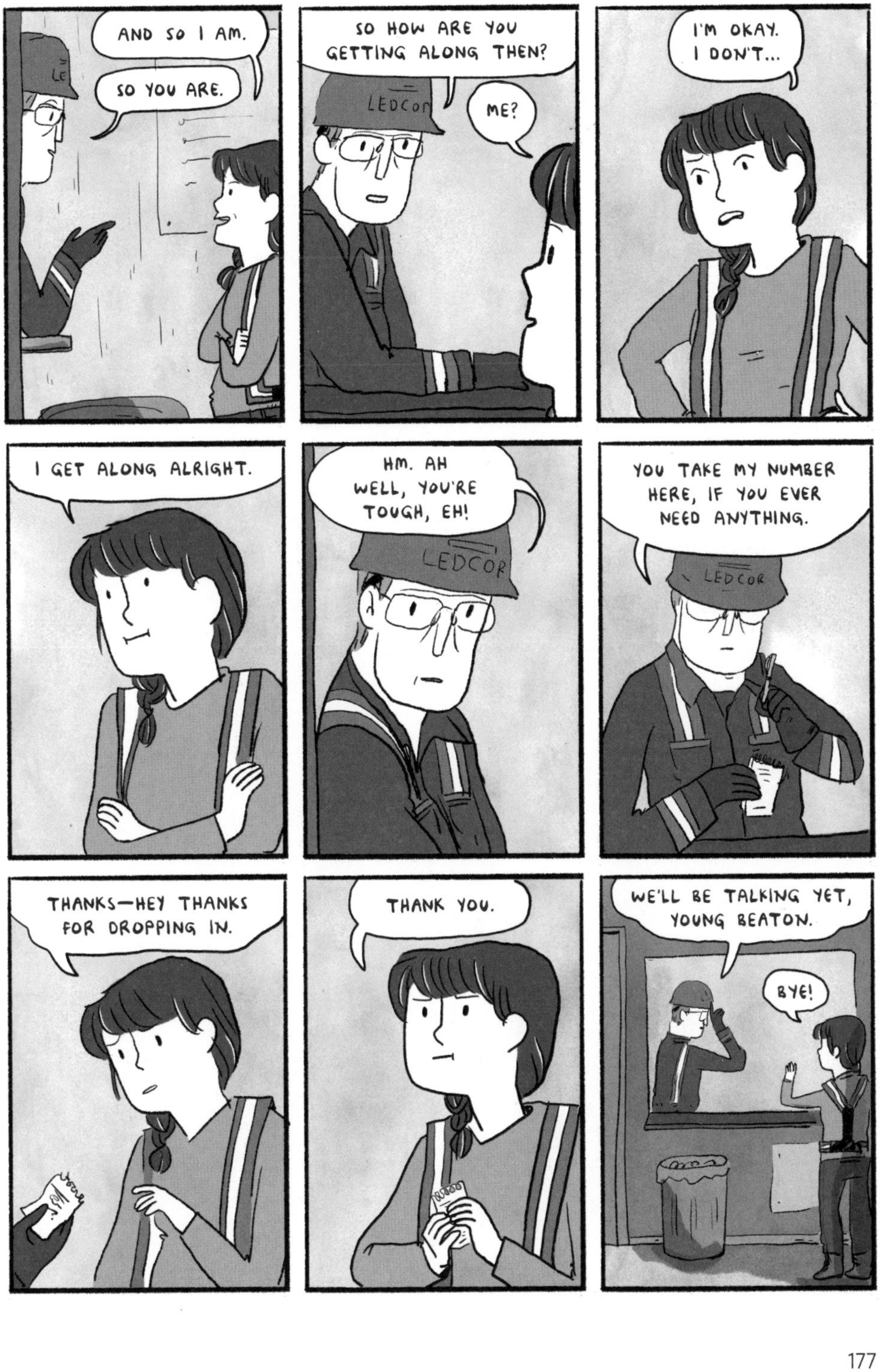
AND SO I AM.
SO YOU ARE.
LE
SO HOW ARE YOU GETTING ALONG THEN?
LEDCOR
ME?
I'M OKAY. I DON'T...
I GET ALONG ALRIGHT.
HM. AH WELL, YOU'RE TOUGH, EH!
LEDCOR
YOU TAKE MY NUMBER HERE, IF YOU EVER NEED ANYTHING.
LEDCOR
THANKS—HEY THANKS FOR DROPPING IN.
THANK YOU.
WE'LL BE TALKING YET, YOUNG BEATON.
BYE!

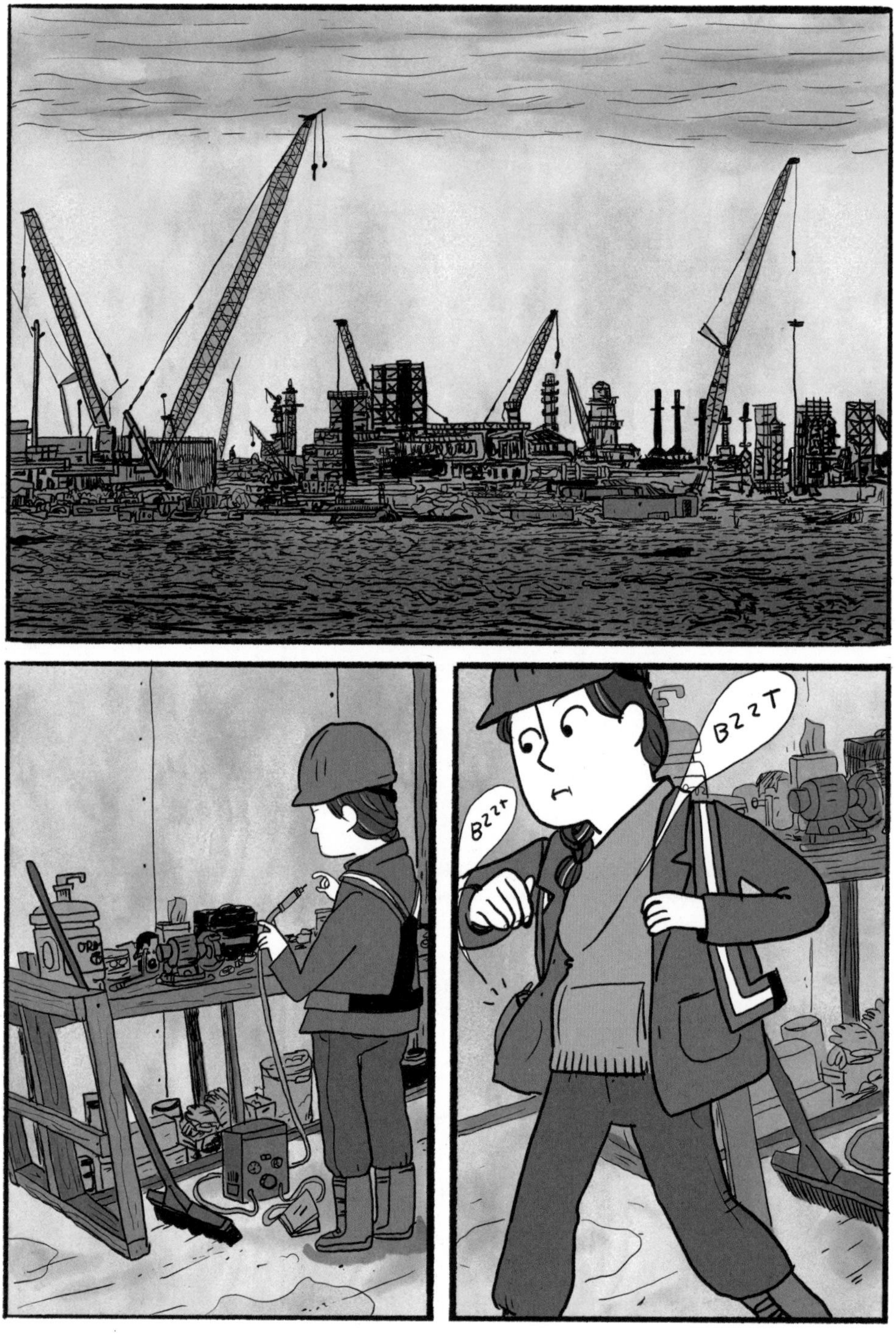
Bzzt
BZZT

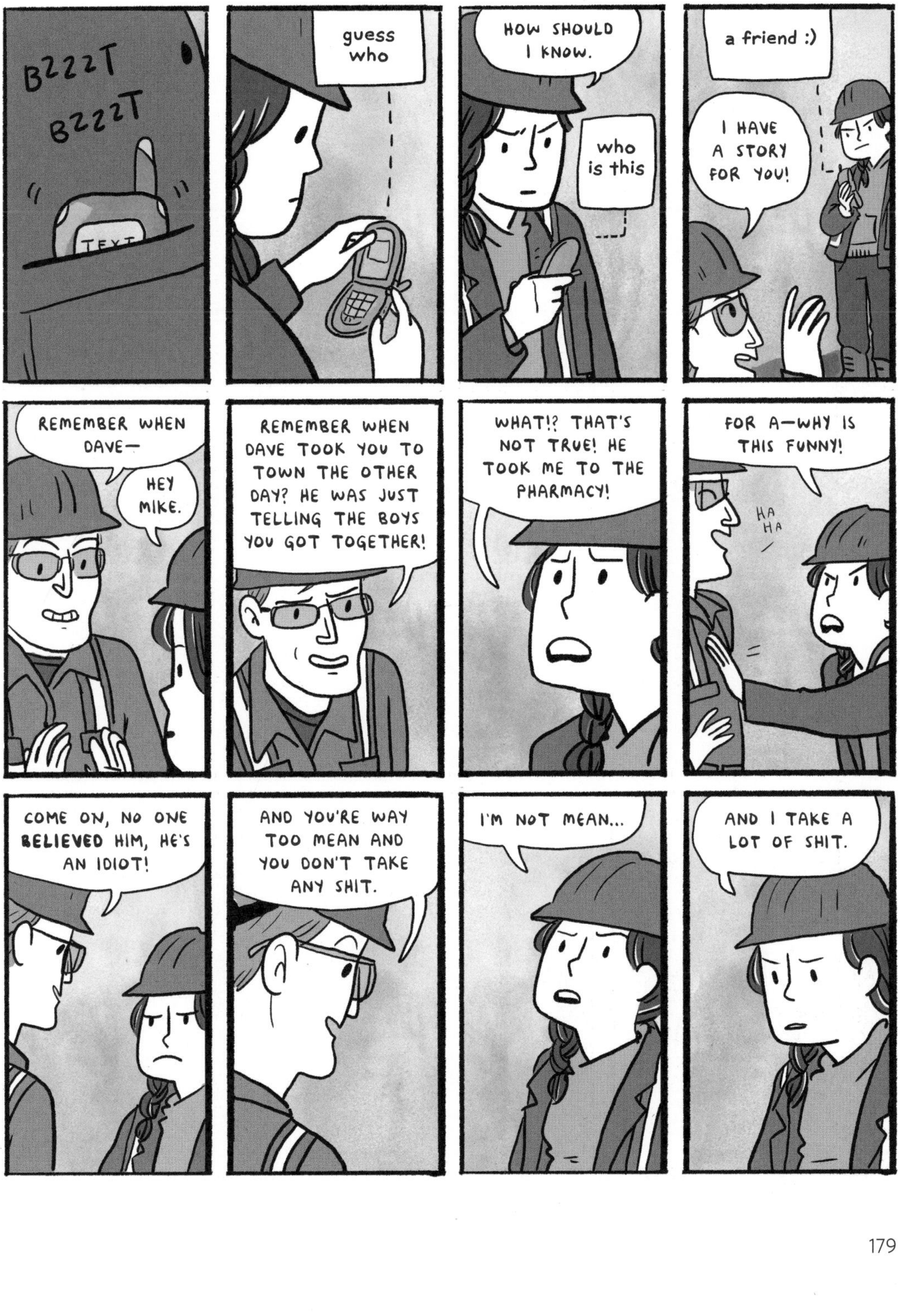
BZZZT
BZZZT
TEXT
guess who
HOW SHOULD I KNOW.
who is this
a friend :)
I HAVE A STORY FOR YOU!
REMEMBER WHEN DAVE—
HEY MIKE.
REMEMBER WHEN DAVE TOOK YOU TO TOWN THE OTHER DAY? HE WAS JUST TELLING THE BOYS YOU GOT TOGETHER!
WHAT!? THAT'S NOT TRUE! HE TOOK ME TO THE PHARMACY!
FOR A—WHY IS THIS FUNNY!
HA HA
COME ON, NO ONE **BELIEVED** HIM, HE'S AN IDIOT!
AND YOU'RE WAY TOO MEAN AND YOU DON'T TAKE ANY SHIT.
I'M NOT MEAN...
AND I TAKE A LOT OF SHIT.

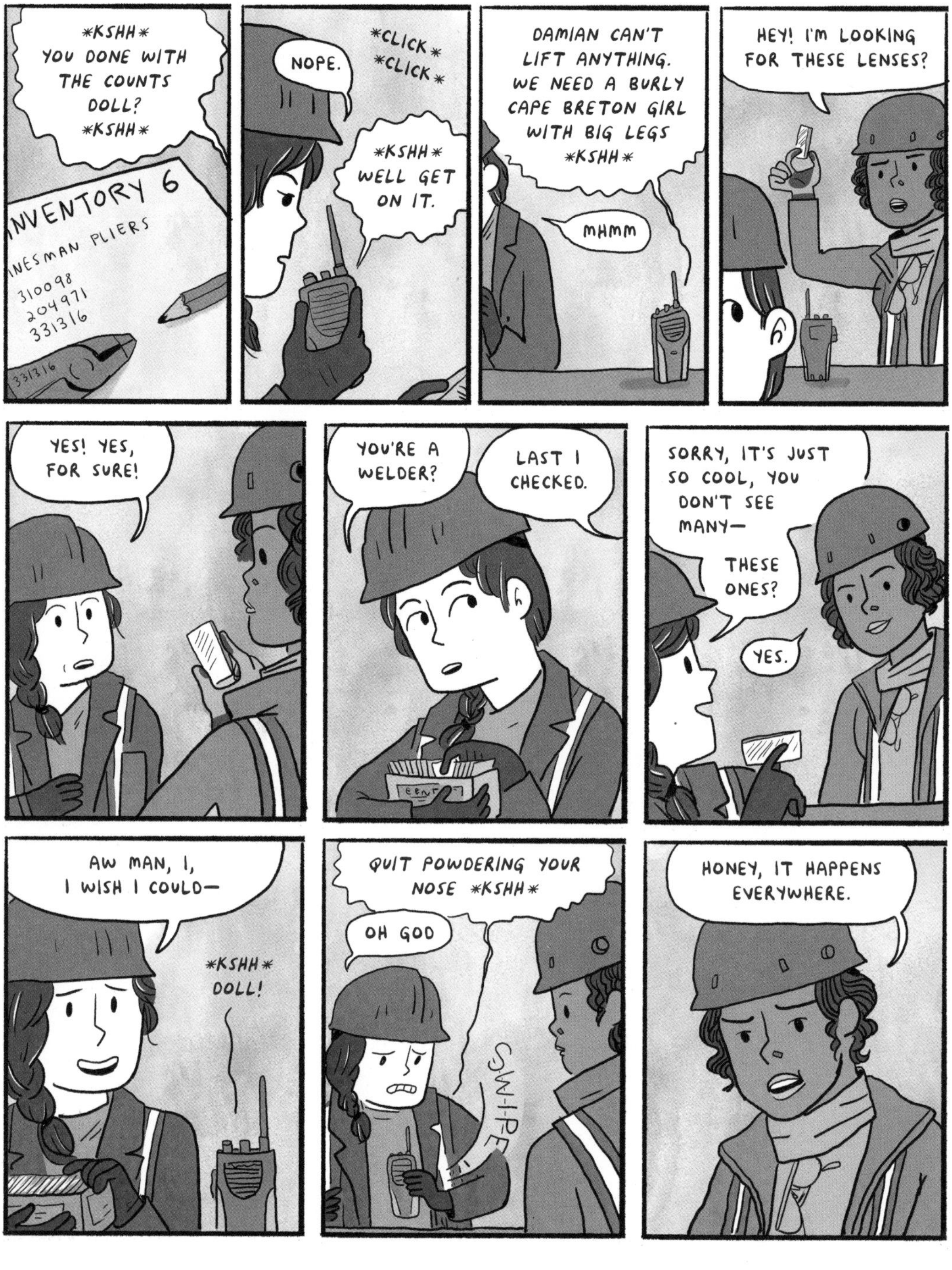
KSHH YOU DONE WITH THE COUNTS DOLL? *KSHH*
INVENTORY 6
NESMAN PLIERS
310098
204971
331316
331316
NOPE.
CLICK *CLICK*
KSHH WELL GET ON IT.
DAMIAN CAN'T LIFT ANYTHING. WE NEED A BURLY CAPE BRETON GIRL WITH BIG LEGS *KSHH*
MHMM
HEY! I'M LOOKING FOR THESE LENSES?
YES! YES, FOR SURE!
YOU'RE A WELDER?
LAST I CHECKED.
SORRY, IT'S JUST SO COOL, YOU DON'T SEE MANY—
THESE ONES?
YES.
AW MAN, I, I WISH I COULD—
KSHH DOLL!
QUIT POWDERING YOUR NOSE *KSHH*
OH GOD
SWIPE
HONEY, IT HAPPENS EVERYWHERE.

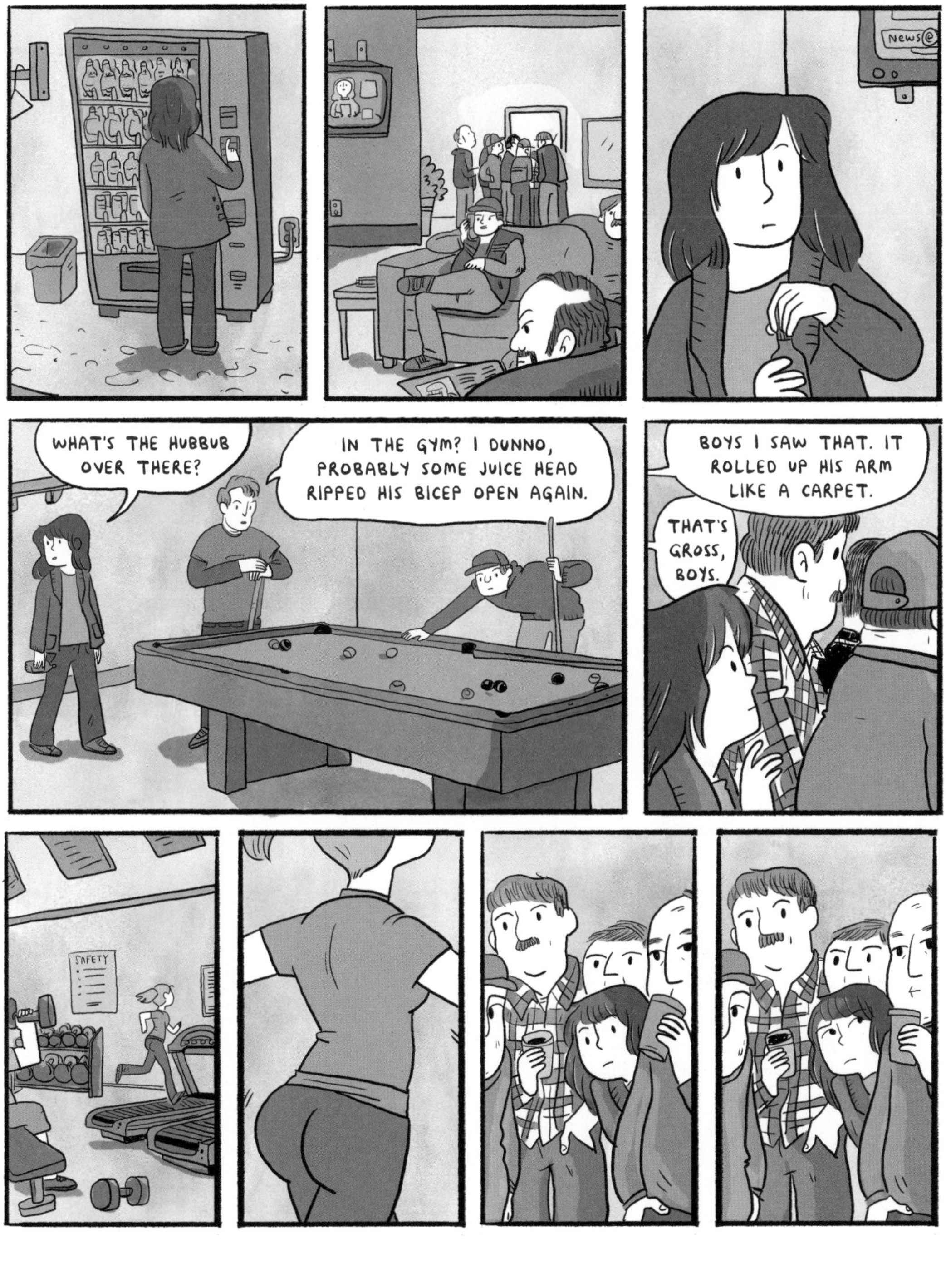
News
WHAT'S THE HUBBUB OVER THERE?
IN THE GYM? I DUNNO, PROBABLY SOME JUICE HEAD RIPPED HIS BICEP OPEN AGAIN.
BOYS I SAW THAT. IT ROLLED UP HIS ARM LIKE A CARPET.
THAT'S GROSS, BOYS.
SAFETY

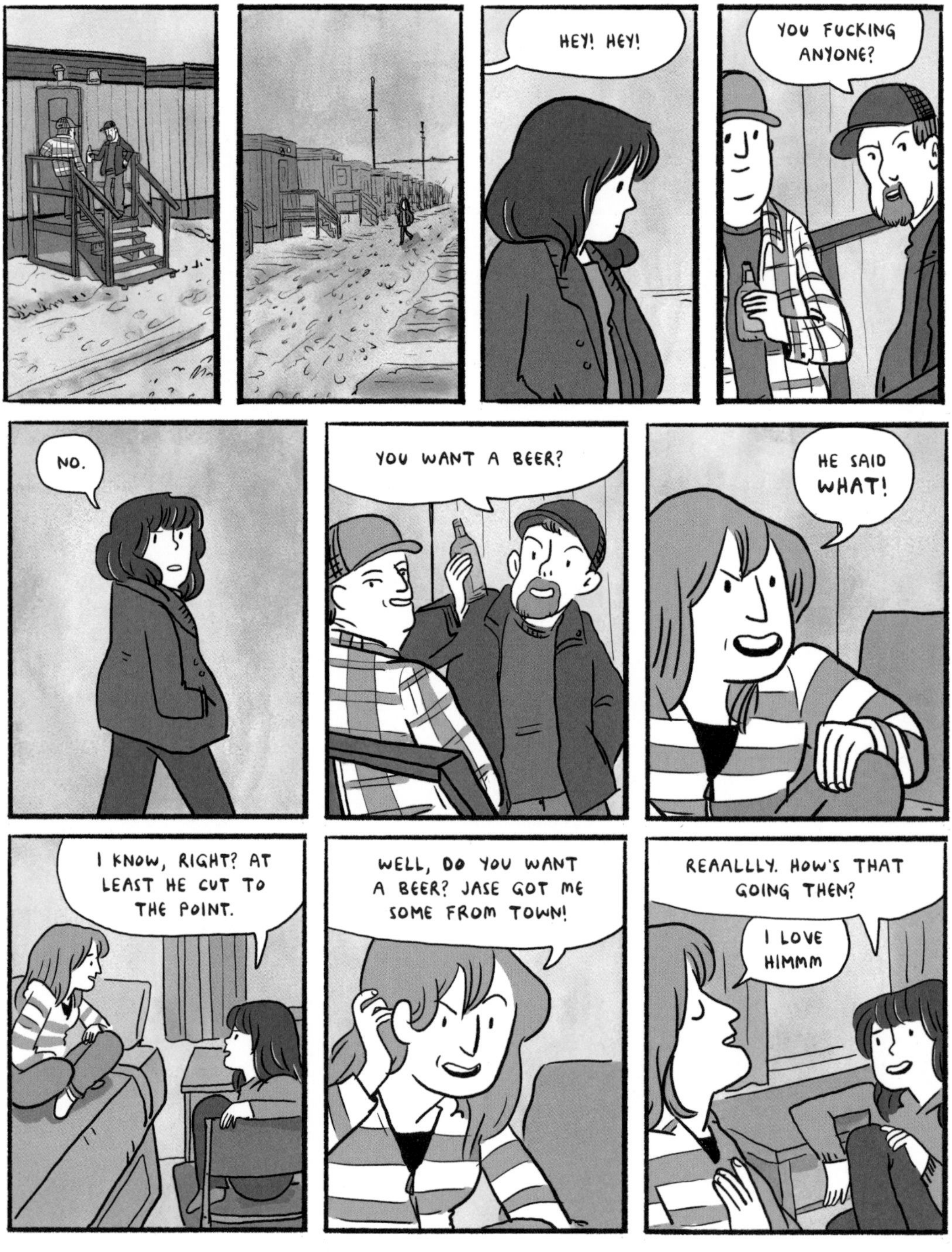
HEY! HEY!
YOU FUCKING ANYONE?
NO.
YOU WANT A BEER?
HE SAID WHAT!
I KNOW, RIGHT? AT LEAST HE CUT TO THE POINT.
WELL, DO YOU WANT A BEER? JASE GOT ME SOME FROM TOWN!
REAALLLY. HOW'S THAT GOING THEN?
I LOVE HIMMM

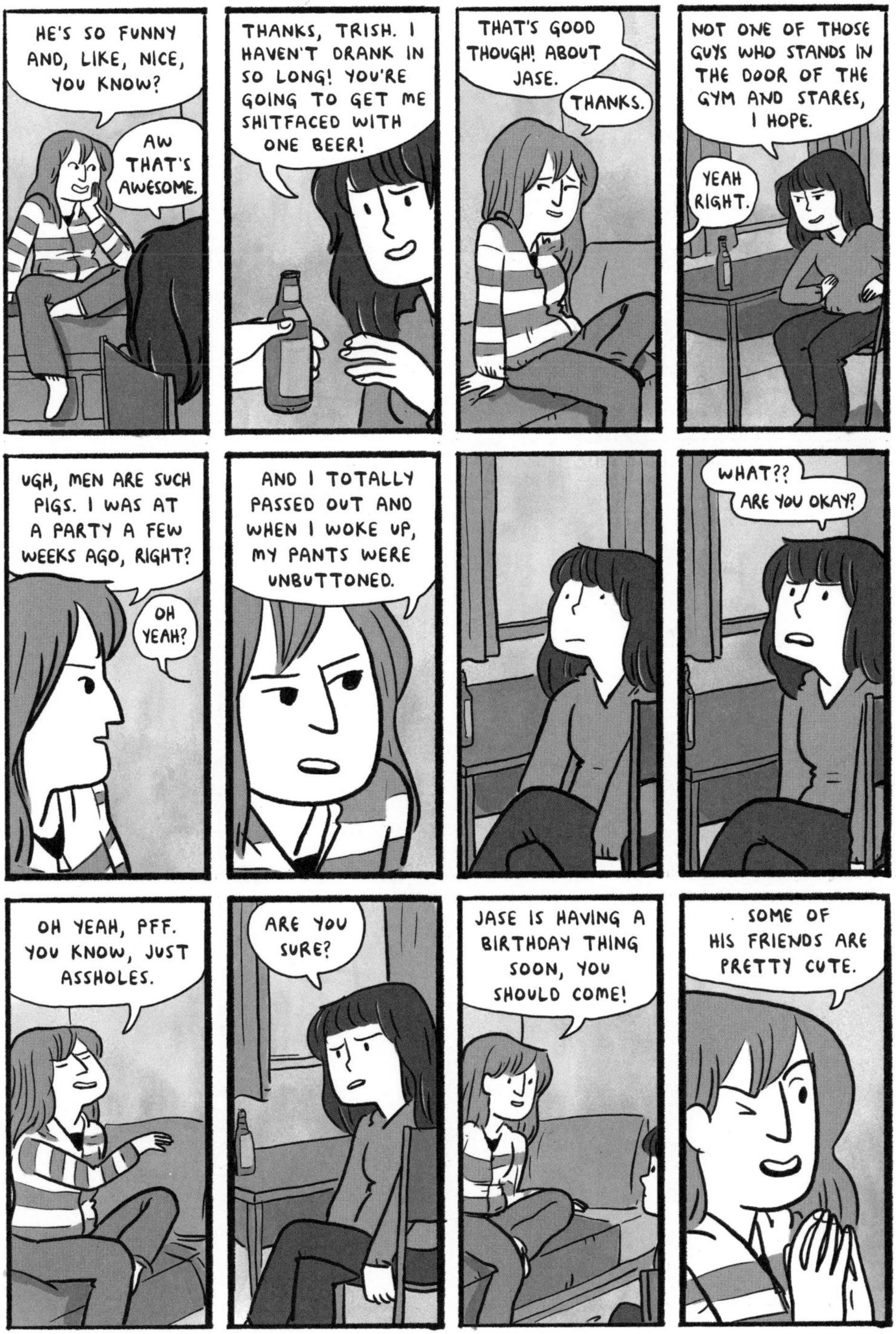
HE'S SO FUNNY AND, LIKE, NICE, YOU KNOW?
AW THAT'S AWESOME.
THANKS, TRISH. I HAVEN'T DRANK IN SO LONG! YOU'RE GOING TO GET ME SHITFACED WITH ONE BEER!
THAT'S GOOD THOUGH! ABOUT JASE.
THANKS.
NOT ONE OF THOSE GUYS WHO STANDS IN THE DOOR OF THE GYM AND STARES, I HOPE.
YEAH RIGHT.
UGH, MEN ARE SUCH PIGS. I WAS AT A PARTY A FEW WEEKS AGO, RIGHT?
OH YEAH?
AND I TOTALLY PASSED OUT AND WHEN I WOKE UP, MY PANTS WERE UNBUTTONED.
WHAT??
ARE YOU OKAY?
OH YEAH, PFF. YOU KNOW, JUST ASSHOLES.
ARE YOU SURE?
JASE IS HAVING A BIRTHDAY THING SOON, YOU SHOULD COME!
SOME OF HIS FRIENDS ARE PRETTY CUTE.

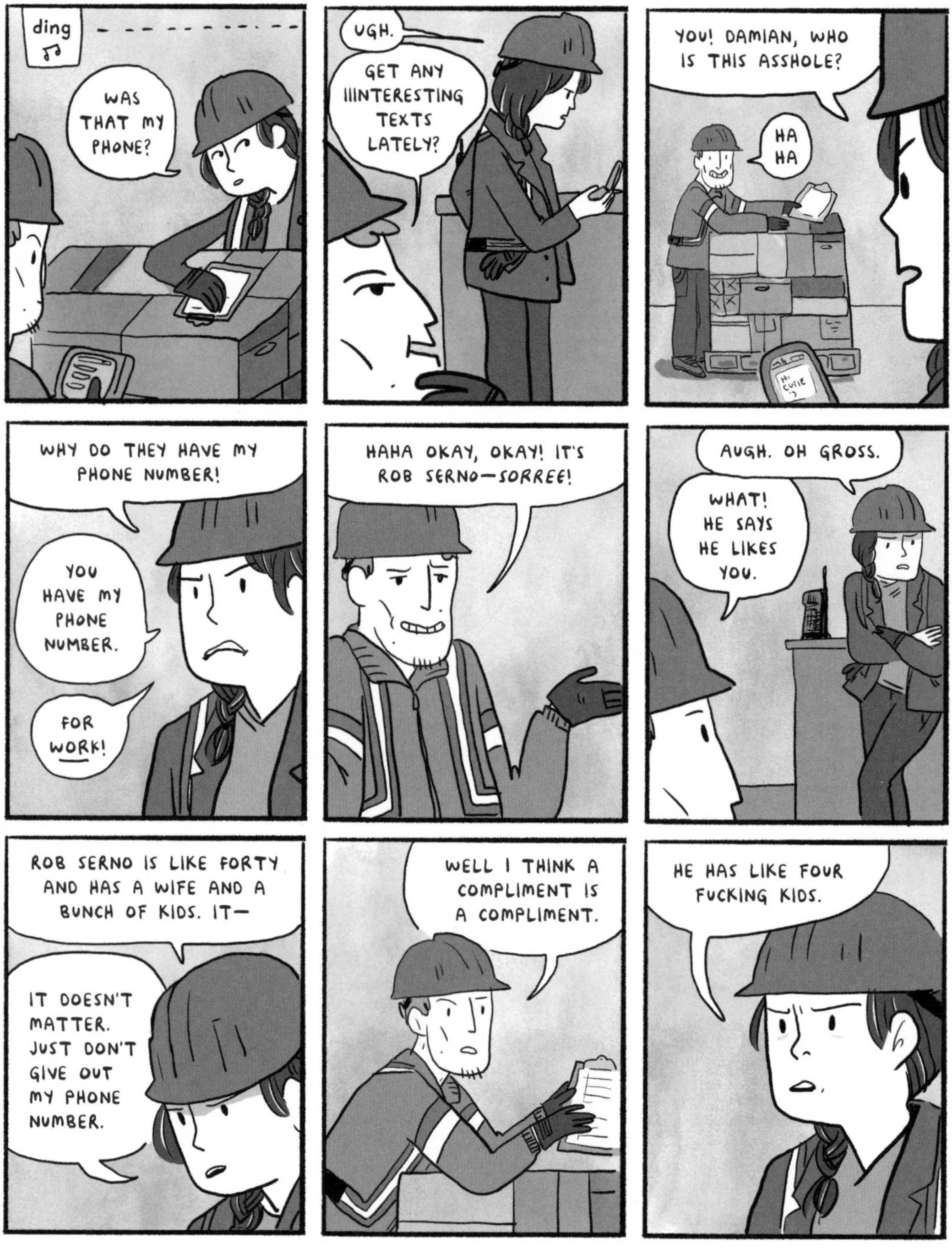
ding
WAS THAT MY PHONE?
UGH.
GET ANY IIIINTERESTING TEXTS LATELY?
YOU! DAMIAN, WHO IS THIS ASSHOLE?
HA HA
WHY DO THEY HAVE MY PHONE NUMBER!
YOU HAVE MY PHONE NUMBER.
FOR WORK!
HAHA OKAY, OKAY! IT'S ROB SERNO—SORREE!
AUGH. OH GROSS.
WHAT! HE SAYS HE LIKES YOU.
ROB SERNO IS LIKE FORTY AND HAS A WIFE AND A BUNCH OF KIDS. IT—
IT DOESN'T MATTER. JUST DON'T GIVE OUT MY PHONE NUMBER.
WELL I THINK A COMPLIMENT IS A COMPLIMENT.
HE HAS LIKE FOUR FUCKING KIDS.

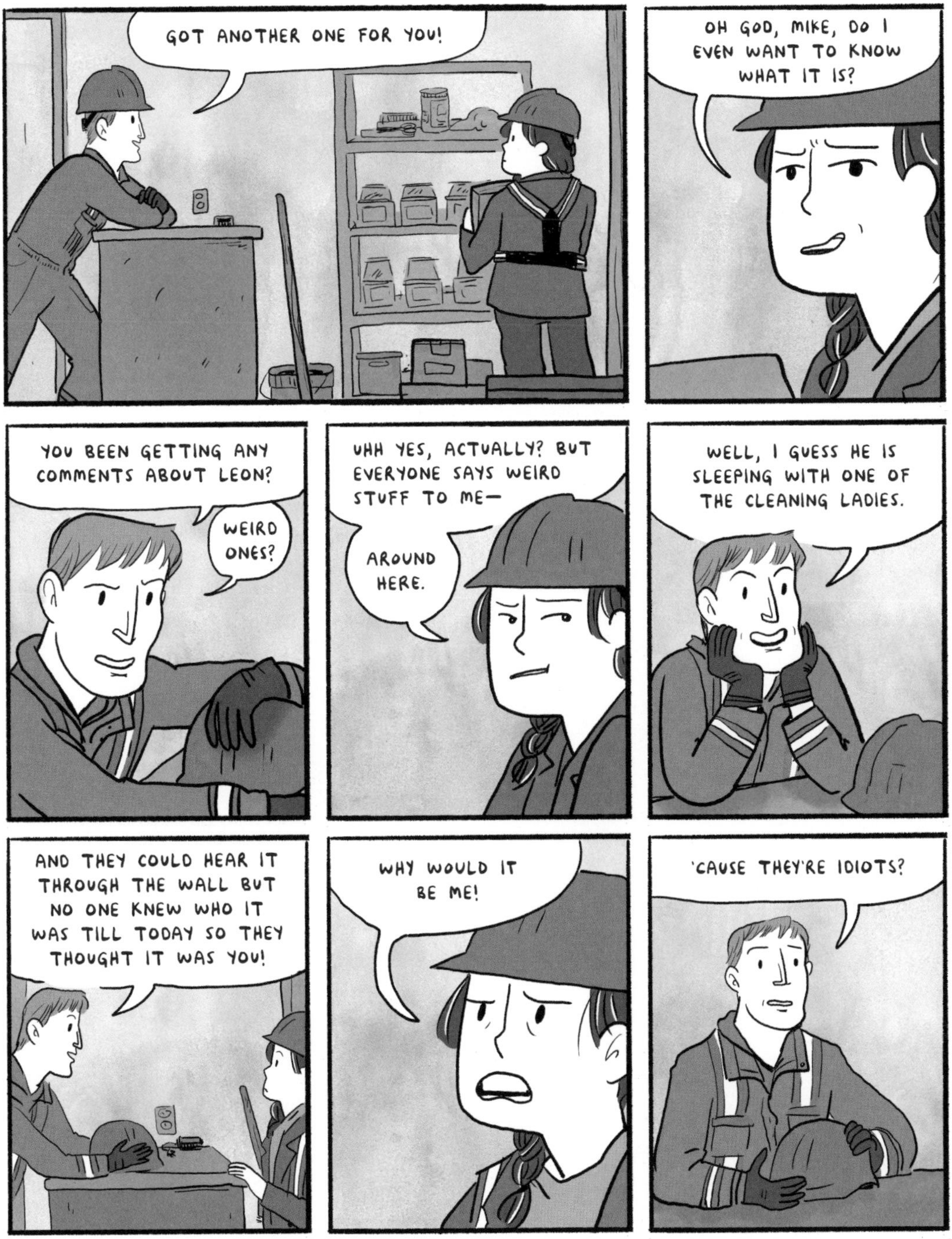
GOT ANOTHER ONE FOR YOU!
OH GOD, MIKE, DO I EVEN WANT TO KNOW WHAT IT IS?
YOU BEEN GETTING ANY COMMENTS ABOUT LEON?
WEIRD ONES?
UHH YES, ACTUALLY? BUT EVERYONE SAYS WEIRD STUFF TO ME—
AROUND HERE.
WELL, I GUESS HE IS SLEEPING WITH ONE OF THE CLEANING LADIES.
AND THEY COULD HEAR IT THROUGH THE WALL BUT NO ONE KNEW WHO IT WAS TILL TODAY SO THEY THOUGHT IT WAS YOU!
WHY WOULD IT BE ME!
'CAUSE THEY'RE IDIOTS?

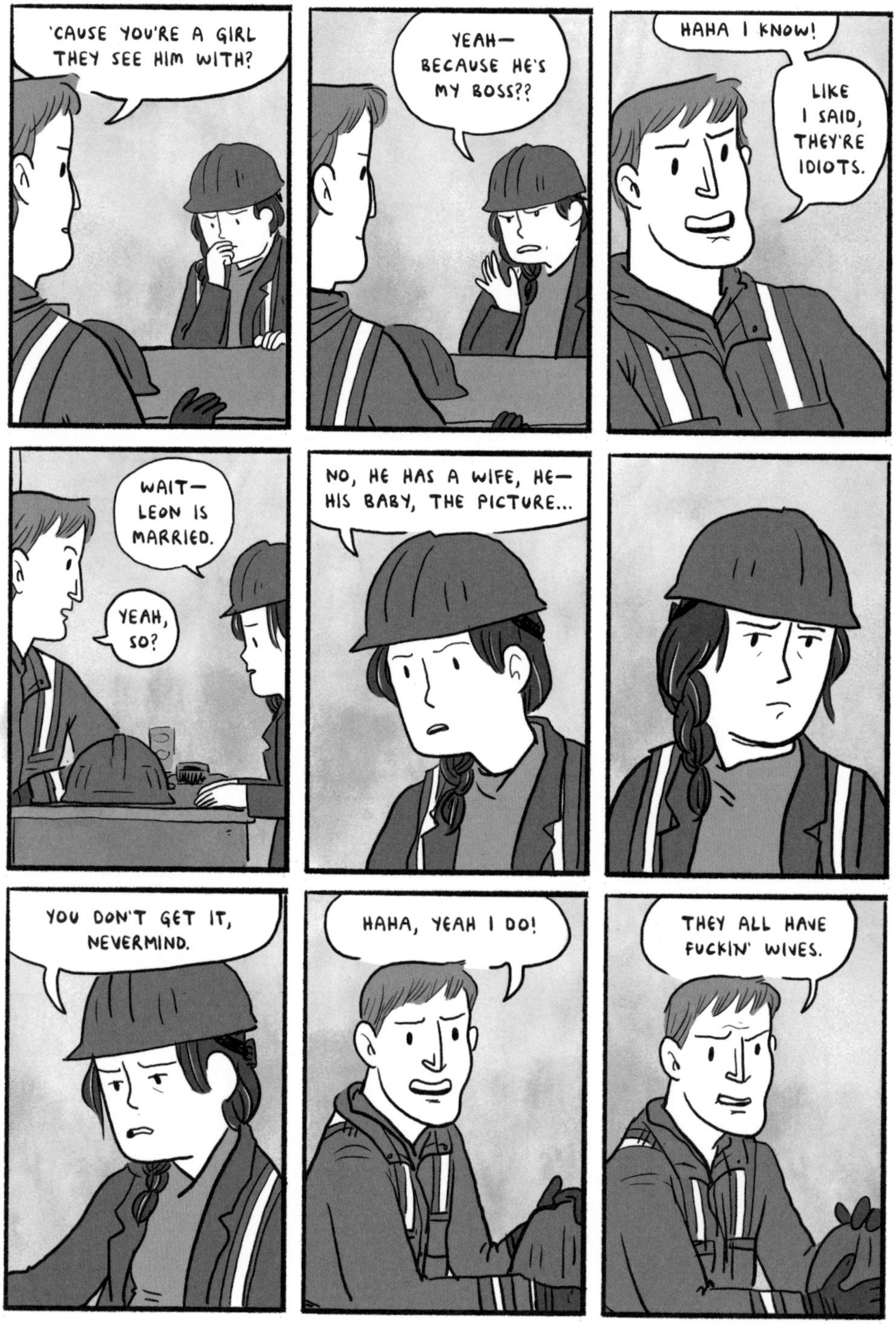
'CAUSE YOU'RE A GIRL THEY SEE HIM WITH?
YEAH— BECAUSE HE'S MY BOSS??
HAHA I KNOW!
LIKE I SAID, THEY'RE IDIOTS.
WAIT— LEON IS MARRIED.
YEAH, SO?
NO, HE HAS A WIFE, HE— HIS BABY, THE PICTURE...
YOU DON'T GET IT, NEVERMIND.
HAHA, YEAH I DO!
THEY ALL HAVE FUCKIN' WIVES.

AMBROSE
780-412-
LOAN
SYNCRUDE vs LONG LAKE
$18/hr
$22/HR
SHIFTS
6 and 6
12 and 2
overtime
random
24h a week
Living in town
- Rent
- food
no expenses
weeks till loan is paid
vs

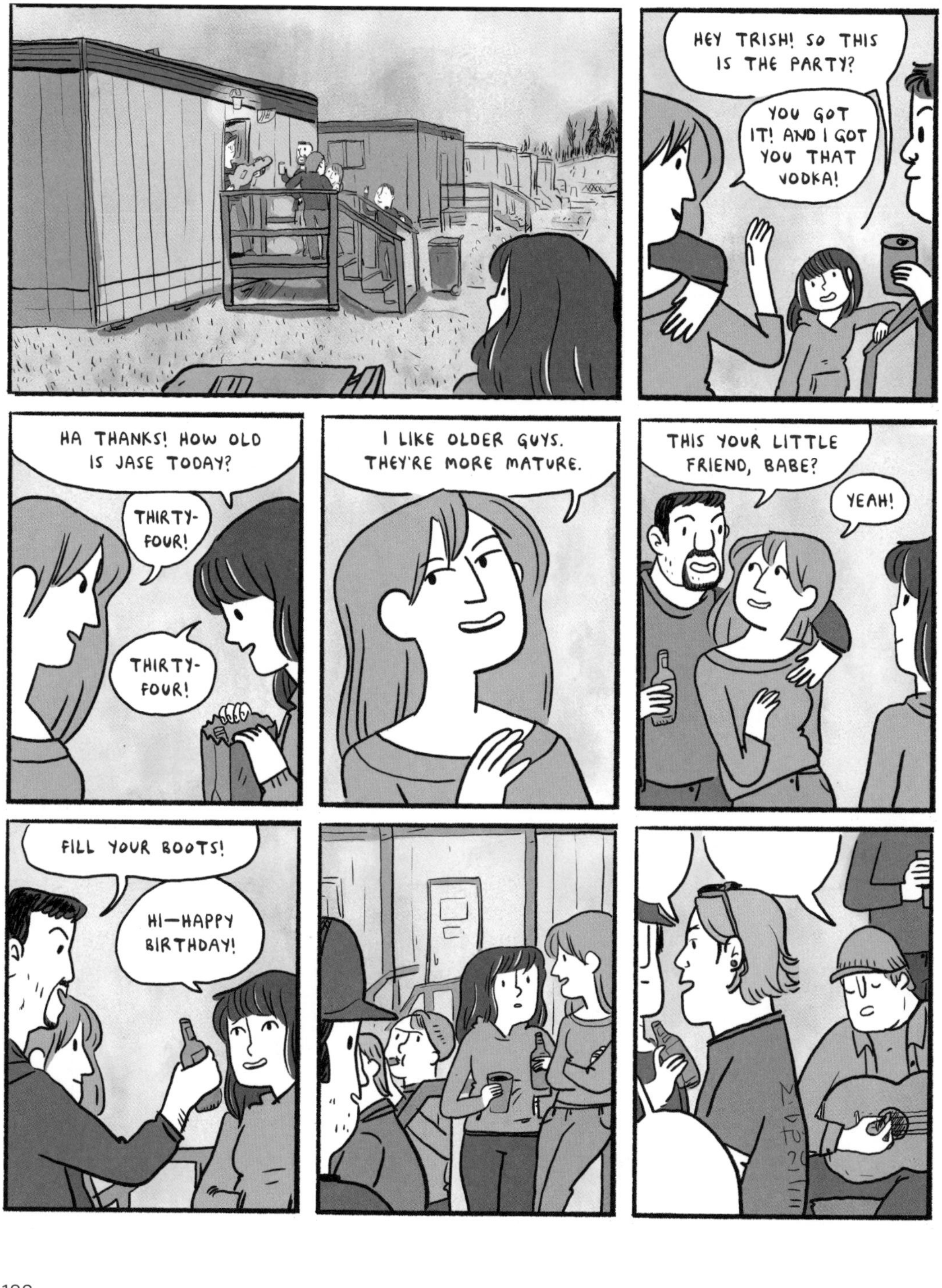
HEY TRISH! SO THIS IS THE PARTY?
YOU GOT IT! AND I GOT YOU THAT VODKA!
HA THANKS! HOW OLD IS JASE TODAY?
THIRTY-FOUR!
THIRTY-FOUR!
I LIKE OLDER GUYS. THEY'RE MORE MATURE.
THIS YOUR LITTLE FRIEND, BABE?
YEAH!
FILL YOUR BOOTS!
HI—HAPPY BIRTHDAY!

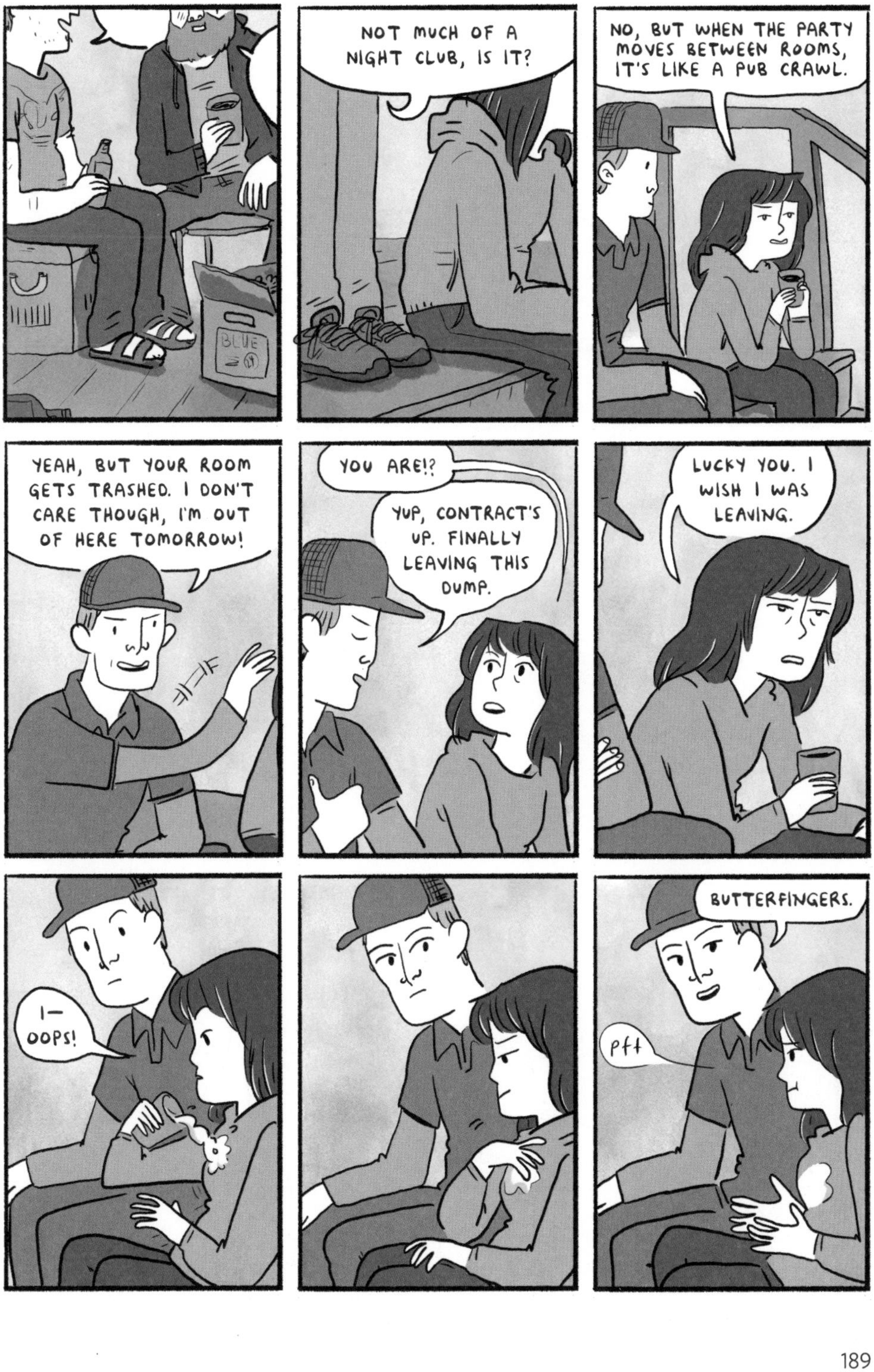
NOT MUCH OF A NIGHT CLUB, IS IT?
NO, BUT WHEN THE PARTY MOVES BETWEEN ROOMS, IT'S LIKE A PUB CRAWL.
YEAH, BUT YOUR ROOM GETS TRASHED. I DON'T CARE THOUGH, I'M OUT OF HERE TOMORROW!
YOU ARE!?
YUP, CONTRACT'S UP. FINALLY LEAVING THIS DUMP.
LUCKY YOU. I WISH I WAS LEAVING.
I— OOPS!
BUTTERFINGERS.
Pft

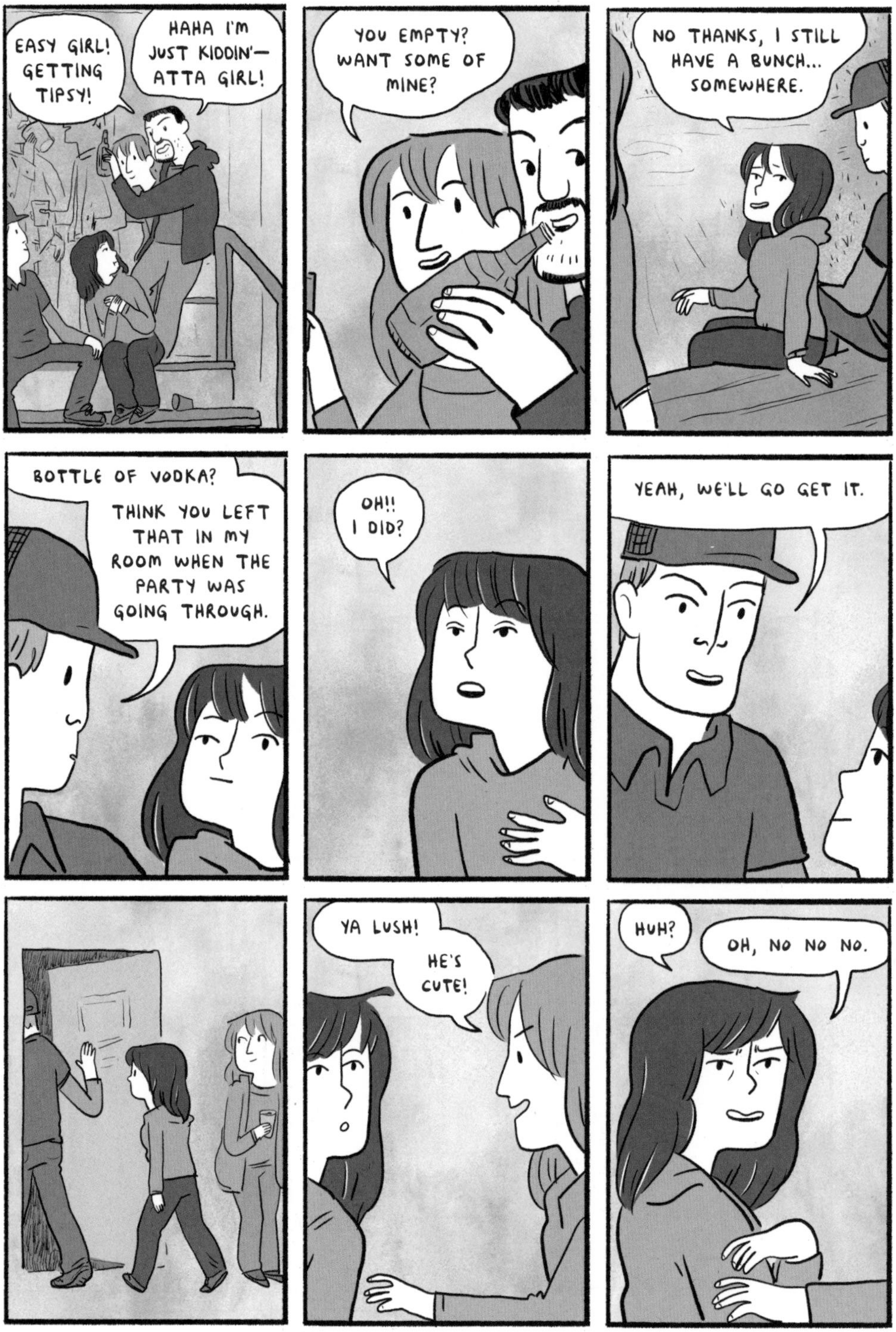
EASY GIRL! GETTING TIPSY!
HAHA I'M JUST KIDDIN'— ATTA GIRL!
YOU EMPTY? WANT SOME OF MINE?
NO THANKS, I STILL HAVE A BUNCH... SOMEWHERE.
BOTTLE OF VODKA?
THINK YOU LEFT THAT IN MY ROOM WHEN THE PARTY WAS GOING THROUGH.
OH!! I DID?
YEAH, WE'LL GO GET IT.
YA LUSH!
HE'S CUTE!
HUH?
OH, NO NO NO.

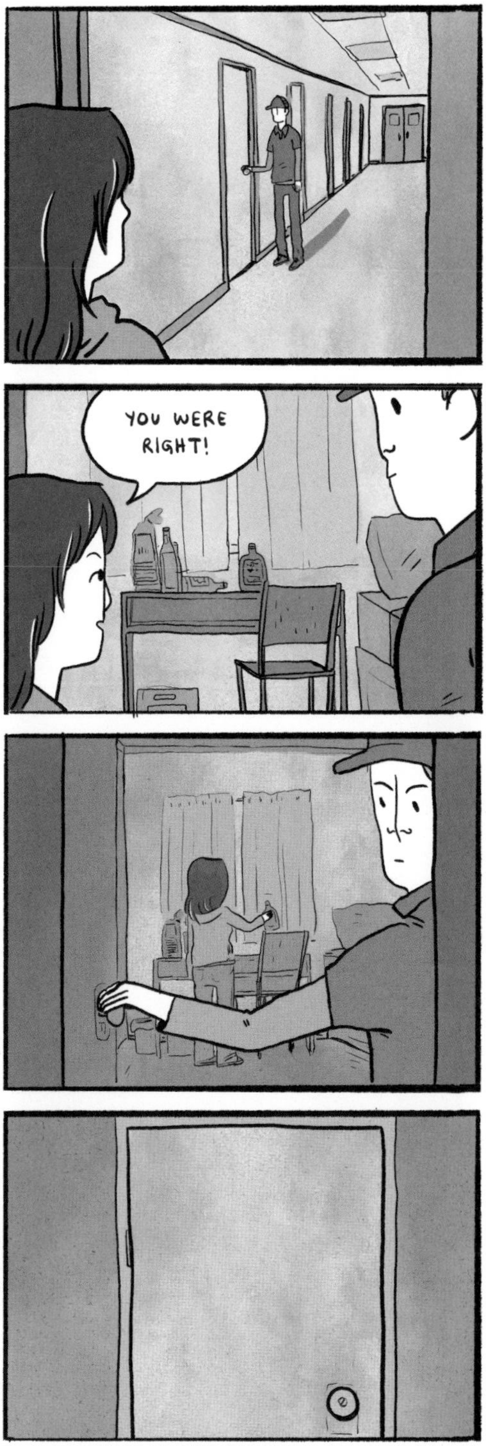
YOU WERE RIGHT!

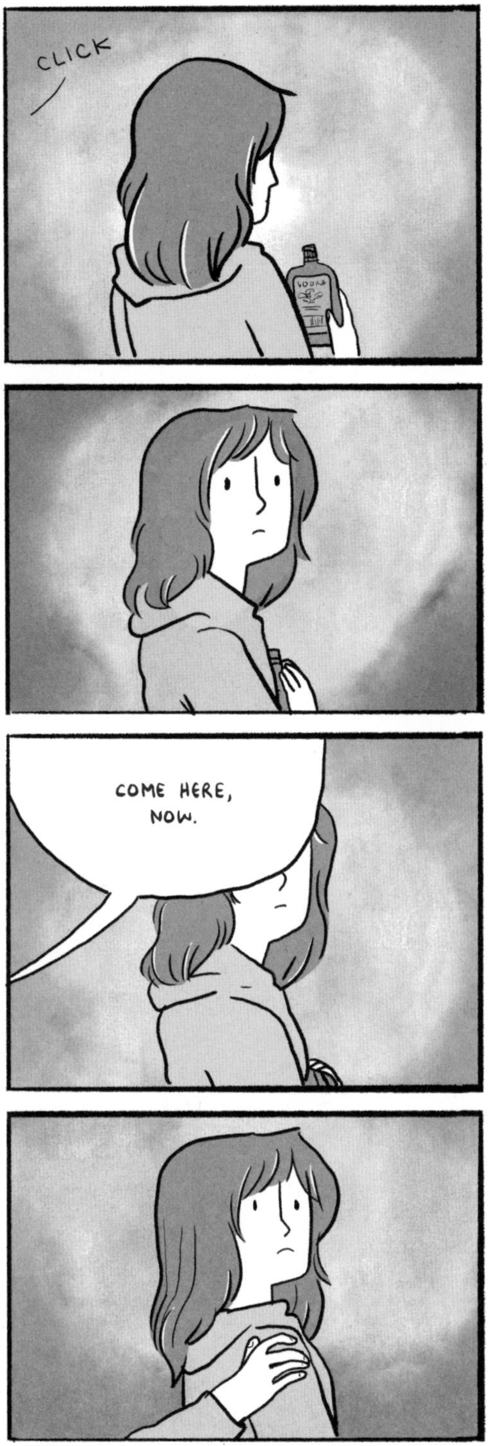
CLICK
VODKA
COME HERE, NOW.

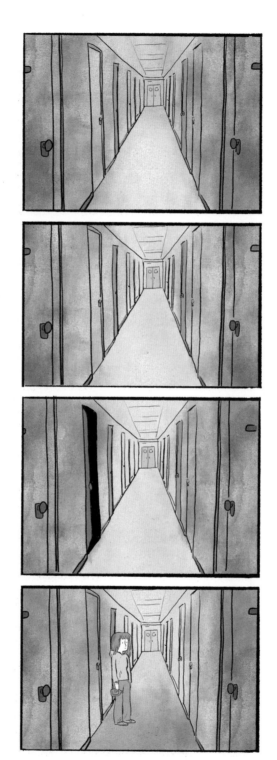

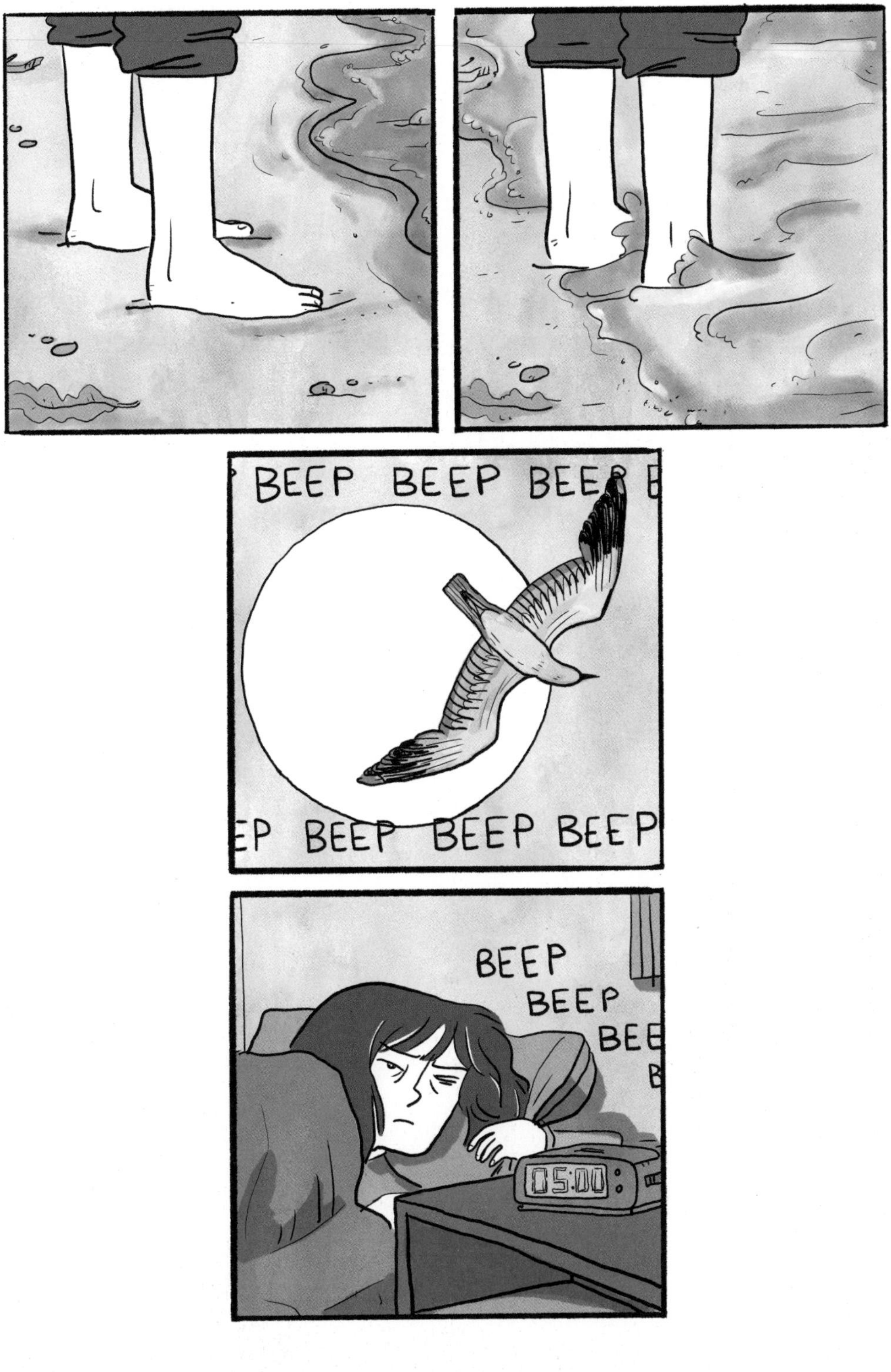
BEEP BEEP BEE
P BEEP BEEP BEEP
BEEP
BEEP
BEE

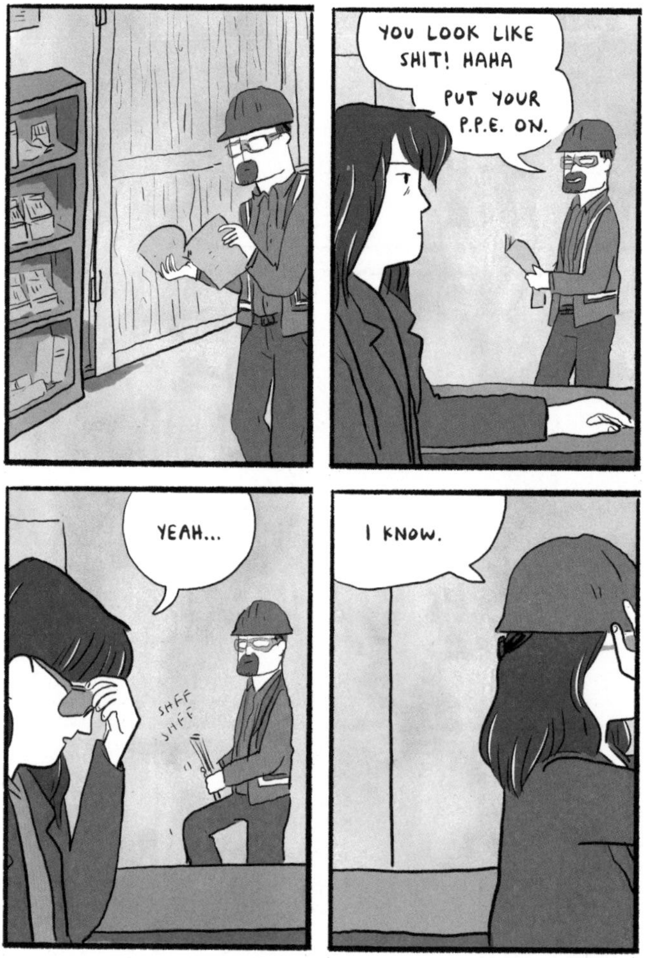
YOU LOOK LIKE SHIT! HAHA
PUT YOUR P.P.E. ON.
SHFF SHFF
YEAH...
I KNOW.

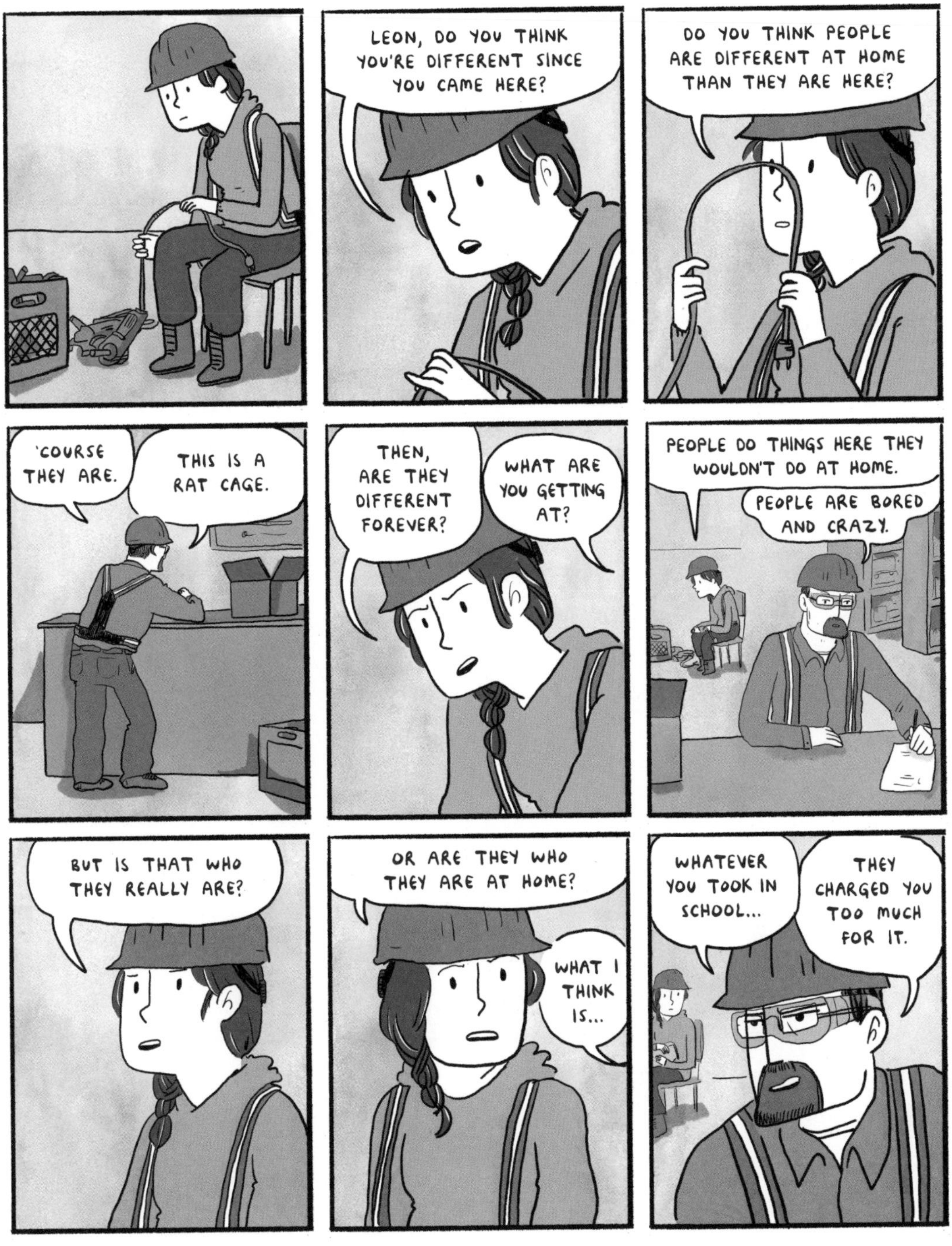
LEON, DO YOU THINK YOU'RE DIFFERENT SINCE YOU CAME HERE?
DO YOU THINK PEOPLE ARE DIFFERENT AT HOME THAN THEY ARE HERE?
'COURSE THEY ARE.
THIS IS A RAT CAGE.
THEN, ARE THEY DIFFERENT FOREVER?
WHAT ARE YOU GETTING AT?
PEOPLE DO THINGS HERE THEY WOULDN'T DO AT HOME.
PEOPLE ARE BORED AND CRAZY.
BUT IS THAT WHO THEY REALLY ARE?
OR ARE THEY WHO THEY ARE AT HOME?
WHAT I THINK IS...
WHATEVER YOU TOOK IN SCHOOL...
THEY CHARGED YOU TOO MUCH FOR IT.

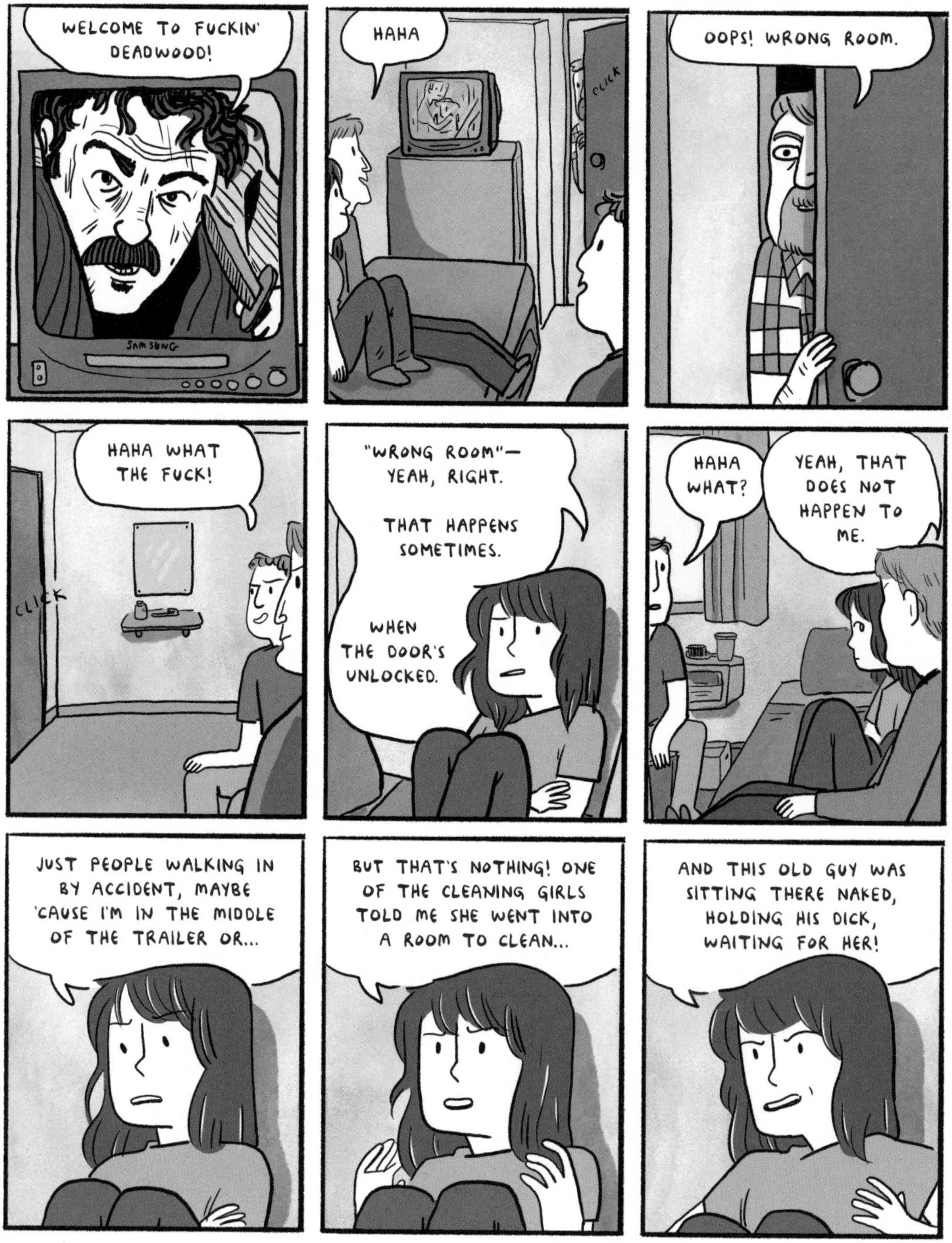
WELCOME TO FUCKIN' DEADWOOD!
SAMSUNG
HAHA
CLICK
OOPS! WRONG ROOM.
HAHA WHAT THE FUCK!
CLICK
"WRONG ROOM"— YEAH, RIGHT.
THAT HAPPENS SOMETIMES.
WHEN THE DOOR'S UNLOCKED.
HAHA WHAT?
YEAH, THAT DOES NOT HAPPEN TO ME.
JUST PEOPLE WALKING IN BY ACCIDENT, MAYBE 'CAUSE I'M IN THE MIDDLE OF THE TRAILER OR...
BUT THAT'S NOTHING! ONE OF THE CLEANING GIRLS TOLD ME SHE WENT INTO A ROOM TO CLEAN...
AND THIS OLD GUY WAS SITTING THERE NAKED, HOLDING HIS DICK, WAITING FOR HER!

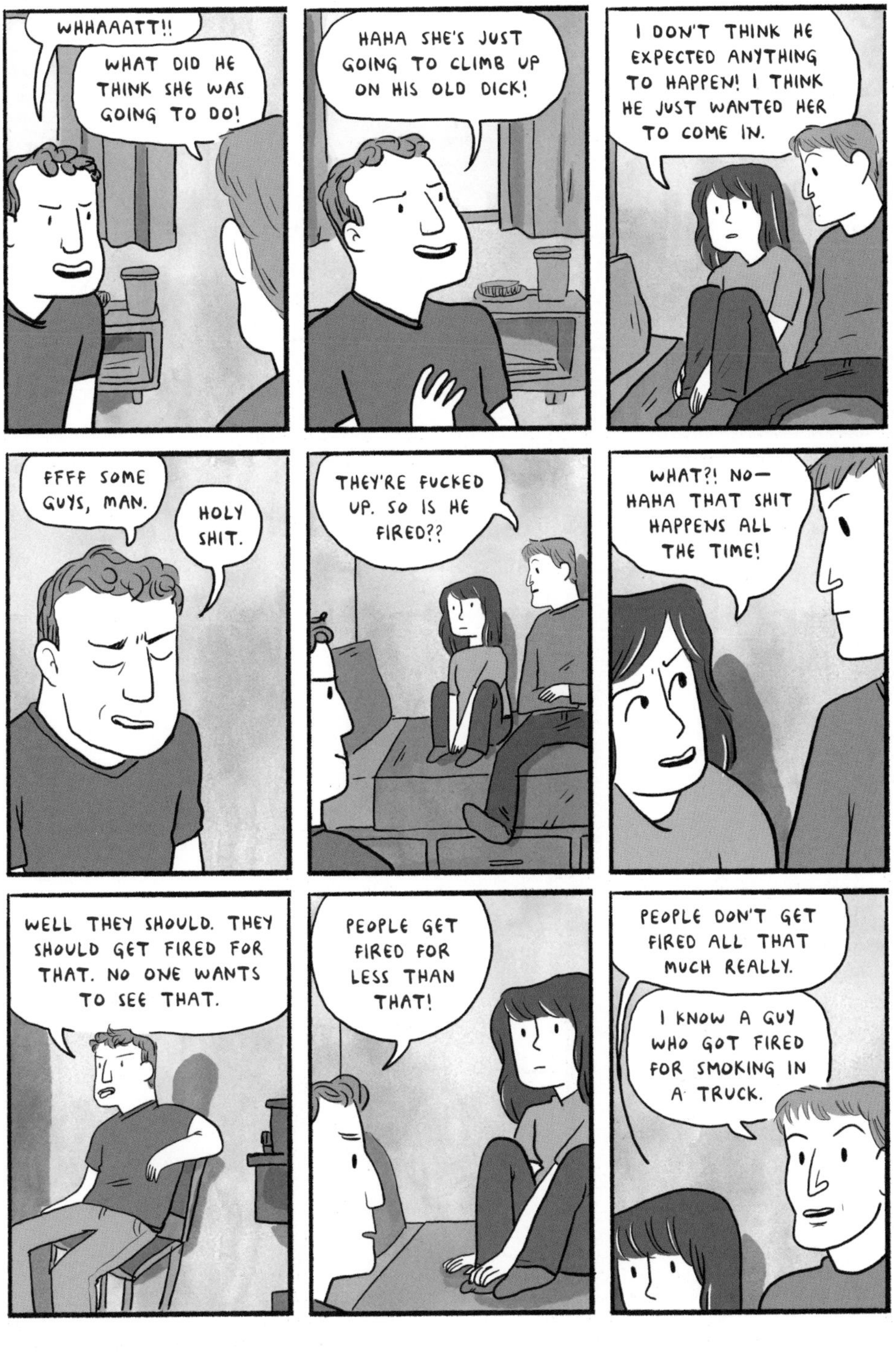
WHHAAATT!!
WHAT DID HE THINK SHE WAS GOING TO DO!
HAHA SHE'S JUST GOING TO CLIMB UP ON HIS OLD DICK!
I DON'T THINK HE EXPECTED ANYTHING TO HAPPEN! I THINK HE JUST WANTED HER TO COME IN.
FFFF SOME GUYS, MAN.
HOLY SHIT.
THEY'RE FUCKED UP. SO IS HE FIRED??
WHAT?! NO— HAHA THAT SHIT HAPPENS ALL THE TIME!
WELL THEY SHOULD. THEY SHOULD GET FIRED FOR THAT. NO ONE WANTS TO SEE THAT.
PEOPLE GET FIRED FOR LESS THAN THAT!
PEOPLE DON'T GET FIRED ALL THAT MUCH REALLY.
I KNOW A GUY WHO GOT FIRED FOR SMOKING IN A TRUCK.

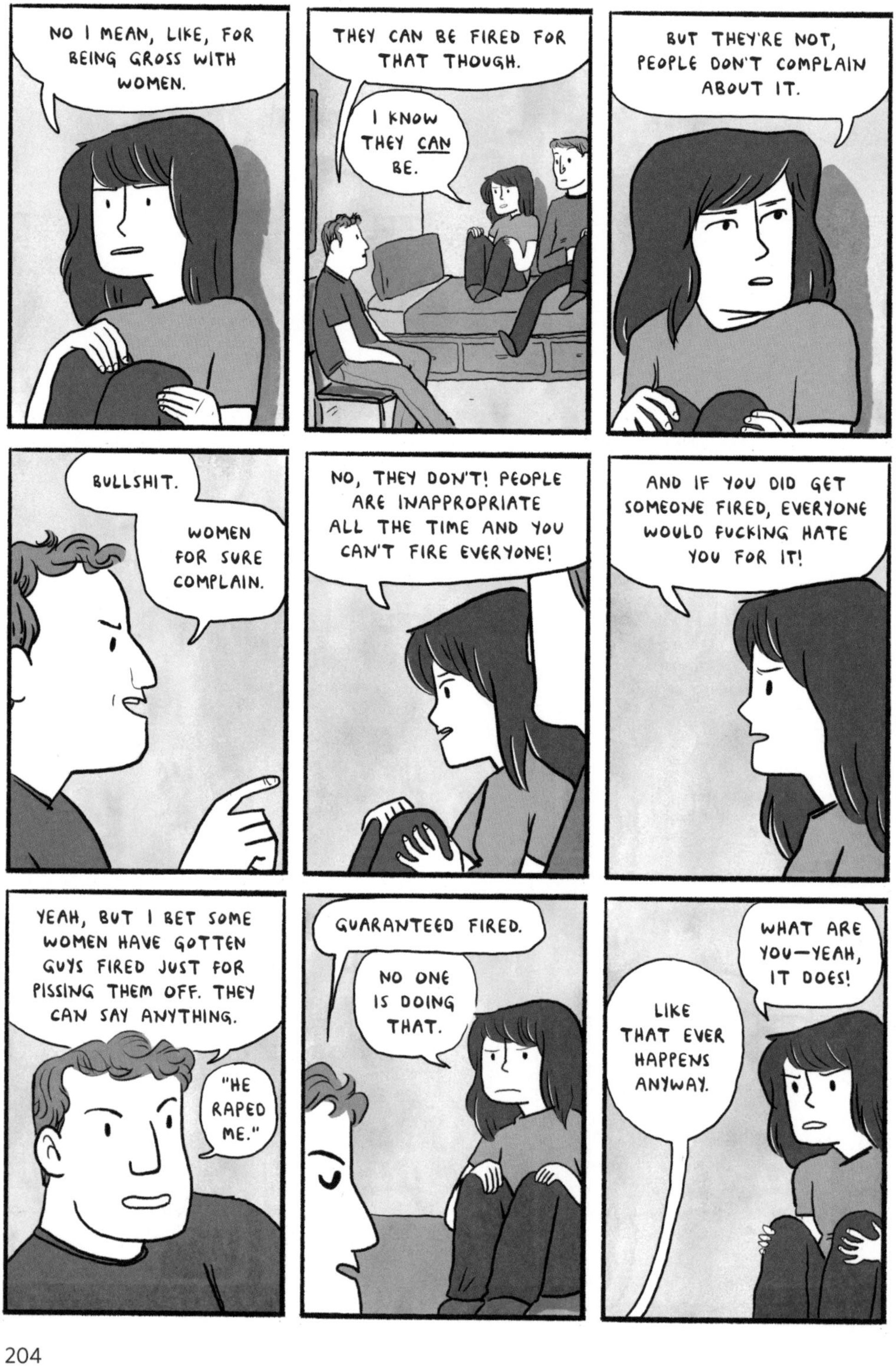
NO I MEAN, LIKE, FOR BEING GROSS WITH WOMEN.
THEY CAN BE FIRED FOR THAT THOUGH.
I KNOW THEY CAN BE.
BUT THEY'RE NOT, PEOPLE DON'T COMPLAIN ABOUT IT.
BULLSHIT.
WOMEN FOR SURE COMPLAIN.
NO, THEY DON'T! PEOPLE ARE INAPPROPRIATE ALL THE TIME AND YOU CAN'T FIRE EVERYONE!
AND IF YOU DID GET SOMEONE FIRED, EVERYONE WOULD FUCKING HATE YOU FOR IT!
YEAH, BUT I BET SOME WOMEN HAVE GOTTEN GUYS FIRED JUST FOR PISSING THEM OFF. THEY CAN SAY ANYTHING.
"HE RAPED ME."
GUARANTEED FIRED.
NO ONE IS DOING THAT.
WHAT ARE YOU—YEAH, IT DOES!
LIKE THAT EVER HAPPENS ANYWAY.

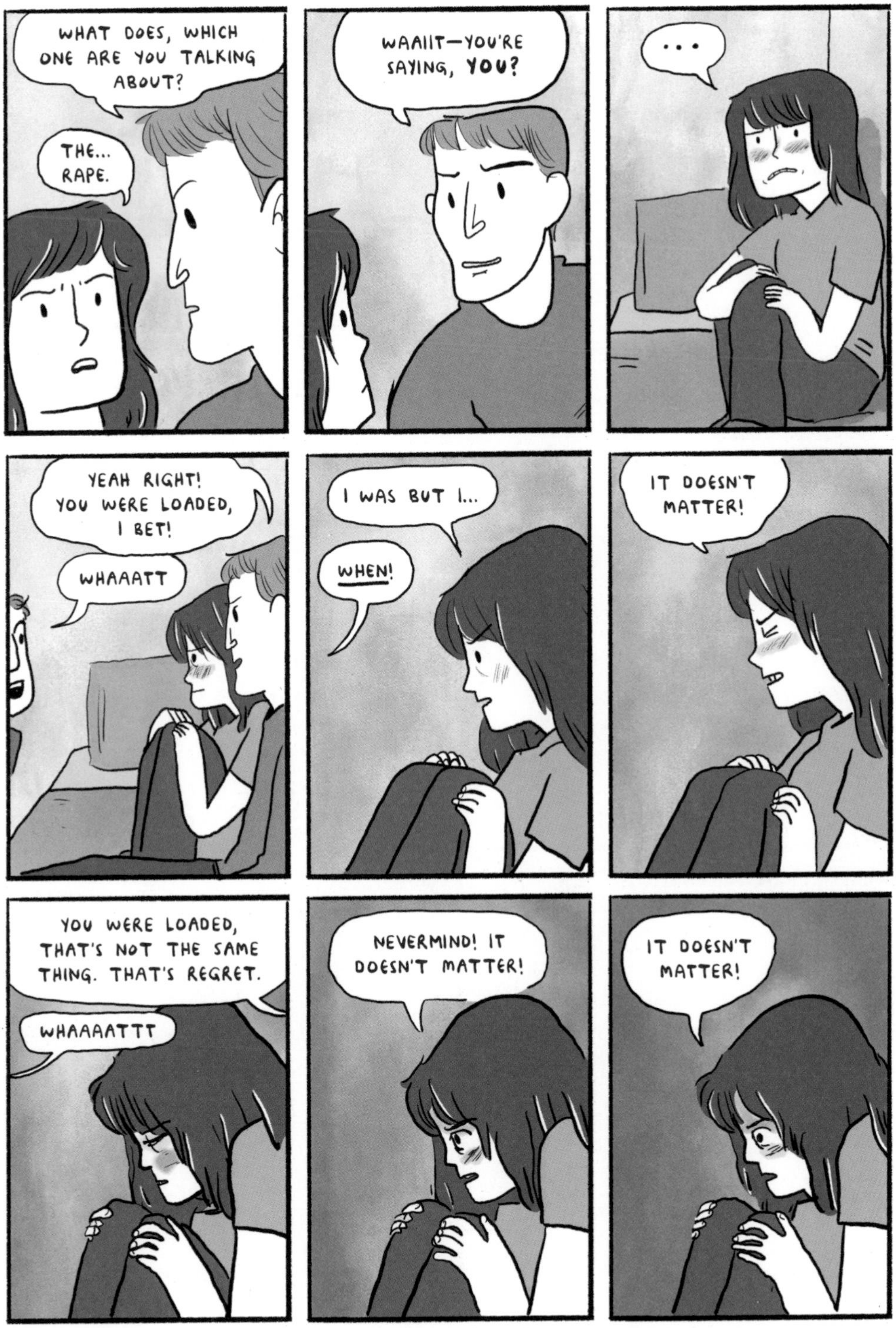
WHAT DOES, WHICH ONE ARE YOU TALKING ABOUT?
THE... RAPE.
WAAIIT—YOU'RE SAYING, YOU?
...
YEAH RIGHT! YOU WERE LOADED, I BET!
WHAAATT
I WAS BUT I...
WHEN!
IT DOESN'T MATTER!
YOU WERE LOADED, THAT'S NOT THE SAME THING. THAT'S REGRET.
WHAAAATTT
NEVERMIND! IT DOESN'T MATTER!
IT DOESN'T MATTER!

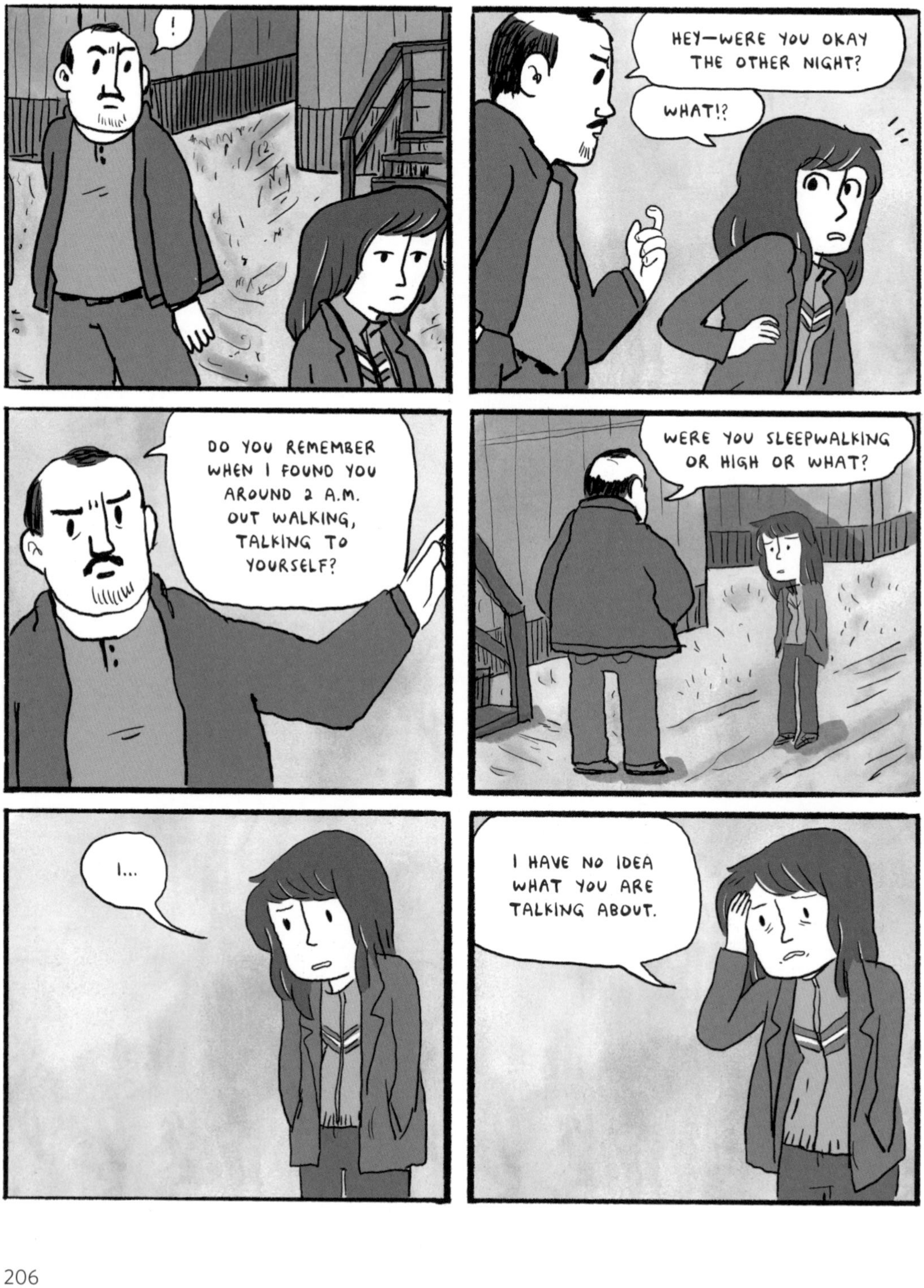
!
HEY—WERE YOU OKAY THE OTHER NIGHT?
WHAT!?
DO YOU REMEMBER WHEN I FOUND YOU AROUND 2 A.M. OUT WALKING, TALKING TO YOURSELF?
WERE YOU SLEEPWALKING OR HIGH OR WHAT?
I...
I HAVE NO IDEA WHAT YOU ARE TALKING ABOUT.

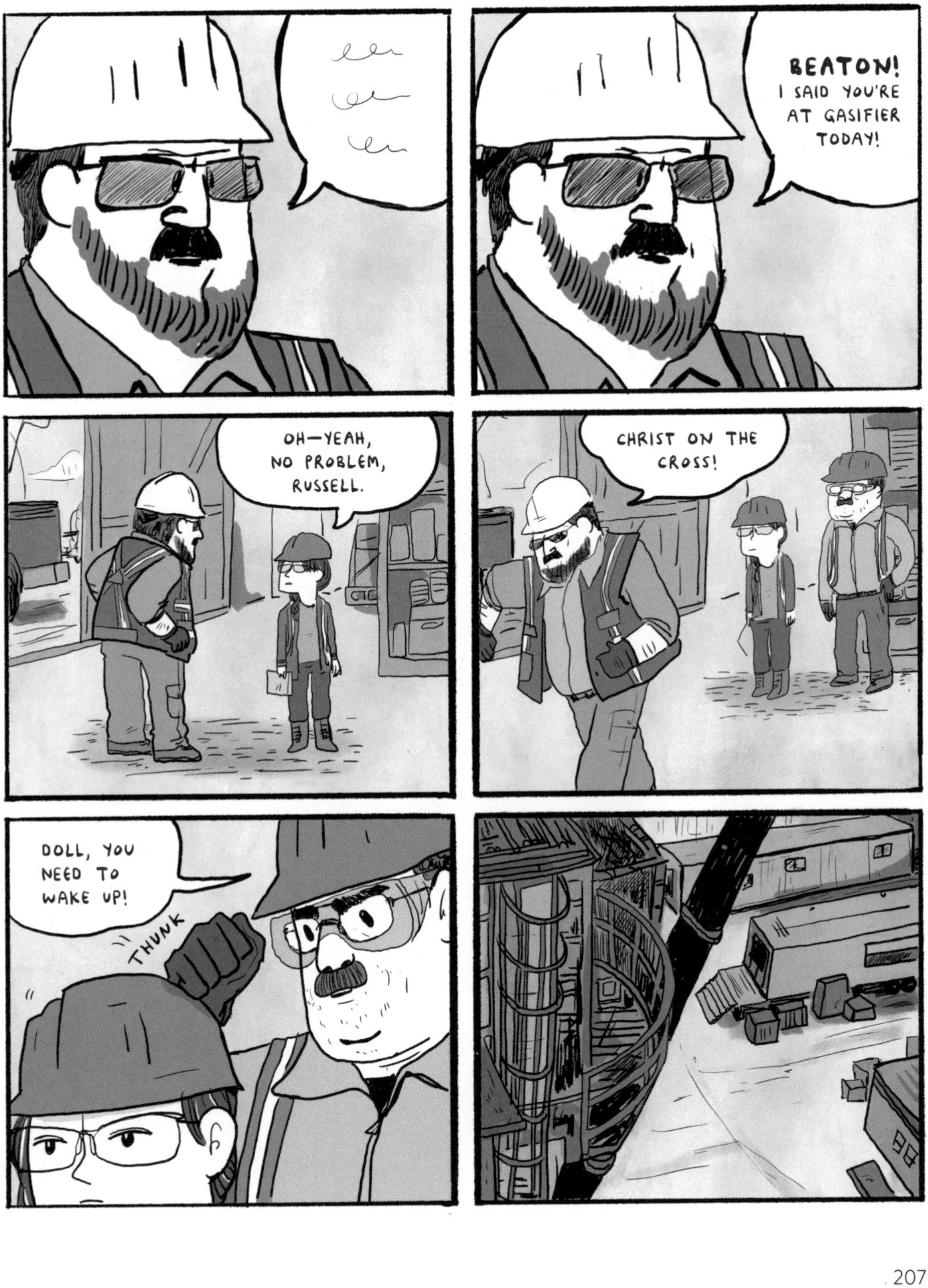
BEATON! I SAID YOU'RE AT GASIFIER TODAY!
OH—YEAH, NO PROBLEM, RUSSELL.
CHRIST ON THE CROSS!
DOLL, YOU NEED TO WAKE UP!
THUNK

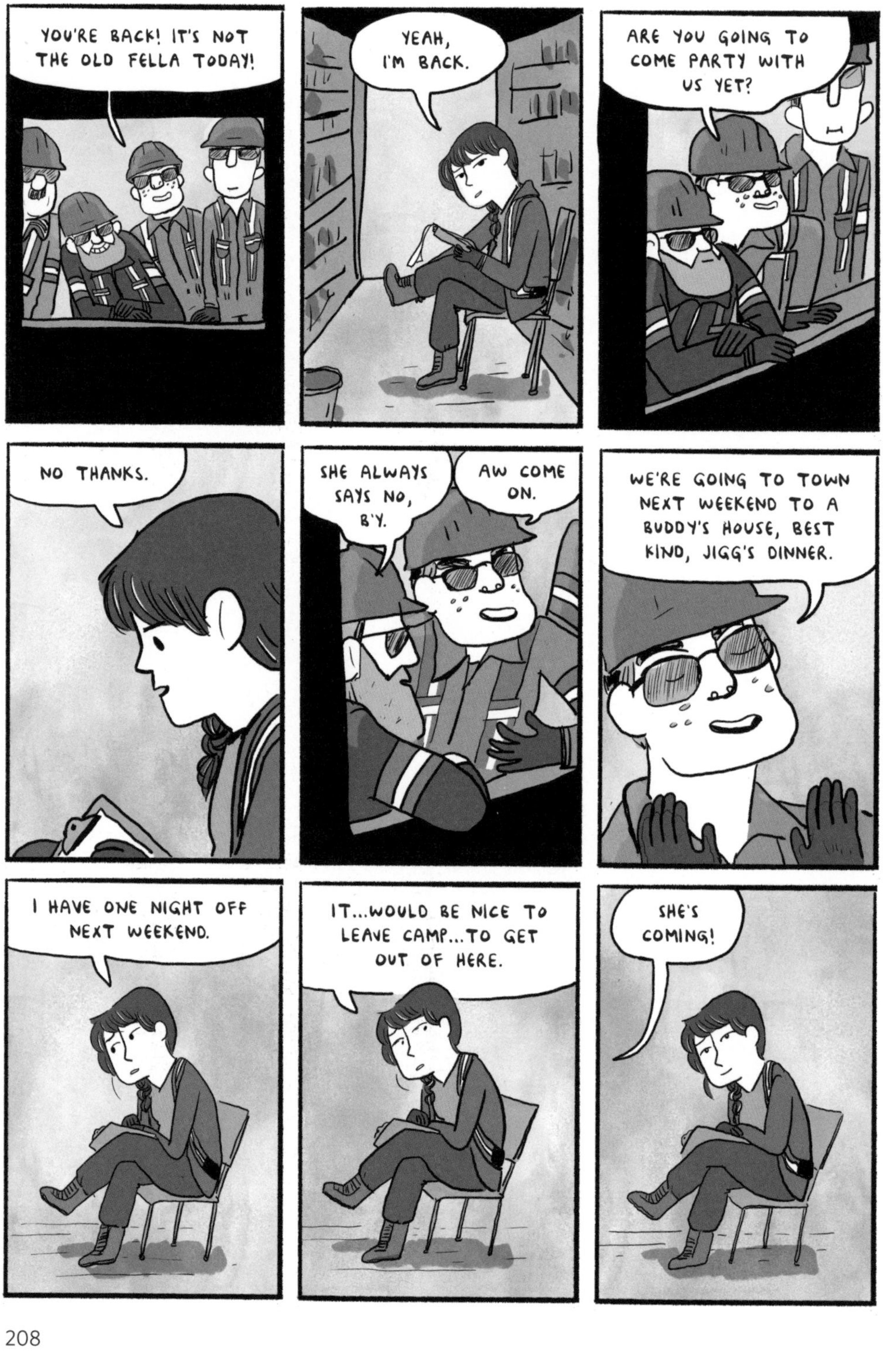
YOU'RE BACK! IT'S NOT THE OLD FELLA TODAY!
YEAH, I'M BACK.
ARE YOU GOING TO COME PARTY WITH US YET?
NO THANKS.
SHE ALWAYS SAYS NO, B'Y.
AW COME ON.
WE'RE GOING TO TOWN NEXT WEEKEND TO A BUDDY'S HOUSE, BEST KIND, JIGG'S DINNER.
I HAVE ONE NIGHT OFF NEXT WEEKEND.
IT...WOULD BE NICE TO LEAVE CAMP...TO GET OUT OF HERE.
SHE'S COMING!

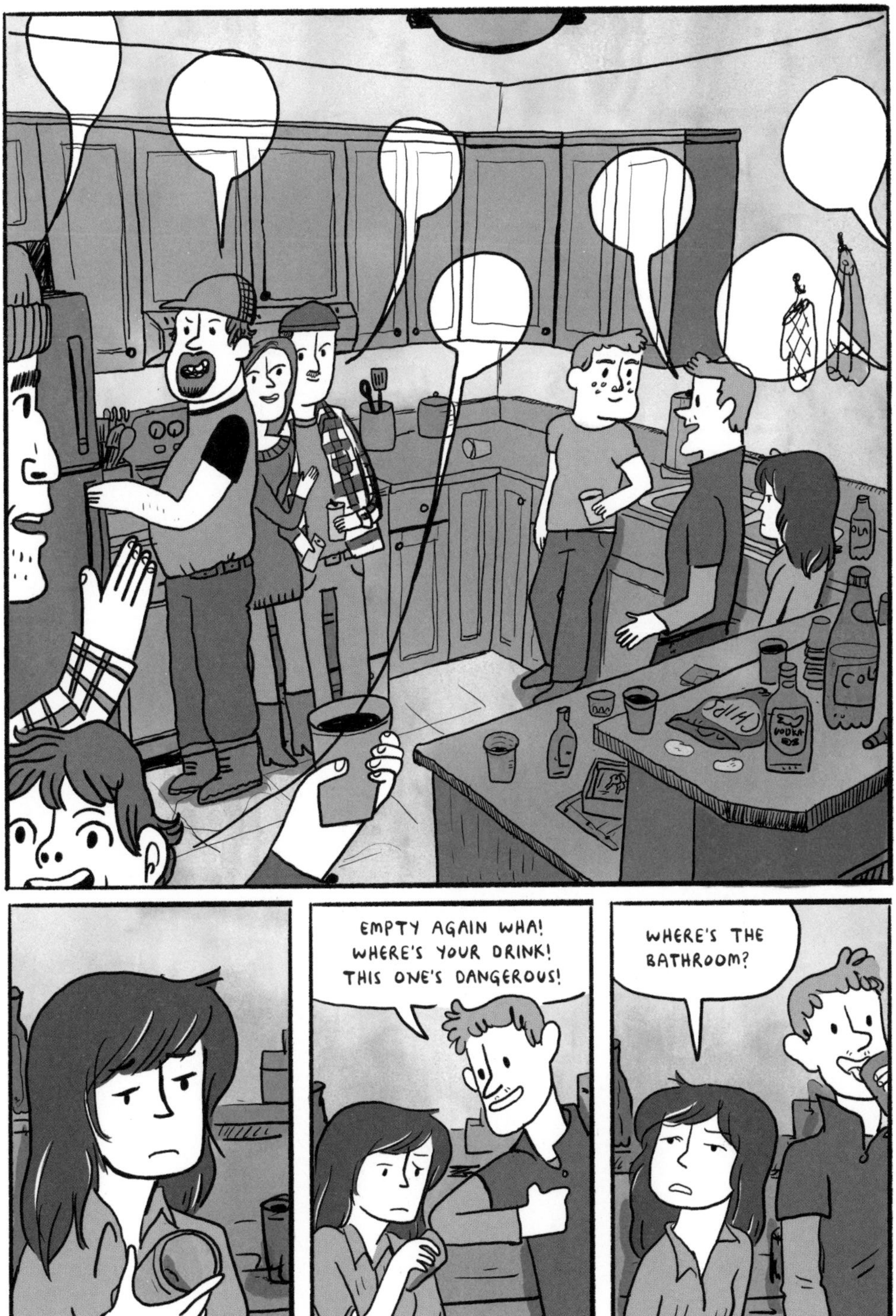
EMPTY AGAIN WHA! WHERE'S YOUR DRINK! THIS ONE'S DANGEROUS!
WHERE'S THE BATHROOM?

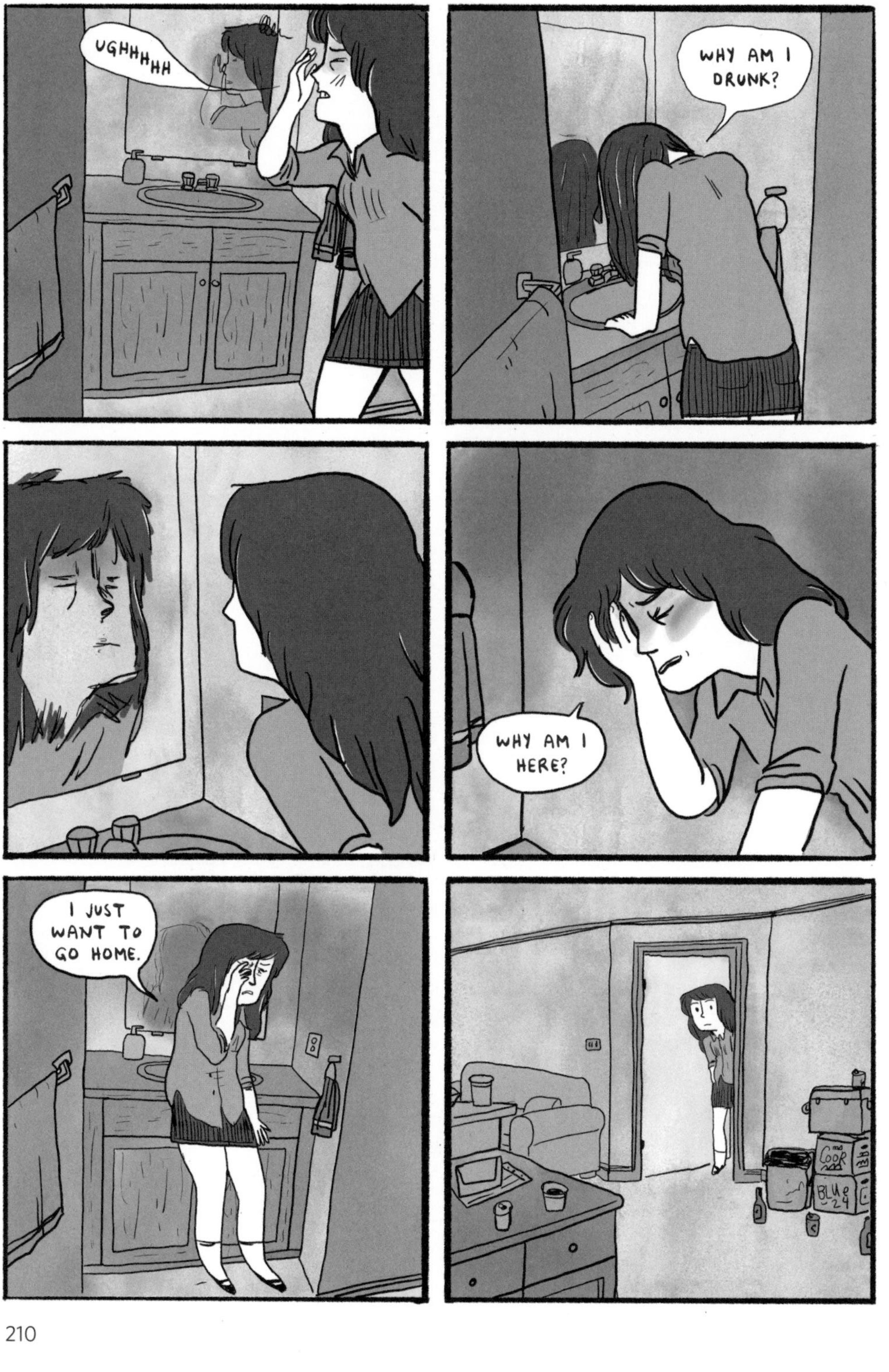
UGHHHHHH
WHY AM I DRUNK?
WHY AM I HERE?
I JUST WANT TO GO HOME.

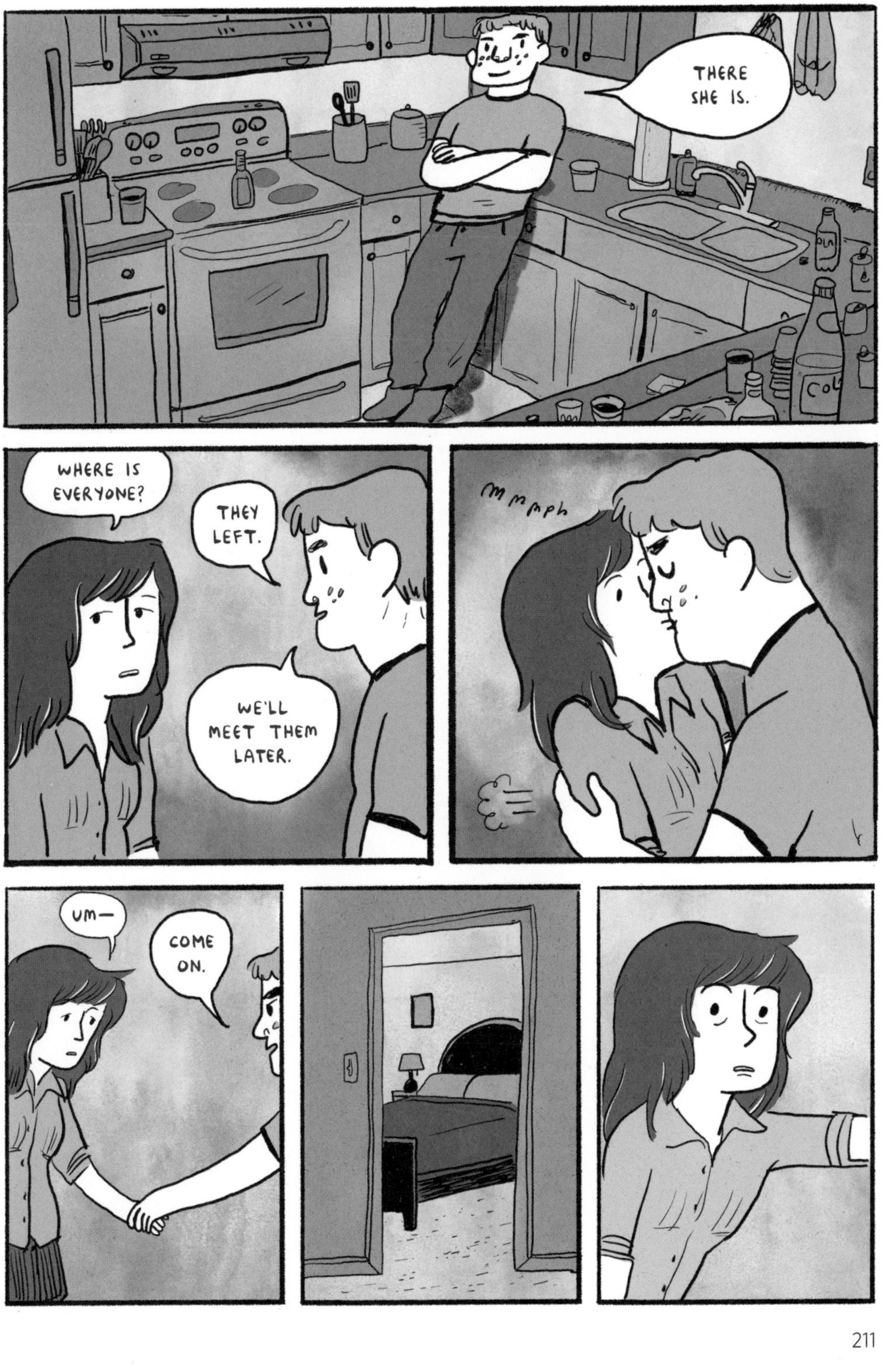
THERE SHE IS.
WHERE IS EVERYONE?
THEY LEFT.
WE'LL MEET THEM LATER.
MMMPH
UM—
COME ON.

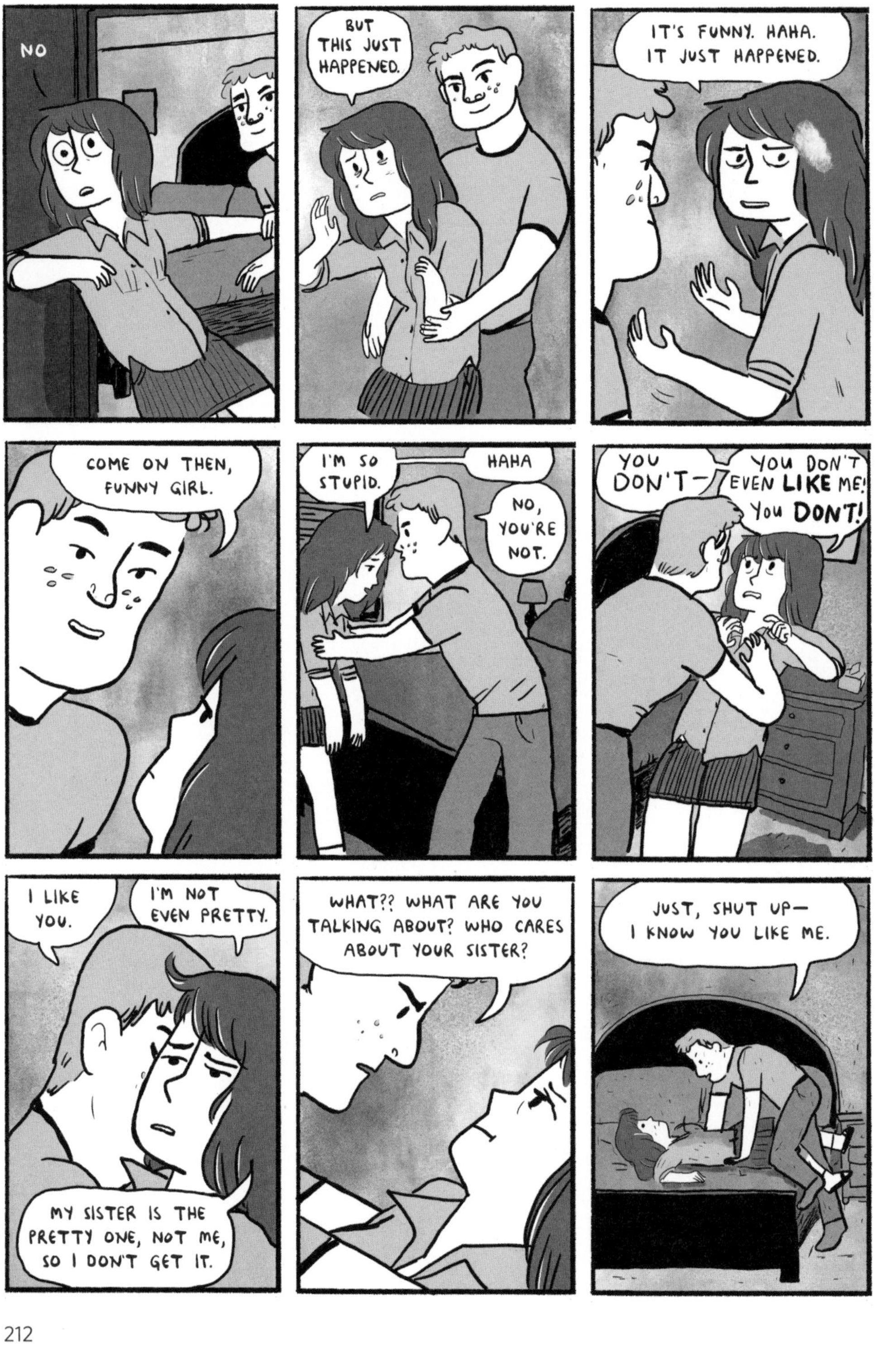
NO
BUT THIS JUST HAPPENED.
IT'S FUNNY. HAHA. IT JUST HAPPENED.
COME ON THEN, FUNNY GIRL.
I'M SO STUPID.
HAHA
NO, YOU'RE NOT.
YOU DON'T—
YOU DON'T EVEN LIKE ME! YOU DON'T!
I LIKE YOU.
I'M NOT EVEN PRETTY.
MY SISTER IS THE PRETTY ONE, NOT ME, SO I DON'T GET IT.
WHAT?? WHAT ARE YOU TALKING ABOUT? WHO CARES ABOUT YOUR SISTER?
JUST, SHUT UP— I KNOW YOU LIKE ME.

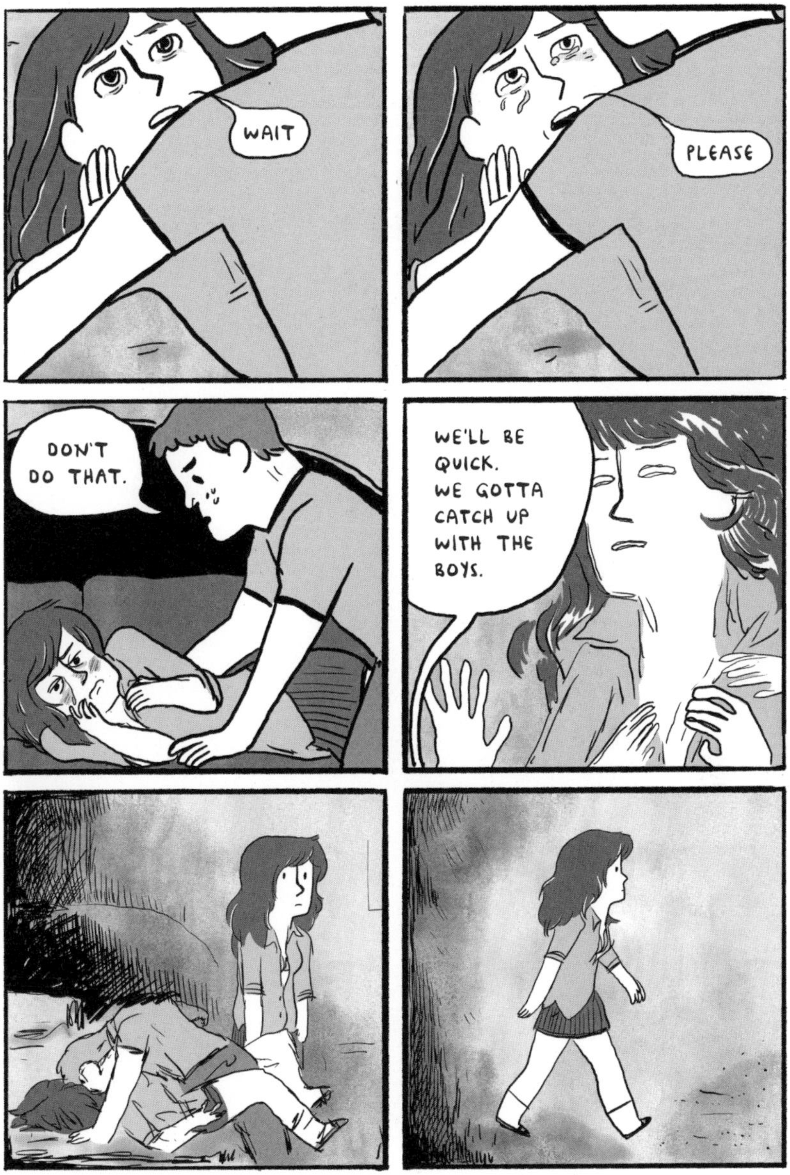
WAIT
PLEASE
DON'T DO THAT.
WE'LL BE QUICK. WE GOTTA CATCH UP WITH THE BOYS.

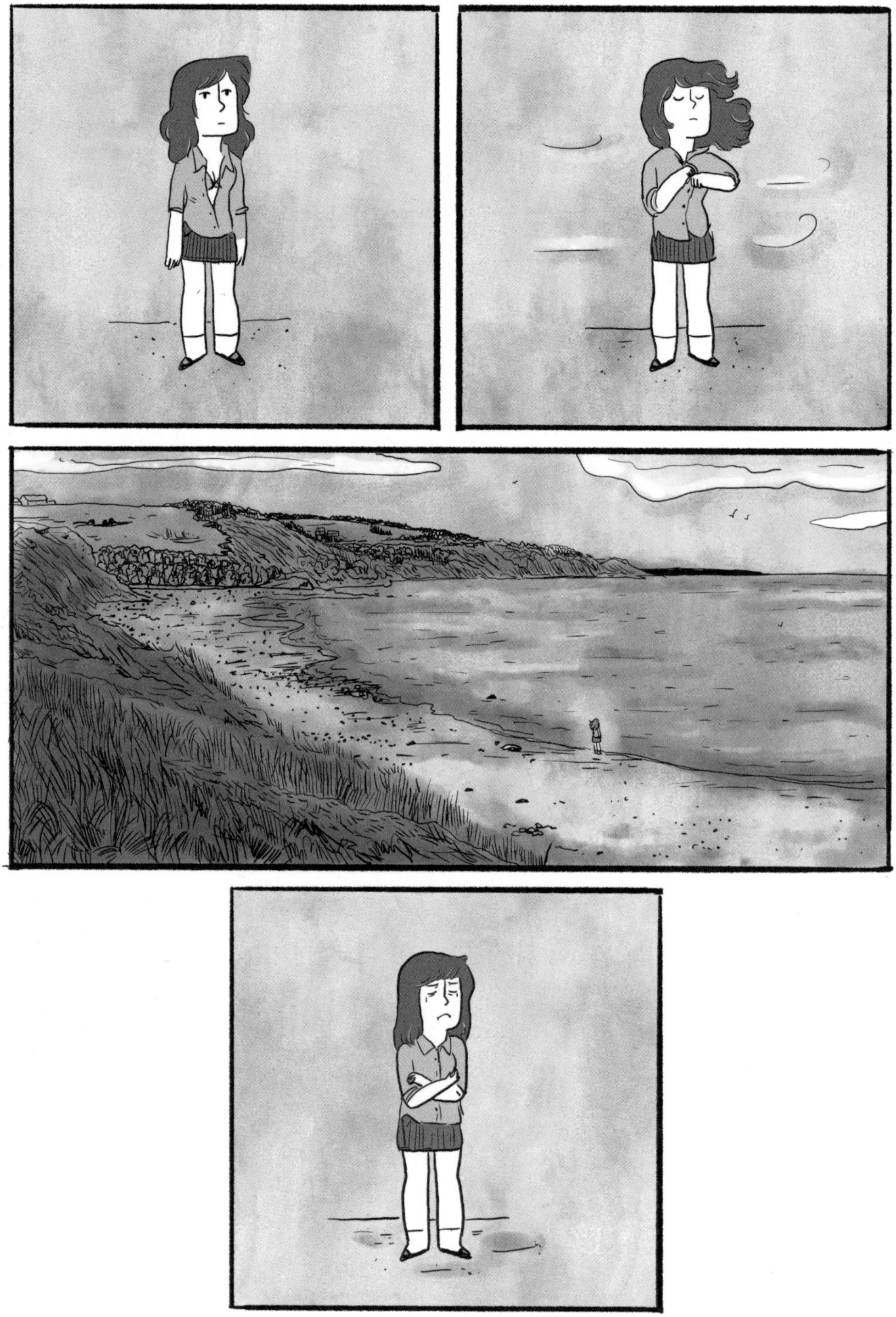

ONE MONTH LATER

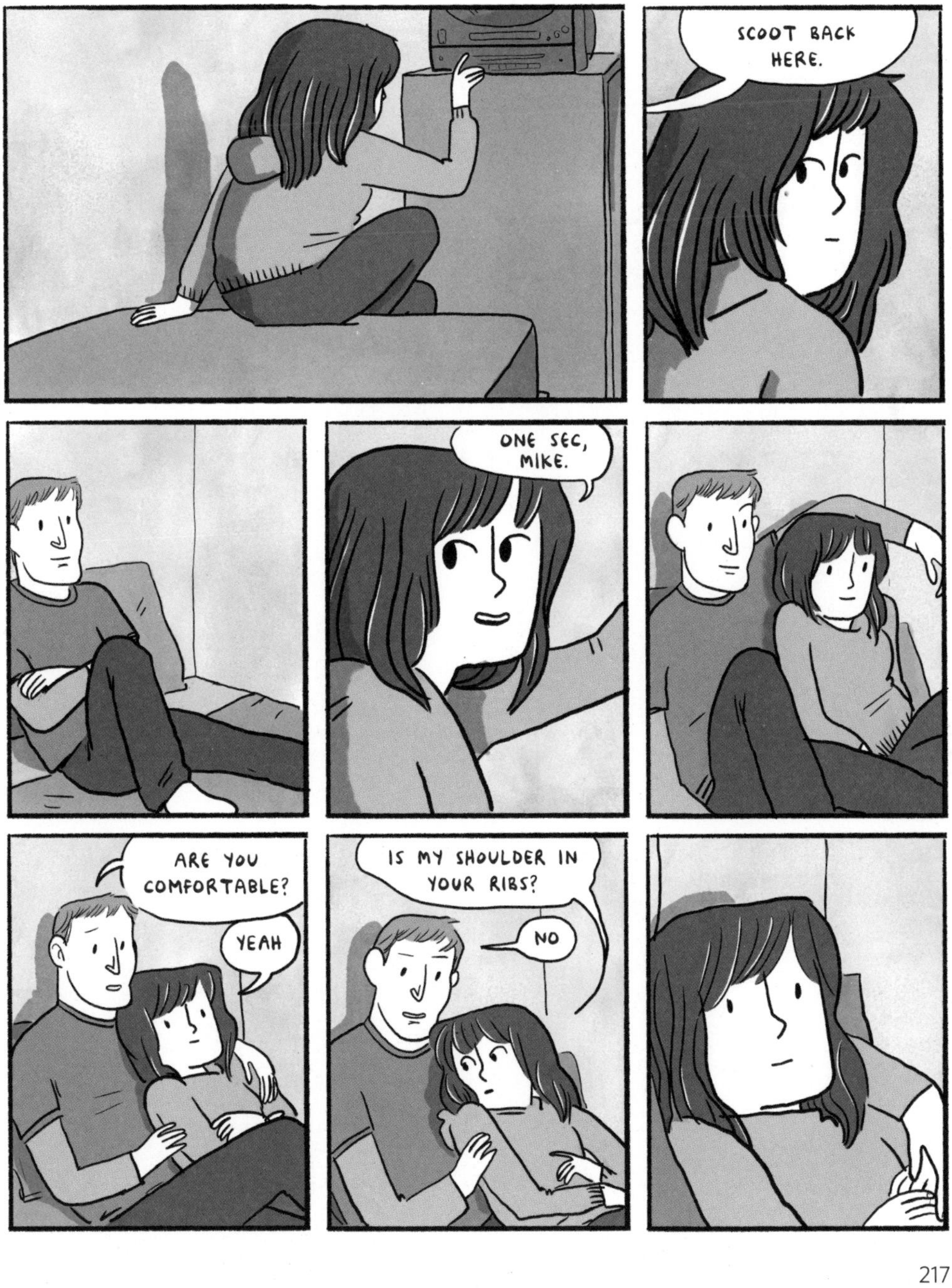
SCOOT BACK HERE.
ONE SEC, MIKE.
ARE YOU COMFORTABLE?
YEAH
IS MY SHOULDER IN YOUR RIBS?
NO

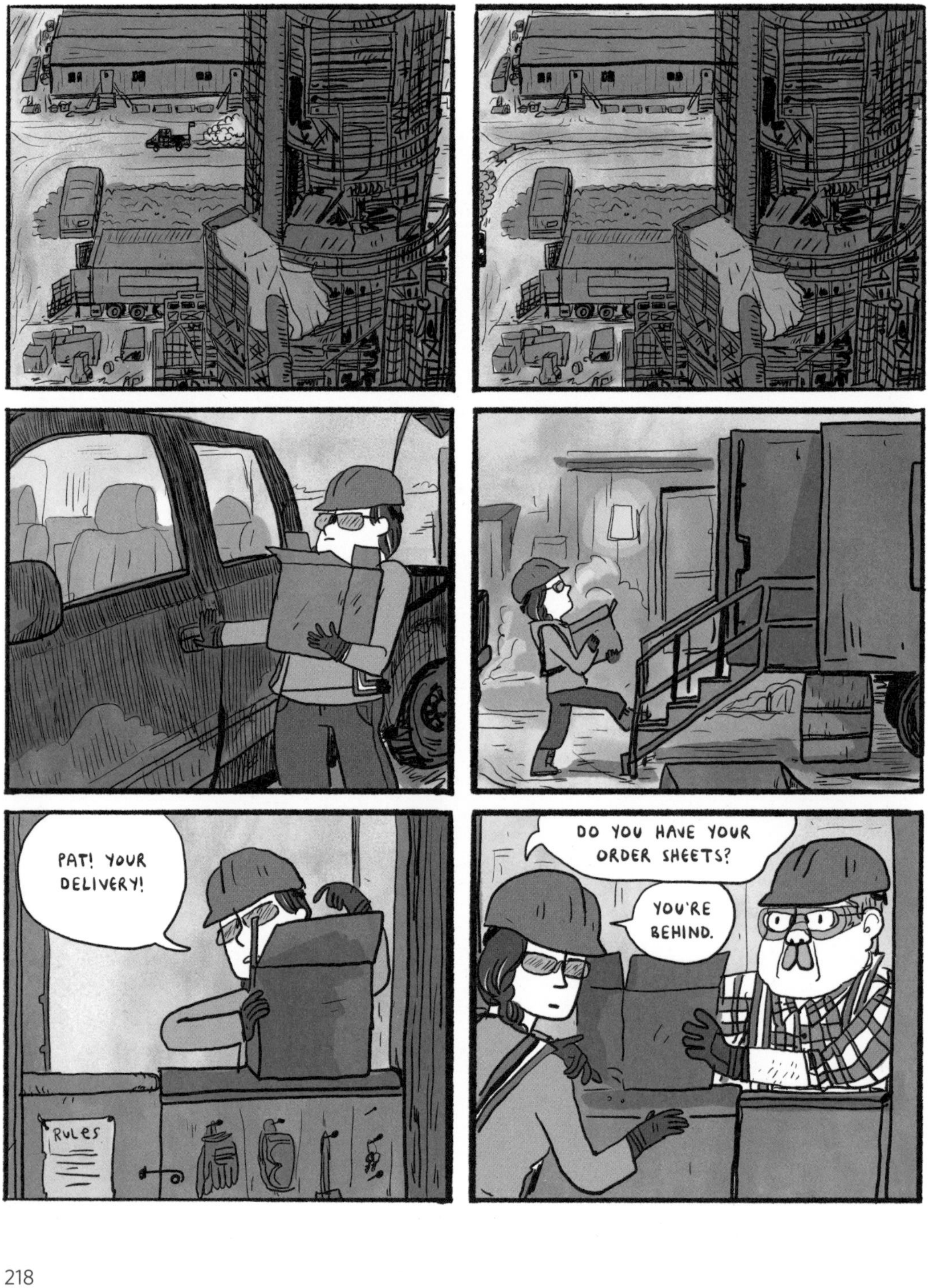
PAT! YOUR DELIVERY!
DO YOU HAVE YOUR ORDER SHEETS?
YOU'RE BEHIND.
RULES

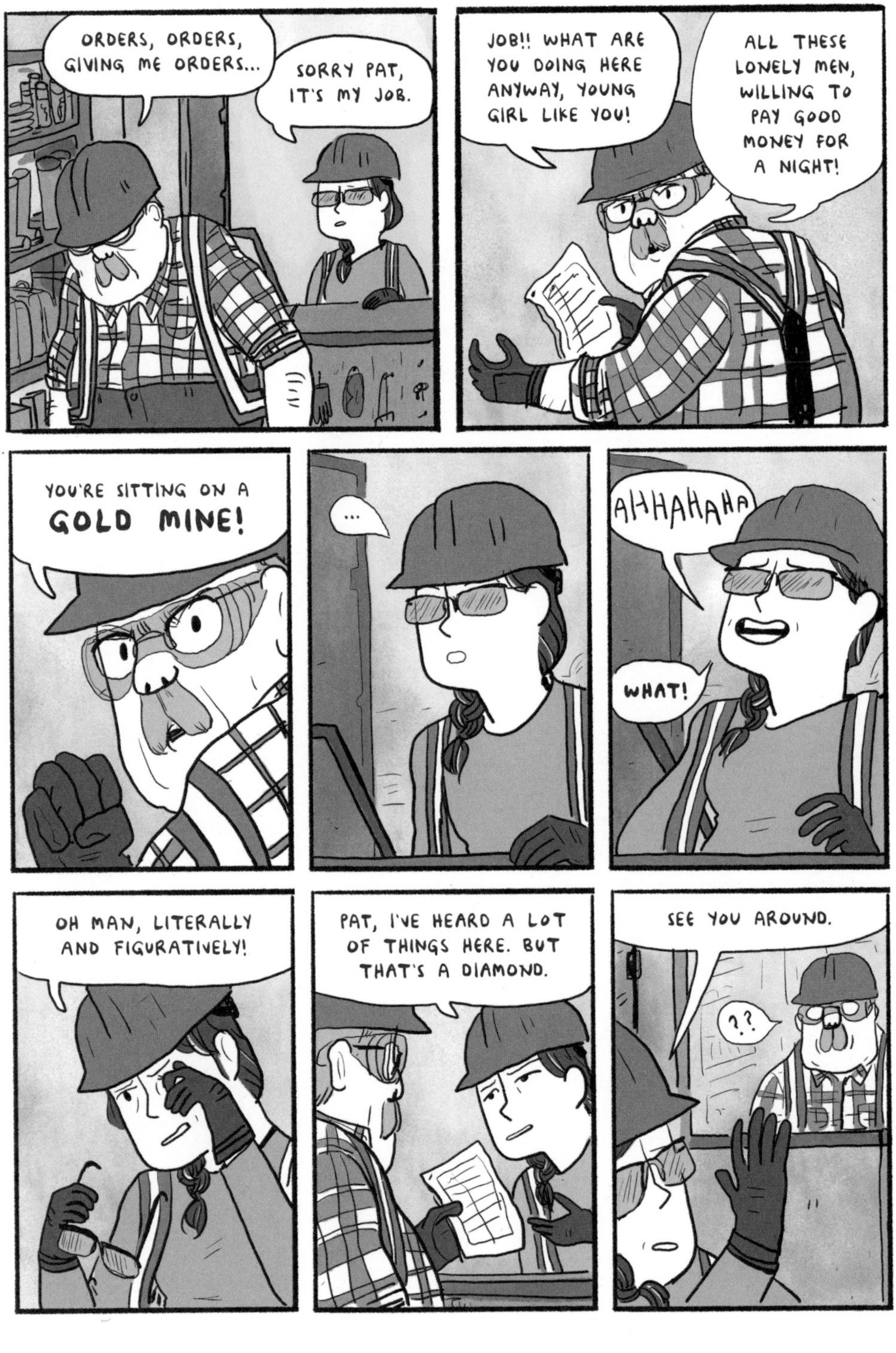
ORDERS, ORDERS, GIVING ME ORDERS...
SORRY PAT, IT'S MY JOB.
JOB!! WHAT ARE YOU DOING HERE ANYWAY, YOUNG GIRL LIKE YOU!
ALL THESE LONELY MEN, WILLING TO PAY GOOD MONEY FOR A NIGHT!
YOU'RE SITTING ON A GOLD MINE!
...
AHHAHAHAHA
WHAT!
OH MAN, LITERALLY AND FIGURATIVELY!
PAT, I'VE HEARD A LOT OF THINGS HERE. BUT THAT'S A DIAMOND.
SEE YOU AROUND.
??

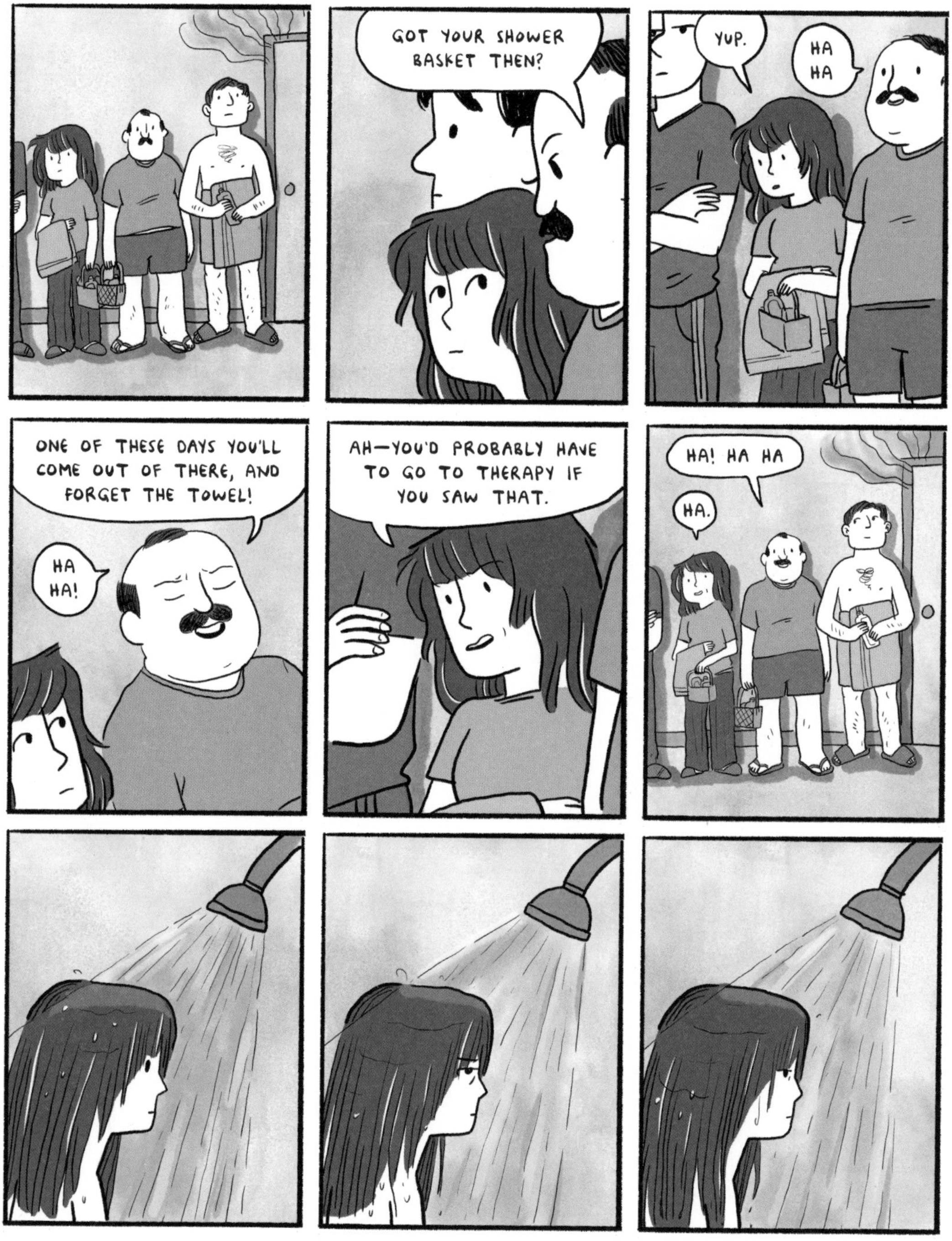
GOT YOUR SHOWER BASKET THEN?
YUP.
HA HA
ONE OF THESE DAYS YOU'LL COME OUT OF THERE, AND FORGET THE TOWEL!
HA HA!
AH—YOU'D PROBABLY HAVE TO GO TO THERAPY IF YOU SAW THAT.
HA! HA HA
HA.

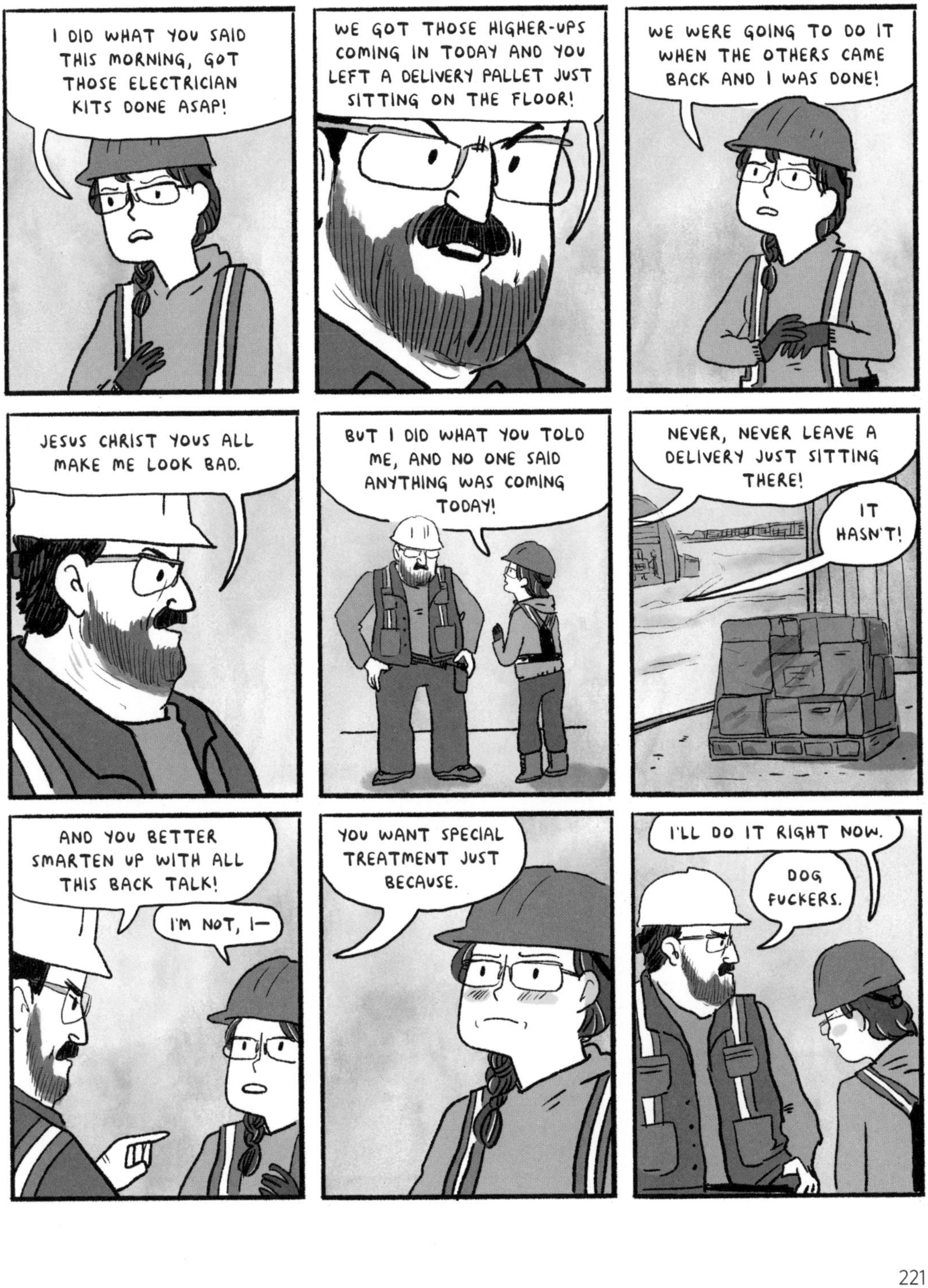
I DID WHAT YOU SAID THIS MORNING, GOT THOSE ELECTRICIAN KITS DONE ASAP!
WE GOT THOSE HIGHER-UPS COMING IN TODAY AND YOU LEFT A DELIVERY PALLET JUST SITTING ON THE FLOOR!
WE WERE GOING TO DO IT WHEN THE OTHERS CAME BACK AND I WAS DONE!
JESUS CHRIST YOUS ALL MAKE ME LOOK BAD.
BUT I DID WHAT YOU TOLD ME, AND NO ONE SAID ANYTHING WAS COMING TODAY!
NEVER, NEVER LEAVE A DELIVERY JUST SITTING THERE!
IT HASN'T!
AND YOU BETTER SMARTEN UP WITH ALL THIS BACK TALK!
I'M NOT, I—
YOU WANT SPECIAL TREATMENT JUST BECAUSE.
I'LL DO IT RIGHT NOW.
DOG FUCKERS.

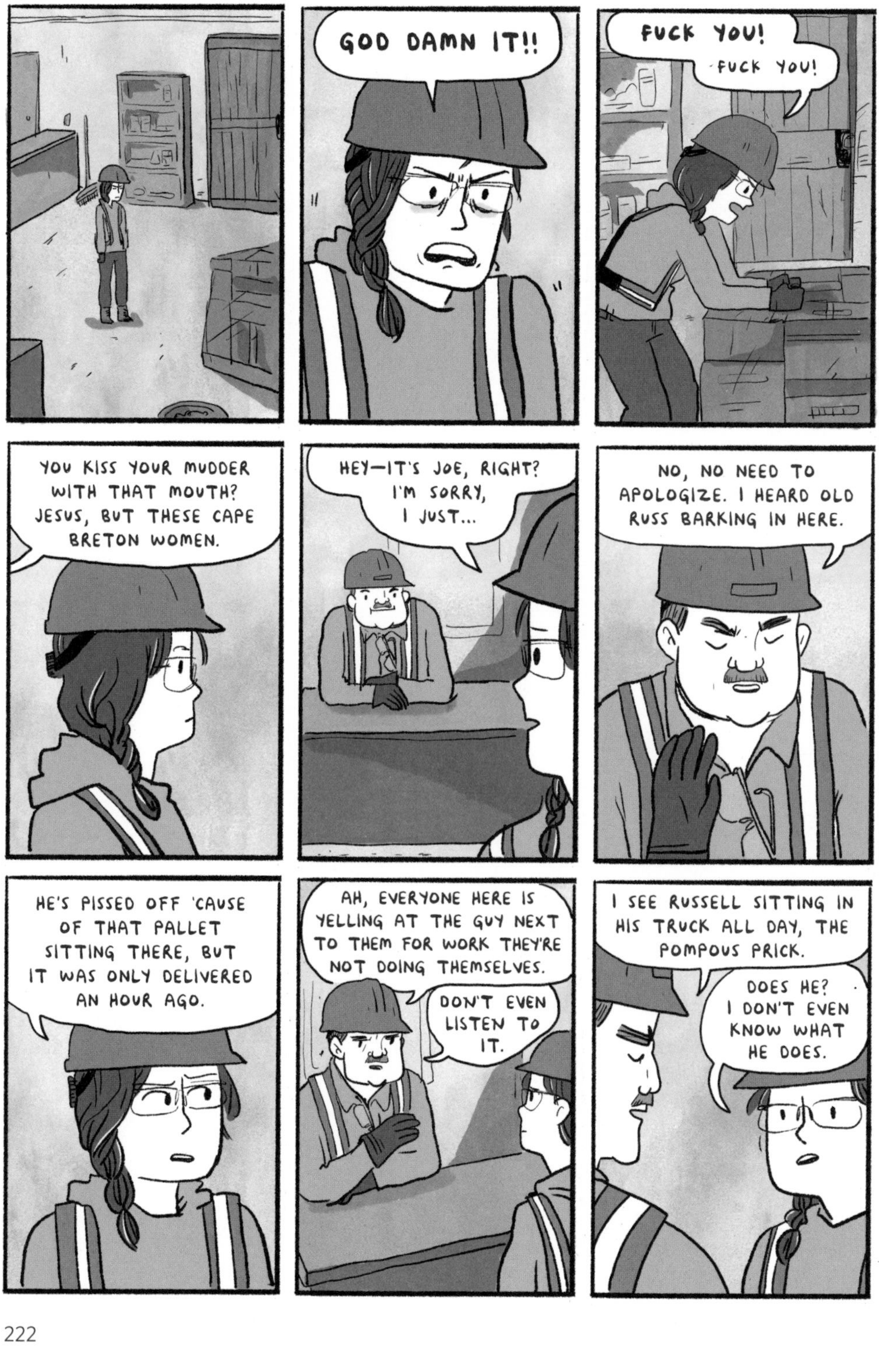
GOD DAMN IT!!
FUCK YOU!
FUCK YOU!
YOU KISS YOUR MUDDER WITH THAT MOUTH? JESUS, BUT THESE CAPE BRETON WOMEN.
HEY—IT'S JOE, RIGHT? I'M SORRY, I JUST...
NO, NO NEED TO APOLOGIZE. I HEARD OLD RUSS BARKING IN HERE.
HE'S PISSED OFF 'CAUSE OF THAT PALLET SITTING THERE, BUT IT WAS ONLY DELIVERED AN HOUR AGO.
AH, EVERYONE HERE IS YELLING AT THE GUY NEXT TO THEM FOR WORK THEY'RE NOT DOING THEMSELVES.
DON'T EVEN LISTEN TO IT.
I SEE RUSSELL SITTING IN HIS TRUCK ALL DAY, THE POMPOUS PRICK.
DOES HE? I DON'T EVEN KNOW WHAT HE DOES.

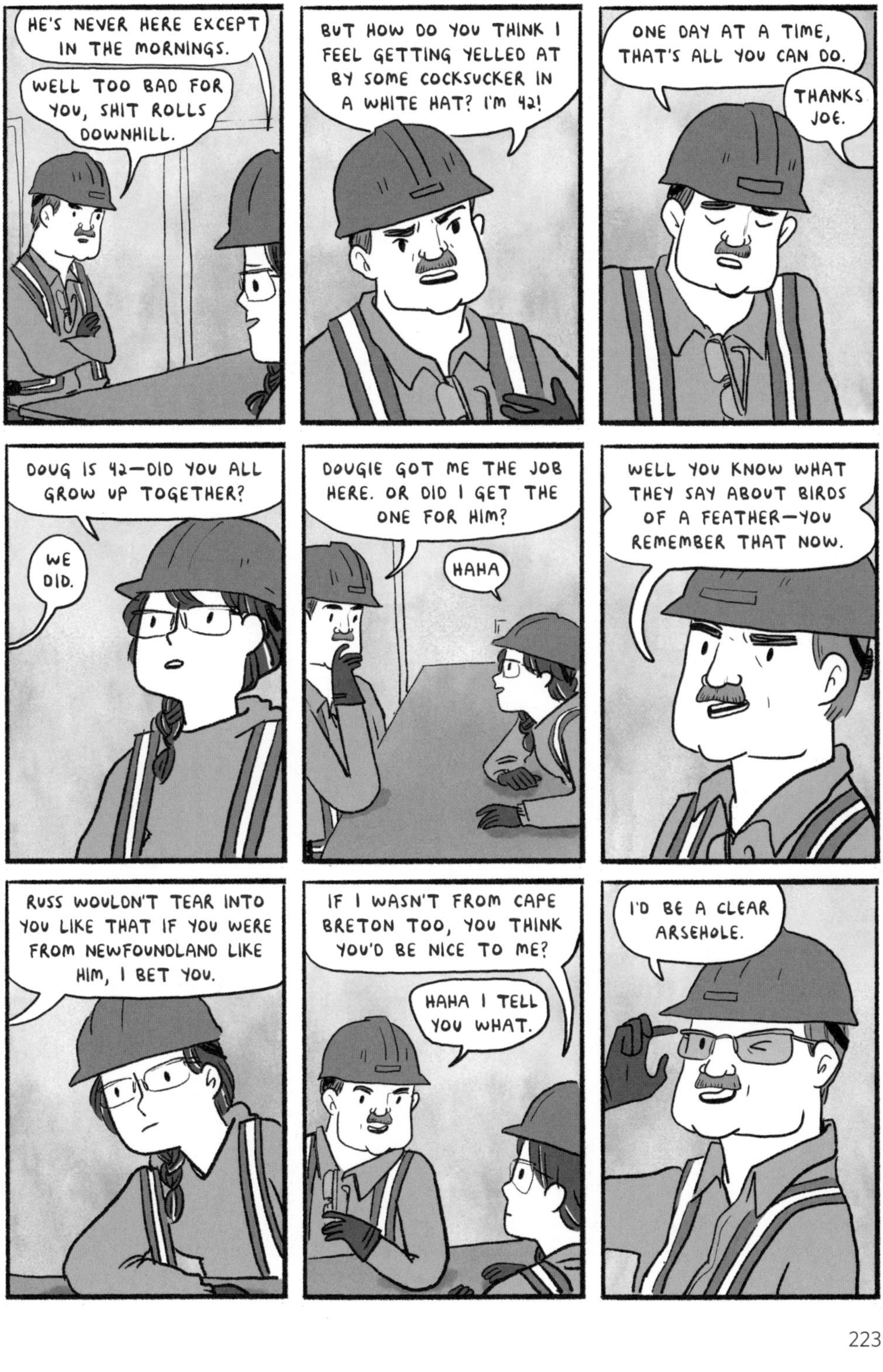
HE'S NEVER HERE EXCEPT IN THE MORNINGS.
WELL TOO BAD FOR YOU, SHIT ROLLS DOWNHILL.
BUT HOW DO YOU THINK I FEEL GETTING YELLED AT BY SOME COCKSUCKER IN A WHITE HAT? I'M 42!
ONE DAY AT A TIME, THAT'S ALL YOU CAN DO.
THANKS JOE.
DOUG IS 42—DID YOU ALL GROW UP TOGETHER?
WE DID.
DOUGIE GOT ME THE JOB HERE. OR DID I GET THE ONE FOR HIM?
HAHA
WELL YOU KNOW WHAT THEY SAY ABOUT BIRDS OF A FEATHER—YOU REMEMBER THAT NOW.
RUSS WOULDN'T TEAR INTO YOU LIKE THAT IF YOU WERE FROM NEWFOUNDLAND LIKE HIM, I BET YOU.
IF I WASN'T FROM CAPE BRETON TOO, YOU THINK YOU'D BE NICE TO ME?
HAHA I TELL YOU WHAT.
I'D BE A CLEAR ARSEHOLE.

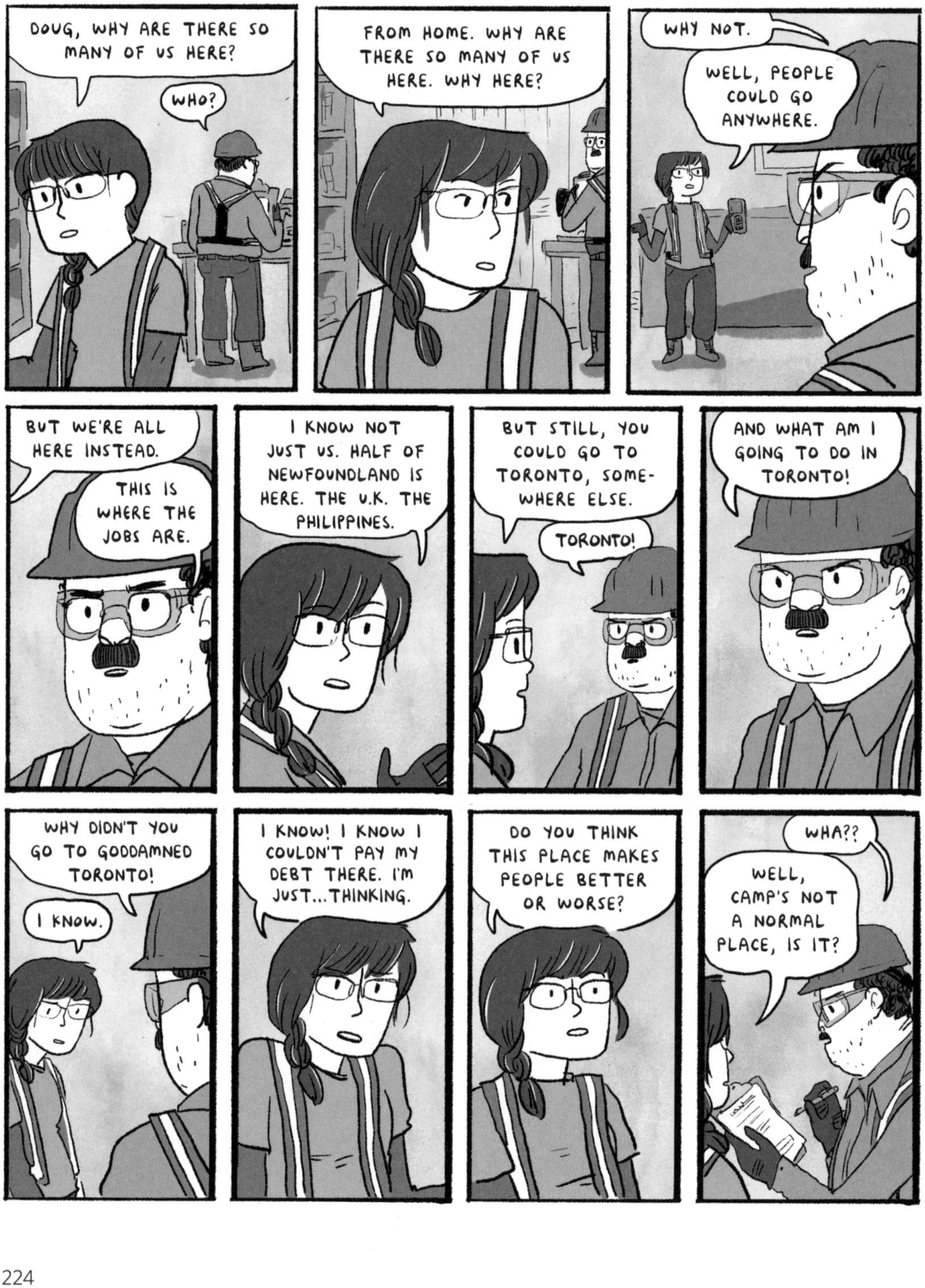
DOUG, WHY ARE THERE SO MANY OF US HERE?
WHO?
FROM HOME. WHY ARE THERE SO MANY OF US HERE. WHY HERE?
WHY NOT.
WELL, PEOPLE COULD GO ANYWHERE.
BUT WE'RE ALL HERE INSTEAD.
THIS IS WHERE THE JOBS ARE.
I KNOW NOT JUST US. HALF OF NEWFOUNDLAND IS HERE. THE U.K. THE PHILIPPINES.
BUT STILL, YOU COULD GO TO TORONTO, SOMEWHERE ELSE.
TORONTO!
AND WHAT AM I GOING TO DO IN TORONTO!
WHY DIDN'T YOU GO TO GODDAMNED TORONTO!
I KNOW.
I KNOW! I KNOW I COULDN'T PAY MY DEBT THERE. I'M JUST...THINKING.
DO YOU THINK THIS PLACE MAKES PEOPLE BETTER OR WORSE?
WHA??
WELL, CAMP'S NOT A NORMAL PLACE, IS IT?

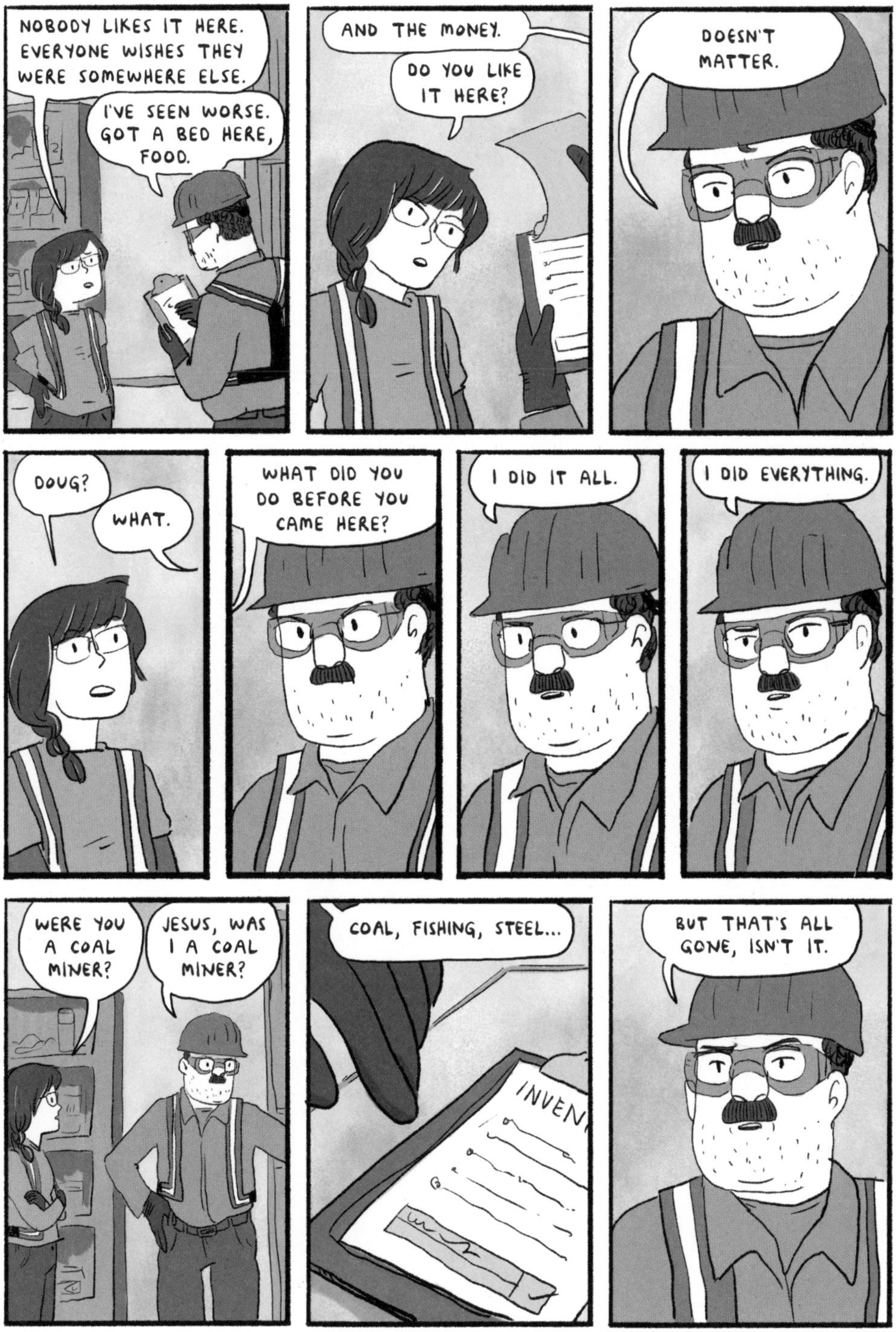
NOBODY LIKES IT HERE. EVERYONE WISHES THEY WERE SOMEWHERE ELSE.
I'VE SEEN WORSE. GOT A BED HERE, FOOD.
AND THE MONEY.
DO YOU LIKE IT HERE?
DOESN'T MATTER.
DOUG?
WHAT.
WHAT DID YOU DO BEFORE YOU CAME HERE?
I DID IT ALL.
I DID EVERYTHING.
WERE YOU A COAL MINER?
JESUS, WAS I A COAL MINER?
COAL, FISHING, STEEL...
INVEN
BUT THAT'S ALL GONE, ISN'T IT.

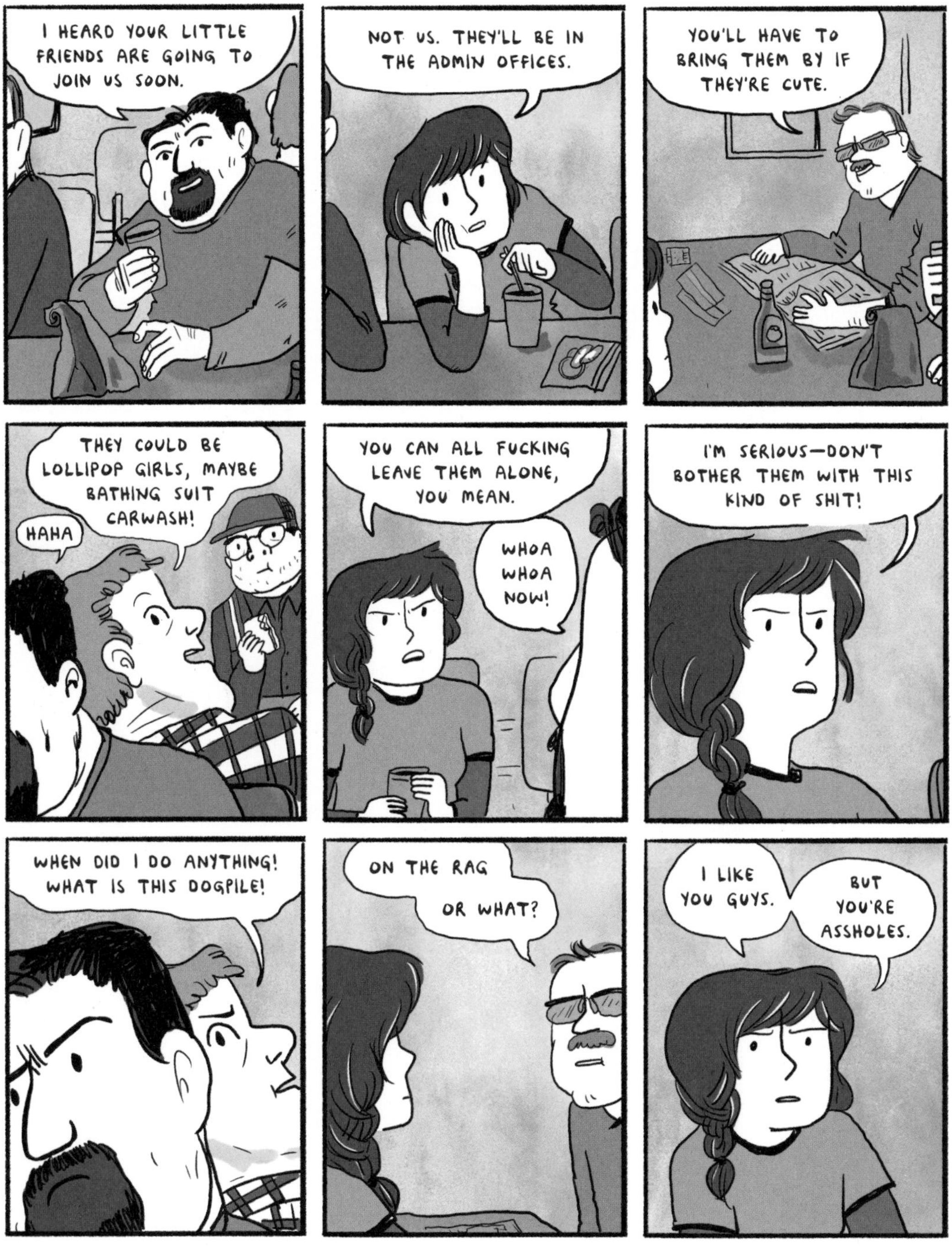
I HEARD YOUR LITTLE FRIENDS ARE GOING TO JOIN US SOON.
NOT US. THEY'LL BE IN THE ADMIN OFFICES.
YOU'LL HAVE TO BRING THEM BY IF THEY'RE CUTE.
THEY COULD BE LOLLIPOP GIRLS, MAYBE BATHING SUIT CARWASH!
HAHA
YOU CAN ALL FUCKING LEAVE THEM ALONE, YOU MEAN.
WHOA WHOA NOW!
I'M SERIOUS—DON'T BOTHER THEM WITH THIS KIND OF SHIT!
WHEN DID I DO ANYTHING! WHAT IS THIS DOGPILE!
ON THE RAG
OR WHAT?
I LIKE YOU GUYS.
BUT YOU'RE ASSHOLES.

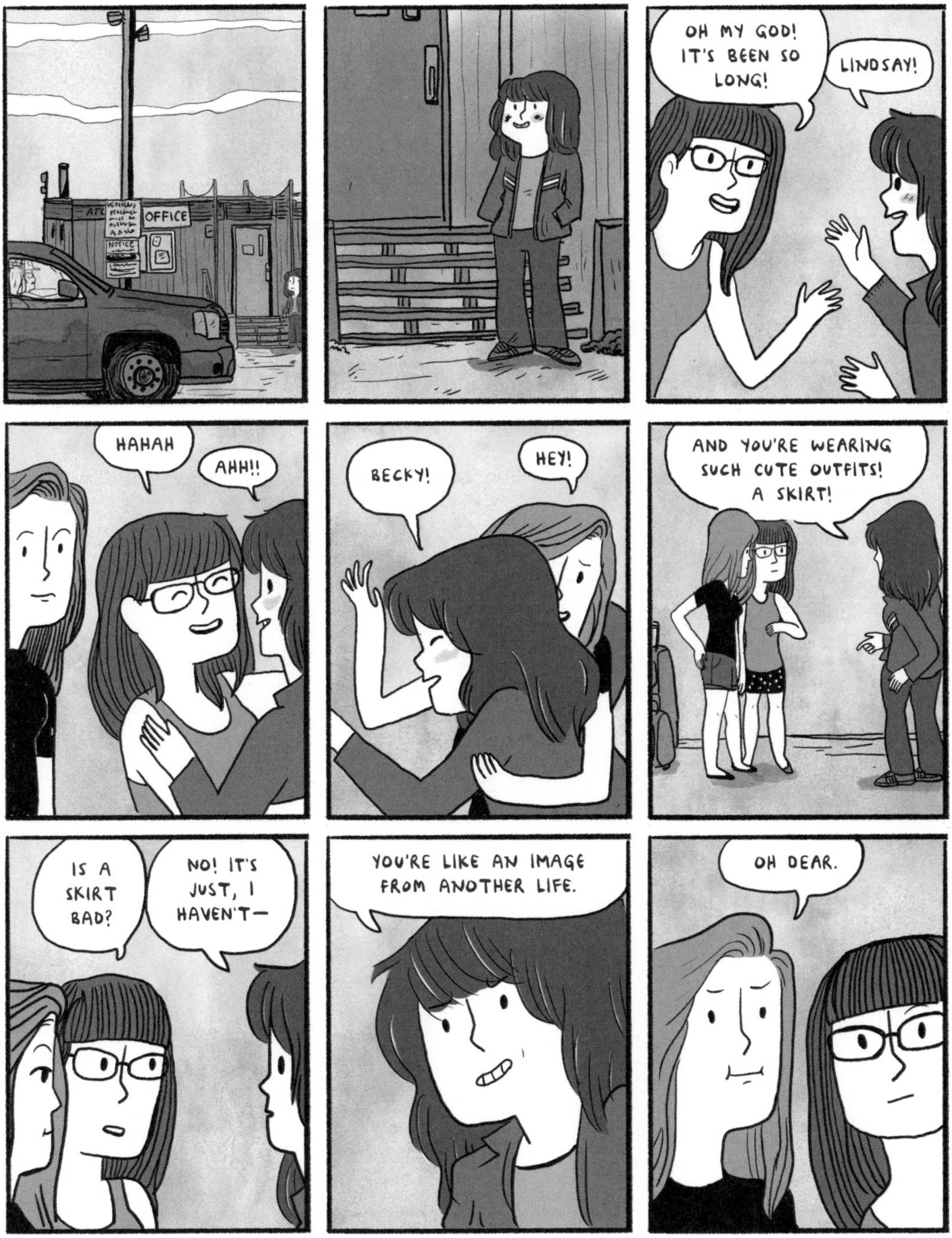
OFFICE
NOTICE
OH MY GOD! IT'S BEEN SO LONG!
LINDSAY!
HAHAH
AHH!!
BECKY!
HEY!
AND YOU'RE WEARING SUCH CUTE OUTFITS! A SKIRT!
IS A SKIRT BAD?
NO! IT'S JUST, I HAVEN'T—
YOU'RE LIKE AN IMAGE FROM ANOTHER LIFE.
OH DEAR.

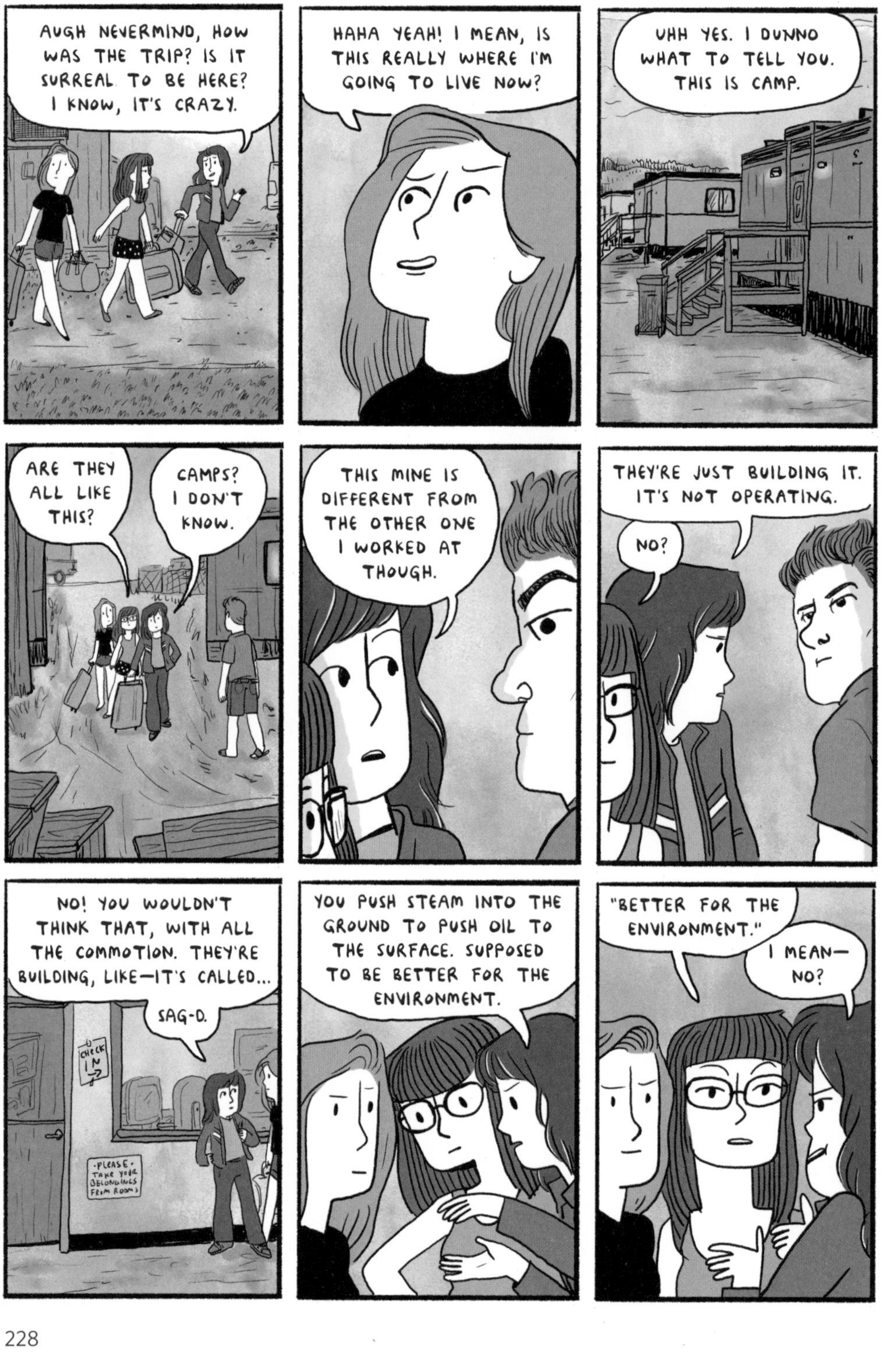
AUGH NEVERMIND, HOW WAS THE TRIP? IS IT SURREAL TO BE HERE? I KNOW, IT'S CRAZY.
HAHA YEAH! I MEAN, IS THIS REALLY WHERE I'M GOING TO LIVE NOW?
UHH YES. I DUNNO WHAT TO TELL YOU. THIS IS CAMP.
ARE THEY ALL LIKE THIS?
CAMPS? I DON'T KNOW.
THIS MINE IS DIFFERENT FROM THE OTHER ONE I WORKED AT THOUGH.
THEY'RE JUST BUILDING IT. IT'S NOT OPERATING.
NO?
NO! YOU WOULDN'T THINK THAT, WITH ALL THE COMMOTION. THEY'RE BUILDING, LIKE—IT'S CALLED...
SAG-D.
CHECK IN
PLEASE TAKE YOUR BELONGINGS FROM ROOMS
YOU PUSH STEAM INTO THE GROUND TO PUSH OIL TO THE SURFACE. SUPPOSED TO BE BETTER FOR THE ENVIRONMENT.
"BETTER FOR THE ENVIRONMENT."
I MEAN— NO?

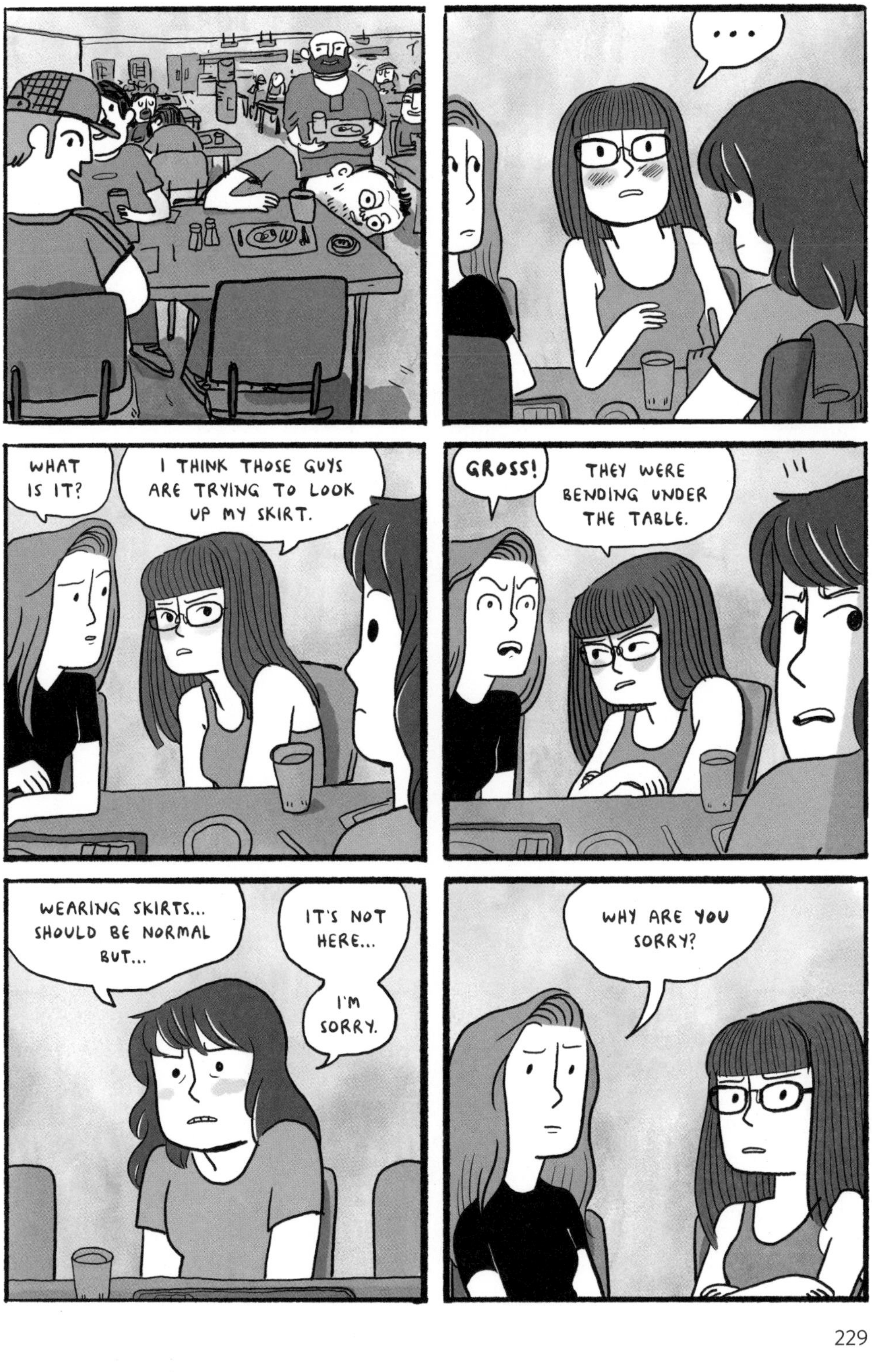
...
WHAT IS IT?
I THINK THOSE GUYS ARE TRYING TO LOOK UP MY SKIRT.
GROSS!
THEY WERE BENDING UNDER THE TABLE.
WEARING SKIRTS... SHOULD BE NORMAL BUT...
IT'S NOT HERE...
I'M SORRY.
WHY ARE YOU SORRY?

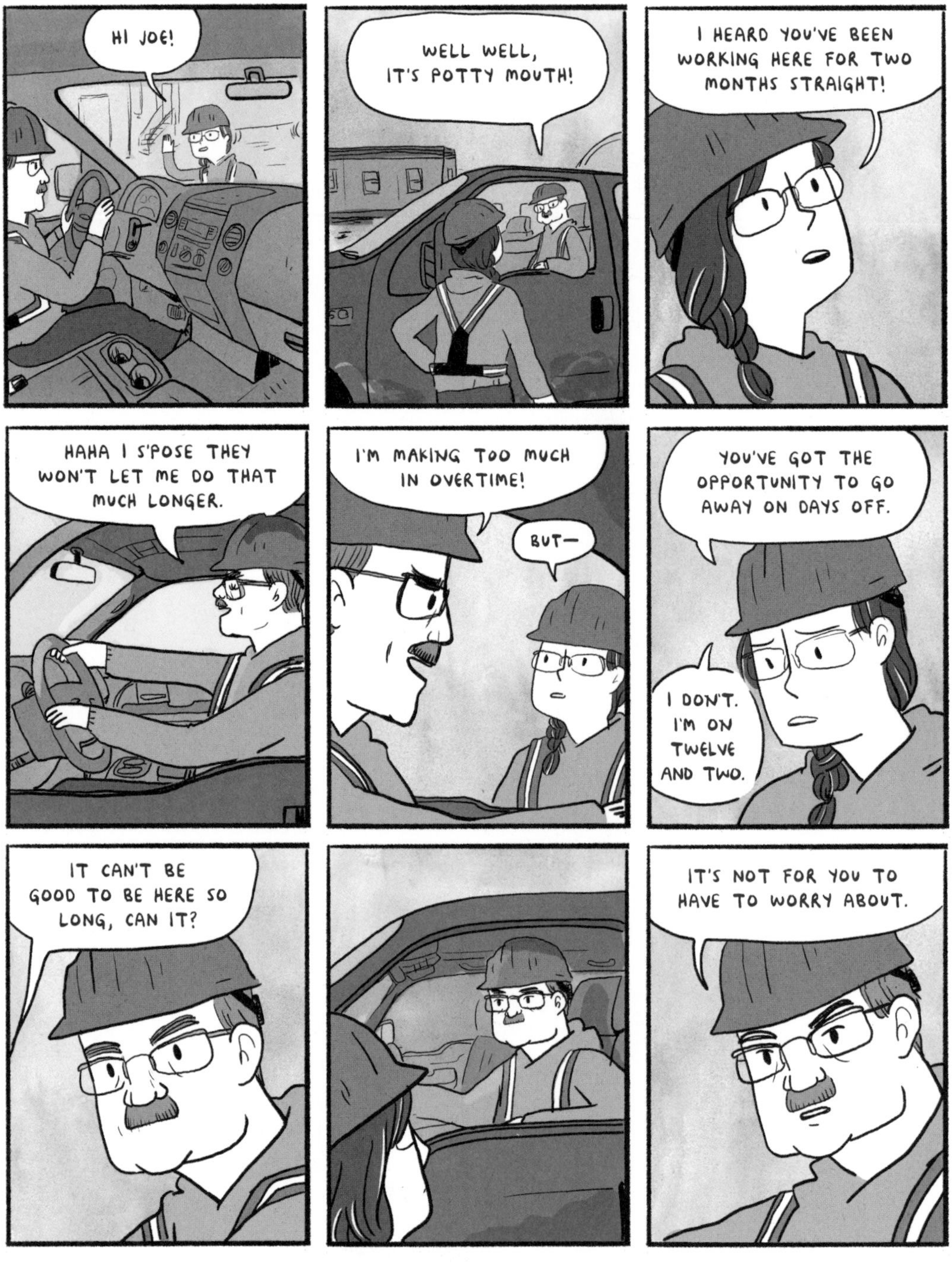
HI JOE!
WELL WELL, IT'S POTTY MOUTH!
I HEARD YOU'VE BEEN WORKING HERE FOR TWO MONTHS STRAIGHT!
HAHA I S'POSE THEY WON'T LET ME DO THAT MUCH LONGER.
I'M MAKING TOO MUCH IN OVERTIME!
BUT—
YOU'VE GOT THE OPPORTUNITY TO GO AWAY ON DAYS OFF.
I DON'T. I'M ON TWELVE AND TWO.
IT CAN'T BE GOOD TO BE HERE SO LONG, CAN IT?
IT'S NOT FOR YOU TO HAVE TO WORRY ABOUT.

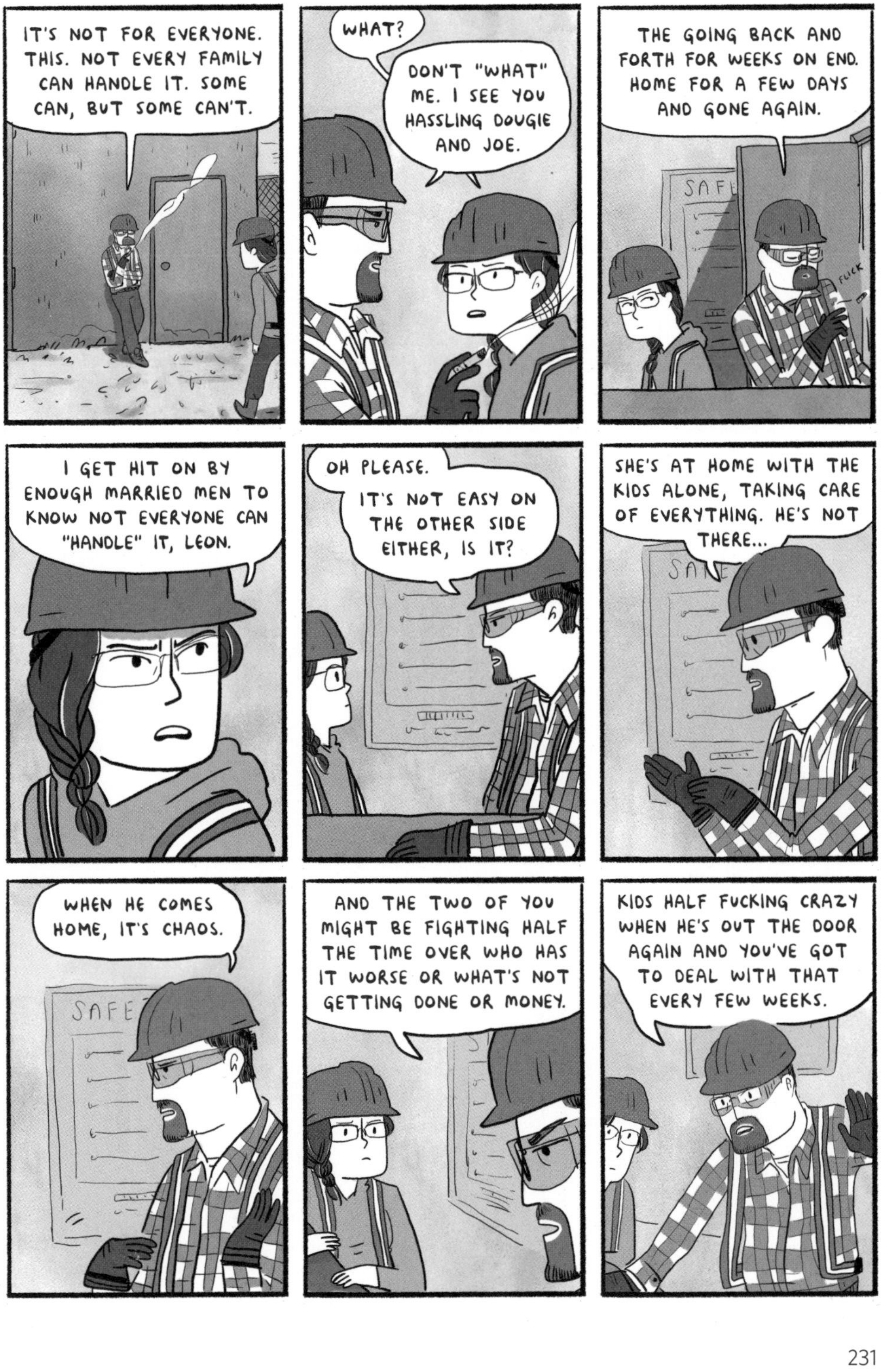
IT'S NOT FOR EVERYONE. THIS. NOT EVERY FAMILY CAN HANDLE IT. SOME CAN, BUT SOME CAN'T.
WHAT?
DON'T "WHAT" ME. I SEE YOU HASSLING DOUGIE AND JOE.
THE GOING BACK AND FORTH FOR WEEKS ON END. HOME FOR A FEW DAYS AND GONE AGAIN.
FLICK
I GET HIT ON BY ENOUGH MARRIED MEN TO KNOW NOT EVERYONE CAN "HANDLE" IT, LEON.
OH PLEASE.
IT'S NOT EASY ON THE OTHER SIDE EITHER, IS IT?
SHE'S AT HOME WITH THE KIDS ALONE, TAKING CARE OF EVERYTHING. HE'S NOT THERE...
WHEN HE COMES HOME, IT'S CHAOS.
AND THE TWO OF YOU MIGHT BE FIGHTING HALF THE TIME OVER WHO HAS IT WORSE OR WHAT'S NOT GETTING DONE OR MONEY.
KIDS HALF FUCKING CRAZY WHEN HE'S OUT THE DOOR AGAIN AND YOU'VE GOT TO DEAL WITH THAT EVERY FEW WEEKS.

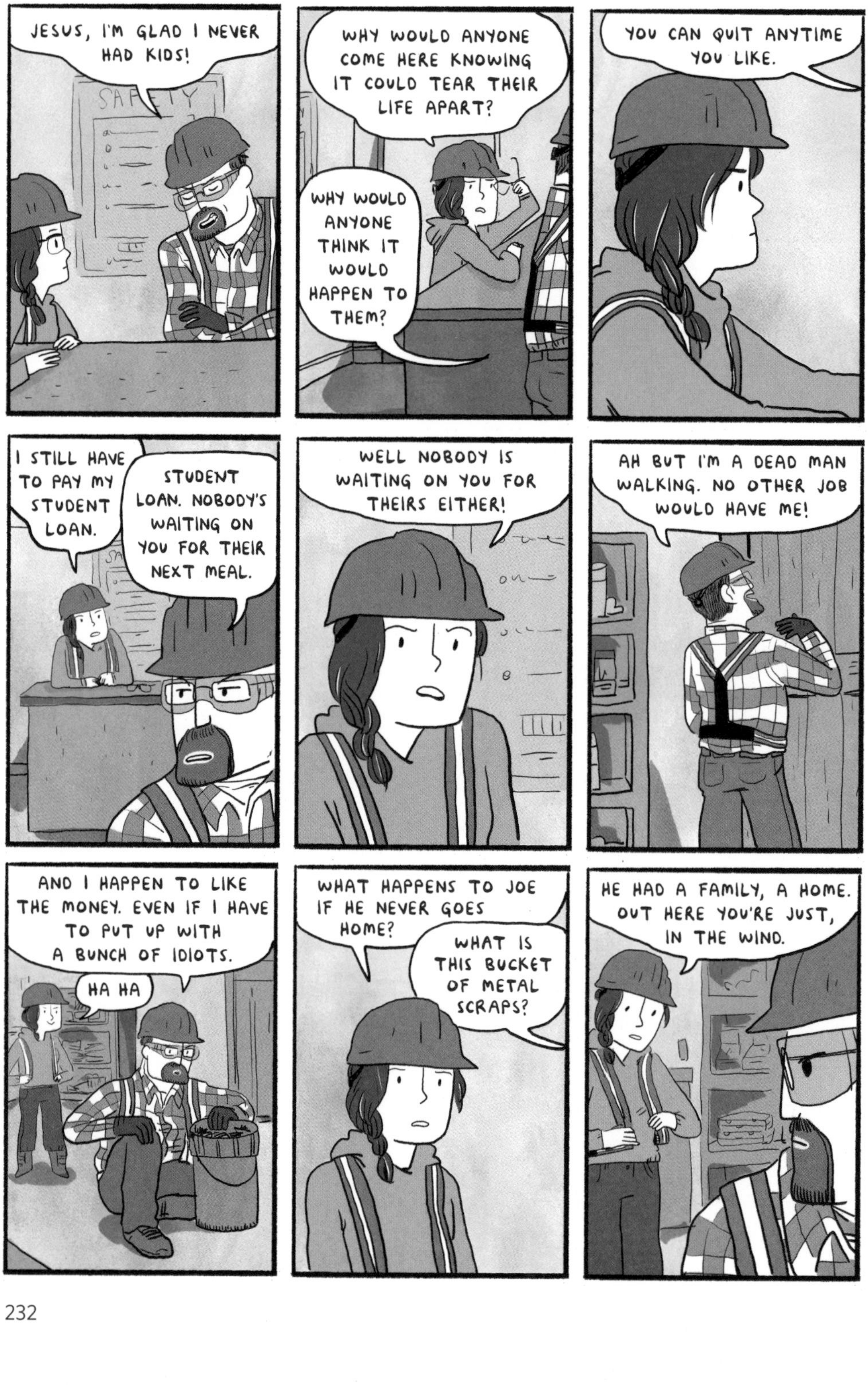
JESUS, I'M GLAD I NEVER HAD KIDS!
SAFETY
WHY WOULD ANYONE COME HERE KNOWING IT COULD TEAR THEIR LIFE APART?
WHY WOULD ANYONE THINK IT WOULD HAPPEN TO THEM?
YOU CAN QUIT ANYTIME YOU LIKE.
I STILL HAVE TO PAY MY STUDENT LOAN.
STUDENT LOAN. NOBODY'S WAITING ON YOU FOR THEIR NEXT MEAL.
WELL NOBODY IS WAITING ON YOU FOR THEIRS EITHER!
AH BUT I'M A DEAD MAN WALKING. NO OTHER JOB WOULD HAVE ME!
AND I HAPPEN TO LIKE THE MONEY. EVEN IF I HAVE TO PUT UP WITH A BUNCH OF IDIOTS.
HA HA
WHAT HAPPENS TO JOE IF HE NEVER GOES HOME?
WHAT IS THIS BUCKET OF METAL SCRAPS?
HE HAD A FAMILY, A HOME. OUT HERE YOU'RE JUST, IN THE WIND.

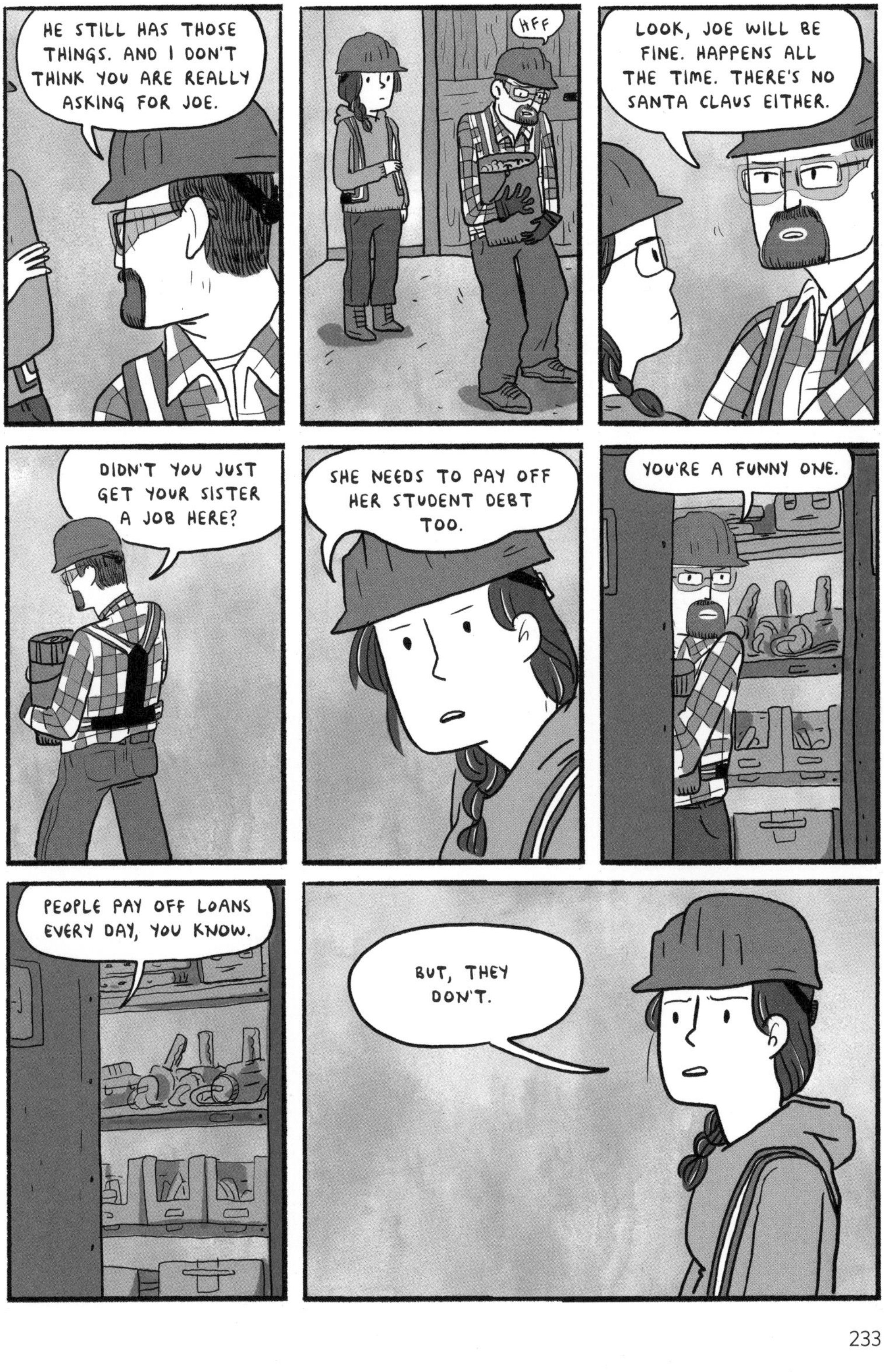
HE STILL HAS THOSE THINGS. AND I DON'T THINK YOU ARE REALLY ASKING FOR JOE.
HFF
LOOK, JOE WILL BE FINE. HAPPENS ALL THE TIME. THERE'S NO SANTA CLAUS EITHER.
DIDN'T YOU JUST GET YOUR SISTER A JOB HERE?
SHE NEEDS TO PAY OFF HER STUDENT DEBT TOO.
YOU'RE A FUNNY ONE.
PEOPLE PAY OFF LOANS EVERY DAY, YOU KNOW.
BUT, THEY DON'T.

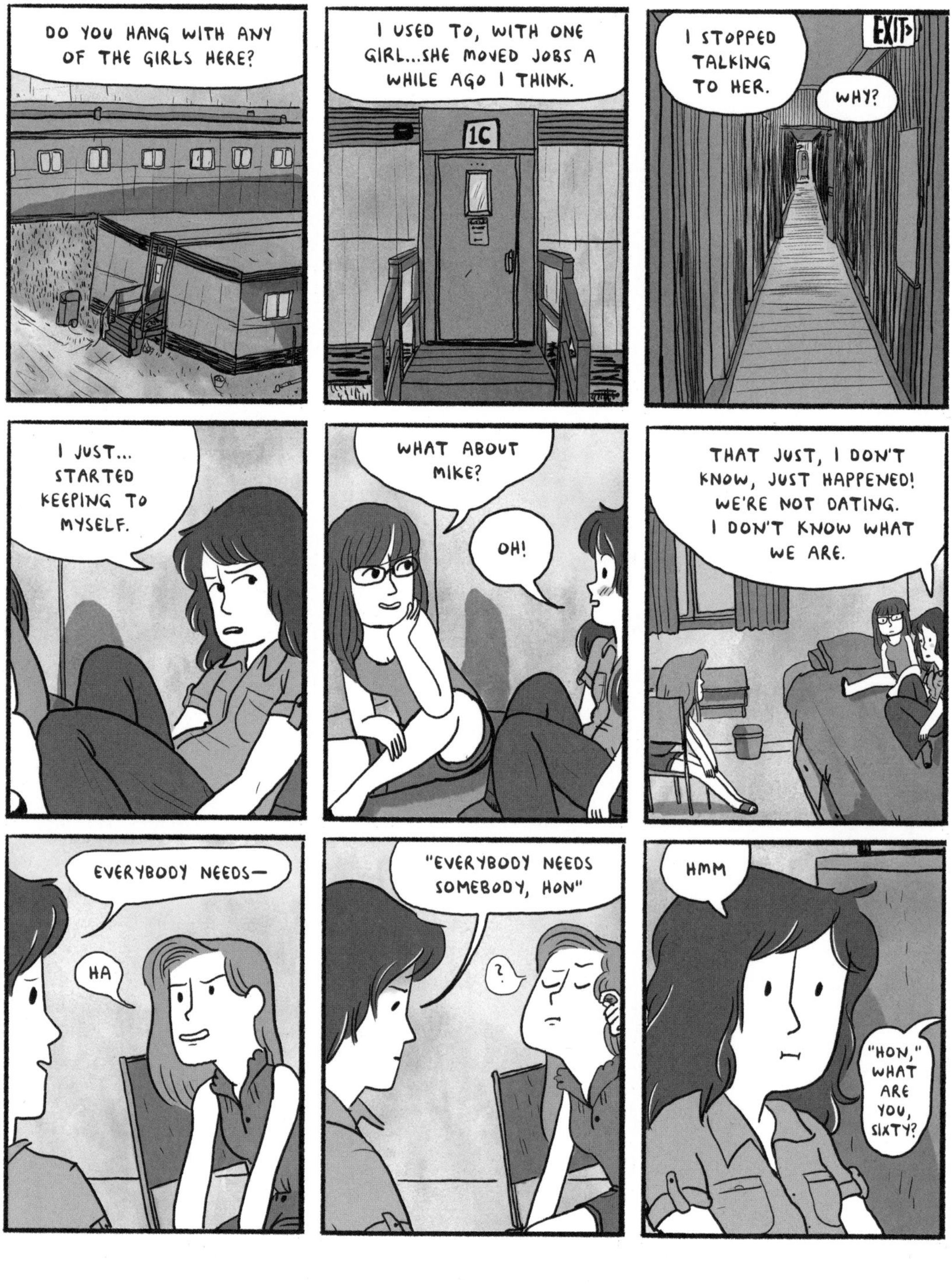
DO YOU HANG WITH ANY OF THE GIRLS HERE?
1C
I USED TO, WITH ONE GIRL...SHE MOVED JOBS A WHILE AGO I THINK.
EXIT
I STOPPED TALKING TO HER.
WHY?
I JUST... STARTED KEEPING TO MYSELF.
WHAT ABOUT MIKE?
OH!
THAT JUST, I DON'T KNOW, JUST HAPPENED! WE'RE NOT DATING. I DON'T KNOW WHAT WE ARE.
EVERYBODY NEEDS—
HA
"EVERYBODY NEEDS SOMEBODY, HON"
?
HMM
"HON," WHAT ARE YOU, SIXTY?

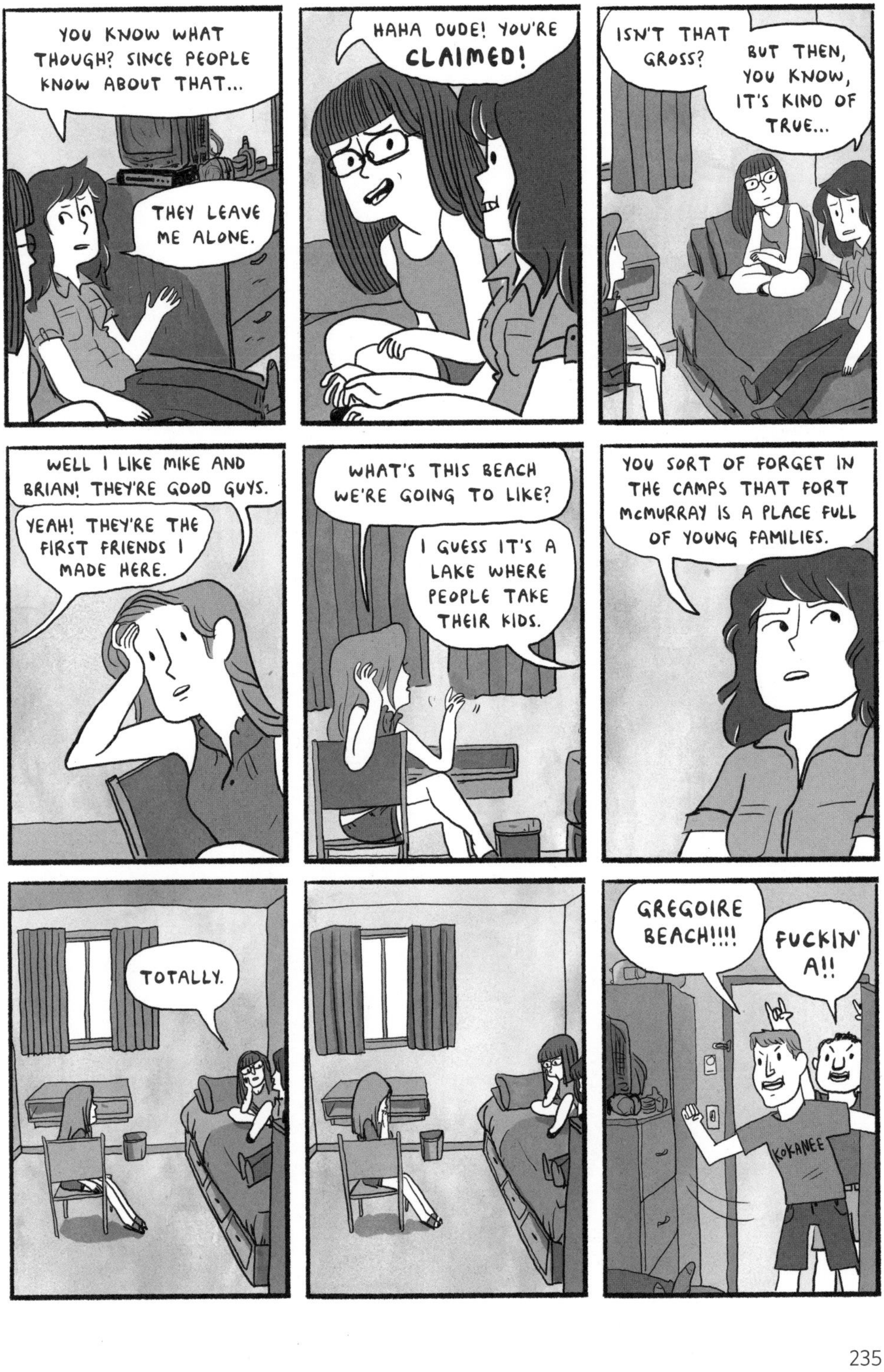
YOU KNOW WHAT THOUGH? SINCE PEOPLE KNOW ABOUT THAT...
THEY LEAVE ME ALONE.
HAHA DUDE! YOU'RE CLAIMED!
ISN'T THAT GROSS?
BUT THEN, YOU KNOW, IT'S KIND OF TRUE...
WELL I LIKE MIKE AND BRIAN! THEY'RE GOOD GUYS.
YEAH! THEY'RE THE FIRST FRIENDS I MADE HERE.
WHAT'S THIS BEACH WE'RE GOING TO LIKE?
I GUESS IT'S A LAKE WHERE PEOPLE TAKE THEIR KIDS.
YOU SORT OF FORGET IN THE CAMPS THAT FORT McMURRAY IS A PLACE FULL OF YOUNG FAMILIES.
TOTALLY.
GREGOIRE BEACH!!!!
FUCKIN' A!!
KOKANEE

♫ tryin to catch me ridin dirty
tryin to catch me ridin dirty ♫

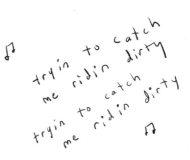

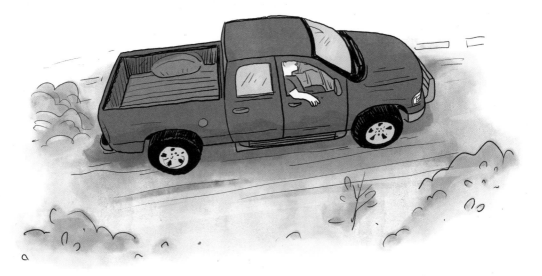

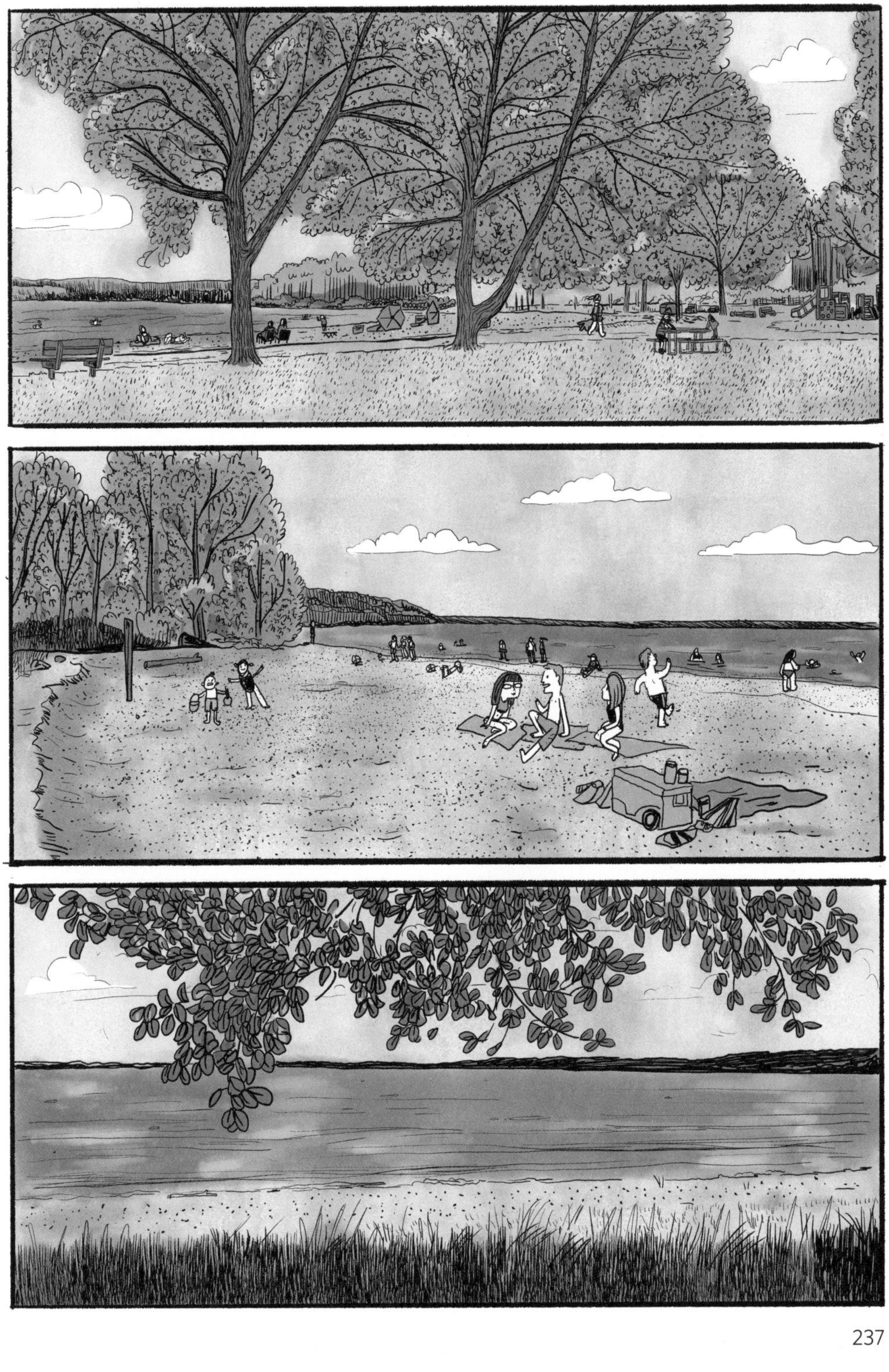

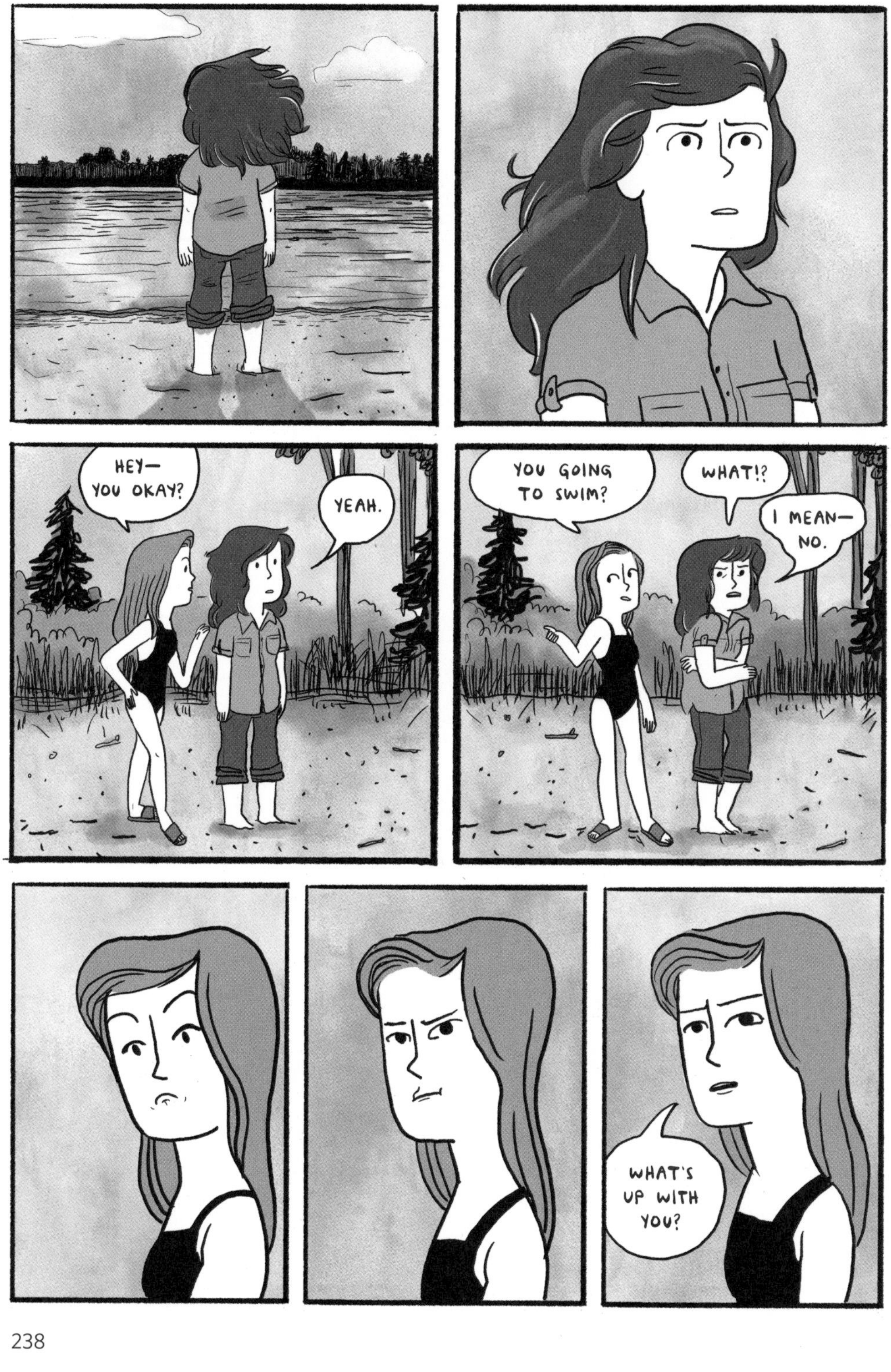
HEY— YOU OKAY?
YEAH.
YOU GOING TO SWIM?
WHAT!?
I MEAN— NO.
WHAT'S UP WITH YOU?

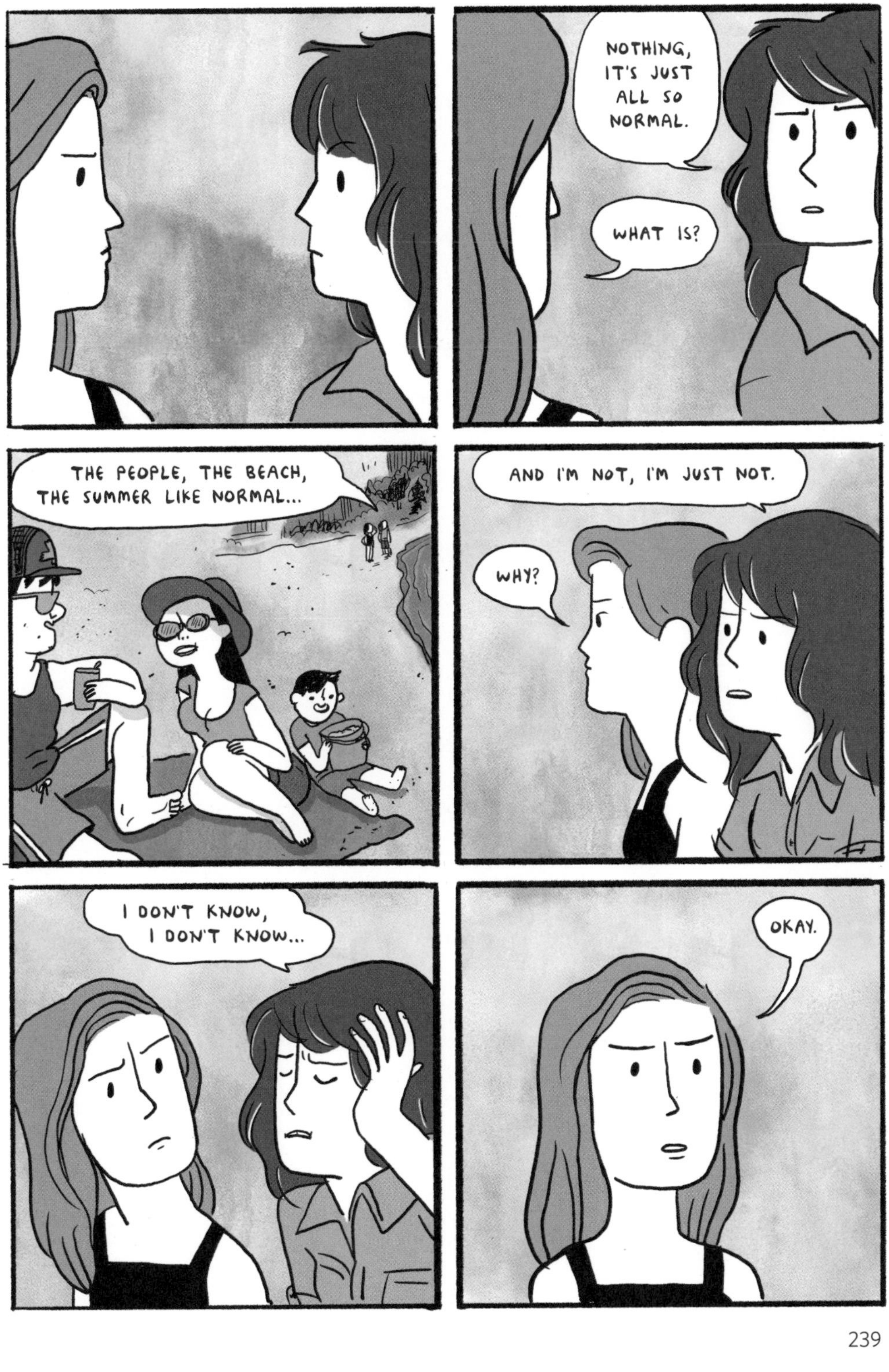
NOTHING, IT'S JUST ALL SO NORMAL.
WHAT IS?
THE PEOPLE, THE BEACH, THE SUMMER LIKE NORMAL...
AND I'M NOT, I'M JUST NOT.
WHY?
I DON'T KNOW, I DON'T KNOW...
OKAY.

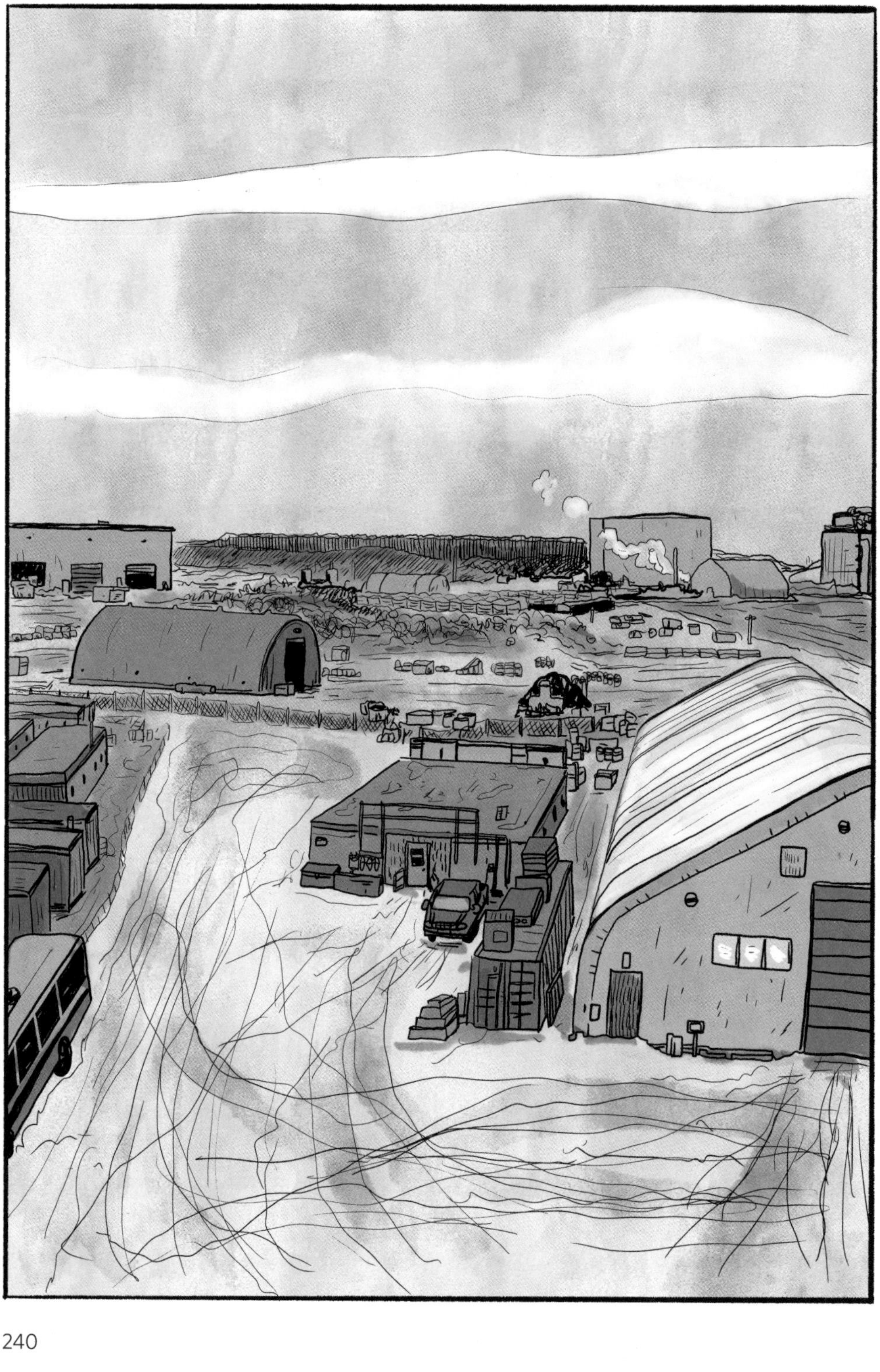

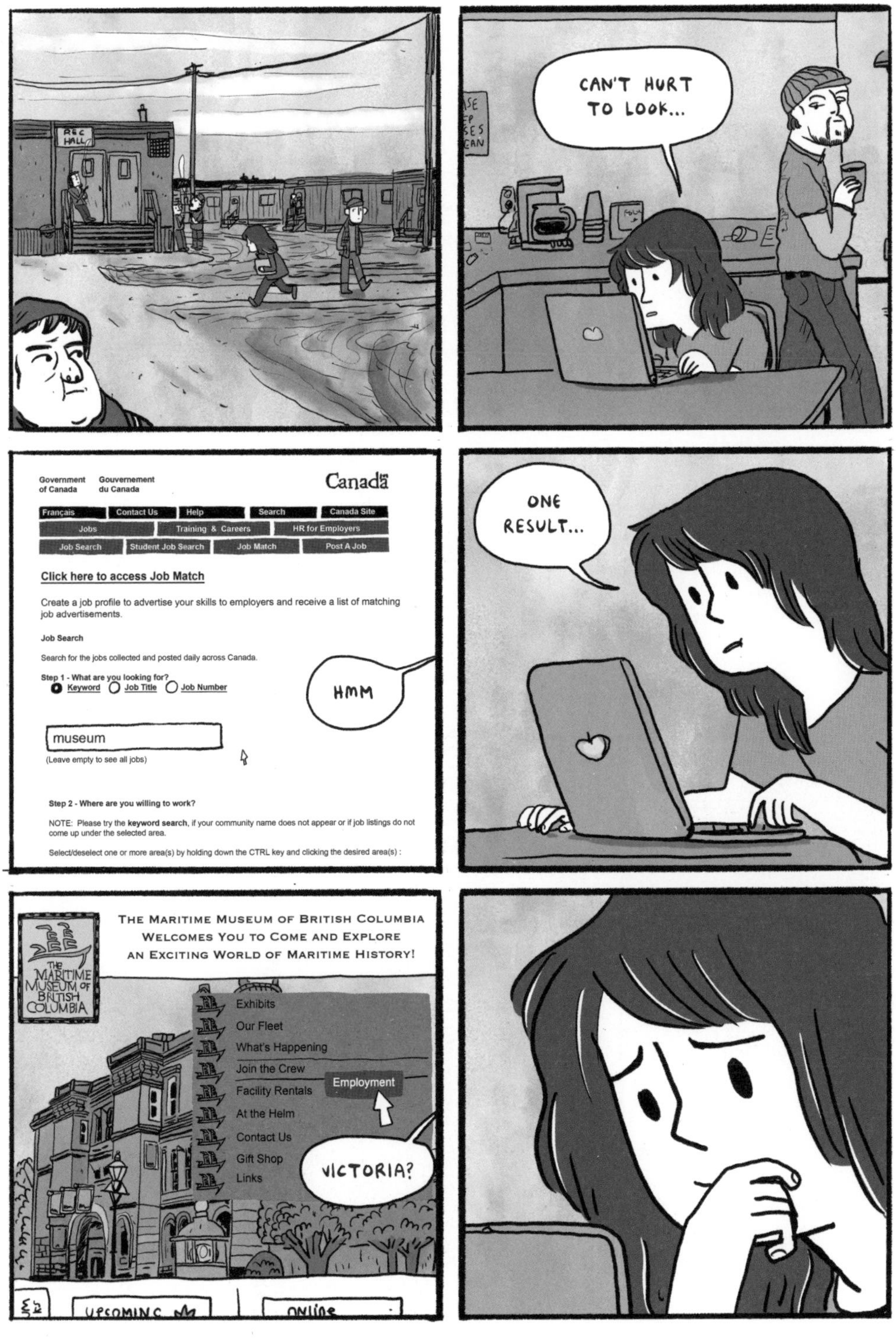
REC HALL
CAN'T HURT TO LOOK...
Government of Canada
Gouvernement du Canada
Canada
Français
Contact Us
Help
Search
Canada Site
Jobs
Training & Careers
HR for Employers
Job Search
Student Job Search
Job Match
Post A Job
Click here to access Job Match
Create a job profile to advertise your skills to employers and receive a list of matching job advertisements.
Job Search
Search for the jobs collected and posted daily across Canada.
Step 1 - What are you looking for?
Keyword
Job Title
Job Number
museum
(Leave empty to see all jobs)
Step 2 - Where are you willing to work?
NOTE: Please try the keyword search, if your community name does not appear or if job listings do not come up under the selected area.
Select/deselect one or more area(s) by holding down the CTRL key and clicking the desired area(s) :
HMM
ONE RESULT...
THE MARITIME MUSEUM OF BRITISH COLUMBIA WELCOMES YOU TO COME AND EXPLORE AN EXCITING WORLD OF MARITIME HISTORY!
THE MARITIME MUSEUM OF BRITISH COLUMBIA
Exhibits
Our Fleet
What's Happening
Join the Crew
Facility Rentals
Employment
At the Helm
Contact Us
Gift Shop
Links
VICTORIA?

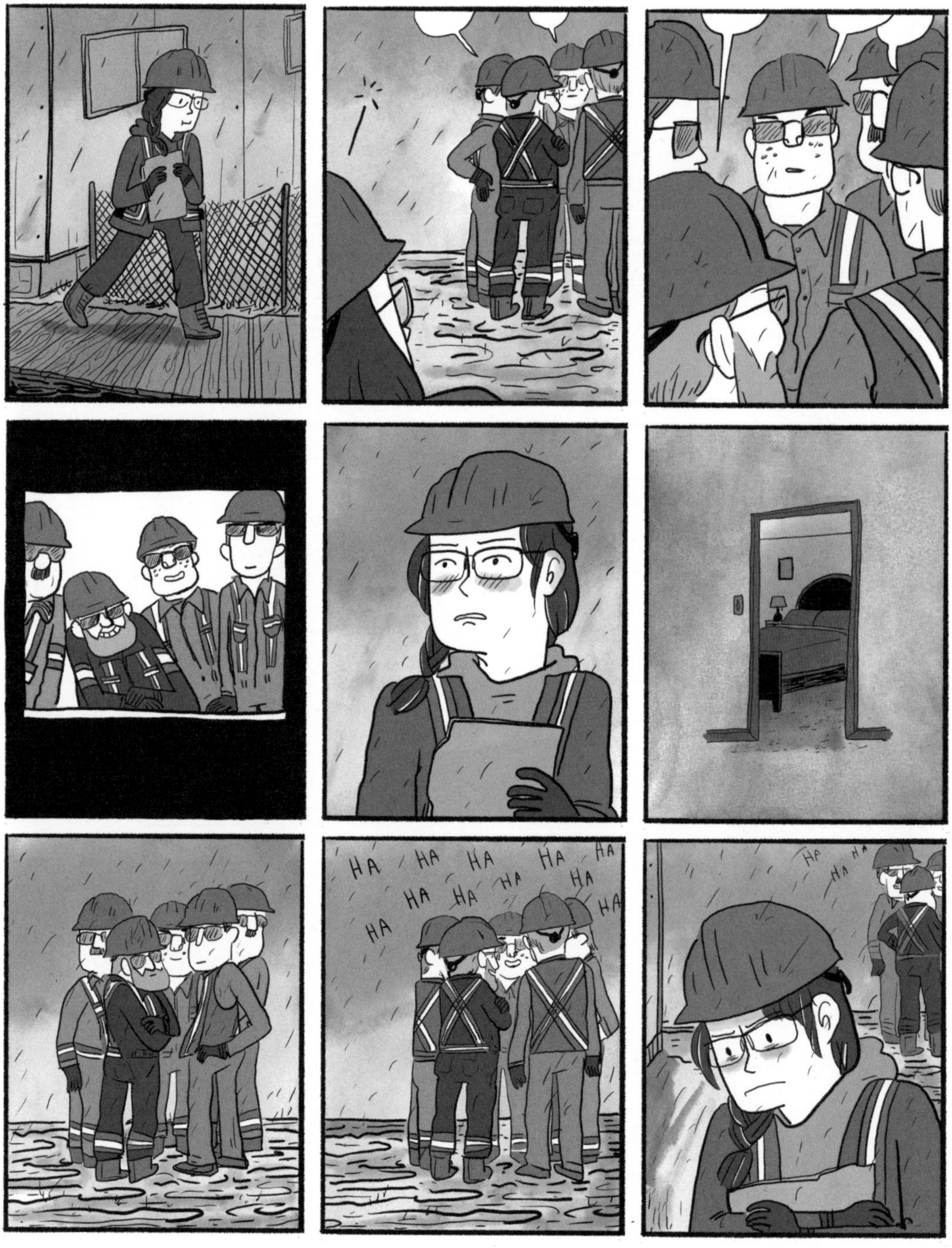
HA HA HA HA HA
HA HA HA HA
HA HA HA
HA HA HA HA

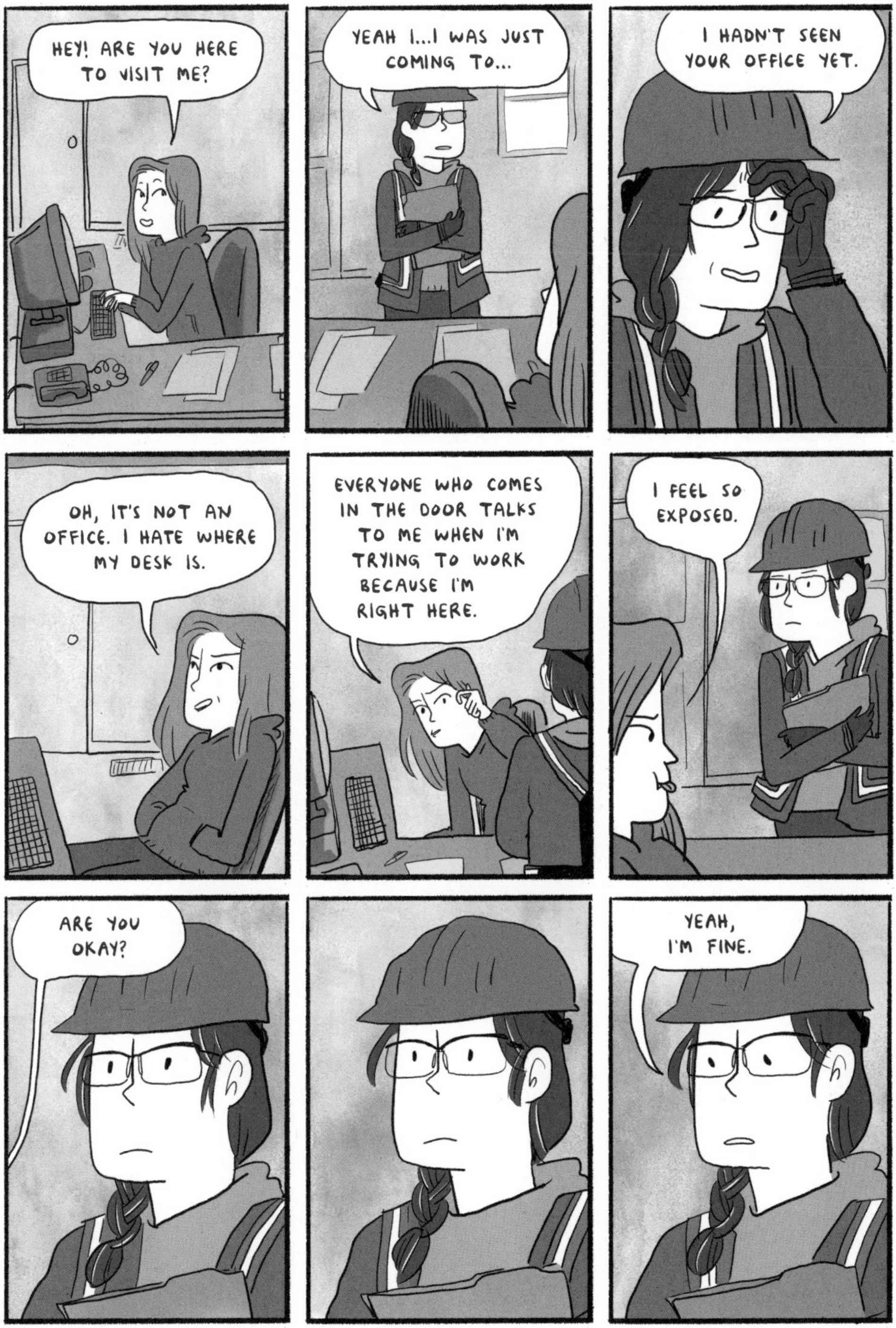
HEY! ARE YOU HERE TO VISIT ME?
YEAH I...I WAS JUST COMING TO...
I HADN'T SEEN YOUR OFFICE YET.
OH, IT'S NOT AN OFFICE. I HATE WHERE MY DESK IS.
EVERYONE WHO COMES IN THE DOOR TALKS TO ME WHEN I'M TRYING TO WORK BECAUSE I'M RIGHT HERE.
I FEEL SO EXPOSED.
ARE YOU OKAY?
YEAH, I'M FINE.

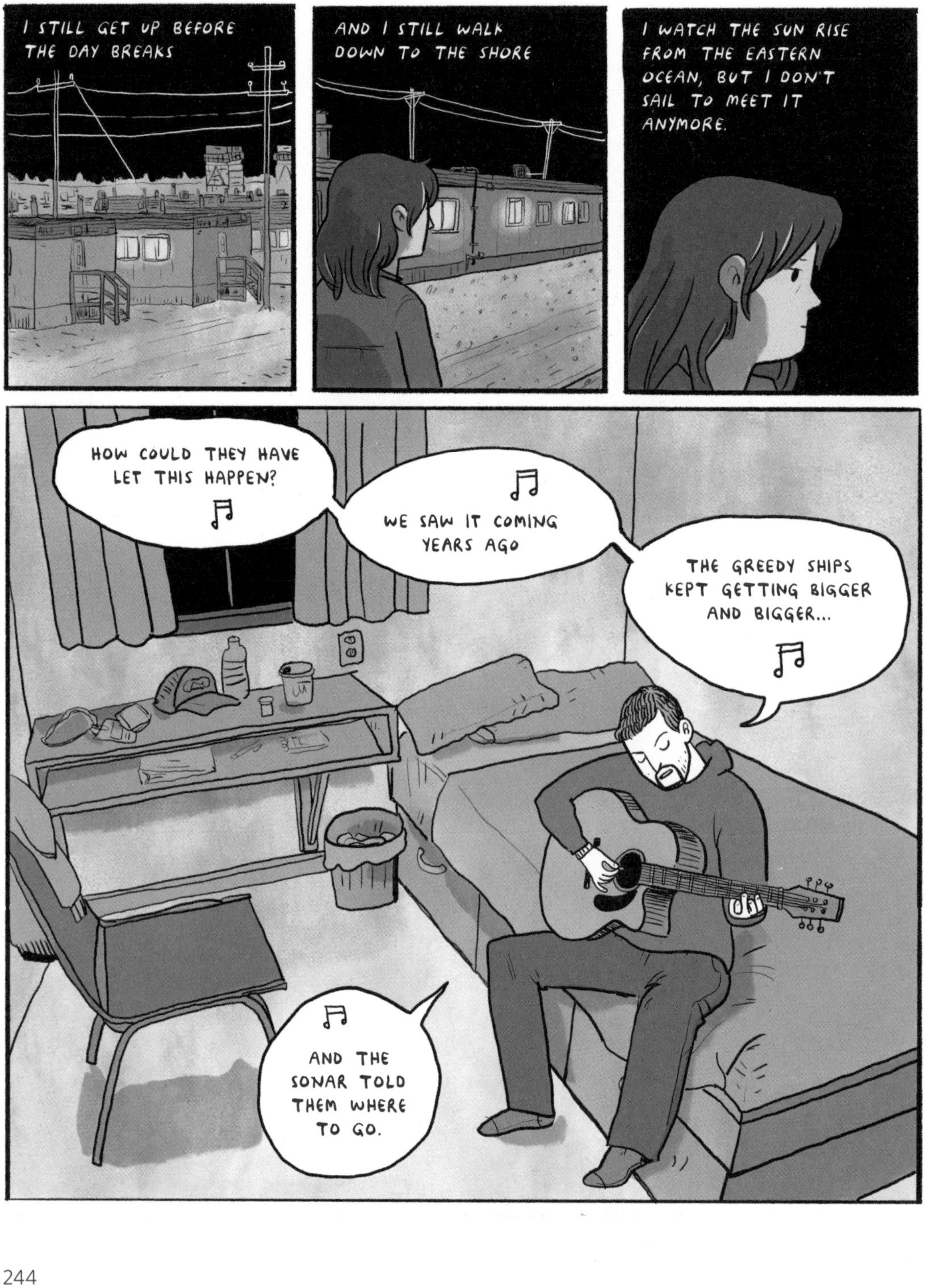
I STILL GET UP BEFORE THE DAY BREAKS
AND I STILL WALK DOWN TO THE SHORE
I WATCH THE SUN RISE FROM THE EASTERN OCEAN, BUT I DON'T SAIL TO MEET IT ANYMORE.
HOW COULD THEY HAVE LET THIS HAPPEN? ♫
♫ WE SAW IT COMING YEARS AGO
THE GREEDY SHIPS KEPT GETTING BIGGER AND BIGGER... ♫
♫ AND THE SONAR TOLD THEM WHERE TO GO.

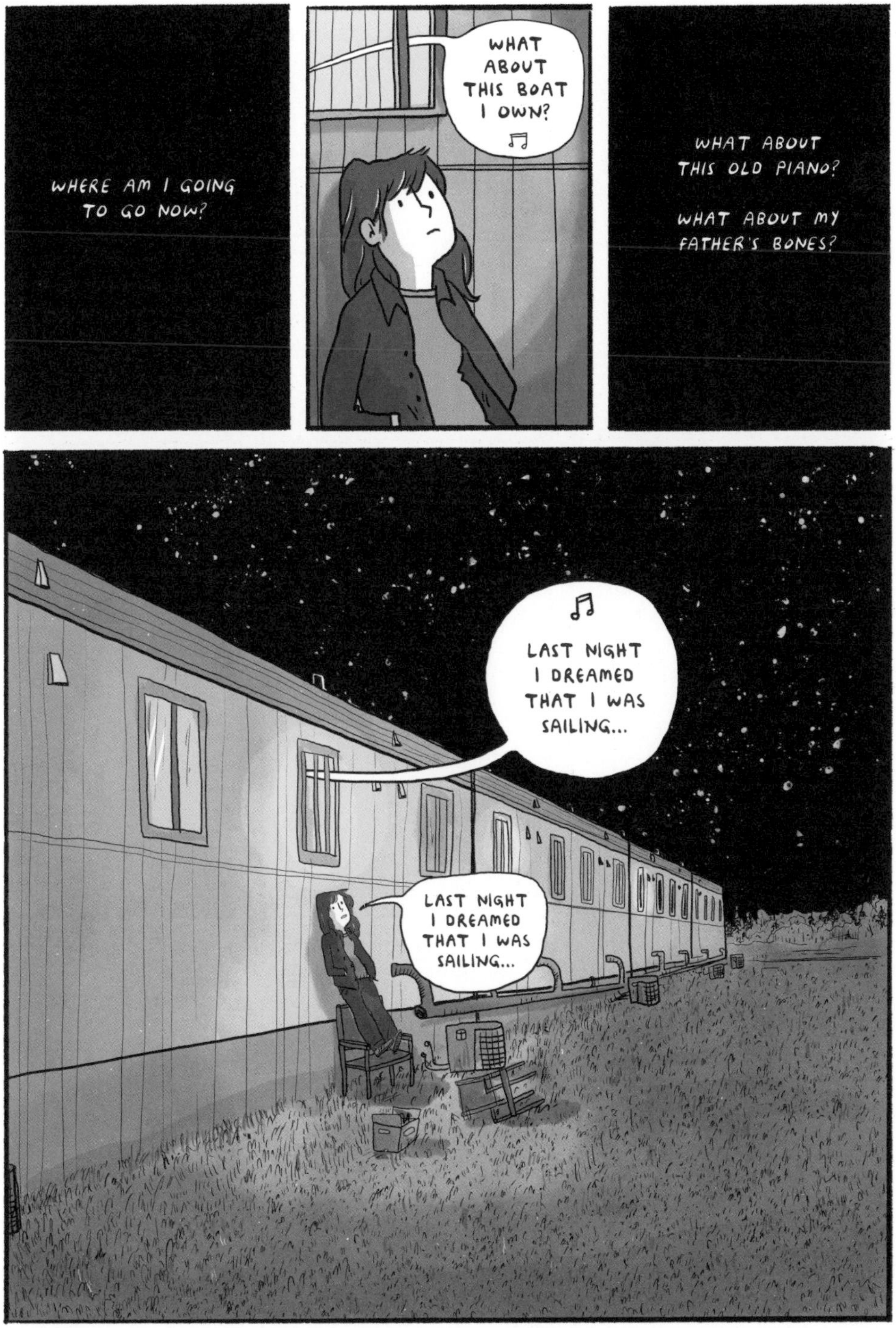
WHERE AM I GOING TO GO NOW?
WHAT ABOUT THIS BOAT I OWN? ♫
WHAT ABOUT THIS OLD PIANO?
WHAT ABOUT MY FATHER'S BONES?
♫ LAST NIGHT I DREAMED THAT I WAS SAILING...
LAST NIGHT I DREAMED THAT I WAS SAILING...

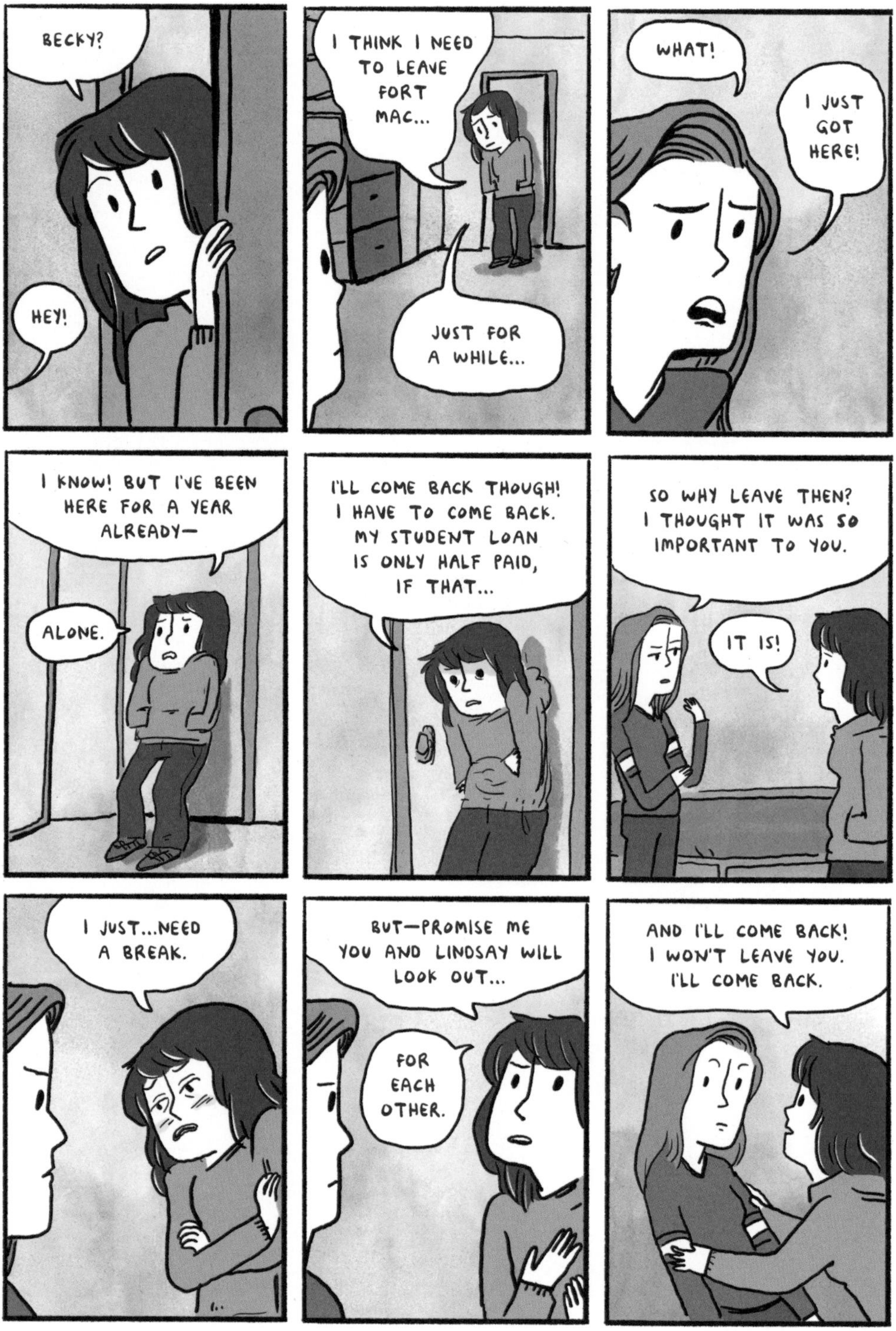
BECKY?
HEY!
I THINK I NEED TO LEAVE FORT MAC...
JUST FOR A WHILE...
WHAT!
I JUST GOT HERE!
I KNOW! BUT I'VE BEEN HERE FOR A YEAR ALREADY—
ALONE.
I'LL COME BACK THOUGH! I HAVE TO COME BACK. MY STUDENT LOAN IS ONLY HALF PAID, IF THAT...
SO WHY LEAVE THEN? I THOUGHT IT WAS SO IMPORTANT TO YOU.
IT IS!
I JUST...NEED A BREAK.
BUT—PROMISE ME YOU AND LINDSAY WILL LOOK OUT...
FOR EACH OTHER.
AND I'LL COME BACK! I WON'T LEAVE YOU. I'LL COME BACK.

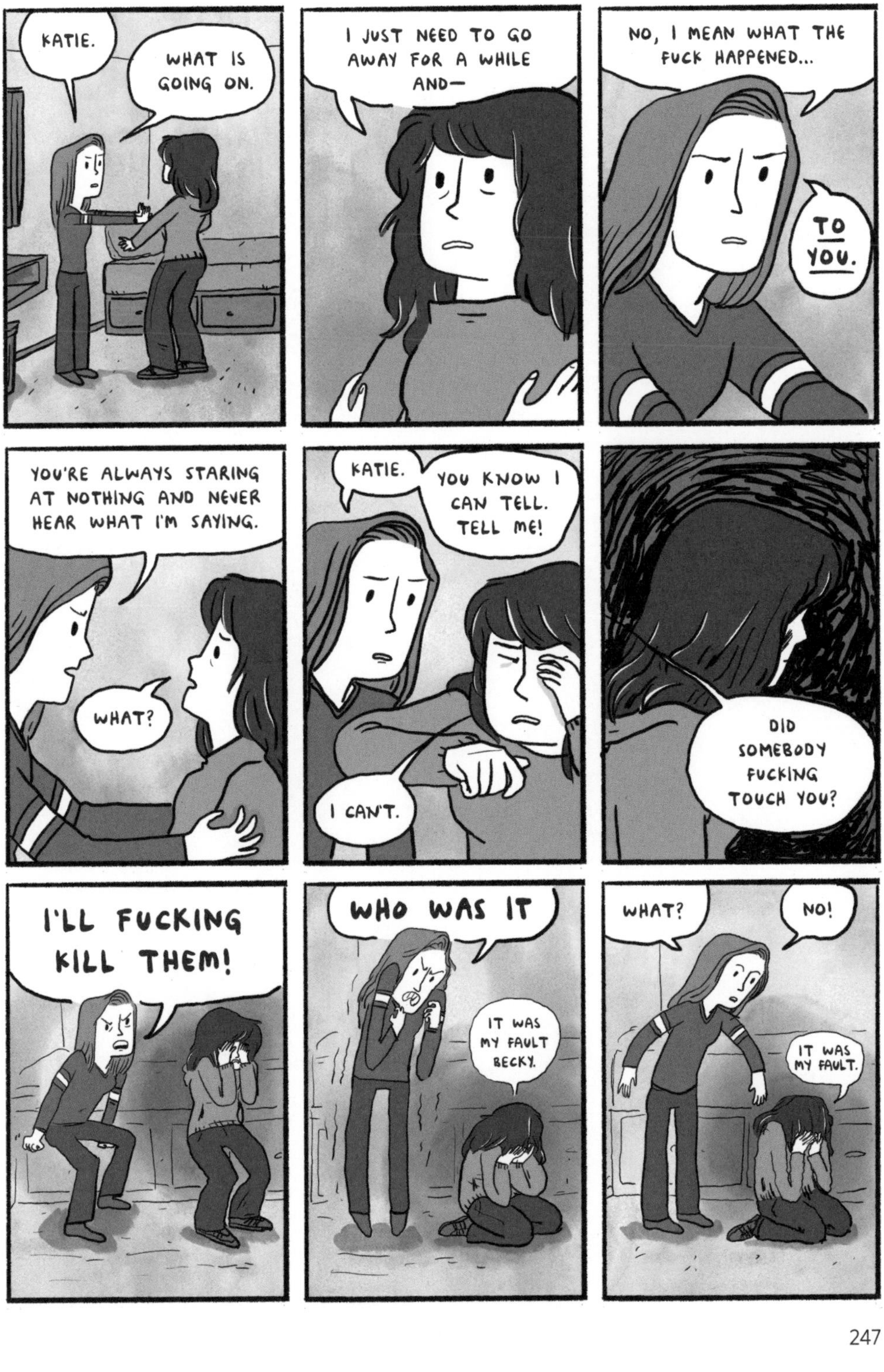
KATIE.
WHAT IS GOING ON.
I JUST NEED TO GO AWAY FOR A WHILE AND—
NO, I MEAN WHAT THE FUCK HAPPENED...
TO YOU.
YOU'RE ALWAYS STARING AT NOTHING AND NEVER HEAR WHAT I'M SAYING.
WHAT?
KATIE.
YOU KNOW I CAN TELL. TELL ME!
I CAN'T.
DID SOMEBODY FUCKING TOUCH YOU?
I'LL FUCKING KILL THEM!
WHO WAS IT
IT WAS MY FAULT BECKY.
WHAT?
NO!
IT WAS MY FAULT.

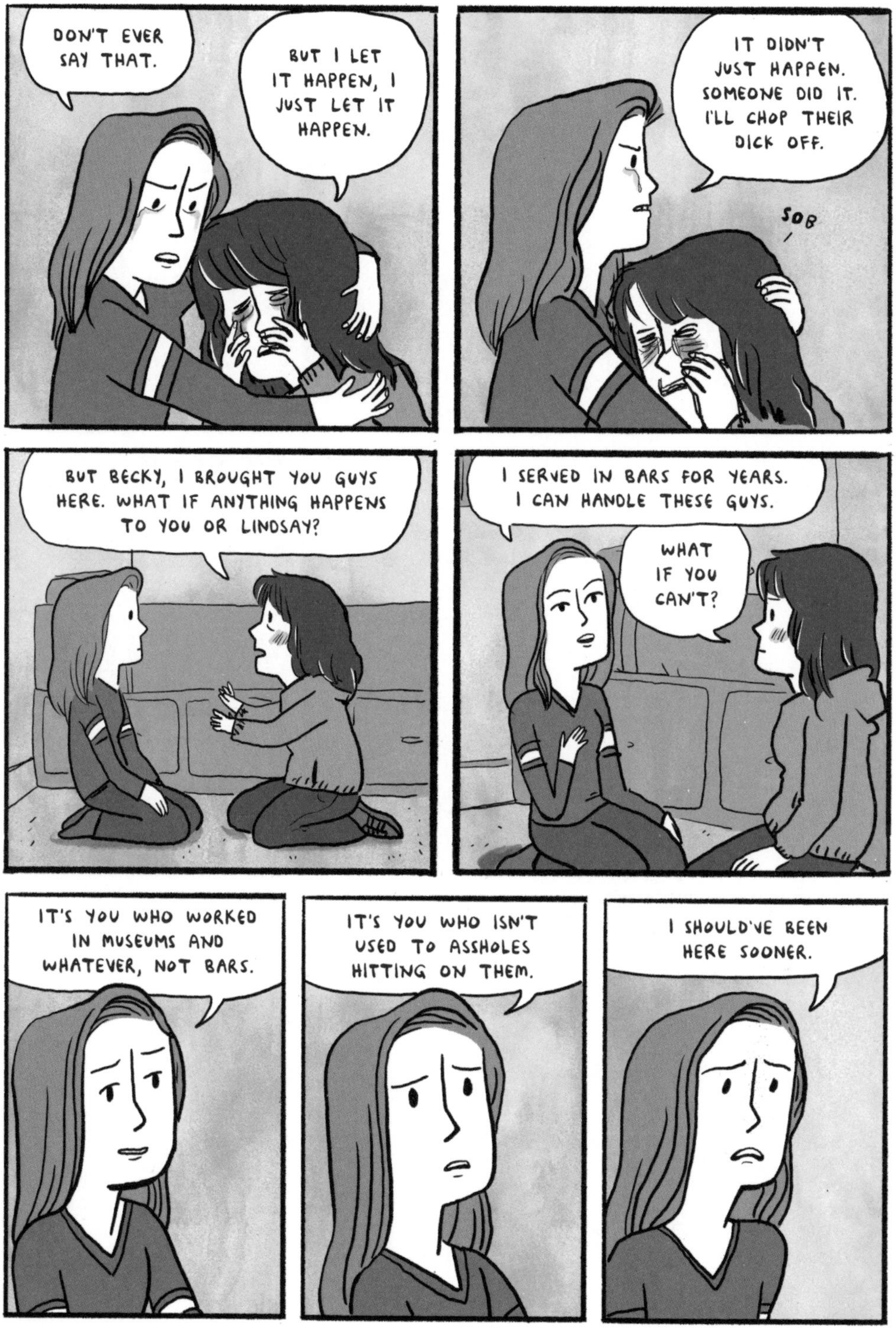
DON'T EVER SAY THAT.
BUT I LET IT HAPPEN, I JUST LET IT HAPPEN.
IT DIDN'T JUST HAPPEN. SOMEONE DID IT. I'LL CHOP THEIR DICK OFF.
SOB
BUT BECKY, I BROUGHT YOU GUYS HERE. WHAT IF ANYTHING HAPPENS TO YOU OR LINDSAY?
I SERVED IN BARS FOR YEARS. I CAN HANDLE THESE GUYS.
WHAT IF YOU CAN'T?
IT'S YOU WHO WORKED IN MUSEUMS AND WHATEVER, NOT BARS.
IT'S YOU WHO ISN'T USED TO ASSHOLES HITTING ON THEM.
I SHOULD'VE BEEN HERE SOONER.

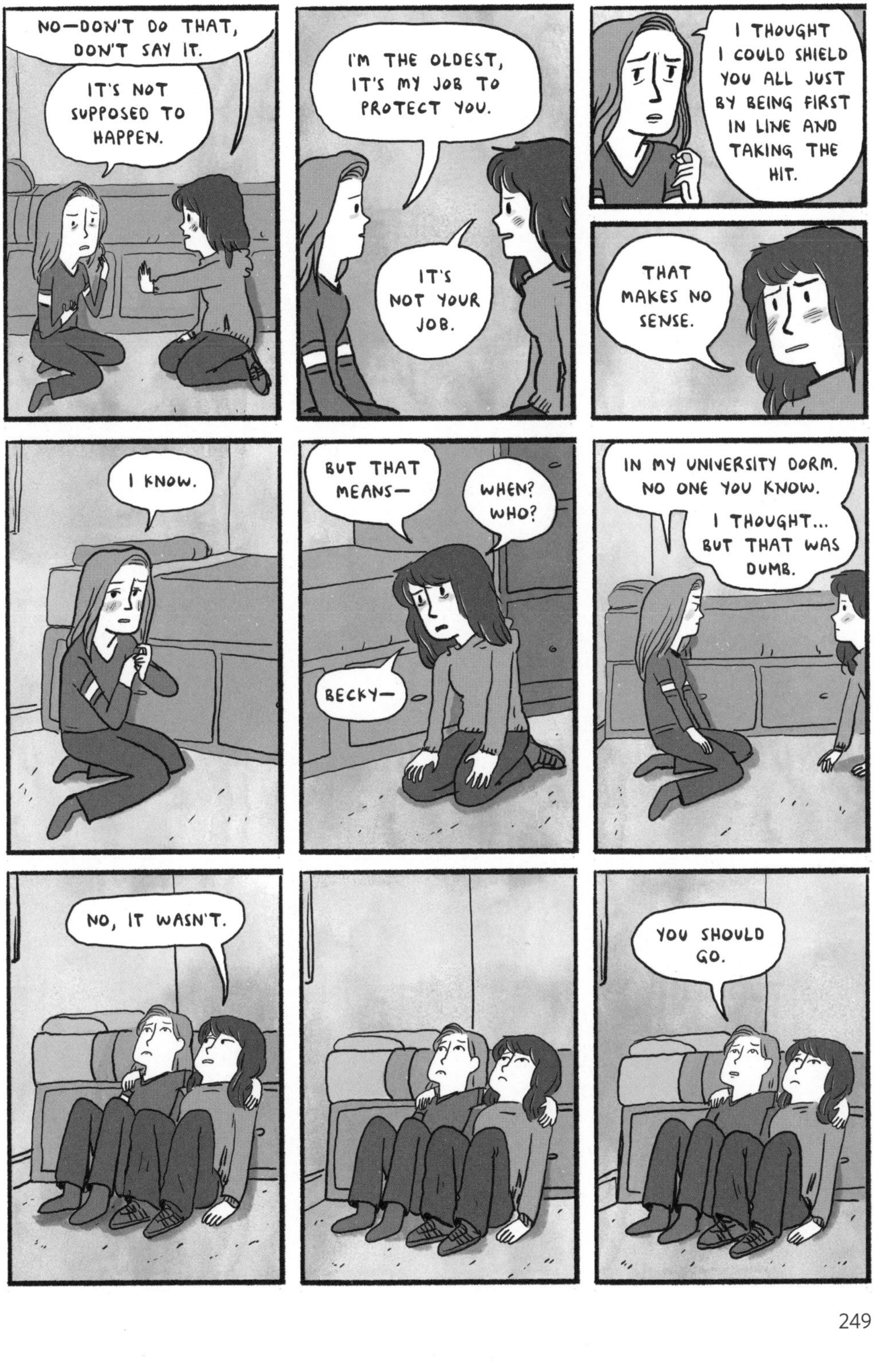
NO—DON'T DO THAT, DON'T SAY IT.
IT'S NOT SUPPOSED TO HAPPEN.
I'M THE OLDEST, IT'S MY JOB TO PROTECT YOU.
IT'S NOT YOUR JOB.
I THOUGHT I COULD SHIELD YOU ALL JUST BY BEING FIRST IN LINE AND TAKING THE HIT.
THAT MAKES NO SENSE.
I KNOW.
BUT THAT MEANS—
WHEN? WHO?
BECKY—
IN MY UNIVERSITY DORM. NO ONE YOU KNOW.
I THOUGHT... BUT THAT WAS DUMB.
NO, IT WASN'T.
YOU SHOULD GO.

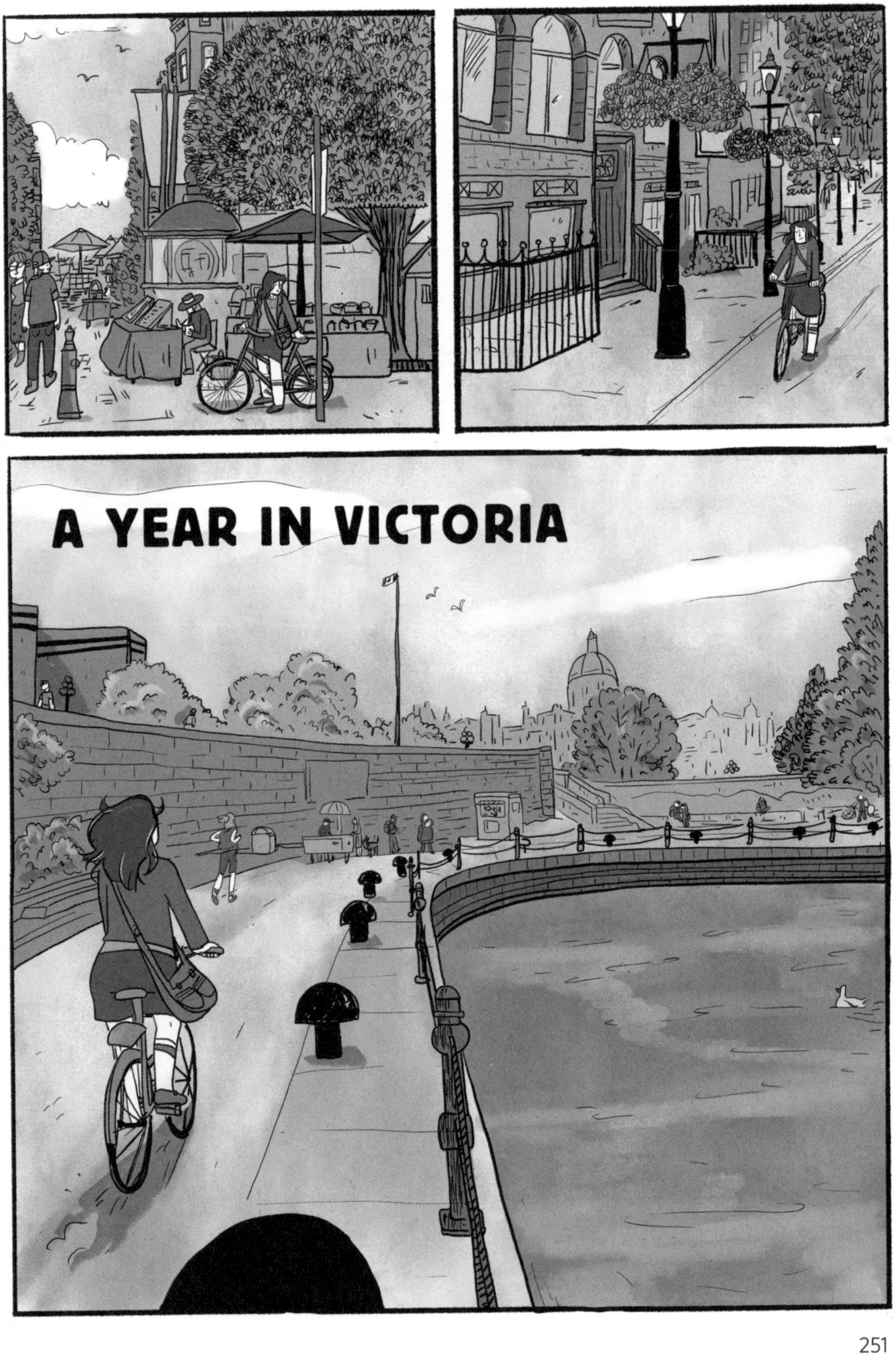
A YEAR IN VICTORIA

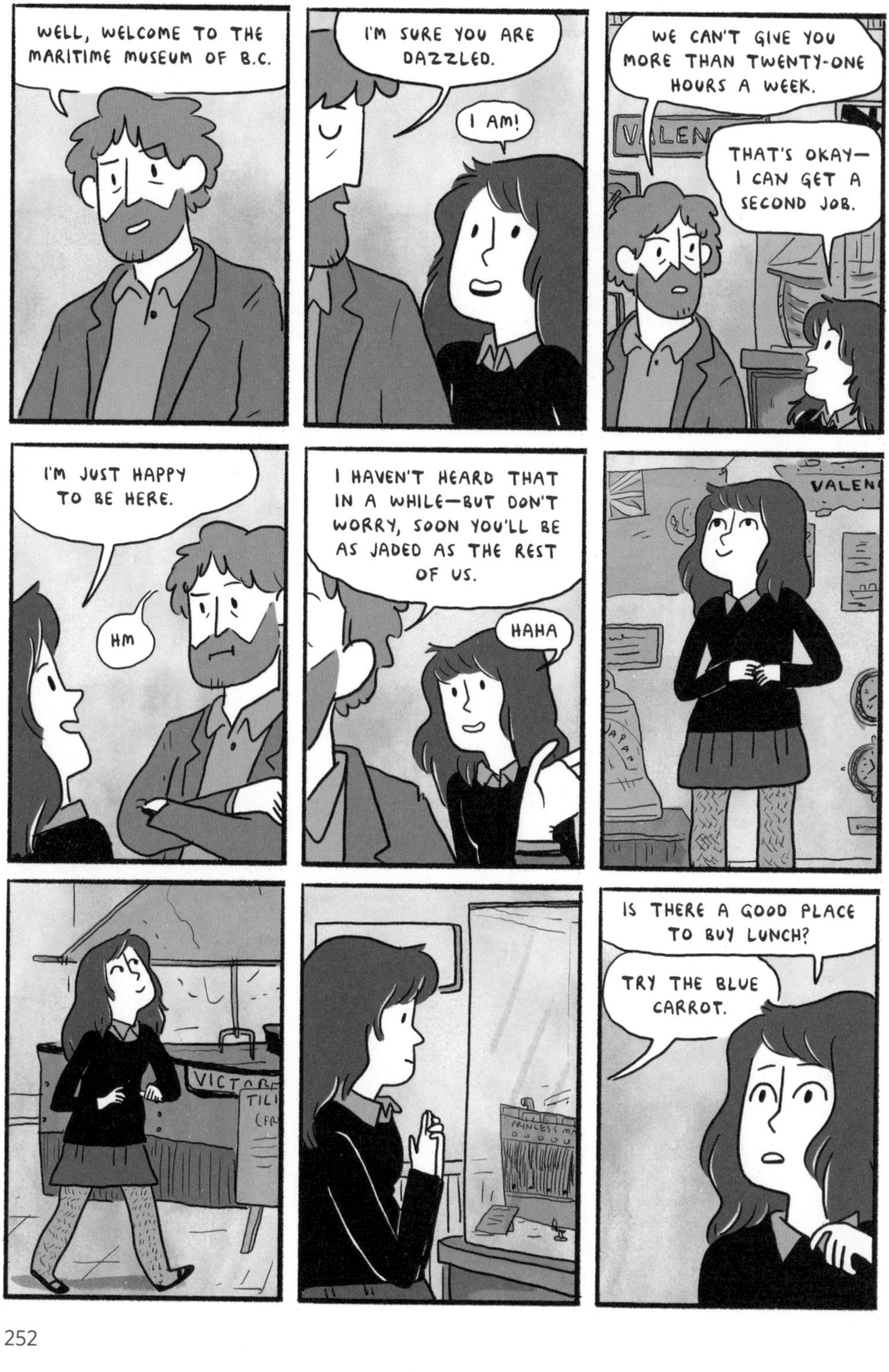
WELL, WELCOME TO THE MARITIME MUSEUM OF B.C.
I'M SURE YOU ARE DAZZLED.
I AM!
WE CAN'T GIVE YOU MORE THAN TWENTY-ONE HOURS A WEEK.
THAT'S OKAY— I CAN GET A SECOND JOB.
I'M JUST HAPPY TO BE HERE.
HM
I HAVEN'T HEARD THAT IN A WHILE—BUT DON'T WORRY, SOON YOU'LL BE AS JADED AS THE REST OF US.
HAHA
IS THERE A GOOD PLACE TO BUY LUNCH?
TRY THE BLUE CARROT.

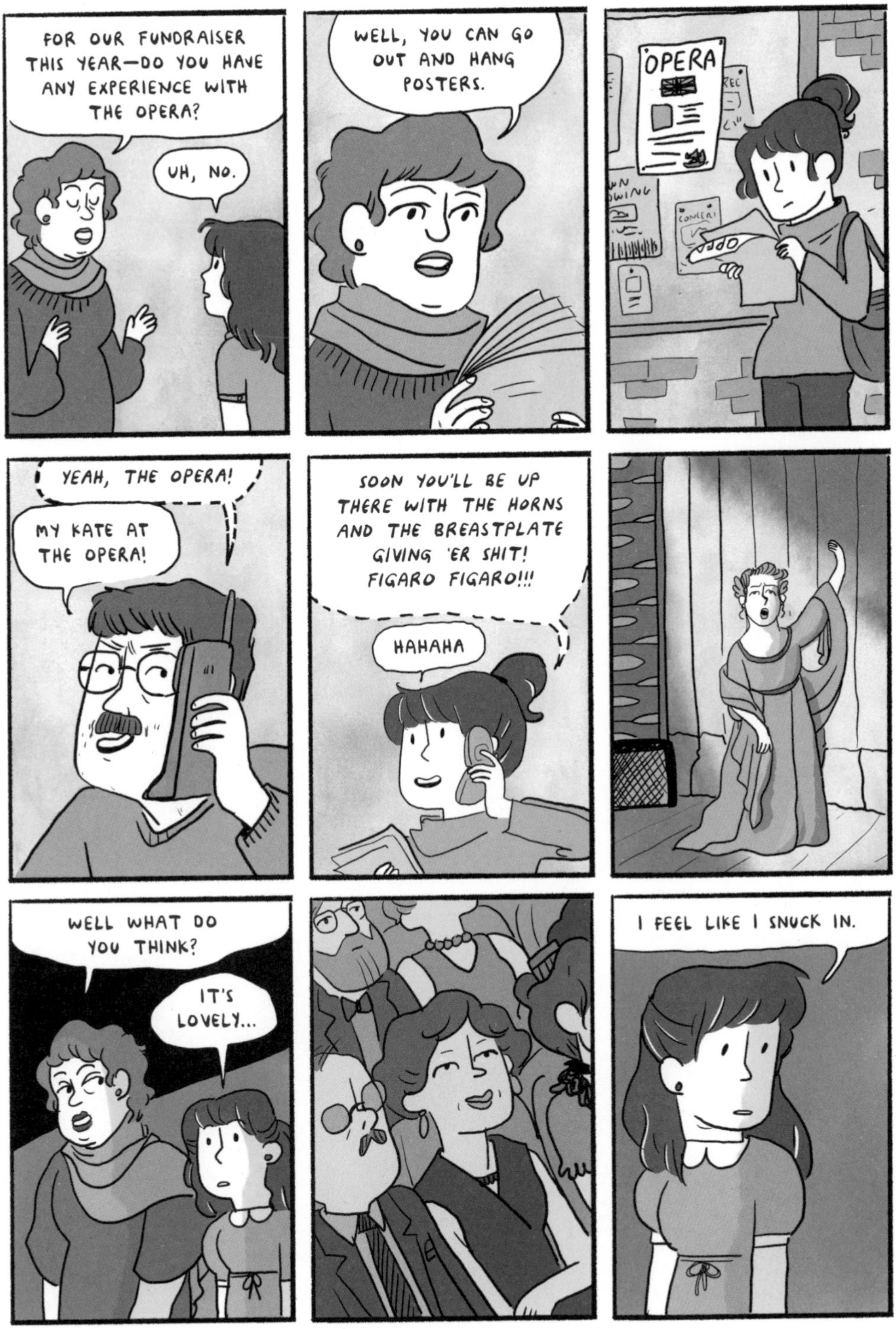
FOR OUR FUNDRAISER THIS YEAR—DO YOU HAVE ANY EXPERIENCE WITH THE OPERA?
UH, NO.
WELL, YOU CAN GO OUT AND HANG POSTERS.
OPERA
YEAH, THE OPERA!
MY KATE AT THE OPERA!
SOON YOU'LL BE UP THERE WITH THE HORNS AND THE BREASTPLATE GIVING 'ER SHIT! FIGARO FIGARO!!!
HAHAHA
WELL WHAT DO YOU THINK?
IT'S LOVELY...
I FEEL LIKE I SNUCK IN.

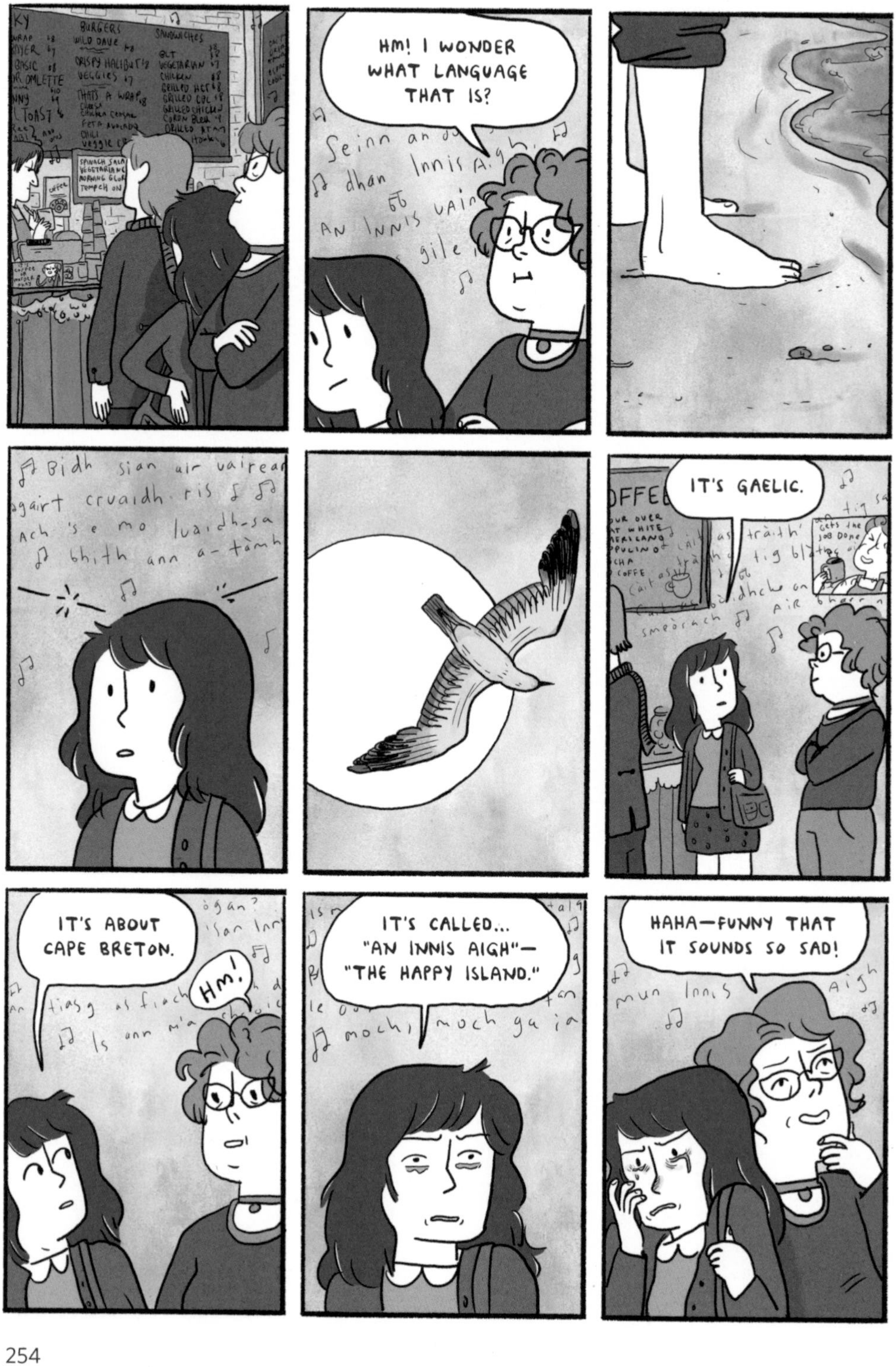
HM! I WONDER WHAT LANGUAGE THAT IS?
IT'S GAELIC.
IT'S ABOUT CAPE BRETON.
HM!
IT'S CALLED... "AN INNIS AIGH"— "THE HAPPY ISLAND."
HAHA—FUNNY THAT IT SOUNDS SO SAD!

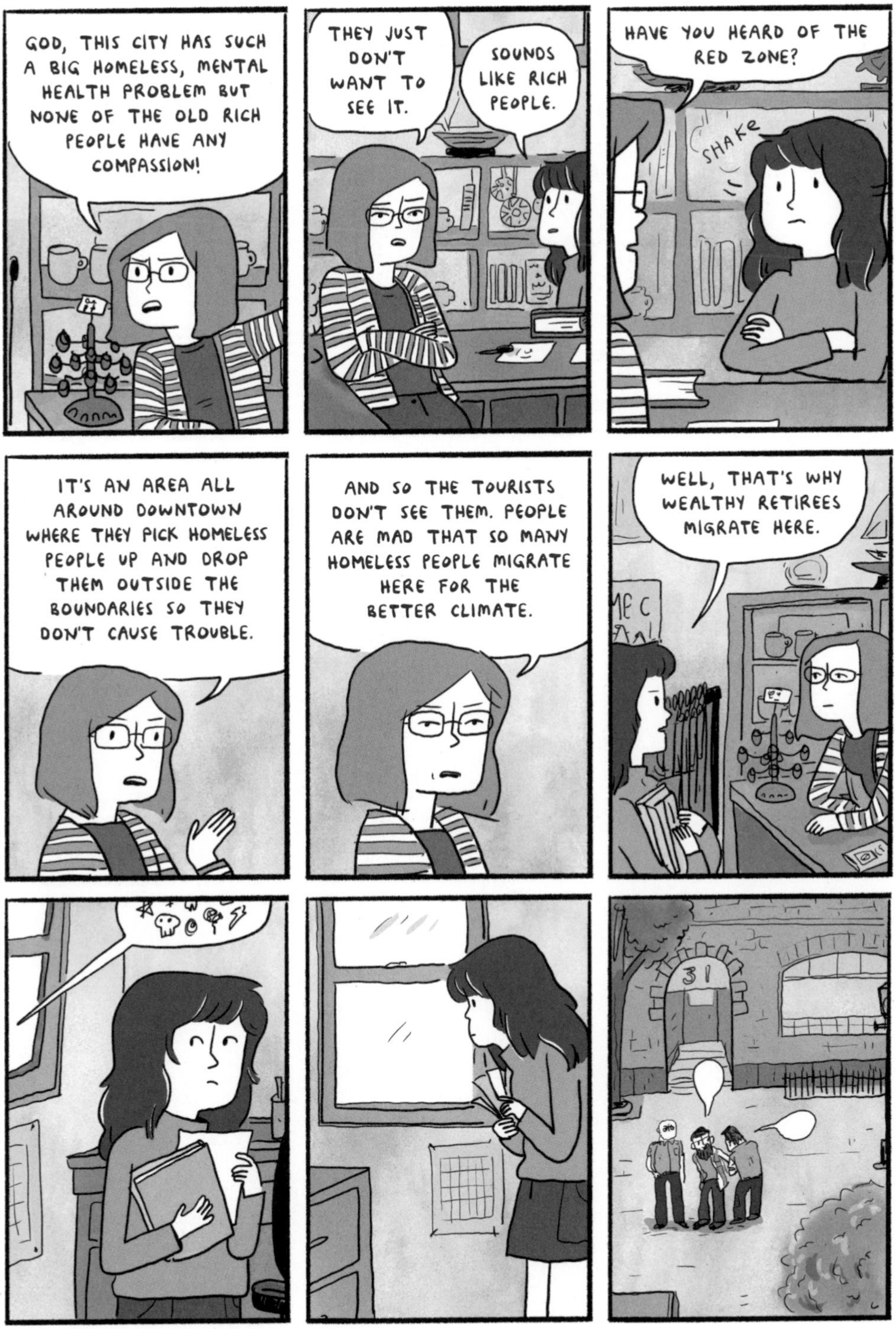
GOD, THIS CITY HAS SUCH A BIG HOMELESS, MENTAL HEALTH PROBLEM BUT NONE OF THE OLD RICH PEOPLE HAVE ANY COMPASSION!
THEY JUST DON'T WANT TO SEE IT.
SOUNDS LIKE RICH PEOPLE.
HAVE YOU HEARD OF THE RED ZONE?
SHAKE
IT'S AN AREA ALL AROUND DOWNTOWN WHERE THEY PICK HOMELESS PEOPLE UP AND DROP THEM OUTSIDE THE BOUNDARIES SO THEY DON'T CAUSE TROUBLE.
AND SO THE TOURISTS DON'T SEE THEM. PEOPLE ARE MAD THAT SO MANY HOMELESS PEOPLE MIGRATE HERE FOR THE BETTER CLIMATE.
WELL, THAT'S WHY WEALTHY RETIREES MIGRATE HERE.
31

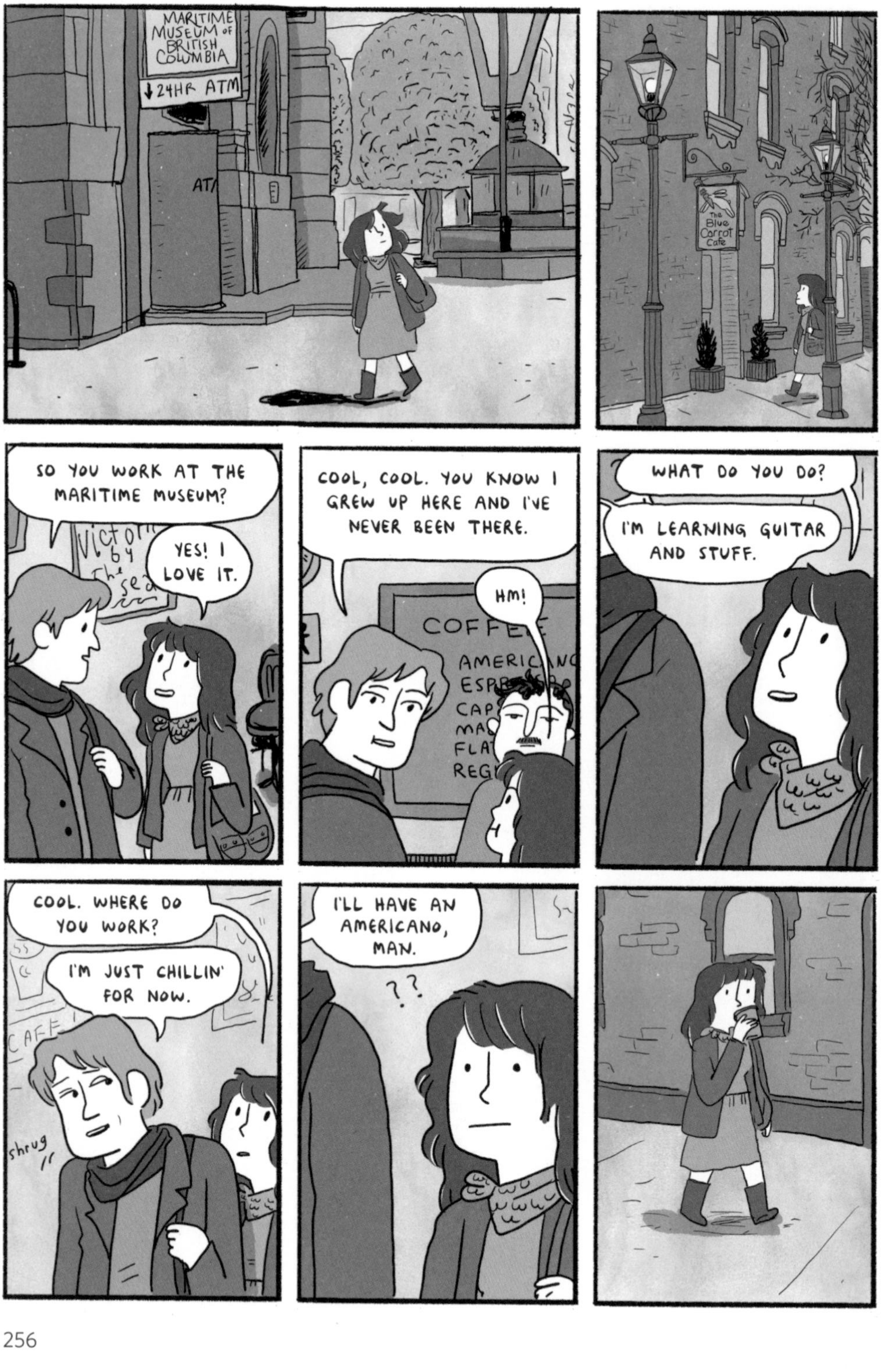
MARITIME MUSEUM OF BRITISH COLUMBIA
↓24HR ATM
The Blue Carrot Cafe
SO YOU WORK AT THE MARITIME MUSEUM?
YES! I LOVE IT.
COOL, COOL. YOU KNOW I GREW UP HERE AND I'VE NEVER BEEN THERE.
HM!
WHAT DO YOU DO?
I'M LEARNING GUITAR AND STUFF.
COOL. WHERE DO YOU WORK?
I'M JUST CHILLIN' FOR NOW.
shrug
I'LL HAVE AN AMERICANO, MAN.
??

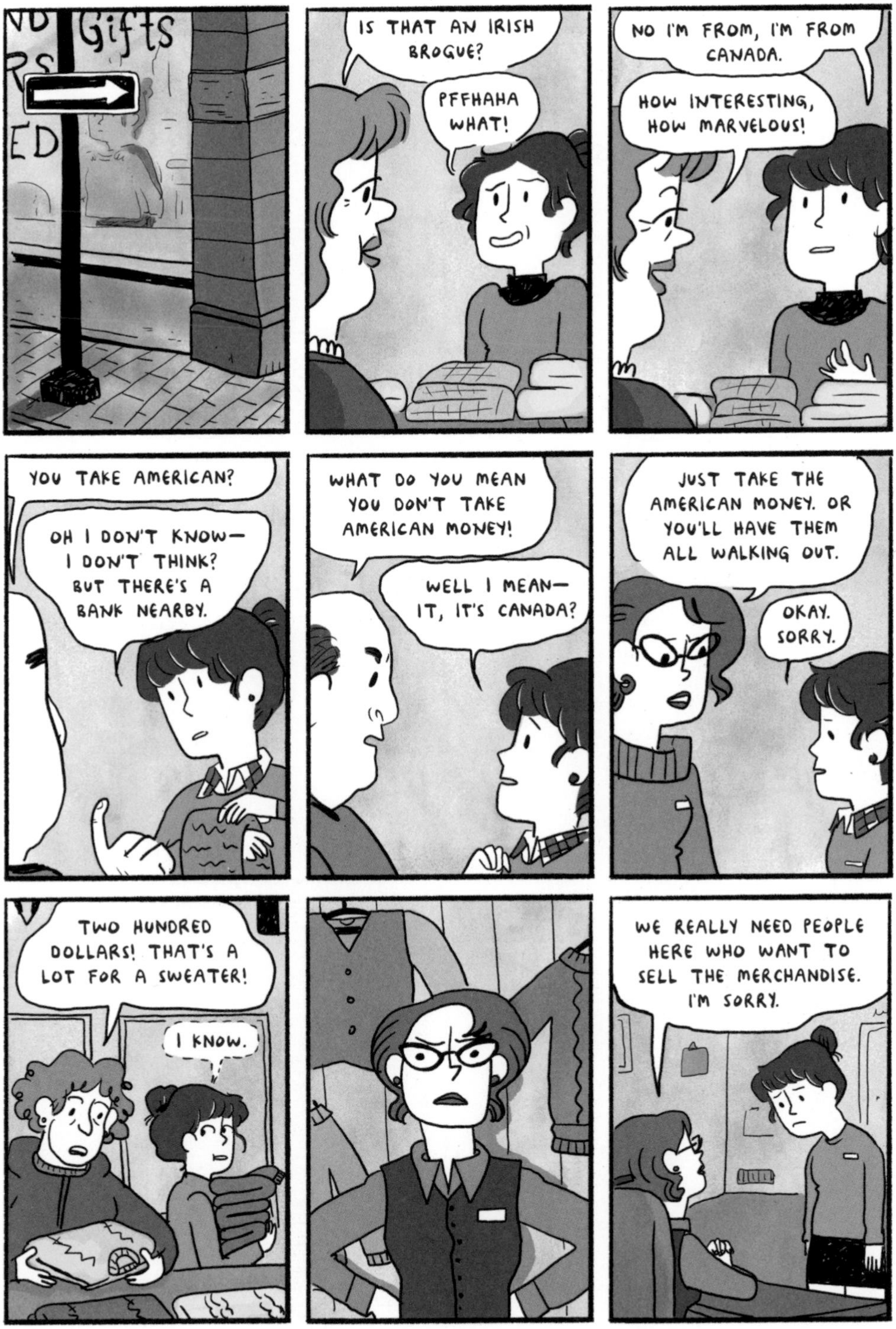
Gifts
IS THAT AN IRISH BROGUE?
PFFHAHA WHAT!
NO I'M FROM, I'M FROM CANADA.
HOW INTERESTING, HOW MARVELOUS!
YOU TAKE AMERICAN?
OH I DON'T KNOW— I DON'T THINK? BUT THERE'S A BANK NEARBY.
WHAT DO YOU MEAN YOU DON'T TAKE AMERICAN MONEY!
WELL I MEAN— IT, IT'S CANADA?
JUST TAKE THE AMERICAN MONEY. OR YOU'LL HAVE THEM ALL WALKING OUT.
OKAY. SORRY.
TWO HUNDRED DOLLARS! THAT'S A LOT FOR A SWEATER!
I KNOW.
WE REALLY NEED PEOPLE HERE WHO WANT TO SELL THE MERCHANDISE. I'M SORRY.

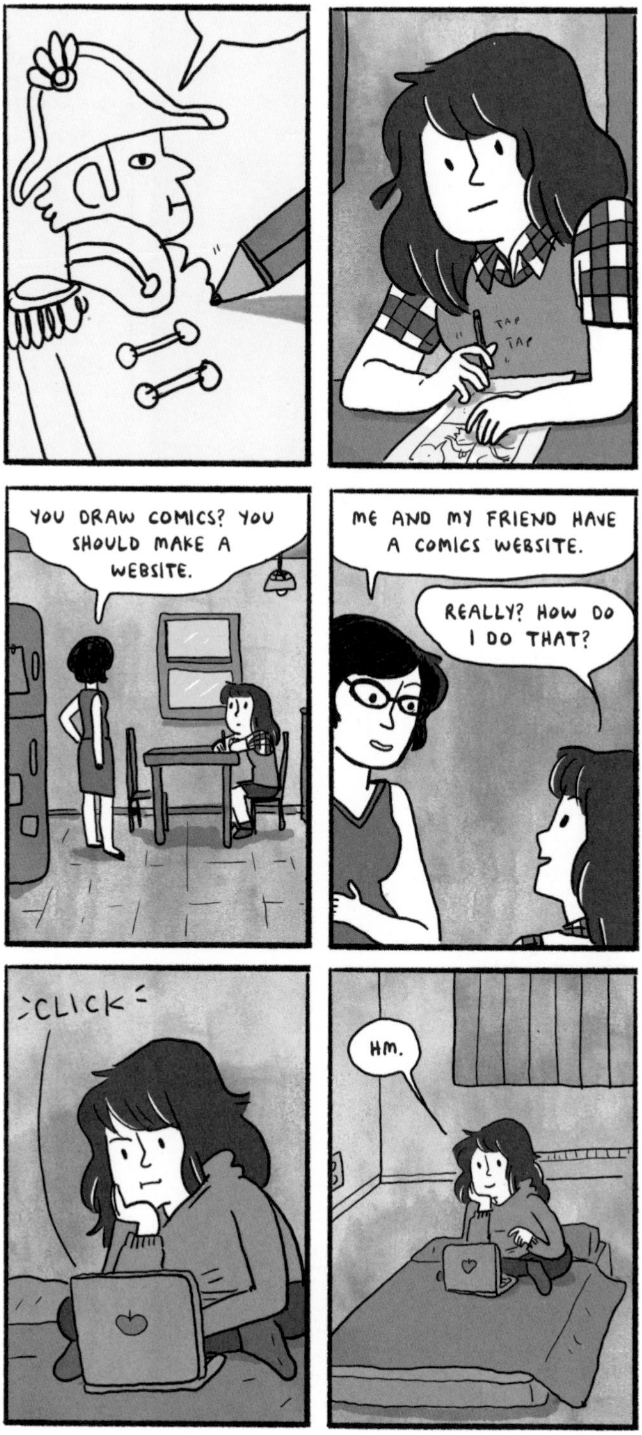
TAP
TAP
YOU DRAW COMICS? YOU SHOULD MAKE A WEBSITE.
ME AND MY FRIEND HAVE A COMICS WEBSITE.
REALLY? HOW DO I DO THAT?
CLICK
HM.

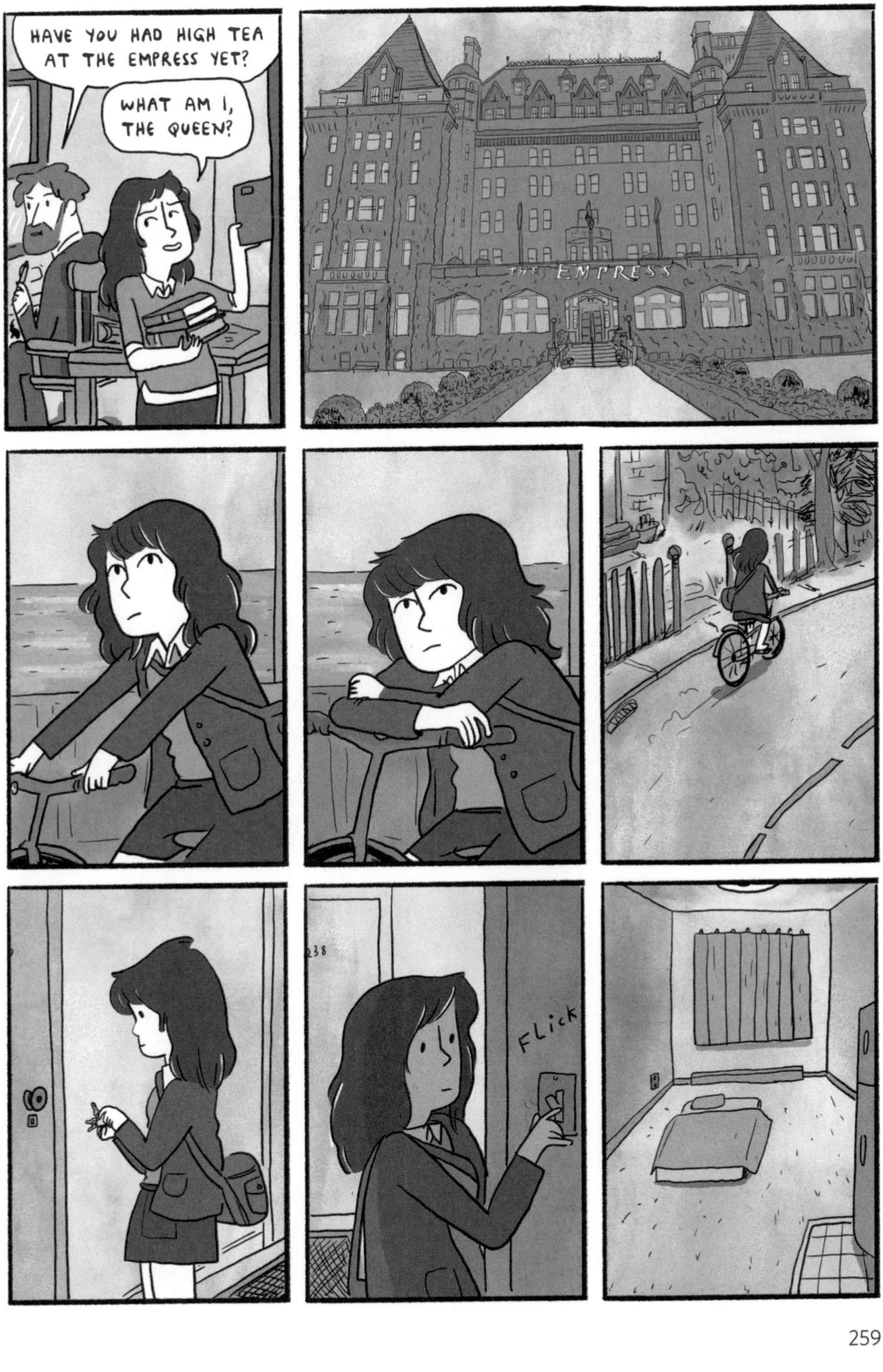
HAVE YOU HAD HIGH TEA AT THE EMPRESS YET?
WHAT AM I, THE QUEEN?
THE EMPRESS
238
FLICK

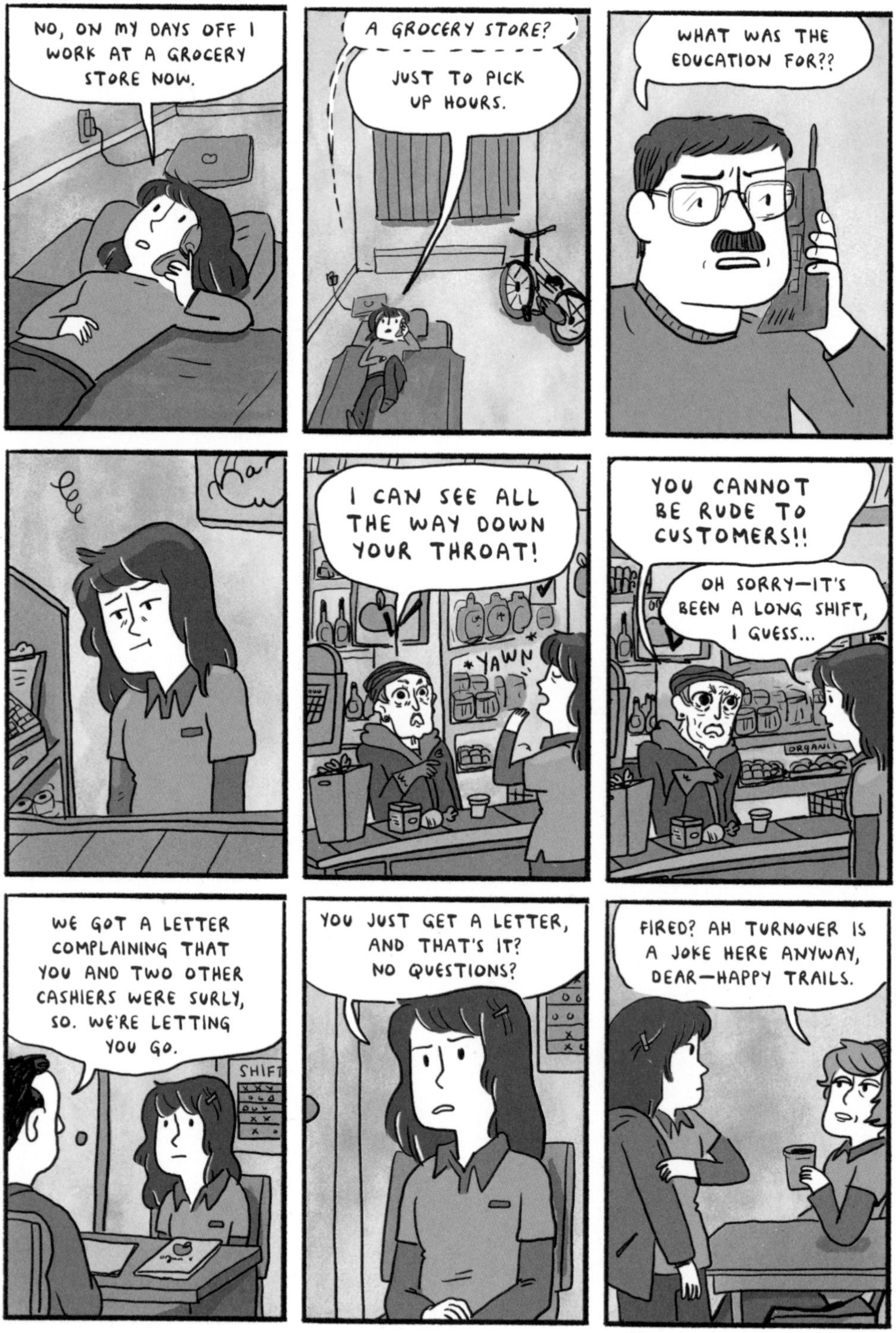
NO, ON MY DAYS OFF I WORK AT A GROCERY STORE NOW.
A GROCERY STORE?
JUST TO PICK UP HOURS.
WHAT WAS THE EDUCATION FOR??
I CAN SEE ALL THE WAY DOWN YOUR THROAT!
YAWN
YOU CANNOT BE RUDE TO CUSTOMERS!!
OH SORRY—IT'S BEEN A LONG SHIFT, I GUESS...
WE GOT A LETTER COMPLAINING THAT YOU AND TWO OTHER CASHIERS WERE SURLY, SO. WE'RE LETTING YOU GO.
SHIFT
YOU JUST GET A LETTER, AND THAT'S IT? NO QUESTIONS?
FIRED? AH TURNOVER IS A JOKE HERE ANYWAY, DEAR—HAPPY TRAILS.

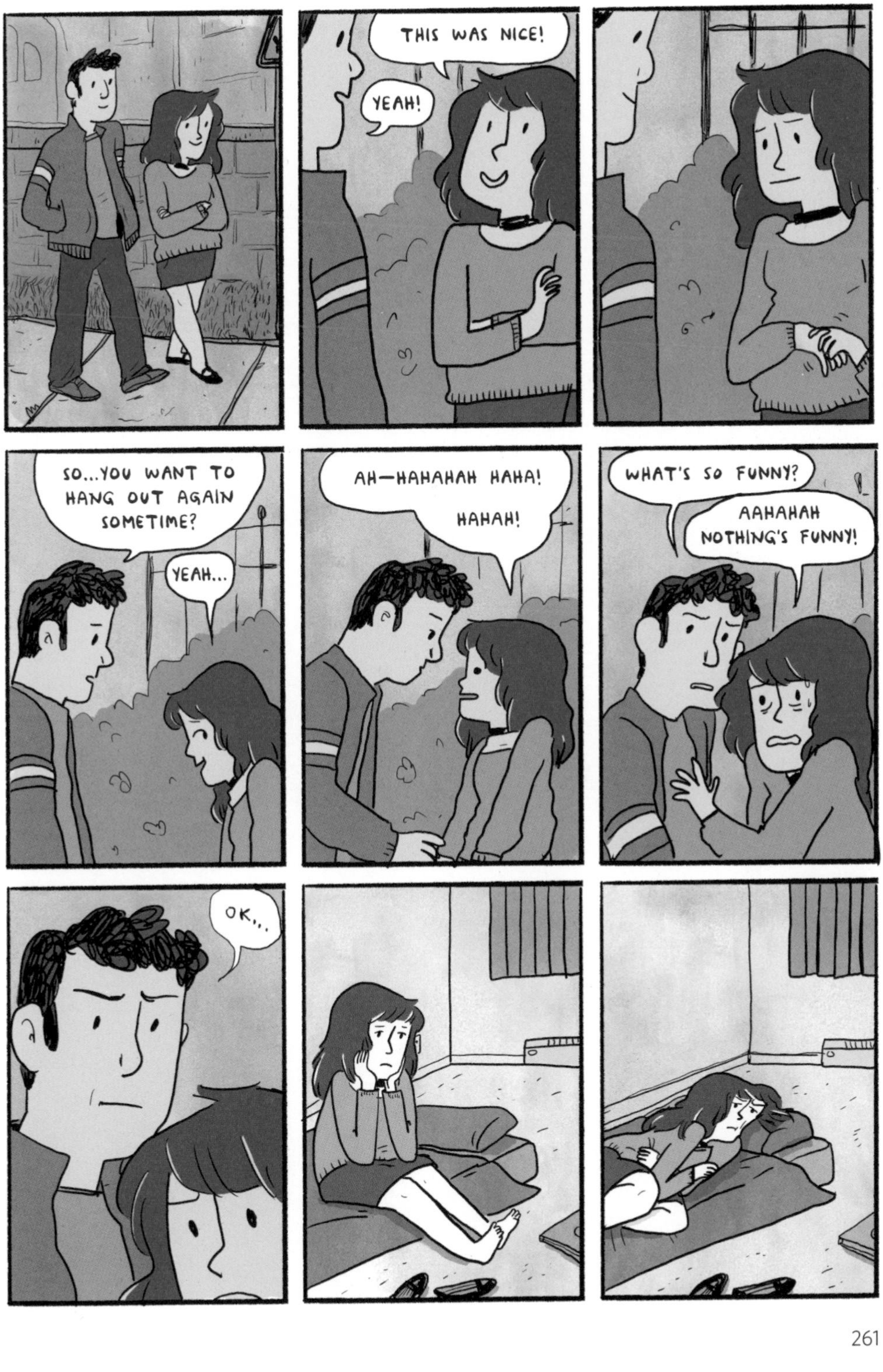
THIS WAS NICE!
YEAH!
SO...YOU WANT TO HANG OUT AGAIN SOMETIME?
YEAH...
AH—HAHAHAH HAHA!
HAHAH!
WHAT'S SO FUNNY?
AAHAHAH NOTHING'S FUNNY!
OK...

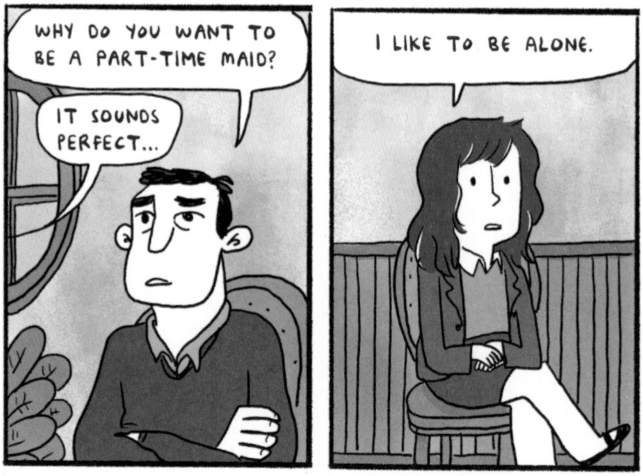
WHY DO YOU WANT TO BE A PART-TIME MAID?
IT SOUNDS PERFECT...
I LIKE TO BE ALONE.

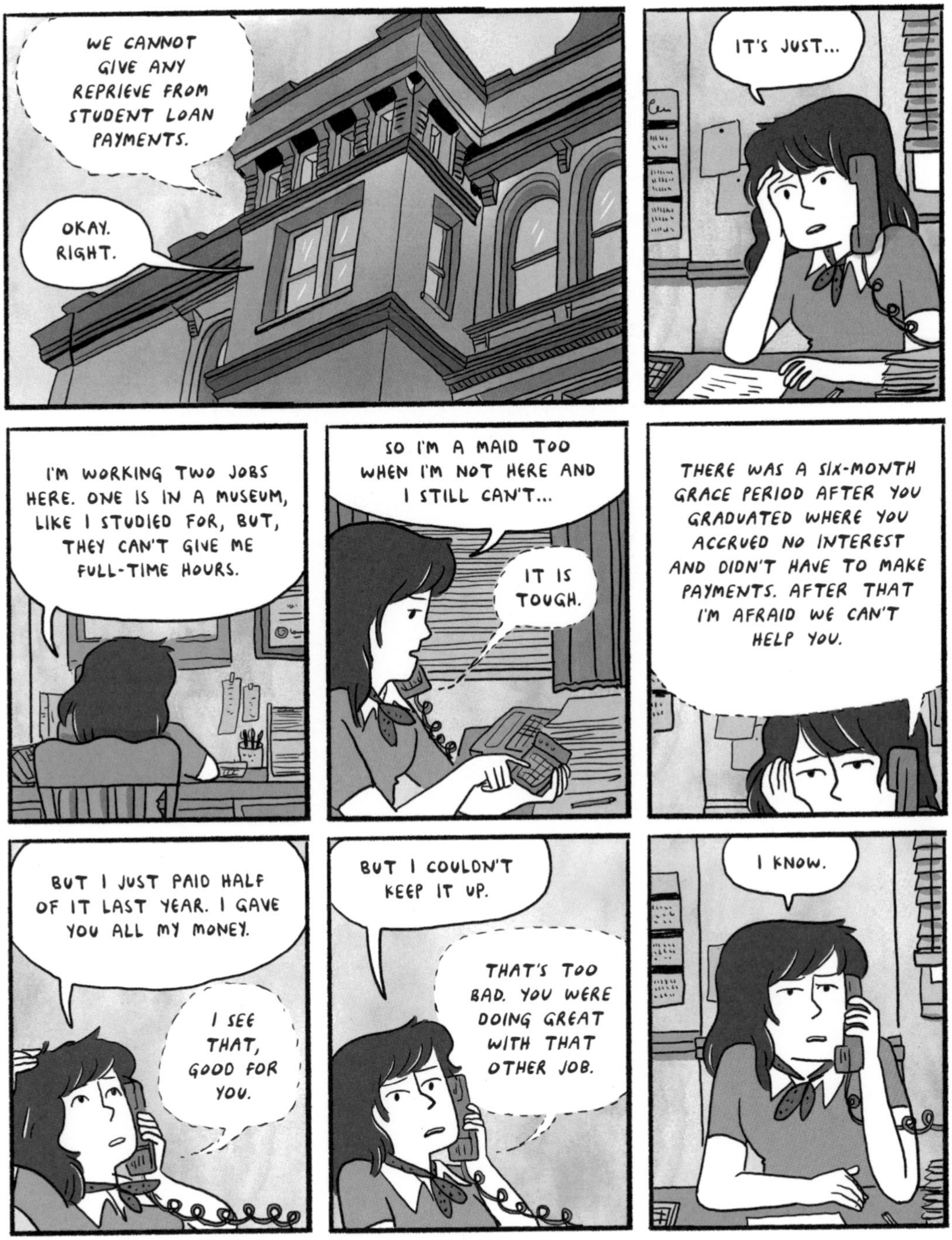
WE CANNOT GIVE ANY REPRIEVE FROM STUDENT LOAN PAYMENTS.
OKAY. RIGHT.
IT'S JUST...
I'M WORKING TWO JOBS HERE. ONE IS IN A MUSEUM, LIKE I STUDIED FOR, BUT, THEY CAN'T GIVE ME FULL-TIME HOURS.
SO I'M A MAID TOO WHEN I'M NOT HERE AND I STILL CAN'T...
IT IS TOUGH.
THERE WAS A SIX-MONTH GRACE PERIOD AFTER YOU GRADUATED WHERE YOU ACCRUED NO INTEREST AND DIDN'T HAVE TO MAKE PAYMENTS. AFTER THAT I'M AFRAID WE CAN'T HELP YOU.
BUT I JUST PAID HALF OF IT LAST YEAR. I GAVE YOU ALL MY MONEY.
I SEE THAT, GOOD FOR YOU.
BUT I COULDN'T KEEP IT UP.
THAT'S TOO BAD. YOU WERE DOING GREAT WITH THAT OTHER JOB.
I KNOW.

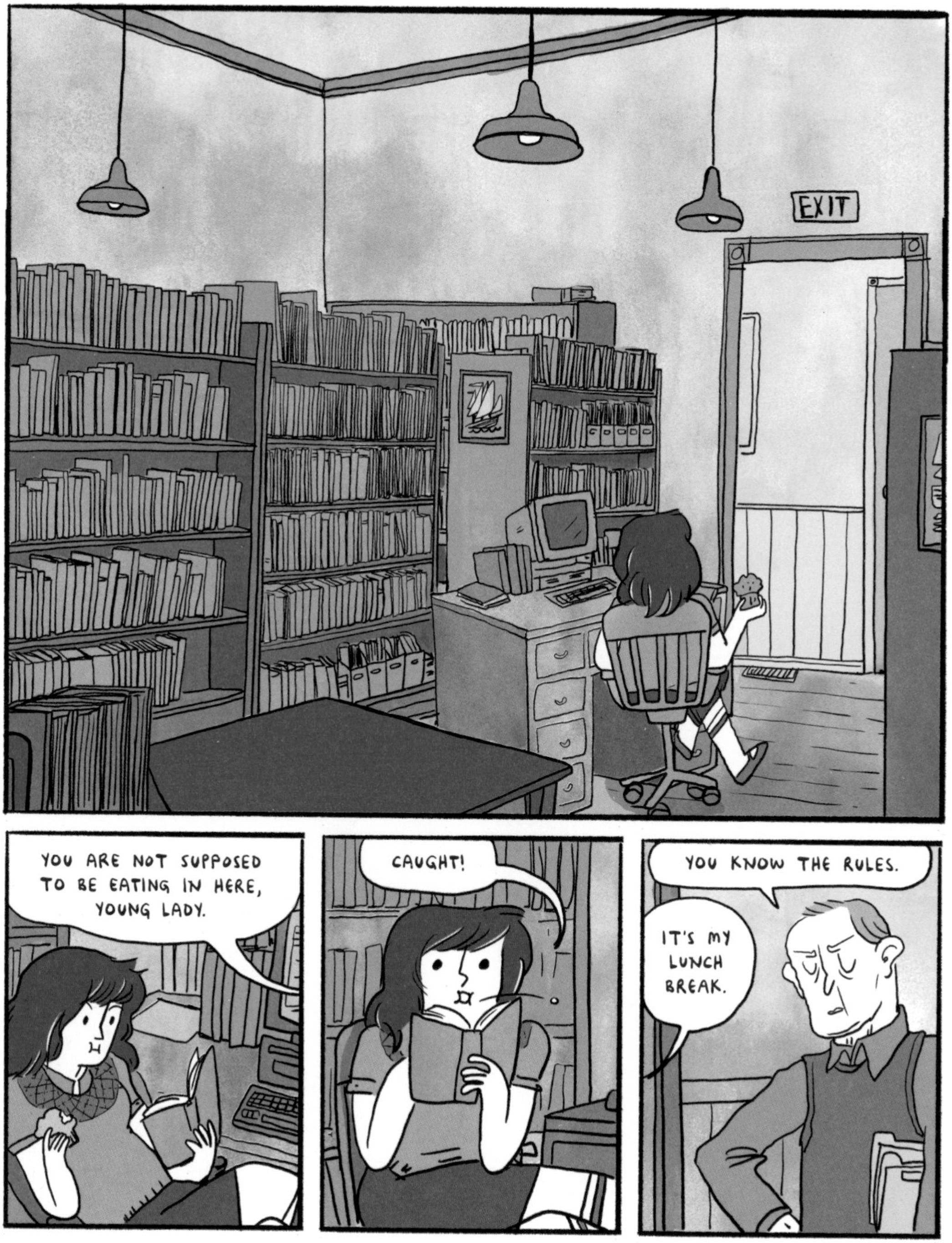
EXIT
YOU ARE NOT SUPPOSED TO BE EATING IN HERE, YOUNG LADY.
CAUGHT!
YOU KNOW THE RULES.
IT'S MY LUNCH BREAK.

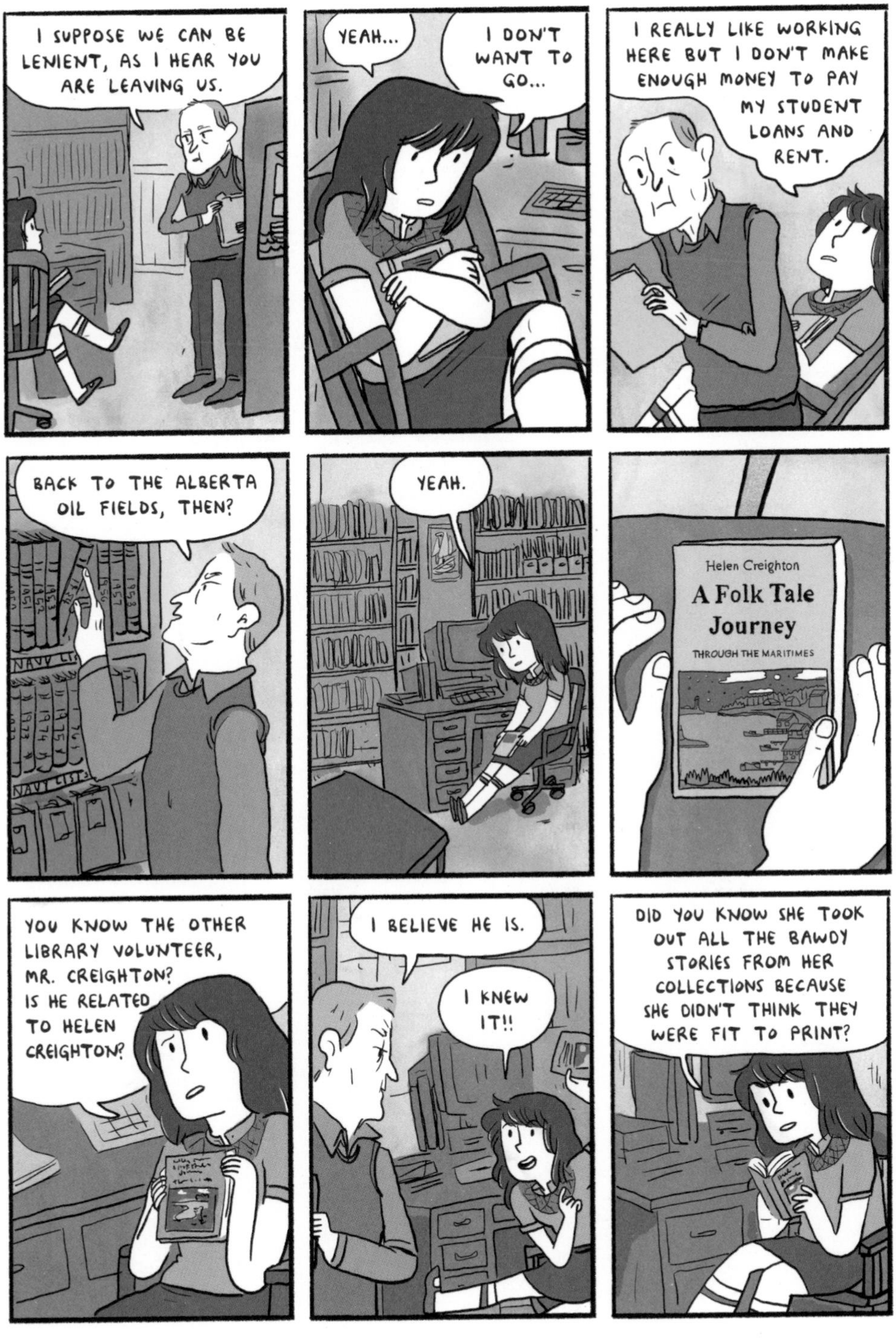
I SUPPOSE WE CAN BE LENIENT, AS I HEAR YOU ARE LEAVING US.
YEAH...
I DON'T WANT TO GO...
I REALLY LIKE WORKING HERE BUT I DON'T MAKE ENOUGH MONEY TO PAY MY STUDENT LOANS AND RENT.
BACK TO THE ALBERTA OIL FIELDS, THEN?
YEAH.
Helen Creighton
A Folk Tale Journey
THROUGH THE MARITIMES
YOU KNOW THE OTHER LIBRARY VOLUNTEER, MR. CREIGHTON? IS HE RELATED TO HELEN CREIGHTON?
I BELIEVE HE IS.
I KNEW IT!!
DID YOU KNOW SHE TOOK OUT ALL THE BAWDY STORIES FROM HER COLLECTIONS BECAUSE SHE DIDN'T THINK THEY WERE FIT TO PRINT?

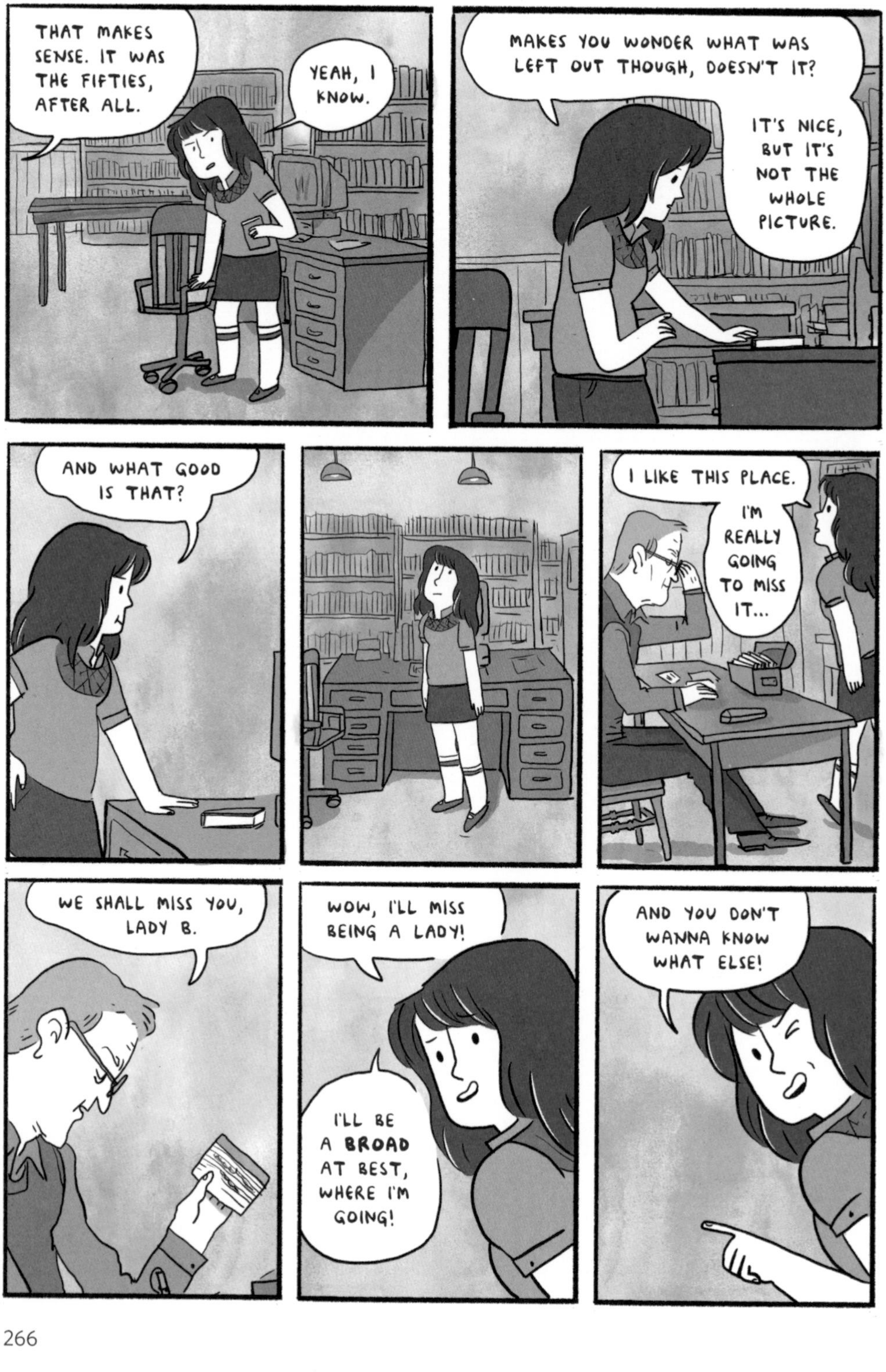

THAT MAKES SENSE. IT WAS THE FIFTIES, AFTER ALL.
YEAH, I KNOW.
MAKES YOU WONDER WHAT WAS LEFT OUT THOUGH, DOESN'T IT?
IT'S NICE, BUT IT'S NOT THE WHOLE PICTURE.
AND WHAT GOOD IS THAT?
I LIKE THIS PLACE.
I'M REALLY GOING TO MISS IT...
WE SHALL MISS YOU, LADY B.
WOW, I'LL MISS BEING A LADY!
I'LL BE A **BROAD** AT BEST, WHERE I'M GOING!
AND YOU DON'T WANNA KNOW WHAT ELSE!

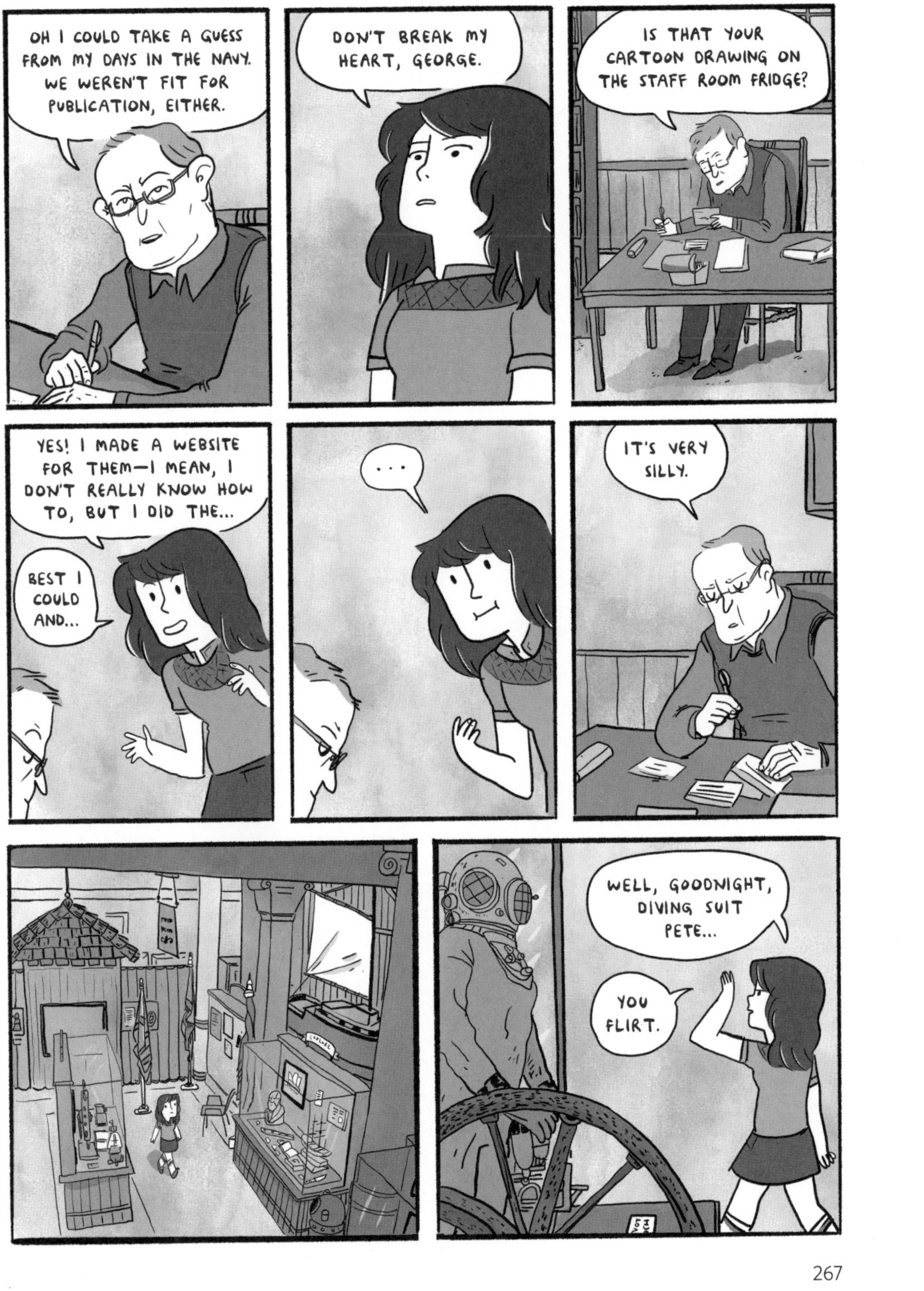
OH I COULD TAKE A GUESS FROM MY DAYS IN THE NAVY. WE WEREN'T FIT FOR PUBLICATION, EITHER.
DON'T BREAK MY HEART, GEORGE.
IS THAT YOUR CARTOON DRAWING ON THE STAFF ROOM FRIDGE?
YES! I MADE A WEBSITE FOR THEM—I MEAN, I DON'T REALLY KNOW HOW TO, BUT I DID THE...
BEST I COULD AND...
...
IT'S VERY SILLY.
WELL, GOODNIGHT, DIVING SUIT PETE...
YOU FLIRT.

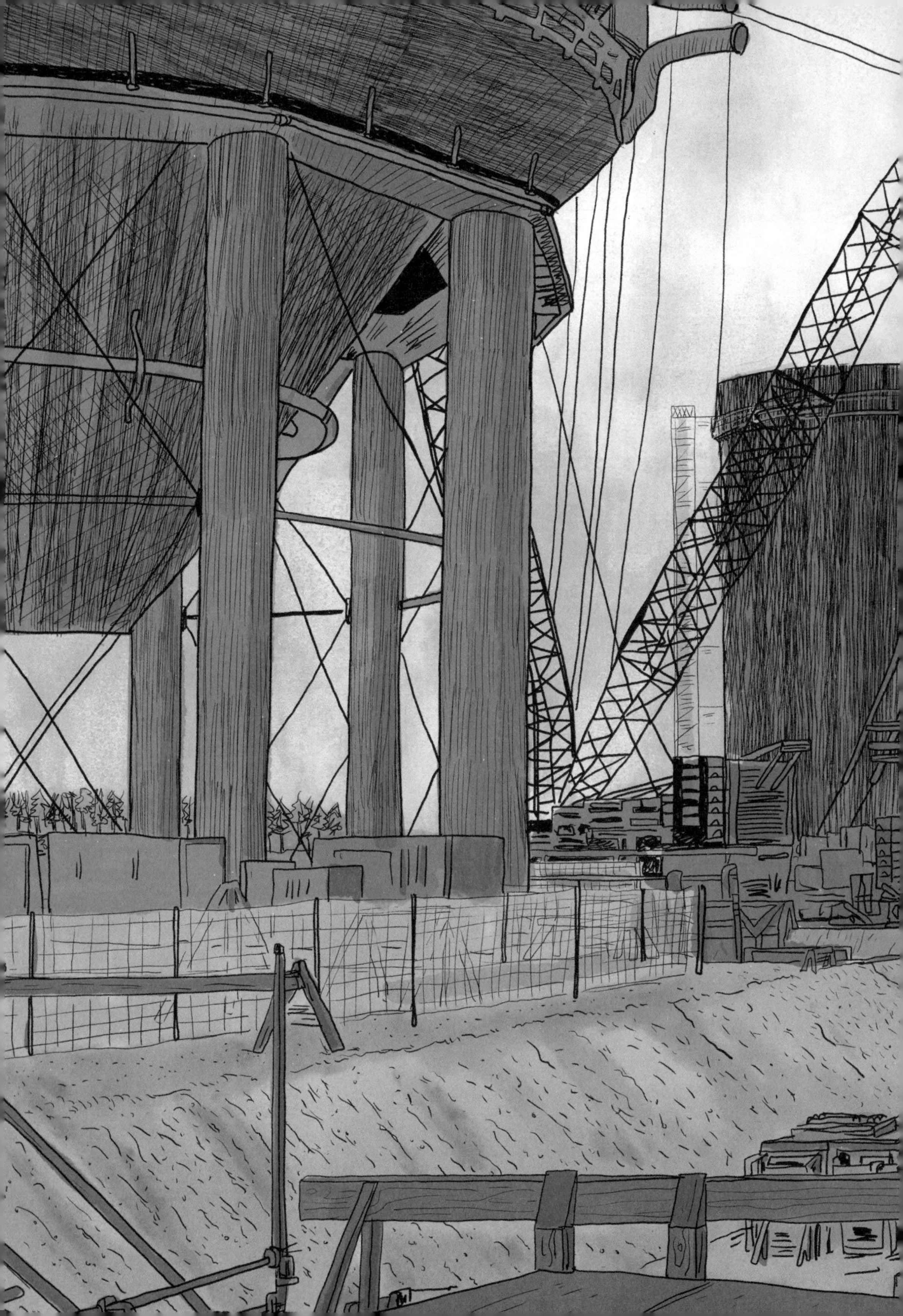

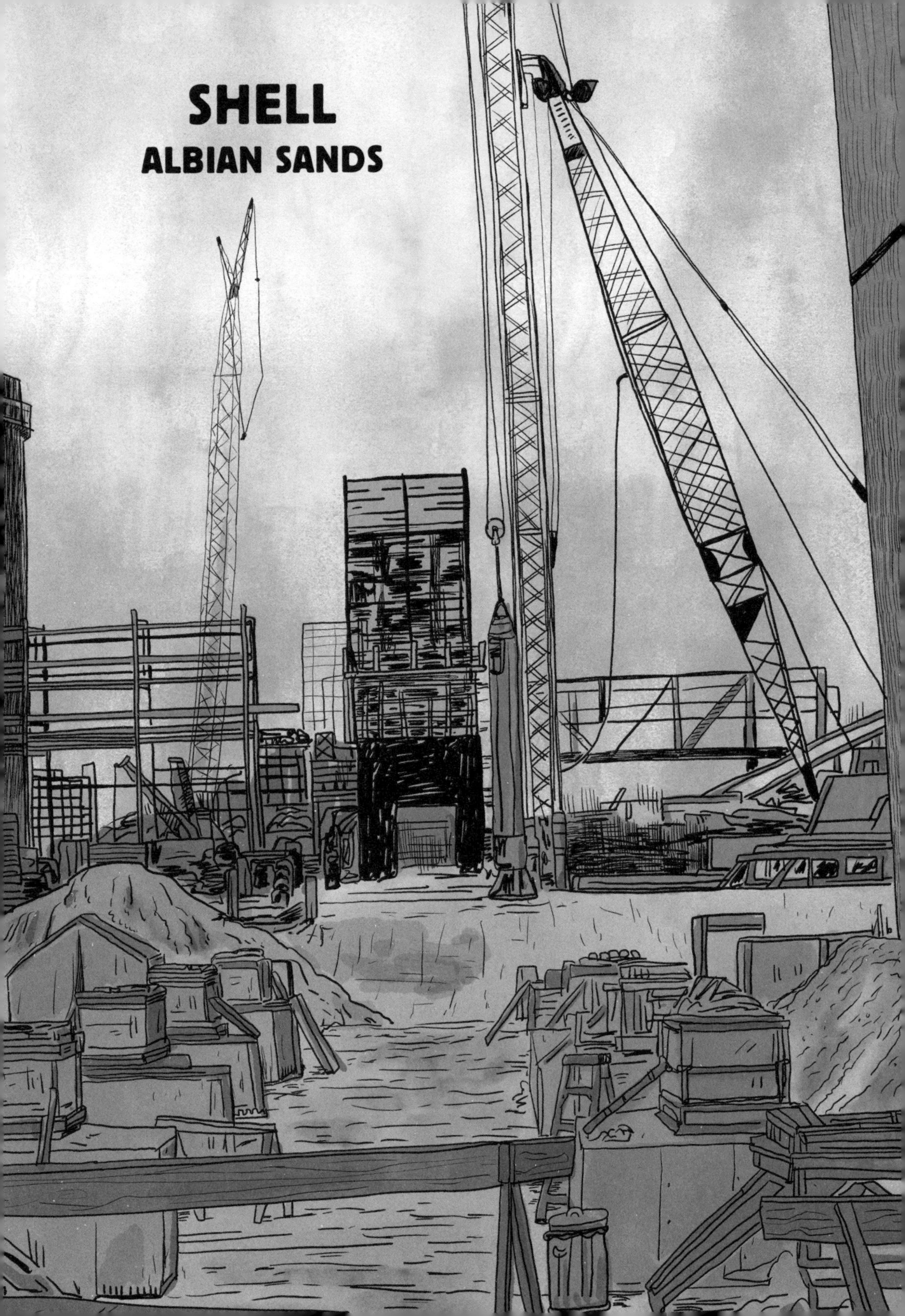
SHELL
ALBIAN SANDS

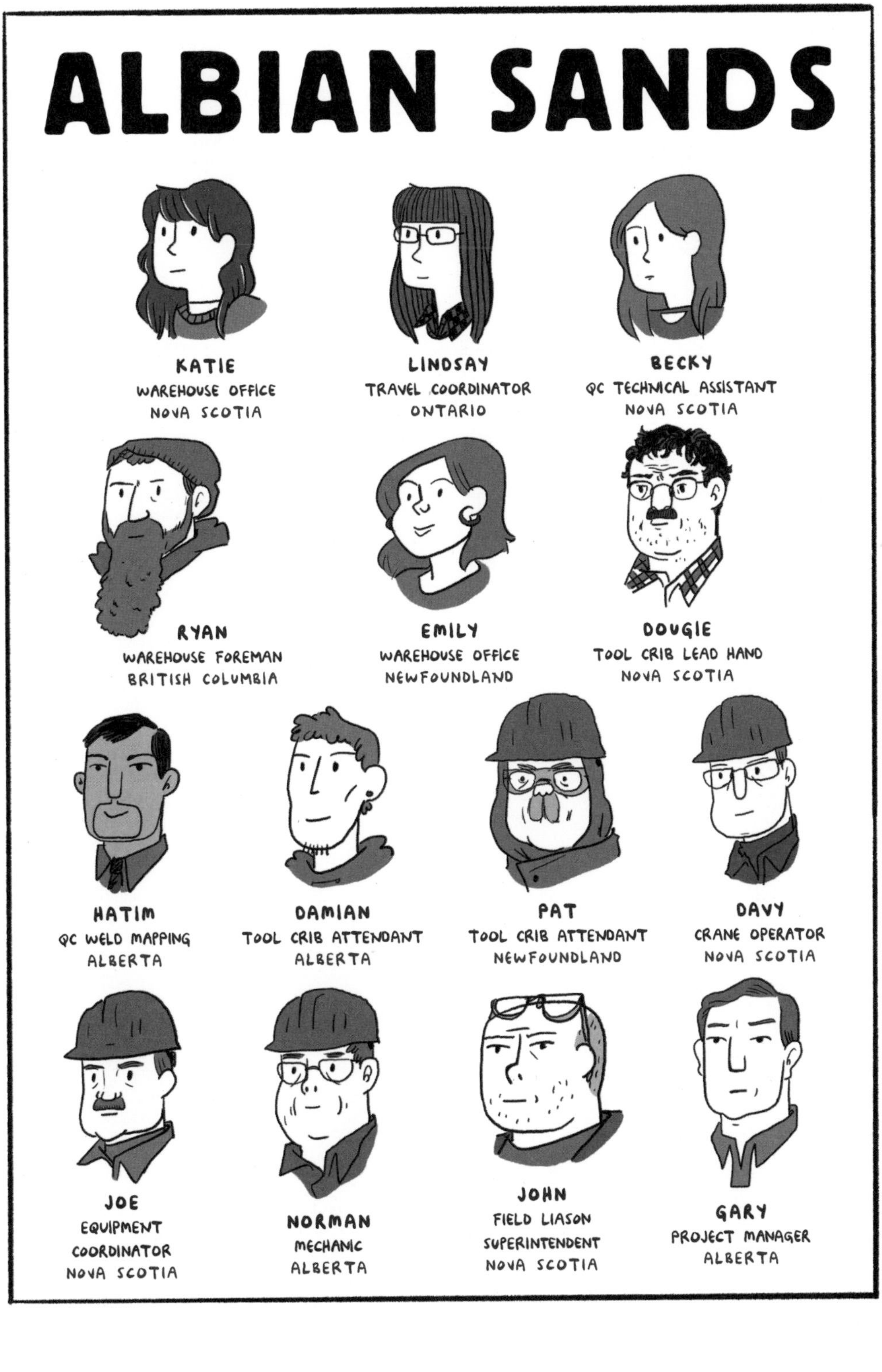
ALBIAN SANDS
KATIE
WAREHOUSE OFFICE
NOVA SCOTIA
LINDSAY
TRAVEL COORDINATOR
ONTARIO
BECKY
QC TECHNICAL ASSISTANT
NOVA SCOTIA
RYAN
WAREHOUSE FOREMAN
BRITISH COLUMBIA
EMILY
WAREHOUSE OFFICE
NEWFOUNDLAND
DOUGIE
TOOL CRIB LEAD HAND
NOVA SCOTIA
HATIM
QC WELD MAPPING
ALBERTA
DAMIAN
TOOL CRIB ATTENDANT
ALBERTA
PAT
TOOL CRIB ATTENDANT
NEWFOUNDLAND
DAVY
CRANE OPERATOR
NOVA SCOTIA
JOE
EQUIPMENT
COORDINATOR
NOVA SCOTIA
NORMAN
MECHANIC
ALBERTA
JOHN
FIELD LIASON
SUPERINTENDENT
NOVA SCOTIA
GARY
PROJECT MANAGER
ALBERTA

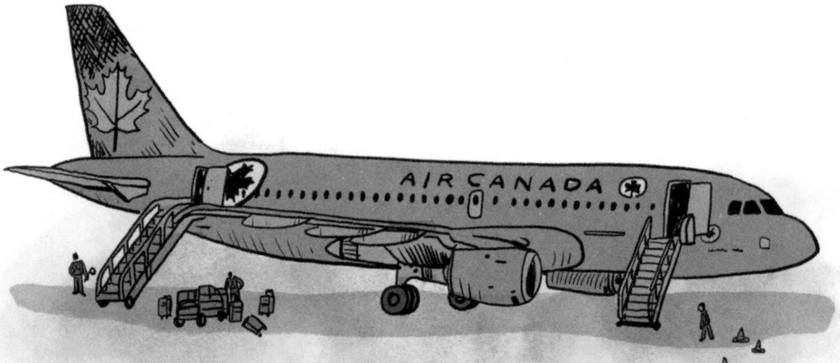
AIR CANADA

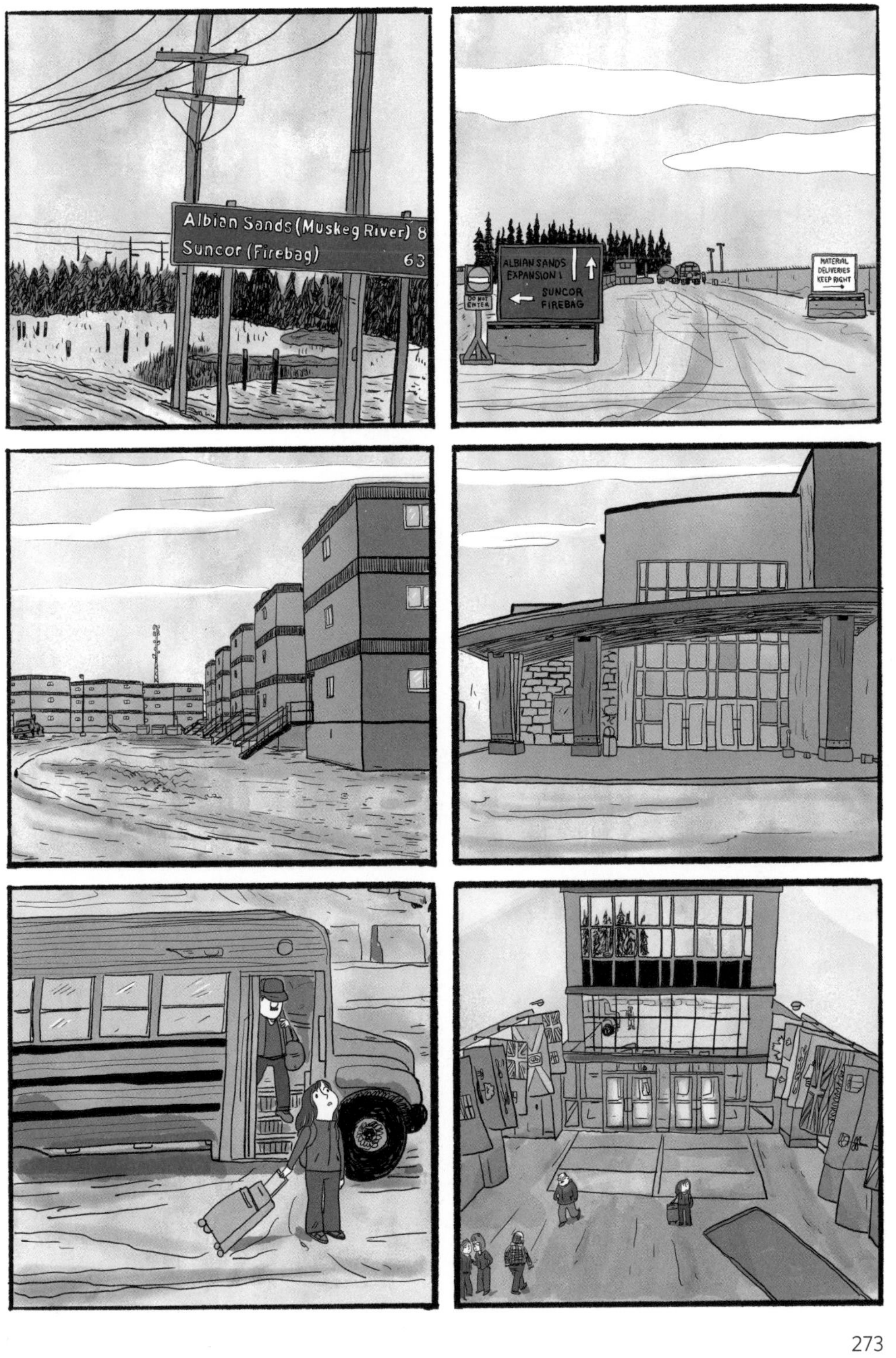
Albian Sands (Muskeg River) 8
Suncor (Firebag) 63
ALBIAN SANDS EXPANSION 1
SUNCOR FIREBAG
DO NOT ENTER
MATERIAL DELIVERIES KEEP RIGHT

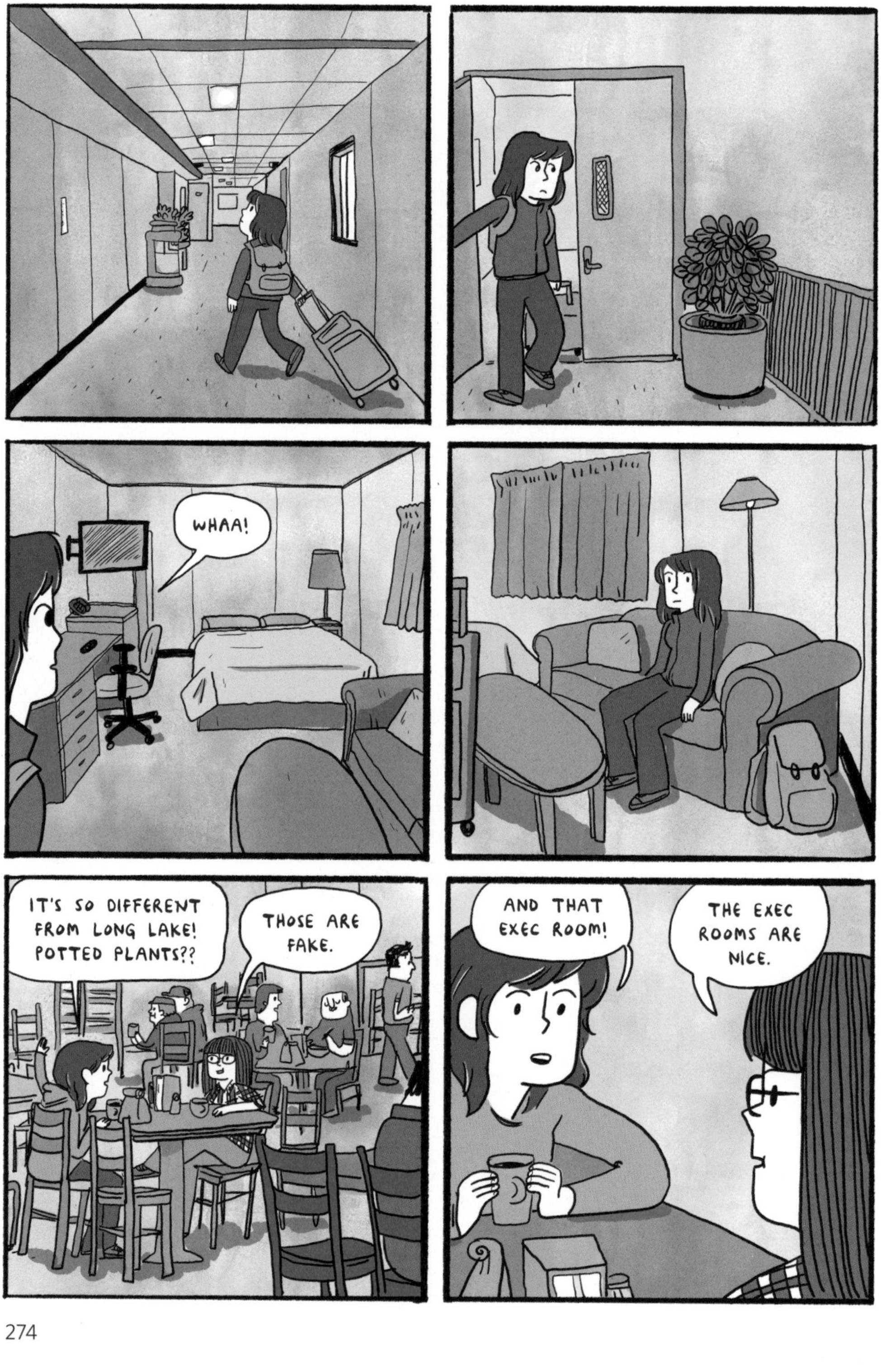
WHAA!
IT'S SO DIFFERENT FROM LONG LAKE! POTTED PLANTS??
THOSE ARE FAKE.
AND THAT EXEC ROOM!
THE EXEC ROOMS ARE NICE.

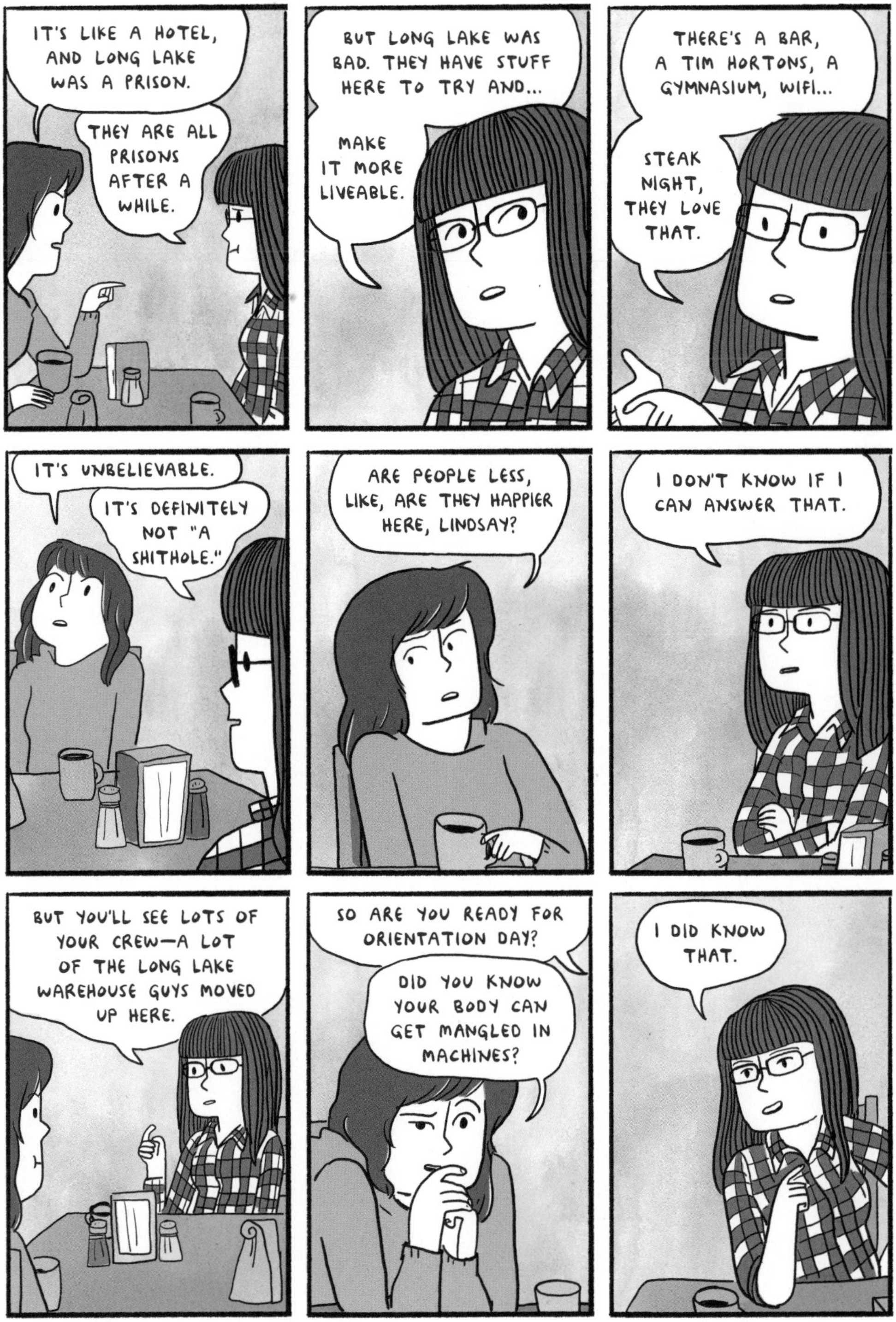
IT'S LIKE A HOTEL, AND LONG LAKE WAS A PRISON.
THEY ARE ALL PRISONS AFTER A WHILE.
BUT LONG LAKE WAS BAD. THEY HAVE STUFF HERE TO TRY AND...
MAKE IT MORE LIVEABLE.
THERE'S A BAR, A TIM HORTONS, A GYMNASIUM, WIFI...
STEAK NIGHT, THEY LOVE THAT.
IT'S UNBELIEVABLE.
IT'S DEFINITELY NOT "A SHITHOLE."
ARE PEOPLE LESS, LIKE, ARE THEY HAPPIER HERE, LINDSAY?
I DON'T KNOW IF I CAN ANSWER THAT.
BUT YOU'LL SEE LOTS OF YOUR CREW—A LOT OF THE LONG LAKE WAREHOUSE GUYS MOVED UP HERE.
SO ARE YOU READY FOR ORIENTATION DAY?
DID YOU KNOW YOUR BODY CAN GET MANGLED IN MACHINES?
I DID KNOW THAT.

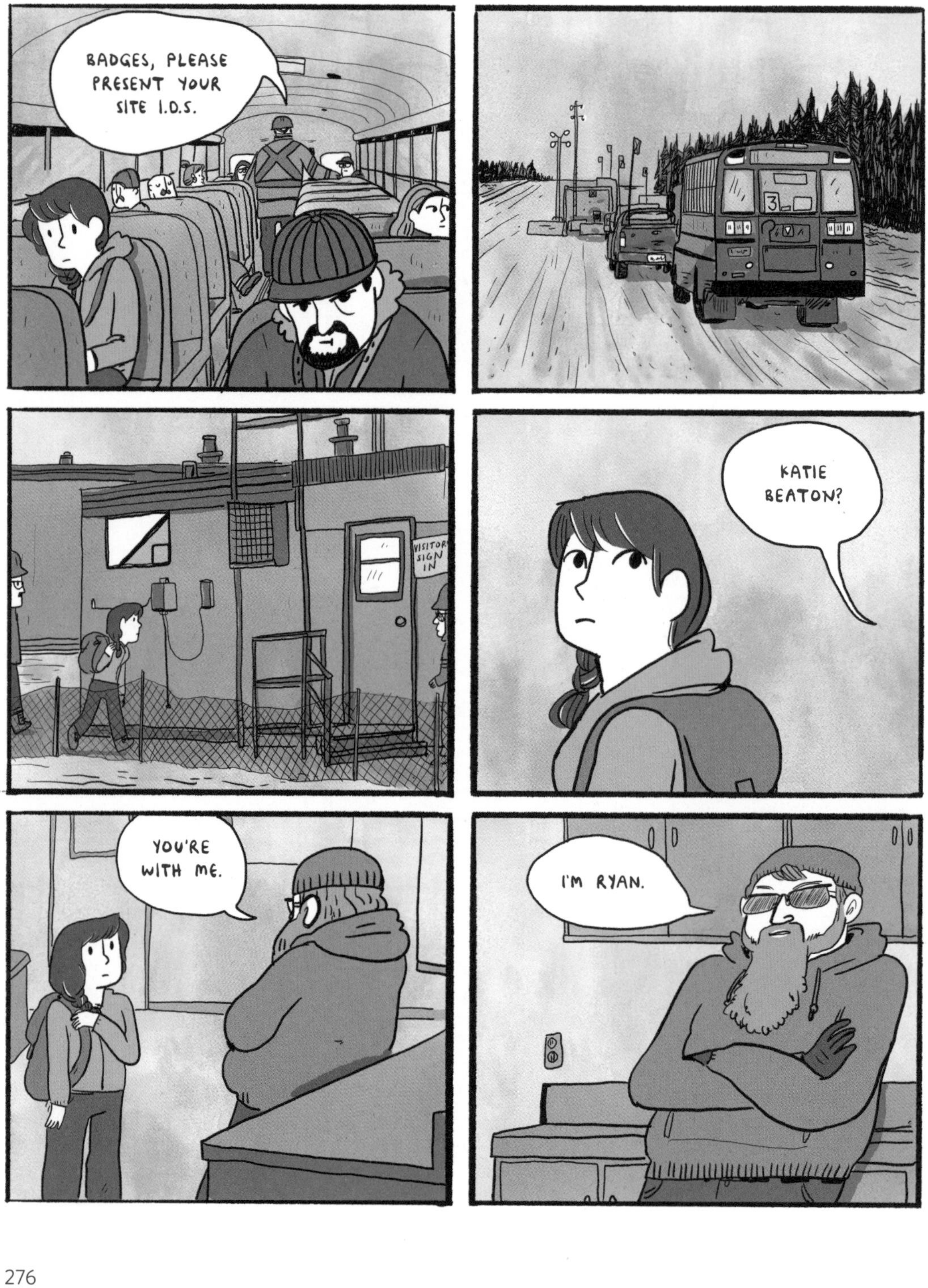
BADGES, PLEASE PRESENT YOUR SITE I.D.S.
VISITORS SIGN IN
KATIE BEATON?
YOU'RE WITH ME.
I'M RYAN.

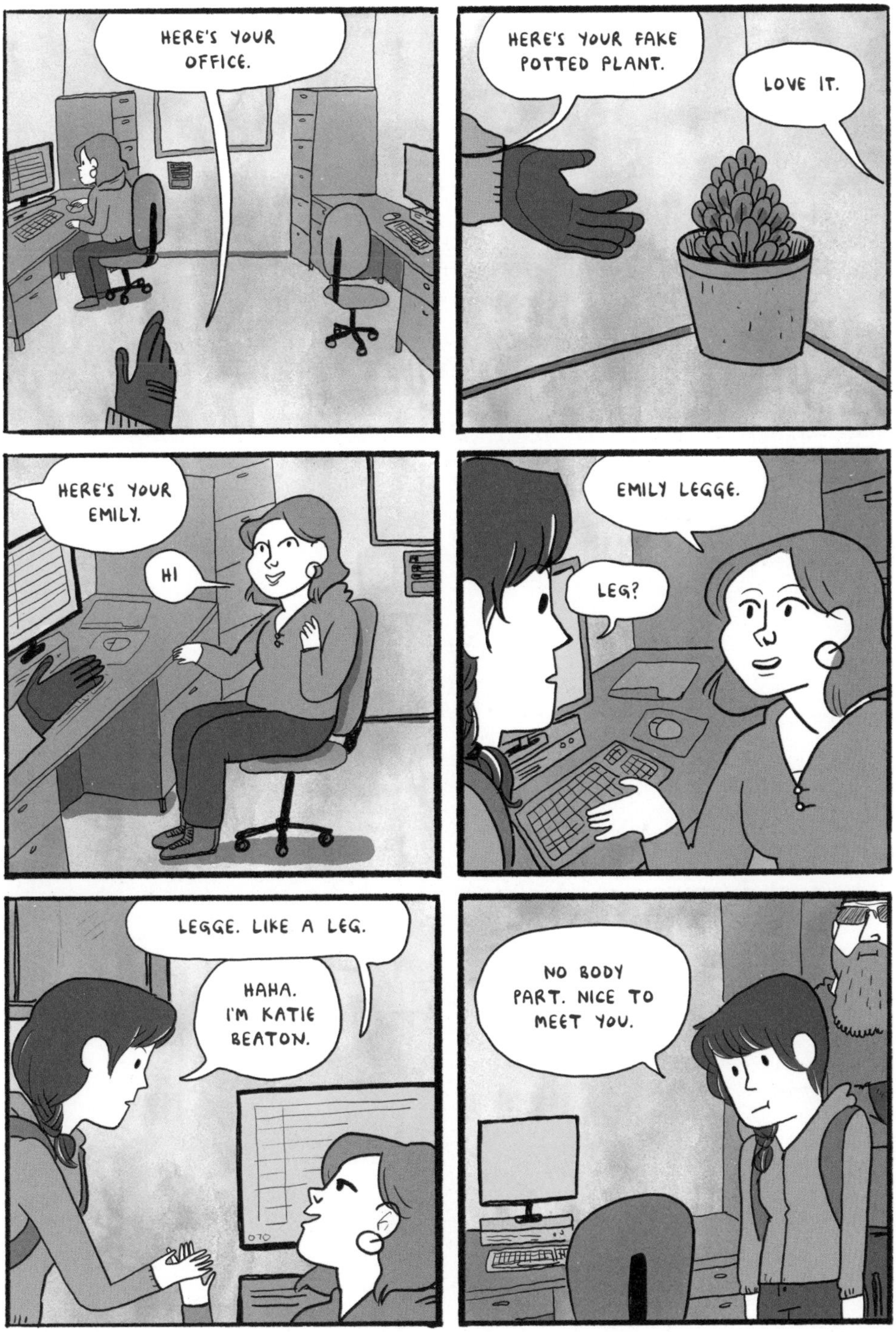
HERE'S YOUR OFFICE.
HERE'S YOUR FAKE POTTED PLANT.
LOVE IT.
HERE'S YOUR EMILY.
HI
EMILY LEGGE.
LEG?
LEGGE. LIKE A LEG.
HAHA. I'M KATIE BEATON.
NO BODY PART. NICE TO MEET YOU.

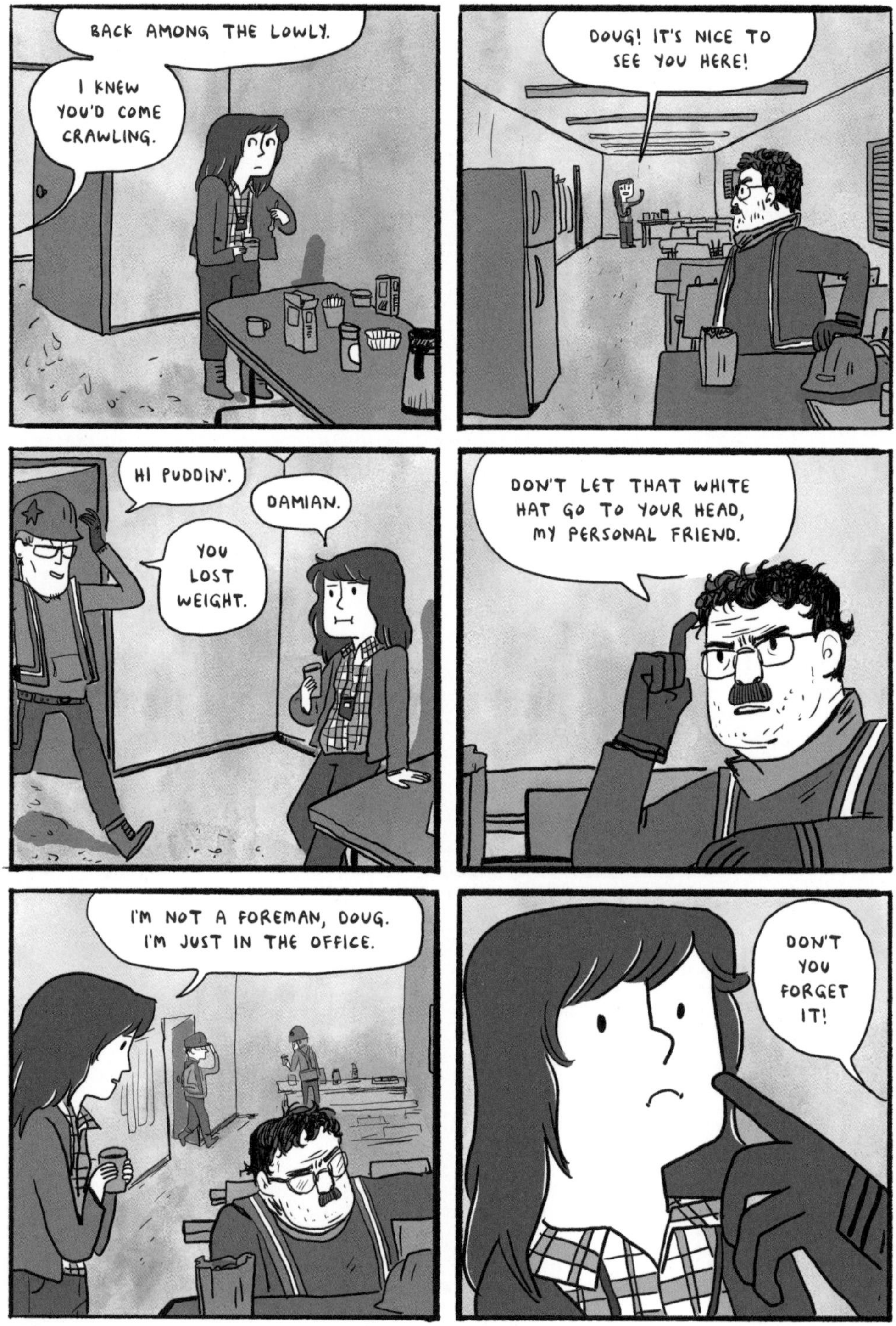
BACK AMONG THE LOWLY.
I KNEW YOU'D COME CRAWLING.
DOUG! IT'S NICE TO SEE YOU HERE!
HI PUDDIN'.
DAMIAN.
YOU LOST WEIGHT.
DON'T LET THAT WHITE HAT GO TO YOUR HEAD, MY PERSONAL FRIEND.
I'M NOT A FOREMAN, DOUG. I'M JUST IN THE OFFICE.
DON'T YOU FORGET IT!

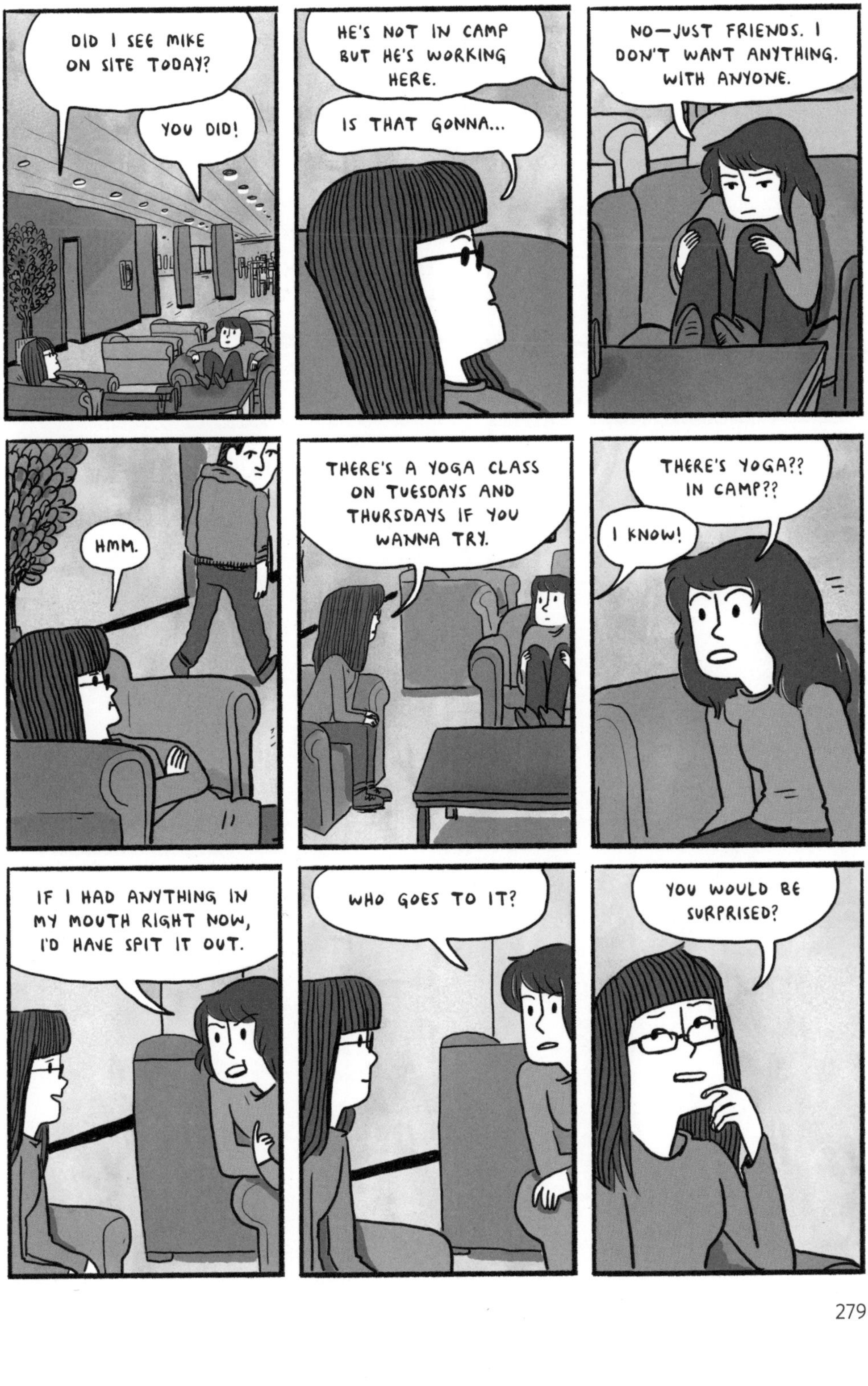
DID I SEE MIKE ON SITE TODAY?
YOU DID!
HE'S NOT IN CAMP BUT HE'S WORKING HERE.
IS THAT GONNA...
NO—JUST FRIENDS. I DON'T WANT ANYTHING. WITH ANYONE.
HMM.
THERE'S A YOGA CLASS ON TUESDAYS AND THURSDAYS IF YOU WANNA TRY.
THERE'S YOGA?? IN CAMP??
I KNOW!
IF I HAD ANYTHING IN MY MOUTH RIGHT NOW, I'D HAVE SPIT IT OUT.
WHO GOES TO IT?
YOU WOULD BE SURPRISED?

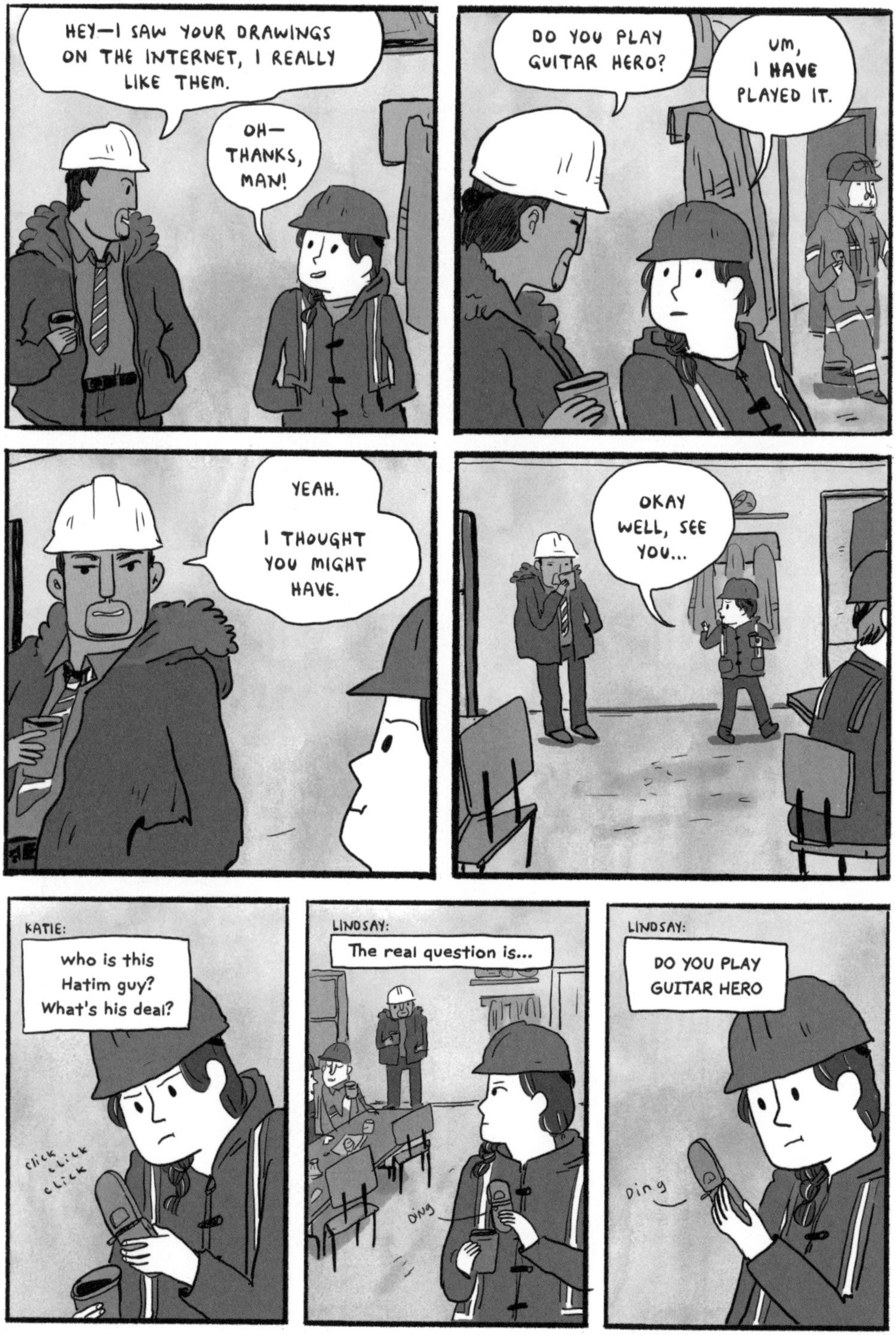
HEY—I SAW YOUR DRAWINGS ON THE INTERNET, I REALLY LIKE THEM.
OH— THANKS, MAN!
DO YOU PLAY GUITAR HERO?
UM, I HAVE PLAYED IT.
YEAH.
I THOUGHT YOU MIGHT HAVE.
OKAY WELL, SEE YOU...
KATIE:
who is this Hatim guy? What's his deal?
click click click
LINDSAY:
The real question is...
DING
LINDSAY:
DO YOU PLAY GUITAR HERO
DING

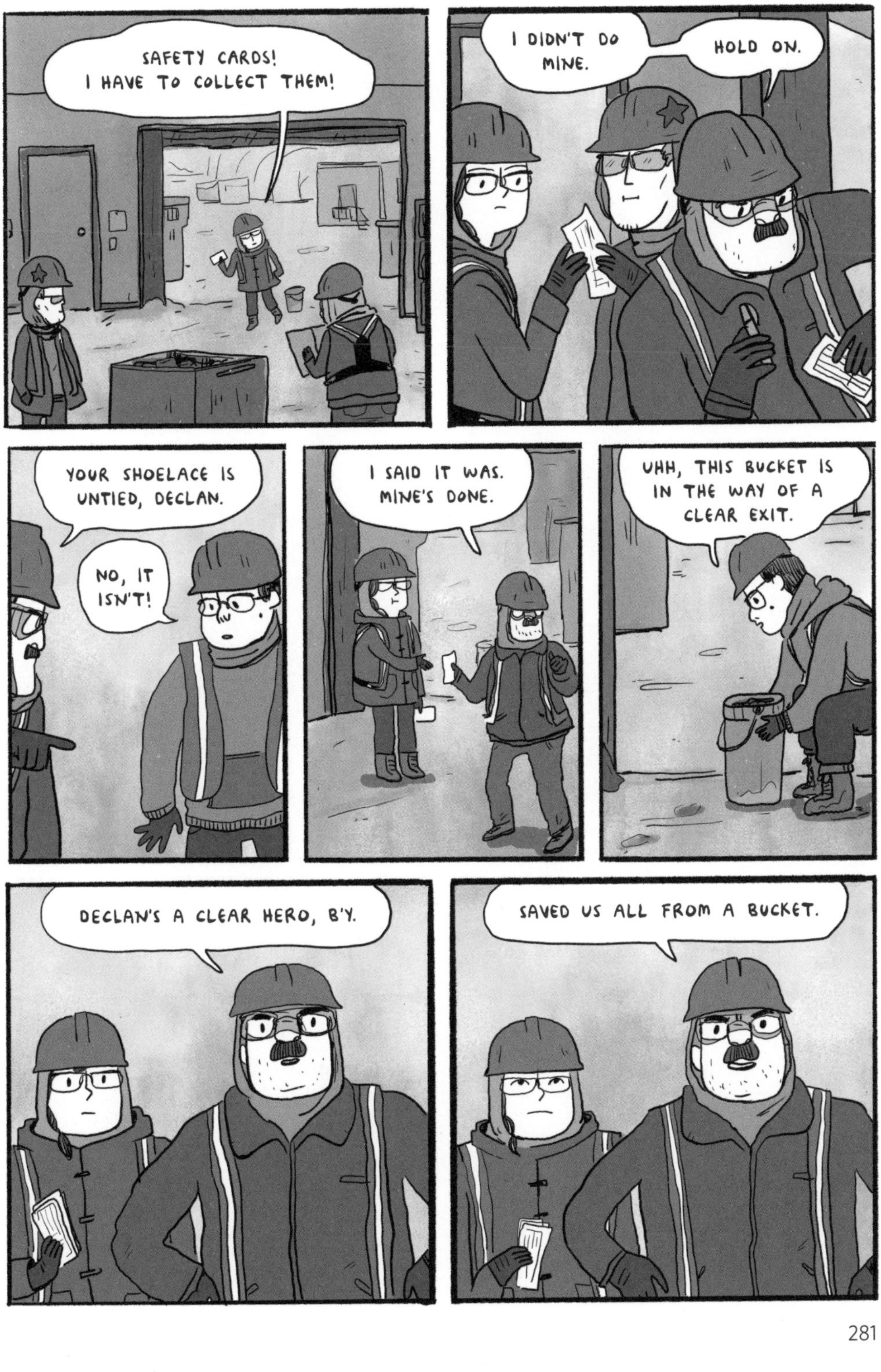
SAFETY CARDS! I HAVE TO COLLECT THEM!
I DIDN'T DO MINE.
HOLD ON.
YOUR SHOELACE IS UNTIED, DECLAN.
NO, IT ISN'T!
I SAID IT WAS. MINE'S DONE.
UHH, THIS BUCKET IS IN THE WAY OF A CLEAR EXIT.
DECLAN'S A CLEAR HERO, B'Y.
SAVED US ALL FROM A BUCKET.

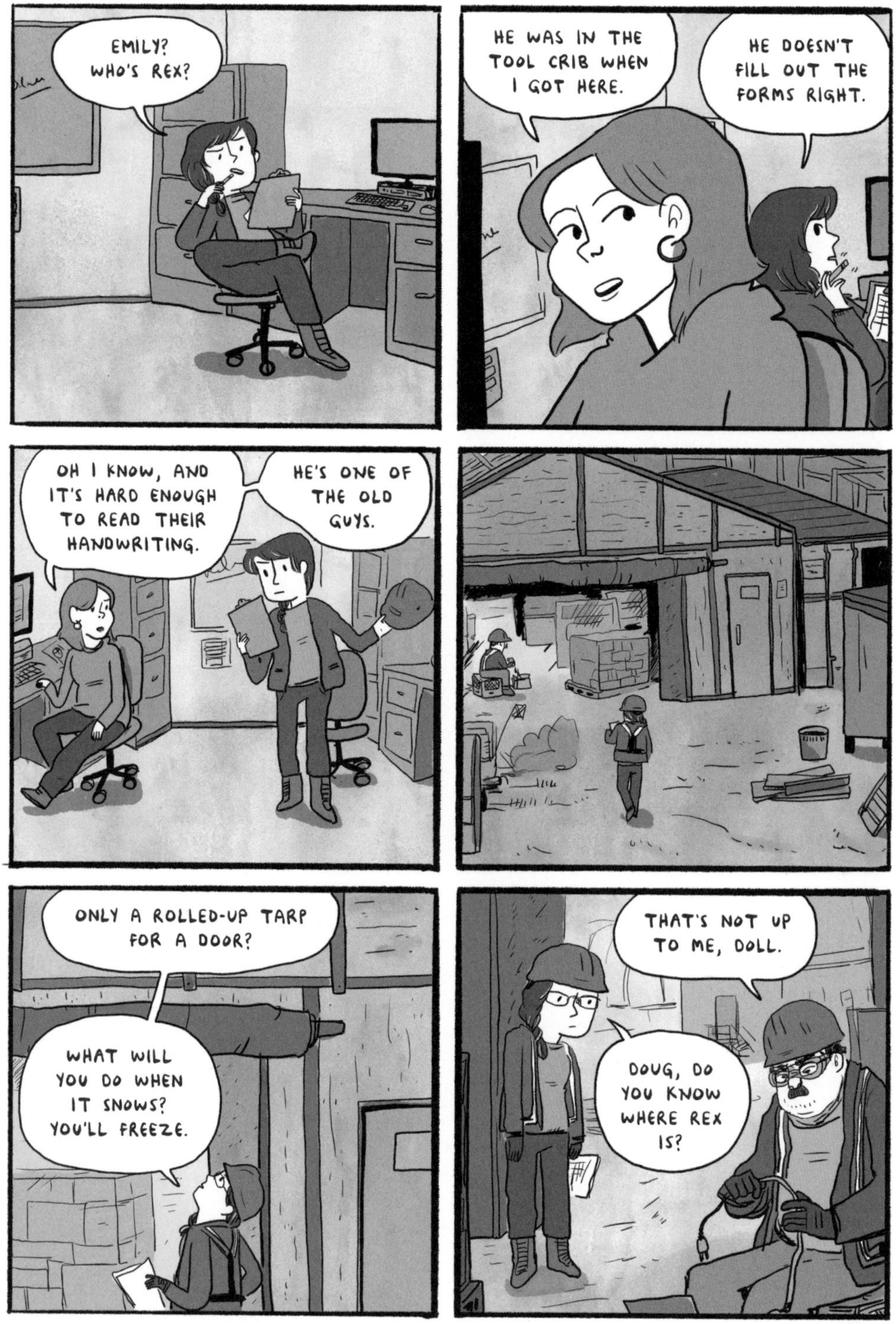
EMILY? WHO'S REX?
HE WAS IN THE TOOL CRIB WHEN I GOT HERE.
HE DOESN'T FILL OUT THE FORMS RIGHT.
OH I KNOW, AND IT'S HARD ENOUGH TO READ THEIR HANDWRITING.
HE'S ONE OF THE OLD GUYS.
ONLY A ROLLED-UP TARP FOR A DOOR?
WHAT WILL YOU DO WHEN IT SNOWS? YOU'LL FREEZE.
THAT'S NOT UP TO ME, DOLL.
DOUG, DO YOU KNOW WHERE REX IS?

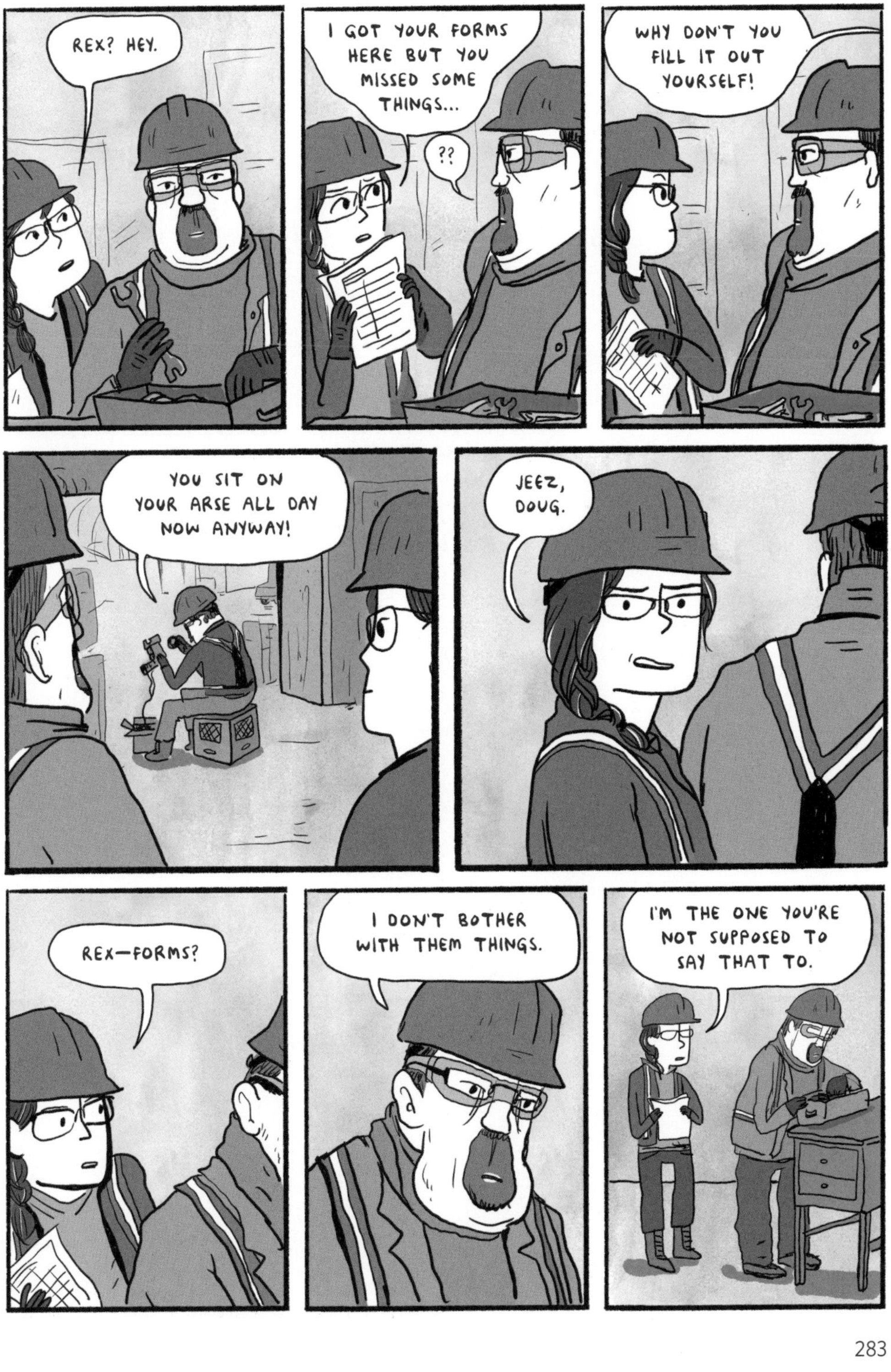
REX? HEY.
I GOT YOUR FORMS HERE BUT YOU MISSED SOME THINGS...
??
WHY DON'T YOU FILL IT OUT YOURSELF!
YOU SIT ON YOUR ARSE ALL DAY NOW ANYWAY!
JEEZ, DOUG.
REX—FORMS?
I DON'T BOTHER WITH THEM THINGS.
I'M THE ONE YOU'RE NOT SUPPOSED TO SAY THAT TO.

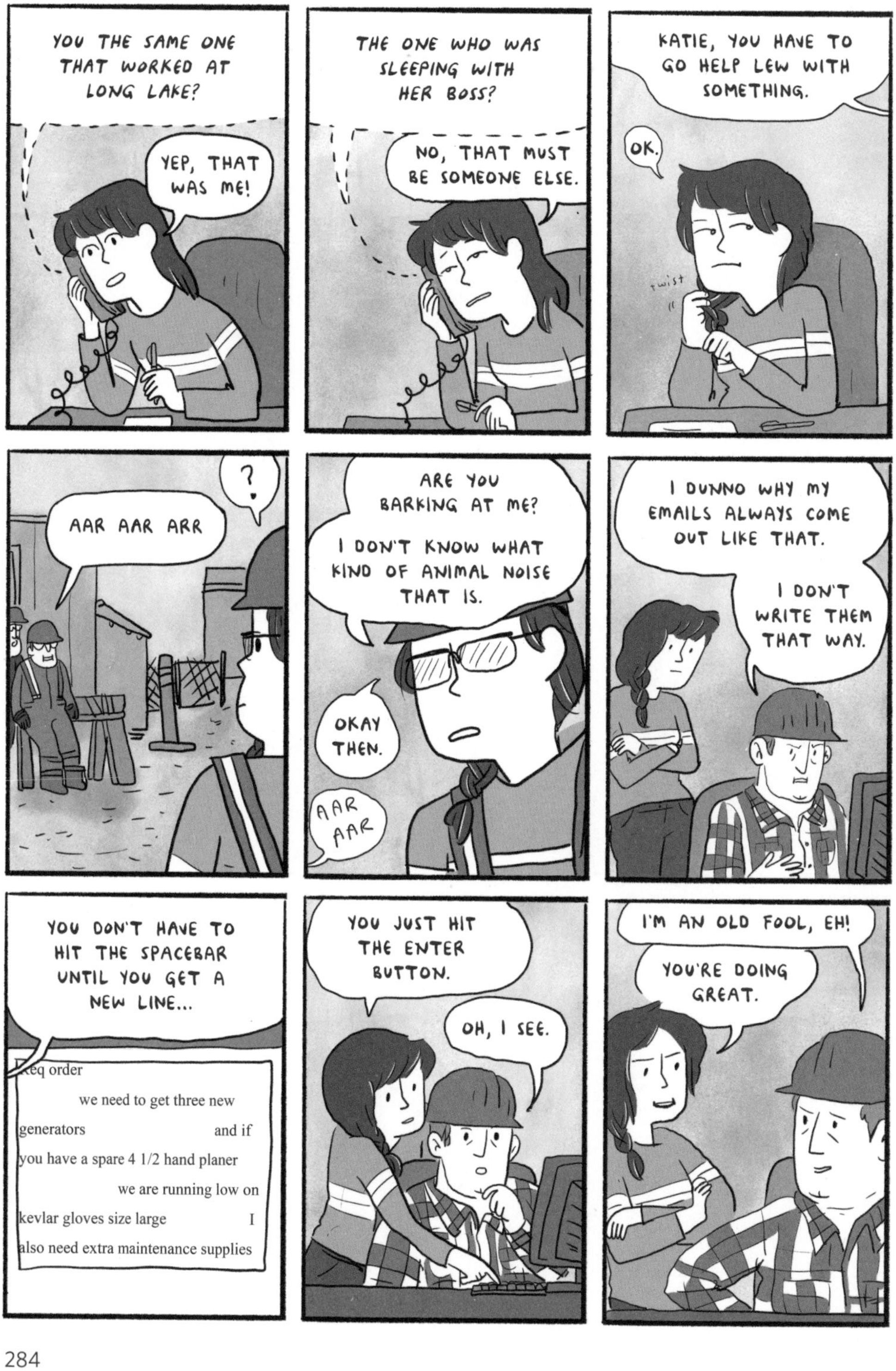
YOU THE SAME ONE THAT WORKED AT LONG LAKE?
YEP, THAT WAS ME!
THE ONE WHO WAS SLEEPING WITH HER BOSS?
NO, THAT MUST BE SOMEONE ELSE.
KATIE, YOU HAVE TO GO HELP LEW WITH SOMETHING.
OK.
twist
AAR AAR ARR
?
ARE YOU BARKING AT ME?
I DON'T KNOW WHAT KIND OF ANIMAL NOISE THAT IS.
OKAY THEN.
AAR AAR
I DUNNO WHY MY EMAILS ALWAYS COME OUT LIKE THAT.
I DON'T WRITE THEM THAT WAY.
YOU DON'T HAVE TO HIT THE SPACEBAR UNTIL YOU GET A NEW LINE...
Req order
we need to get three new
generators and if
you have a spare 4 1/2 hand planer
we are running low on
kevlar gloves size large I
also need extra maintenance supplies
YOU JUST HIT THE ENTER BUTTON.
OH, I SEE.
I'M AN OLD FOOL, EH!
YOU'RE DOING GREAT.

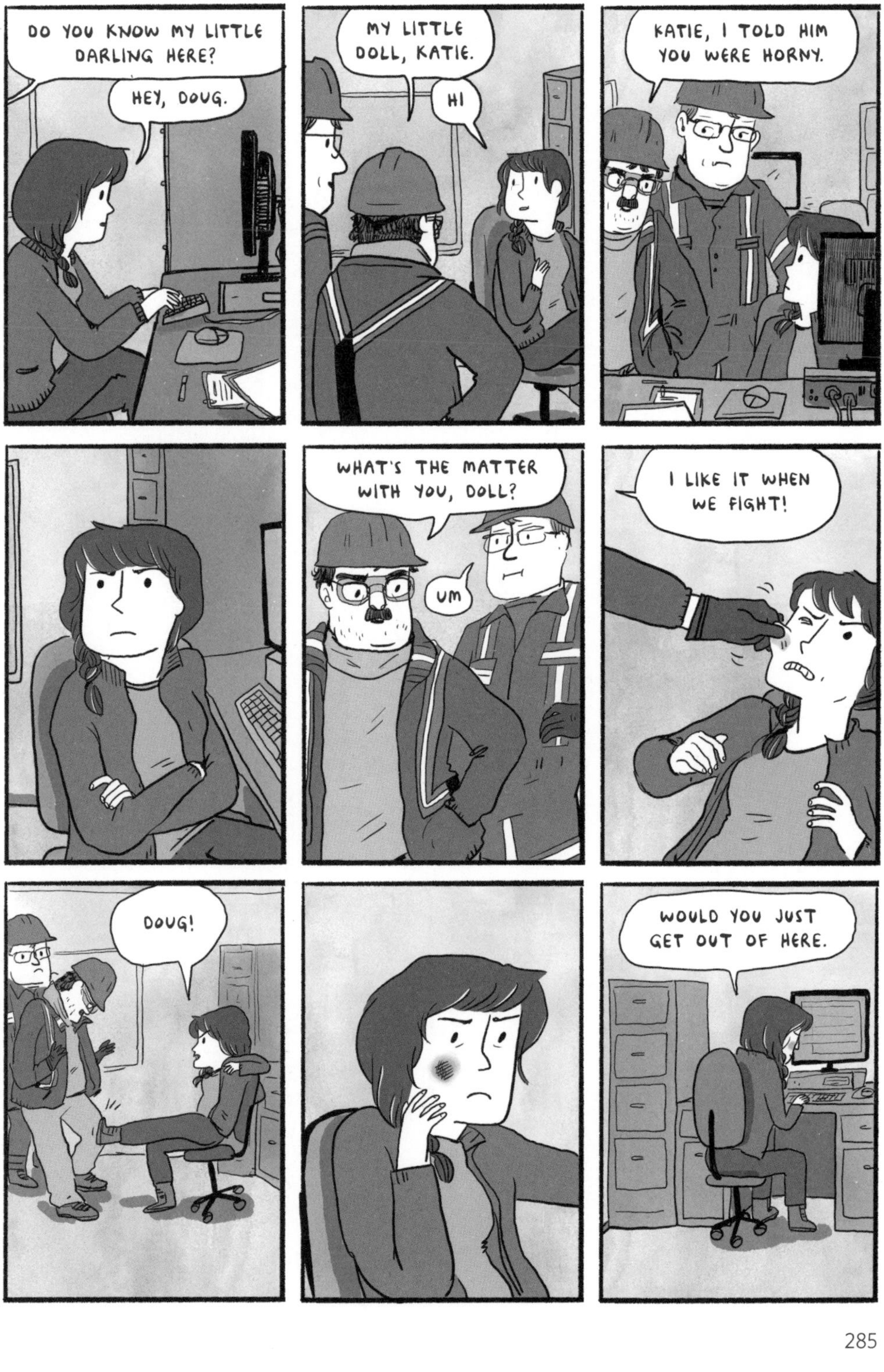
DO YOU KNOW MY LITTLE DARLING HERE?
HEY, DOUG.
MY LITTLE DOLL, KATIE.
HI
KATIE, I TOLD HIM YOU WERE HORNY.
WHAT'S THE MATTER WITH YOU, DOLL?
UM
I LIKE IT WHEN WE FIGHT!
DOUG!
WOULD YOU JUST GET OUT OF HERE.

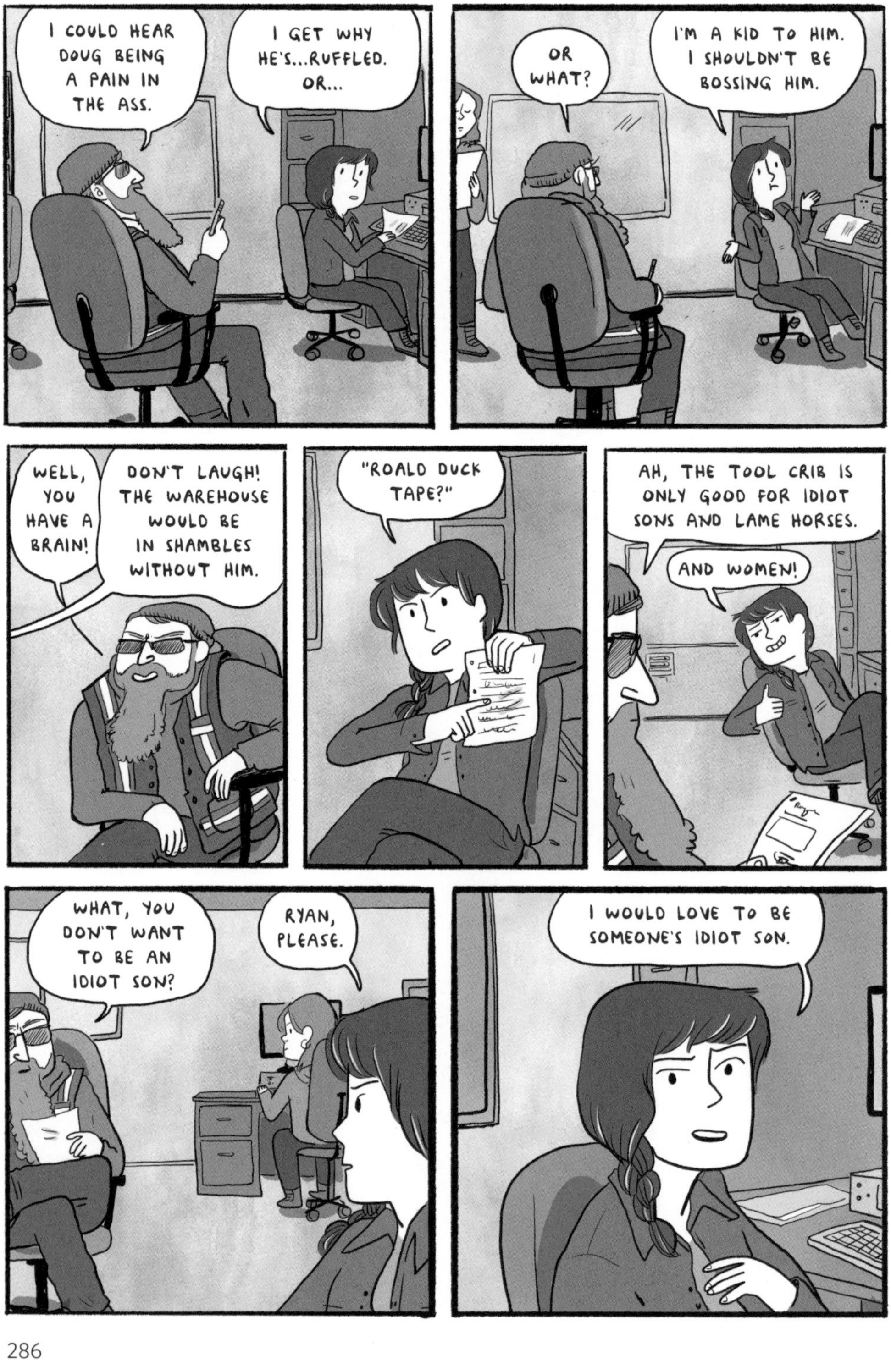
I COULD HEAR DOUG BEING A PAIN IN THE ASS.
I GET WHY HE'S...RUFFLED. OR...
OR WHAT?
I'M A KID TO HIM. I SHOULDN'T BE BOSSING HIM.
WELL, YOU HAVE A BRAIN!
DON'T LAUGH! THE WAREHOUSE WOULD BE IN SHAMBLES WITHOUT HIM.
"ROALD DUCK TAPE?"
AH, THE TOOL CRIB IS ONLY GOOD FOR IDIOT SONS AND LAME HORSES.
AND WOMEN!
WHAT, YOU DON'T WANT TO BE AN IDIOT SON?
RYAN, PLEASE.
I WOULD LOVE TO BE SOMEONE'S IDIOT SON.

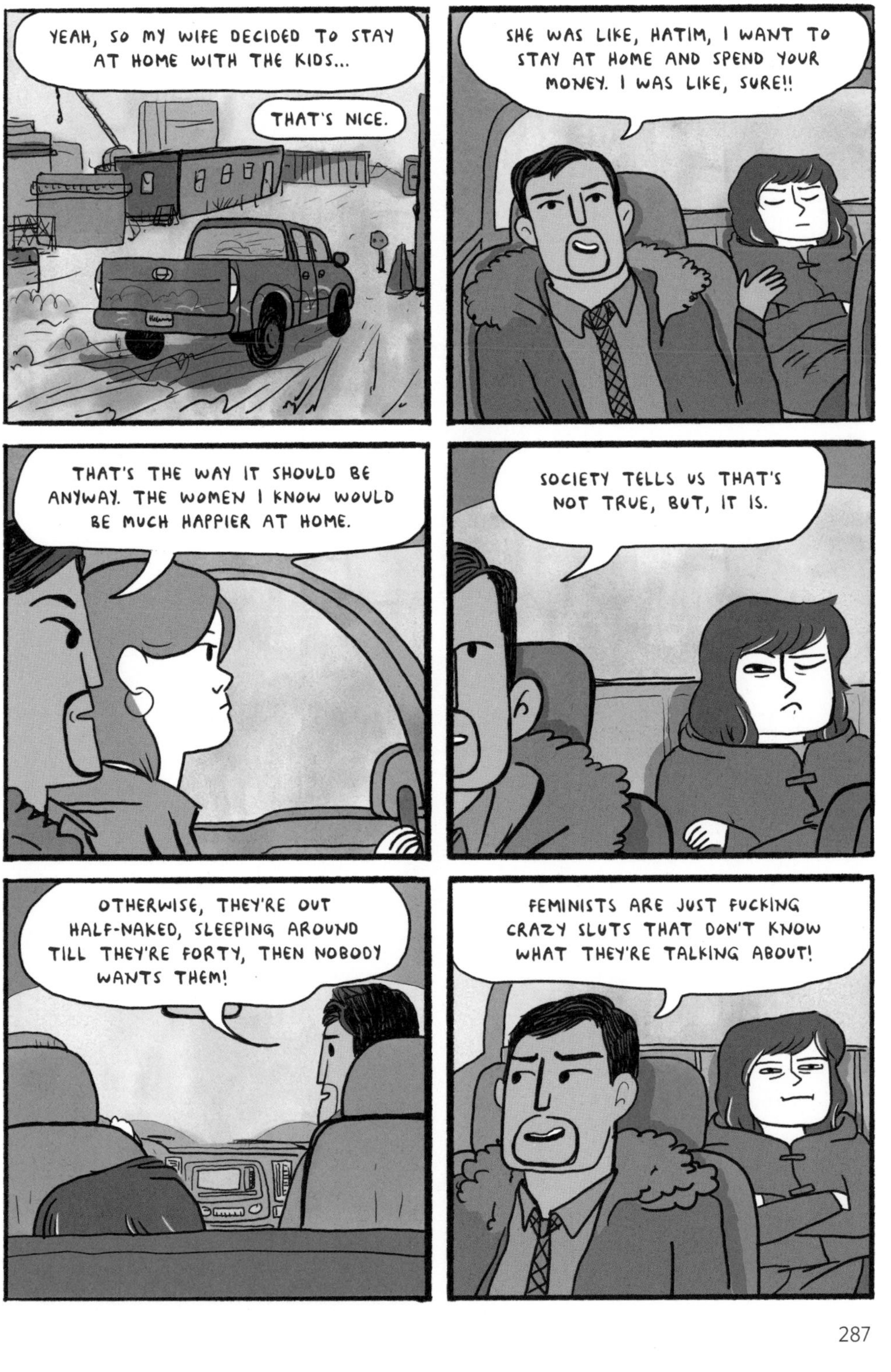
YEAH, SO MY WIFE DECIDED TO STAY AT HOME WITH THE KIDS...
THAT'S NICE.
SHE WAS LIKE, HATIM, I WANT TO STAY AT HOME AND SPEND YOUR MONEY. I WAS LIKE, SURE!!
THAT'S THE WAY IT SHOULD BE ANYWAY. THE WOMEN I KNOW WOULD BE MUCH HAPPIER AT HOME.
SOCIETY TELLS US THAT'S NOT TRUE, BUT, IT IS.
OTHERWISE, THEY'RE OUT HALF-NAKED, SLEEPING AROUND TILL THEY'RE FORTY, THEN NOBODY WANTS THEM!
FEMINISTS ARE JUST FUCKING CRAZY SLUTS THAT DON'T KNOW WHAT THEY'RE TALKING ABOUT!

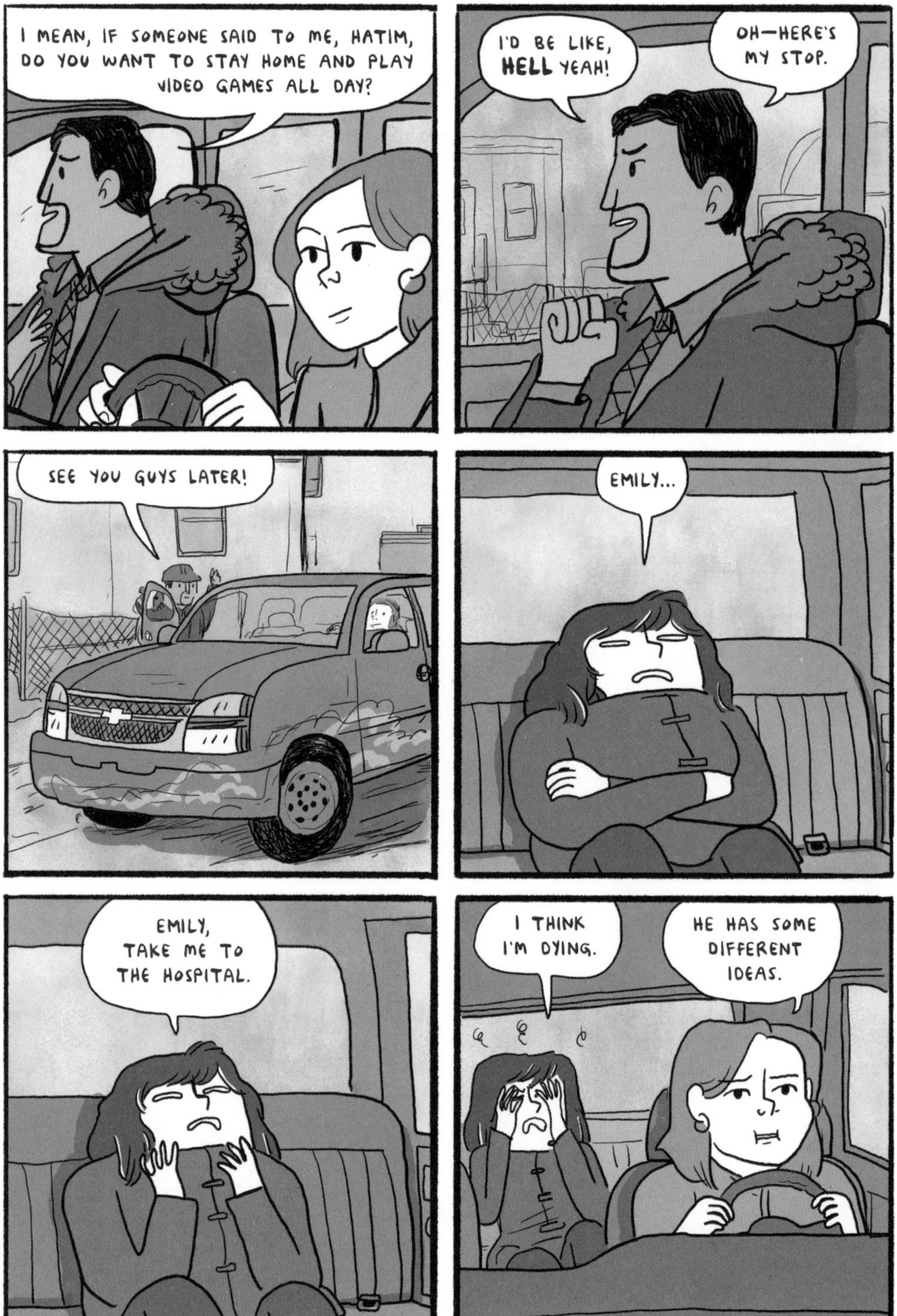
I MEAN, IF SOMEONE SAID TO ME, HATIM, DO YOU WANT TO STAY HOME AND PLAY VIDEO GAMES ALL DAY?
I'D BE LIKE, **HELL** YEAH!
OH—HERE'S MY STOP.
SEE YOU GUYS LATER!
EMILY...
EMILY, TAKE ME TO THE HOSPITAL.
I THINK I'M DYING.
HE HAS SOME DIFFERENT IDEAS.

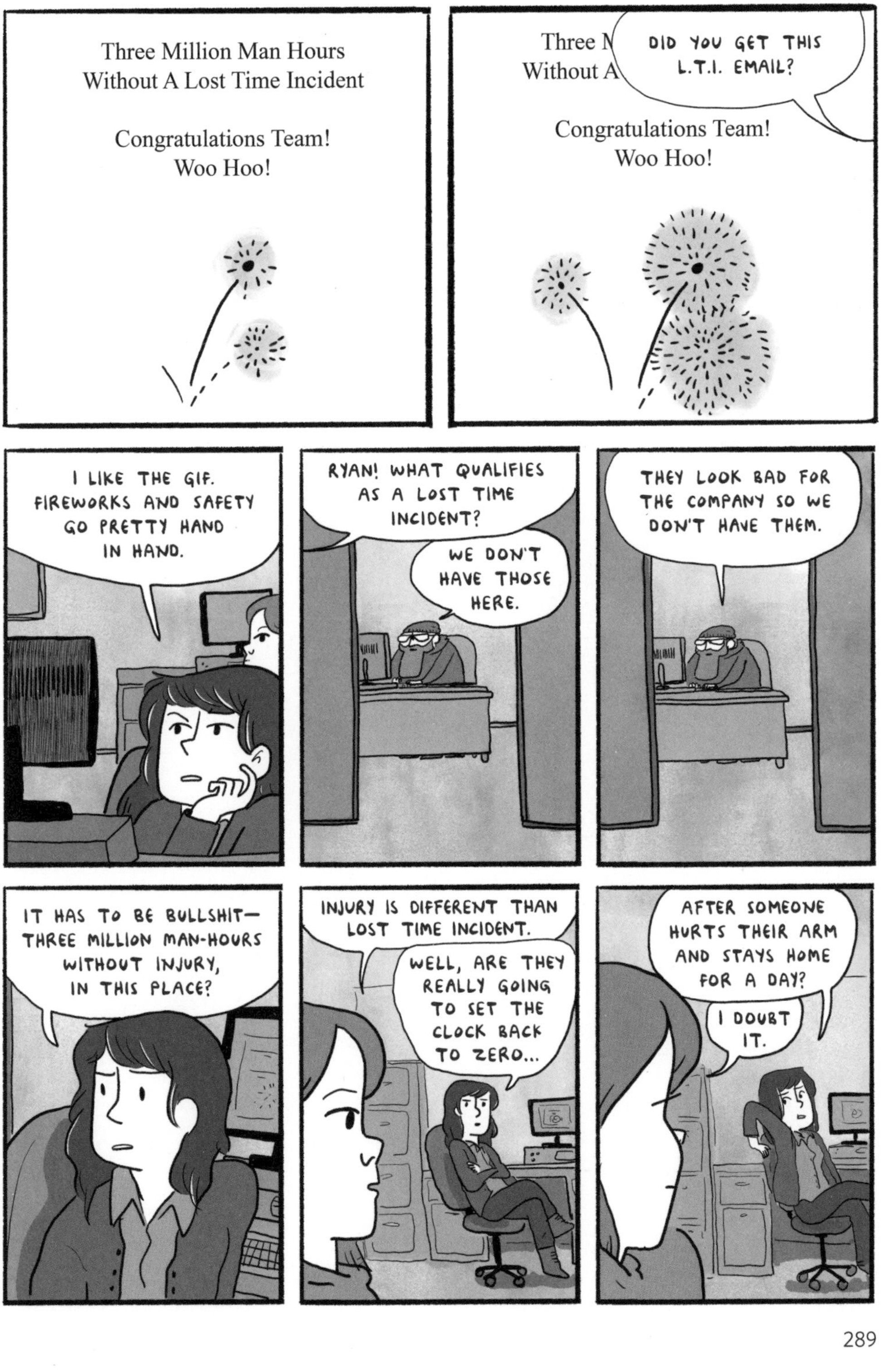
Three Million Man Hours
Without A Lost Time Incident
Congratulations Team!
Woo Hoo!
DID YOU GET THIS L.T.I. EMAIL?
I LIKE THE GIF. FIREWORKS AND SAFETY GO PRETTY HAND IN HAND.
RYAN! WHAT QUALIFIES AS A LOST TIME INCIDENT?
WE DON'T HAVE THOSE HERE.
THEY LOOK BAD FOR THE COMPANY SO WE DON'T HAVE THEM.
IT HAS TO BE BULLSHIT— THREE MILLION MAN-HOURS WITHOUT INJURY, IN THIS PLACE?
INJURY IS DIFFERENT THAN LOST TIME INCIDENT.
WELL, ARE THEY REALLY GOING TO SET THE CLOCK BACK TO ZERO...
AFTER SOMEONE HURTS THEIR ARM AND STAYS HOME FOR A DAY?
I DOUBT IT.

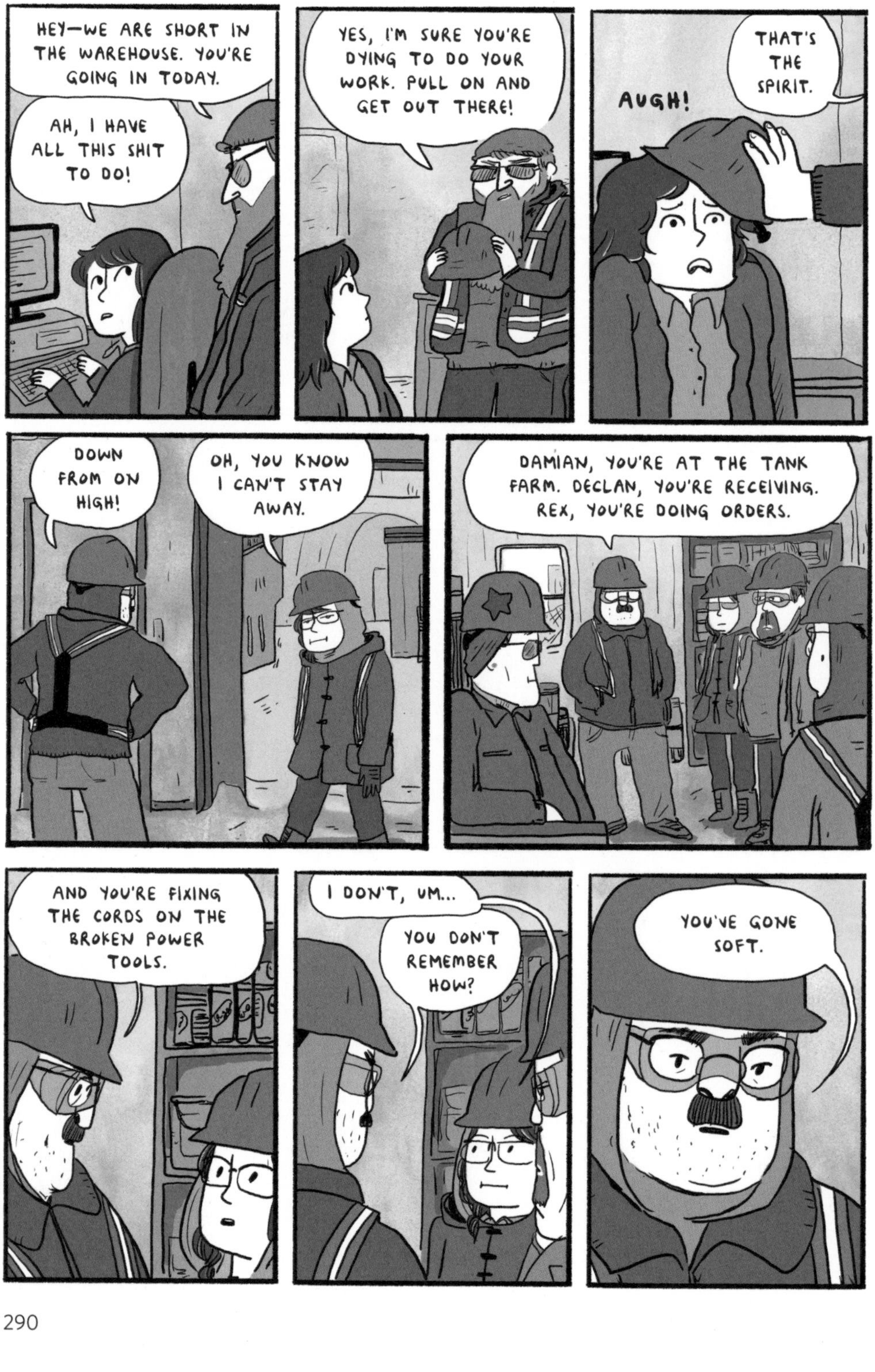
HEY—WE ARE SHORT IN THE WAREHOUSE. YOU'RE GOING IN TODAY.
AH, I HAVE ALL THIS SHIT TO DO!
YES, I'M SURE YOU'RE DYING TO DO YOUR WORK. PULL ON AND GET OUT THERE!
AUGH!
THAT'S THE SPIRIT.
DOWN FROM ON HIGH!
OH, YOU KNOW I CAN'T STAY AWAY.
DAMIAN, YOU'RE AT THE TANK FARM. DECLAN, YOU'RE RECEIVING. REX, YOU'RE DOING ORDERS.
AND YOU'RE FIXING THE CORDS ON THE BROKEN POWER TOOLS.
I DON'T, UM...
YOU DON'T REMEMBER HOW?
YOU'VE GONE SOFT.

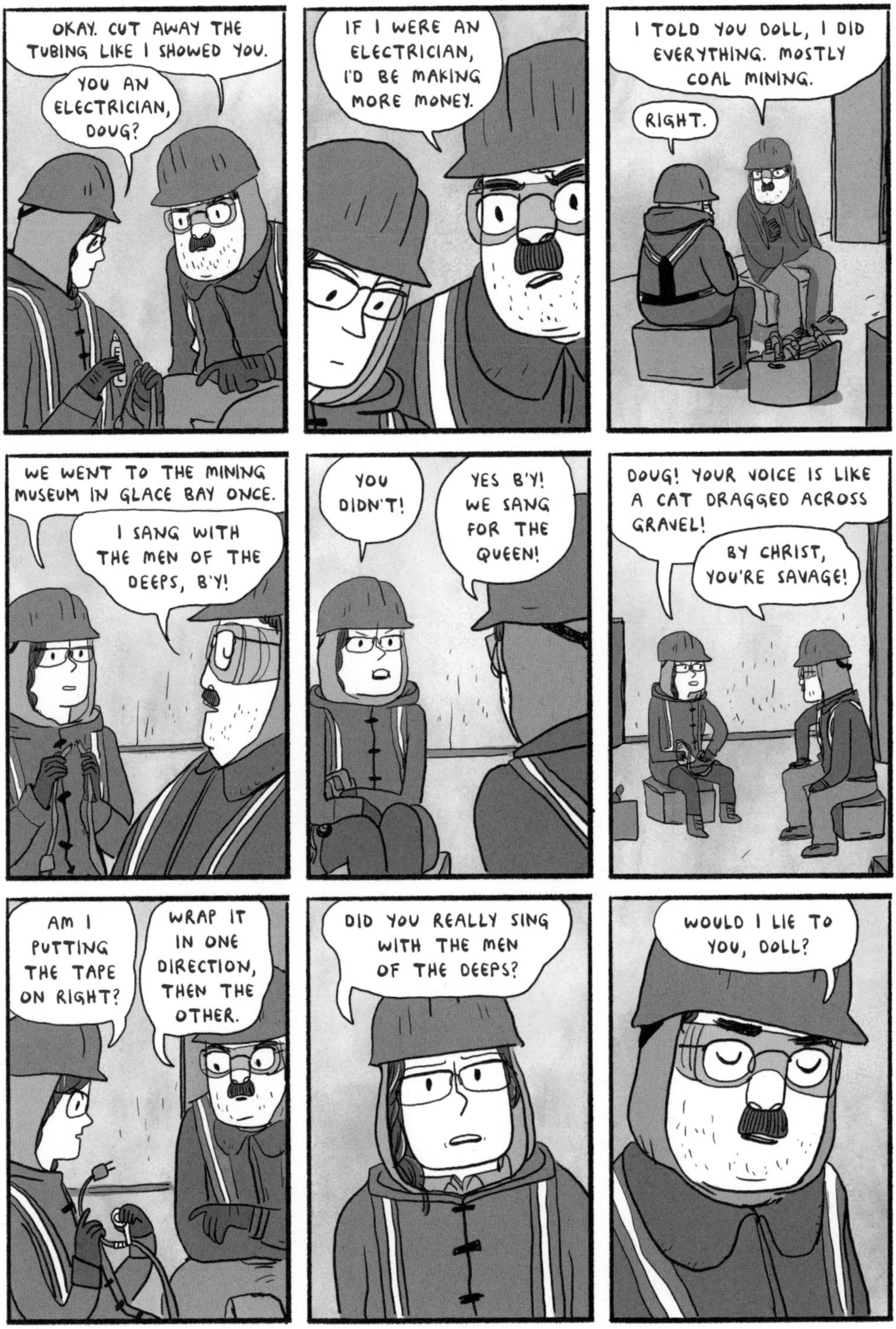
OKAY. CUT AWAY THE TUBING LIKE I SHOWED YOU.
YOU AN ELECTRICIAN, DOUG?
IF I WERE AN ELECTRICIAN, I'D BE MAKING MORE MONEY.
I TOLD YOU DOLL, I DID EVERYTHING. MOSTLY COAL MINING.
RIGHT.
WE WENT TO THE MINING MUSEUM IN GLACE BAY ONCE.
I SANG WITH THE MEN OF THE DEEPS, B'Y!
YOU DIDN'T!
YES B'Y! WE SANG FOR THE QUEEN!
DOUG! YOUR VOICE IS LIKE A CAT DRAGGED ACROSS GRAVEL!
BY CHRIST, YOU'RE SAVAGE!
AM I PUTTING THE TAPE ON RIGHT?
WRAP IT IN ONE DIRECTION, THEN THE OTHER.
DID YOU REALLY SING WITH THE MEN OF THE DEEPS?
WOULD I LIE TO YOU, DOLL?

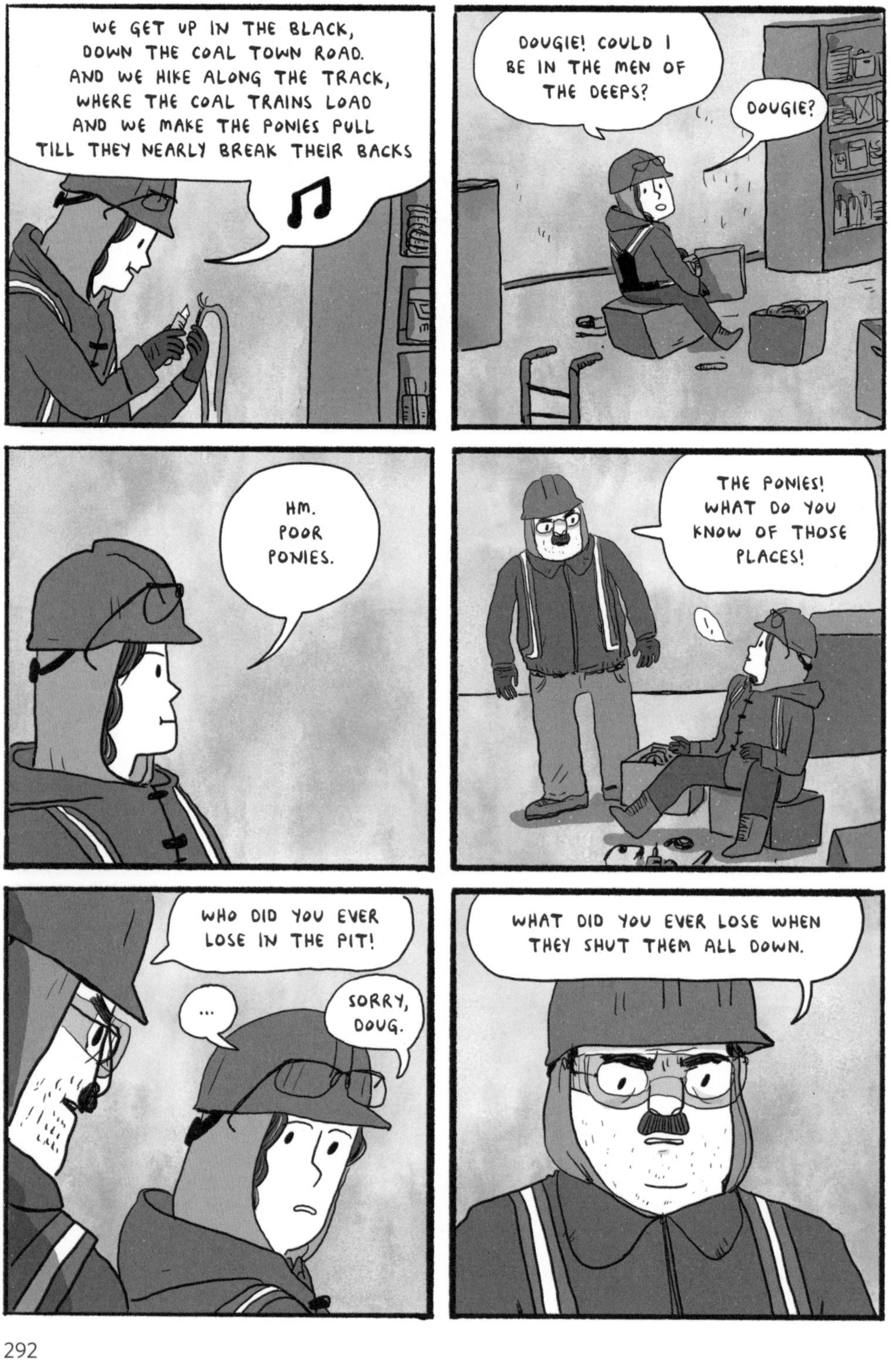
WE GET UP IN THE BLACK, DOWN THE COAL TOWN ROAD. AND WE HIKE ALONG THE TRACK, WHERE THE COAL TRAINS LOAD AND WE MAKE THE PONIES PULL TILL THEY NEARLY BREAK THEIR BACKS
DOUGIE! COULD I BE IN THE MEN OF THE DEEPS?
DOUGIE?
HM. POOR PONIES.
THE PONIES! WHAT DO YOU KNOW OF THOSE PLACES!
!
WHO DID YOU EVER LOSE IN THE PIT!
...
SORRY, DOUG.
WHAT DID YOU EVER LOSE WHEN THEY SHUT THEM ALL DOWN.

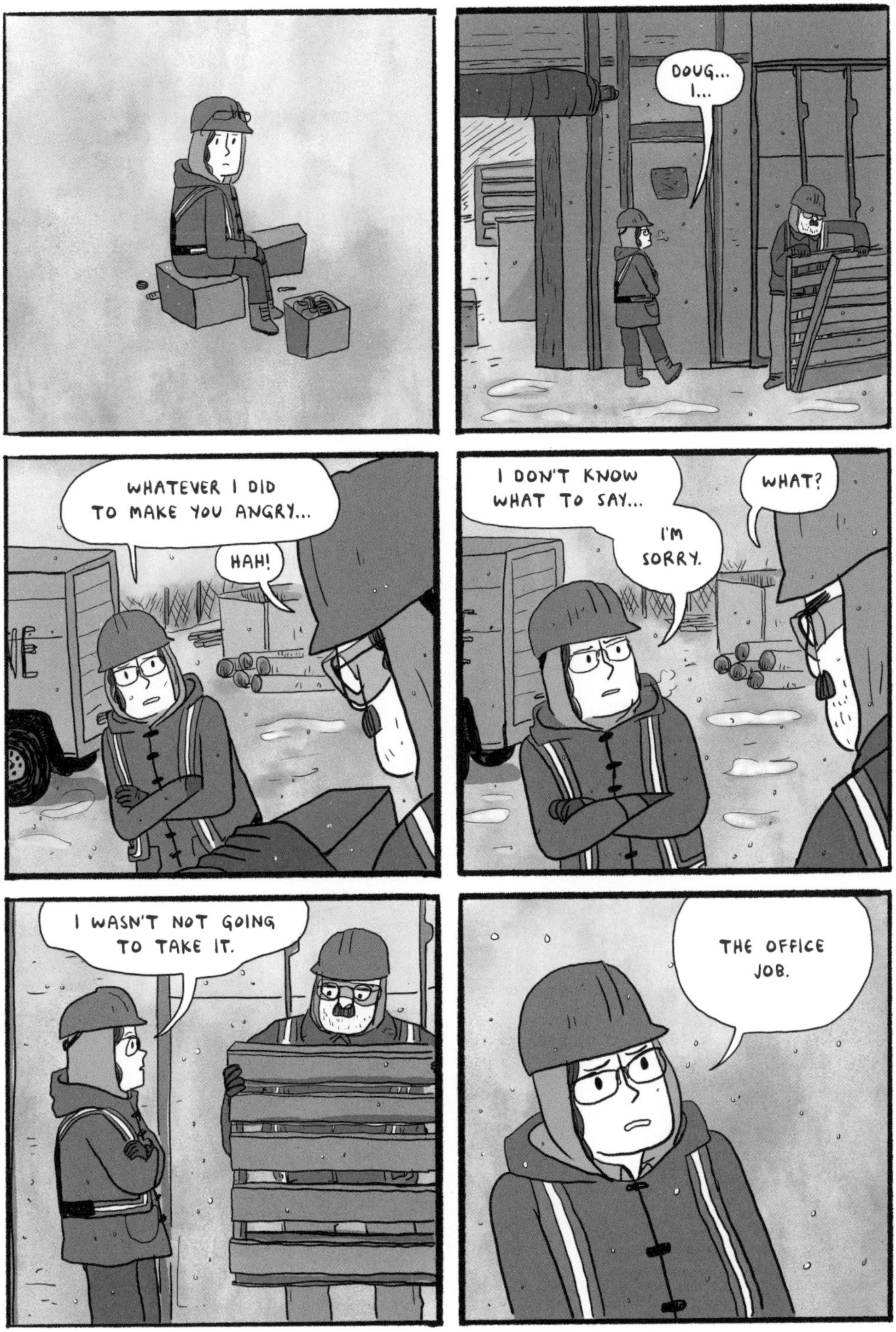
DOUG...
I...
WHATEVER I DID TO MAKE YOU ANGRY...
HAH!
I DON'T KNOW WHAT TO SAY...
I'M SORRY.
WHAT?
I WASN'T NOT GOING TO TAKE IT.
THE OFFICE JOB.

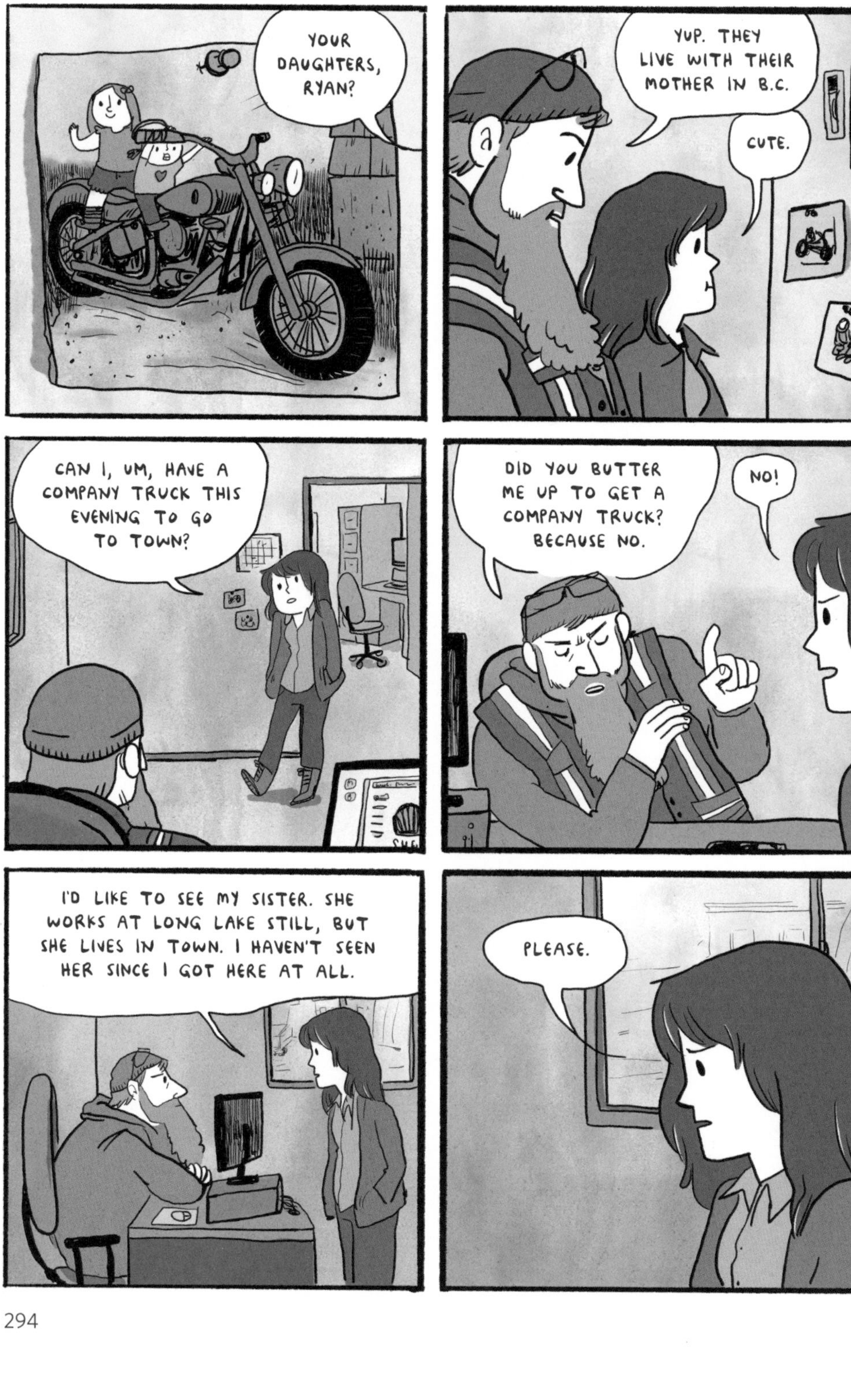
YOUR DAUGHTERS, RYAN?
YUP. THEY LIVE WITH THEIR MOTHER IN B.C.
CUTE.
CAN I, UM, HAVE A COMPANY TRUCK THIS EVENING TO GO TO TOWN?
DID YOU BUTTER ME UP TO GET A COMPANY TRUCK? BECAUSE NO.
NO!
I'D LIKE TO SEE MY SISTER. SHE WORKS AT LONG LAKE STILL, BUT SHE LIVES IN TOWN. I HAVEN'T SEEN HER SINCE I GOT HERE AT ALL.
PLEASE.

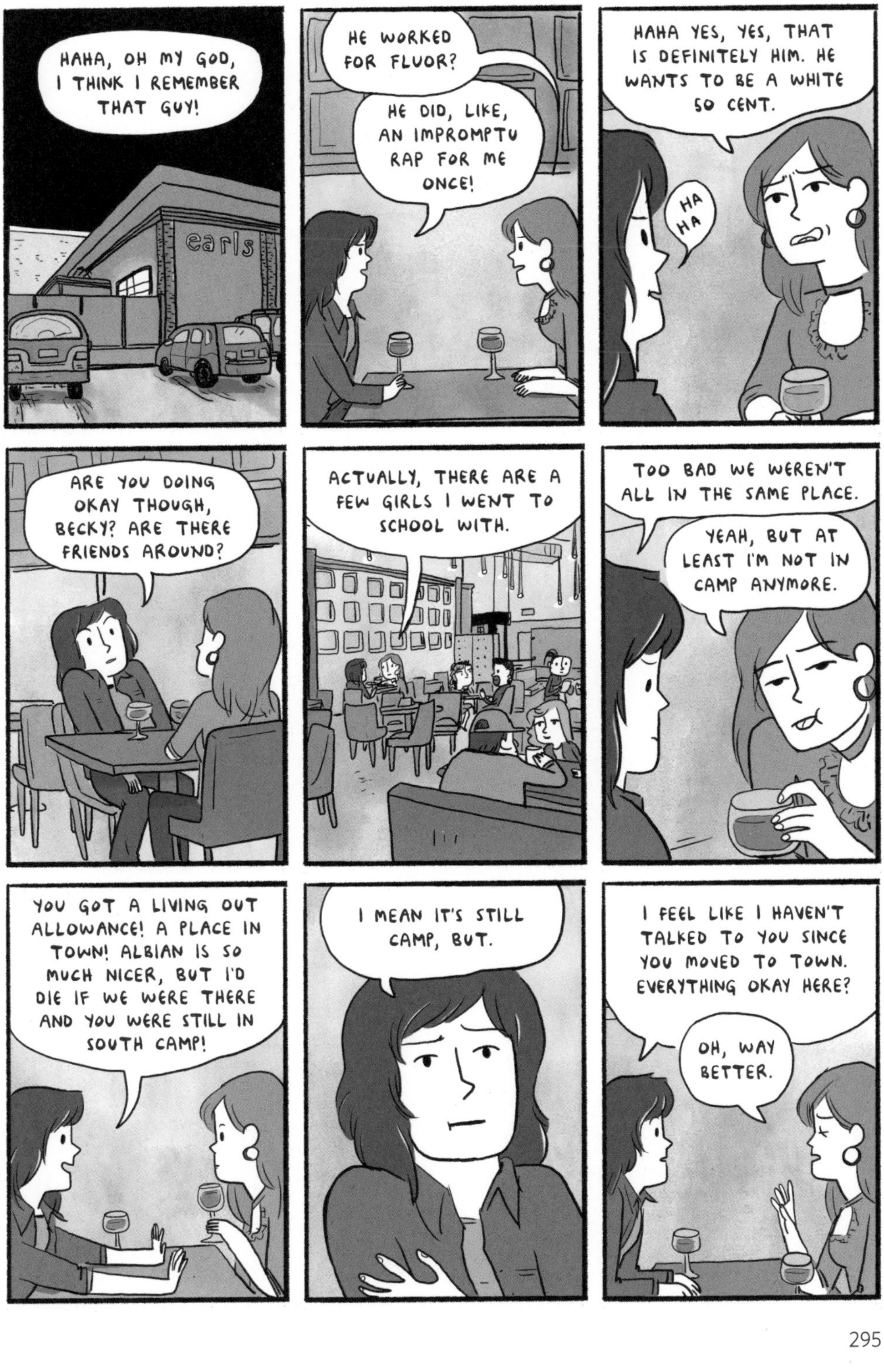
HAHA, OH MY GOD, I THINK I REMEMBER THAT GUY!
earls
HE WORKED FOR FLUOR?
HE DID, LIKE, AN IMPROMPTU RAP FOR ME ONCE!
HAHA YES, YES, THAT IS DEFINITELY HIM. HE WANTS TO BE A WHITE 50 CENT.
HA HA
ARE YOU DOING OKAY THOUGH, BECKY? ARE THERE FRIENDS AROUND?
ACTUALLY, THERE ARE A FEW GIRLS I WENT TO SCHOOL WITH.
TOO BAD WE WEREN'T ALL IN THE SAME PLACE.
YEAH, BUT AT LEAST I'M NOT IN CAMP ANYMORE.
YOU GOT A LIVING OUT ALLOWANCE! A PLACE IN TOWN! ALBIAN IS SO MUCH NICER, BUT I'D DIE IF WE WERE THERE AND YOU WERE STILL IN SOUTH CAMP!
I MEAN IT'S STILL CAMP, BUT.
I FEEL LIKE I HAVEN'T TALKED TO YOU SINCE YOU MOVED TO TOWN. EVERYTHING OKAY HERE?
OH, WAY BETTER.

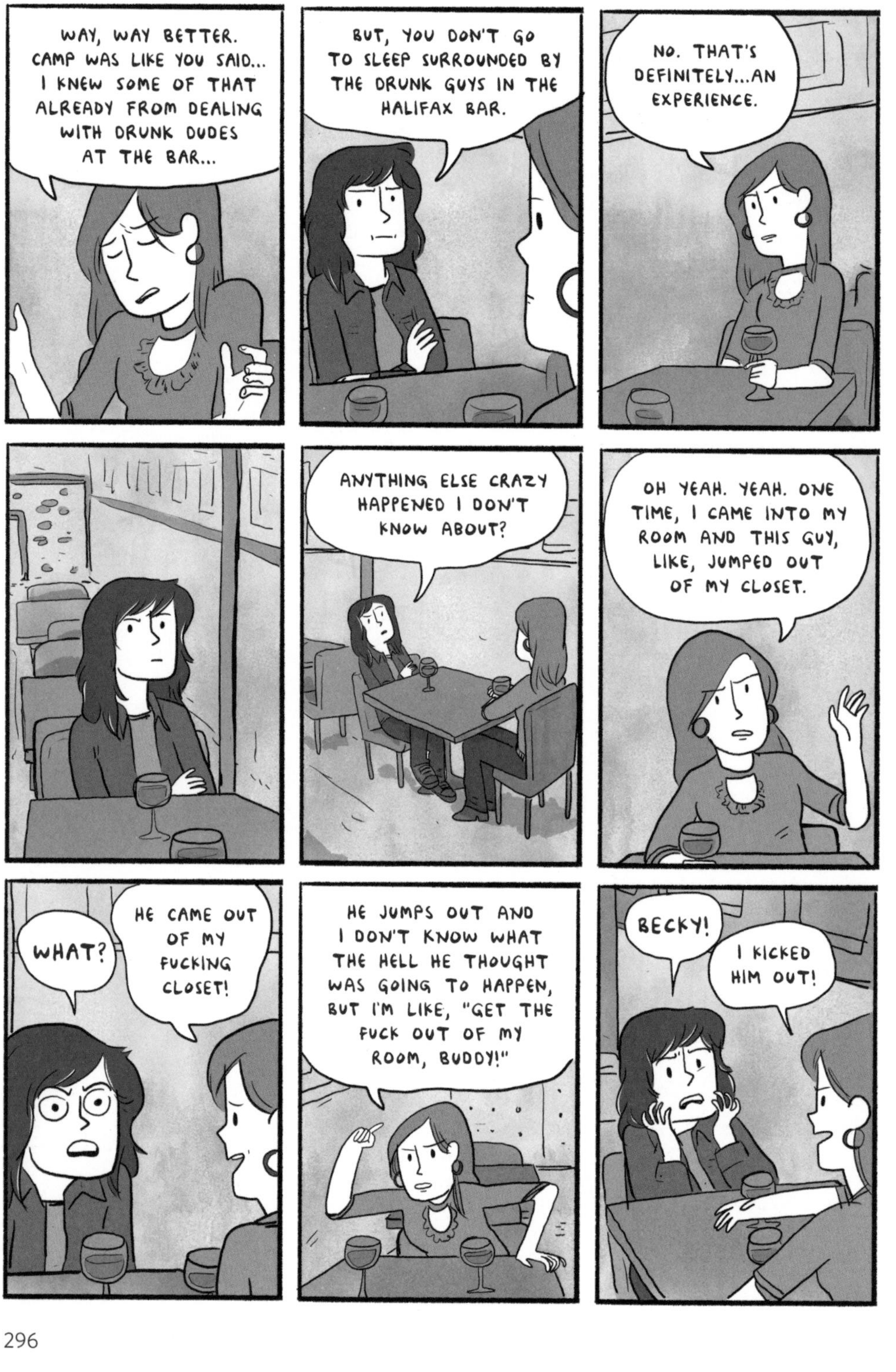
WAY, WAY BETTER. CAMP WAS LIKE YOU SAID... I KNEW SOME OF THAT ALREADY FROM DEALING WITH DRUNK DUDES AT THE BAR...
BUT, YOU DON'T GO TO SLEEP SURROUNDED BY THE DRUNK GUYS IN THE HALIFAX BAR.
NO. THAT'S DEFINITELY...AN EXPERIENCE.
ANYTHING ELSE CRAZY HAPPENED I DON'T KNOW ABOUT?
OH YEAH. YEAH. ONE TIME, I CAME INTO MY ROOM AND THIS GUY, LIKE, JUMPED OUT OF MY CLOSET.
WHAT?
HE CAME OUT OF MY FUCKING CLOSET!
HE JUMPS OUT AND I DON'T KNOW WHAT THE HELL HE THOUGHT WAS GOING TO HAPPEN, BUT I'M LIKE, "GET THE FUCK OUT OF MY ROOM, BUDDY!"
BECKY!
I KICKED HIM OUT!

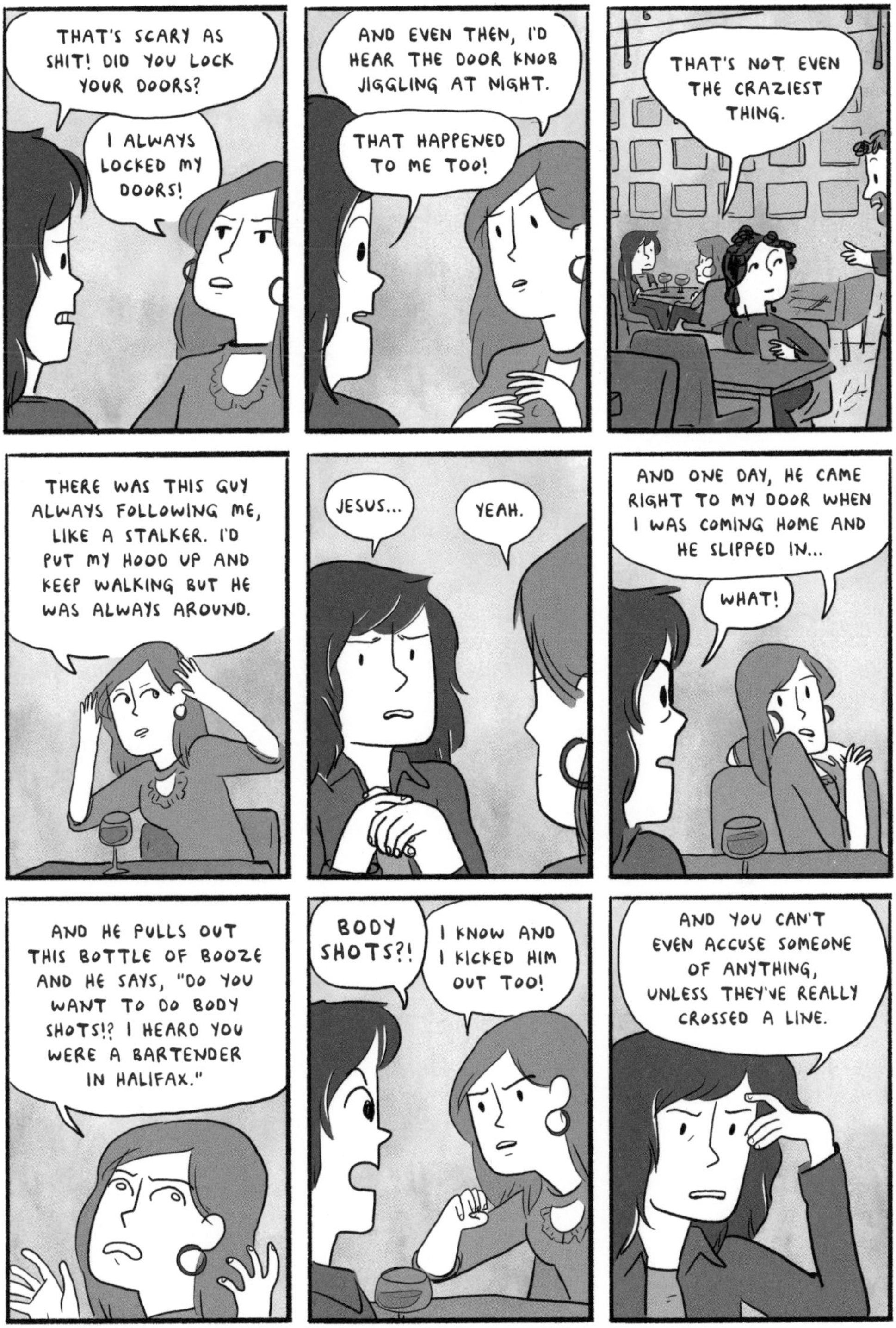
THAT'S SCARY AS SHIT! DID YOU LOCK YOUR DOORS?
I ALWAYS LOCKED MY DOORS!
AND EVEN THEN, I'D HEAR THE DOOR KNOB JIGGLING AT NIGHT.
THAT HAPPENED TO ME TOO!
THAT'S NOT EVEN THE CRAZIEST THING.
THERE WAS THIS GUY ALWAYS FOLLOWING ME, LIKE A STALKER. I'D PUT MY HOOD UP AND KEEP WALKING BUT HE WAS ALWAYS AROUND.
JESUS...
YEAH.
AND ONE DAY, HE CAME RIGHT TO MY DOOR WHEN I WAS COMING HOME AND HE SLIPPED IN...
WHAT!
AND HE PULLS OUT THIS BOTTLE OF BOOZE AND HE SAYS, "DO YOU WANT TO DO BODY SHOTS!? I HEARD YOU WERE A BARTENDER IN HALIFAX."
BODY SHOTS?!
I KNOW AND I KICKED HIM OUT TOO!
AND YOU CAN'T EVEN ACCUSE SOMEONE OF ANYTHING, UNLESS THEY'VE REALLY CROSSED A LINE.

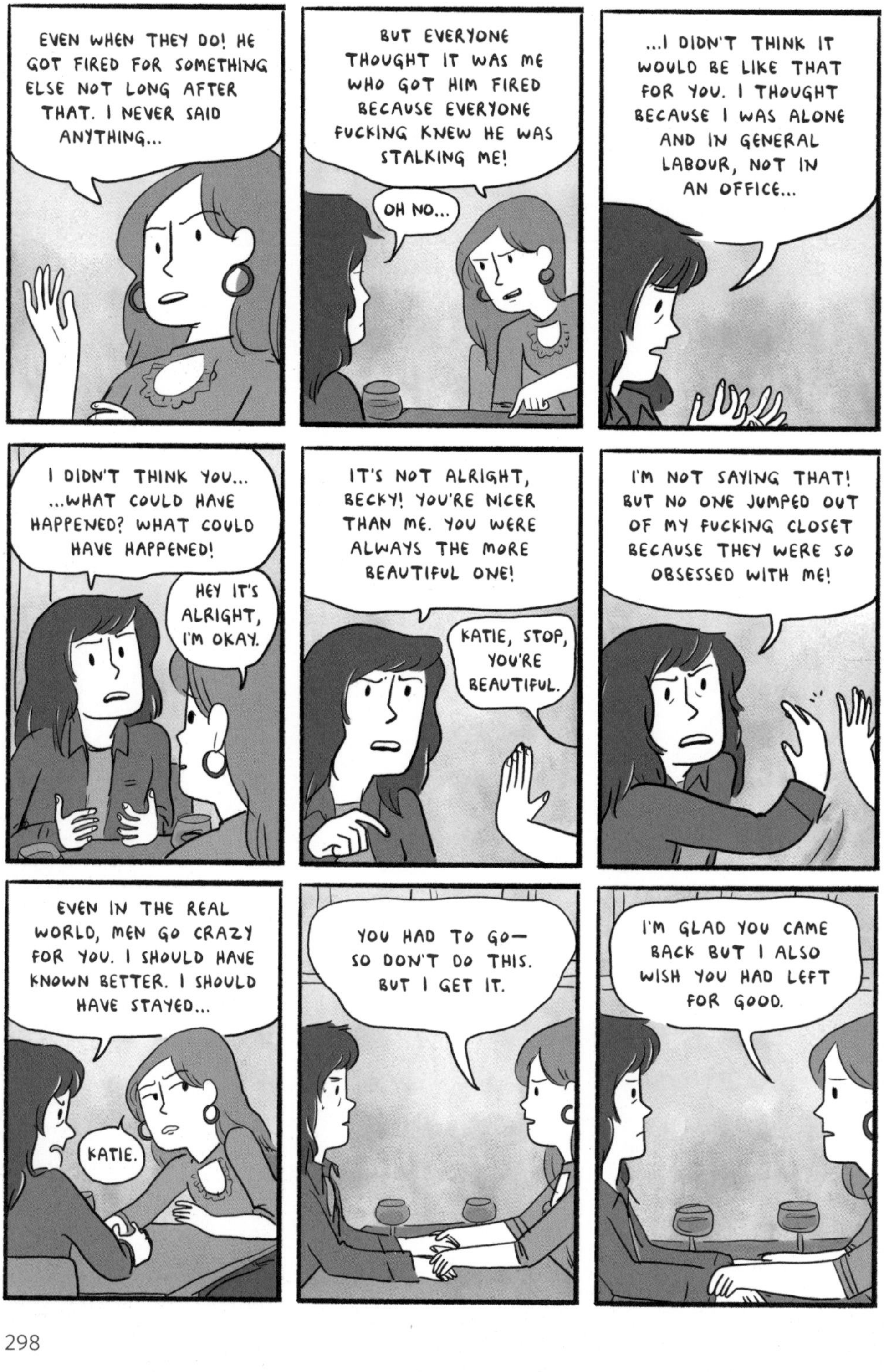
EVEN WHEN THEY DO! HE GOT FIRED FOR SOMETHING ELSE NOT LONG AFTER THAT. I NEVER SAID ANYTHING...
BUT EVERYONE THOUGHT IT WAS ME WHO GOT HIM FIRED BECAUSE EVERYONE FUCKING KNEW HE WAS STALKING ME!
OH NO...
...I DIDN'T THINK IT WOULD BE LIKE THAT FOR YOU. I THOUGHT BECAUSE I WAS ALONE AND IN GENERAL LABOUR, NOT IN AN OFFICE...
I DIDN'T THINK YOU... ...WHAT COULD HAVE HAPPENED? WHAT COULD HAVE HAPPENED!
HEY IT'S ALRIGHT, I'M OKAY.
IT'S NOT ALRIGHT, BECKY! YOU'RE NICER THAN ME. YOU WERE ALWAYS THE MORE BEAUTIFUL ONE!
KATIE, STOP, YOU'RE BEAUTIFUL.
I'M NOT SAYING THAT! BUT NO ONE JUMPED OUT OF MY FUCKING CLOSET BECAUSE THEY WERE SO OBSESSED WITH ME!
EVEN IN THE REAL WORLD, MEN GO CRAZY FOR YOU. I SHOULD HAVE KNOWN BETTER. I SHOULD HAVE STAYED...
KATIE.
YOU HAD TO GO— SO DON'T DO THIS. BUT I GET IT.
I'M GLAD YOU CAME BACK BUT I ALSO WISH YOU HAD LEFT FOR GOOD.

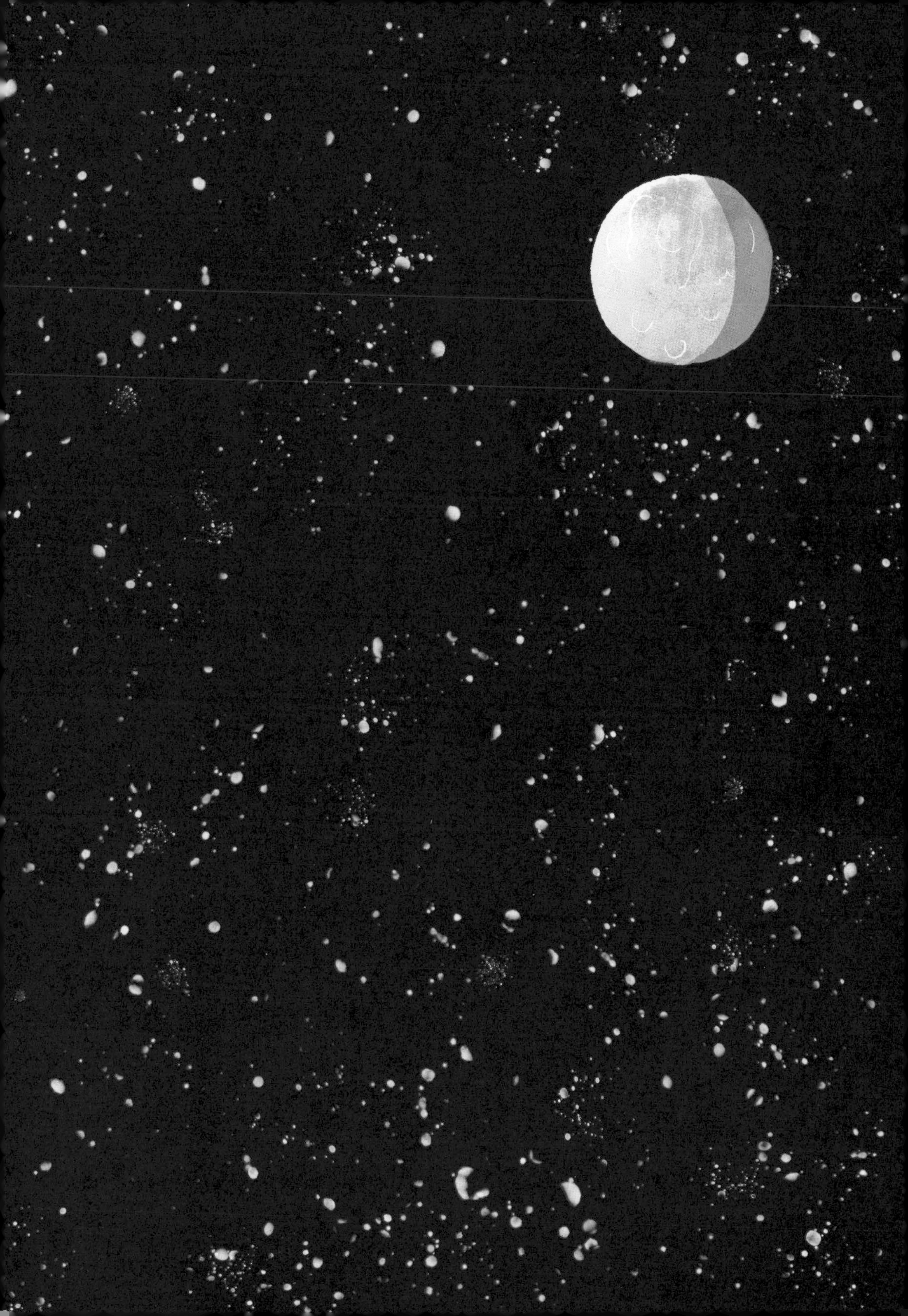

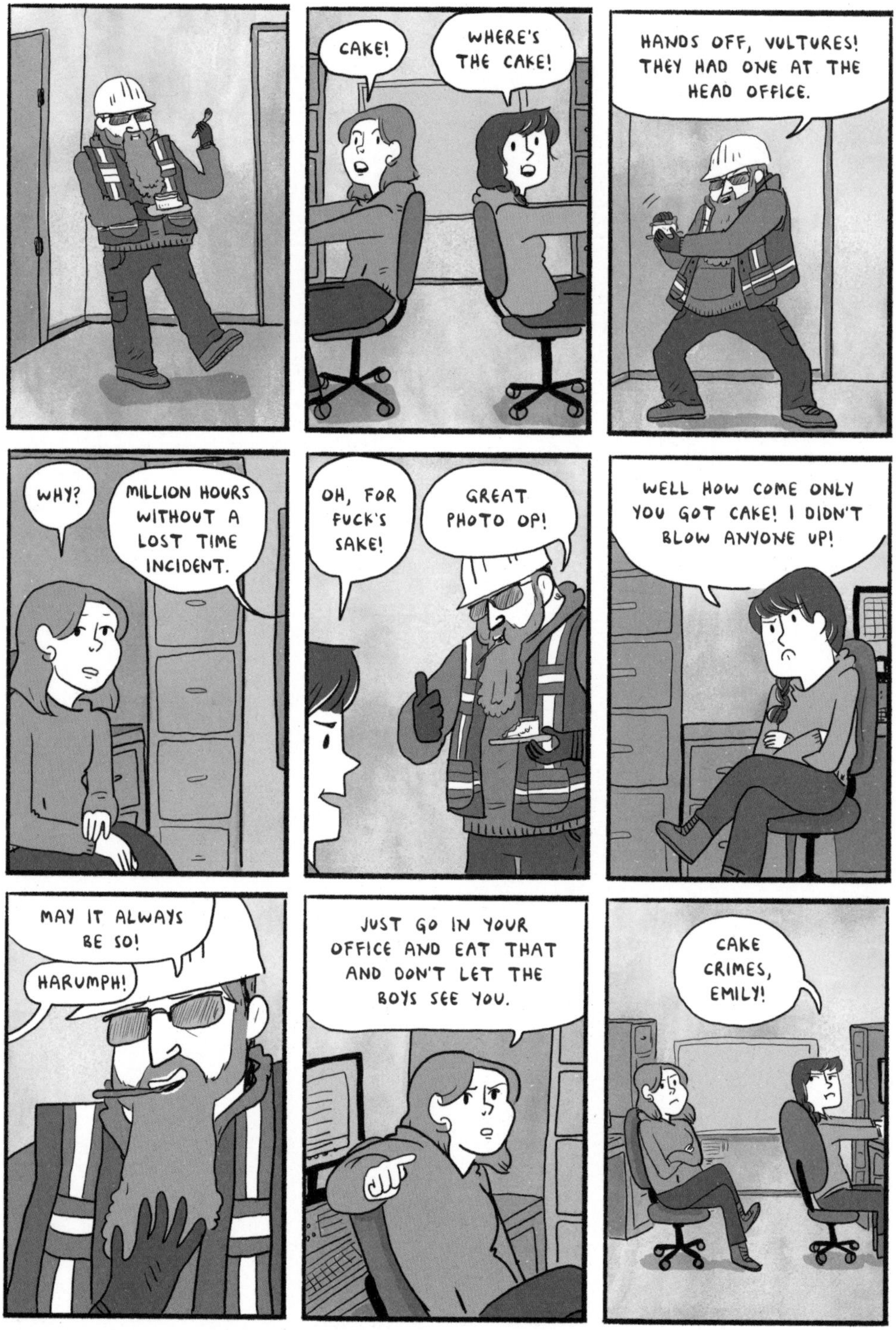
CAKE!
WHERE'S THE CAKE!
HANDS OFF, VULTURES! THEY HAD ONE AT THE HEAD OFFICE.
WHY?
MILLION HOURS WITHOUT A LOST TIME INCIDENT.
OH, FOR FUCK'S SAKE!
GREAT PHOTO OP!
WELL HOW COME ONLY YOU GOT CAKE! I DIDN'T BLOW ANYONE UP!
MAY IT ALWAYS BE SO!
HARUMPH!
JUST GO IN YOUR OFFICE AND EAT THAT AND DON'T LET THE BOYS SEE YOU.
CAKE CRIMES, EMILY!

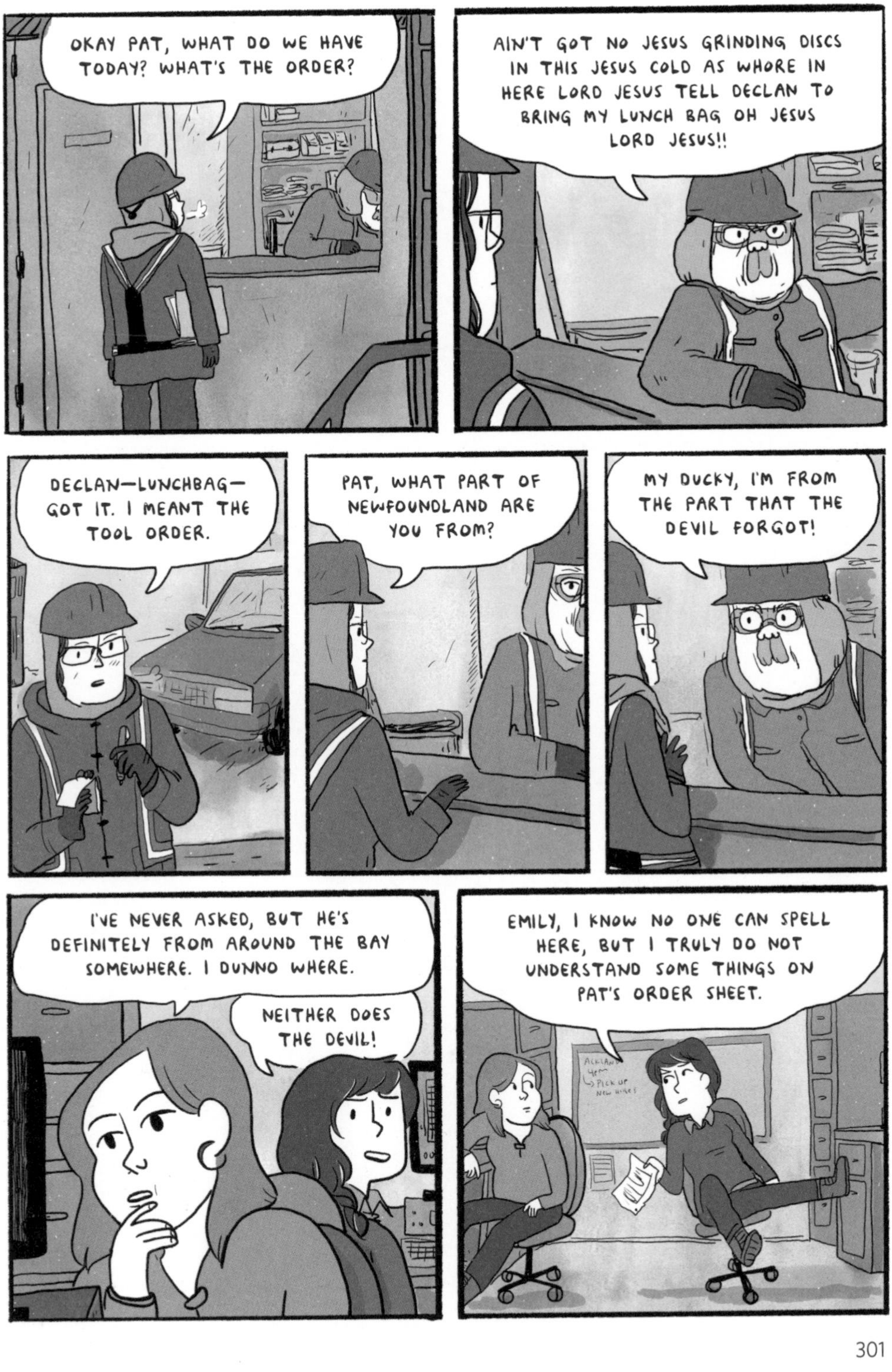

OKAY PAT, WHAT DO WE HAVE TODAY? WHAT'S THE ORDER?
AIN'T GOT NO JESUS GRINDING DISCS IN THIS JESUS COLD AS WHORE IN HERE LORD JESUS TELL DECLAN TO BRING MY LUNCH BAG OH JESUS LORD JESUS!!
DECLAN—LUNCHBAG—GOT IT. I MEANT THE TOOL ORDER.
PAT, WHAT PART OF NEWFOUNDLAND ARE YOU FROM?
MY DUCKY, I'M FROM THE PART THAT THE DEVIL FORGOT!
I'VE NEVER ASKED, BUT HE'S DEFINITELY FROM AROUND THE BAY SOMEWHERE. I DUNNO WHERE.
NEITHER DOES THE DEVIL!
EMILY, I KNOW NO ONE CAN SPELL HERE, BUT I TRULY DO NOT UNDERSTAND SOME THINGS ON PAT'S ORDER SHEET.

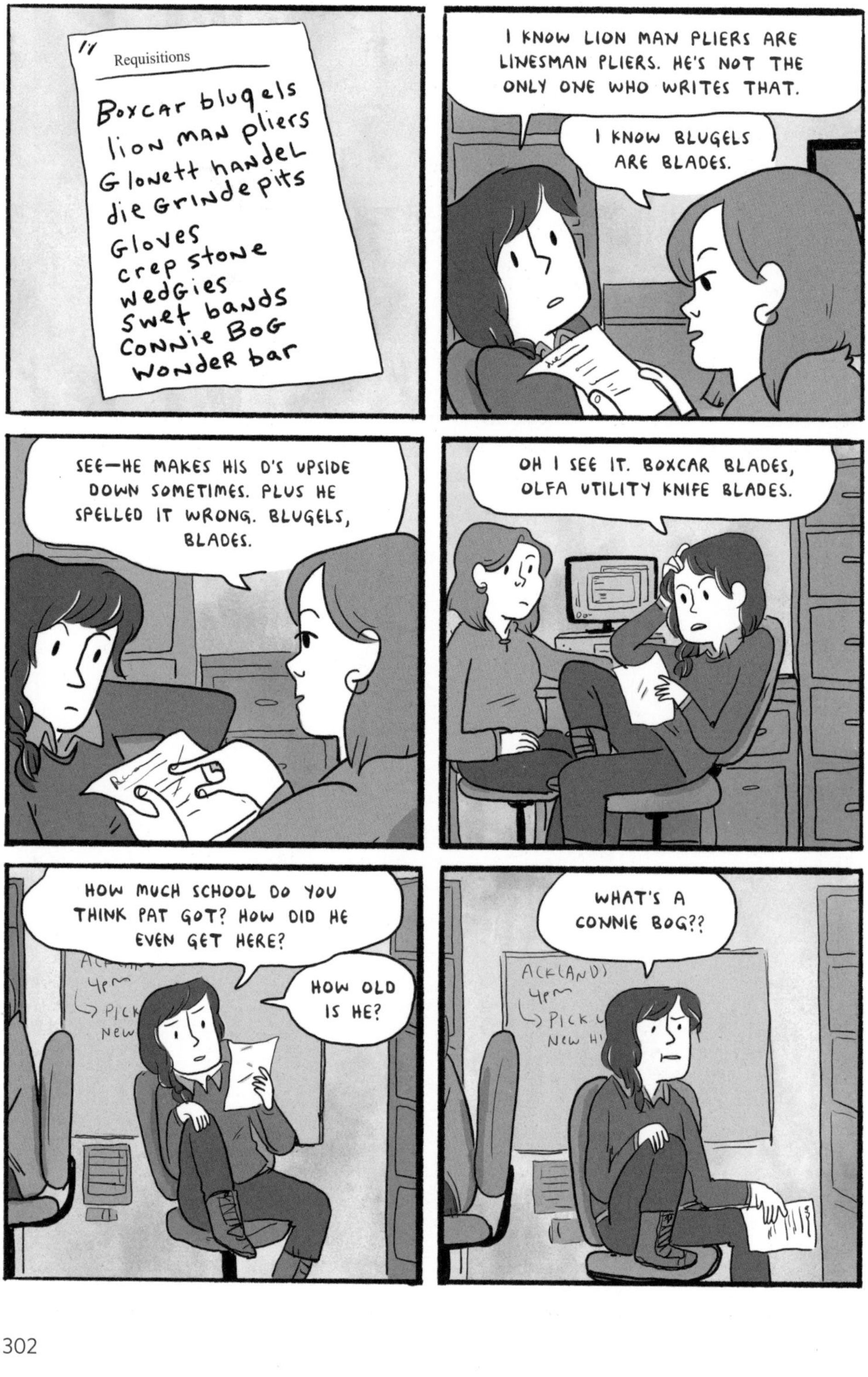
Requisitions
Boxcar blugels
lion man pliers
Glonett handel
die Grinde pits
Gloves
crep stone
wedgies
Swet bands
Connie Bog
Wonder bar
I KNOW LION MAN PLIERS ARE LINESMAN PLIERS. HE'S NOT THE ONLY ONE WHO WRITES THAT.
I KNOW BLUGELS ARE BLADES.
SEE—HE MAKES HIS D'S UPSIDE DOWN SOMETIMES. PLUS HE SPELLED IT WRONG. BLUGELS, BLADES.
OH I SEE IT. BOXCAR BLADES, OLFA UTILITY KNIFE BLADES.
HOW MUCH SCHOOL DO YOU THINK PAT GOT? HOW DID HE EVEN GET HERE?
HOW OLD IS HE?
WHAT'S A CONNIE BOG??

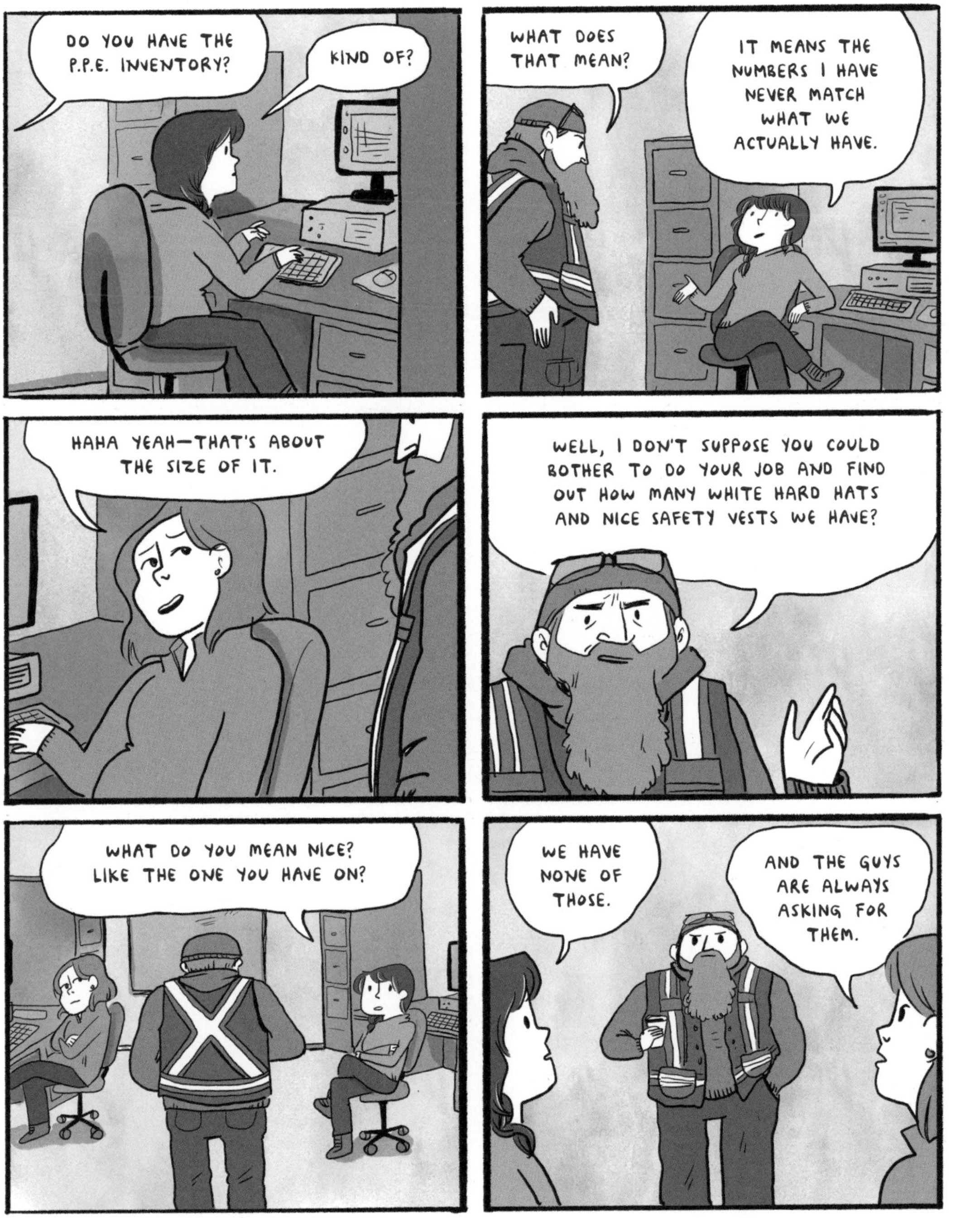
DO YOU HAVE THE P.P.E. INVENTORY?
KIND OF?
WHAT DOES THAT MEAN?
IT MEANS THE NUMBERS I HAVE NEVER MATCH WHAT WE ACTUALLY HAVE.
HAHA YEAH—THAT'S ABOUT THE SIZE OF IT.
WELL, I DON'T SUPPOSE YOU COULD BOTHER TO DO YOUR JOB AND FIND OUT HOW MANY WHITE HARD HATS AND NICE SAFETY VESTS WE HAVE?
WHAT DO YOU MEAN NICE? LIKE THE ONE YOU HAVE ON?
WE HAVE NONE OF THOSE.
AND THE GUYS ARE ALWAYS ASKING FOR THEM.

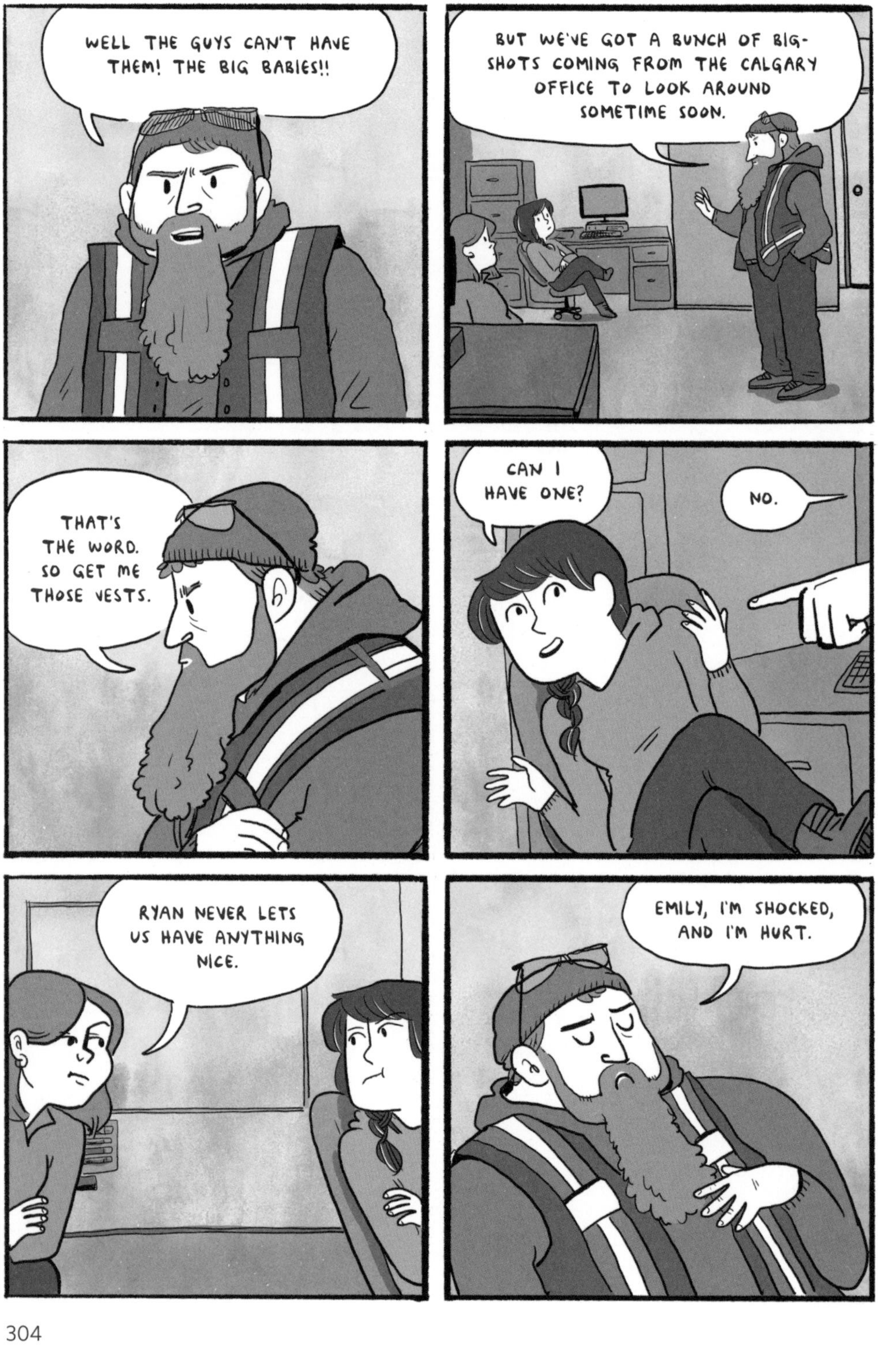
WELL THE GUYS CAN'T HAVE THEM! THE BIG BABIES!!
BUT WE'VE GOT A BUNCH OF BIG-SHOTS COMING FROM THE CALGARY OFFICE TO LOOK AROUND SOMETIME SOON.
THAT'S THE WORD. SO GET ME THOSE VESTS.
CAN I HAVE ONE?
NO.
RYAN NEVER LETS US HAVE ANYTHING NICE.
EMILY, I'M SHOCKED, AND I'M HURT.

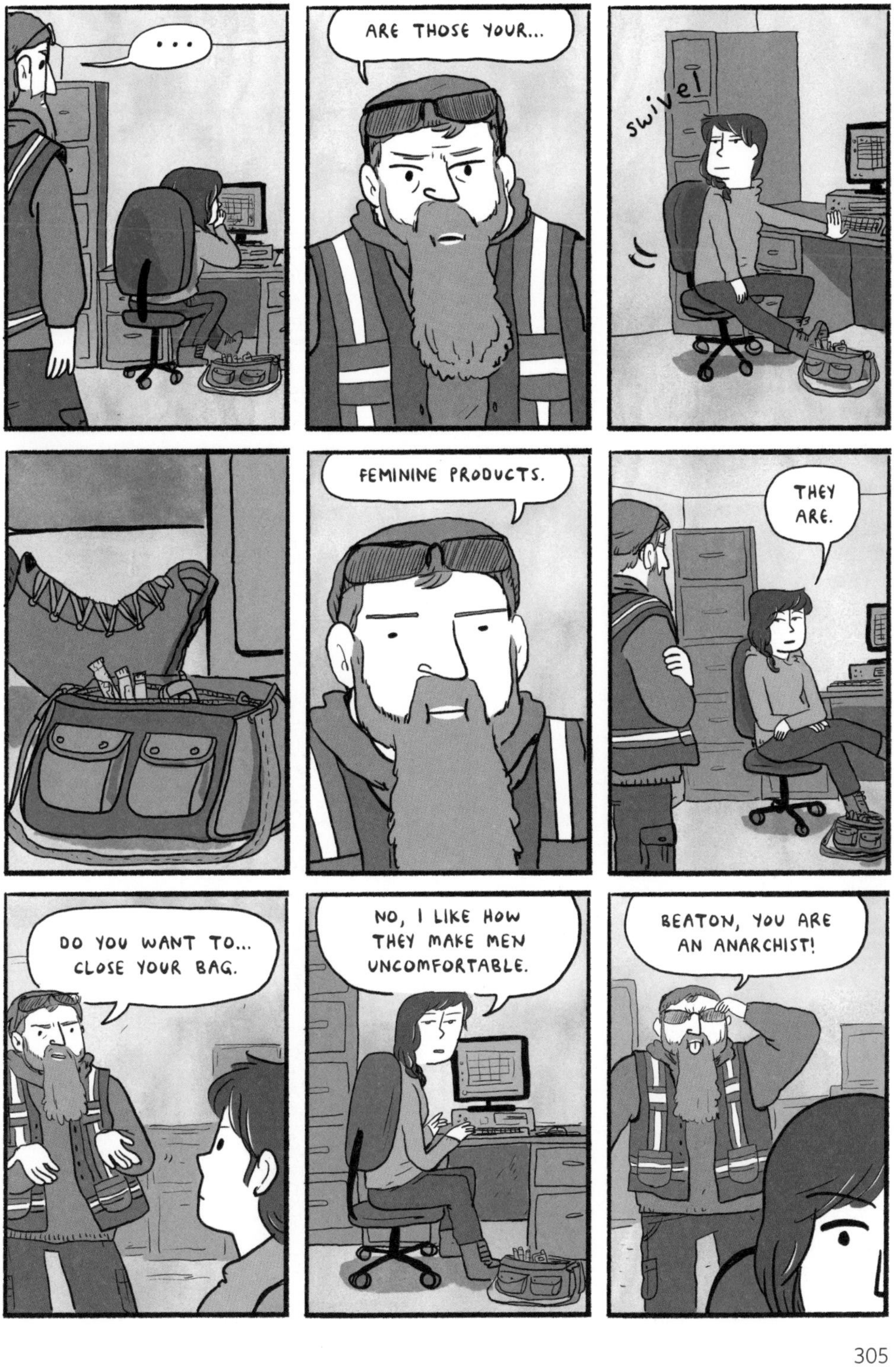
. . .
ARE THOSE YOUR...
swivel
FEMININE PRODUCTS.
THEY ARE.
DO YOU WANT TO... CLOSE YOUR BAG.
NO, I LIKE HOW THEY MAKE MEN UNCOMFORTABLE.
BEATON, YOU ARE AN ANARCHIST!

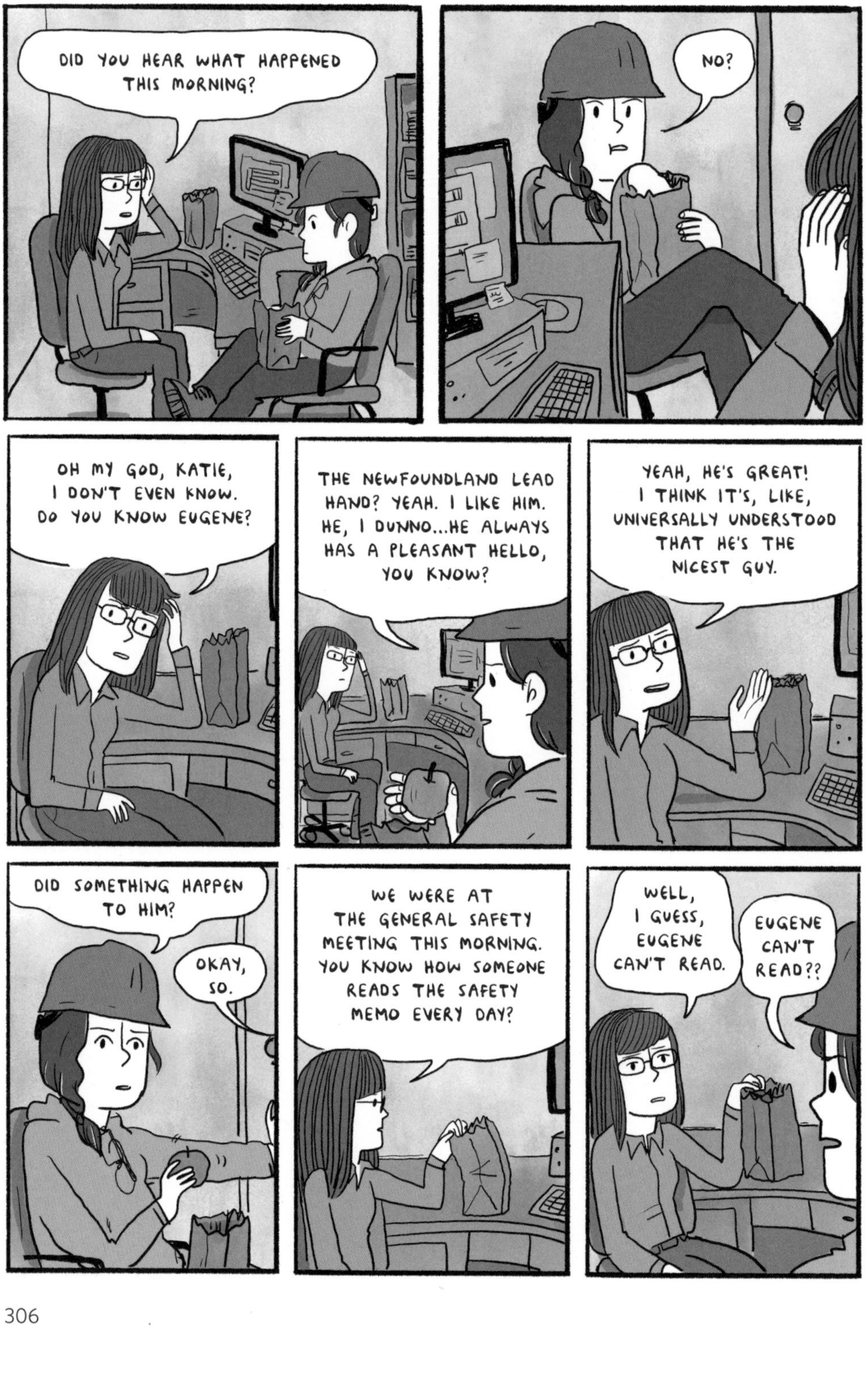
DID YOU HEAR WHAT HAPPENED THIS MORNING?
NO?
OH MY GOD, KATIE, I DON'T EVEN KNOW. DO YOU KNOW EUGENE?
THE NEWFOUNDLAND LEAD HAND? YEAH. I LIKE HIM. HE, I DUNNO...HE ALWAYS HAS A PLEASANT HELLO, YOU KNOW?
YEAH, HE'S GREAT! I THINK IT'S, LIKE, UNIVERSALLY UNDERSTOOD THAT HE'S THE NICEST GUY.
DID SOMETHING HAPPEN TO HIM?
OKAY, SO.
WE WERE AT THE GENERAL SAFETY MEETING THIS MORNING. YOU KNOW HOW SOMEONE READS THE SAFETY MEMO EVERY DAY?
WELL, I GUESS, EUGENE CAN'T READ.
EUGENE CAN'T READ??

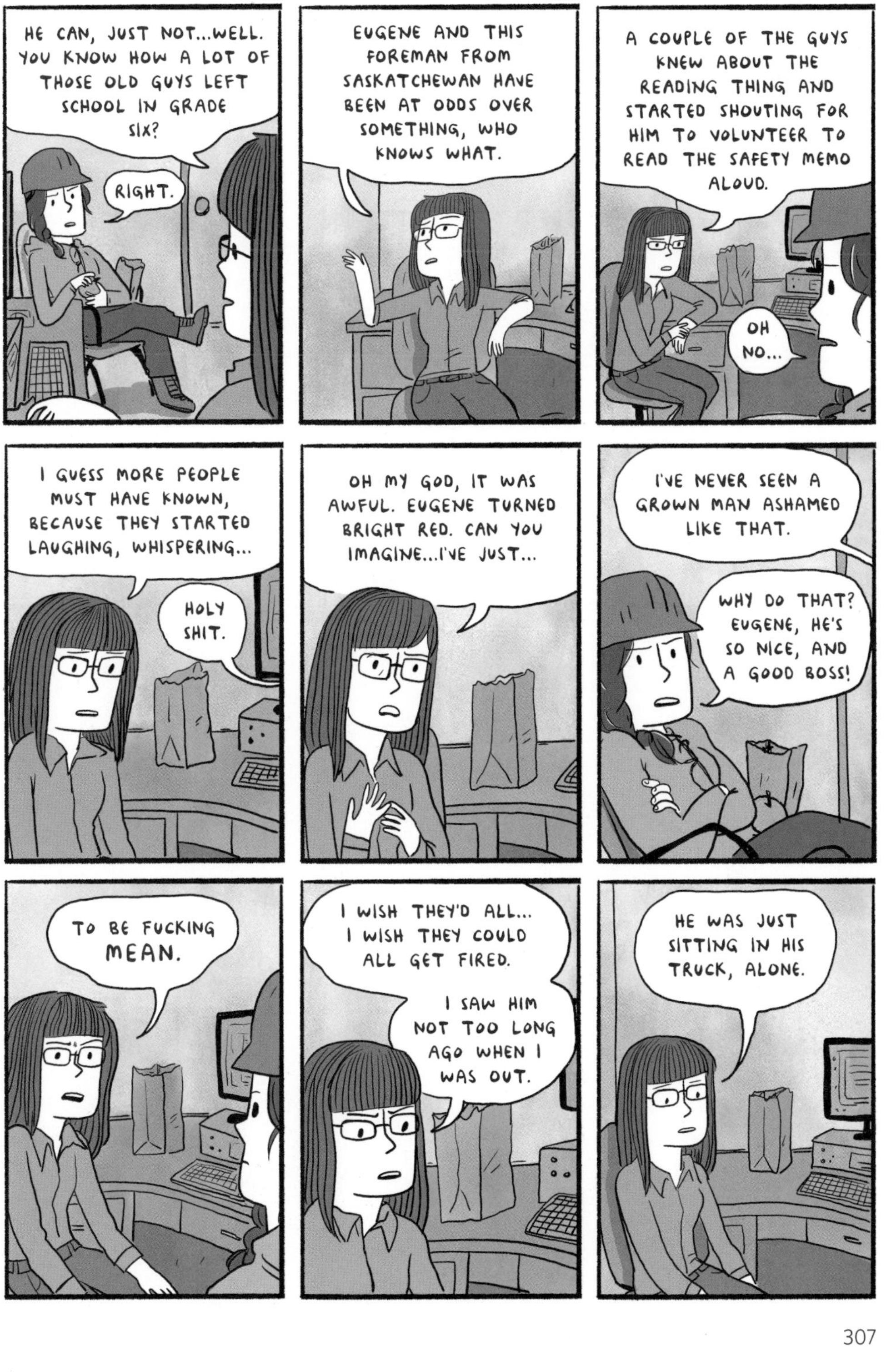
HE CAN, JUST NOT...WELL. YOU KNOW HOW A LOT OF THOSE OLD GUYS LEFT SCHOOL IN GRADE SIX?
RIGHT.
EUGENE AND THIS FOREMAN FROM SASKATCHEWAN HAVE BEEN AT ODDS OVER SOMETHING, WHO KNOWS WHAT.
A COUPLE OF THE GUYS KNEW ABOUT THE READING THING AND STARTED SHOUTING FOR HIM TO VOLUNTEER TO READ THE SAFETY MEMO ALOUD.
OH NO...
I GUESS MORE PEOPLE MUST HAVE KNOWN, BECAUSE THEY STARTED LAUGHING, WHISPERING...
HOLY SHIT.
OH MY GOD, IT WAS AWFUL. EUGENE TURNED BRIGHT RED. CAN YOU IMAGINE...I'VE JUST...
I'VE NEVER SEEN A GROWN MAN ASHAMED LIKE THAT.
WHY DO THAT? EUGENE, HE'S SO NICE, AND A GOOD BOSS!
TO BE FUCKING MEAN.
I WISH THEY'D ALL... I WISH THEY COULD ALL GET FIRED.
I SAW HIM NOT TOO LONG AGO WHEN I WAS OUT.
HE WAS JUST SITTING IN HIS TRUCK, ALONE.

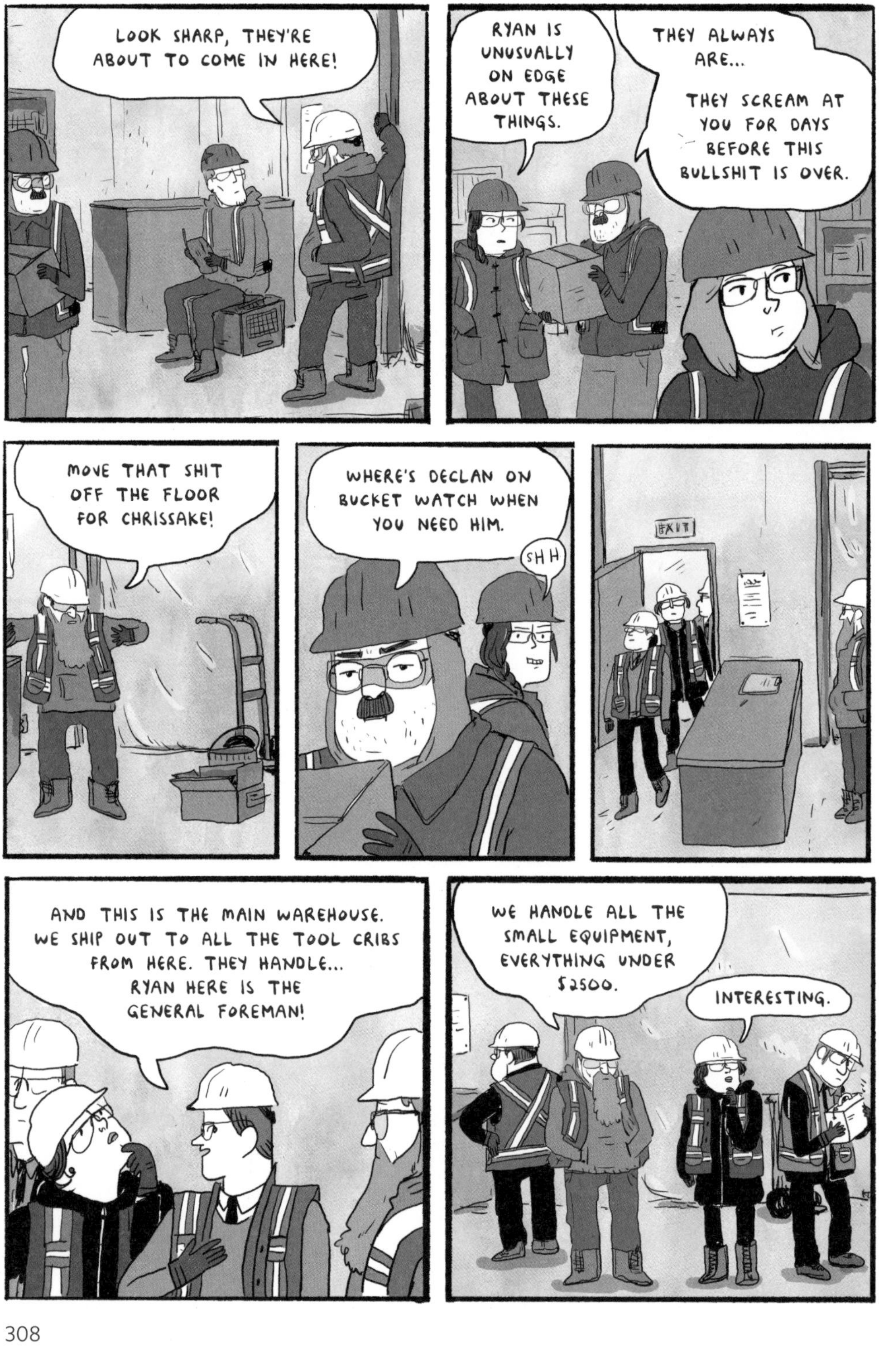
LOOK SHARP, THEY'RE ABOUT TO COME IN HERE!
RYAN IS UNUSUALLY ON EDGE ABOUT THESE THINGS.
THEY ALWAYS ARE...
THEY SCREAM AT YOU FOR DAYS BEFORE THIS BULLSHIT IS OVER.
MOVE THAT SHIT OFF THE FLOOR FOR CHRISSAKE!
WHERE'S DECLAN ON BUCKET WATCH WHEN YOU NEED HIM.
SHH
EXIT
AND THIS IS THE MAIN WAREHOUSE. WE SHIP OUT TO ALL THE TOOL CRIBS FROM HERE. THEY HANDLE... RYAN HERE IS THE GENERAL FOREMAN!
WE HANDLE ALL THE SMALL EQUIPMENT, EVERYTHING UNDER $2500.
INTERESTING.

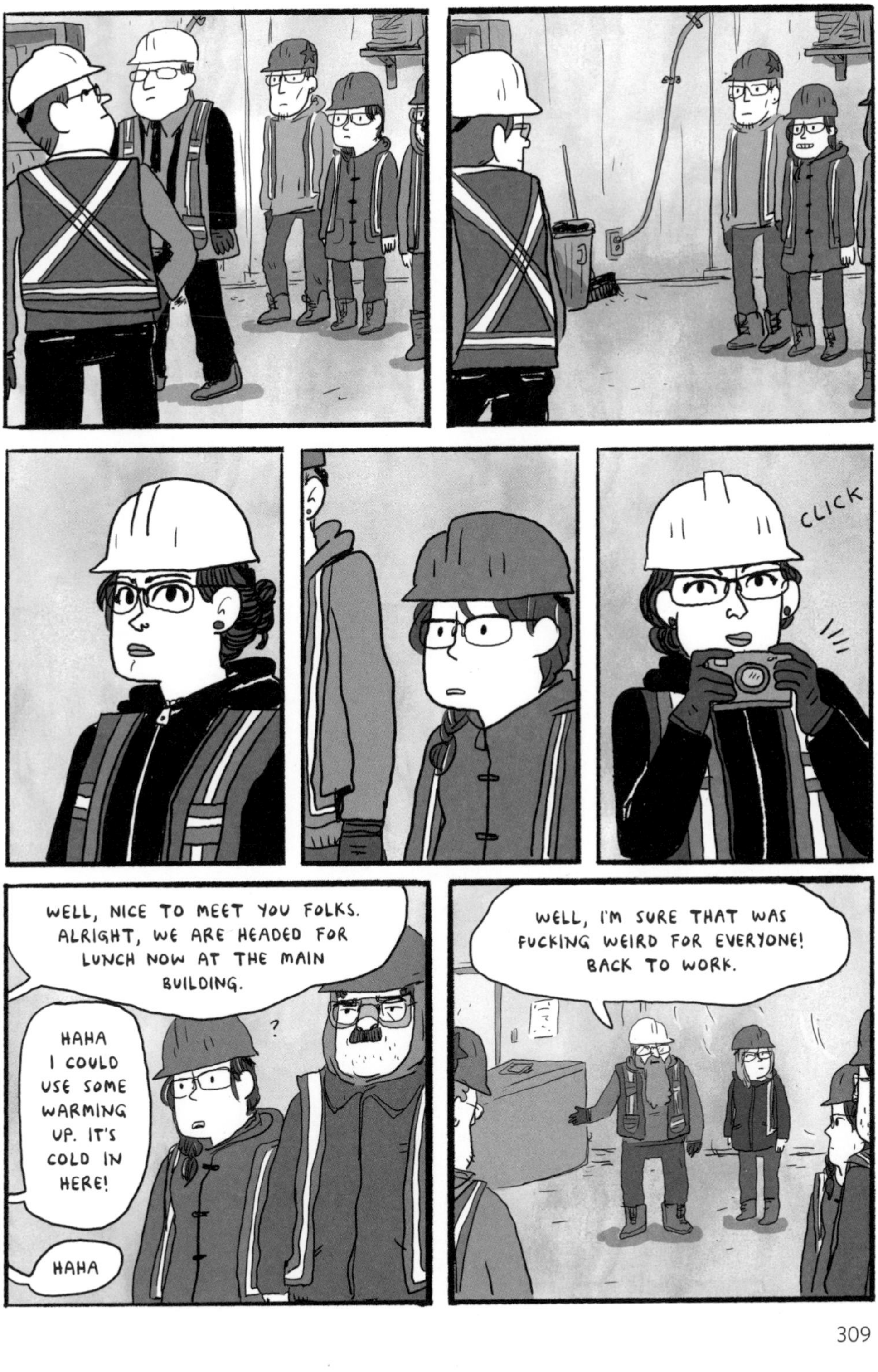
CLICK
WELL, NICE TO MEET YOU FOLKS. ALRIGHT, WE ARE HEADED FOR LUNCH NOW AT THE MAIN BUILDING.
HAHA I COULD USE SOME WARMING UP. IT'S COLD IN HERE!
HAHA
?
WELL, I'M SURE THAT WAS FUCKING WEIRD FOR EVERYONE! BACK TO WORK.

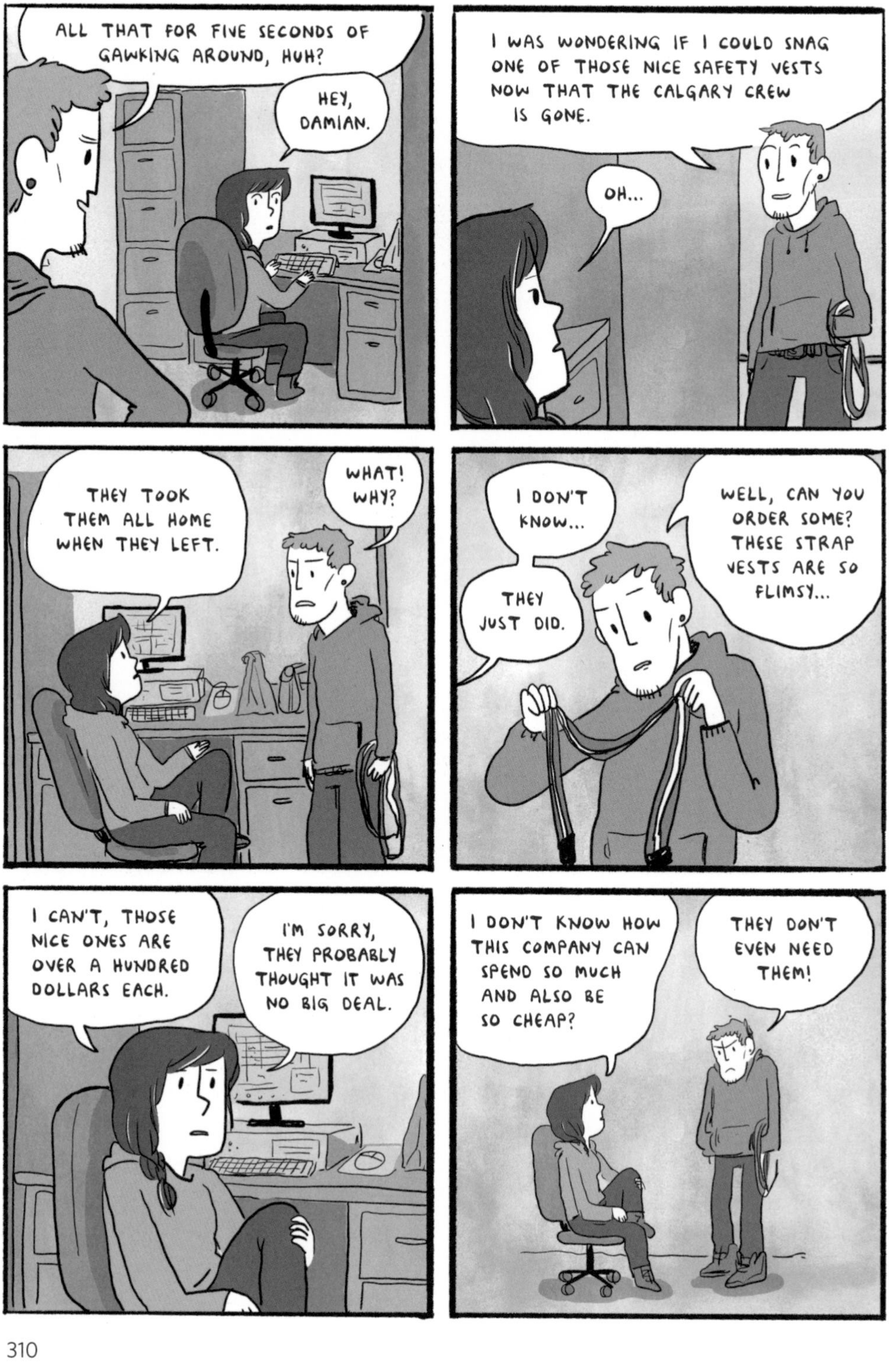
ALL THAT FOR FIVE SECONDS OF GAWKING AROUND, HUH?
HEY, DAMIAN.
I WAS WONDERING IF I COULD SNAG ONE OF THOSE NICE SAFETY VESTS NOW THAT THE CALGARY CREW IS GONE.
OH...
THEY TOOK THEM ALL HOME WHEN THEY LEFT.
WHAT! WHY?
I DON'T KNOW...
THEY JUST DID.
WELL, CAN YOU ORDER SOME? THESE STRAP VESTS ARE SO FLIMSY...
I CAN'T, THOSE NICE ONES ARE OVER A HUNDRED DOLLARS EACH.
I'M SORRY, THEY PROBABLY THOUGHT IT WAS NO BIG DEAL.
I DON'T KNOW HOW THIS COMPANY CAN SPEND SO MUCH AND ALSO BE SO CHEAP?
THEY DON'T EVEN NEED THEM!

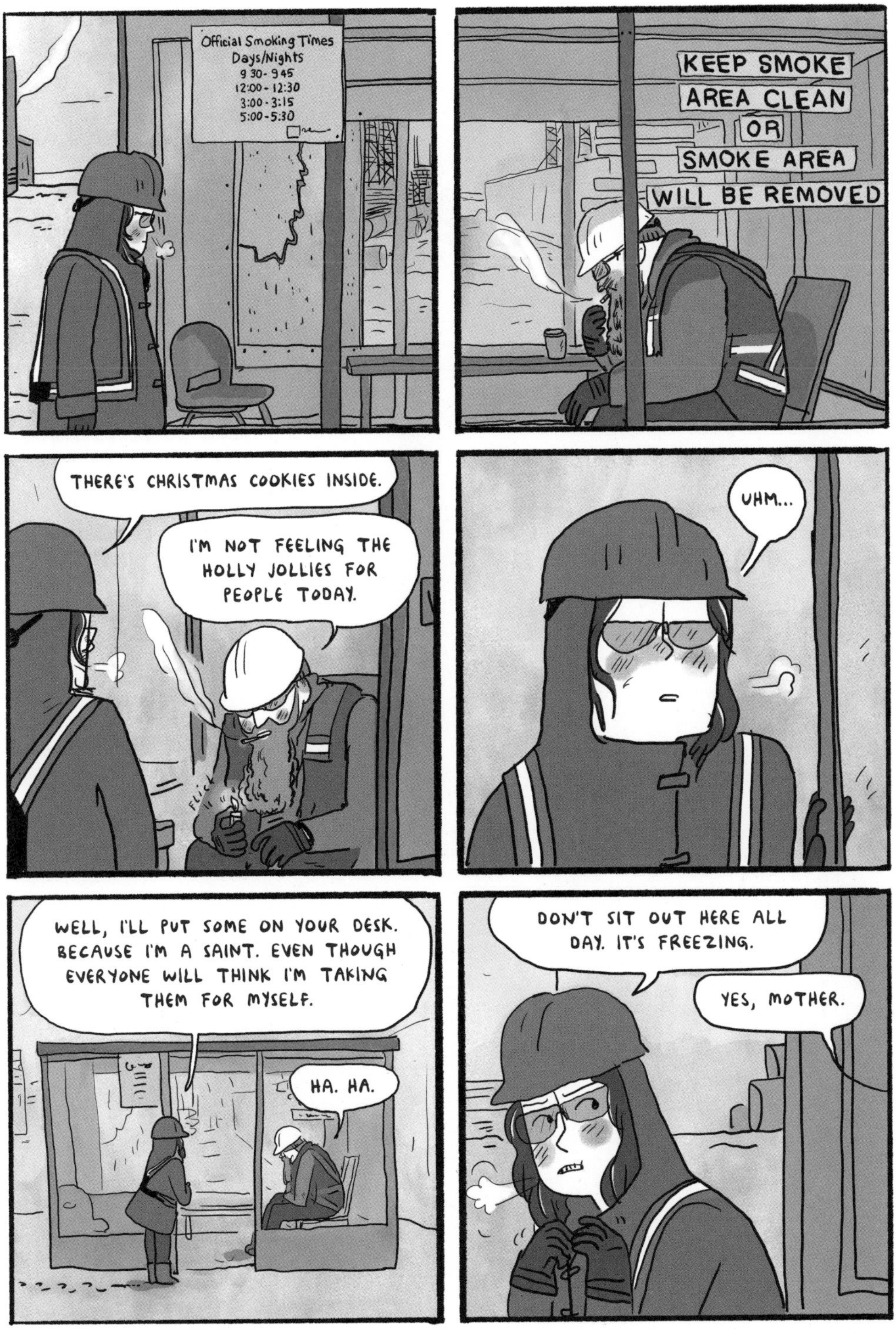

Official Smoking Times
Days/Nights
9 30 - 9 45
12:00 - 12:30
3:00 - 3:15
5:00 - 5:30
KEEP SMOKE
AREA CLEAN
OR
SMOKE AREA
WILL BE REMOVED
THERE'S CHRISTMAS COOKIES INSIDE.
I'M NOT FEELING THE HOLLY JOLLIES FOR PEOPLE TODAY.
FLICK
UHM...
WELL, I'LL PUT SOME ON YOUR DESK. BECAUSE I'M A SAINT. EVEN THOUGH EVERYONE WILL THINK I'M TAKING THEM FOR MYSELF.
HA. HA.
DON'T SIT OUT HERE ALL DAY. IT'S FREEZING.
YES, MOTHER.

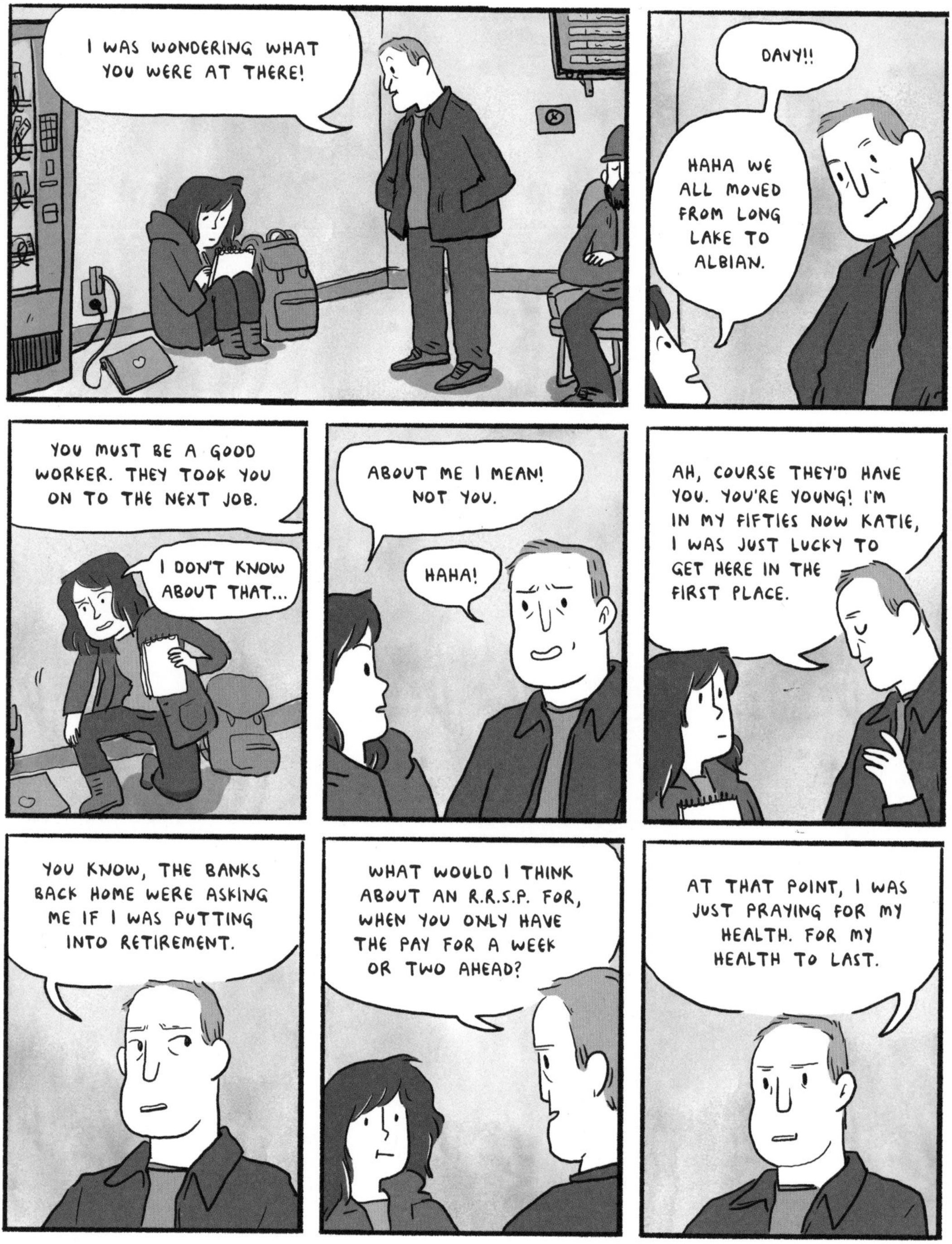
I WAS WONDERING WHAT YOU WERE AT THERE!
DAVY!!
HAHA WE ALL MOVED FROM LONG LAKE TO ALBIAN.
YOU MUST BE A GOOD WORKER. THEY TOOK YOU ON TO THE NEXT JOB.
I DON'T KNOW ABOUT THAT...
ABOUT ME I MEAN! NOT YOU.
HAHA!
AH, COURSE THEY'D HAVE YOU. YOU'RE YOUNG! I'M IN MY FIFTIES NOW KATIE, I WAS JUST LUCKY TO GET HERE IN THE FIRST PLACE.
YOU KNOW, THE BANKS BACK HOME WERE ASKING ME IF I WAS PUTTING INTO RETIREMENT.
WHAT WOULD I THINK ABOUT AN R.R.S.P. FOR, WHEN YOU ONLY HAVE THE PAY FOR A WEEK OR TWO AHEAD?
AT THAT POINT, I WAS JUST PRAYING FOR MY HEALTH. FOR MY HEALTH TO LAST.

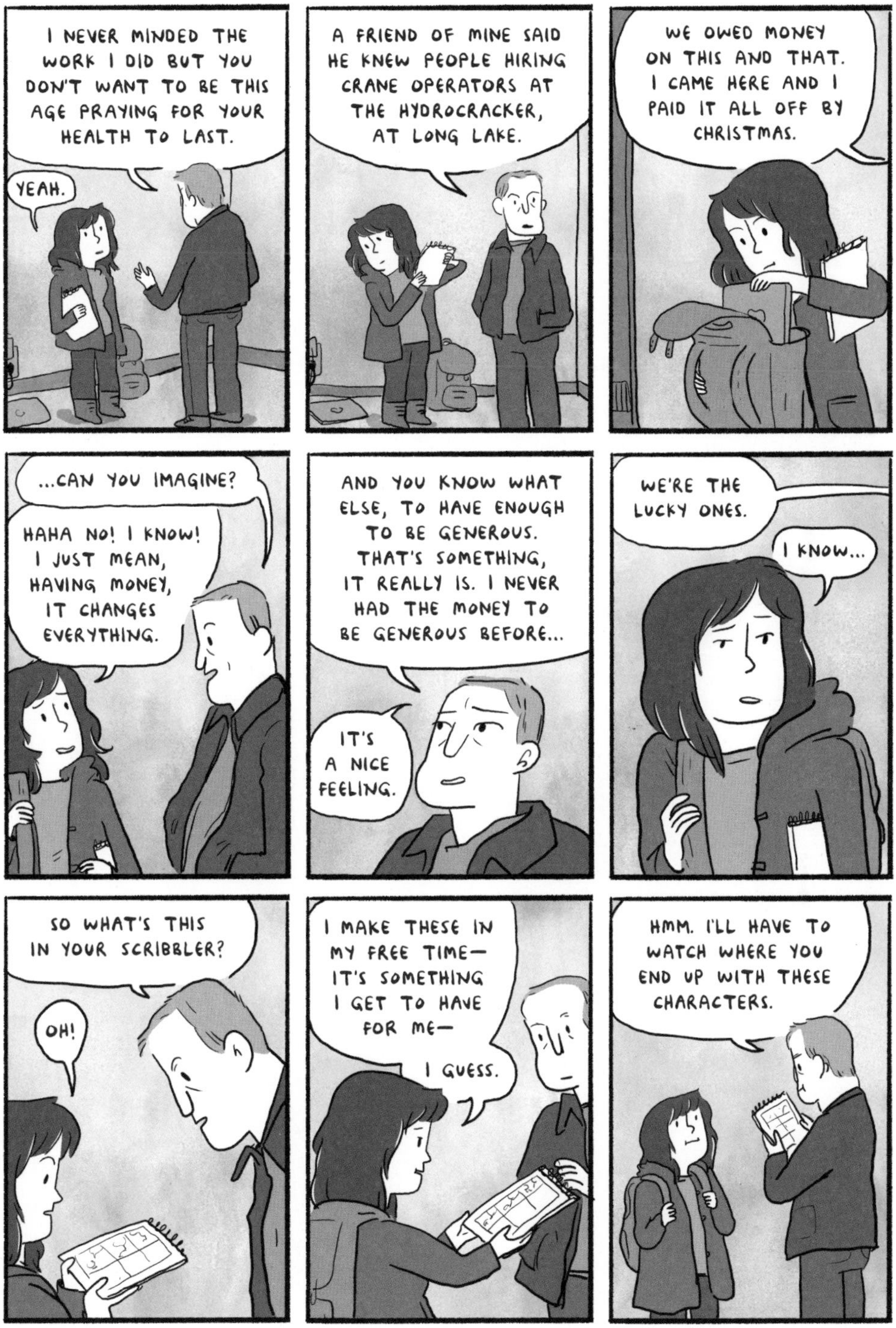
I NEVER MINDED THE WORK I DID BUT YOU DON'T WANT TO BE THIS AGE PRAYING FOR YOUR HEALTH TO LAST.
YEAH.
A FRIEND OF MINE SAID HE KNEW PEOPLE HIRING CRANE OPERATORS AT THE HYDROCRACKER, AT LONG LAKE.
WE OWED MONEY ON THIS AND THAT. I CAME HERE AND I PAID IT ALL OFF BY CHRISTMAS.
...CAN YOU IMAGINE?
HAHA NO! I KNOW! I JUST MEAN, HAVING MONEY, IT CHANGES EVERYTHING.
AND YOU KNOW WHAT ELSE, TO HAVE ENOUGH TO BE GENEROUS. THAT'S SOMETHING, IT REALLY IS. I NEVER HAD THE MONEY TO BE GENEROUS BEFORE...
IT'S A NICE FEELING.
WE'RE THE LUCKY ONES.
I KNOW...
SO WHAT'S THIS IN YOUR SCRIBBLER?
OH!
I MAKE THESE IN MY FREE TIME— IT'S SOMETHING I GET TO HAVE FOR ME—
I GUESS.
HMM. I'LL HAVE TO WATCH WHERE YOU END UP WITH THESE CHARACTERS.

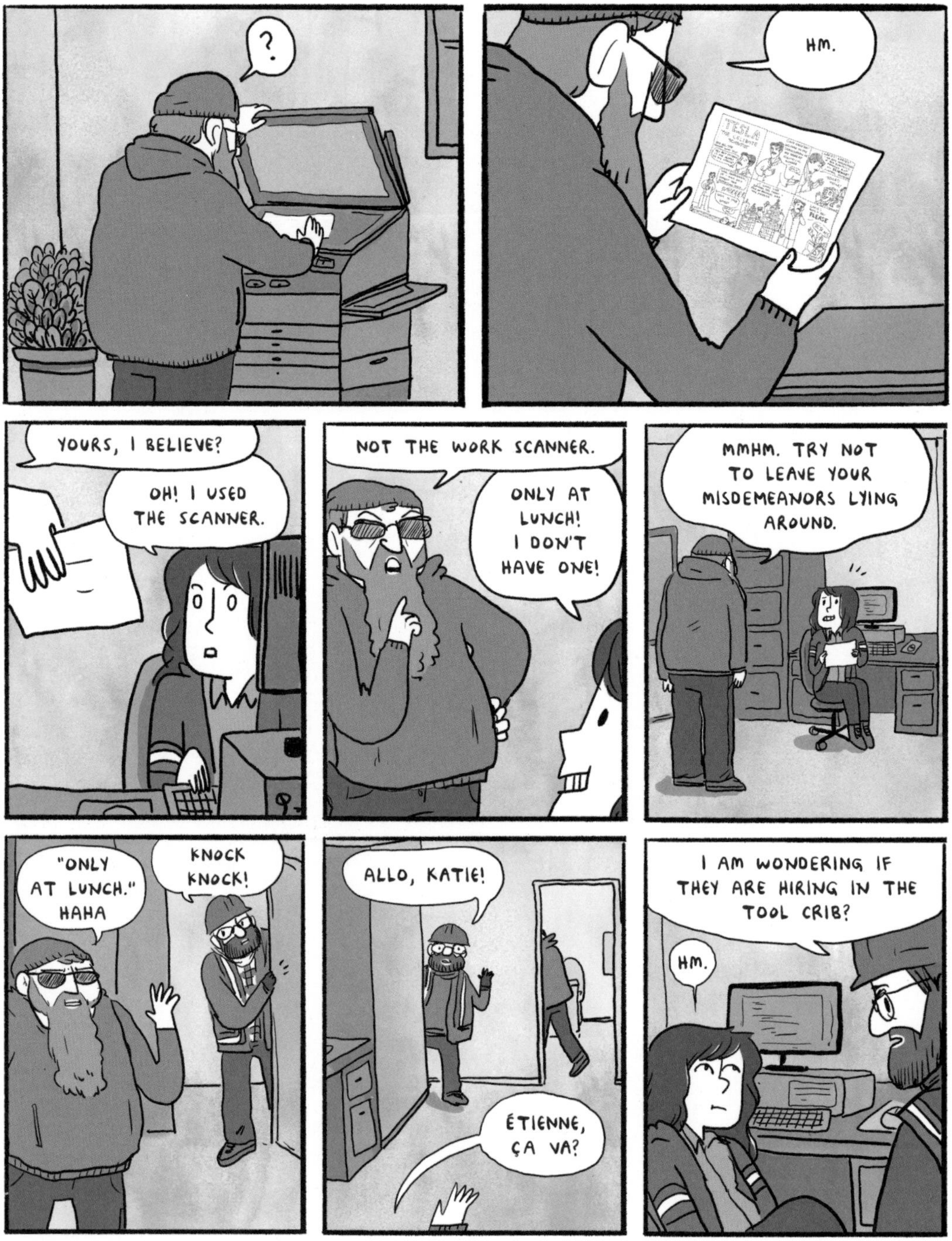
?
HM.
YOURS, I BELIEVE?
OH! I USED THE SCANNER.
NOT THE WORK SCANNER.
ONLY AT LUNCH! I DON'T HAVE ONE!
MMHM. TRY NOT TO LEAVE YOUR MISDEMEANORS LYING AROUND.
"ONLY AT LUNCH." HAHA
KNOCK KNOCK!
ALLO, KATIE!
ÉTIENNE, ÇA VA?
I AM WONDERING IF THEY ARE HIRING IN THE TOOL CRIB?
HM.

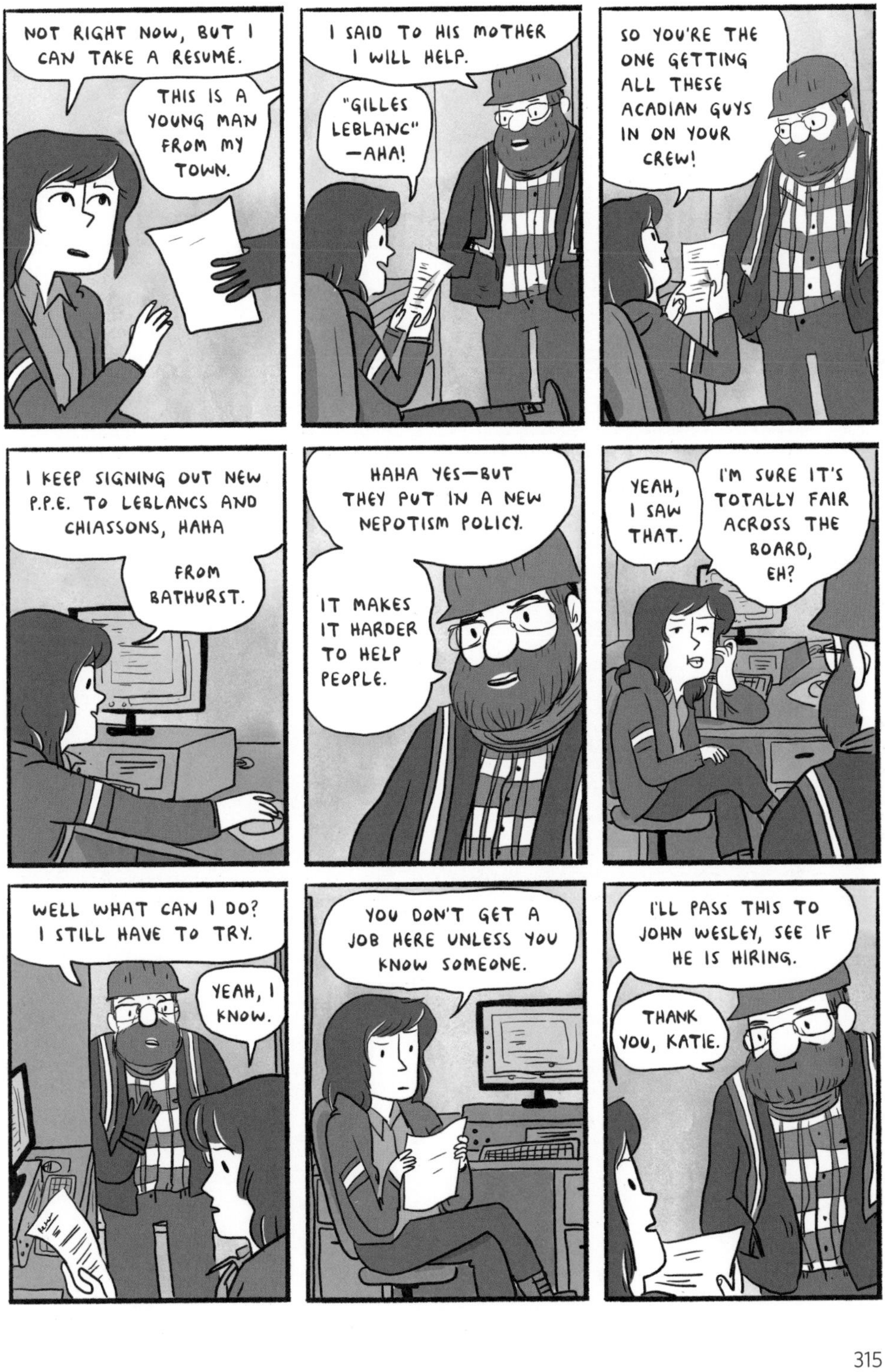
NOT RIGHT NOW, BUT I CAN TAKE A RESUMÉ.
THIS IS A YOUNG MAN FROM MY TOWN.
I SAID TO HIS MOTHER I WILL HELP.
"GILLES LEBLANC" —AHA!
SO YOU'RE THE ONE GETTING ALL THESE ACADIAN GUYS IN ON YOUR CREW!
I KEEP SIGNING OUT NEW P.P.E. TO LEBLANCS AND CHIASSONS, HAHA
FROM BATHURST.
HAHA YES—BUT THEY PUT IN A NEW NEPOTISM POLICY.
IT MAKES IT HARDER TO HELP PEOPLE.
YEAH, I SAW THAT.
I'M SURE IT'S TOTALLY FAIR ACROSS THE BOARD, EH?
WELL WHAT CAN I DO? I STILL HAVE TO TRY.
YEAH, I KNOW.
YOU DON'T GET A JOB HERE UNLESS YOU KNOW SOMEONE.
I'LL PASS THIS TO JOHN WESLEY, SEE IF HE IS HIRING.
THANK YOU, KATIE.

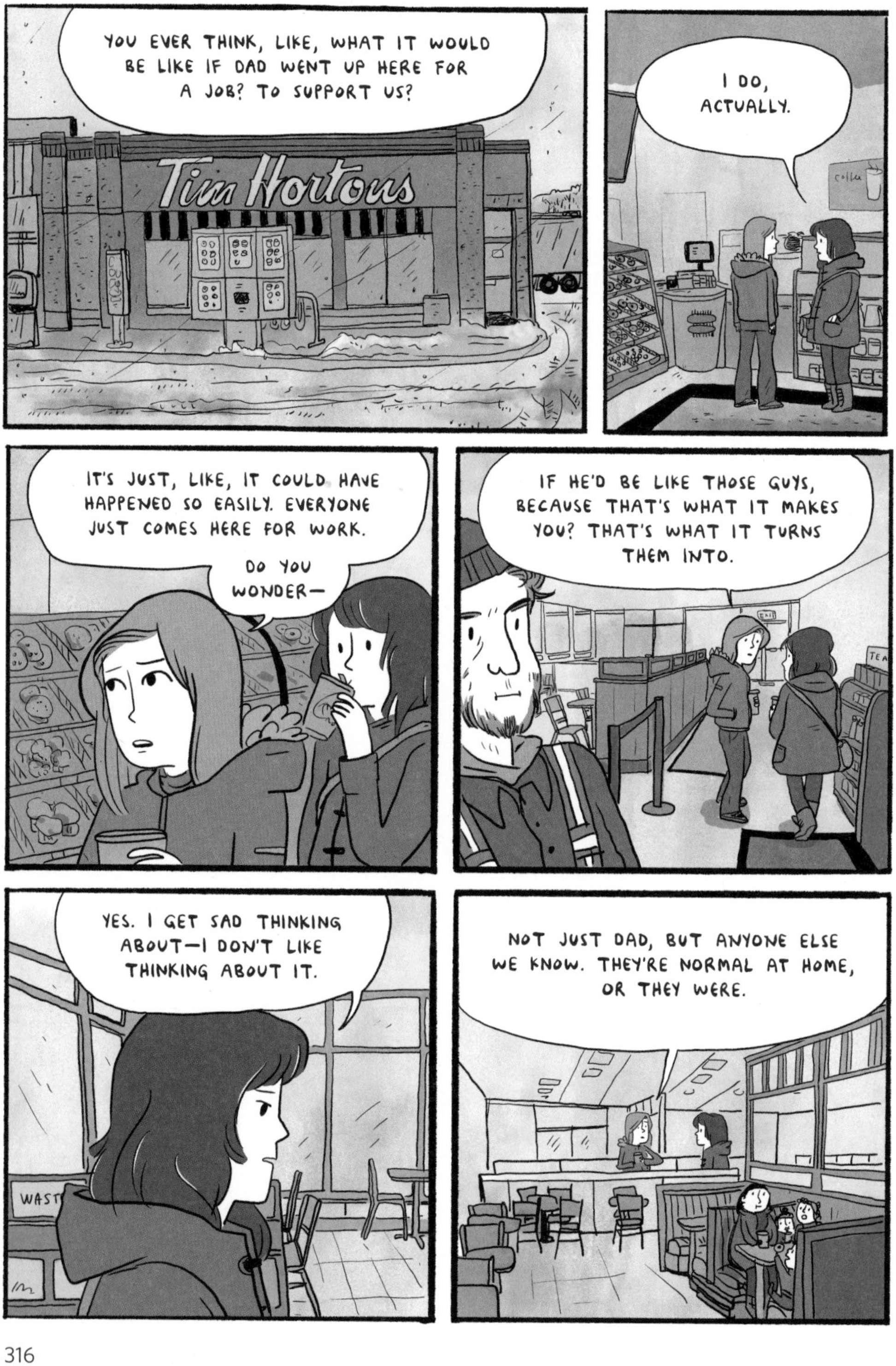
YOU EVER THINK, LIKE, WHAT IT WOULD BE LIKE IF DAD WENT UP HERE FOR A JOB? TO SUPPORT US?
Tim Hortons
I DO, ACTUALLY.
IT'S JUST, LIKE, IT COULD HAVE HAPPENED SO EASILY. EVERYONE JUST COMES HERE FOR WORK.
DO YOU WONDER—
IF HE'D BE LIKE THOSE GUYS, BECAUSE THAT'S WHAT IT MAKES YOU? THAT'S WHAT IT TURNS THEM INTO.
YES. I GET SAD THINKING ABOUT—I DON'T LIKE THINKING ABOUT IT.
NOT JUST DAD, BUT ANYONE ELSE WE KNOW. THEY'RE NORMAL AT HOME, OR THEY WERE.

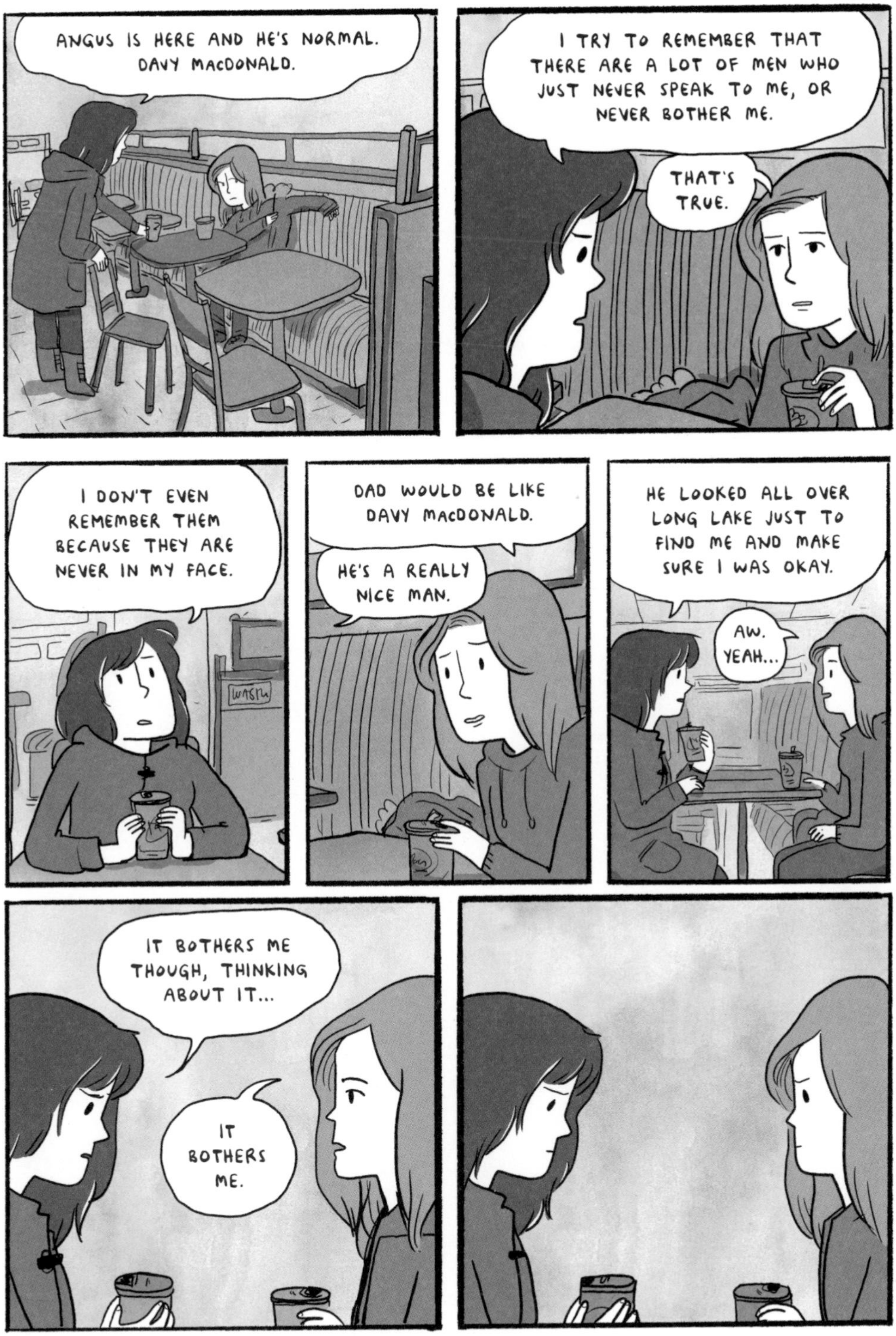
ANGUS IS HERE AND HE'S NORMAL. DAVY MACDONALD.
I TRY TO REMEMBER THAT THERE ARE A LOT OF MEN WHO JUST NEVER SPEAK TO ME, OR NEVER BOTHER ME.
THAT'S TRUE.
I DON'T EVEN REMEMBER THEM BECAUSE THEY ARE NEVER IN MY FACE.
DAD WOULD BE LIKE DAVY MACDONALD.
HE'S A REALLY NICE MAN.
HE LOOKED ALL OVER LONG LAKE JUST TO FIND ME AND MAKE SURE I WAS OKAY.
AW. YEAH...
IT BOTHERS ME THOUGH, THINKING ABOUT IT...
IT BOTHERS ME.

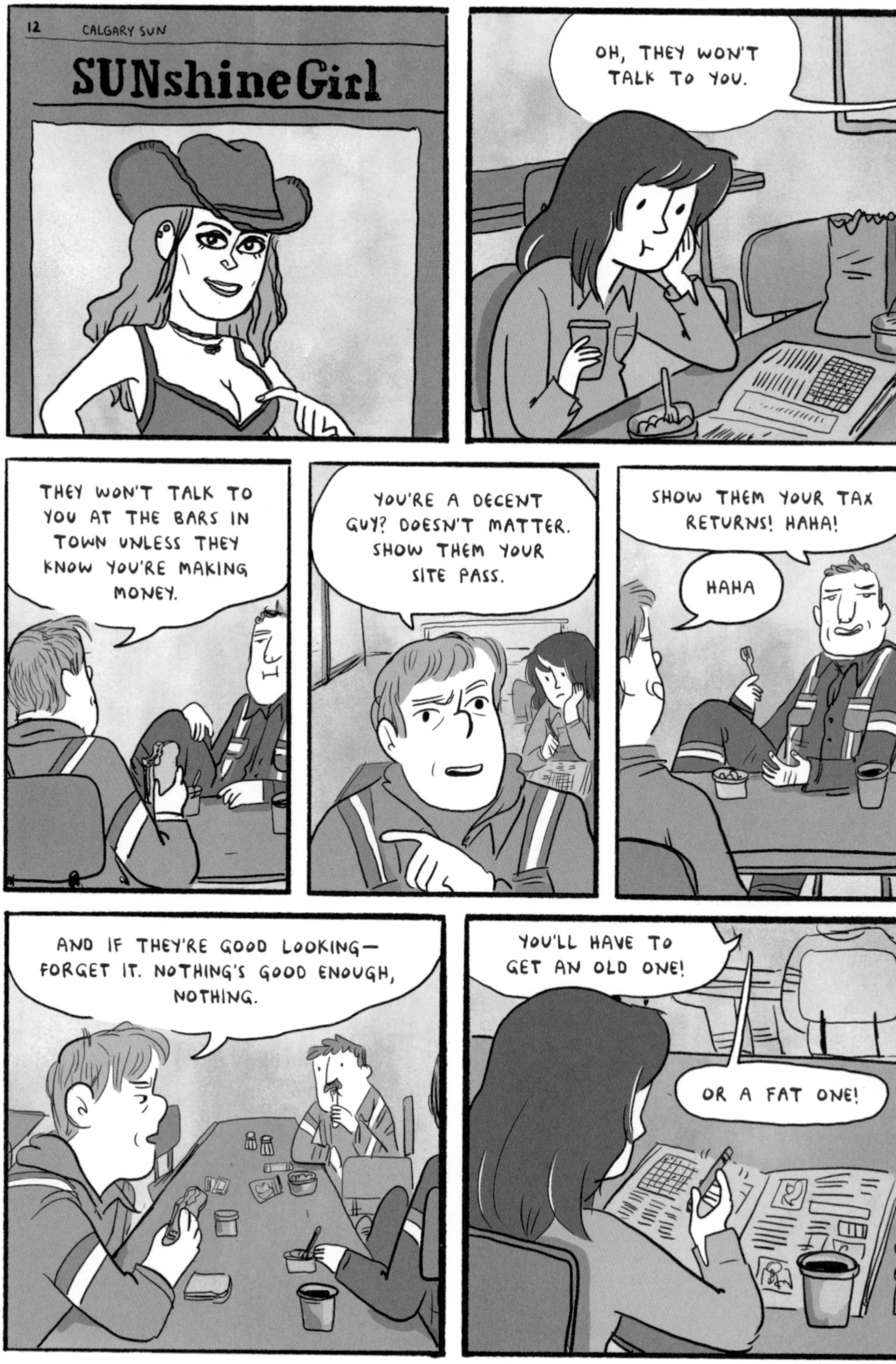
12
CALGARY SUN
SUNshine Girl
OH, THEY WON'T TALK TO YOU.
THEY WON'T TALK TO YOU AT THE BARS IN TOWN UNLESS THEY KNOW YOU'RE MAKING MONEY.
YOU'RE A DECENT GUY? DOESN'T MATTER. SHOW THEM YOUR SITE PASS.
SHOW THEM YOUR TAX RETURNS! HAHA!
HAHA
AND IF THEY'RE GOOD LOOKING— FORGET IT. NOTHING'S GOOD ENOUGH, NOTHING.
YOU'LL HAVE TO GET AN OLD ONE!
OR A FAT ONE!

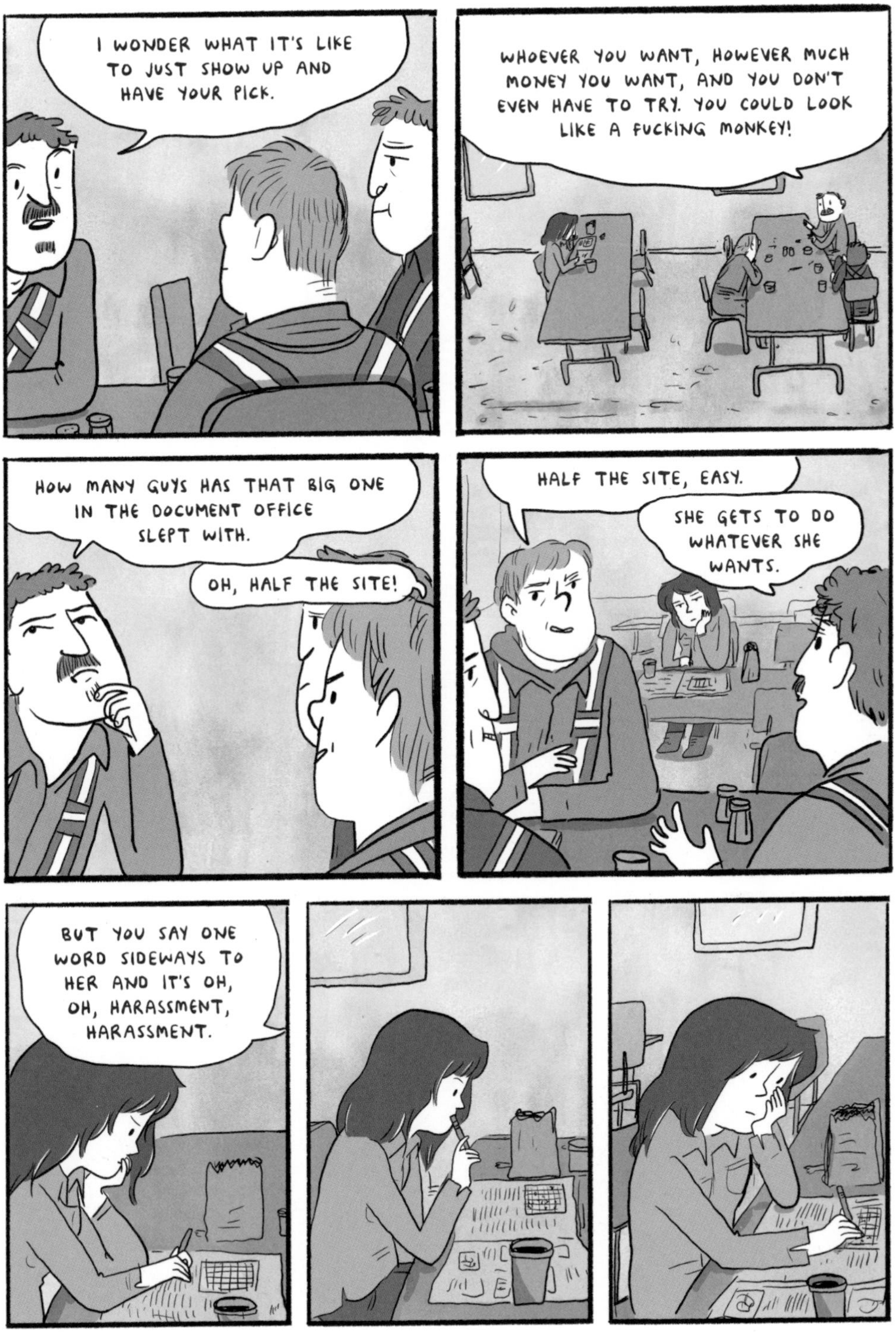
I WONDER WHAT IT'S LIKE TO JUST SHOW UP AND HAVE YOUR PICK.
WHOEVER YOU WANT, HOWEVER MUCH MONEY YOU WANT, AND YOU DON'T EVEN HAVE TO TRY. YOU COULD LOOK LIKE A FUCKING MONKEY!
HOW MANY GUYS HAS THAT BIG ONE IN THE DOCUMENT OFFICE SLEPT WITH.
OH, HALF THE SITE!
HALF THE SITE, EASY.
SHE GETS TO DO WHATEVER SHE WANTS.
BUT YOU SAY ONE WORD SIDEWAYS TO HER AND IT'S OH, OH, HARASSMENT, HARASSMENT.

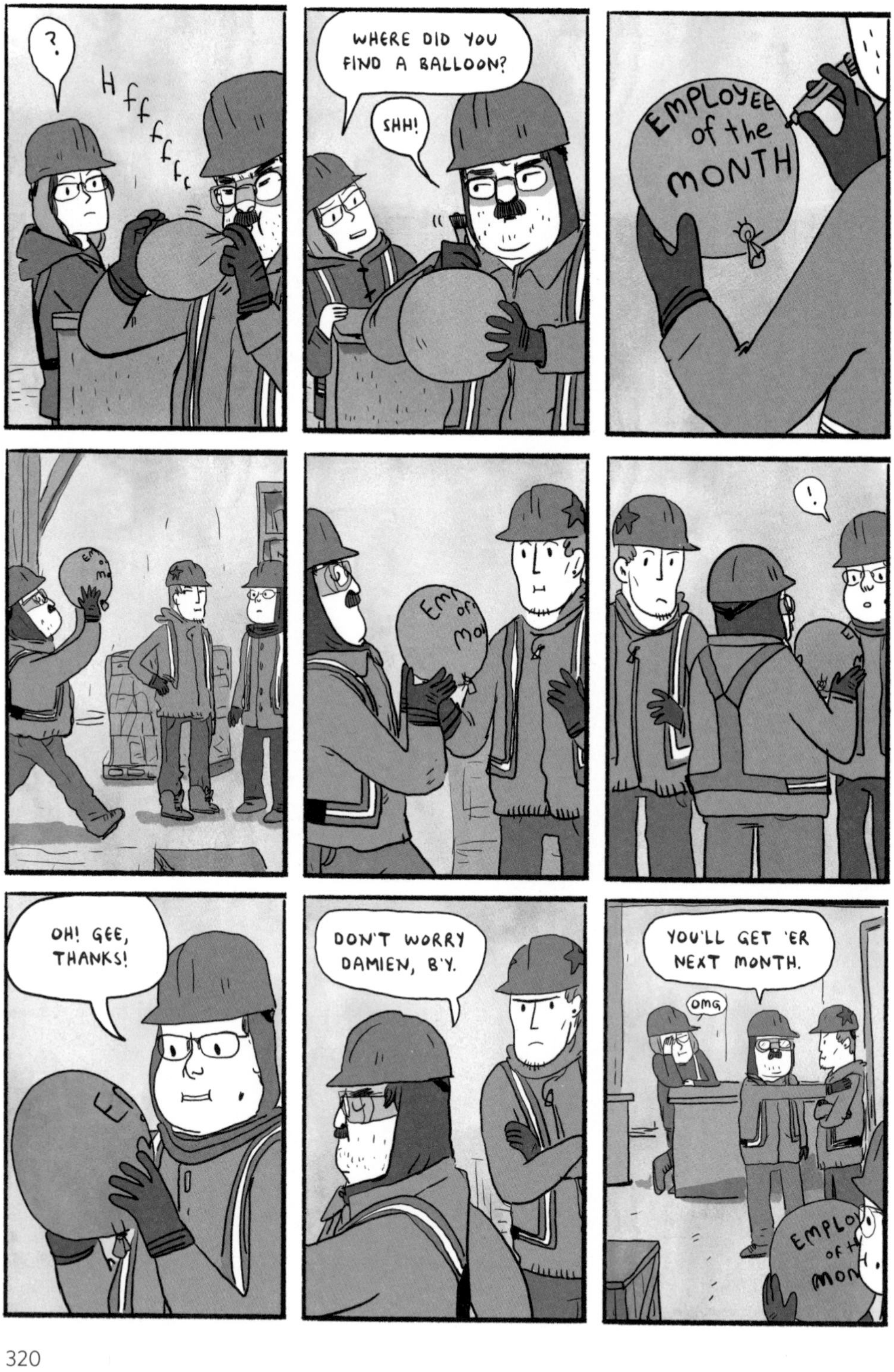
?
Hfffffff
WHERE DID YOU FIND A BALLOON?
SHH!
EMPLOYEE of the MONTH
!
OH! GEE, THANKS!
DON'T WORRY DAMIEN, B'Y.
YOU'LL GET 'ER NEXT MONTH.
OMG

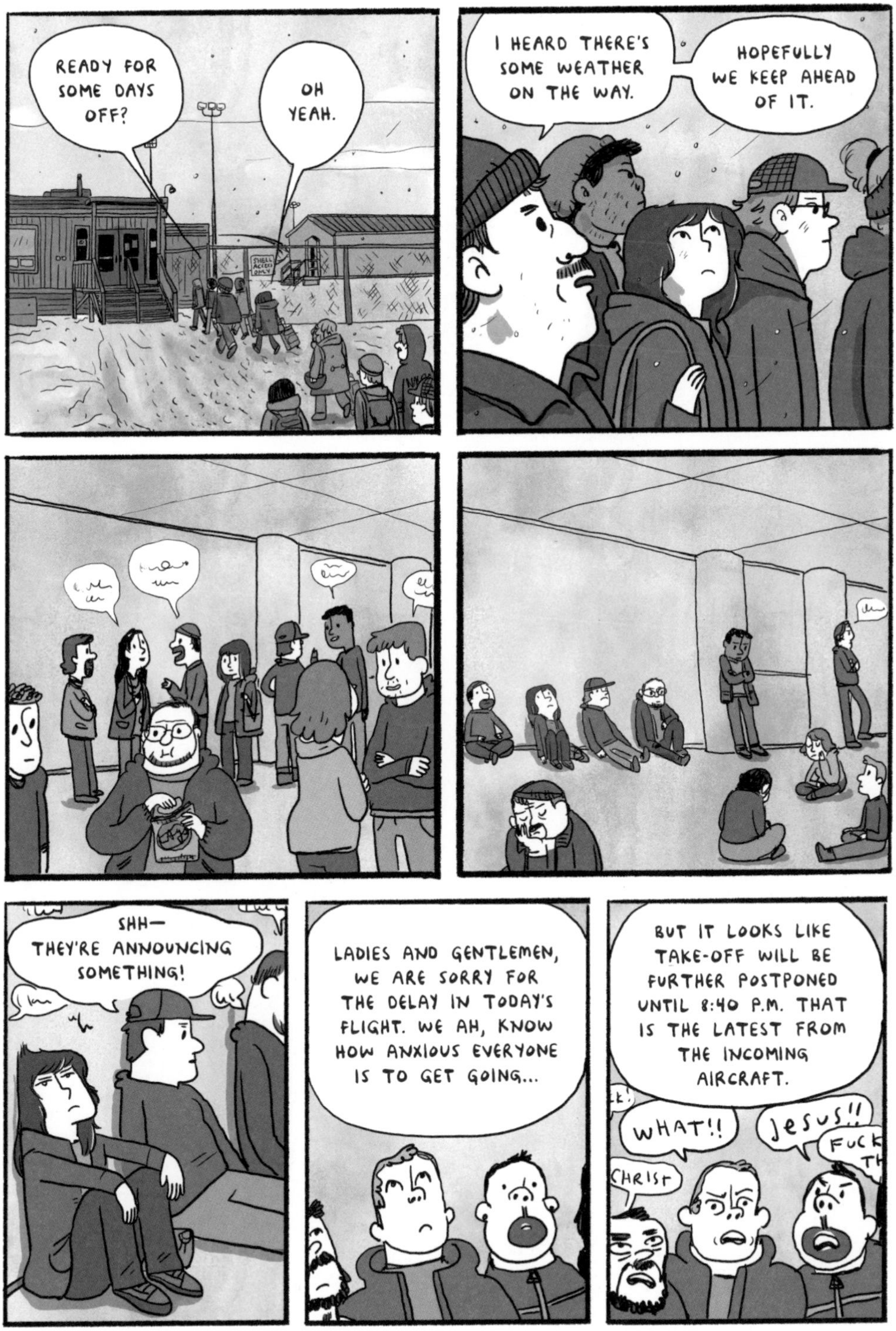
READY FOR SOME DAYS OFF?
OH YEAH.
I HEARD THERE'S SOME WEATHER ON THE WAY.
HOPEFULLY WE KEEP AHEAD OF IT.
SHH— THEY'RE ANNOUNCING SOMETHING!
LADIES AND GENTLEMEN, WE ARE SORRY FOR THE DELAY IN TODAY'S FLIGHT. WE AH, KNOW HOW ANXIOUS EVERYONE IS TO GET GOING...
BUT IT LOOKS LIKE TAKE-OFF WILL BE FURTHER POSTPONED UNTIL 8:40 P.M. THAT IS THE LATEST FROM THE INCOMING AIRCRAFT.
WHAT!!
JESUS!!
CHRIST

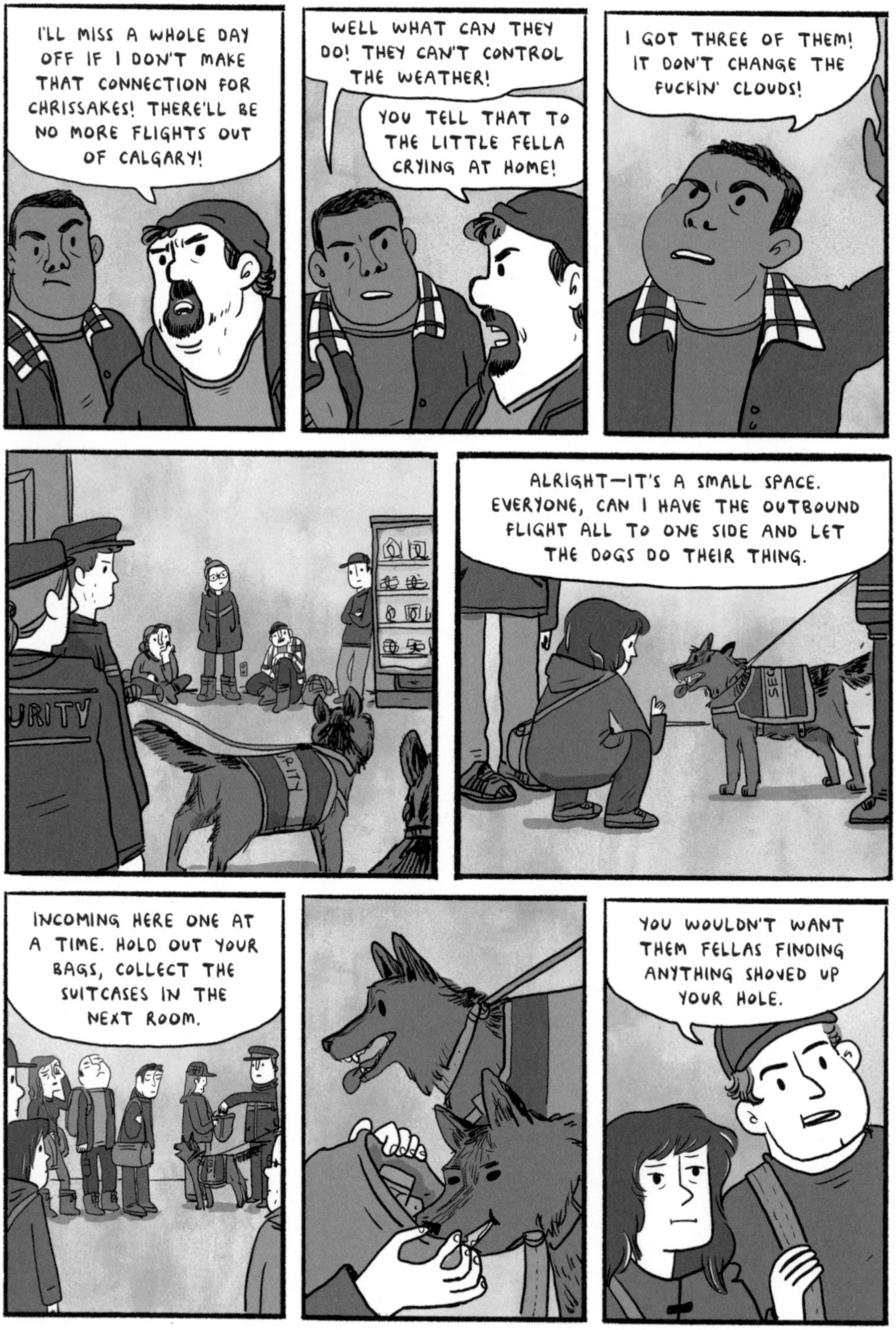
I'LL MISS A WHOLE DAY OFF IF I DON'T MAKE THAT CONNECTION FOR CHRISSAKES! THERE'LL BE NO MORE FLIGHTS OUT OF CALGARY!
WELL WHAT CAN THEY DO! THEY CAN'T CONTROL THE WEATHER!
YOU TELL THAT TO THE LITTLE FELLA CRYING AT HOME!
I GOT THREE OF THEM! IT DON'T CHANGE THE FUCKIN' CLOUDS!
URITY
ALRIGHT—IT'S A SMALL SPACE. EVERYONE, CAN I HAVE THE OUTBOUND FLIGHT ALL TO ONE SIDE AND LET THE DOGS DO THEIR THING.
INCOMING HERE ONE AT A TIME. HOLD OUT YOUR BAGS, COLLECT THE SUITCASES IN THE NEXT ROOM.
YOU WOULDN'T WANT THEM FELLAS FINDING ANYTHING SHOVED UP YOUR HOLE.

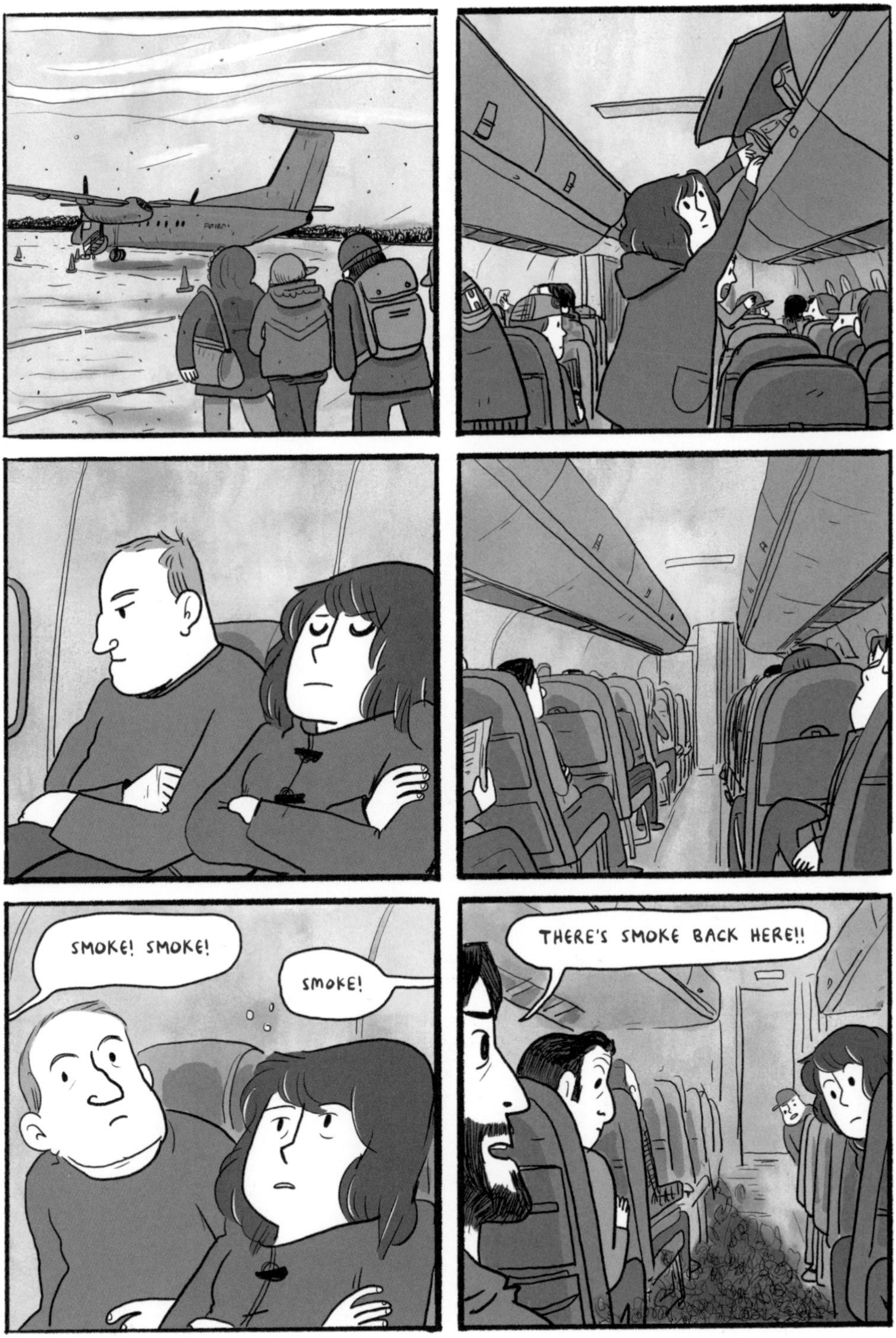
SMOKE! SMOKE!
SMOKE!
THERE'S SMOKE BACK HERE!!

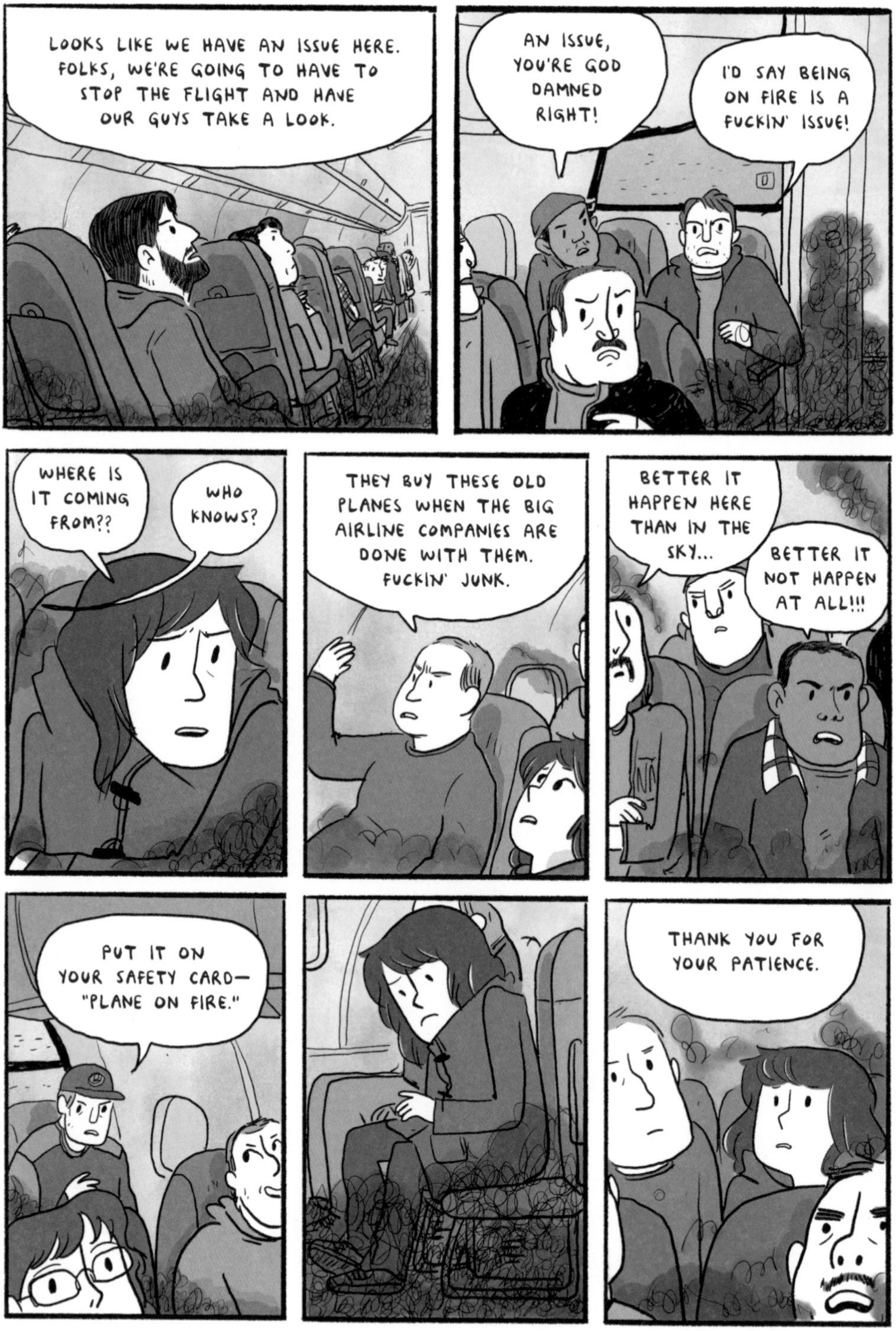
LOOKS LIKE WE HAVE AN ISSUE HERE. FOLKS, WE'RE GOING TO HAVE TO STOP THE FLIGHT AND HAVE OUR GUYS TAKE A LOOK.
AN ISSUE, YOU'RE GOD DAMNED RIGHT!
I'D SAY BEING ON FIRE IS A FUCKIN' ISSUE!
WHERE IS IT COMING FROM??
WHO KNOWS?
THEY BUY THESE OLD PLANES WHEN THE BIG AIRLINE COMPANIES ARE DONE WITH THEM. FUCKIN' JUNK.
BETTER IT HAPPEN HERE THAN IN THE SKY...
BETTER IT NOT HAPPEN AT ALL!!!
PUT IT ON YOUR SAFETY CARD— "PLANE ON FIRE."
THANK YOU FOR YOUR PATIENCE.

THIS IS YOUR BOARDING PASS
DO NOT THROW AWAY
FLAIR
Airlines
SCARE
AIR
Departure time
10:15
Boarding
09:45

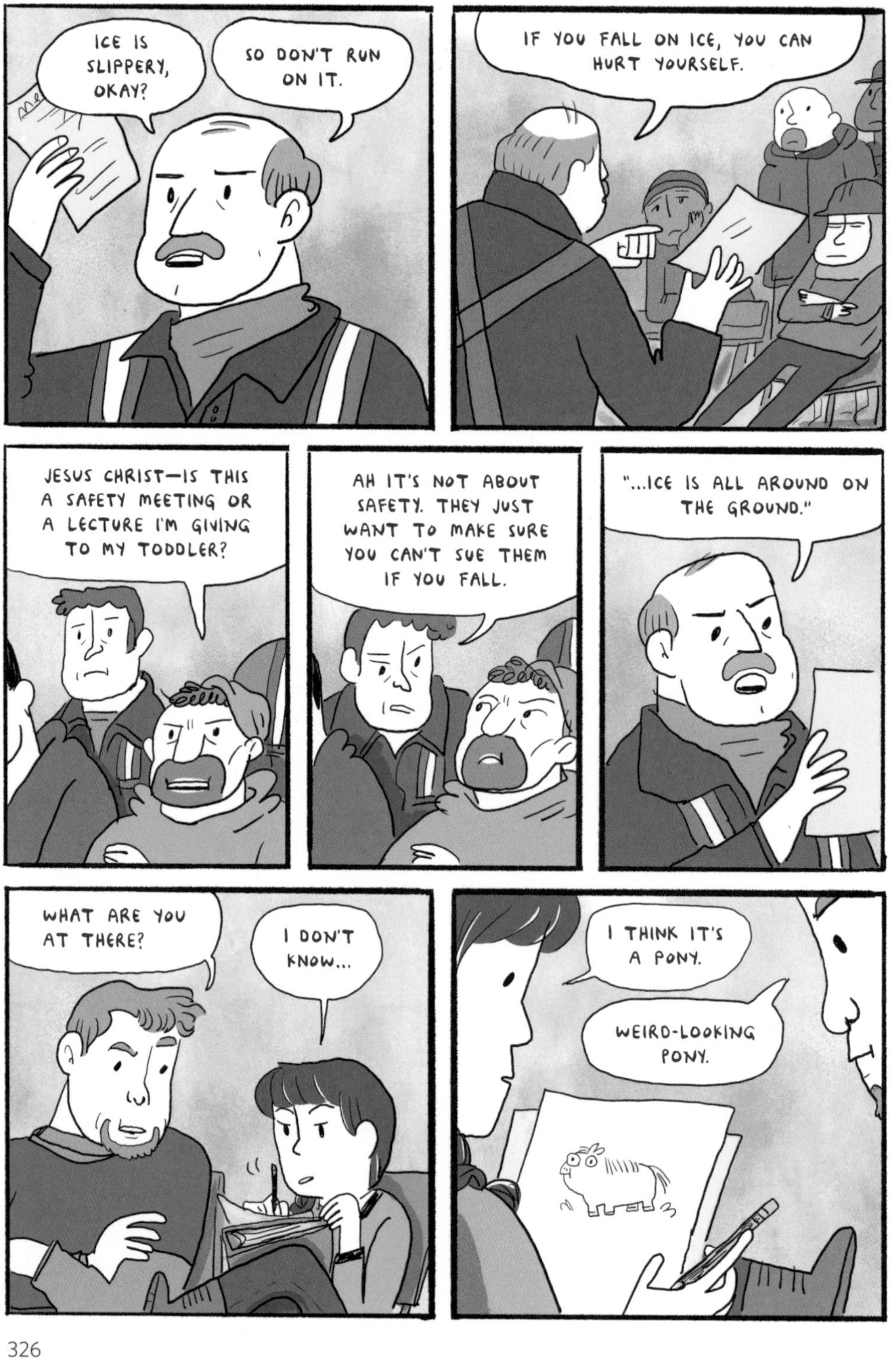
ICE IS SLIPPERY, OKAY?
SO DON'T RUN ON IT.
IF YOU FALL ON ICE, YOU CAN HURT YOURSELF.
JESUS CHRIST—IS THIS A SAFETY MEETING OR A LECTURE I'M GIVING TO MY TODDLER?
AH IT'S NOT ABOUT SAFETY. THEY JUST WANT TO MAKE SURE YOU CAN'T SUE THEM IF YOU FALL.
"...ICE IS ALL AROUND ON THE GROUND."
WHAT ARE YOU AT THERE?
I DON'T KNOW...
I THINK IT'S A PONY.
WEIRD-LOOKING PONY.

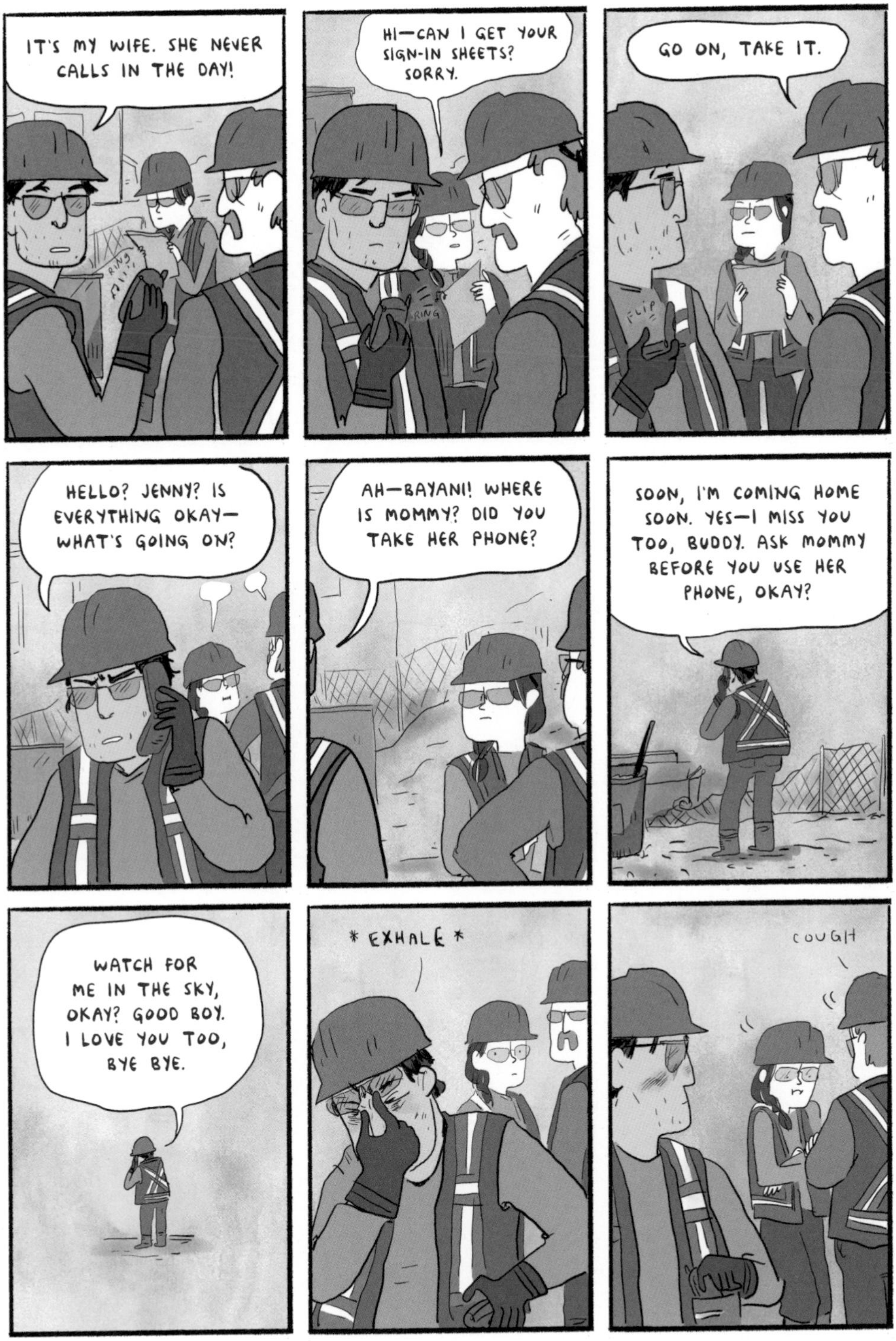
IT'S MY WIFE. SHE NEVER CALLS IN THE DAY!
RING
HI—CAN I GET YOUR SIGN-IN SHEETS? SORRY.
RING
GO ON, TAKE IT.
FLIP
HELLO? JENNY? IS EVERYTHING OKAY— WHAT'S GOING ON?
AH—BAYANI! WHERE IS MOMMY? DID YOU TAKE HER PHONE?
SOON, I'M COMING HOME SOON. YES—I MISS YOU TOO, BUDDY. ASK MOMMY BEFORE YOU USE HER PHONE, OKAY?
WATCH FOR ME IN THE SKY, OKAY? GOOD BOY. I LOVE YOU TOO, BYE BYE.
* EXHALE *
COUGH

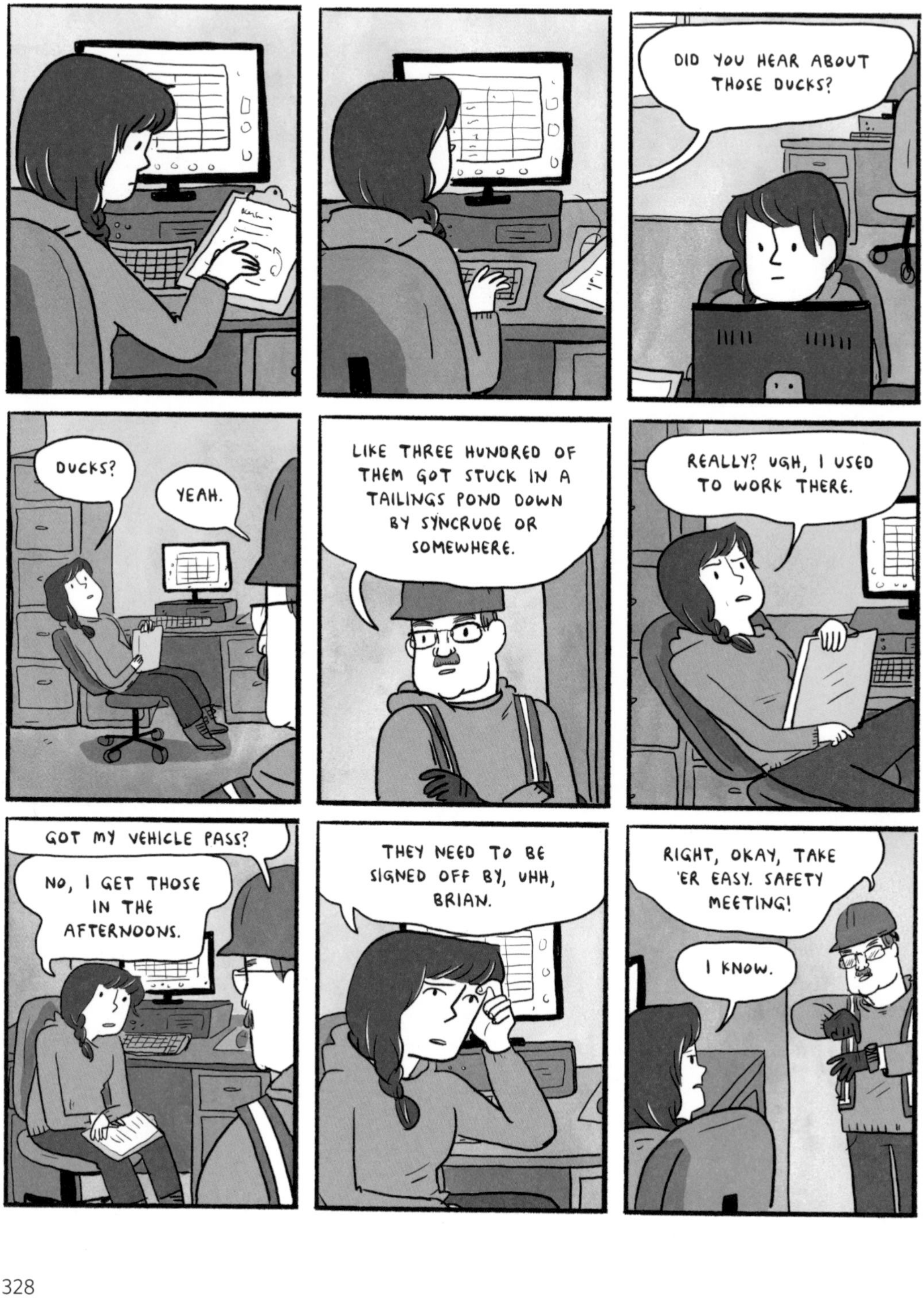
DID YOU HEAR ABOUT THOSE DUCKS?
DUCKS?
YEAH.
LIKE THREE HUNDRED OF THEM GOT STUCK IN A TAILINGS POND DOWN BY SYNCRUDE OR SOMEWHERE.
REALLY? UGH, I USED TO WORK THERE.
GOT MY VEHICLE PASS?
NO, I GET THOSE IN THE AFTERNOONS.
THEY NEED TO BE SIGNED OFF BY, UHH, BRIAN.
RIGHT, OKAY, TAKE 'ER EASY. SAFETY MEETING!
I KNOW.

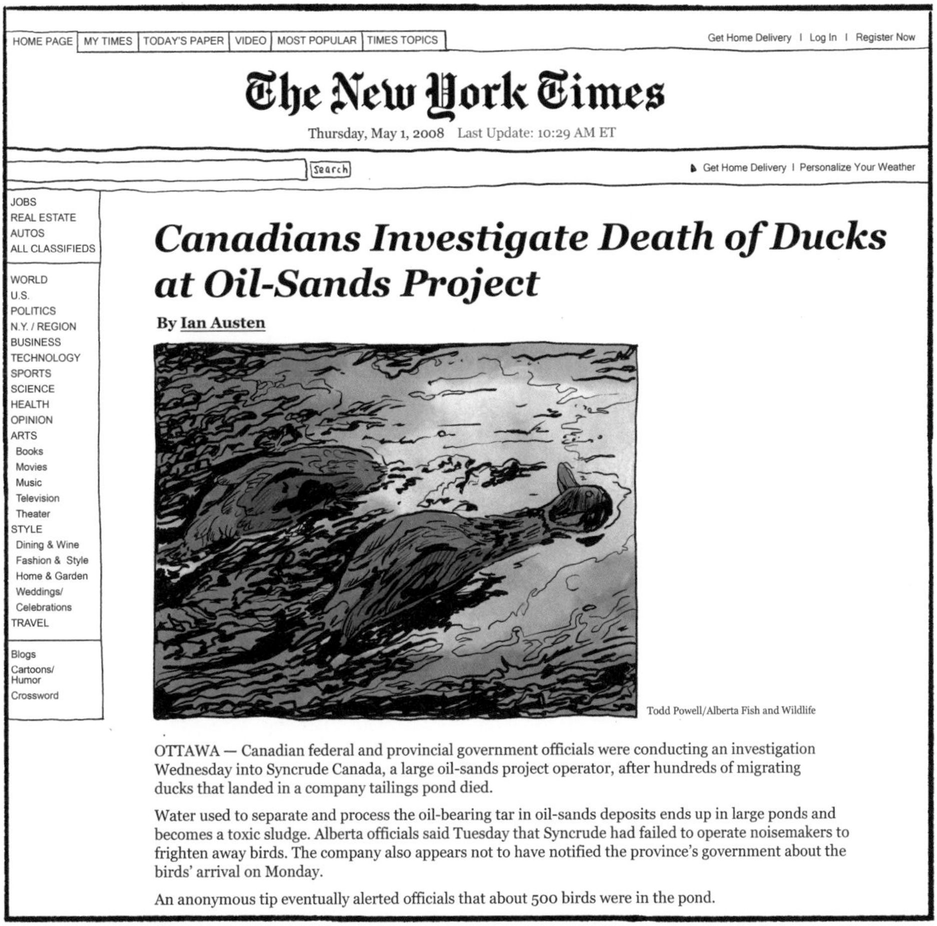
HOME PAGE | MY TIMES | TODAY'S PAPER | VIDEO | MOST POPULAR | TIMES TOPICS

Get Home Delivery | Log In | Register Now

The New York Times

Thursday, May 1, 2008 Last Update: 10:29 AM ET

Search

Get Home Delivery | Personalize Your Weather

JOBS
REAL ESTATE
AUTOS
ALL CLASSIFIEDS

WORLD
U.S.
POLITICS
N.Y. / REGION
BUSINESS
TECHNOLOGY
SPORTS
SCIENCE
HEALTH
OPINION
ARTS
Books
Movies
Music
Television
Theater
STYLE
Dining & Wine
Fashion & Style
Home & Garden
Weddings/ Celebrations
TRAVEL

Blogs
Cartoons/ Humor
Crossword

Canadians Investigate Death of Ducks at Oil-Sands Project

By Ian Austen

Todd Powell/Alberta Fish and Wildlife

OTTAWA — Canadian federal and provincial government officials were conducting an investigation Wednesday into Syncrude Canada, a large oil-sands project operator, after hundreds of migrating ducks that landed in a company tailings pond died.

Water used to separate and process the oil-bearing tar in oil-sands deposits ends up in large ponds and becomes a toxic sludge. Alberta officials said Tuesday that Syncrude had failed to operate noisemakers to frighten away birds. The company also appears not to have notified the province's government about the birds' arrival on Monday.

An anonymous tip eventually alerted officials that about 500 birds were in the pond.

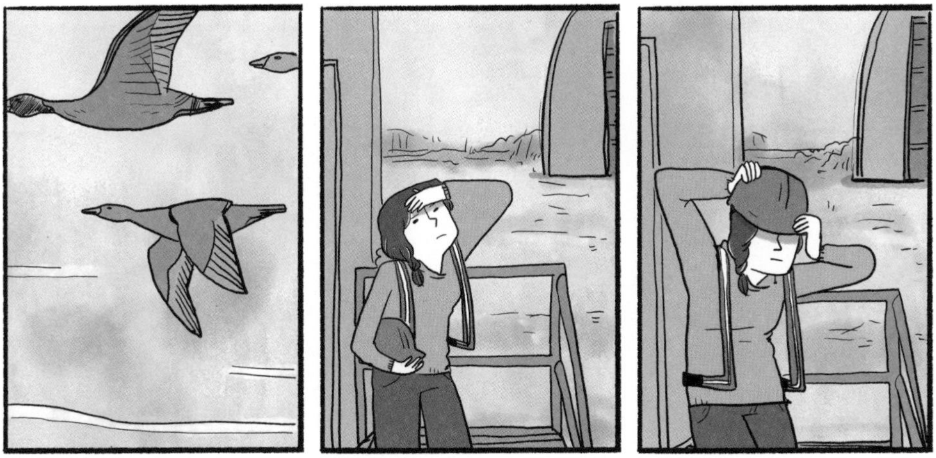

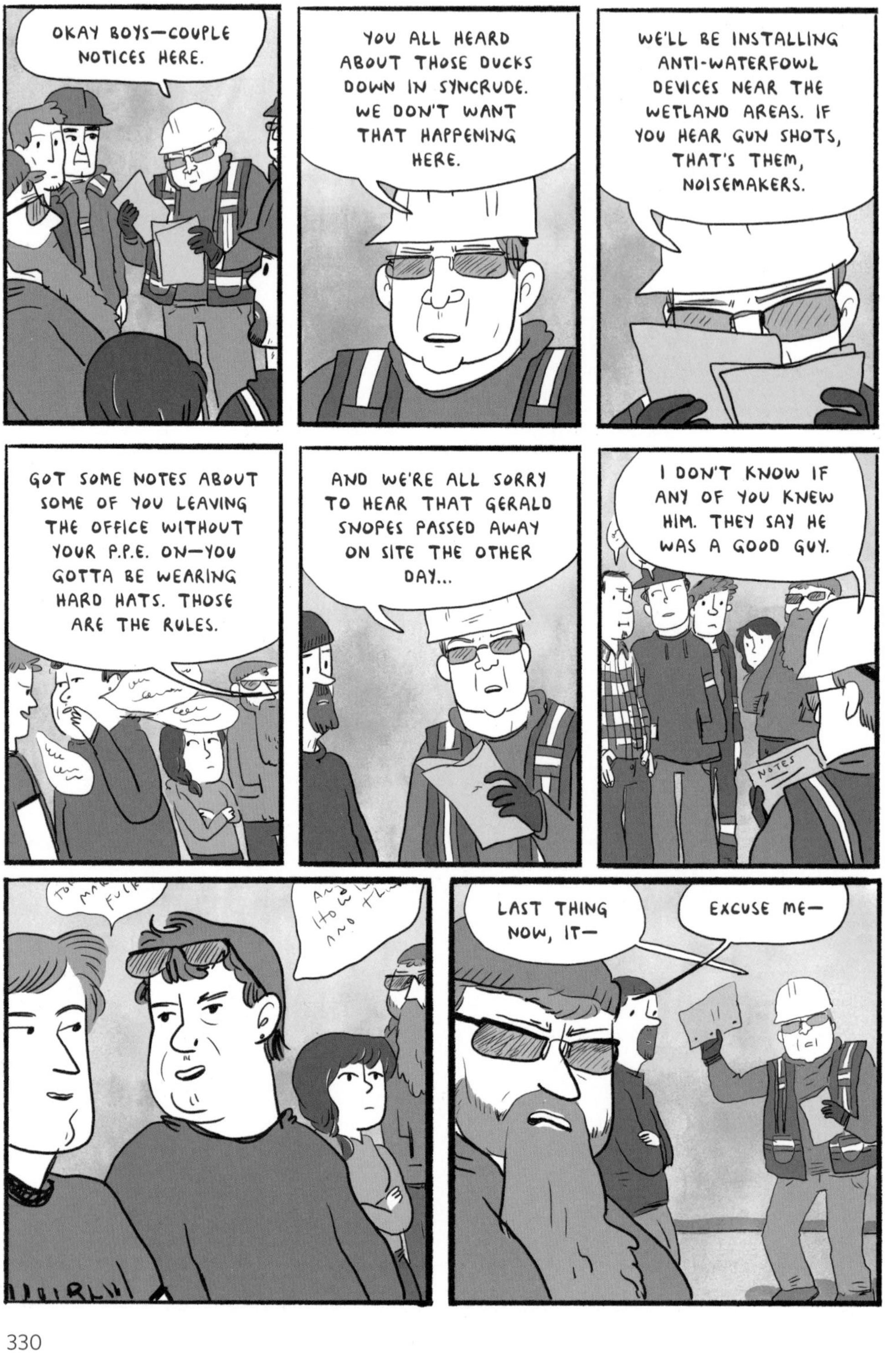
OKAY BOYS—COUPLE NOTICES HERE.
YOU ALL HEARD ABOUT THOSE DUCKS DOWN IN SYNCRUDE. WE DON'T WANT THAT HAPPENING HERE.
WE'LL BE INSTALLING ANTI-WATERFOWL DEVICES NEAR THE WETLAND AREAS. IF YOU HEAR GUN SHOTS, THAT'S THEM, NOISEMAKERS.
GOT SOME NOTES ABOUT SOME OF YOU LEAVING THE OFFICE WITHOUT YOUR P.P.E. ON—YOU GOTTA BE WEARING HARD HATS. THOSE ARE THE RULES.
AND WE'RE ALL SORRY TO HEAR THAT GERALD SNOPES PASSED AWAY ON SITE THE OTHER DAY...
I DON'T KNOW IF ANY OF YOU KNEW HIM. THEY SAY HE WAS A GOOD GUY.
NOTES
LAST THING NOW, IT—
EXCUSE ME—

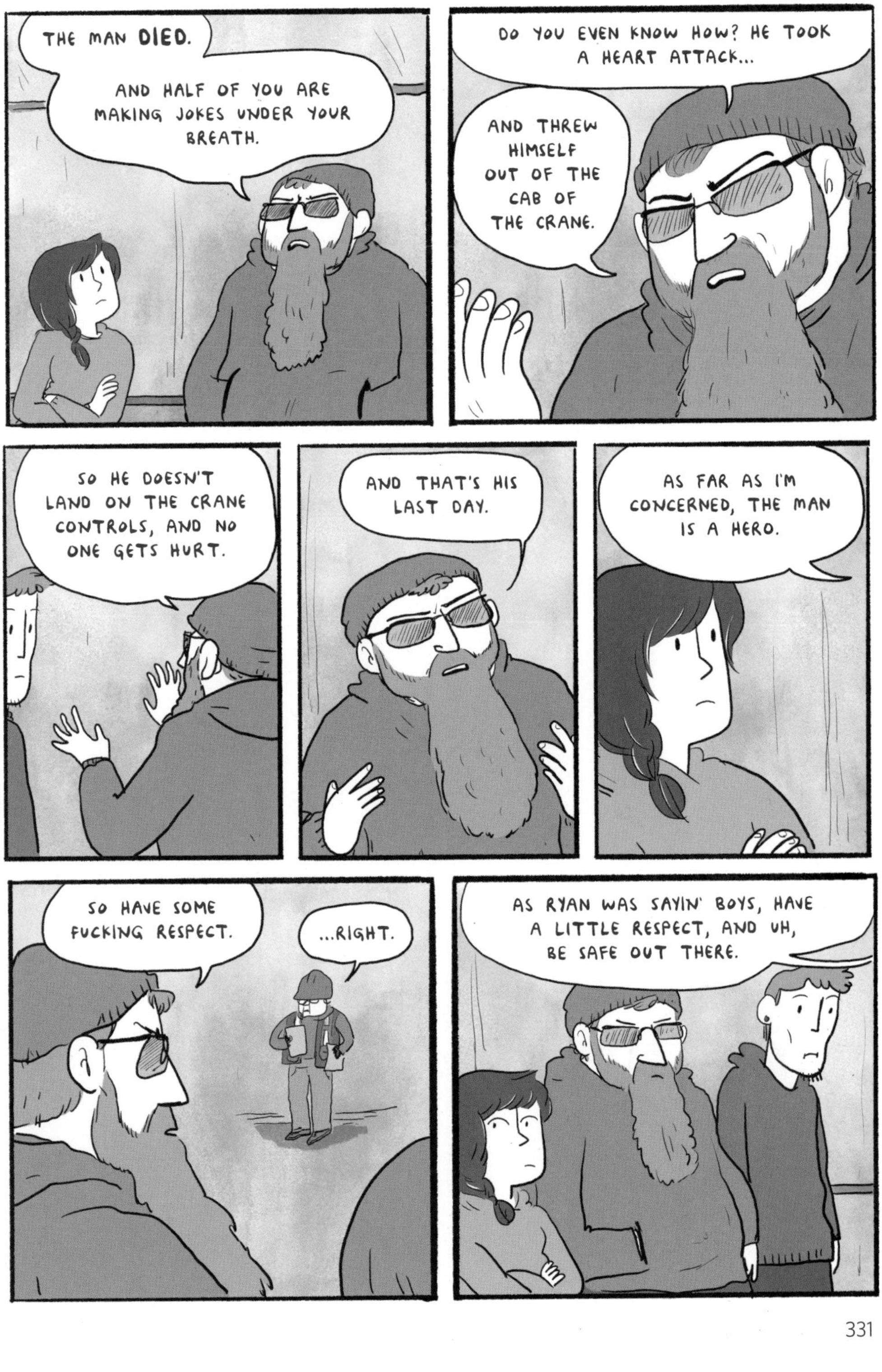
THE MAN DIED.
AND HALF OF YOU ARE MAKING JOKES UNDER YOUR BREATH.
DO YOU EVEN KNOW HOW? HE TOOK A HEART ATTACK...
AND THREW HIMSELF OUT OF THE CAB OF THE CRANE.
SO HE DOESN'T LAND ON THE CRANE CONTROLS, AND NO ONE GETS HURT.
AND THAT'S HIS LAST DAY.
AS FAR AS I'M CONCERNED, THE MAN IS A HERO.
SO HAVE SOME FUCKING RESPECT.
...RIGHT.
AS RYAN WAS SAYIN' BOYS, HAVE A LITTLE RESPECT, AND UH, BE SAFE OUT THERE.

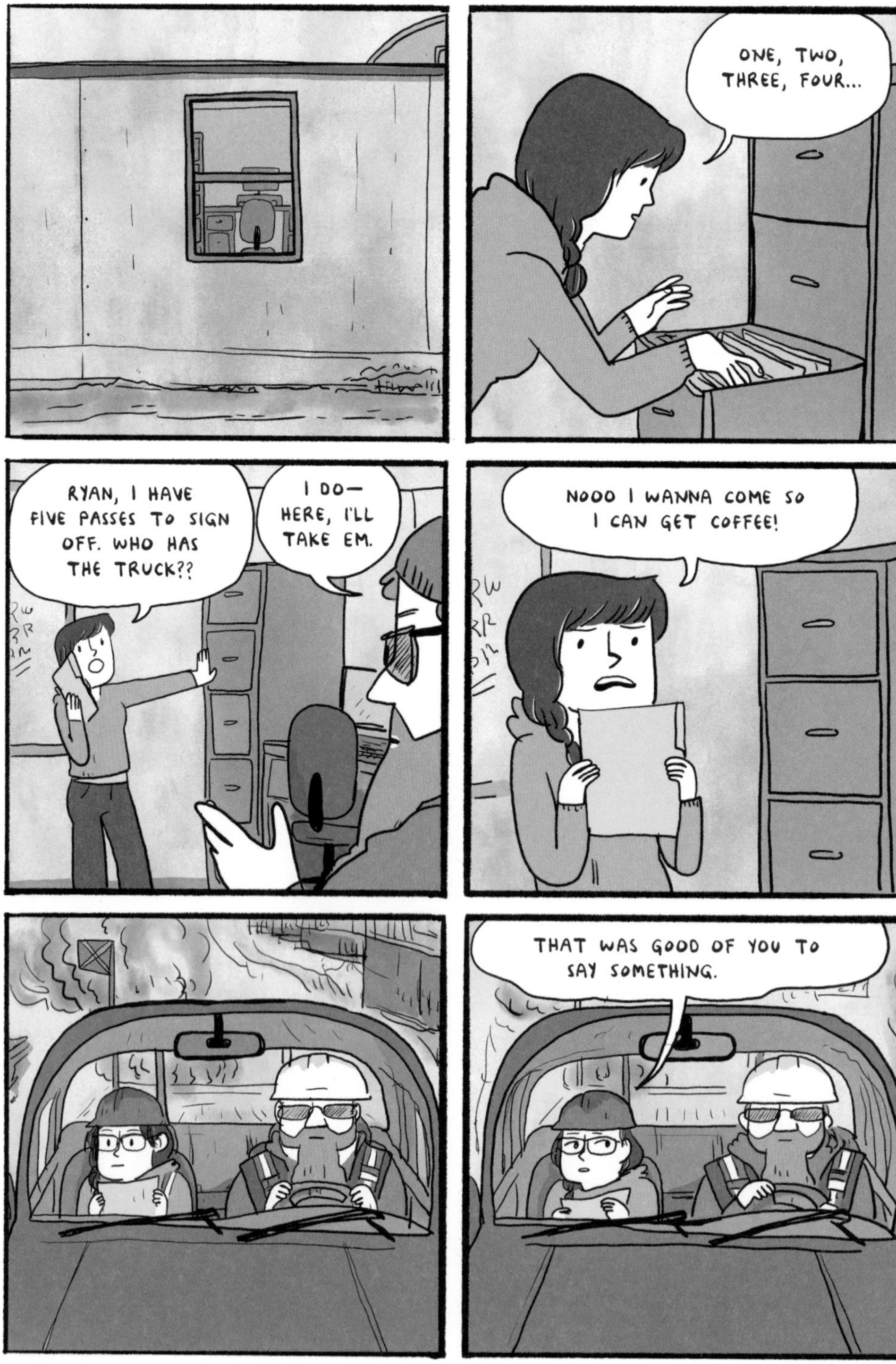
ONE, TWO, THREE, FOUR...
RYAN, I HAVE FIVE PASSES TO SIGN OFF. WHO HAS THE TRUCK??
I DO— HERE, I'LL TAKE EM.
NOOO I WANNA COME SO I CAN GET COFFEE!
THAT WAS GOOD OF YOU TO SAY SOMETHING.

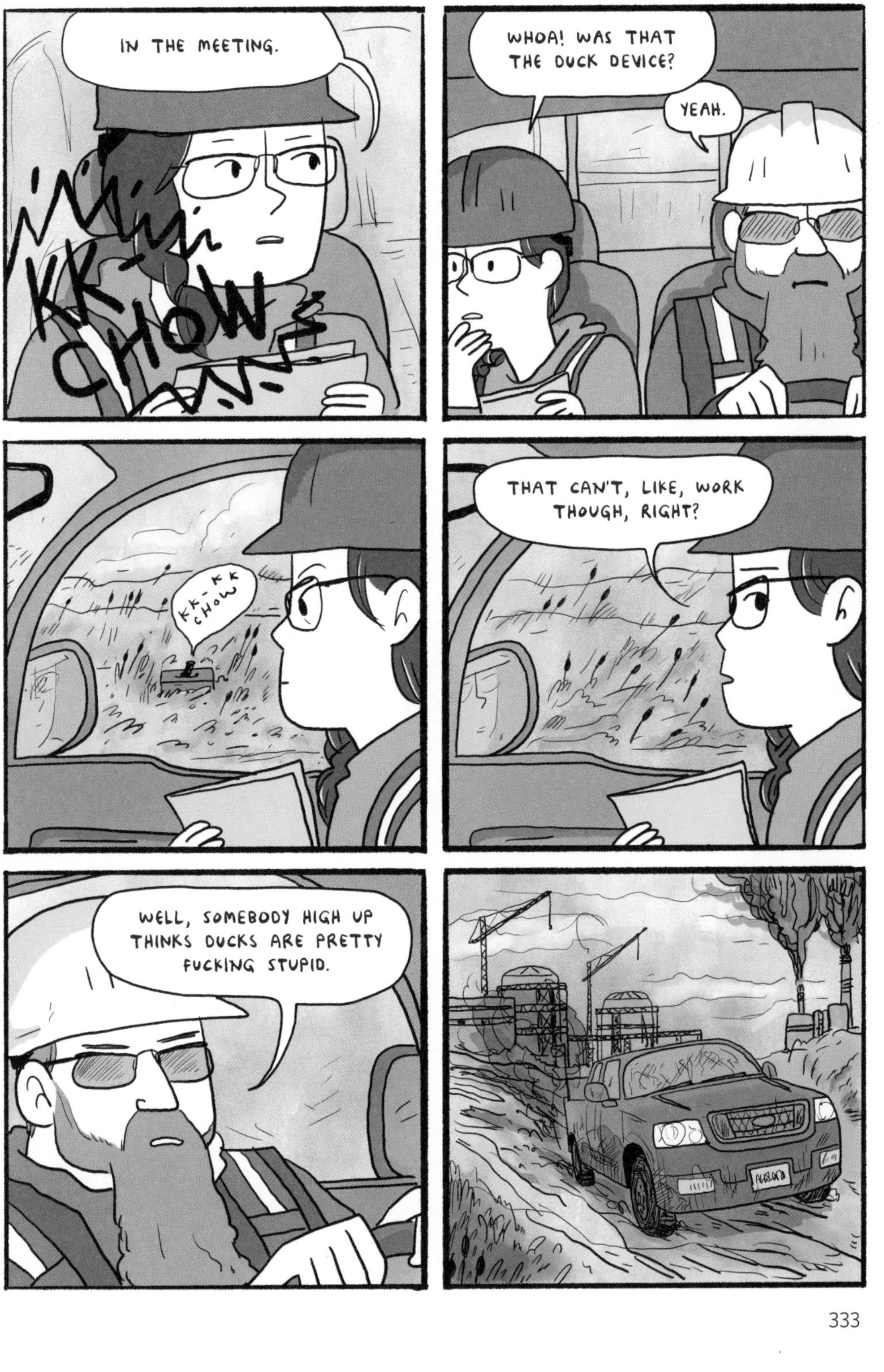
IN THE MEETING.
KK-CHOW
WHOA! WAS THAT THE DUCK DEVICE?
YEAH.
KK-KK CHOW
THAT CAN'T, LIKE, WORK THOUGH, RIGHT?
WELL, SOMEBODY HIGH UP THINKS DUCKS ARE PRETTY FUCKING STUPID.

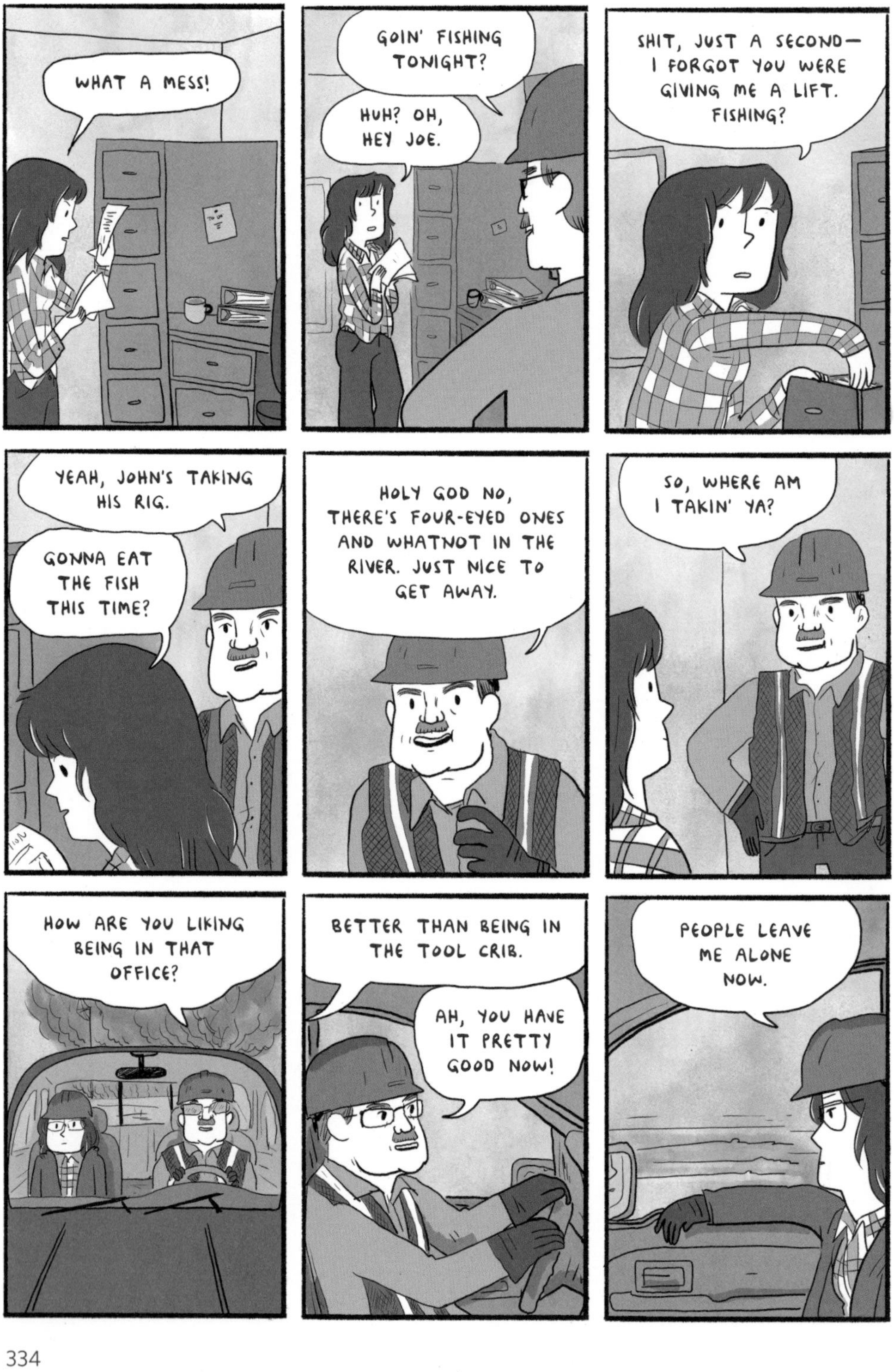
WHAT A MESS!
GOIN' FISHING TONIGHT?
HUH? OH, HEY JOE.
SHIT, JUST A SECOND— I FORGOT YOU WERE GIVING ME A LIFT. FISHING?
YEAH, JOHN'S TAKING HIS RIG.
GONNA EAT THE FISH THIS TIME?
HOLY GOD NO, THERE'S FOUR-EYED ONES AND WHATNOT IN THE RIVER. JUST NICE TO GET AWAY.
SO, WHERE AM I TAKIN' YA?
HOW ARE YOU LIKING BEING IN THAT OFFICE?
BETTER THAN BEING IN THE TOOL CRIB.
AH, YOU HAVE IT PRETTY GOOD NOW!
PEOPLE LEAVE ME ALONE NOW.

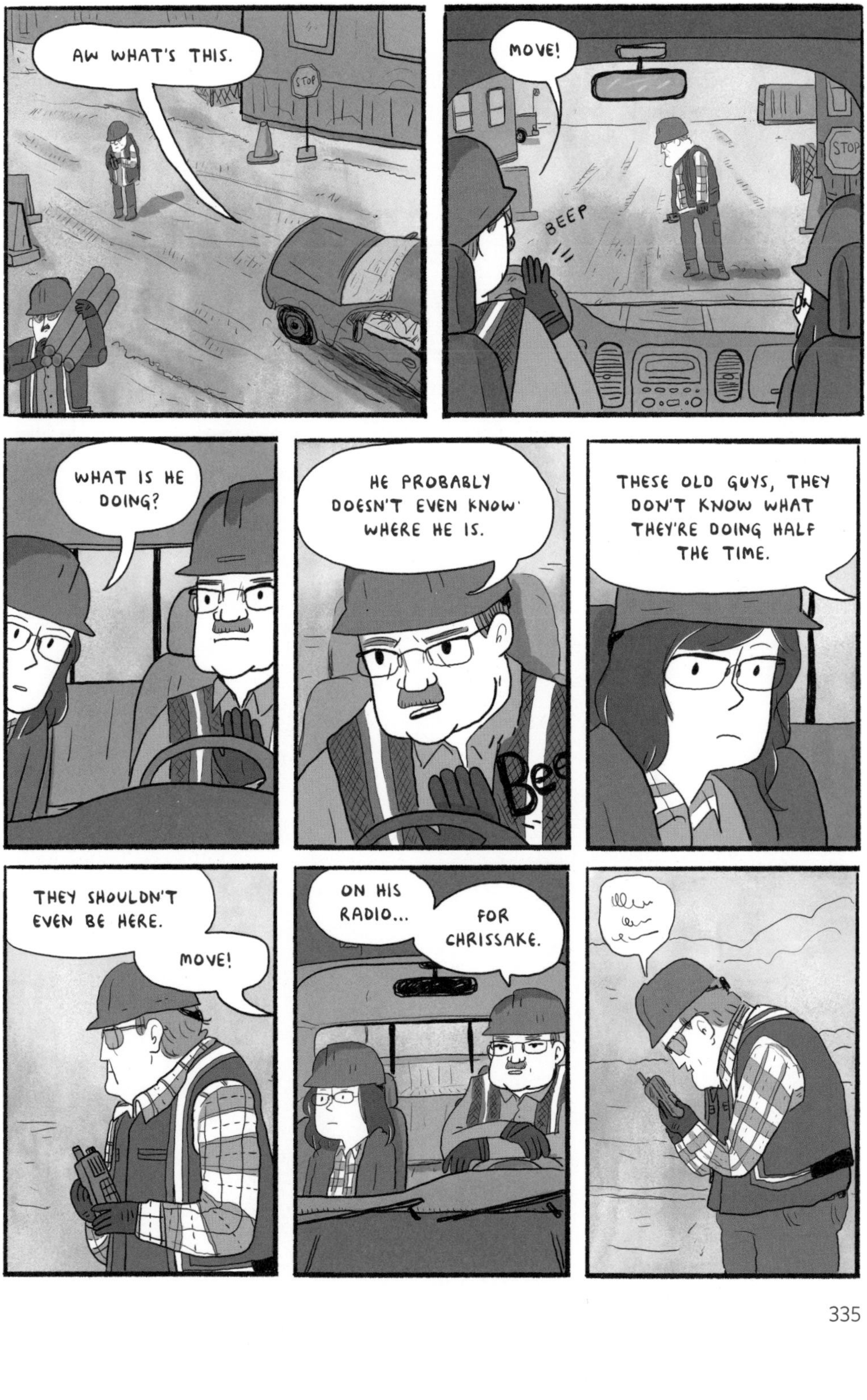
AW WHAT'S THIS.
MOVE!
BEEP
WHAT IS HE DOING?
HE PROBABLY DOESN'T EVEN KNOW WHERE HE IS.
THESE OLD GUYS, THEY DON'T KNOW WHAT THEY'RE DOING HALF THE TIME.
THEY SHOULDN'T EVEN BE HERE.
MOVE!
ON HIS RADIO...
FOR CHRISSAKE.

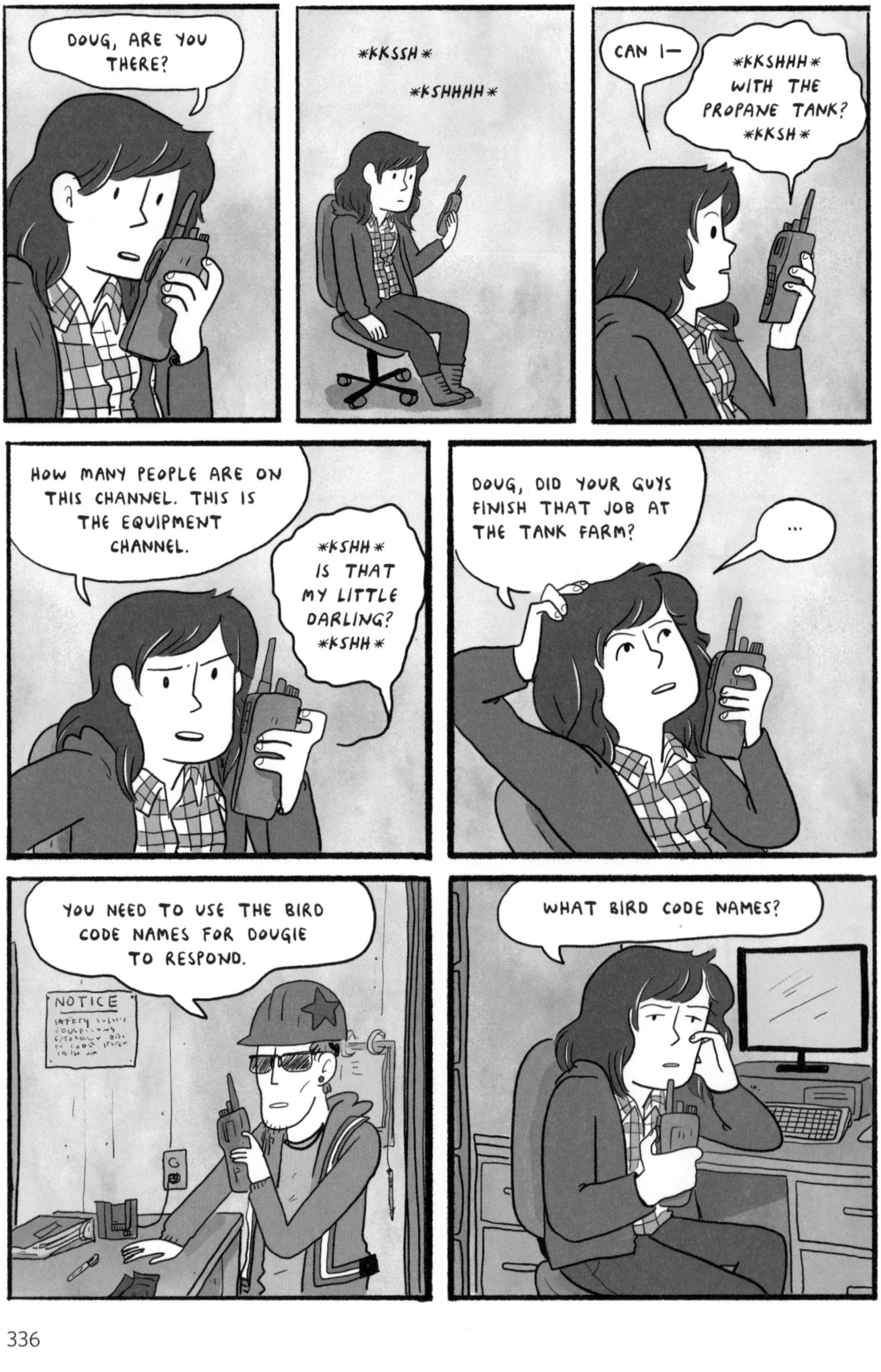
DOUG, ARE YOU THERE?
KKSSH
KSHHHH
CAN I—
KKSHHH WITH THE PROPANE TANK? *KKSH*
HOW MANY PEOPLE ARE ON THIS CHANNEL. THIS IS THE EQUIPMENT CHANNEL.
KSHH IS THAT MY LITTLE DARLING? *KSHH*
DOUG, DID YOUR GUYS FINISH THAT JOB AT THE TANK FARM?
...
YOU NEED TO USE THE BIRD CODE NAMES FOR DOUGIE TO RESPOND.
NOTICE
WHAT BIRD CODE NAMES?

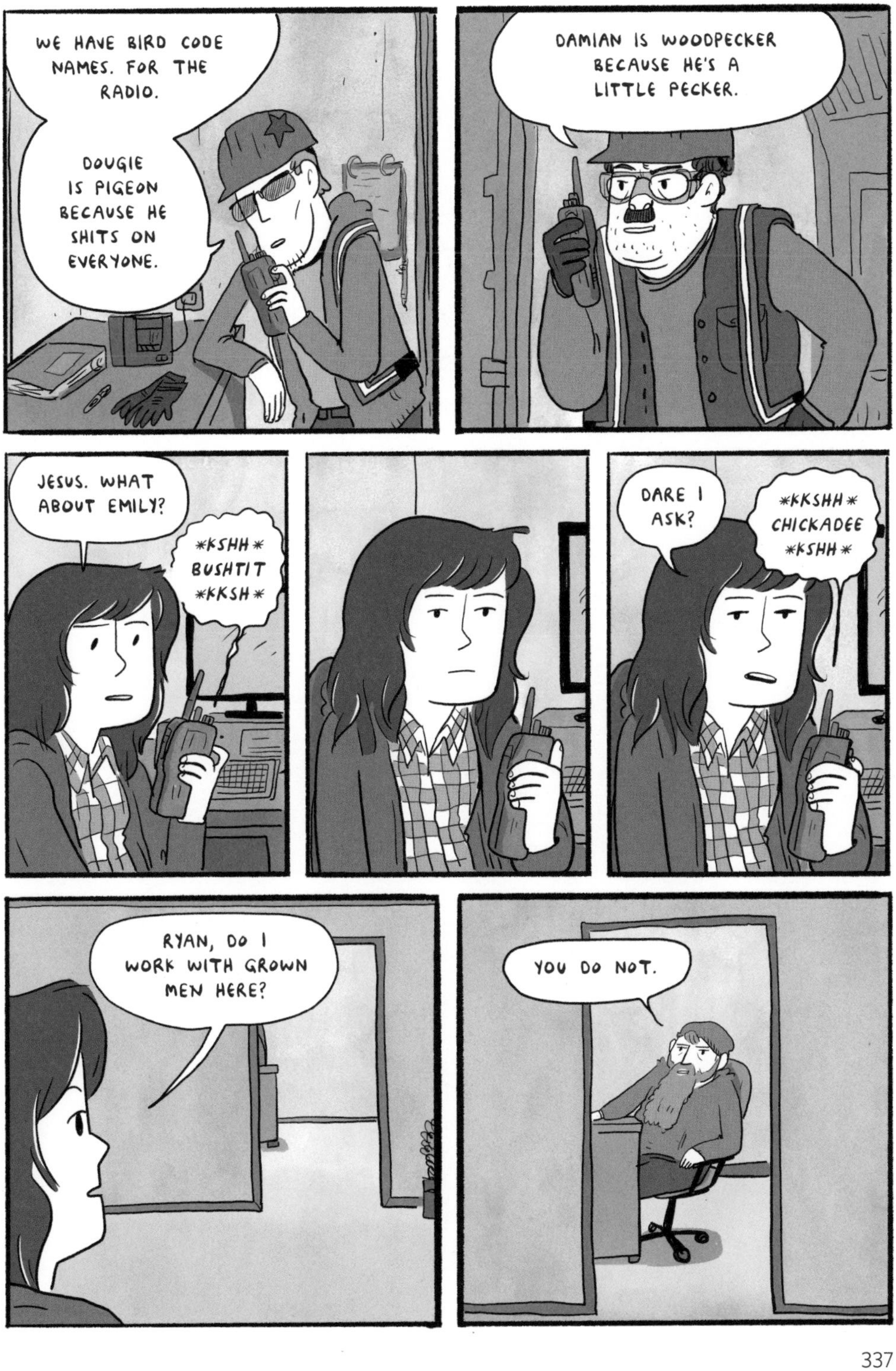
WE HAVE BIRD CODE NAMES. FOR THE RADIO.
DOUGIE IS PIGEON BECAUSE HE SHITS ON EVERYONE.
DAMIAN IS WOODPECKER BECAUSE HE'S A LITTLE PECKER.
JESUS. WHAT ABOUT EMILY?
KSHH BUSHTIT *KKSH*
DARE I ASK?
KKSHH CHICKADEE *KSHH*
RYAN, DO I WORK WITH GROWN MEN HERE?
YOU DO NOT.

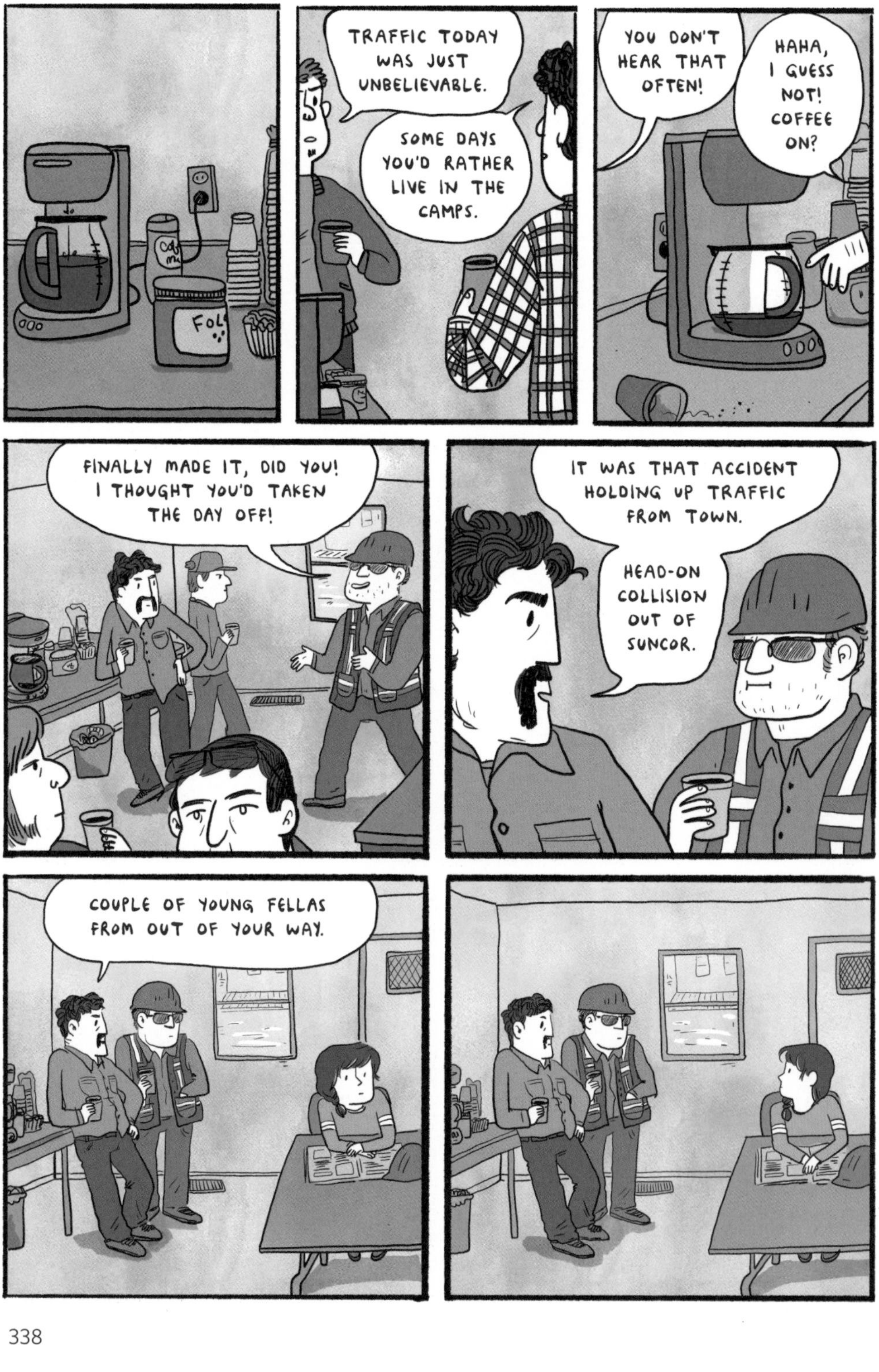
TRAFFIC TODAY WAS JUST UNBELIEVABLE.
SOME DAYS YOU'D RATHER LIVE IN THE CAMPS.
YOU DON'T HEAR THAT OFTEN!
HAHA, I GUESS NOT! COFFEE ON?
FINALLY MADE IT, DID YOU! I THOUGHT YOU'D TAKEN THE DAY OFF!
IT WAS THAT ACCIDENT HOLDING UP TRAFFIC FROM TOWN.
HEAD-ON COLLISION OUT OF SUNCOR.
COUPLE OF YOUNG FELLAS FROM OUT OF YOUR WAY.

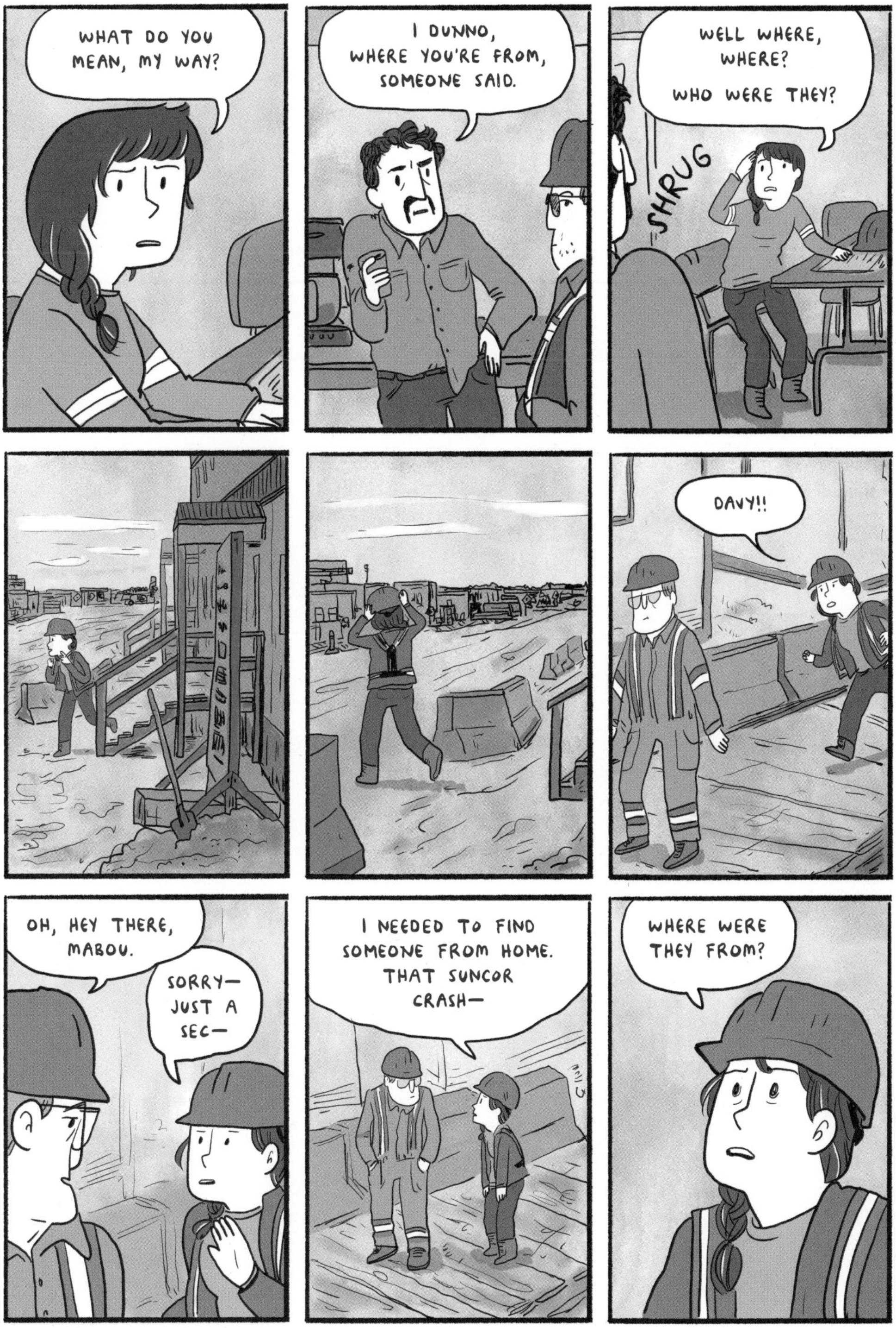
WHAT DO YOU MEAN, MY WAY?
I DUNNO, WHERE YOU'RE FROM, SOMEONE SAID.
WELL WHERE, WHERE?
WHO WERE THEY?
SHRUG
DAVY!!
OH, HEY THERE, MABOU.
SORRY— JUST A SEC—
I NEEDED TO FIND SOMEONE FROM HOME. THAT SUNCOR CRASH—
WHERE WERE THEY FROM?

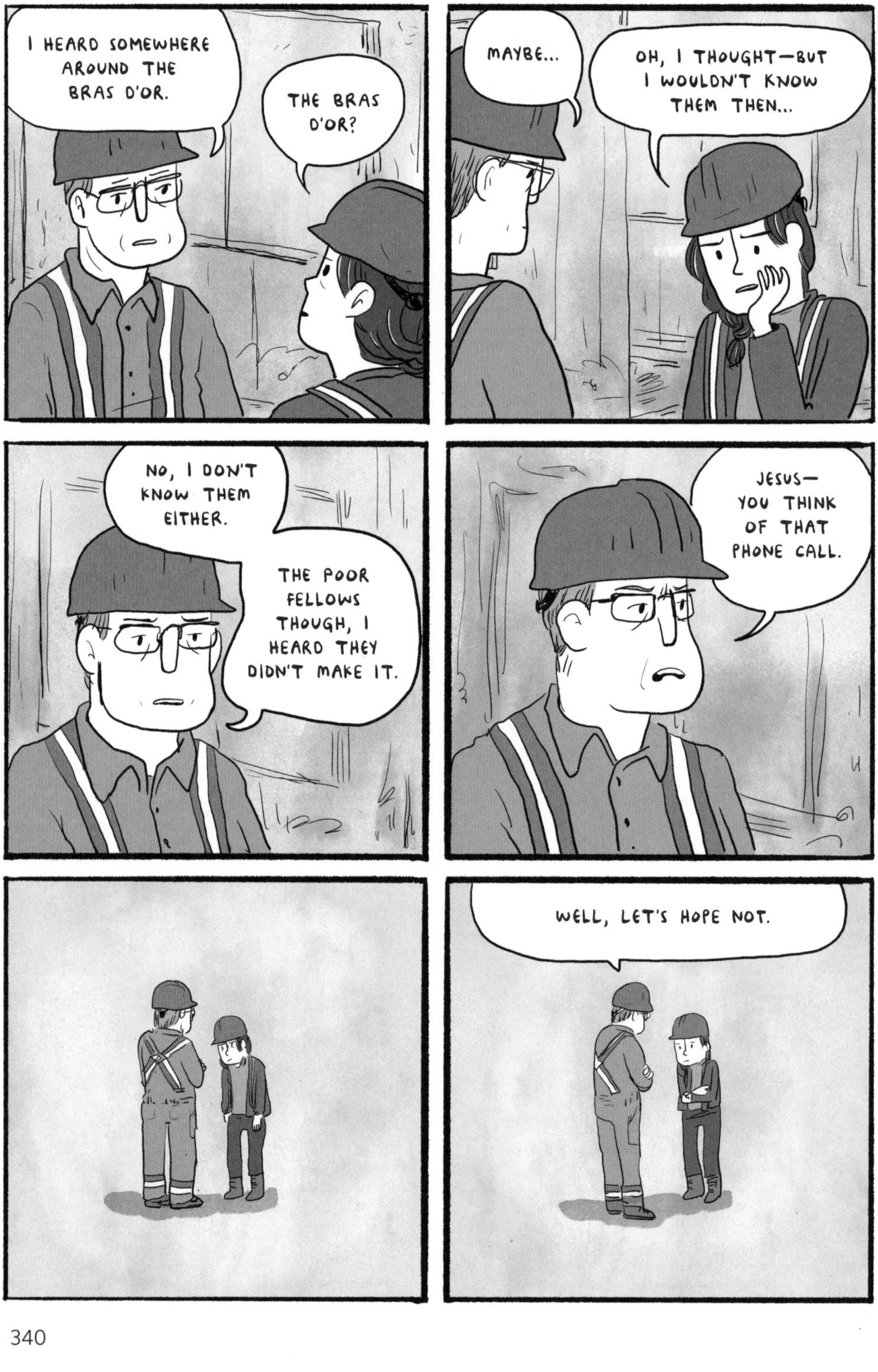
I HEARD SOMEWHERE AROUND THE BRAS D'OR.
THE BRAS D'OR?
MAYBE...
OH, I THOUGHT—BUT I WOULDN'T KNOW THEM THEN...
NO, I DON'T KNOW THEM EITHER.
THE POOR FELLOWS THOUGH, I HEARD THEY DIDN'T MAKE IT.
JESUS— YOU THINK OF THAT PHONE CALL.
WELL, LET'S HOPE NOT.

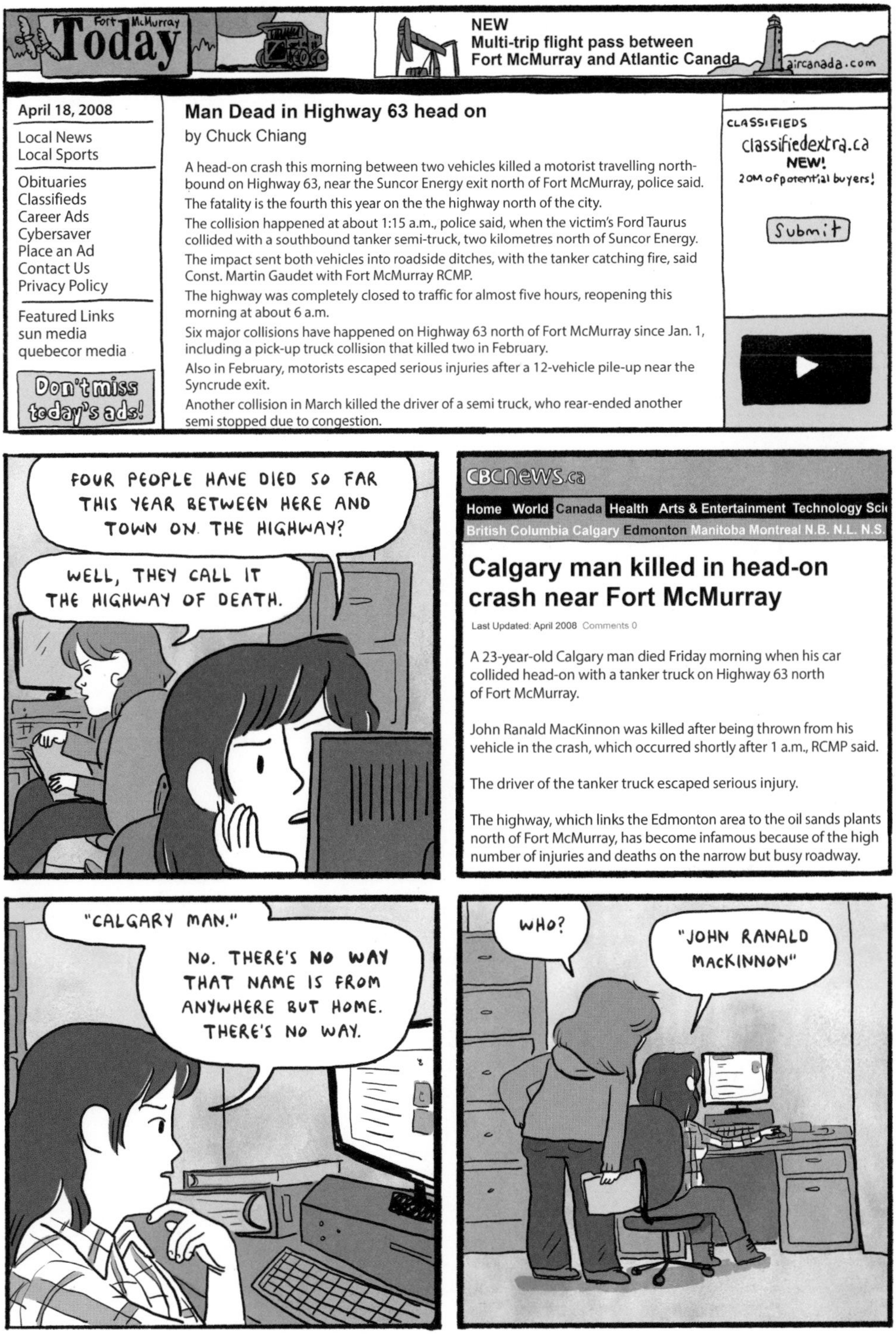

Fort McMurray Today

NEW
Multi-trip flight pass between
Fort McMurray and Atlantic Canada
aircanada.com

April 18, 2008

Local News
Local Sports
Obituaries
Classifieds
Career Ads
Cybersaver
Place an Ad
Contact Us
Privacy Policy
Featured Links
sun media
quebecor media

Don't miss today's ads!

Man Dead in Highway 63 head on

by Chuck Chiang

A head-on crash this morning between two vehicles killed a motorist travelling north-bound on Highway 63, near the Suncor Energy exit north of Fort McMurray, police said.

The fatality is the fourth this year on the the highway north of the city.

The collision happened at about 1:15 a.m., police said, when the victim's Ford Taurus collided with a southbound tanker semi-truck, two kilometres north of Suncor Energy.

The impact sent both vehicles into roadside ditches, with the tanker catching fire, said Const. Martin Gaudet with Fort McMurray RCMP.

The highway was completely closed to traffic for almost five hours, reopening this morning at about 6 a.m.

Six major collisions have happened on Highway 63 north of Fort McMurray since Jan. 1, including a pick-up truck collision that killed two in February.

Also in February, motorists escaped serious injuries after a 12-vehicle pile-up near the Syncrude exit.

Another collision in March killed the driver of a semi truck, who rear-ended another semi stopped due to congestion.

CLASSIFIEDS
classifiedextra.ca
NEW!
2OM of potential buyers!
Submit

FOUR PEOPLE HAVE DIED SO FAR THIS YEAR BETWEEN HERE AND TOWN ON THE HIGHWAY?
WELL, THEY CALL IT THE HIGHWAY OF DEATH.

CBCnews.ca

Home World Canada Health Arts & Entertainment Technology Sci

British Columbia Calgary Edmonton Manitoba Montreal N.B. N.L. N.S.

Calgary man killed in head-on crash near Fort McMurray

Last Updated: April 2008 Comments 0

A 23-year-old Calgary man died Friday morning when his car collided head-on with a tanker truck on Highway 63 north of Fort McMurray.

John Ranald MacKinnon was killed after being thrown from his vehicle in the crash, which occurred shortly after 1 a.m., RCMP said.

The driver of the tanker truck escaped serious injury.

The highway, which links the Edmonton area to the oil sands plants north of Fort McMurray, has become infamous because of the high number of injuries and deaths on the narrow but busy roadway.

"CALGARY MAN."
NO. THERE'S NO WAY THAT NAME IS FROM ANYWHERE BUT HOME. THERE'S NO WAY.
WHO?
"JOHN RANALD MACKINNON"

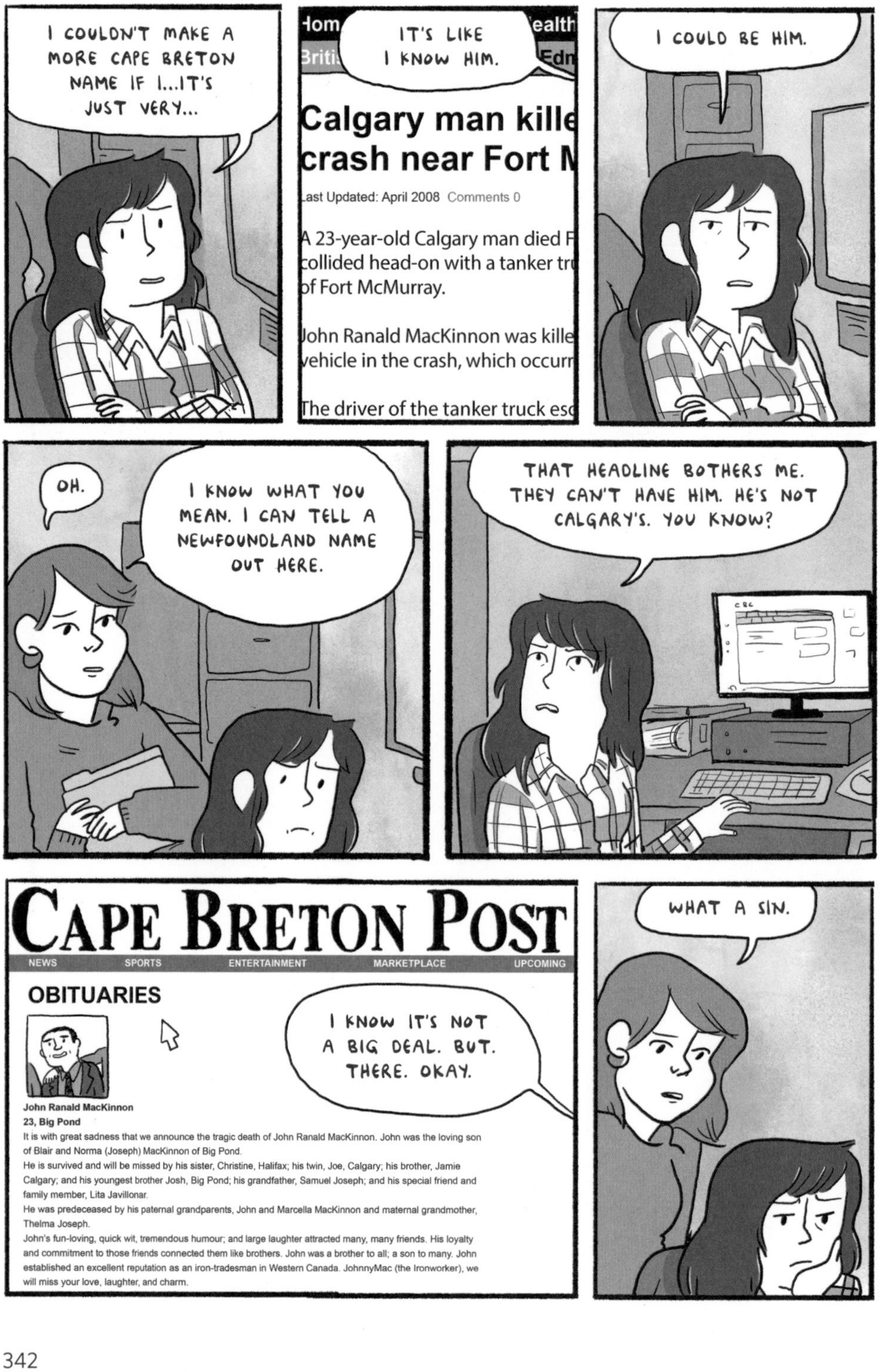
I COULDN'T MAKE A MORE CAPE BRETON NAME IF I...IT'S JUST VERY...
IT'S LIKE I KNOW HIM.
Calgary man kille
crash near Fort M
ast Updated: April 2008 Comments 0
A 23-year-old Calgary man died F
collided head-on with a tanker tr
of Fort McMurray.
John Ranald MacKinnon was kille
vehicle in the crash, which occurr
The driver of the tanker truck esc
I COULD BE HIM.
OH.
I KNOW WHAT YOU MEAN. I CAN TELL A NEWFOUNDLAND NAME OUT HERE.
THAT HEADLINE BOTHERS ME. THEY CAN'T HAVE HIM. HE'S NOT CALGARY'S. YOU KNOW?
CAPE BRETON POST
NEWS SPORTS ENTERTAINMENT MARKETPLACE UPCOMING
OBITUARIES
John Ranald MacKinnon
23, Big Pond
It is with great sadness that we announce the tragic death of John Ranald MacKinnon. John was the loving son of Blair and Norma (Joseph) MacKinnon of Big Pond.
He is survived and will be missed by his sister, Christine, Halifax; his twin, Joe, Calgary; his brother, Jamie Calgary; and his youngest brother Josh, Big Pond; his grandfather, Samuel Joseph; and his special friend and family member, Lita Javillonar.
He was predeceased by his paternal grandparents, John and Marcella MacKinnon and maternal grandmother, Thelma Joseph.
John's fun-loving, quick wit, tremendous humour; and large laughter attracted many, many friends. His loyalty and commitment to those friends connected them like brothers. John was a brother to all; a son to many. John established an excellent reputation as an iron-tradesman in Western Canada. JohnnyMac (the Ironworker), we will miss your love, laughter, and charm.
I KNOW IT'S NOT A BIG DEAL. BUT. THERE. OKAY.
WHAT A SIN.

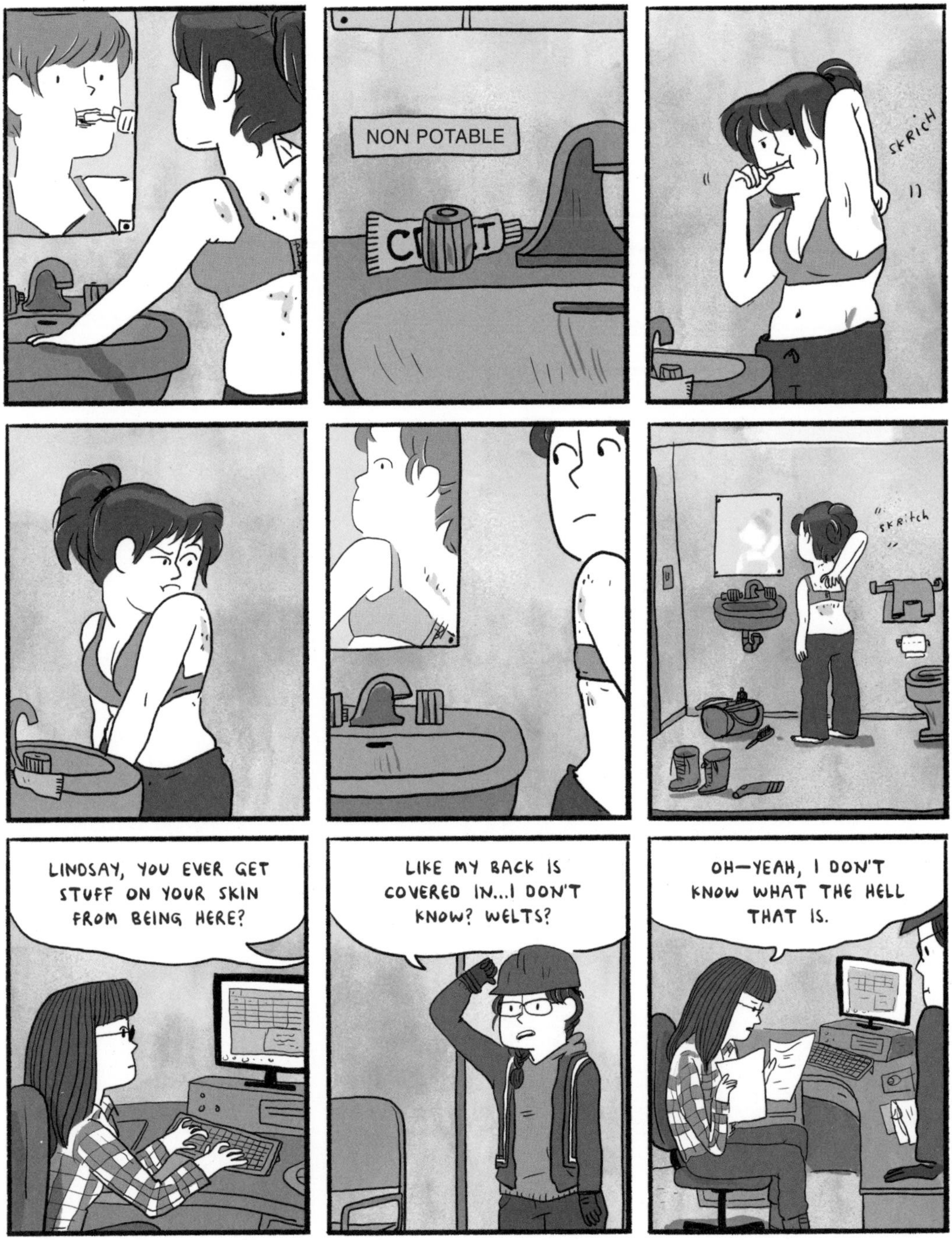
NON POTABLE
SKRICH
SKRITCH
LINDSAY, YOU EVER GET STUFF ON YOUR SKIN FROM BEING HERE?
LIKE MY BACK IS COVERED IN...I DON'T KNOW? WELTS?
OH—YEAH, I DON'T KNOW WHAT THE HELL THAT IS.

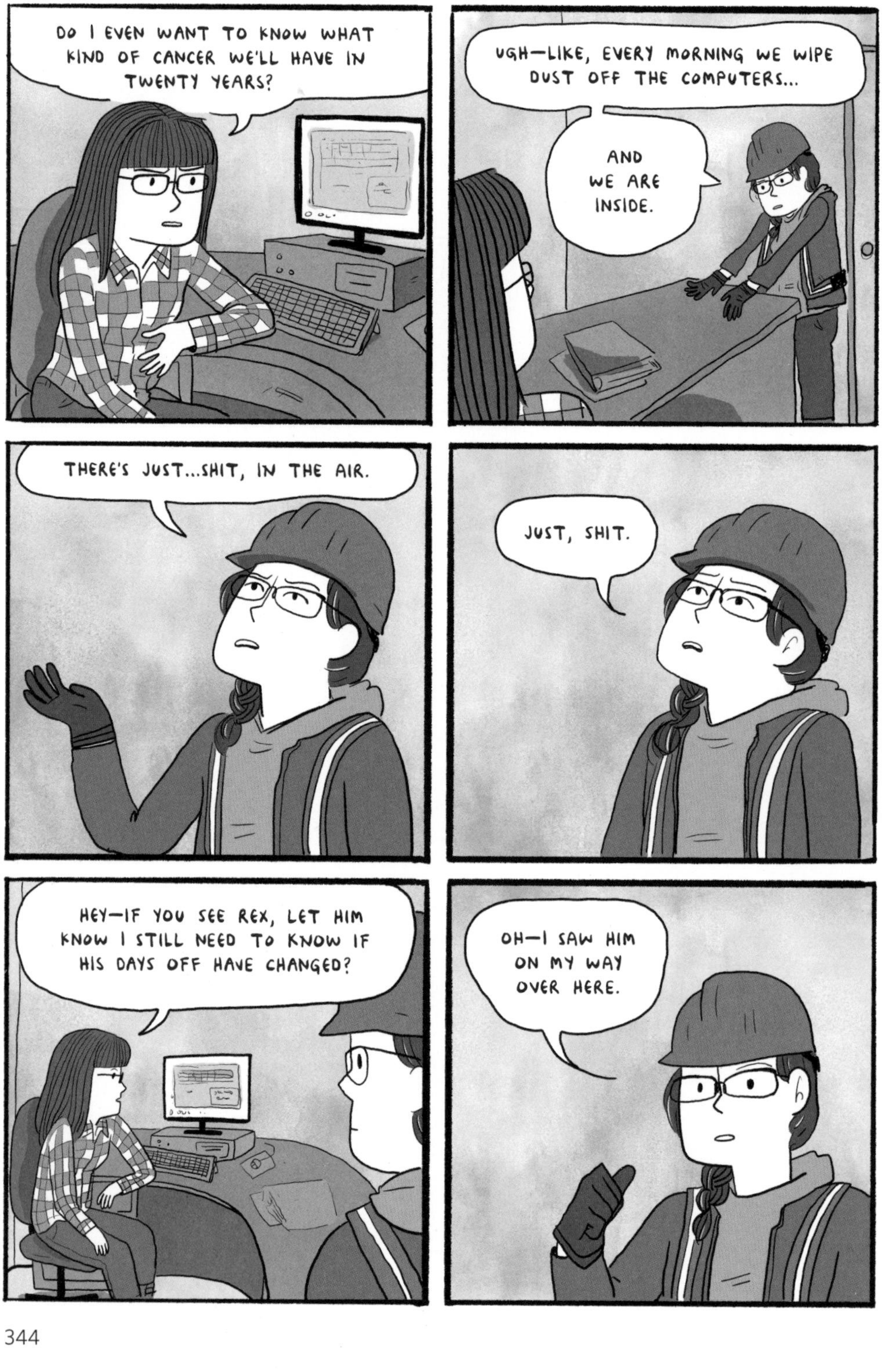
DO I EVEN WANT TO KNOW WHAT KIND OF CANCER WE'LL HAVE IN TWENTY YEARS?
UGH—LIKE, EVERY MORNING WE WIPE DUST OFF THE COMPUTERS...
AND WE ARE INSIDE.
THERE'S JUST...SHIT, IN THE AIR.
JUST, SHIT.
HEY—IF YOU SEE REX, LET HIM KNOW I STILL NEED TO KNOW IF HIS DAYS OFF HAVE CHANGED?
OH—I SAW HIM ON MY WAY OVER HERE.

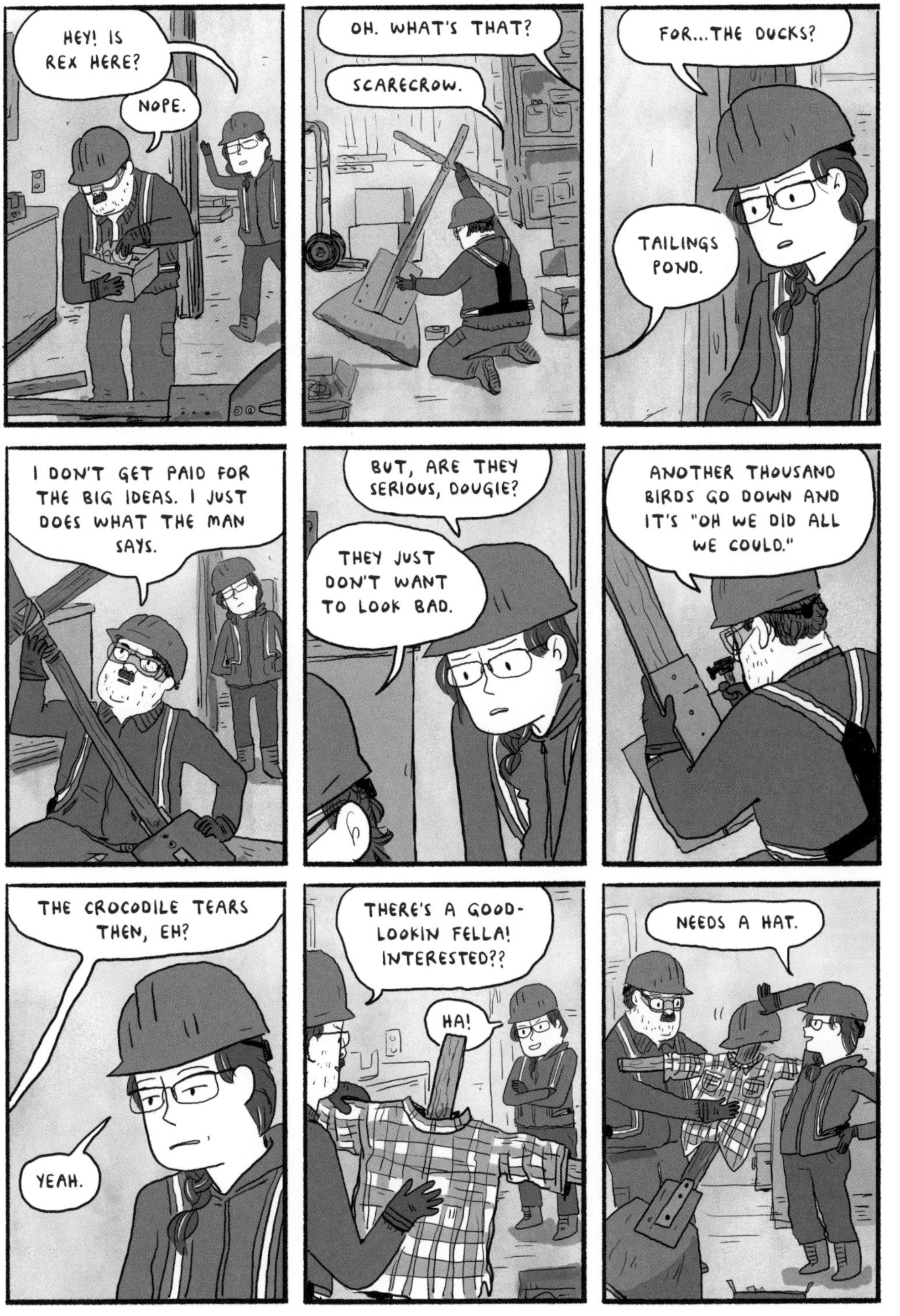
HEY! IS REX HERE?
NOPE.
OH. WHAT'S THAT?
SCARECROW.
FOR...THE DUCKS?
TAILINGS POND.
I DON'T GET PAID FOR THE BIG IDEAS. I JUST DOES WHAT THE MAN SAYS.
BUT, ARE THEY SERIOUS, DOUGIE?
THEY JUST DON'T WANT TO LOOK BAD.
ANOTHER THOUSAND BIRDS GO DOWN AND IT'S "OH WE DID ALL WE COULD."
THE CROCODILE TEARS THEN, EH?
YEAH.
THERE'S A GOOD-LOOKIN FELLA! INTERESTED??
HA!
NEEDS A HAT.

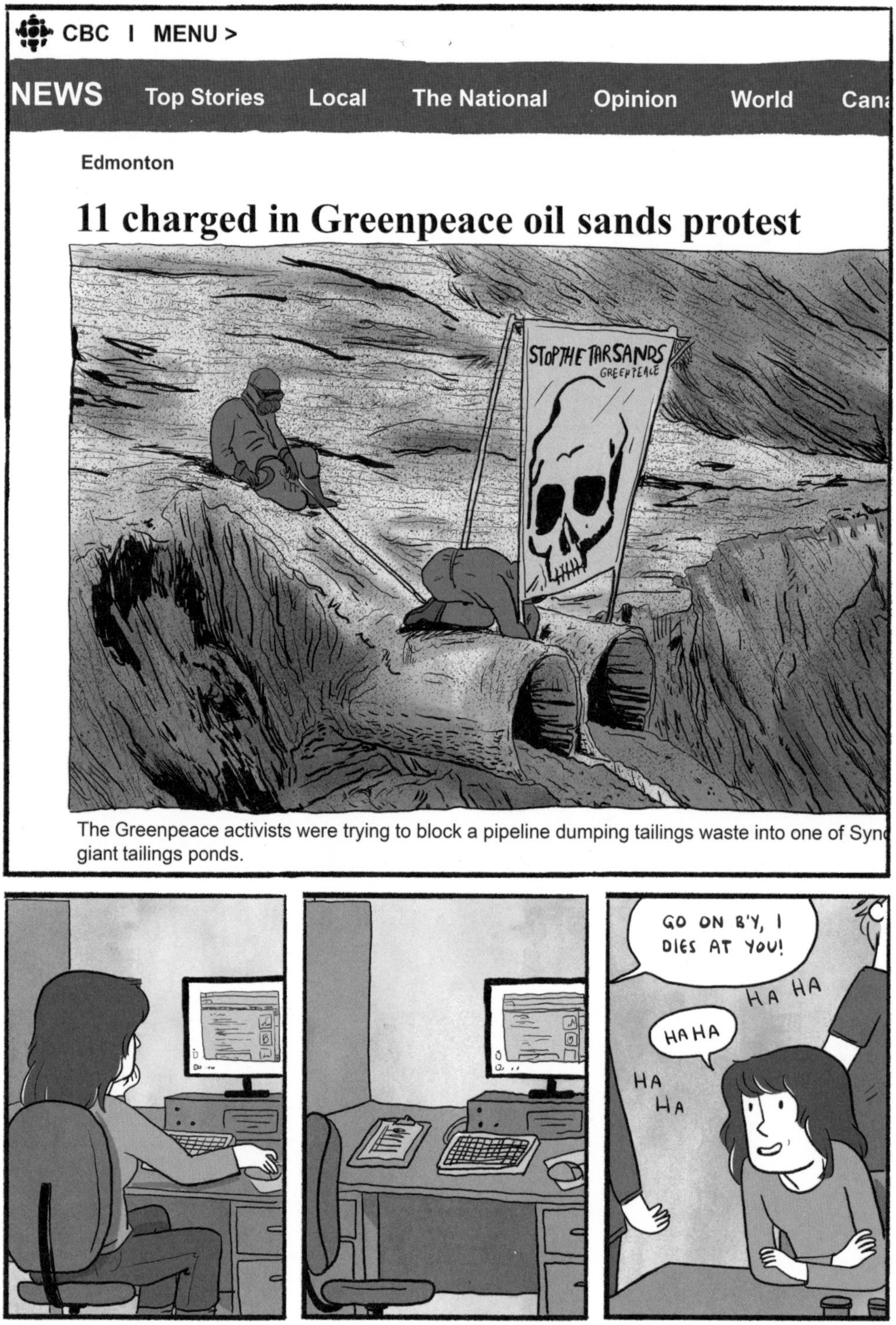
CBC I MENU >
NEWS Top Stories Local The National Opinion World Can
Edmonton
11 charged in Greenpeace oil sands protest
STOP THE TAR SANDS
GREENPEACE
The Greenpeace activists were trying to block a pipeline dumping tailings waste into one of Syn
giant tailings ponds.
GO ON B'Y, I DIES AT YOU!
HA HA
HAHA
HA HA

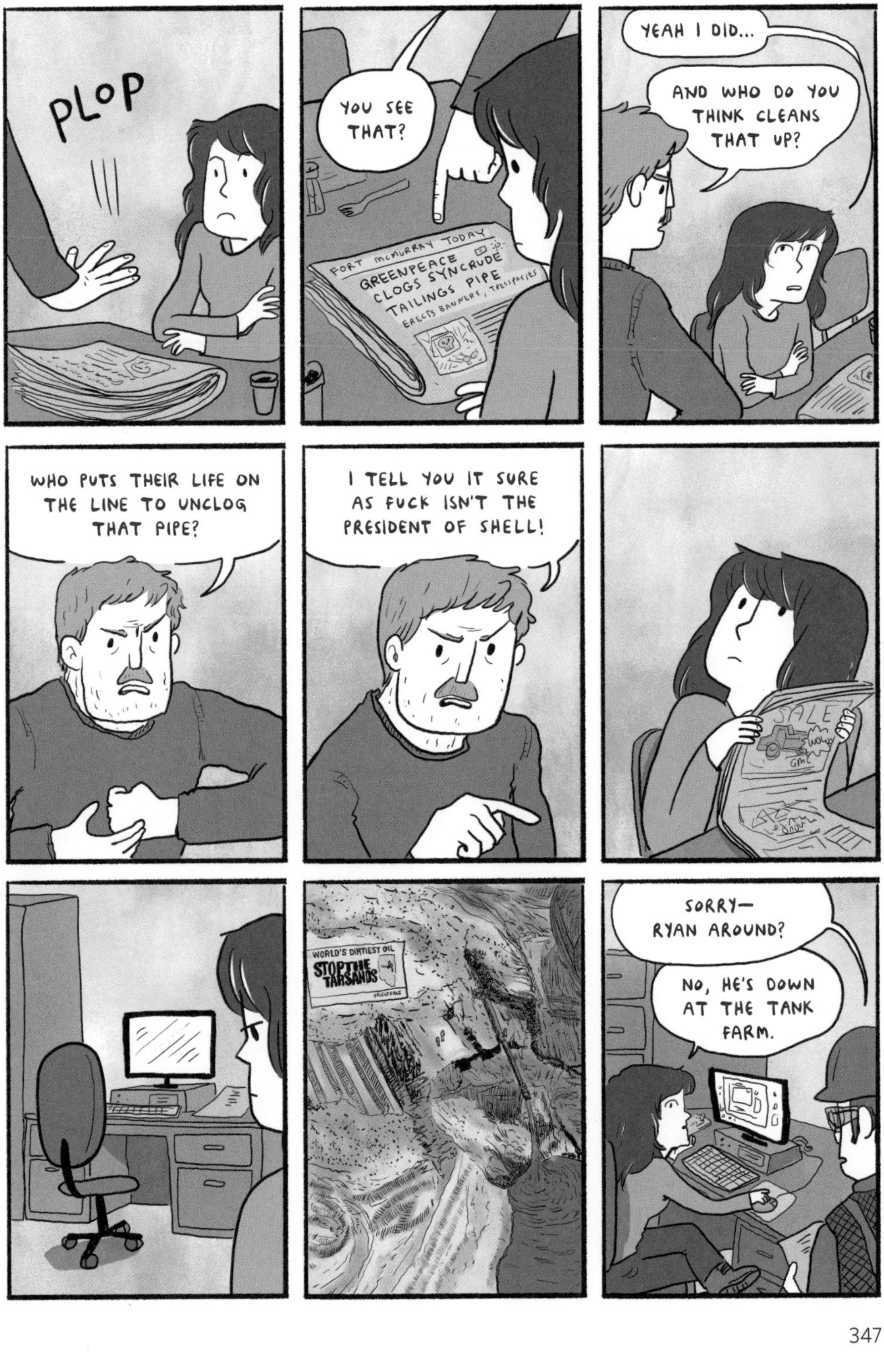
PLOP
YOU SEE THAT?
FORT McMURRAY TODAY
GREENPEACE CLOGS SYNCRUDE TAILINGS PIPE
ERECTS BANNERS, TRESPASSES
YEAH I DID...
AND WHO DO YOU THINK CLEANS THAT UP?
WHO PUTS THEIR LIFE ON THE LINE TO UNCLOG THAT PIPE?
I TELL YOU IT SURE AS FUCK ISN'T THE PRESIDENT OF SHELL!
SALE
WORLD'S DIRTIEST OIL
STOP THE TARSANDS
SORRY— RYAN AROUND?
NO, HE'S DOWN AT THE TANK FARM.

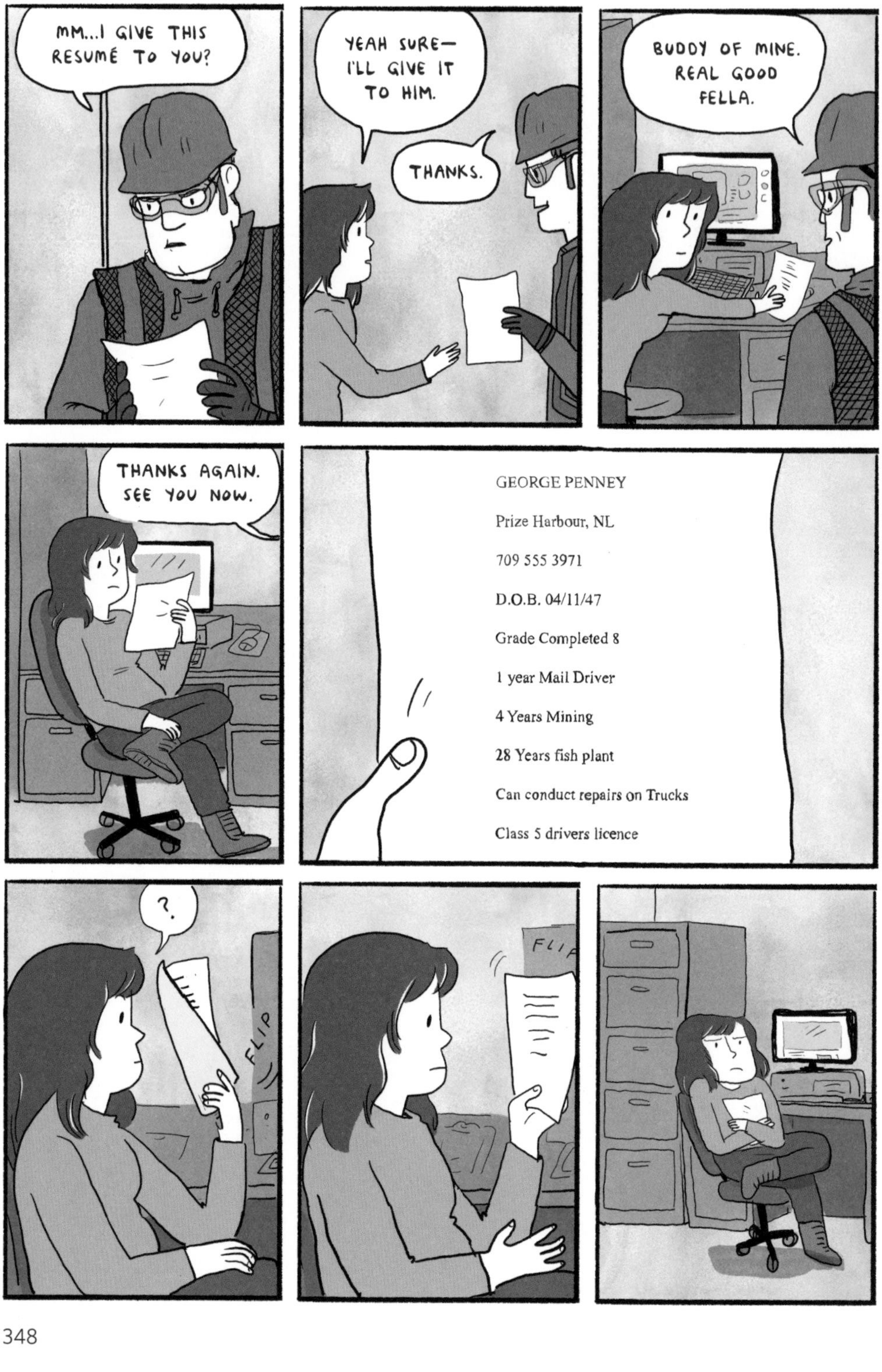
MM...I GIVE THIS RESUMÉ TO YOU?
YEAH SURE— I'LL GIVE IT TO HIM.
THANKS.
BUDDY OF MINE. REAL GOOD FELLA.
THANKS AGAIN. SEE YOU NOW.
GEORGE PENNEY
Prize Harbour, NL
709 555 3971
D.O.B. 04/11/47
Grade Completed 8
1 year Mail Driver
4 Years Mining
28 Years fish plant
Can conduct repairs on Trucks
Class 5 drivers licence
?
FLIP
FLIP

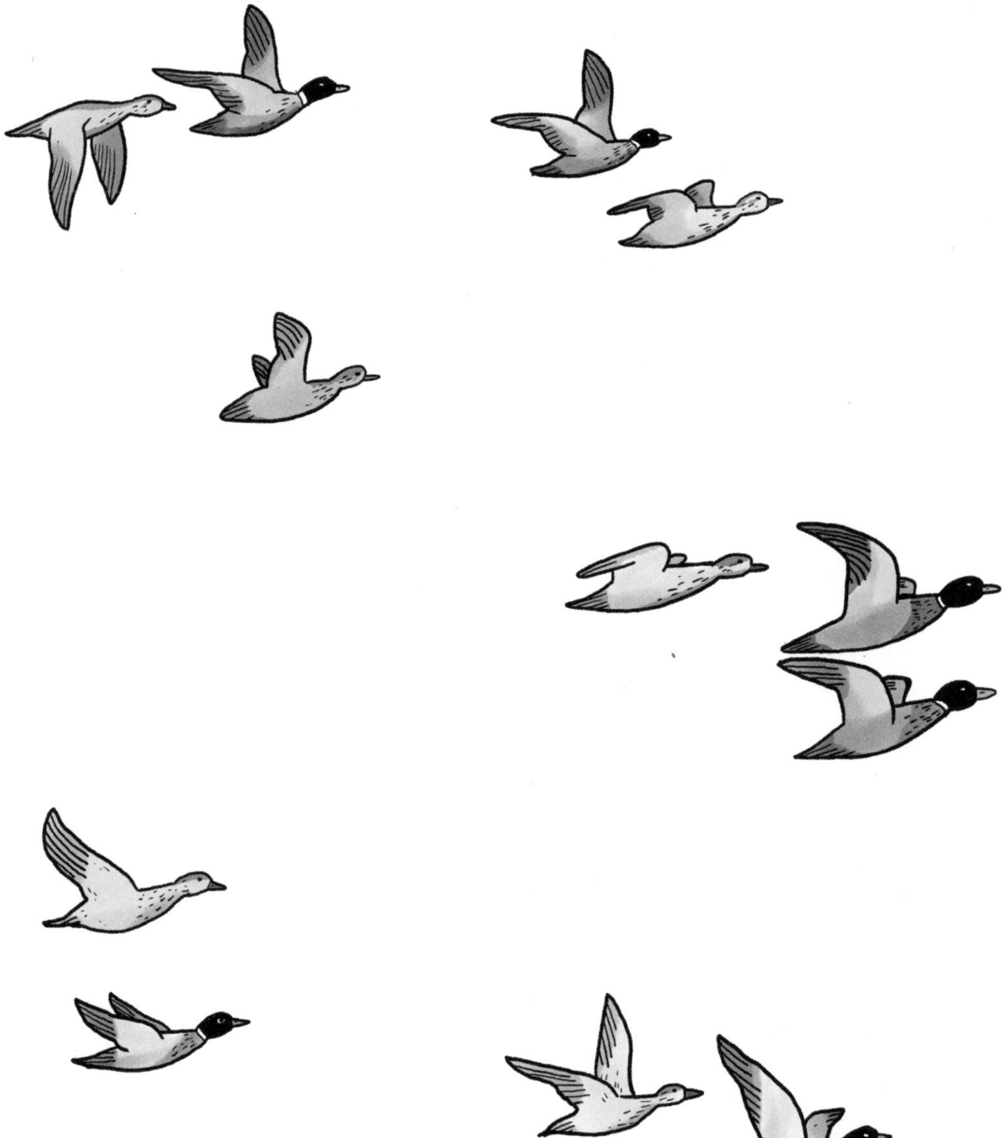

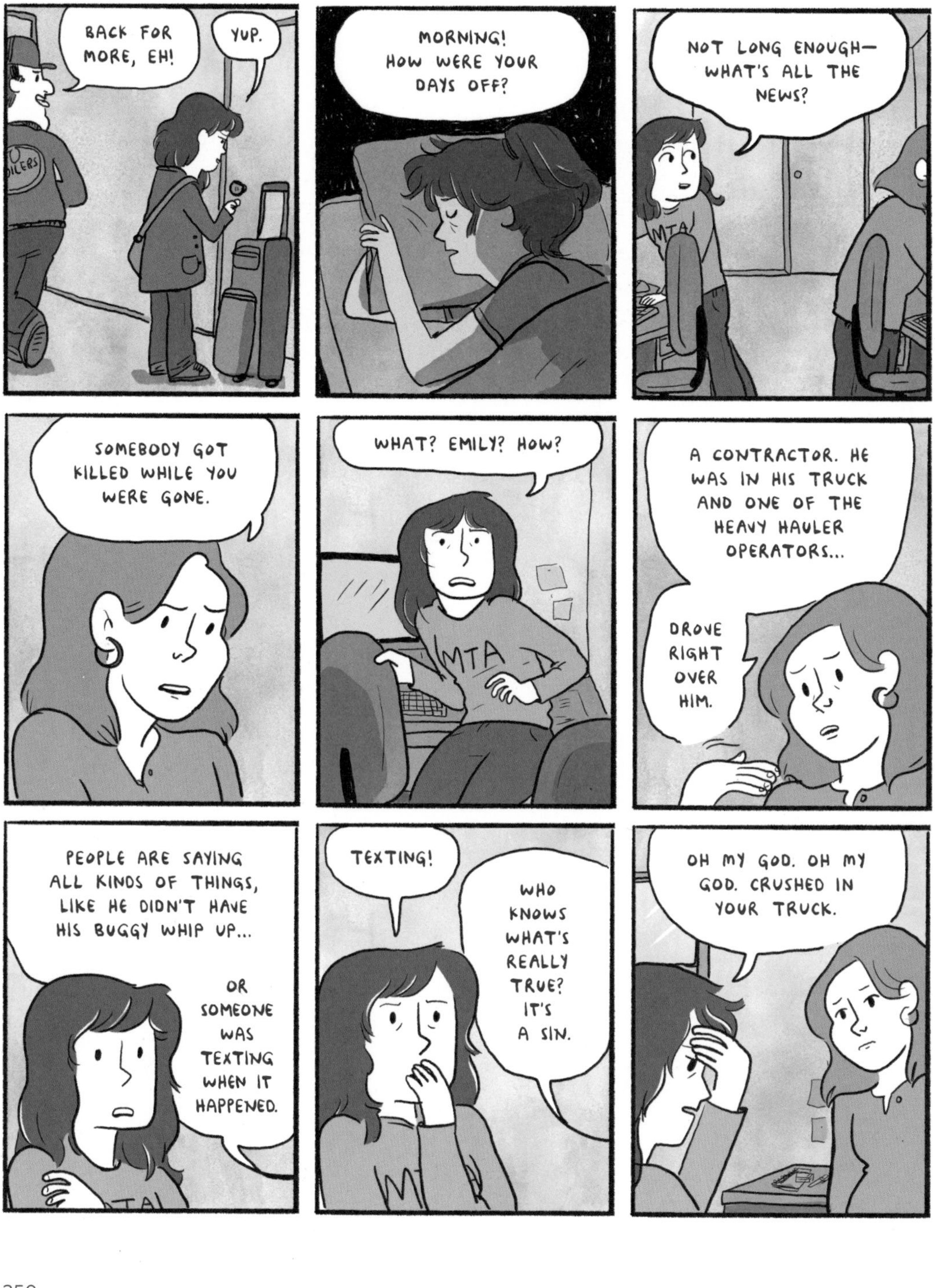
BACK FOR MORE, EH!
YUP.
MORNING! HOW WERE YOUR DAYS OFF?
NOT LONG ENOUGH— WHAT'S ALL THE NEWS?
SOMEBODY GOT KILLED WHILE YOU WERE GONE.
WHAT? EMILY? HOW?
A CONTRACTOR. HE WAS IN HIS TRUCK AND ONE OF THE HEAVY HAULER OPERATORS...
DROVE RIGHT OVER HIM.
PEOPLE ARE SAYING ALL KINDS OF THINGS, LIKE HE DIDN'T HAVE HIS BUGGY WHIP UP...
OR SOMEONE WAS TEXTING WHEN IT HAPPENED.
TEXTING!
WHO KNOWS WHAT'S REALLY TRUE? IT'S A SIN.
OH MY GOD. OH MY GOD. CRUSHED IN YOUR TRUCK.

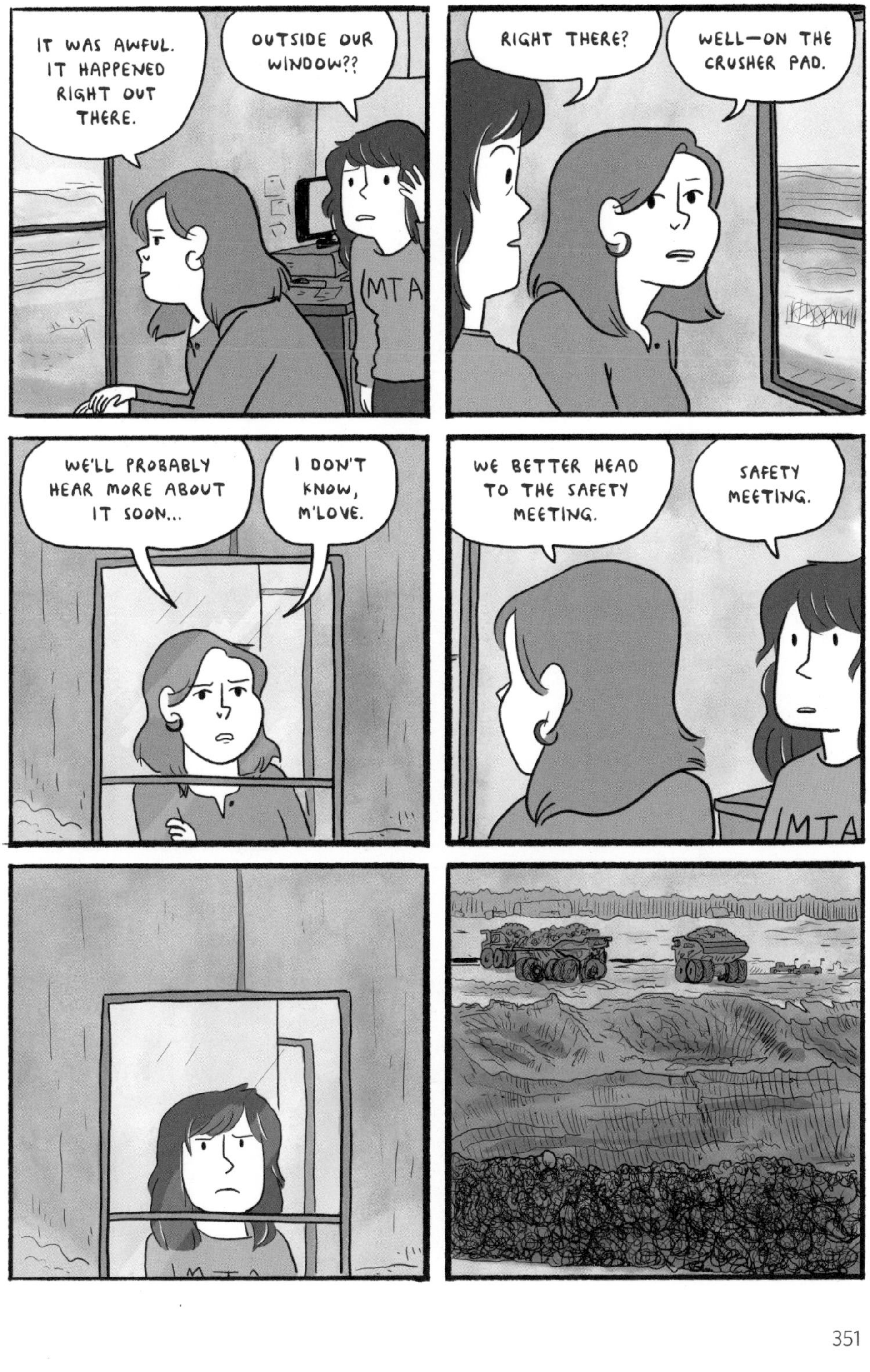
IT WAS AWFUL. IT HAPPENED RIGHT OUT THERE.
OUTSIDE OUR WINDOW??
MTA
RIGHT THERE?
WELL—ON THE CRUSHER PAD.
WE'LL PROBABLY HEAR MORE ABOUT IT SOON...
I DON'T KNOW, M'LOVE.
WE BETTER HEAD TO THE SAFETY MEETING.
SAFETY MEETING.
MTA

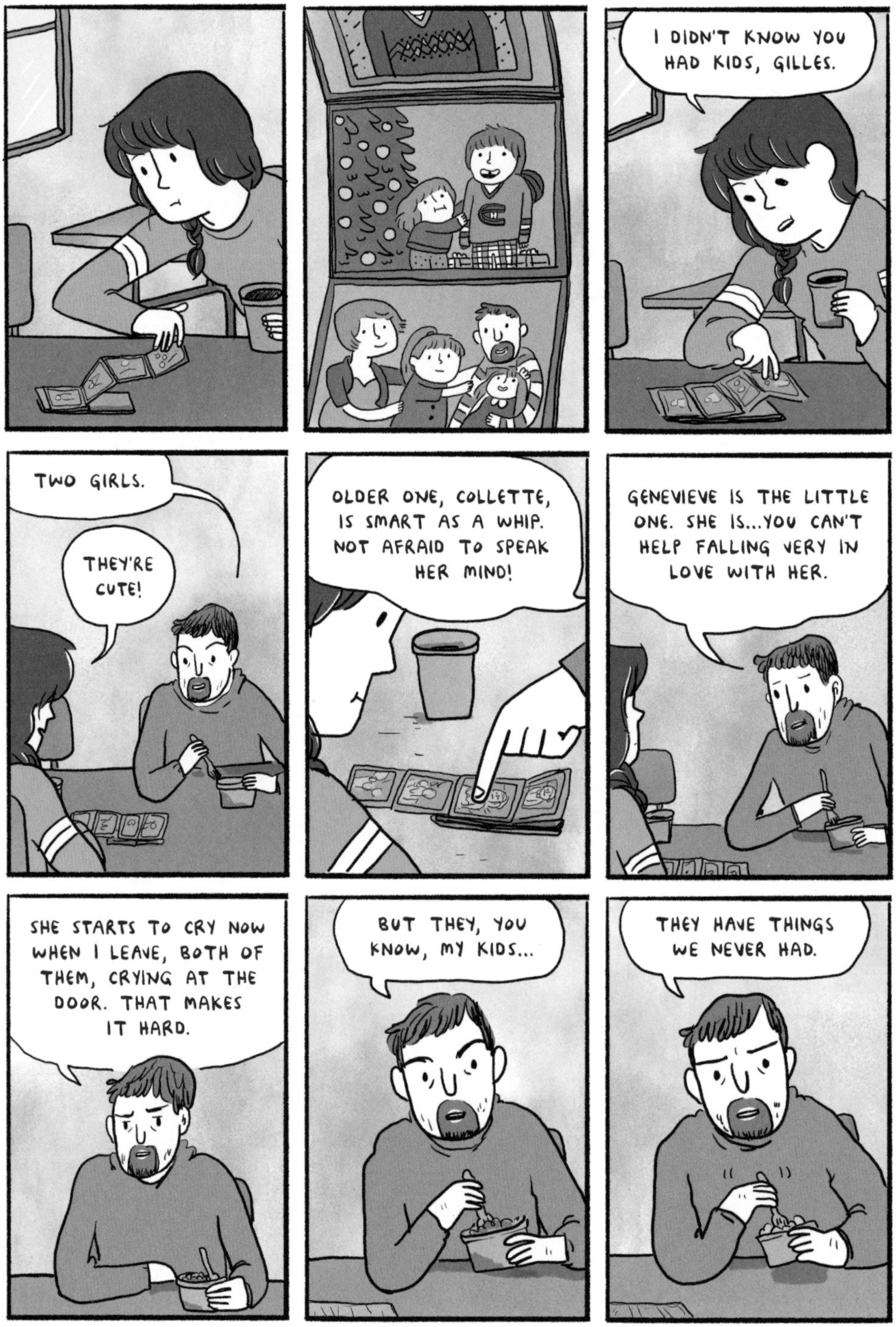
I DIDN'T KNOW YOU HAD KIDS, GILLES.
TWO GIRLS.
THEY'RE CUTE!
OLDER ONE, COLLETTE, IS SMART AS A WHIP. NOT AFRAID TO SPEAK HER MIND!
GENEVIEVE IS THE LITTLE ONE. SHE IS...YOU CAN'T HELP FALLING VERY IN LOVE WITH HER.
SHE STARTS TO CRY NOW WHEN I LEAVE, BOTH OF THEM, CRYING AT THE DOOR. THAT MAKES IT HARD.
BUT THEY, YOU KNOW, MY KIDS...
THEY HAVE THINGS WE NEVER HAD.

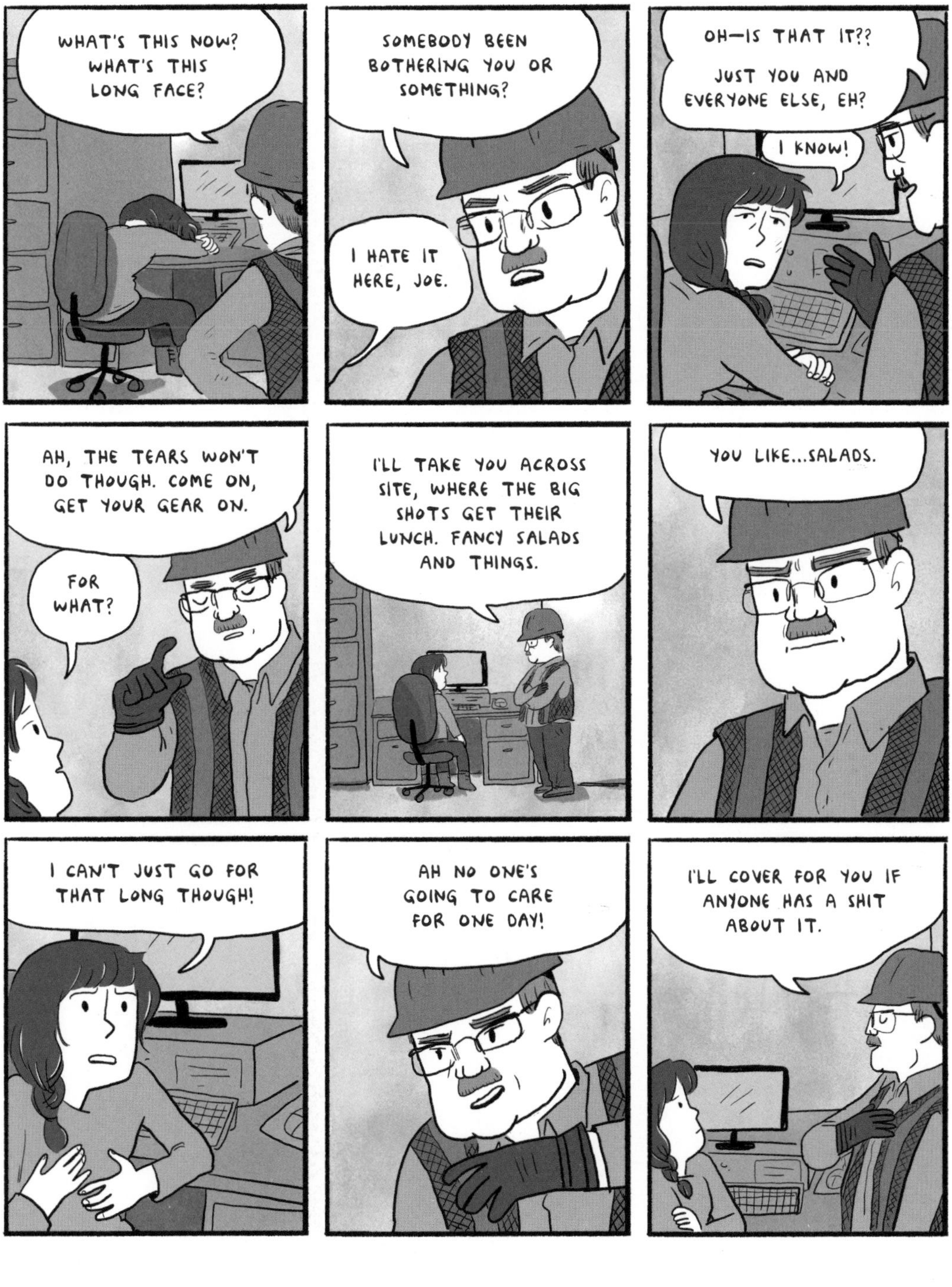
WHAT'S THIS NOW? WHAT'S THIS LONG FACE?
SOMEBODY BEEN BOTHERING YOU OR SOMETHING?
I HATE IT HERE, JOE.
OH—IS THAT IT??
JUST YOU AND EVERYONE ELSE, EH?
I KNOW!
AH, THE TEARS WON'T DO THOUGH. COME ON, GET YOUR GEAR ON.
FOR WHAT?
I'LL TAKE YOU ACROSS SITE, WHERE THE BIG SHOTS GET THEIR LUNCH. FANCY SALADS AND THINGS.
YOU LIKE...SALADS.
I CAN'T JUST GO FOR THAT LONG THOUGH!
AH NO ONE'S GOING TO CARE FOR ONE DAY!
I'LL COVER FOR YOU IF ANYONE HAS A SHIT ABOUT IT.

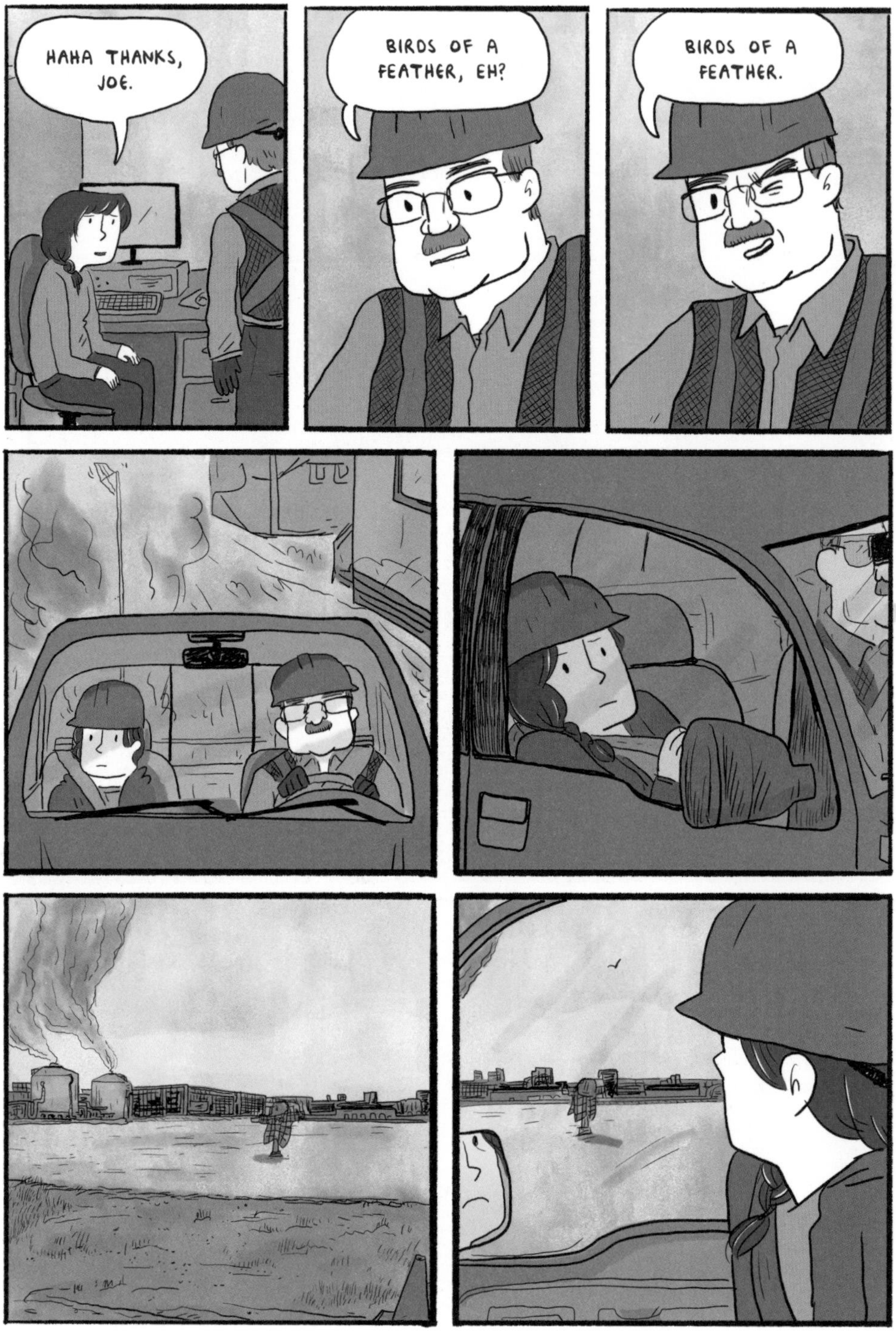
HAHA THANKS, JOE.
BIRDS OF A FEATHER, EH?
BIRDS OF A FEATHER.

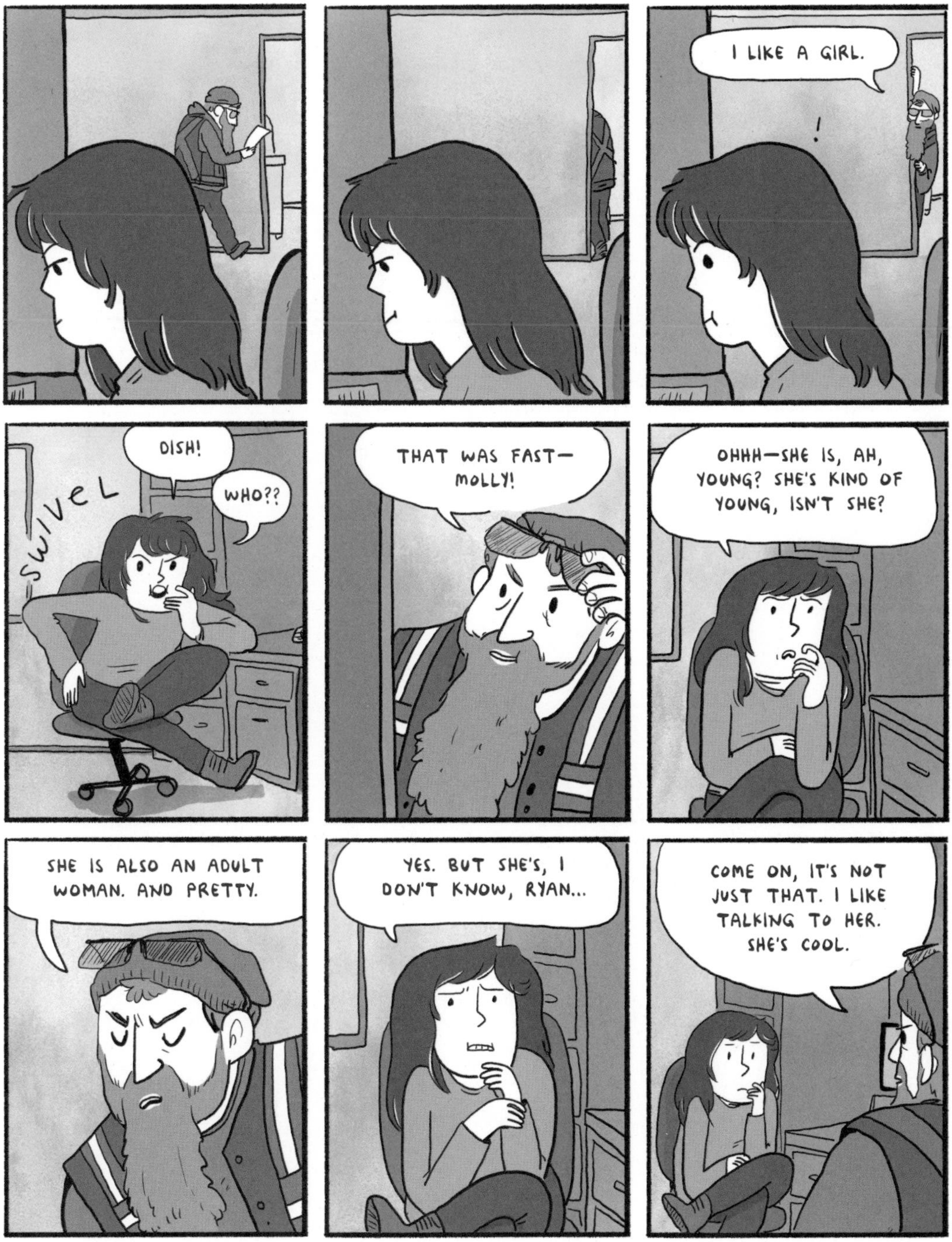
I LIKE A GIRL.
!
SWIVEL
DISH!
WHO??
THAT WAS FAST— MOLLY!
OHHH—SHE IS, AH, YOUNG? SHE'S KIND OF YOUNG, ISN'T SHE?
SHE IS ALSO AN ADULT WOMAN. AND PRETTY.
YES. BUT SHE'S, I DON'T KNOW, RYAN...
COME ON, IT'S NOT JUST THAT. I LIKE TALKING TO HER. SHE'S COOL.

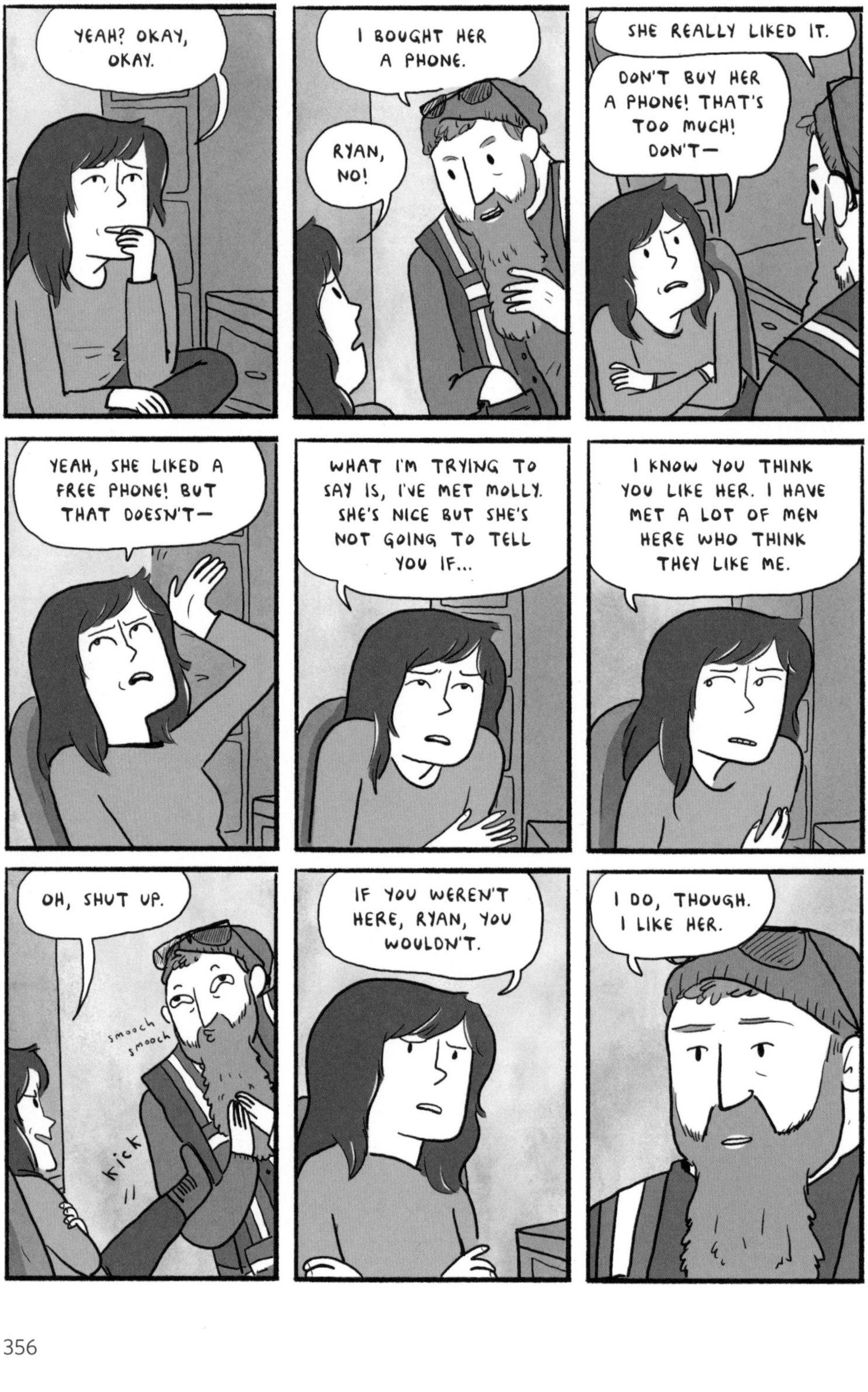
YEAH? OKAY, OKAY.
I BOUGHT HER A PHONE.
RYAN, NO!
SHE REALLY LIKED IT.
DON'T BUY HER A PHONE! THAT'S TOO MUCH! DON'T—
YEAH, SHE LIKED A FREE PHONE! BUT THAT DOESN'T—
WHAT I'M TRYING TO SAY IS, I'VE MET MOLLY. SHE'S NICE BUT SHE'S NOT GOING TO TELL YOU IF...
I KNOW YOU THINK YOU LIKE HER. I HAVE MET A LOT OF MEN HERE WHO THINK THEY LIKE ME.
OH, SHUT UP.
smooch smooch
kick
IF YOU WEREN'T HERE, RYAN, YOU WOULDN'T.
I DO, THOUGH. I LIKE HER.

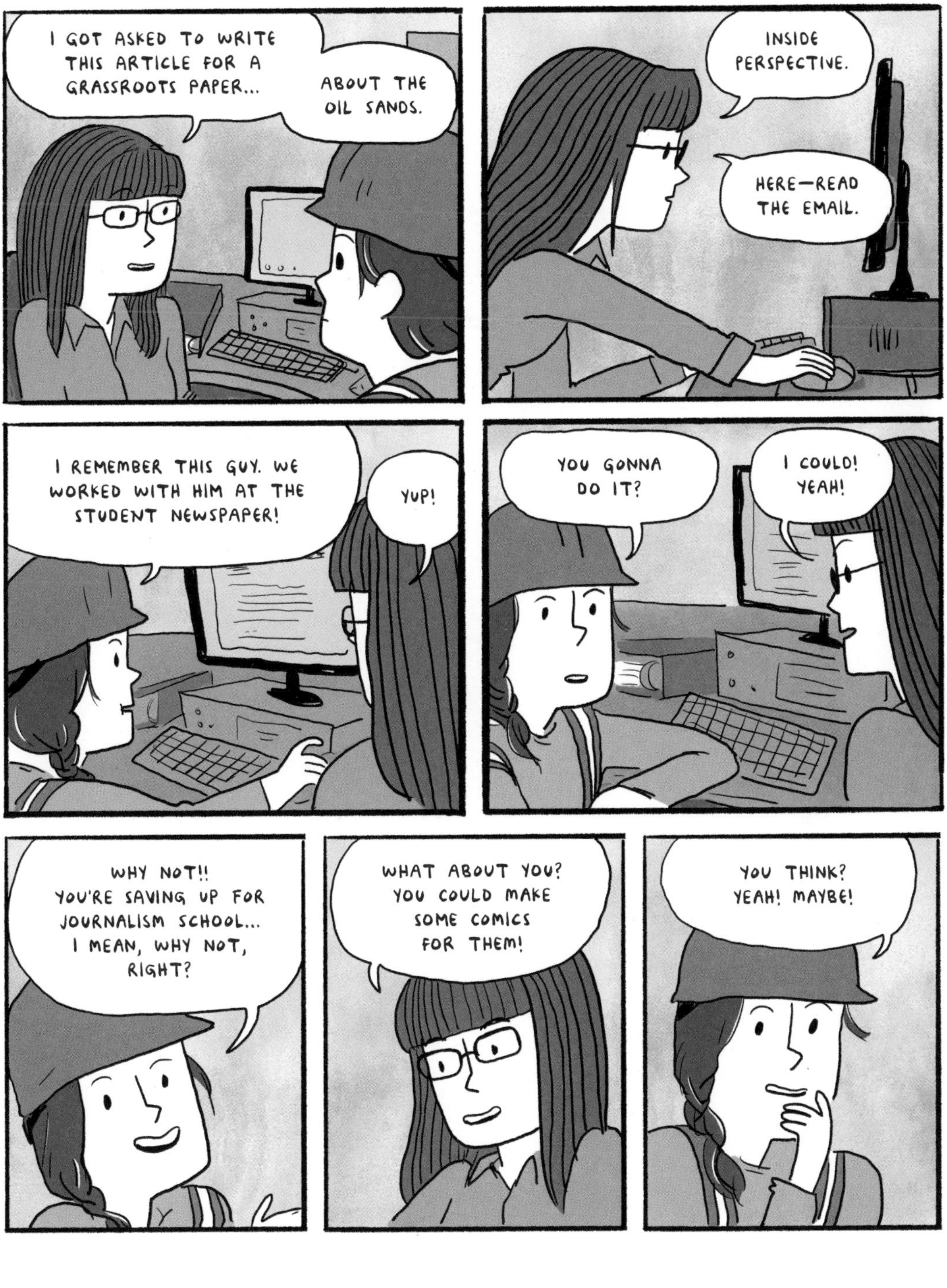
I GOT ASKED TO WRITE THIS ARTICLE FOR A GRASSROOTS PAPER...
ABOUT THE OIL SANDS.
INSIDE PERSPECTIVE.
HERE—READ THE EMAIL.
I REMEMBER THIS GUY. WE WORKED WITH HIM AT THE STUDENT NEWSPAPER!
YUP!
YOU GONNA DO IT?
I COULD! YEAH!
WHY NOT!! YOU'RE SAVING UP FOR JOURNALISM SCHOOL... I MEAN, WHY NOT, RIGHT?
WHAT ABOUT YOU? YOU COULD MAKE SOME COMICS FOR THEM!
YOU THINK? YEAH! MAYBE!

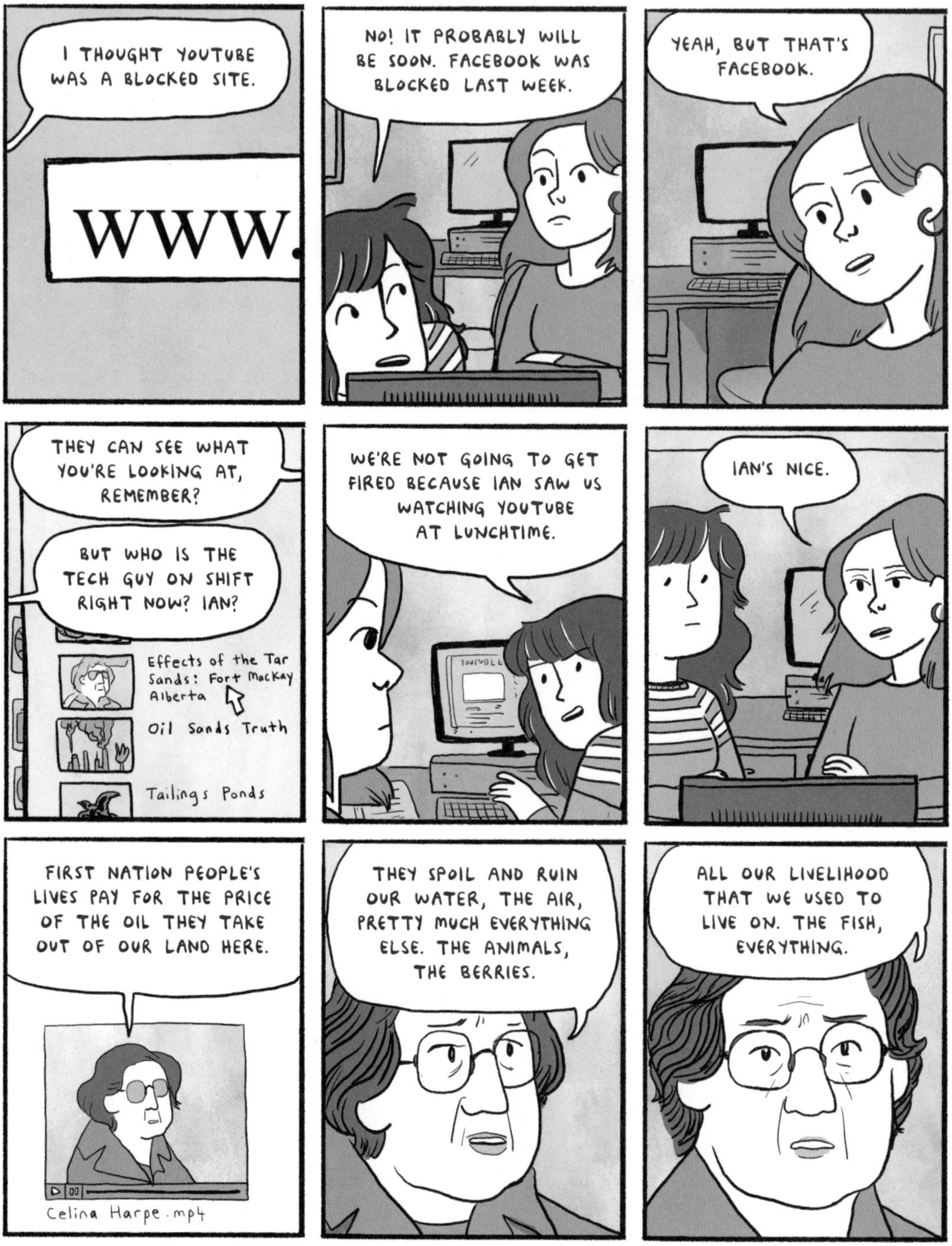
I THOUGHT YOUTUBE WAS A BLOCKED SITE.
WWW.
NO! IT PROBABLY WILL BE SOON. FACEBOOK WAS BLOCKED LAST WEEK.
YEAH, BUT THAT'S FACEBOOK.
THEY CAN SEE WHAT YOU'RE LOOKING AT, REMEMBER?
BUT WHO IS THE TECH GUY ON SHIFT RIGHT NOW? IAN?
Effects of the Tar Sands: Fort MacKay Alberta
Oil Sands Truth
Tailings Ponds
WE'RE NOT GOING TO GET FIRED BECAUSE IAN SAW US WATCHING YOUTUBE AT LUNCHTIME.
IAN'S NICE.
FIRST NATION PEOPLE'S LIVES PAY FOR THE PRICE OF THE OIL THEY TAKE OUT OF OUR LAND HERE.
Celina Harpe.mp4
THEY SPOIL AND RUIN OUR WATER, THE AIR, PRETTY MUCH EVERYTHING ELSE. THE ANIMALS, THE BERRIES.
ALL OUR LIVELIHOOD THAT WE USED TO LIVE ON. THE FISH, EVERYTHING.

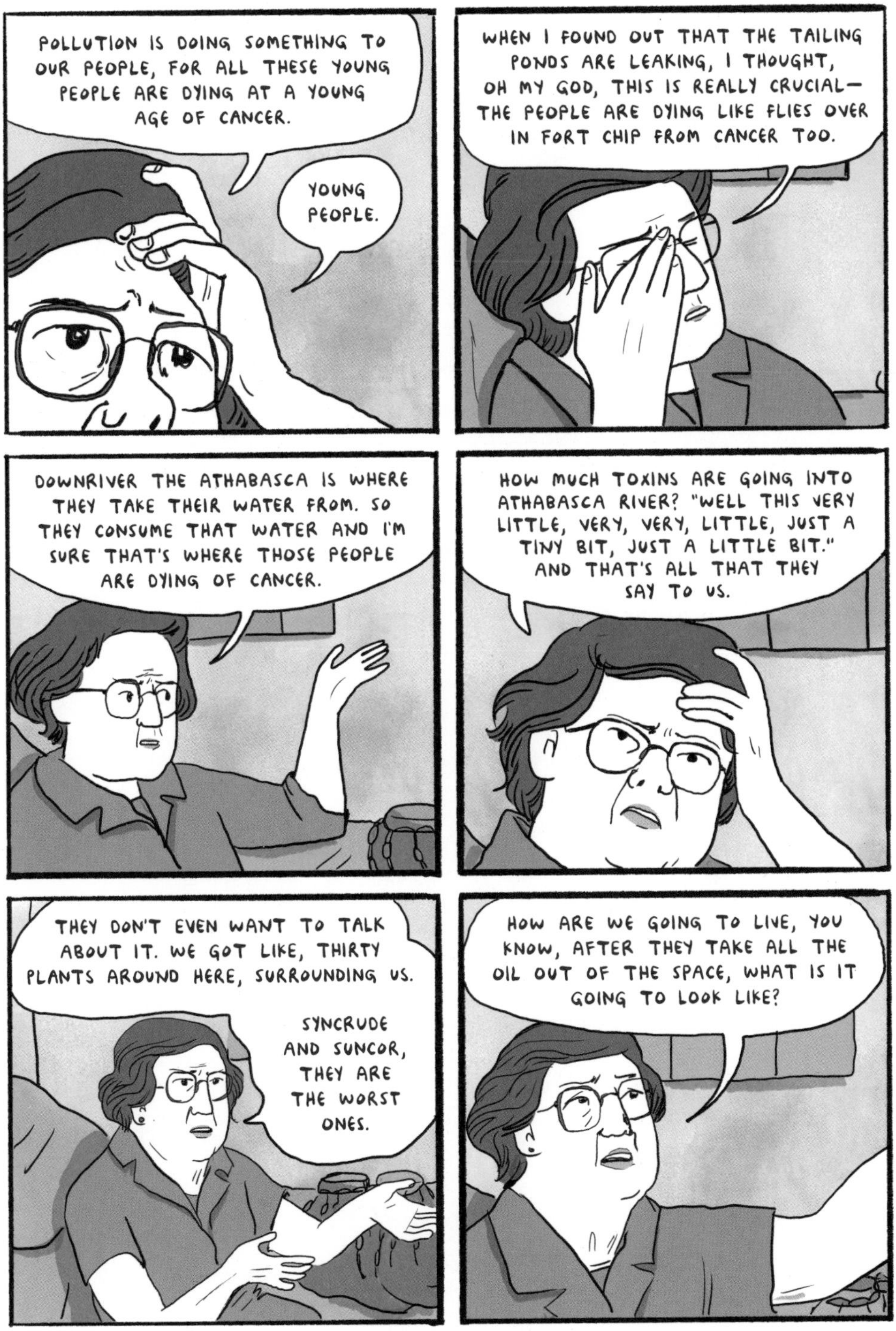
POLLUTION IS DOING SOMETHING TO OUR PEOPLE, FOR ALL THESE YOUNG PEOPLE ARE DYING AT A YOUNG AGE OF CANCER.
YOUNG PEOPLE.
WHEN I FOUND OUT THAT THE TAILING PONDS ARE LEAKING, I THOUGHT, OH MY GOD, THIS IS REALLY CRUCIAL— THE PEOPLE ARE DYING LIKE FLIES OVER IN FORT CHIP FROM CANCER TOO.
DOWNRIVER THE ATHABASCA IS WHERE THEY TAKE THEIR WATER FROM. SO THEY CONSUME THAT WATER AND I'M SURE THAT'S WHERE THOSE PEOPLE ARE DYING OF CANCER.
HOW MUCH TOXINS ARE GOING INTO ATHABASCA RIVER? "WELL THIS VERY LITTLE, VERY, VERY, LITTLE, JUST A TINY BIT, JUST A LITTLE BIT." AND THAT'S ALL THAT THEY SAY TO US.
THEY DON'T EVEN WANT TO TALK ABOUT IT. WE GOT LIKE, THIRTY PLANTS AROUND HERE, SURROUNDING US.
SYNCRUDE AND SUNCOR, THEY ARE THE WORST ONES.
HOW ARE WE GOING TO LIVE, YOU KNOW, AFTER THEY TAKE ALL THE OIL OUT OF THE SPACE, WHAT IS IT GOING TO LOOK LIKE?

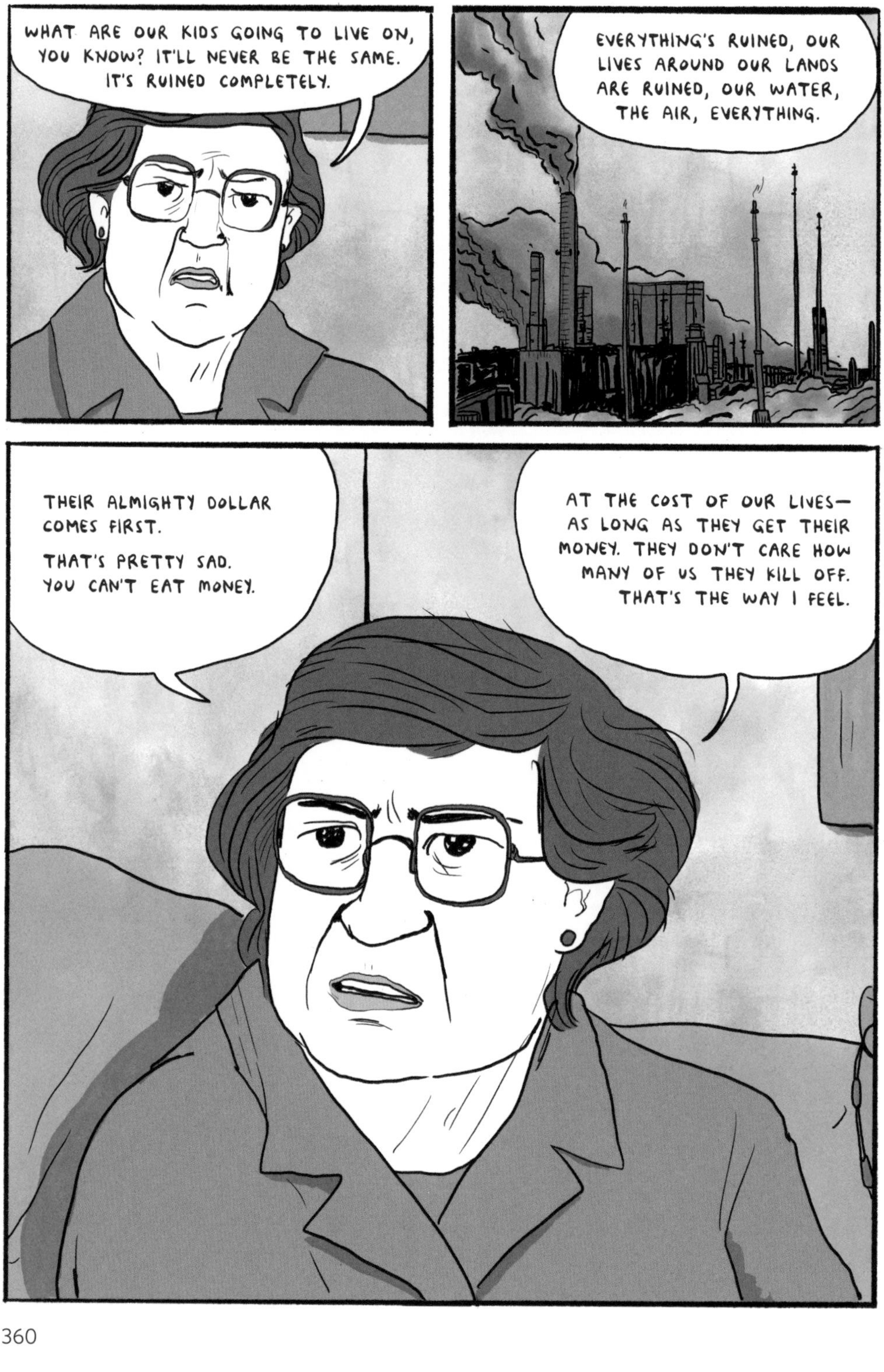

WHAT ARE OUR KIDS GOING TO LIVE ON, YOU KNOW? IT'LL NEVER BE THE SAME. IT'S RUINED COMPLETELY.
EVERYTHING'S RUINED, OUR LIVES AROUND OUR LANDS ARE RUINED, OUR WATER, THE AIR, EVERYTHING.
THEIR ALMIGHTY DOLLAR COMES FIRST.
THAT'S PRETTY SAD. YOU CAN'T EAT MONEY.
AT THE COST OF OUR LIVES— AS LONG AS THEY GET THEIR MONEY. THEY DON'T CARE HOW MANY OF US THEY KILL OFF. THAT'S THE WAY I FEEL.

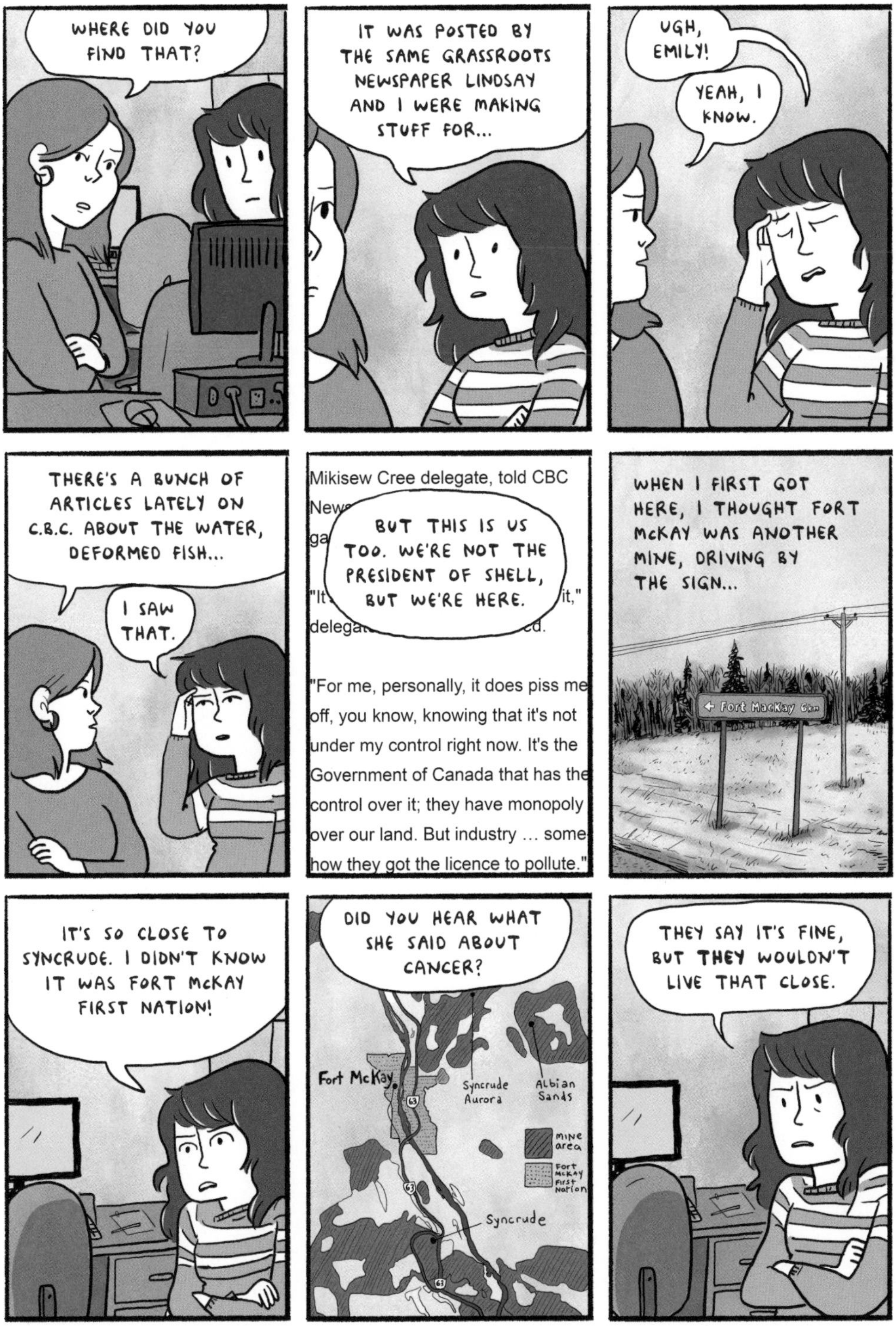
WHERE DID YOU FIND THAT?
IT WAS POSTED BY THE SAME GRASSROOTS NEWSPAPER LINDSAY AND I WERE MAKING STUFF FOR...
UGH, EMILY!
YEAH, I KNOW.
THERE'S A BUNCH OF ARTICLES LATELY ON C.B.C. ABOUT THE WATER, DEFORMED FISH...
I SAW THAT.
Mikisew Cree delegate, told CBC
News
ga
"It
it,"
delega
cd.
BUT THIS IS US TOO. WE'RE NOT THE PRESIDENT OF SHELL, BUT WE'RE HERE.
"For me, personally, it does piss me off, you know, knowing that it's not under my control right now. It's the Government of Canada that has the control over it; they have monopoly over our land. But industry … somehow they got the licence to pollute."
WHEN I FIRST GOT HERE, I THOUGHT FORT McKAY WAS ANOTHER MINE, DRIVING BY THE SIGN...
Fort MacKay 6km
IT'S SO CLOSE TO SYNCRUDE. I DIDN'T KNOW IT WAS FORT McKAY FIRST NATION!
DID YOU HEAR WHAT SHE SAID ABOUT CANCER?
Fort McKay
Syncrude Aurora
Albian Sands
mine area
Fort McKay First Nation
Syncrude
63
THEY SAY IT'S FINE, BUT THEY WOULDN'T LIVE THAT CLOSE.

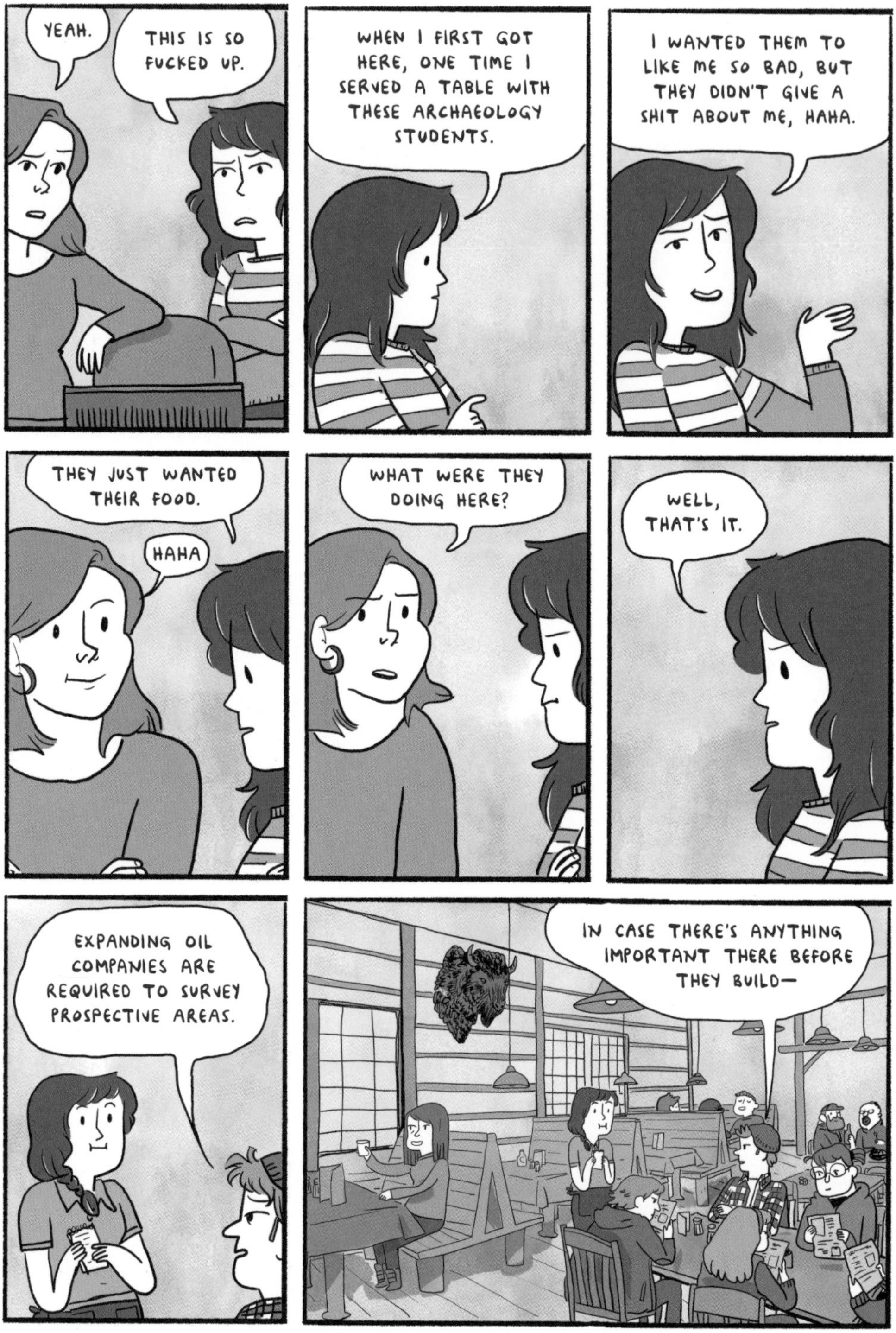
YEAH.
THIS IS SO FUCKED UP.
WHEN I FIRST GOT HERE, ONE TIME I SERVED A TABLE WITH THESE ARCHAEOLOGY STUDENTS.
I WANTED THEM TO LIKE ME SO BAD, BUT THEY DIDN'T GIVE A SHIT ABOUT ME, HAHA.
THEY JUST WANTED THEIR FOOD.
HAHA
WHAT WERE THEY DOING HERE?
WELL, THAT'S IT.
EXPANDING OIL COMPANIES ARE REQUIRED TO SURVEY PROSPECTIVE AREAS.
IN CASE THERE'S ANYTHING IMPORTANT THERE BEFORE THEY BUILD—

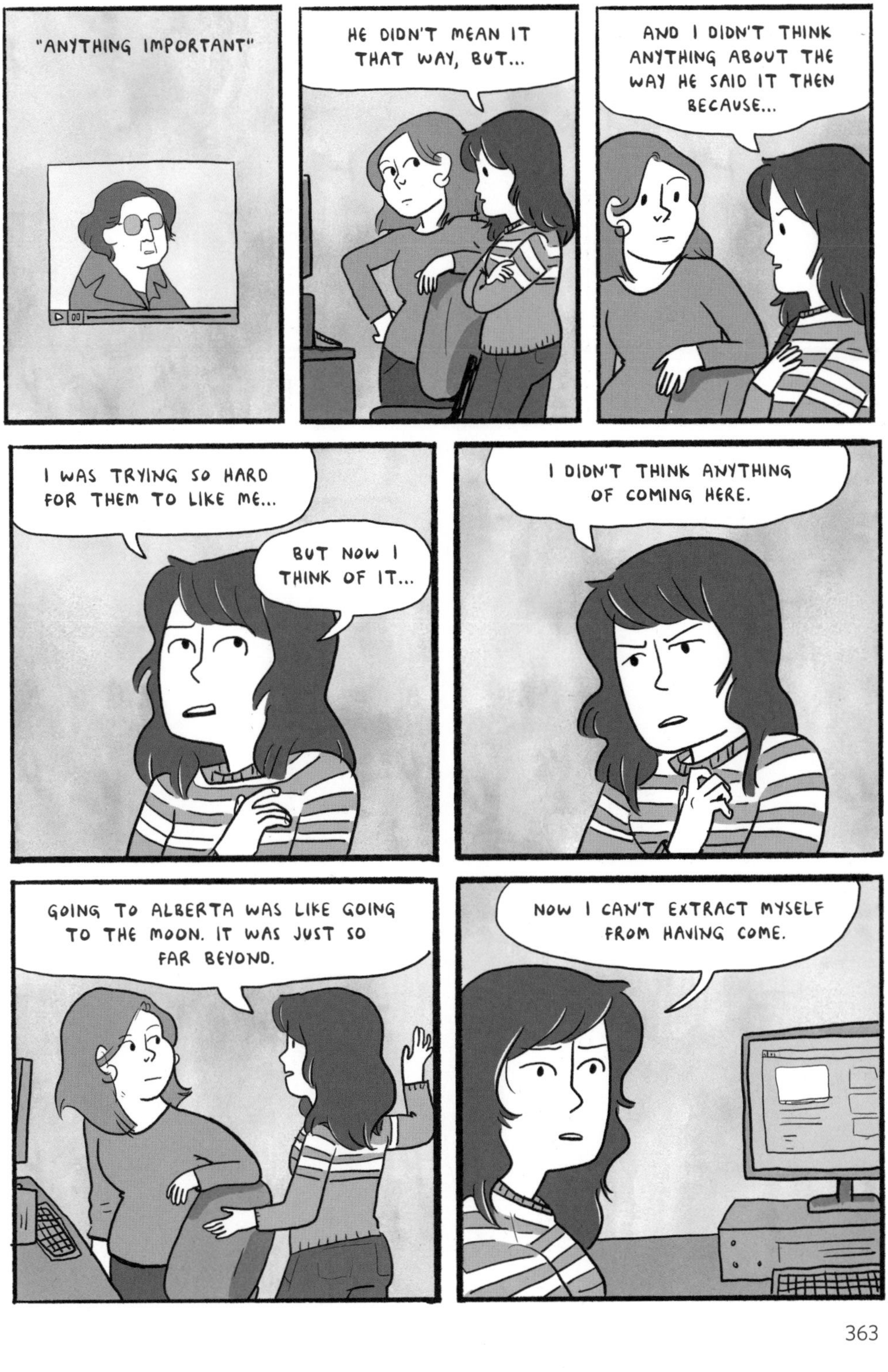
"ANYTHING IMPORTANT"
HE DIDN'T MEAN IT THAT WAY, BUT...
AND I DIDN'T THINK ANYTHING ABOUT THE WAY HE SAID IT THEN BECAUSE...
I WAS TRYING SO HARD FOR THEM TO LIKE ME...
BUT NOW I THINK OF IT...
I DIDN'T THINK ANYTHING OF COMING HERE.
GOING TO ALBERTA WAS LIKE GOING TO THE MOON. IT WAS JUST SO FAR BEYOND.
NOW I CAN'T EXTRACT MYSELF FROM HAVING COME.

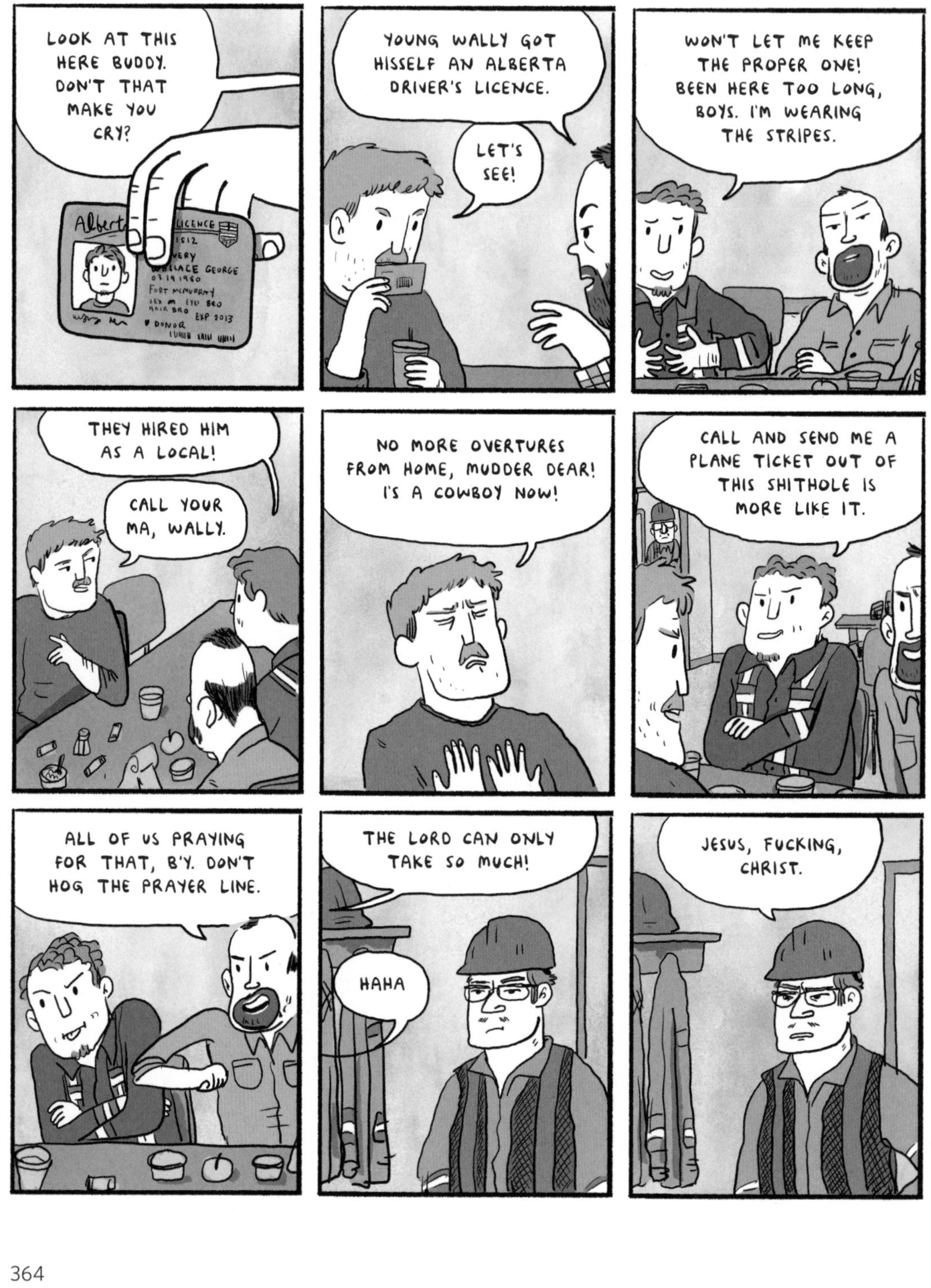
LOOK AT THIS HERE BUDDY. DON'T THAT MAKE YOU CRY?
YOUNG WALLY GOT HISSELF AN ALBERTA DRIVER'S LICENCE.
LET'S SEE!
WON'T LET ME KEEP THE PROPER ONE! BEEN HERE TOO LONG, BOYS. I'M WEARING THE STRIPES.
THEY HIRED HIM AS A LOCAL!
CALL YOUR MA, WALLY.
NO MORE OVERTURES FROM HOME, MUDDER DEAR! I'S A COWBOY NOW!
CALL AND SEND ME A PLANE TICKET OUT OF THIS SHITHOLE IS MORE LIKE IT.
ALL OF US PRAYING FOR THAT, B'Y. DON'T HOG THE PRAYER LINE.
THE LORD CAN ONLY TAKE SO MUCH!
HAHA
JESUS, FUCKING, CHRIST.

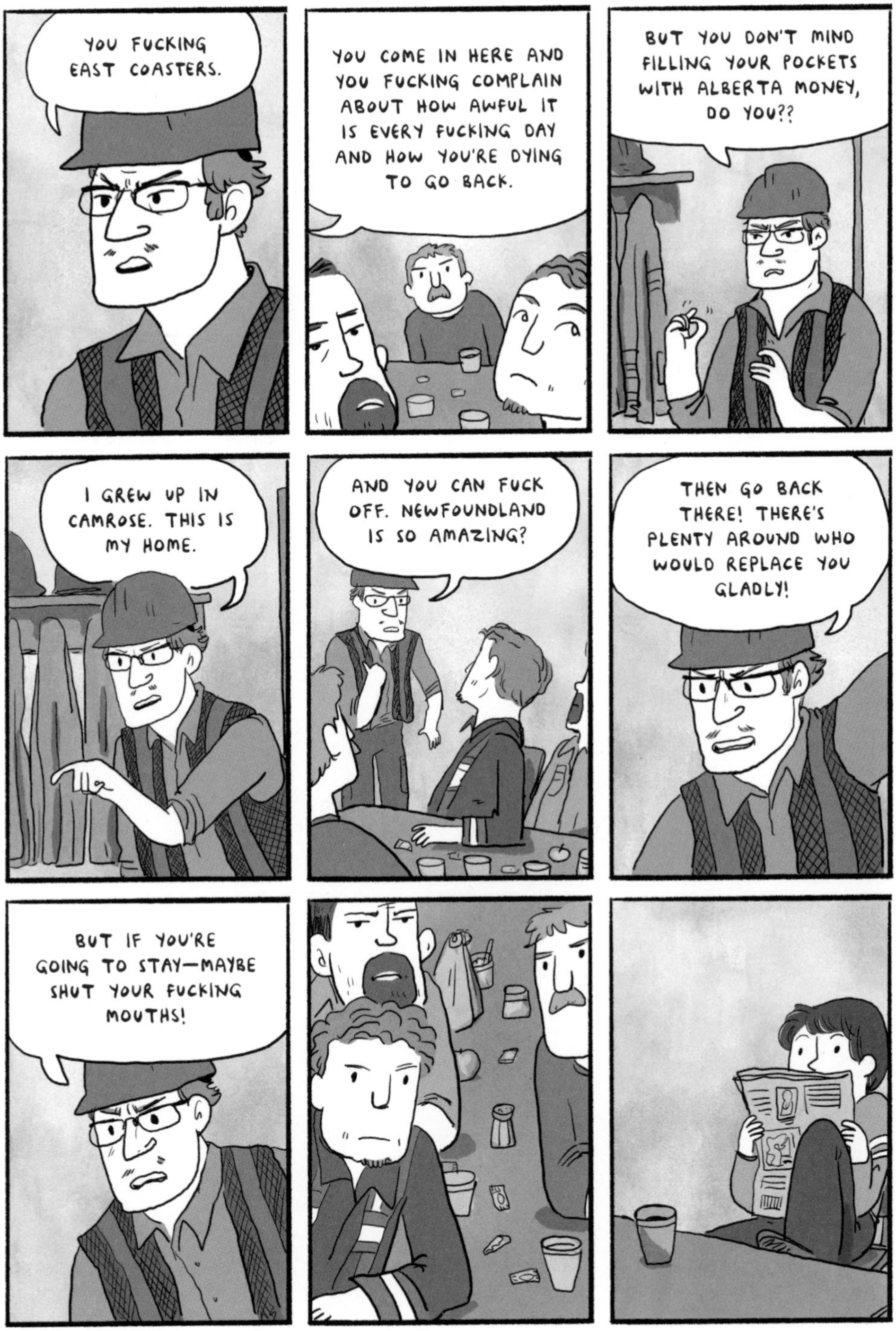
YOU FUCKING EAST COASTERS.
YOU COME IN HERE AND YOU FUCKING COMPLAIN ABOUT HOW AWFUL IT IS EVERY FUCKING DAY AND HOW YOU'RE DYING TO GO BACK.
BUT YOU DON'T MIND FILLING YOUR POCKETS WITH ALBERTA MONEY, DO YOU??
I GREW UP IN CAMROSE. THIS IS MY HOME.
AND YOU CAN FUCK OFF. NEWFOUNDLAND IS SO AMAZING?
THEN GO BACK THERE! THERE'S PLENTY AROUND WHO WOULD REPLACE YOU GLADLY!
BUT IF YOU'RE GOING TO STAY—MAYBE SHUT YOUR FUCKING MOUTHS!

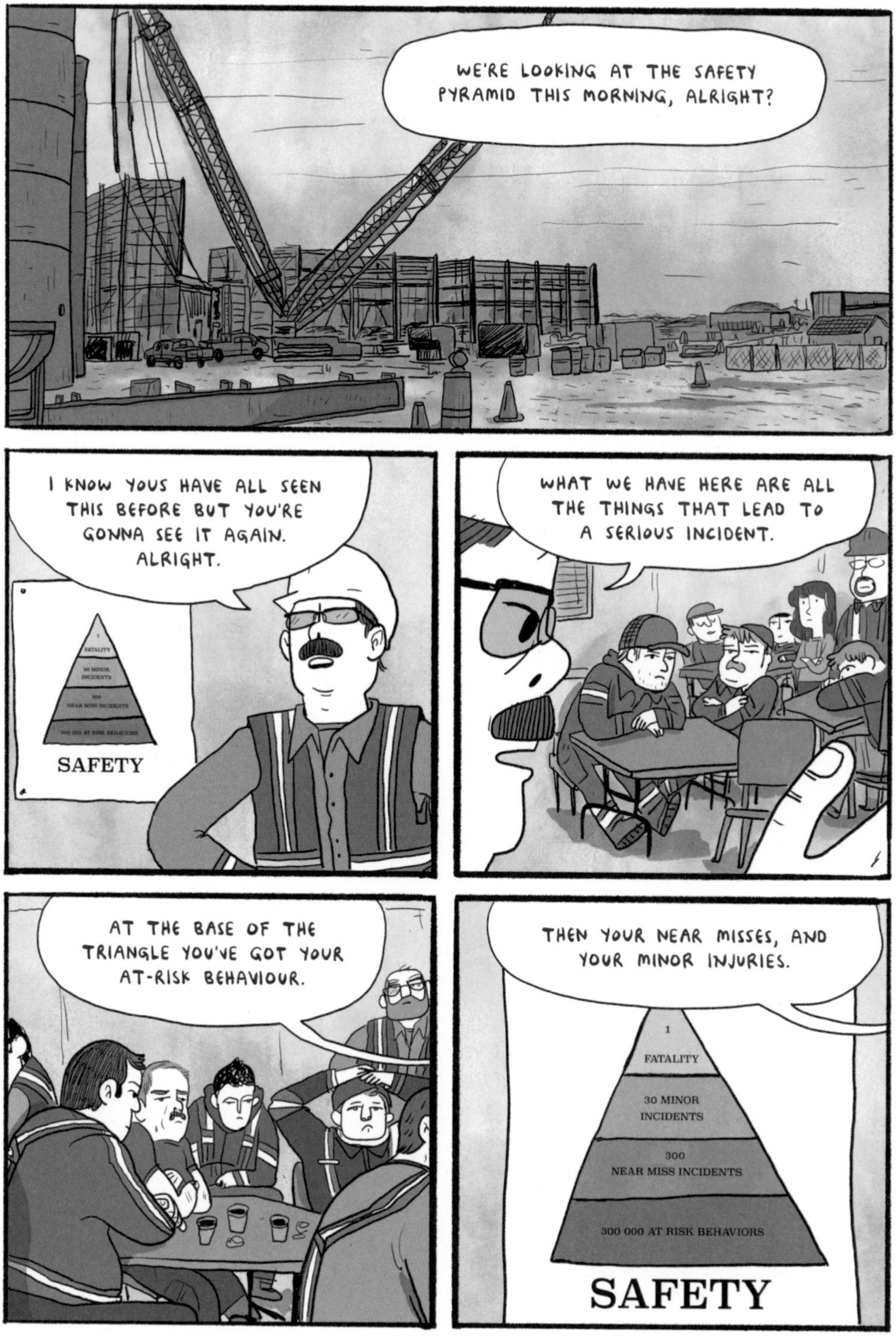
WE'RE LOOKING AT THE SAFETY PYRAMID THIS MORNING, ALRIGHT?
I KNOW YOUS HAVE ALL SEEN THIS BEFORE BUT YOU'RE GONNA SEE IT AGAIN. ALRIGHT.
1
FATALITY
30 MINOR INCIDENTS
300 NEAR MISS INCIDENTS
300 000 AT RISK BEHAVIORS
SAFETY
WHAT WE HAVE HERE ARE ALL THE THINGS THAT LEAD TO A SERIOUS INCIDENT.
AT THE BASE OF THE TRIANGLE YOU'VE GOT YOUR AT-RISK BEHAVIOUR.
THEN YOUR NEAR MISSES, AND YOUR MINOR INJURIES.
1
FATALITY
30 MINOR INCIDENTS
300 NEAR MISS INCIDENTS
300 000 AT RISK BEHAVIORS
SAFETY

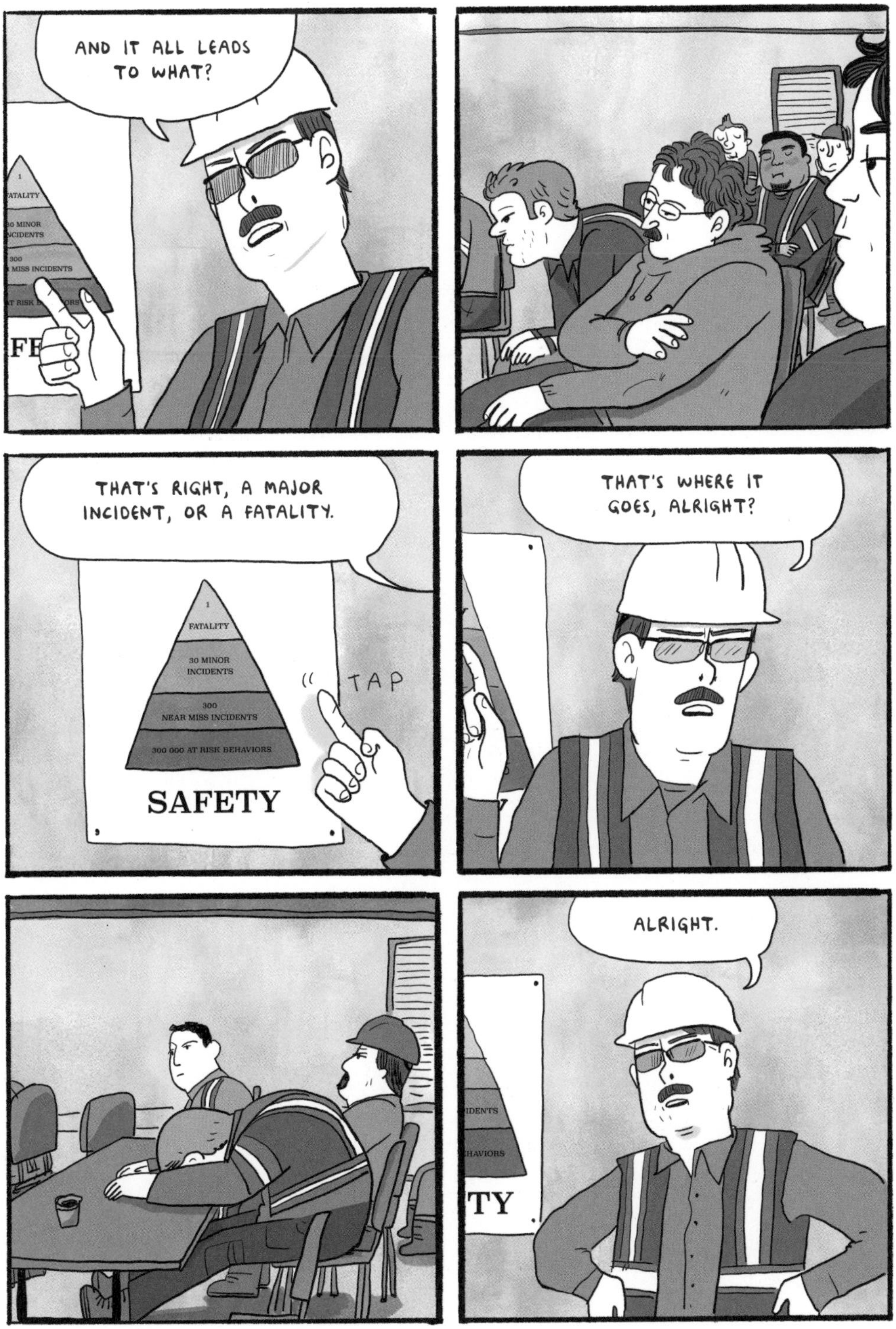
AND IT ALL LEADS TO WHAT?
THAT'S RIGHT, A MAJOR INCIDENT, OR A FATALITY.
1
FATALITY
30 MINOR INCIDENTS
300 NEAR MISS INCIDENTS
300 000 AT RISK BEHAVIORS
SAFETY
TAP
THAT'S WHERE IT GOES, ALRIGHT?
ALRIGHT.

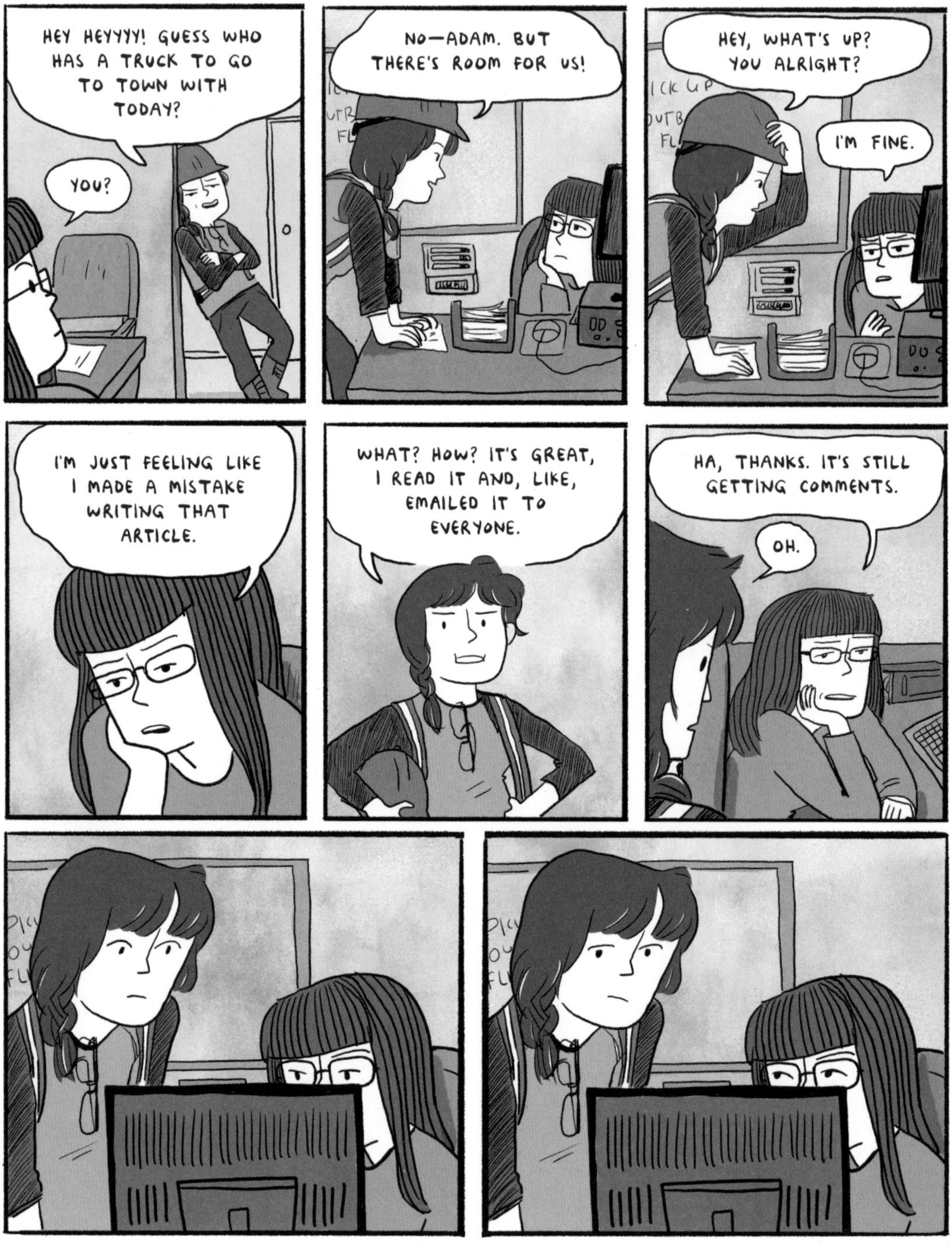
HEY HEYYYY! GUESS WHO HAS A TRUCK TO GO TO TOWN WITH TODAY?
YOU?
NO—ADAM. BUT THERE'S ROOM FOR US!
HEY, WHAT'S UP? YOU ALRIGHT?
I'M FINE.
I'M JUST FEELING LIKE I MADE A MISTAKE WRITING THAT ARTICLE.
WHAT? HOW? IT'S GREAT, I READ IT AND, LIKE, EMAILED IT TO EVERYONE.
HA, THANKS. IT'S STILL GETTING COMMENTS.
OH.

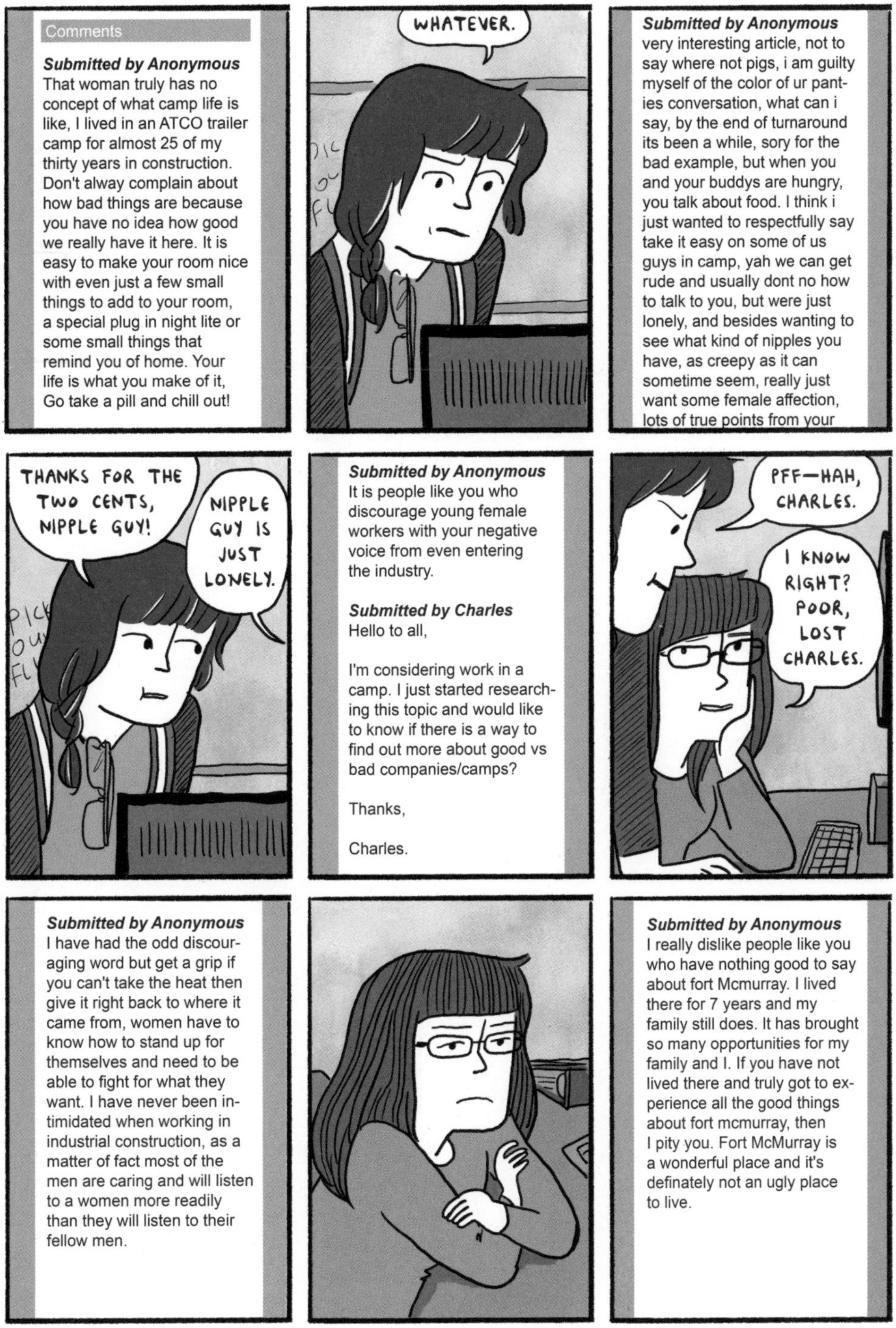
Comments
Submitted by Anonymous
That woman truly has no concept of what camp life is like, I lived in an ATCO trailer camp for almost 25 of my thirty years in construction. Don't alway complain about how bad things are because you have no idea how good we really have it here. It is easy to make your room nice with even just a few small things to add to your room, a special plug in night lite or some small things that remind you of home. Your life is what you make of it, Go take a pill and chill out!
WHATEVER.
Submitted by Anonymous
very interesting article, not to say where not pigs, i am guilty myself of the color of ur panties conversation, what can i say, by the end of turnaround its been a while, sory for the bad example, but when you and your buddys are hungry, you talk about food. I think i just wanted to respectfully say take it easy on some of us guys in camp, yah we can get rude and usually dont no how to talk to you, but were just lonely, and besides wanting to see what kind of nipples you have, as creepy as it can sometime seem, really just want some female affection, lots of true points from your
THANKS FOR THE TWO CENTS, NIPPLE GUY!
NIPPLE GUY IS JUST LONELY.
Submitted by Anonymous
It is people like you who discourage young female workers with your negative voice from even entering the industry.
Submitted by Charles
Hello to all,
I'm considering work in a camp. I just started researching this topic and would like to know if there is a way to find out more about good vs bad companies/camps?
Thanks,
Charles.
PFF—HAH, CHARLES.
I KNOW RIGHT? POOR, LOST CHARLES.
Submitted by Anonymous
I have had the odd discouraging word but get a grip if you can't take the heat then give it right back to where it came from, women have to know how to stand up for themselves and need to be able to fight for what they want. I have never been intimidated when working in industrial construction, as a matter of fact most of the men are caring and will listen to a women more readily than they will listen to their fellow men.
Submitted by Anonymous
I really dislike people like you who have nothing good to say about fort Mcmurray. I lived there for 7 years and my family still does. It has brought so many opportunities for my family and I. If you have not lived there and truly got to experience all the good things about fort mcmurray, then I pity you. Fort McMurray is a wonderful place and it's definately not an ugly place to live.

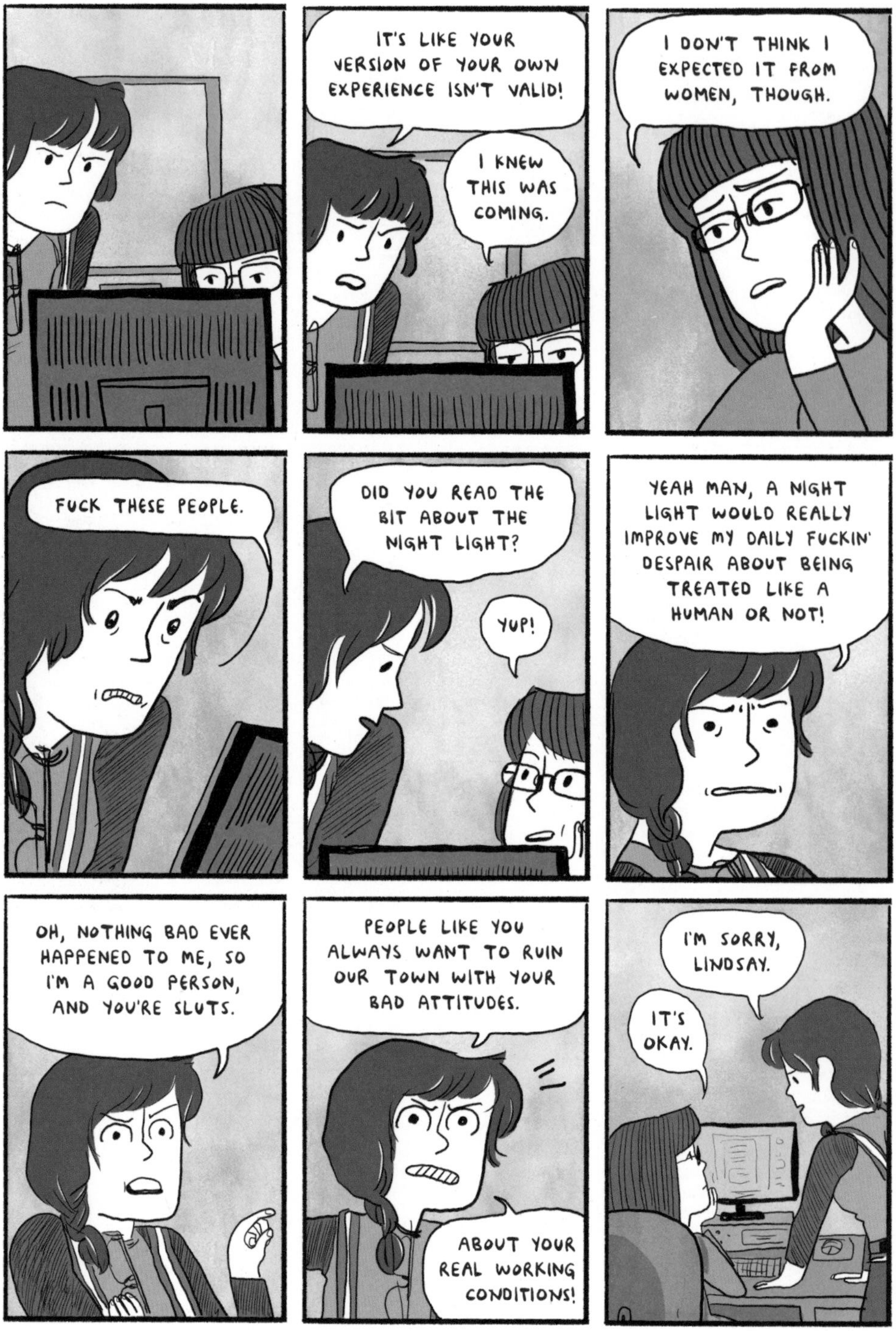
IT'S LIKE YOUR VERSION OF YOUR OWN EXPERIENCE ISN'T VALID!
I KNEW THIS WAS COMING.
I DON'T THINK I EXPECTED IT FROM WOMEN, THOUGH.
FUCK THESE PEOPLE.
DID YOU READ THE BIT ABOUT THE NIGHT LIGHT?
YUP!
YEAH MAN, A NIGHT LIGHT WOULD REALLY IMPROVE MY DAILY FUCKIN' DESPAIR ABOUT BEING TREATED LIKE A HUMAN OR NOT!
OH, NOTHING BAD EVER HAPPENED TO ME, SO I'M A GOOD PERSON, AND YOU'RE SLUTS.
PEOPLE LIKE YOU ALWAYS WANT TO RUIN OUR TOWN WITH YOUR BAD ATTITUDES.
ABOUT YOUR REAL WORKING CONDITIONS!
I'M SORRY, LINDSAY.
IT'S OKAY.

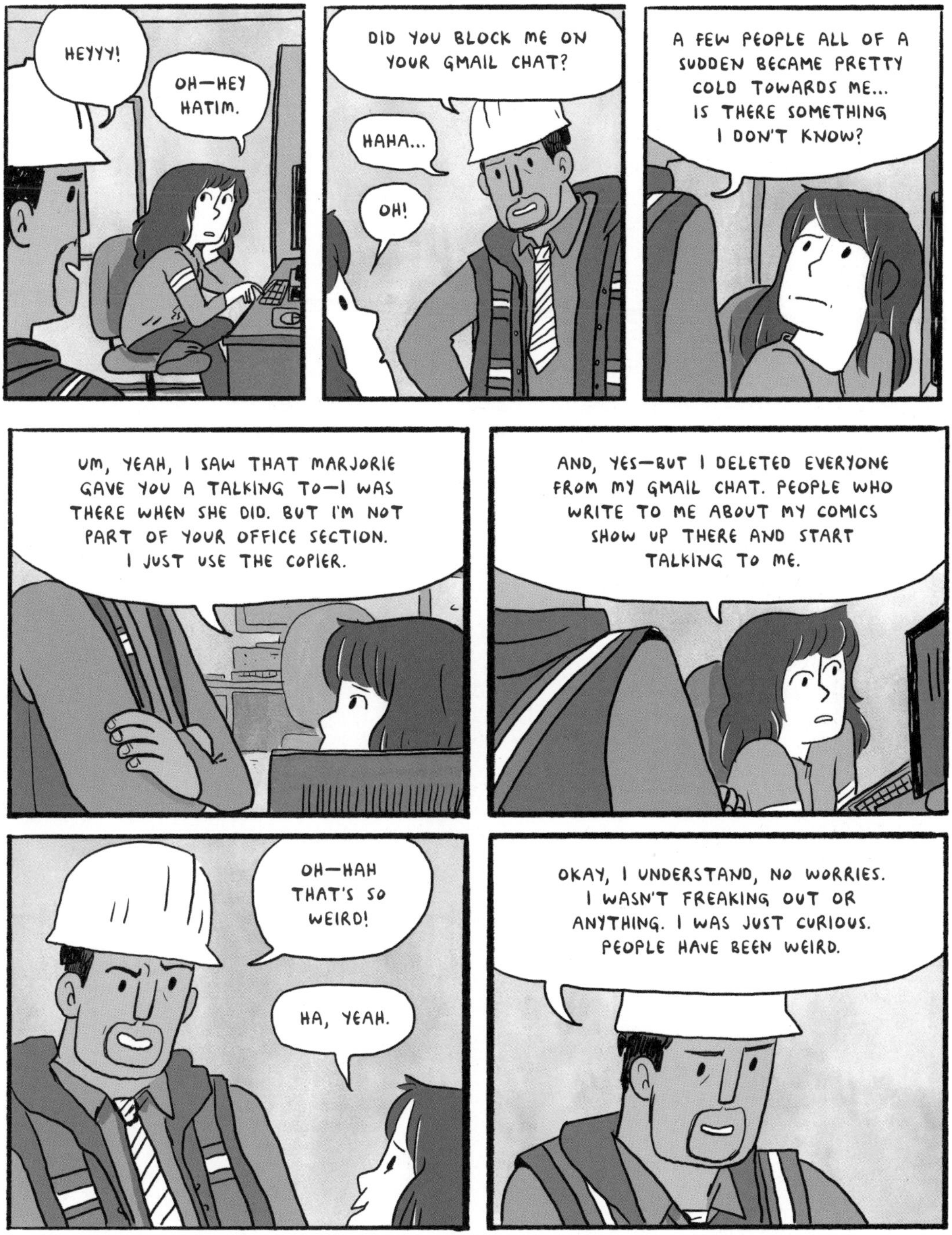
HEYYY!
OH—HEY HATIM.
DID YOU BLOCK ME ON YOUR GMAIL CHAT?
HAHA...
OH!
A FEW PEOPLE ALL OF A SUDDEN BECAME PRETTY COLD TOWARDS ME... IS THERE SOMETHING I DON'T KNOW?
UM, YEAH, I SAW THAT MARJORIE GAVE YOU A TALKING TO—I WAS THERE WHEN SHE DID. BUT I'M NOT PART OF YOUR OFFICE SECTION. I JUST USE THE COPIER.
AND, YES—BUT I DELETED EVERYONE FROM MY GMAIL CHAT. PEOPLE WHO WRITE TO ME ABOUT MY COMICS SHOW UP THERE AND START TALKING TO ME.
OH—HAH THAT'S SO WEIRD!
HA, YEAH.
OKAY, I UNDERSTAND, NO WORRIES. I WASN'T FREAKING OUT OR ANYTHING. I WAS JUST CURIOUS. PEOPLE HAVE BEEN WEIRD.

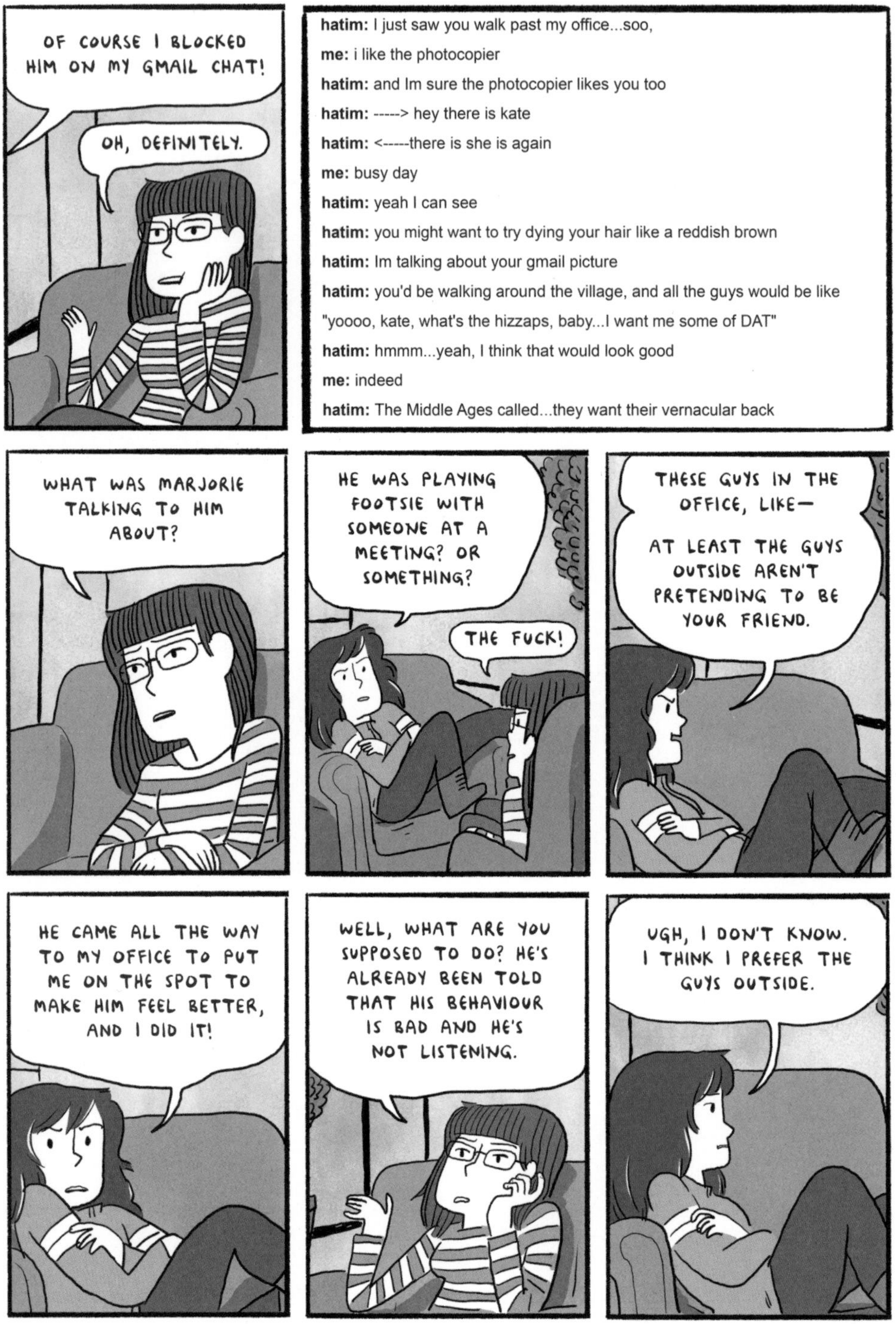
OF COURSE I BLOCKED HIM ON MY GMAIL CHAT!
OH, DEFINITELY.
hatim: I just saw you walk past my office...soo,
me: i like the photocopier
hatim: and Im sure the photocopier likes you too
hatim: -----> hey there is kate
hatim: <-----there is she is again
me: busy day
hatim: yeah I can see
hatim: you might want to try dying your hair like a reddish brown
hatim: Im talking about your gmail picture
hatim: you'd be walking around the village, and all the guys would be like "yoooo, kate, what's the hizzaps, baby...I want me some of DAT"
hatim: hmmm...yeah, I think that would look good
me: indeed
hatim: The Middle Ages called...they want their vernacular back
WHAT WAS MARJORIE TALKING TO HIM ABOUT?
HE WAS PLAYING FOOTSIE WITH SOMEONE AT A MEETING? OR SOMETHING?
THE FUCK!
THESE GUYS IN THE OFFICE, LIKE—
AT LEAST THE GUYS OUTSIDE AREN'T PRETENDING TO BE YOUR FRIEND.
HE CAME ALL THE WAY TO MY OFFICE TO PUT ME ON THE SPOT TO MAKE HIM FEEL BETTER, AND I DID IT!
WELL, WHAT ARE YOU SUPPOSED TO DO? HE'S ALREADY BEEN TOLD THAT HIS BEHAVIOUR IS BAD AND HE'S NOT LISTENING.
UGH, I DON'T KNOW. I THINK I PREFER THE GUYS OUTSIDE.

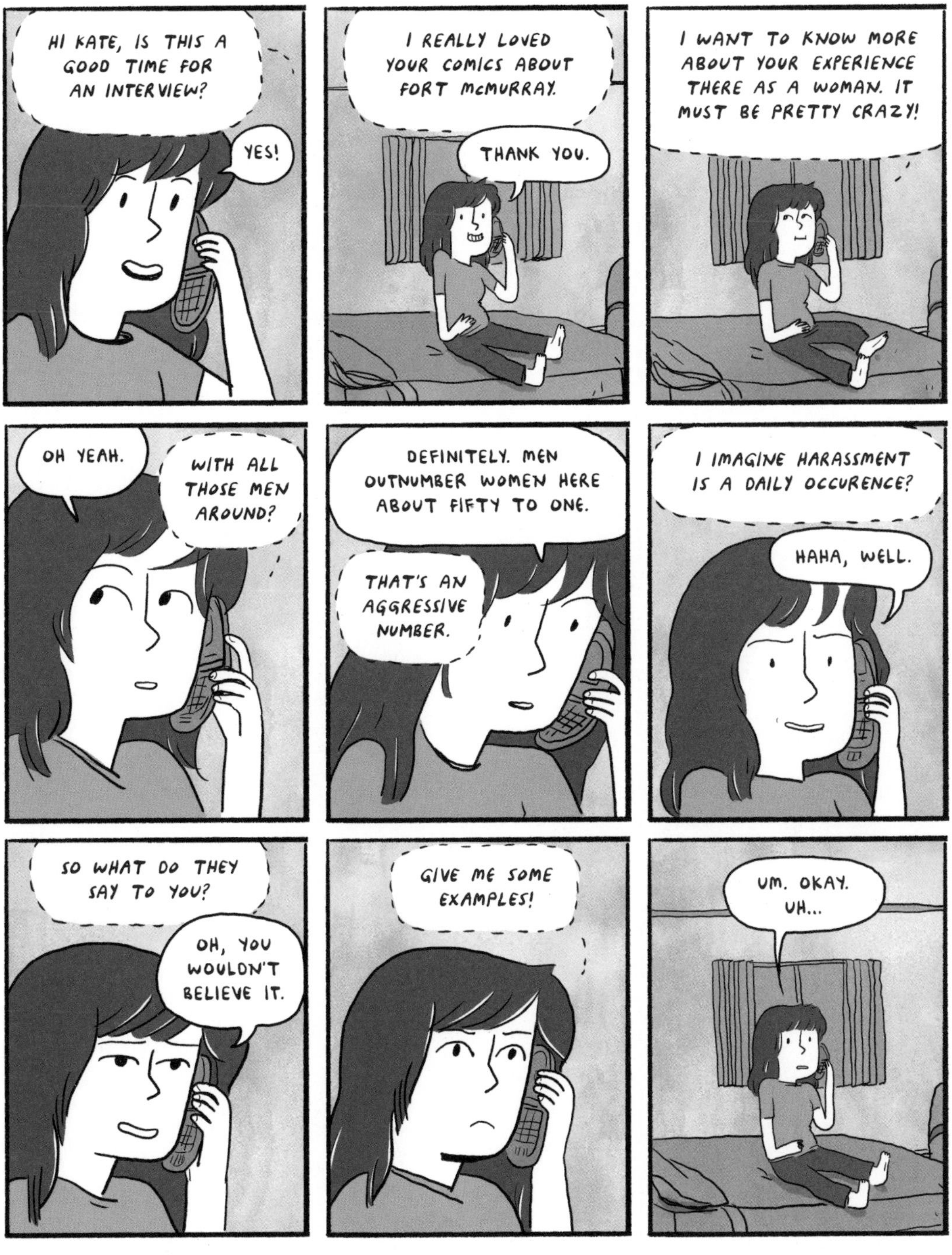
HI KATE, IS THIS A GOOD TIME FOR AN INTERVIEW?
YES!
I REALLY LOVED YOUR COMICS ABOUT FORT McMURRAY.
THANK YOU.
I WANT TO KNOW MORE ABOUT YOUR EXPERIENCE THERE AS A WOMAN. IT MUST BE PRETTY CRAZY!
OH YEAH.
WITH ALL THOSE MEN AROUND?
DEFINITELY. MEN OUTNUMBER WOMEN HERE ABOUT FIFTY TO ONE.
THAT'S AN AGGRESSIVE NUMBER.
I IMAGINE HARASSMENT IS A DAILY OCCURENCE?
HAHA, WELL.
SO WHAT DO THEY SAY TO YOU?
OH, YOU WOULDN'T BELIEVE IT.
GIVE ME SOME EXAMPLES!
UM. OKAY. UH...

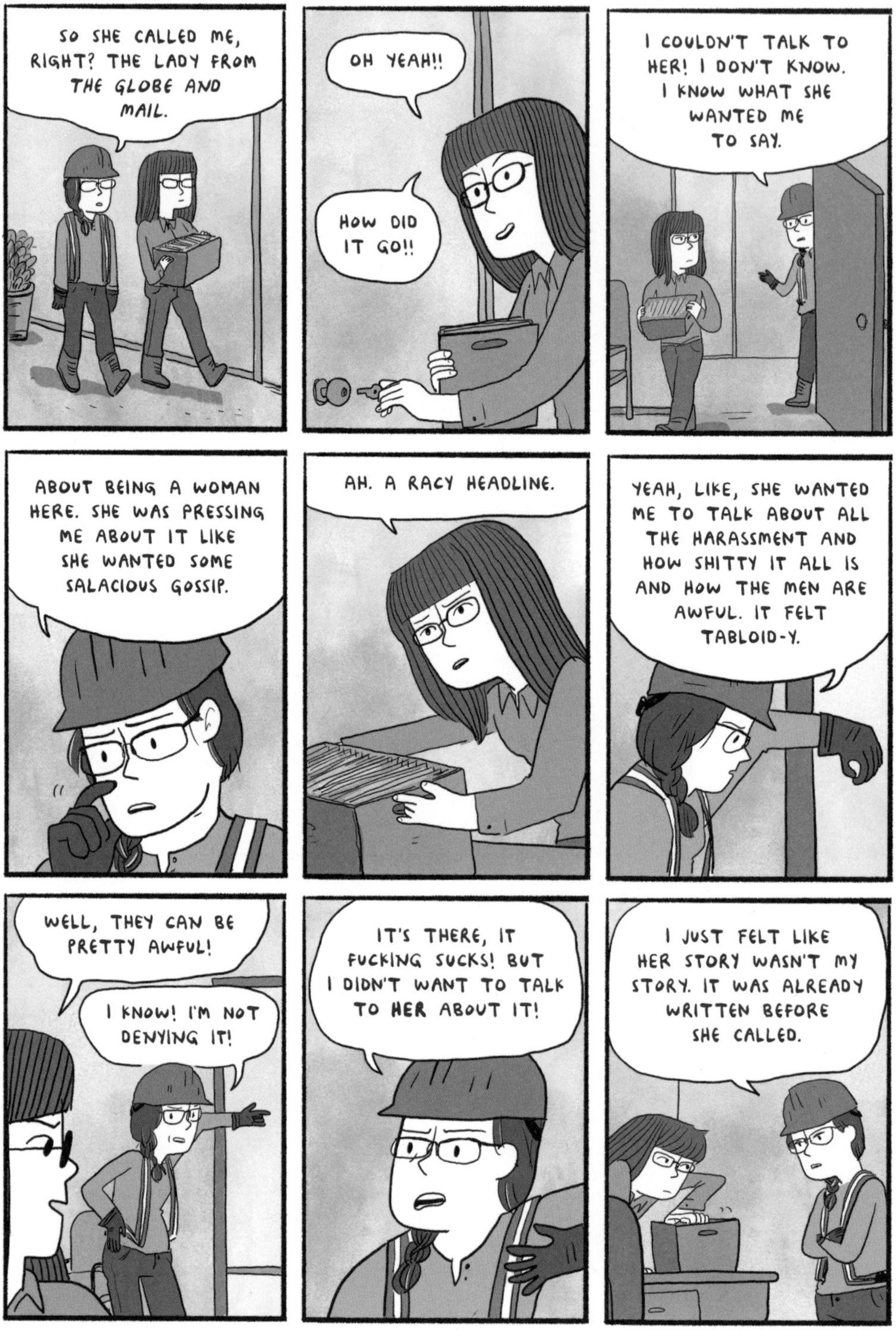
SO SHE CALLED ME, RIGHT? THE LADY FROM THE GLOBE AND MAIL.
OH YEAH!!
HOW DID IT GO!!
I COULDN'T TALK TO HER! I DON'T KNOW. I KNOW WHAT SHE WANTED ME TO SAY.
ABOUT BEING A WOMAN HERE. SHE WAS PRESSING ME ABOUT IT LIKE SHE WANTED SOME SALACIOUS GOSSIP.
AH. A RACY HEADLINE.
YEAH, LIKE, SHE WANTED ME TO TALK ABOUT ALL THE HARASSMENT AND HOW SHITTY IT ALL IS AND HOW THE MEN ARE AWFUL. IT FELT TABLOID-Y.
WELL, THEY CAN BE PRETTY AWFUL!
I KNOW! I'M NOT DENYING IT!
IT'S THERE, IT FUCKING SUCKS! BUT I DIDN'T WANT TO TALK TO HER ABOUT IT!
I JUST FELT LIKE HER STORY WASN'T MY STORY. IT WAS ALREADY WRITTEN BEFORE SHE CALLED.

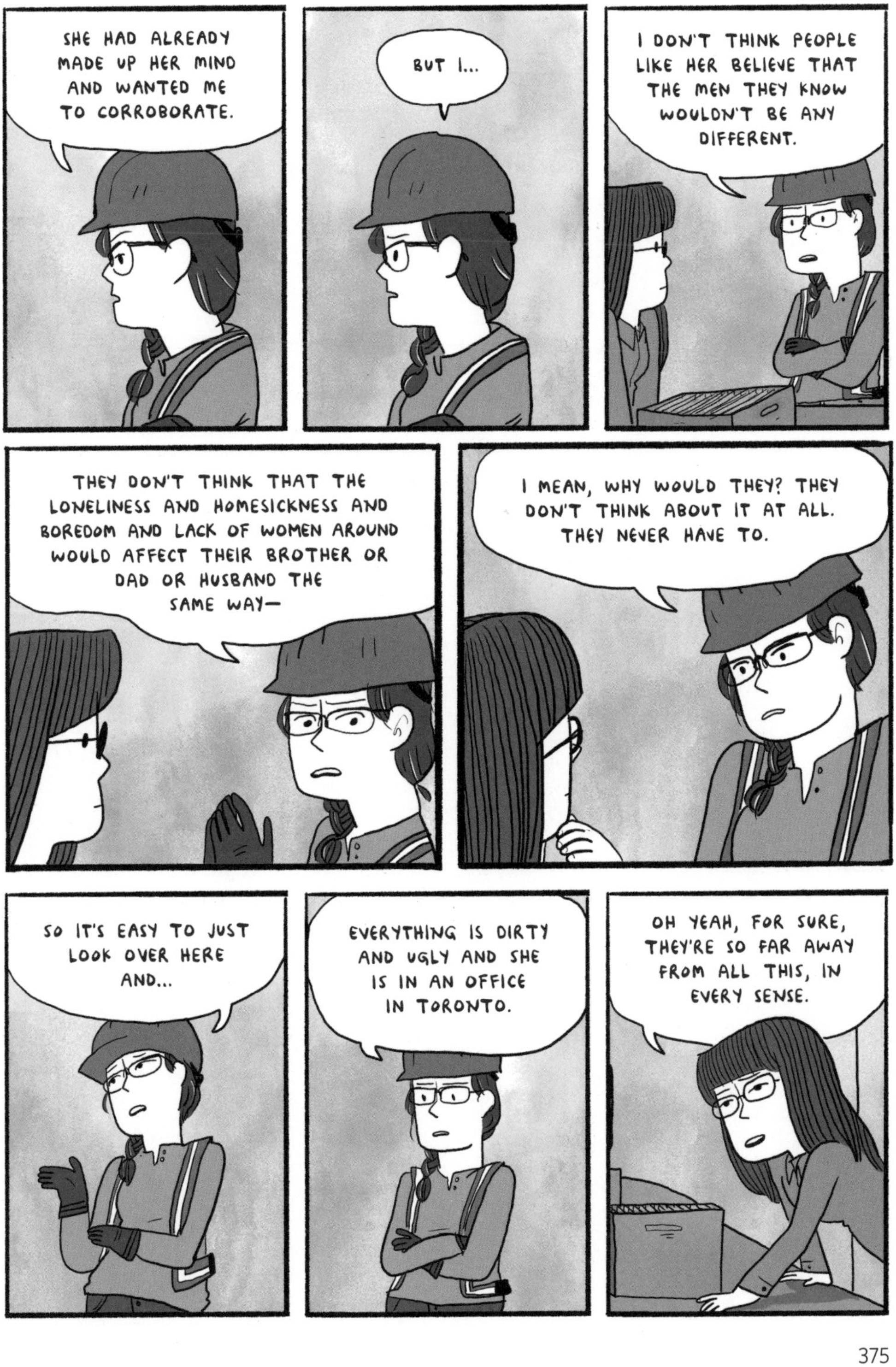
SHE HAD ALREADY MADE UP HER MIND AND WANTED ME TO CORROBORATE.
BUT I...
I DON'T THINK PEOPLE LIKE HER BELIEVE THAT THE MEN THEY KNOW WOULDN'T BE ANY DIFFERENT.
THEY DON'T THINK THAT THE LONELINESS AND HOMESICKNESS AND BOREDOM AND LACK OF WOMEN AROUND WOULD AFFECT THEIR BROTHER OR DAD OR HUSBAND THE SAME WAY—
I MEAN, WHY WOULD THEY? THEY DON'T THINK ABOUT IT AT ALL. THEY NEVER HAVE TO.
SO IT'S EASY TO JUST LOOK OVER HERE AND...
EVERYTHING IS DIRTY AND UGLY AND SHE IS IN AN OFFICE IN TORONTO.
OH YEAH, FOR SURE, THEY'RE SO FAR AWAY FROM ALL THIS, IN EVERY SENSE.

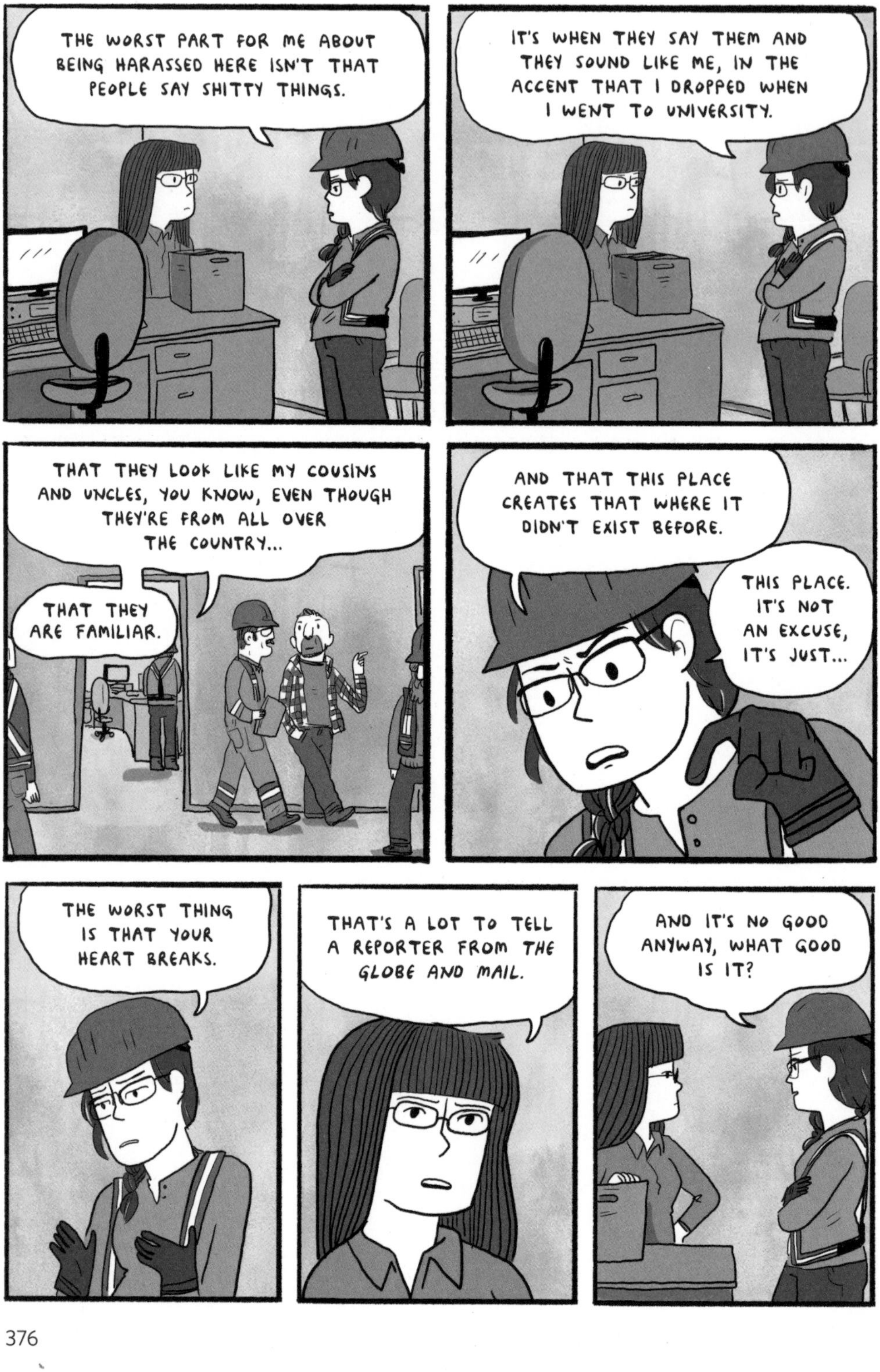
THE WORST PART FOR ME ABOUT BEING HARASSED HERE ISN'T THAT PEOPLE SAY SHITTY THINGS.
IT'S WHEN THEY SAY THEM AND THEY SOUND LIKE ME, IN THE ACCENT THAT I DROPPED WHEN I WENT TO UNIVERSITY.
THAT THEY LOOK LIKE MY COUSINS AND UNCLES, YOU KNOW, EVEN THOUGH THEY'RE FROM ALL OVER THE COUNTRY...
THAT THEY ARE FAMILIAR.
AND THAT THIS PLACE CREATES THAT WHERE IT DIDN'T EXIST BEFORE.
THIS PLACE. IT'S NOT AN EXCUSE, IT'S JUST...
THE WORST THING IS THAT YOUR HEART BREAKS.
THAT'S A LOT TO TELL A REPORTER FROM *THE GLOBE AND MAIL*.
AND IT'S NO GOOD ANYWAY, WHAT GOOD IS IT?

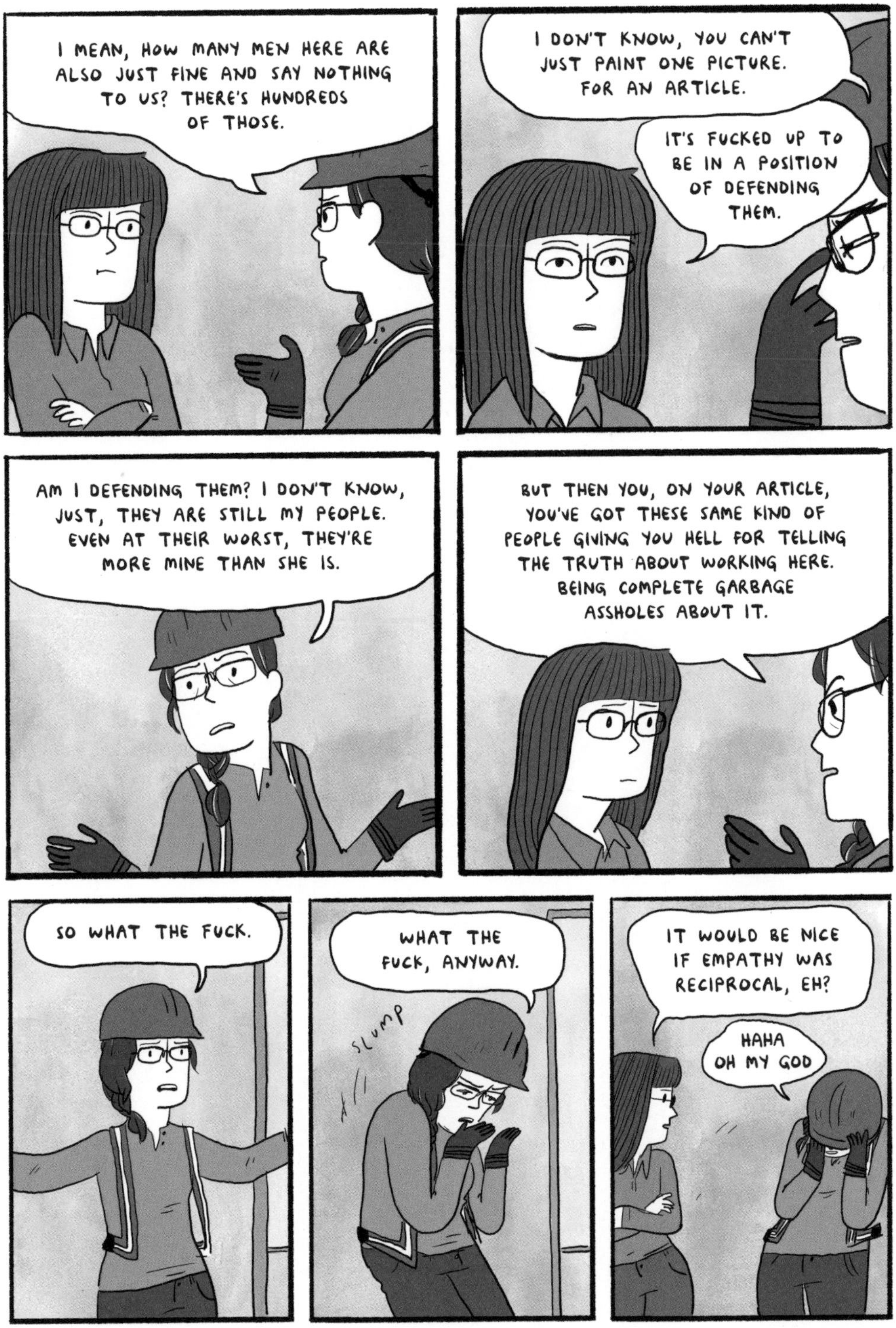
I MEAN, HOW MANY MEN HERE ARE ALSO JUST FINE AND SAY NOTHING TO US? THERE'S HUNDREDS OF THOSE.
I DON'T KNOW, YOU CAN'T JUST PAINT ONE PICTURE. FOR AN ARTICLE.
IT'S FUCKED UP TO BE IN A POSITION OF DEFENDING THEM.
AM I DEFENDING THEM? I DON'T KNOW, JUST, THEY ARE STILL MY PEOPLE. EVEN AT THEIR WORST, THEY'RE MORE MINE THAN SHE IS.
BUT THEN YOU, ON YOUR ARTICLE, YOU'VE GOT THESE SAME KIND OF PEOPLE GIVING YOU HELL FOR TELLING THE TRUTH ABOUT WORKING HERE. BEING COMPLETE GARBAGE ASSHOLES ABOUT IT.
SO WHAT THE FUCK.
WHAT THE FUCK, ANYWAY.
SLUMP
IT WOULD BE NICE IF EMPATHY WAS RECIPROCAL, EH?
HAHA OH MY GOD

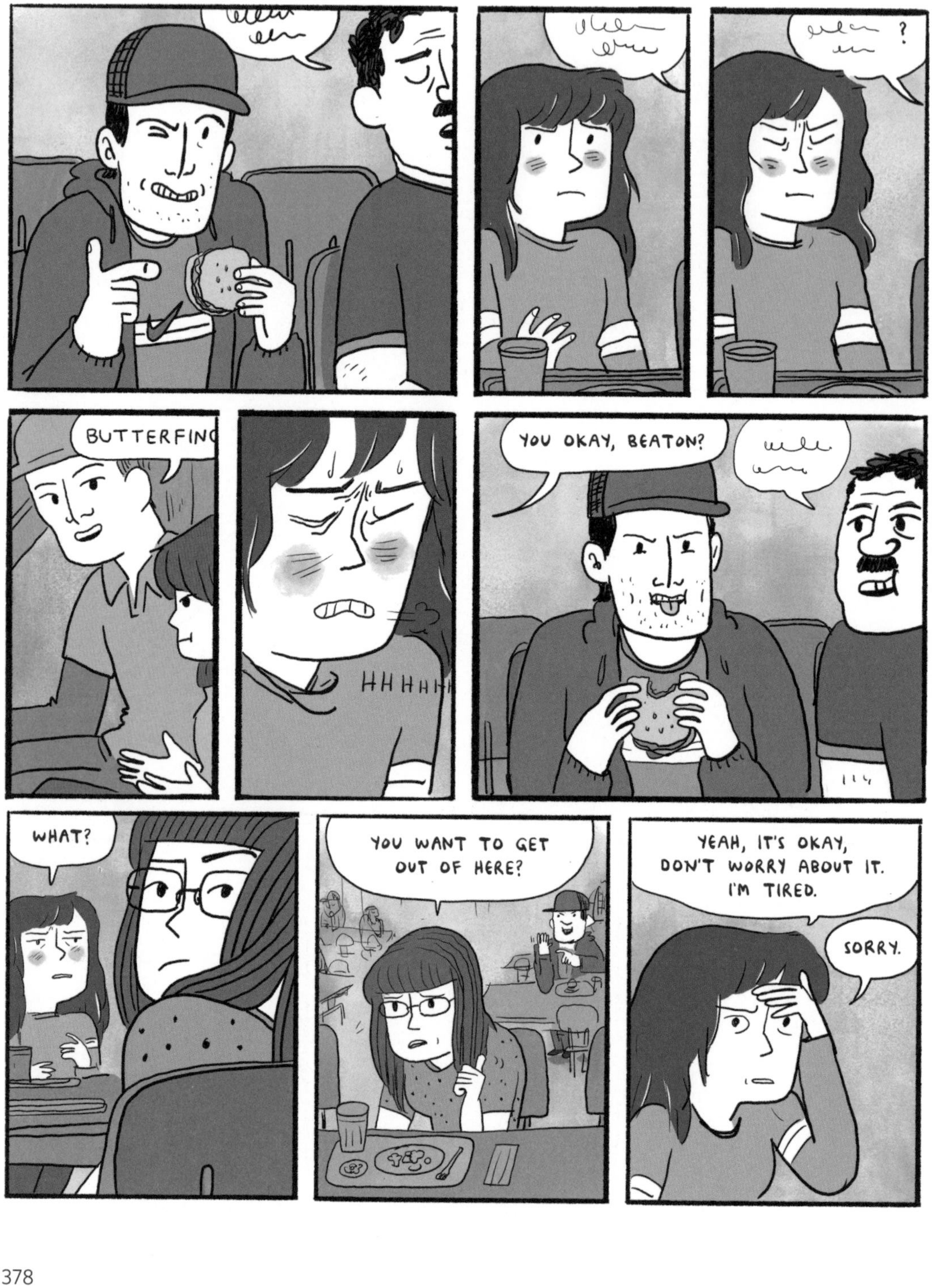
BUTTERFING
YOU OKAY, BEATON?
WHAT?
YOU WANT TO GET OUT OF HERE?
YEAH, IT'S OKAY, DON'T WORRY ABOUT IT. I'M TIRED.
SORRY.

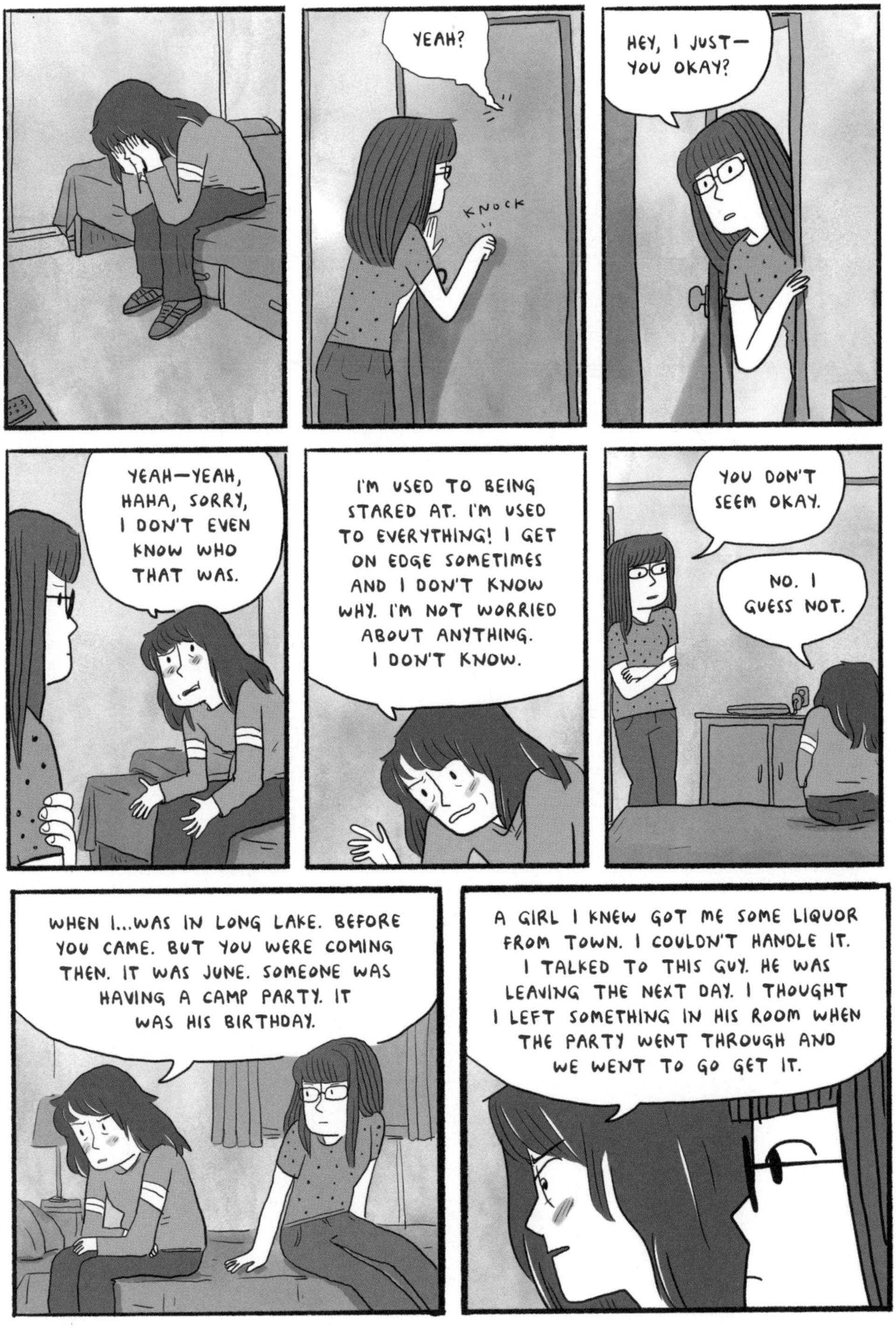

YEAH?
KNOCK
HEY, I JUST—
YOU OKAY?
YEAH—YEAH, HAHA, SORRY, I DON'T EVEN KNOW WHO THAT WAS.
I'M USED TO BEING STARED AT. I'M USED TO EVERYTHING! I GET ON EDGE SOMETIMES AND I DON'T KNOW WHY. I'M NOT WORRIED ABOUT ANYTHING. I DON'T KNOW.
YOU DON'T SEEM OKAY.
NO. I GUESS NOT.
WHEN I...WAS IN LONG LAKE. BEFORE YOU CAME. BUT YOU WERE COMING THEN. IT WAS JUNE. SOMEONE WAS HAVING A CAMP PARTY. IT WAS HIS BIRTHDAY.
A GIRL I KNEW GOT ME SOME LIQUOR FROM TOWN. I COULDN'T HANDLE IT. I TALKED TO THIS GUY. HE WAS LEAVING THE NEXT DAY. I THOUGHT I LEFT SOMETHING IN HIS ROOM WHEN THE PARTY WENT THROUGH AND WE WENT TO GO GET IT.

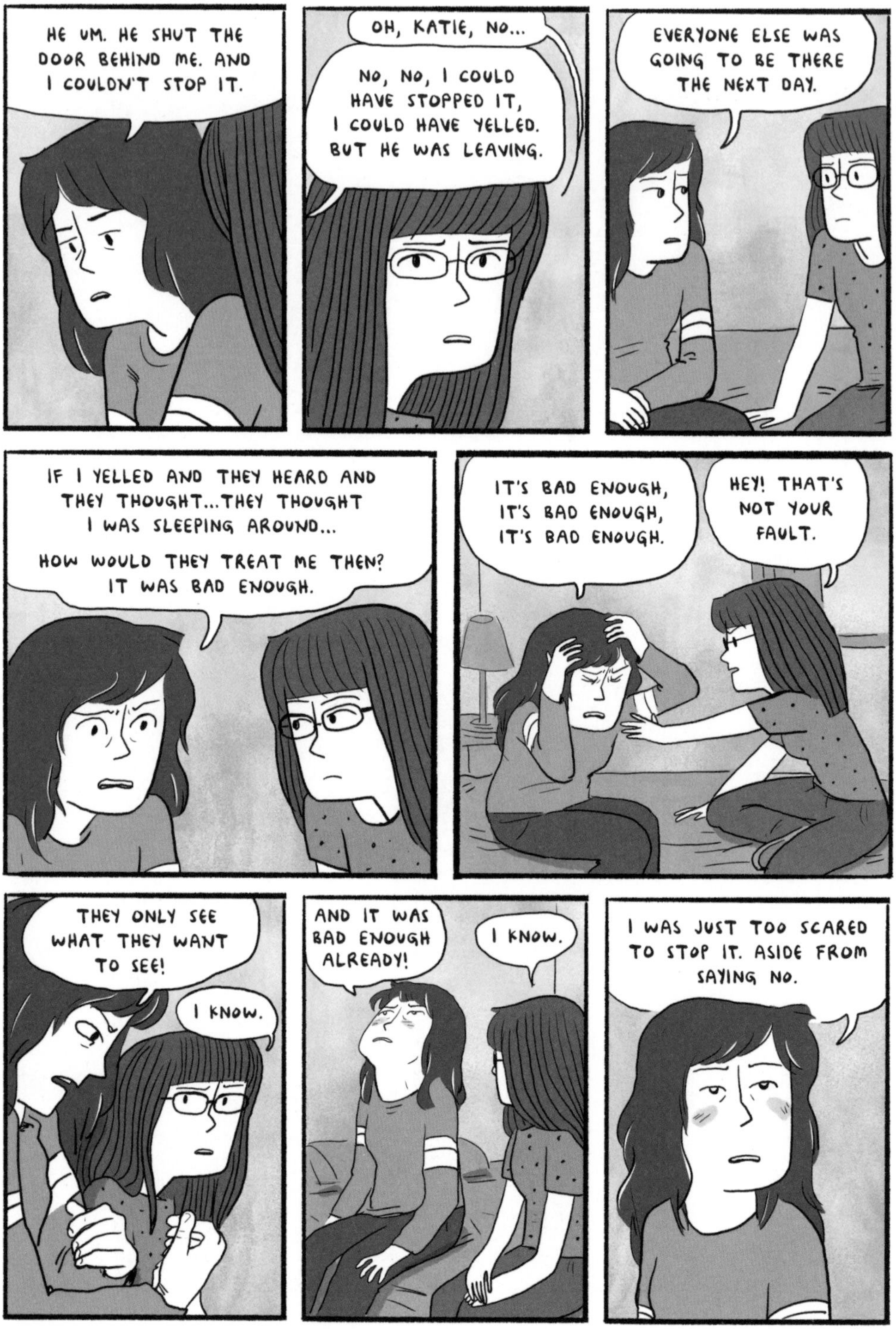
HE UM. HE SHUT THE DOOR BEHIND ME. AND I COULDN'T STOP IT.
OH, KATIE, NO...
NO, NO, I COULD HAVE STOPPED IT, I COULD HAVE YELLED. BUT HE WAS LEAVING.
EVERYONE ELSE WAS GOING TO BE THERE THE NEXT DAY.
IF I YELLED AND THEY HEARD AND THEY THOUGHT...THEY THOUGHT I WAS SLEEPING AROUND...
HOW WOULD THEY TREAT ME THEN? IT WAS BAD ENOUGH.
IT'S BAD ENOUGH, IT'S BAD ENOUGH, IT'S BAD ENOUGH.
HEY! THAT'S NOT YOUR FAULT.
THEY ONLY SEE WHAT THEY WANT TO SEE!
I KNOW.
AND IT WAS BAD ENOUGH ALREADY!
I KNOW.
I WAS JUST TOO SCARED TO STOP IT. ASIDE FROM SAYING NO.

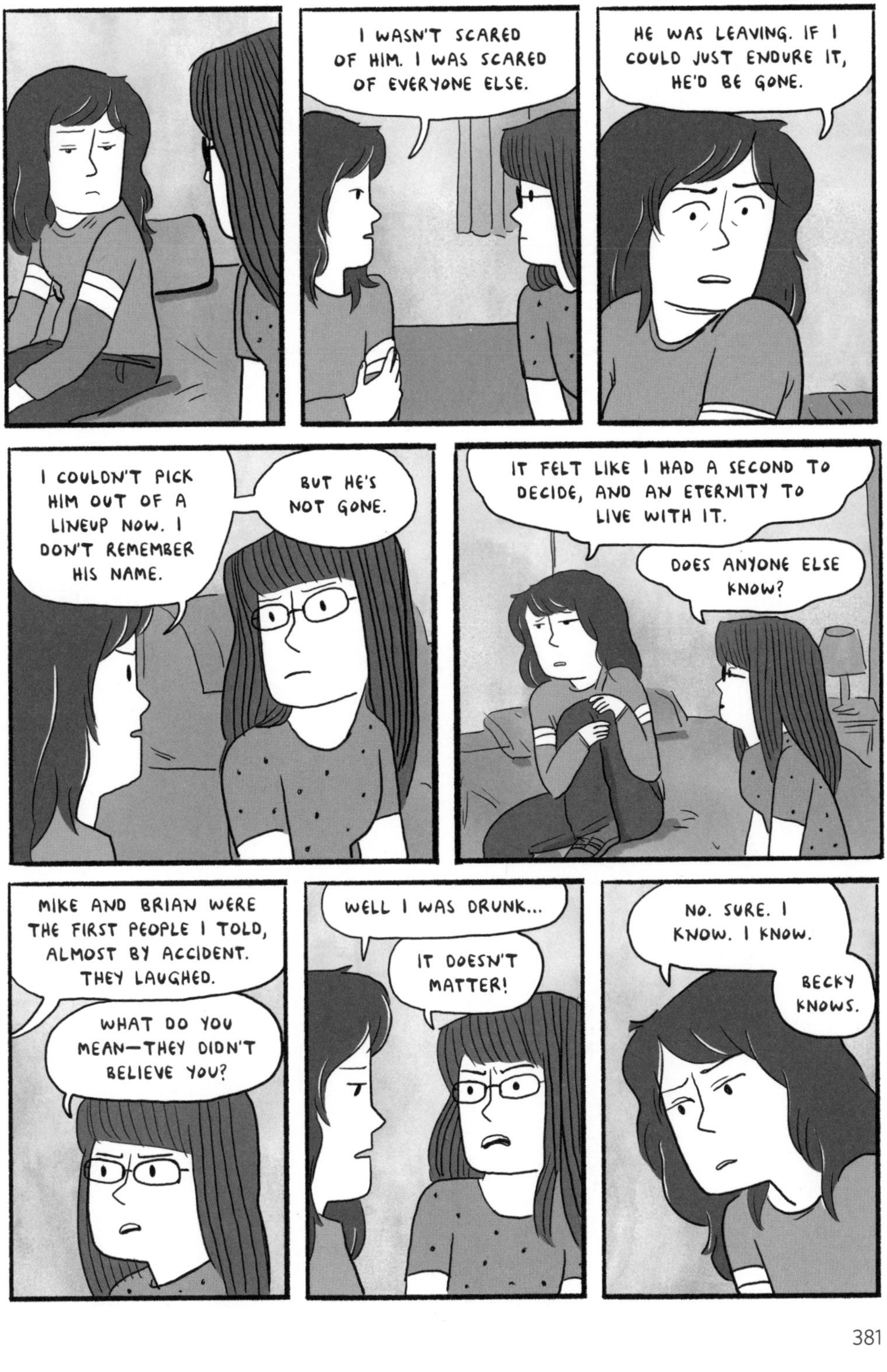

I WASN'T SCARED OF HIM. I WAS SCARED OF EVERYONE ELSE.
HE WAS LEAVING. IF I COULD JUST ENDURE IT, HE'D BE GONE.
I COULDN'T PICK HIM OUT OF A LINEUP NOW. I DON'T REMEMBER HIS NAME.
BUT HE'S NOT GONE.
IT FELT LIKE I HAD A SECOND TO DECIDE, AND AN ETERNITY TO LIVE WITH IT.
DOES ANYONE ELSE KNOW?
MIKE AND BRIAN WERE THE FIRST PEOPLE I TOLD, ALMOST BY ACCIDENT. THEY LAUGHED.
WHAT DO YOU MEAN—THEY DIDN'T BELIEVE YOU?
WELL I WAS DRUNK...
IT DOESN'T MATTER!
NO. SURE. I KNOW. I KNOW.
BECKY KNOWS.

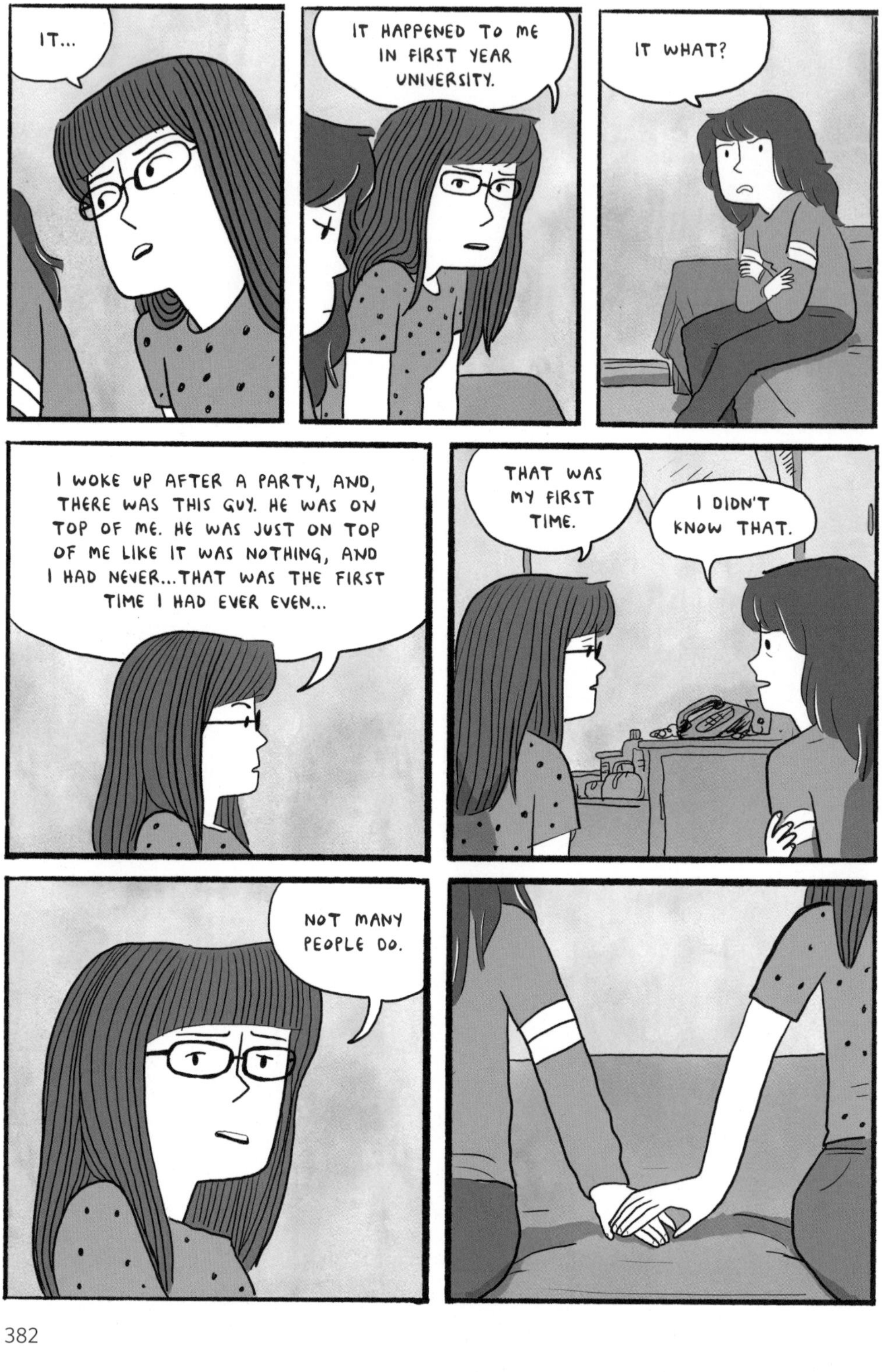
IT...
IT HAPPENED TO ME IN FIRST YEAR UNIVERSITY.
IT WHAT?
I WOKE UP AFTER A PARTY, AND, THERE WAS THIS GUY. HE WAS ON TOP OF ME. HE WAS JUST ON TOP OF ME LIKE IT WAS NOTHING, AND I HAD NEVER...THAT WAS THE FIRST TIME I HAD EVER EVEN...
THAT WAS MY FIRST TIME.
I DIDN'T KNOW THAT.
NOT MANY PEOPLE DO.

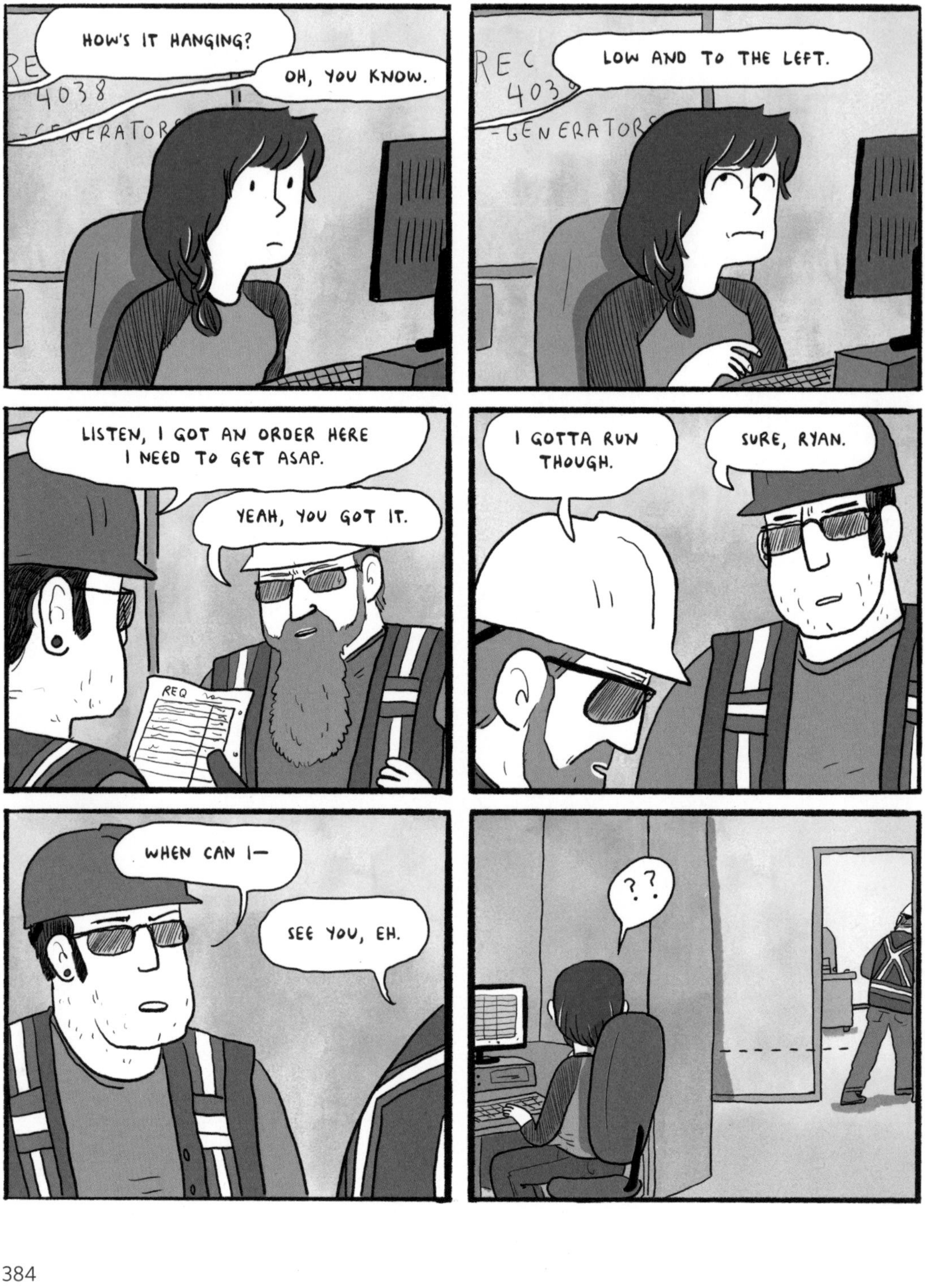
HOW'S IT HANGING?
OH, YOU KNOW.
LOW AND TO THE LEFT.
LISTEN, I GOT AN ORDER HERE I NEED TO GET ASAP.
YEAH, YOU GOT IT.
REQ
I GOTTA RUN THOUGH.
SURE, RYAN.
WHEN CAN I—
SEE YOU, EH.
??

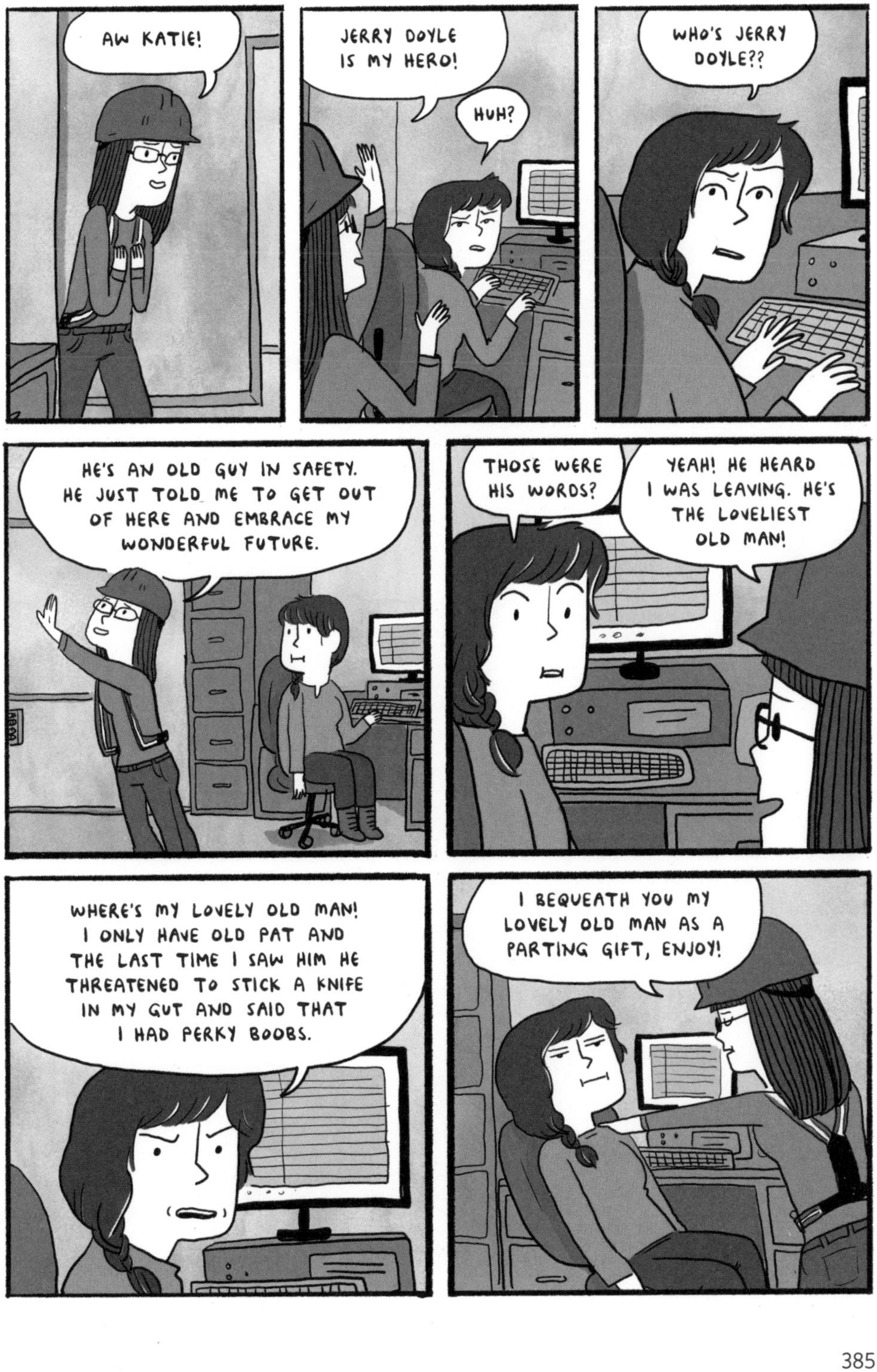
AW KATIE!
JERRY DOYLE IS MY HERO!
HUH?
WHO'S JERRY DOYLE??
HE'S AN OLD GUY IN SAFETY. HE JUST TOLD ME TO GET OUT OF HERE AND EMBRACE MY WONDERFUL FUTURE.
THOSE WERE HIS WORDS?
YEAH! HE HEARD I WAS LEAVING. HE'S THE LOVELIEST OLD MAN!
WHERE'S MY LOVELY OLD MAN! I ONLY HAVE OLD PAT AND THE LAST TIME I SAW HIM HE THREATENED TO STICK A KNIFE IN MY GUT AND SAID THAT I HAD PERKY BOOBS.
I BEQUEATH YOU MY LOVELY OLD MAN AS A PARTING GIFT, ENJOY!

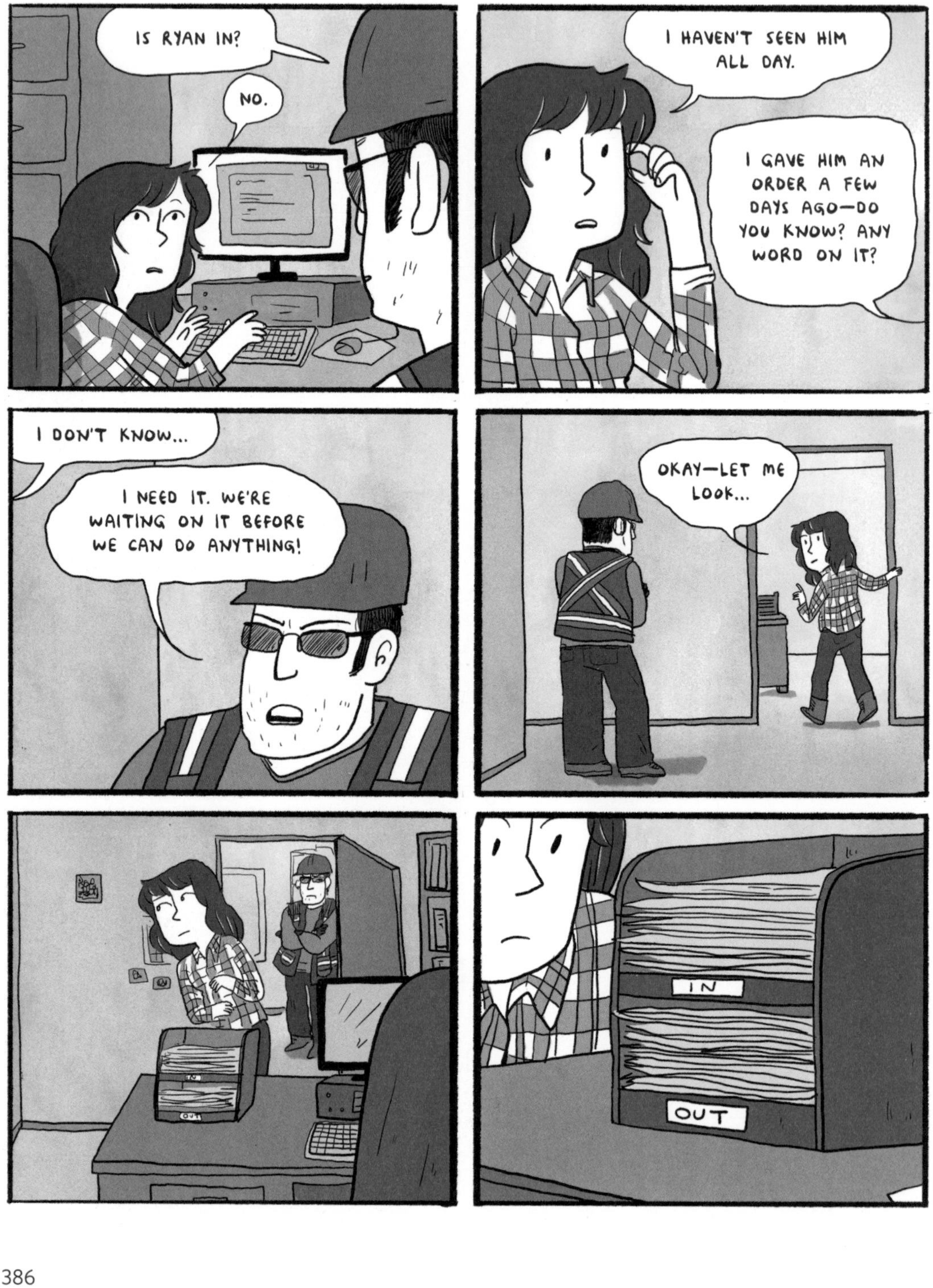
IS RYAN IN?
NO.
I HAVEN'T SEEN HIM ALL DAY.
I GAVE HIM AN ORDER A FEW DAYS AGO—DO YOU KNOW? ANY WORD ON IT?
I DON'T KNOW...
I NEED IT. WE'RE WAITING ON IT BEFORE WE CAN DO ANYTHING!
OKAY—LET ME LOOK...
IN
OUT
IN
OUT

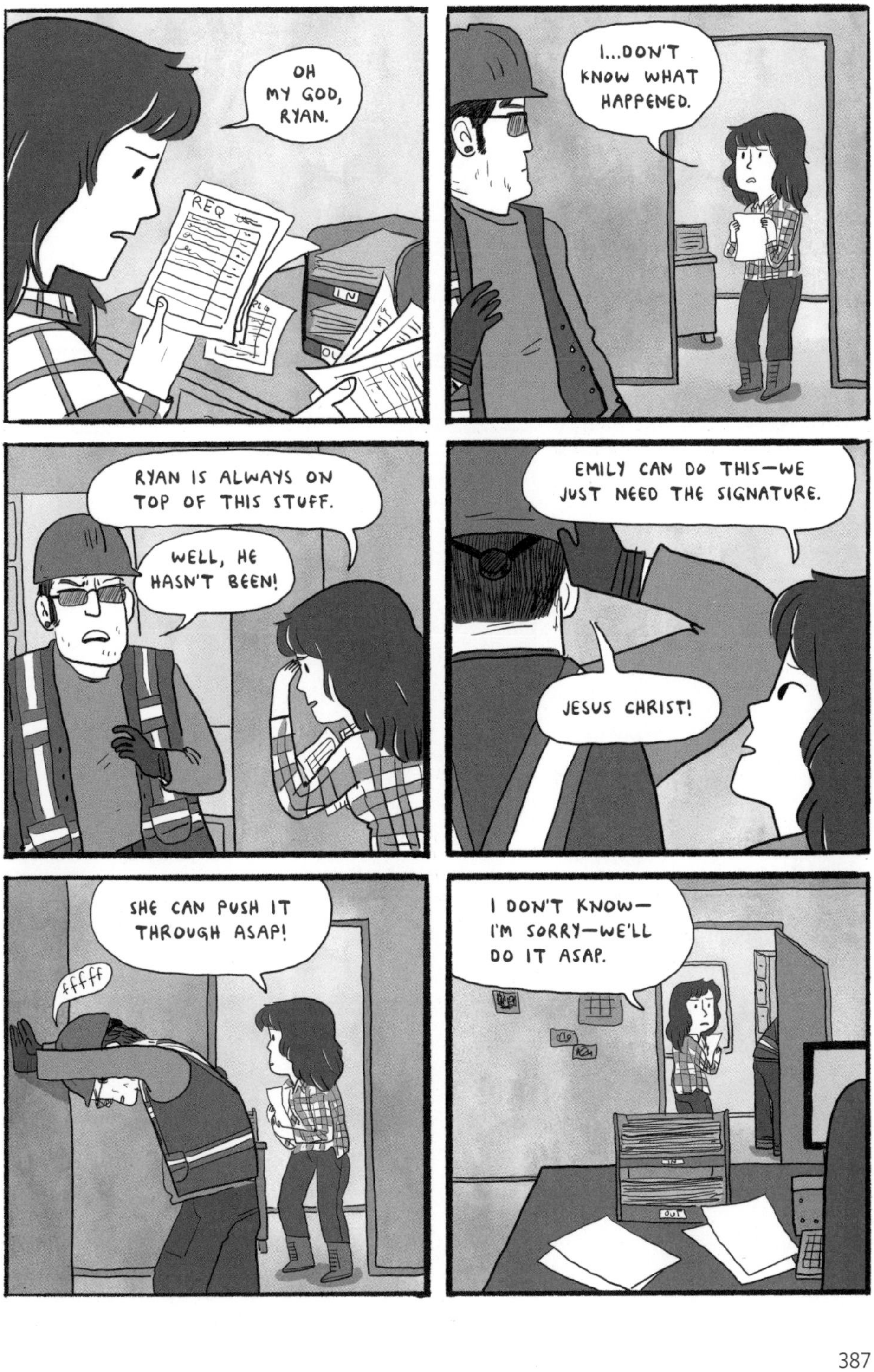
OH MY GOD, RYAN.
I...DON'T KNOW WHAT HAPPENED.
RYAN IS ALWAYS ON TOP OF THIS STUFF.
WELL, HE HASN'T BEEN!
EMILY CAN DO THIS—WE JUST NEED THE SIGNATURE.
JESUS CHRIST!
SHE CAN PUSH IT THROUGH ASAP!
fffff
I DON'T KNOW—I'M SORRY—WE'LL DO IT ASAP.

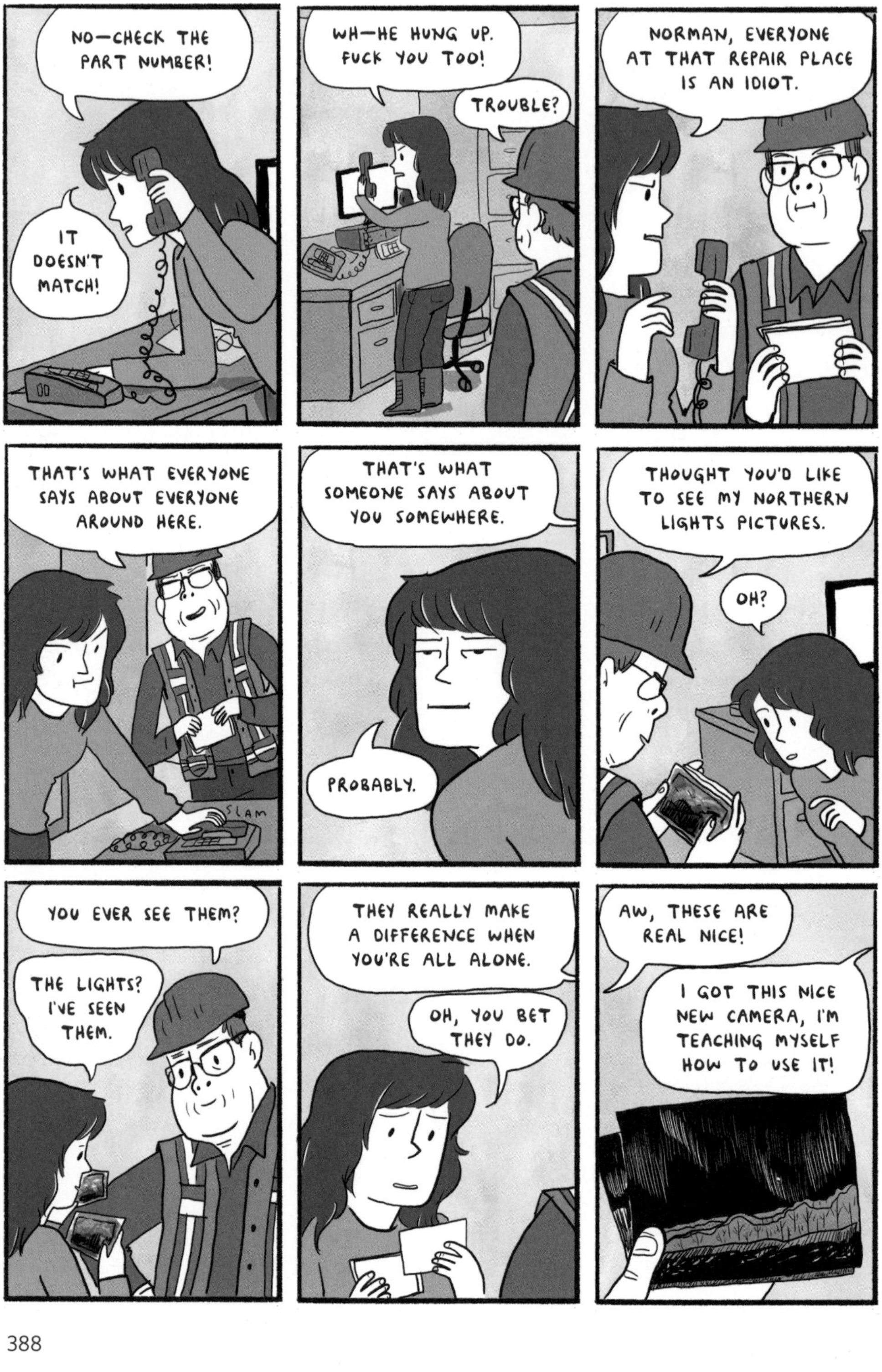
NO—CHECK THE PART NUMBER!
IT DOESN'T MATCH!
WH—HE HUNG UP. FUCK YOU TOO!
TROUBLE?
NORMAN, EVERYONE AT THAT REPAIR PLACE IS AN IDIOT.
THAT'S WHAT EVERYONE SAYS ABOUT EVERYONE AROUND HERE.
SLAM
THAT'S WHAT SOMEONE SAYS ABOUT YOU SOMEWHERE.
PROBABLY.
THOUGHT YOU'D LIKE TO SEE MY NORTHERN LIGHTS PICTURES.
OH?
YOU EVER SEE THEM?
THE LIGHTS? I'VE SEEN THEM.
THEY REALLY MAKE A DIFFERENCE WHEN YOU'RE ALL ALONE.
OH, YOU BET THEY DO.
AW, THESE ARE REAL NICE!
I GOT THIS NICE NEW CAMERA, I'M TEACHING MYSELF HOW TO USE IT!

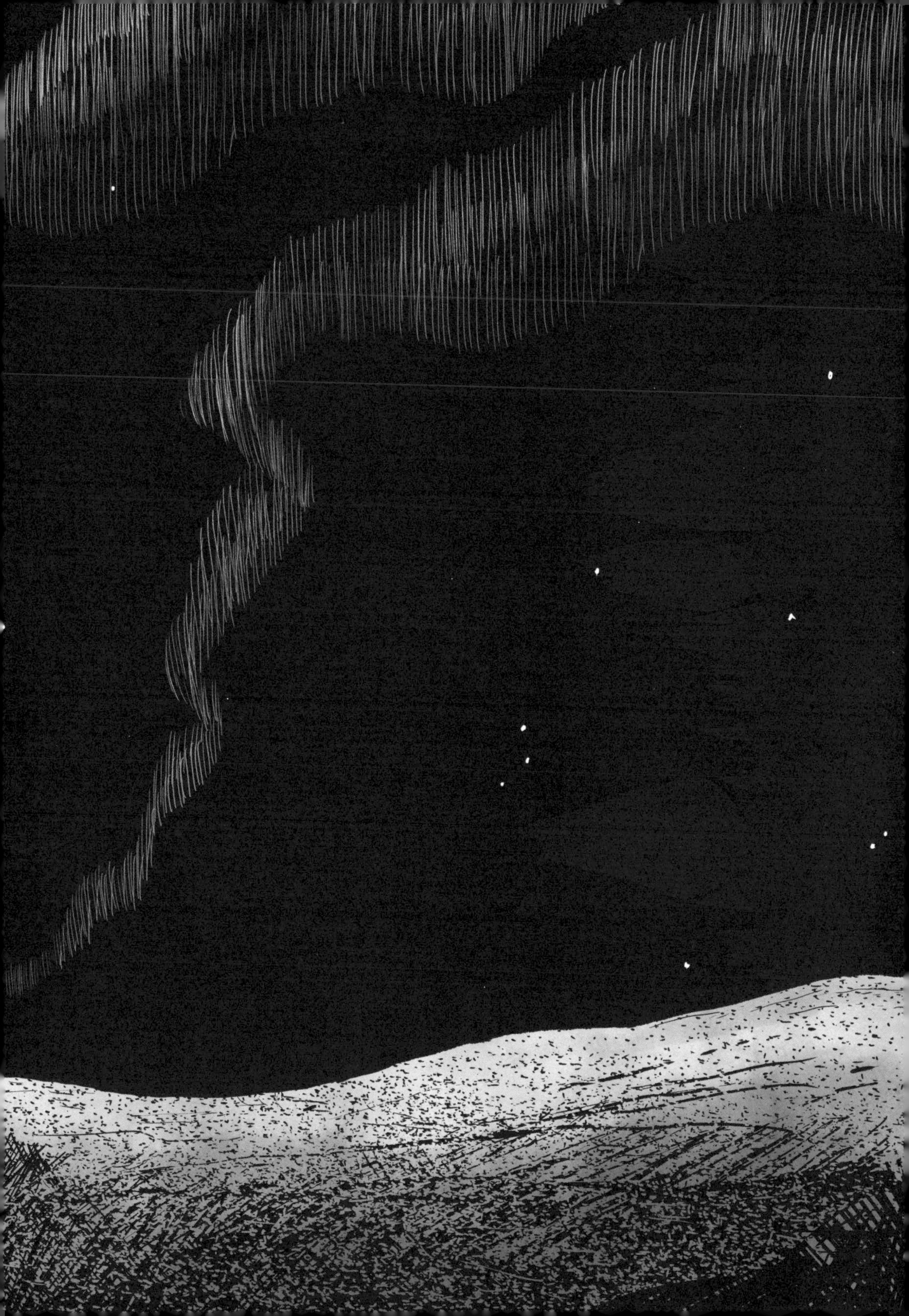

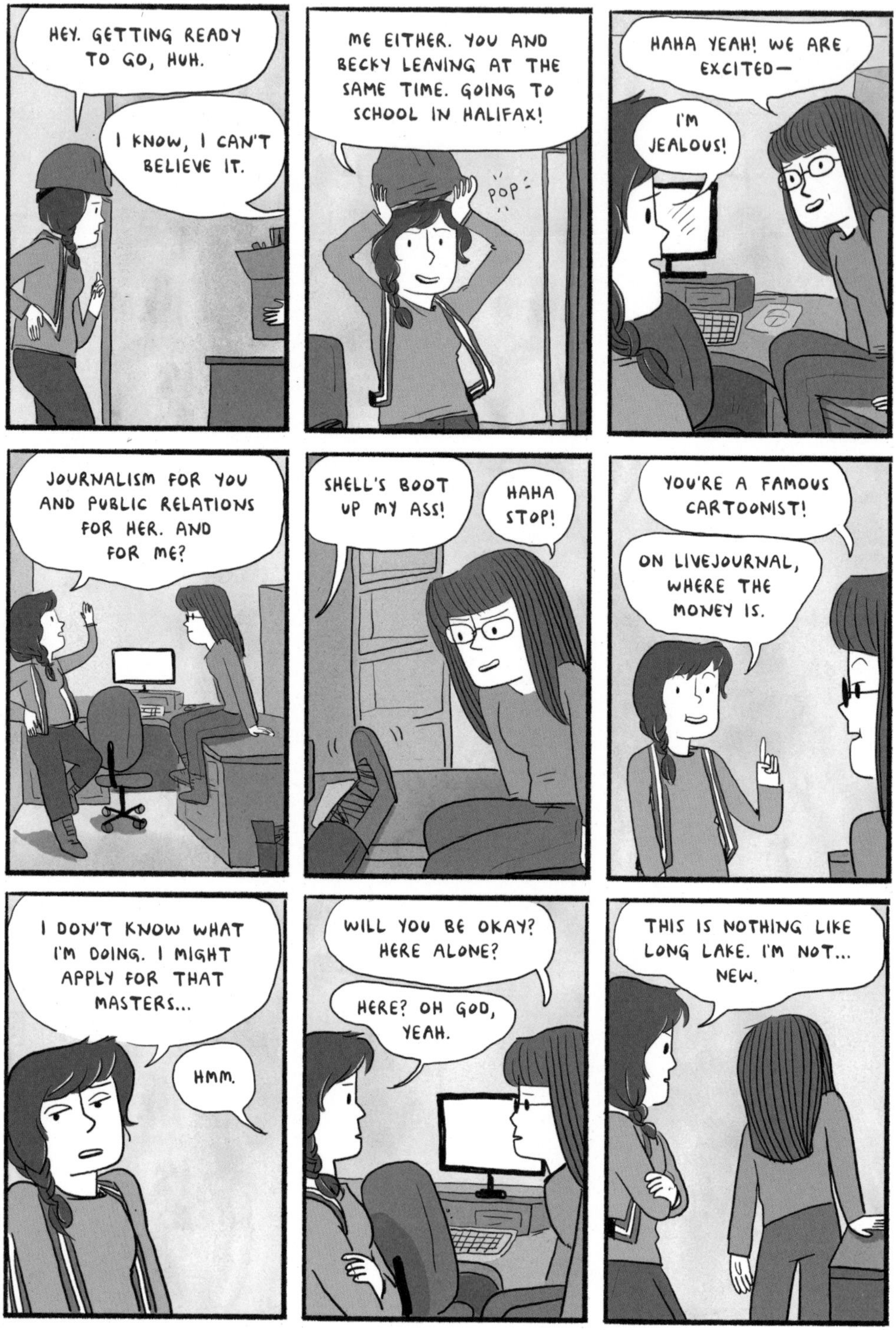
HEY. GETTING READY TO GO, HUH.
I KNOW, I CAN'T BELIEVE IT.
ME EITHER. YOU AND BECKY LEAVING AT THE SAME TIME. GOING TO SCHOOL IN HALIFAX!
POP
HAHA YEAH! WE ARE EXCITED—
I'M JEALOUS!
JOURNALISM FOR YOU AND PUBLIC RELATIONS FOR HER. AND FOR ME?
SHELL'S BOOT UP MY ASS!
HAHA STOP!
YOU'RE A FAMOUS CARTOONIST!
ON LIVEJOURNAL, WHERE THE MONEY IS.
I DON'T KNOW WHAT I'M DOING. I MIGHT APPLY FOR THAT MASTERS...
HMM.
WILL YOU BE OKAY? HERE ALONE?
HERE? OH GOD, YEAH.
THIS IS NOTHING LIKE LONG LAKE. I'M NOT... NEW.

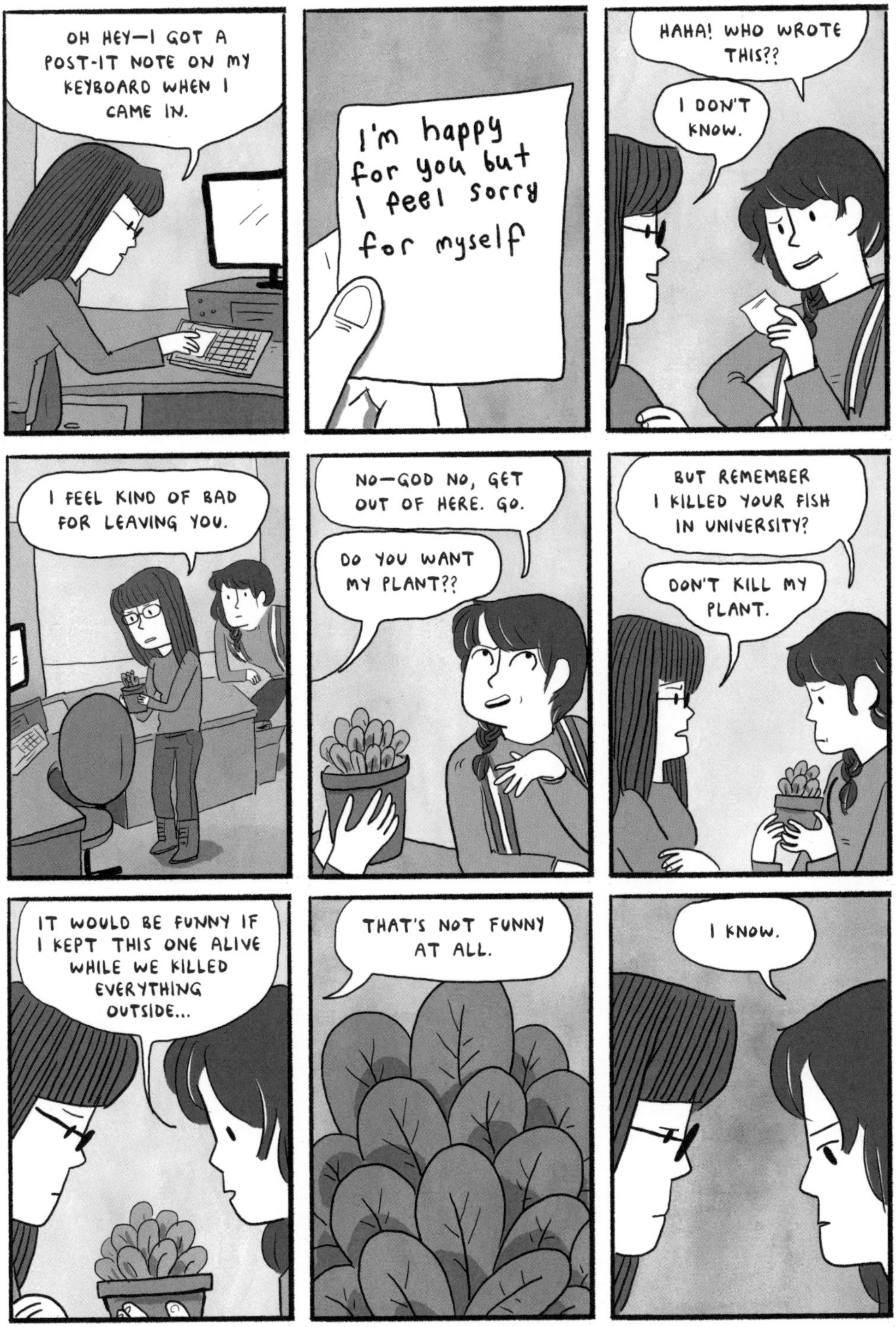
OH HEY—I GOT A POST-IT NOTE ON MY KEYBOARD WHEN I CAME IN.
I'm happy for you but I feel sorry for myself
HAHA! WHO WROTE THIS??
I DON'T KNOW.
I FEEL KIND OF BAD FOR LEAVING YOU.
NO—GOD NO, GET OUT OF HERE. GO.
DO YOU WANT MY PLANT??
BUT REMEMBER I KILLED YOUR FISH IN UNIVERSITY?
DON'T KILL MY PLANT.
IT WOULD BE FUNNY IF I KEPT THIS ONE ALIVE WHILE WE KILLED EVERYTHING OUTSIDE...
THAT'S NOT FUNNY AT ALL.
I KNOW.

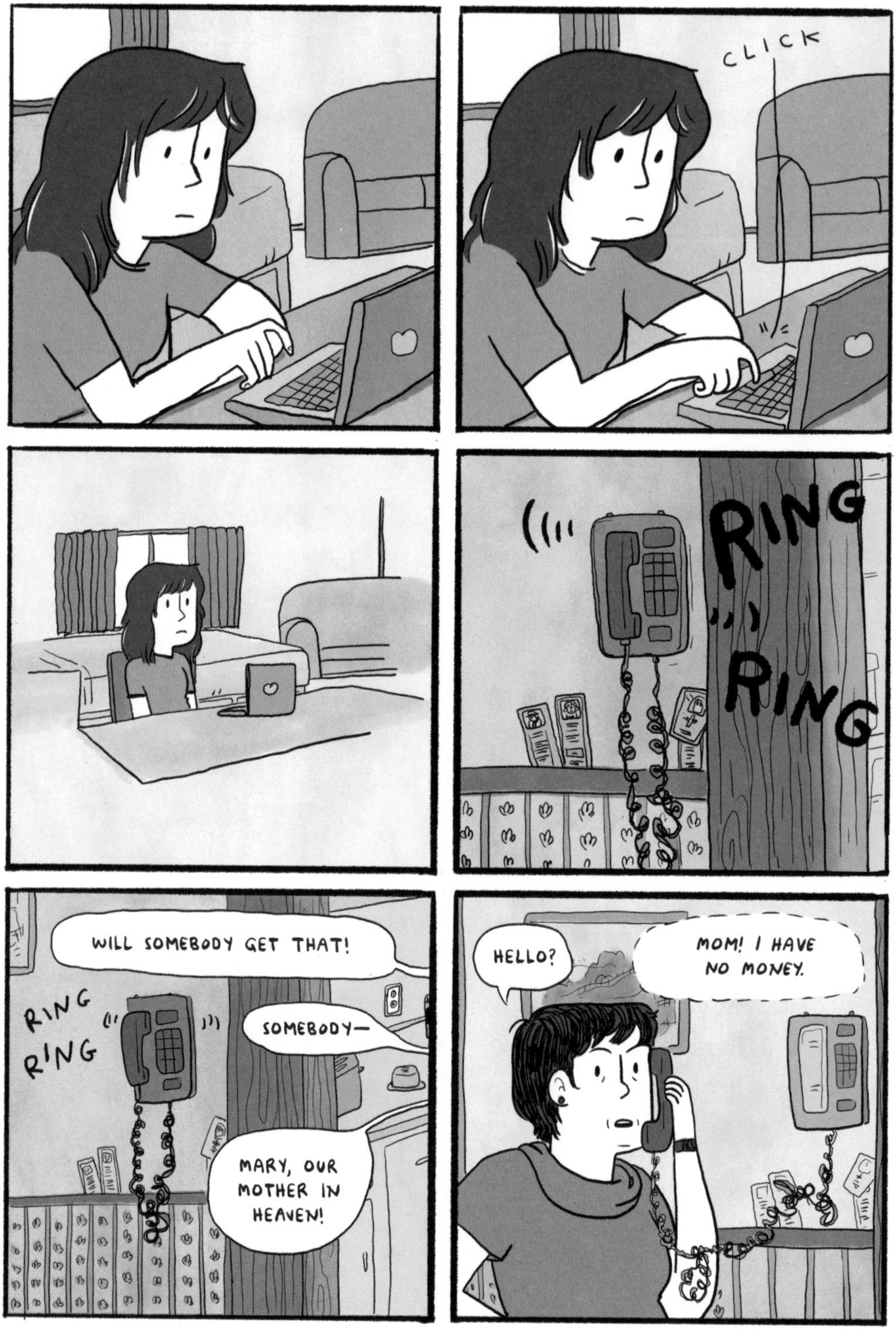
CLICK
RING
RING
WILL SOMEBODY GET THAT!
RING
RING
SOMEBODY—
MARY, OUR MOTHER IN HEAVEN!
HELLO?
MOM! I HAVE NO MONEY.

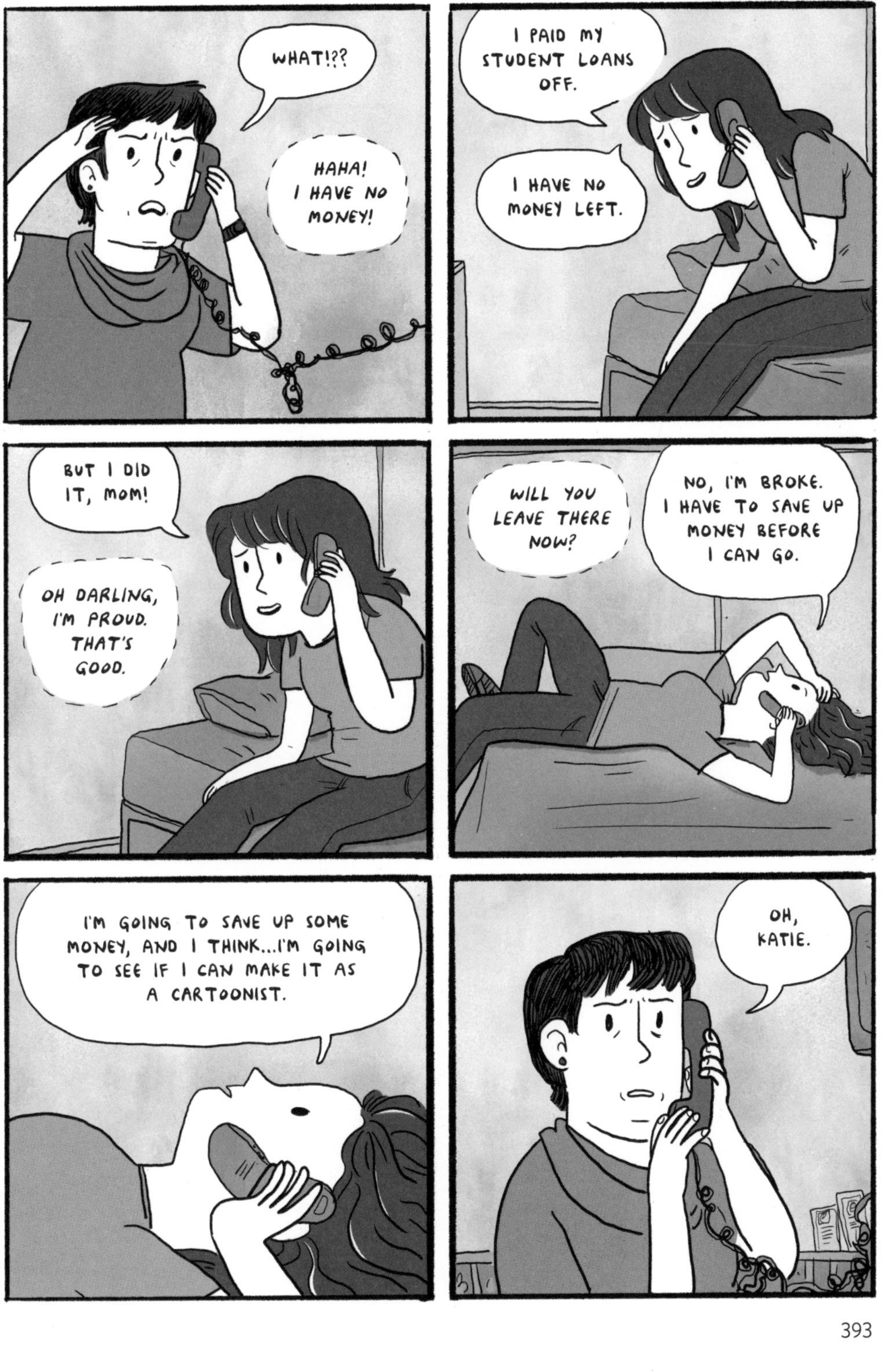
WHAT!??
HAHA! I HAVE NO MONEY!
I PAID MY STUDENT LOANS OFF.
I HAVE NO MONEY LEFT.
BUT I DID IT, MOM!
OH DARLING, I'M PROUD. THAT'S GOOD.
WILL YOU LEAVE THERE NOW?
NO, I'M BROKE. I HAVE TO SAVE UP MONEY BEFORE I CAN GO.
I'M GOING TO SAVE UP SOME MONEY, AND I THINK...I'M GOING TO SEE IF I CAN MAKE IT AS A CARTOONIST.
OH, KATIE.

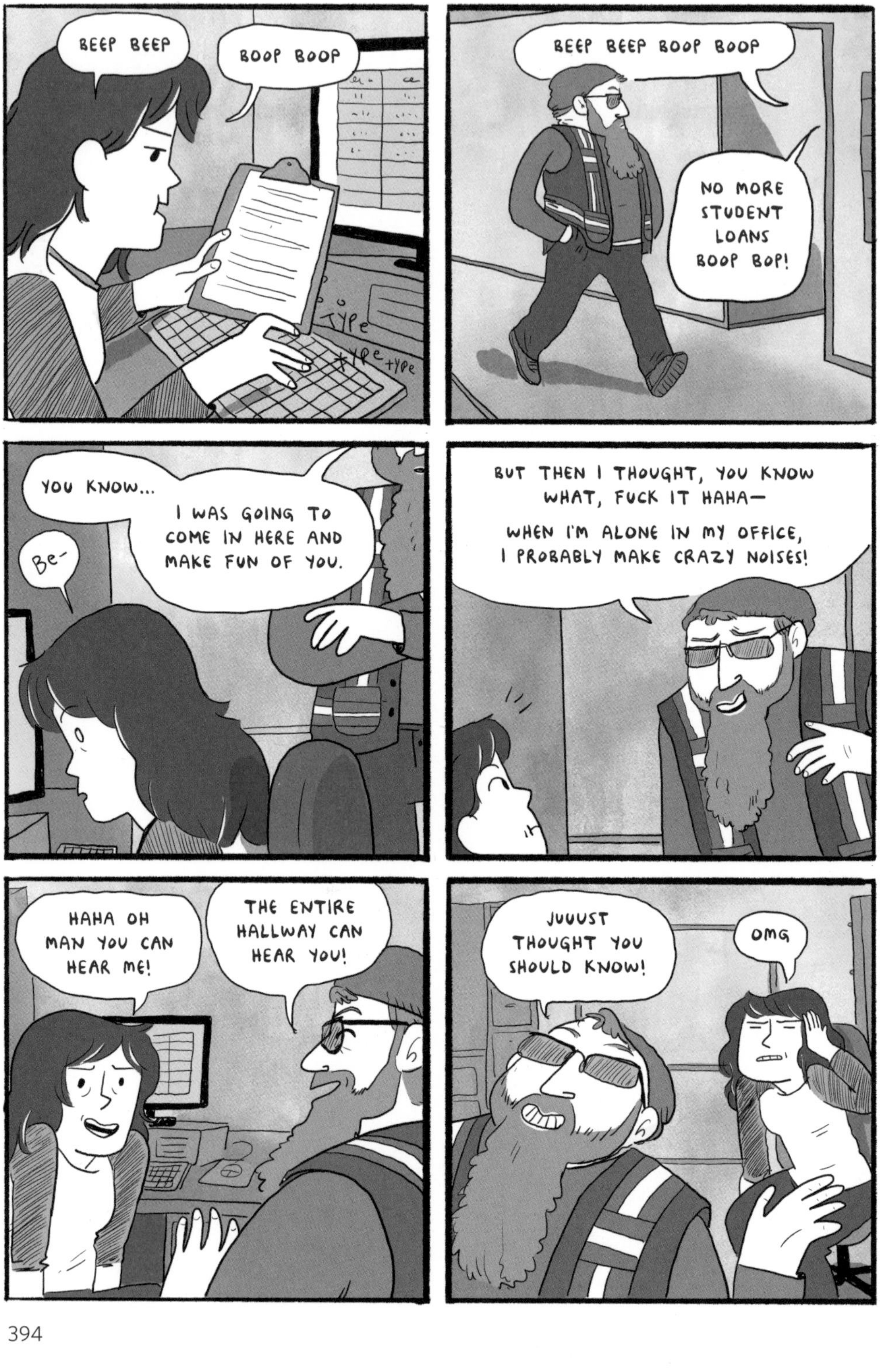
BEEP BEEP
BOOP BOOP
type
type type
BEEP BEEP BOOP BOOP
NO MORE STUDENT LOANS BOOP BOP!
YOU KNOW...
I WAS GOING TO COME IN HERE AND MAKE FUN OF YOU.
Be-
BUT THEN I THOUGHT, YOU KNOW WHAT, FUCK IT HAHA—
WHEN I'M ALONE IN MY OFFICE, I PROBABLY MAKE CRAZY NOISES!
HAHA OH MAN YOU CAN HEAR ME!
THE ENTIRE HALLWAY CAN HEAR YOU!
JUUUST THOUGHT YOU SHOULD KNOW!
OMG

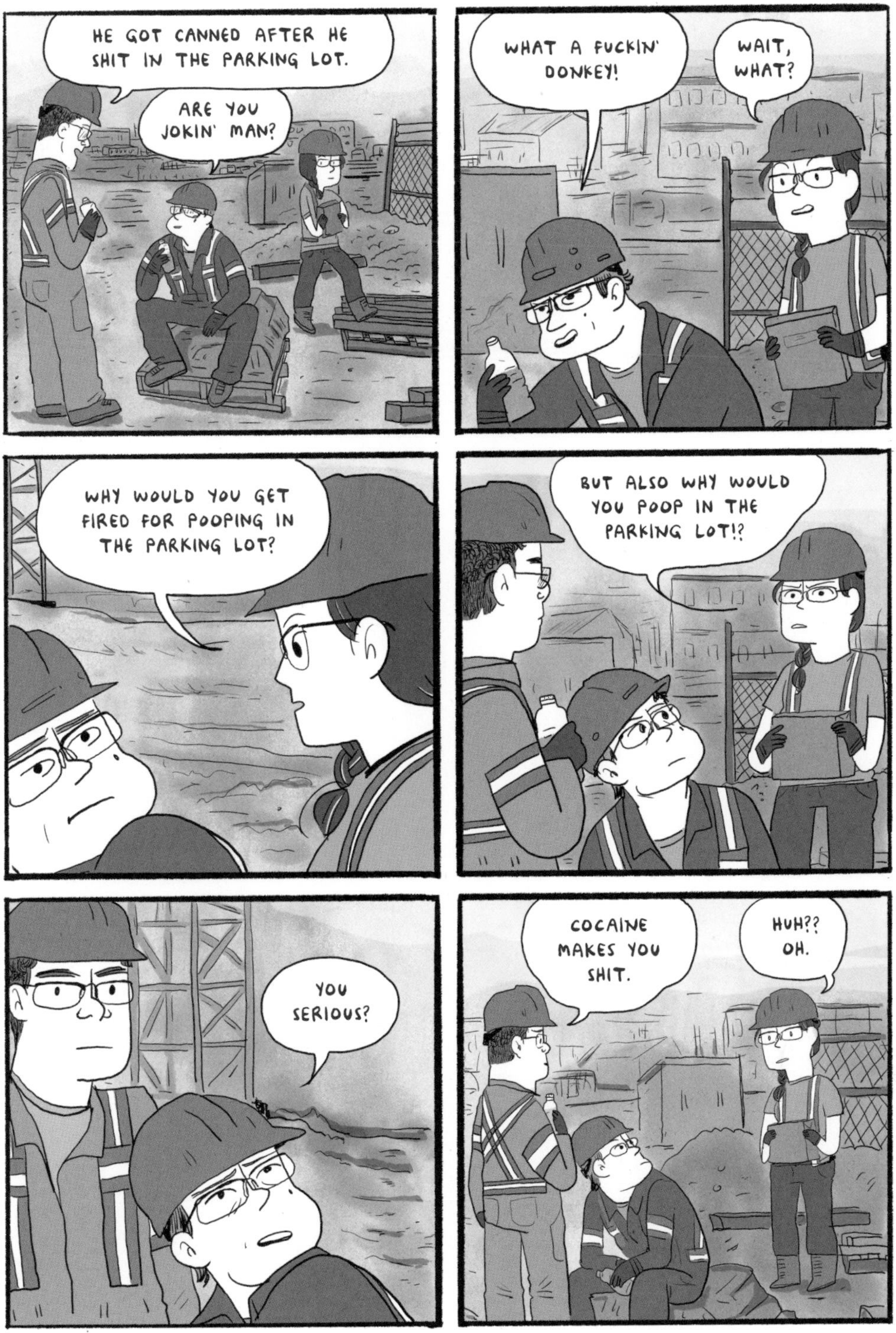
HE GOT CANNED AFTER HE SHIT IN THE PARKING LOT.
ARE YOU JOKIN' MAN?
WHAT A FUCKIN' DONKEY!
WAIT, WHAT?
WHY WOULD YOU GET FIRED FOR POOPING IN THE PARKING LOT?
BUT ALSO WHY WOULD YOU POOP IN THE PARKING LOT!?
YOU SERIOUS?
COCAINE MAKES YOU SHIT.
HUH?? OH.

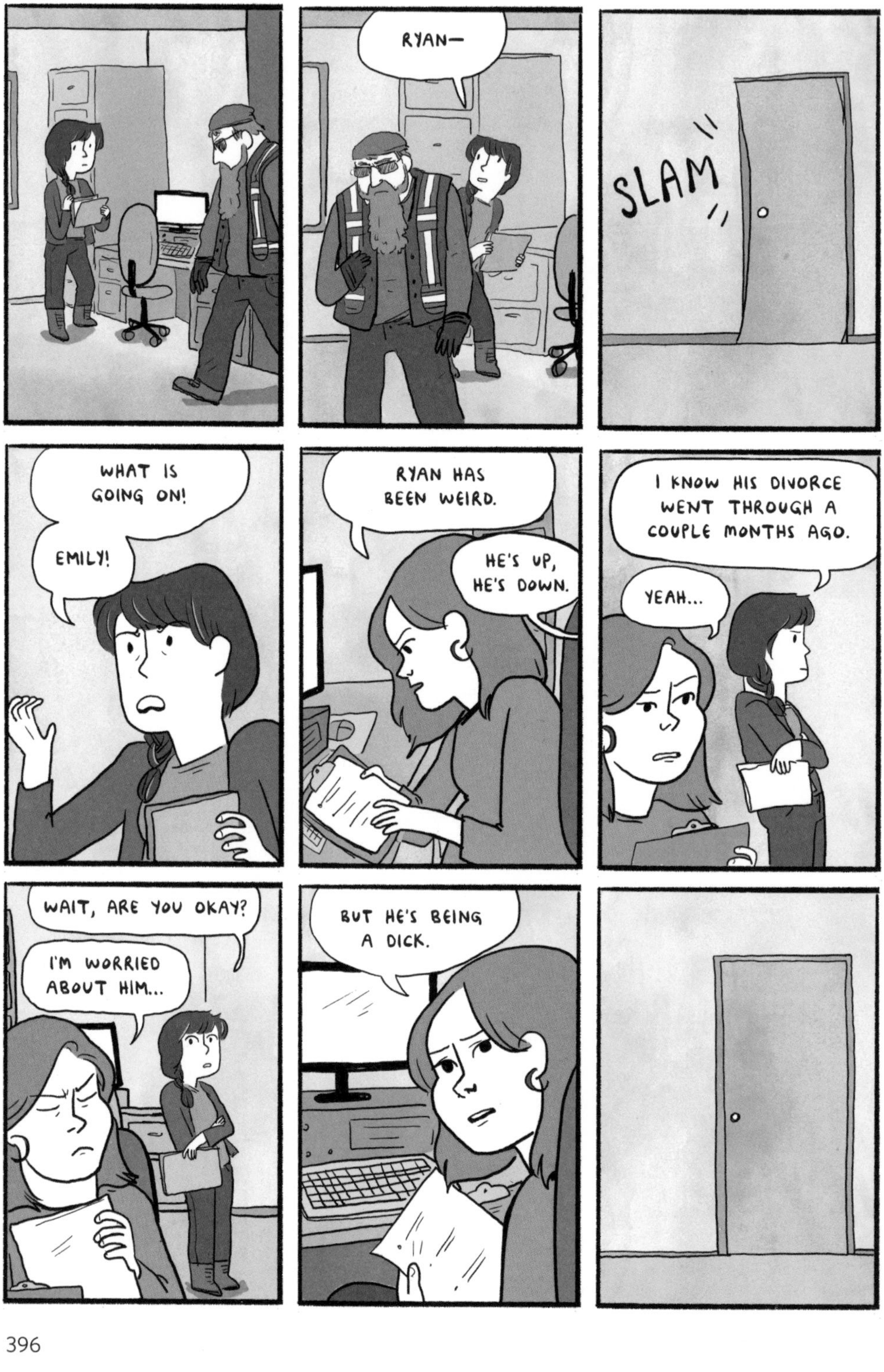
RYAN—
SLAM
WHAT IS GOING ON!
EMILY!
RYAN HAS BEEN WEIRD.
HE'S UP, HE'S DOWN.
I KNOW HIS DIVORCE WENT THROUGH A COUPLE MONTHS AGO.
YEAH...
WAIT, ARE YOU OKAY?
I'M WORRIED ABOUT HIM...
BUT HE'S BEING A DICK.

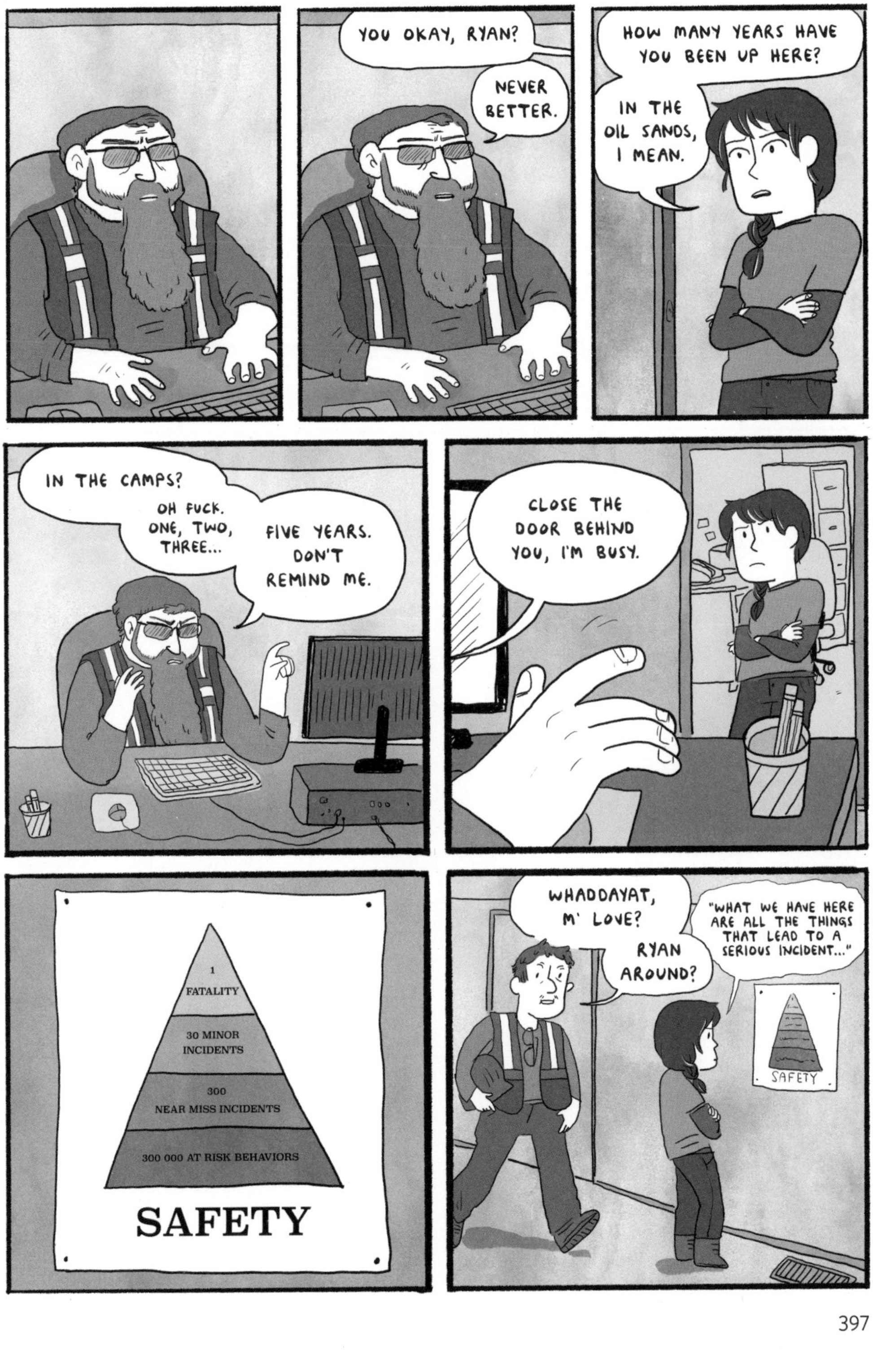
YOU OKAY, RYAN?
NEVER BETTER.
HOW MANY YEARS HAVE YOU BEEN UP HERE?
IN THE OIL SANDS, I MEAN.
IN THE CAMPS?
OH FUCK. ONE, TWO, THREE...
FIVE YEARS. DON'T REMIND ME.
CLOSE THE DOOR BEHIND YOU, I'M BUSY.
1
FATALITY
30 MINOR INCIDENTS
300
NEAR MISS INCIDENTS
300 000 AT RISK BEHAVIORS
SAFETY
WHADDAYAT, M' LOVE?
RYAN AROUND?
"WHAT WE HAVE HERE ARE ALL THE THINGS THAT LEAD TO A SERIOUS INCIDENT..."
SAFETY

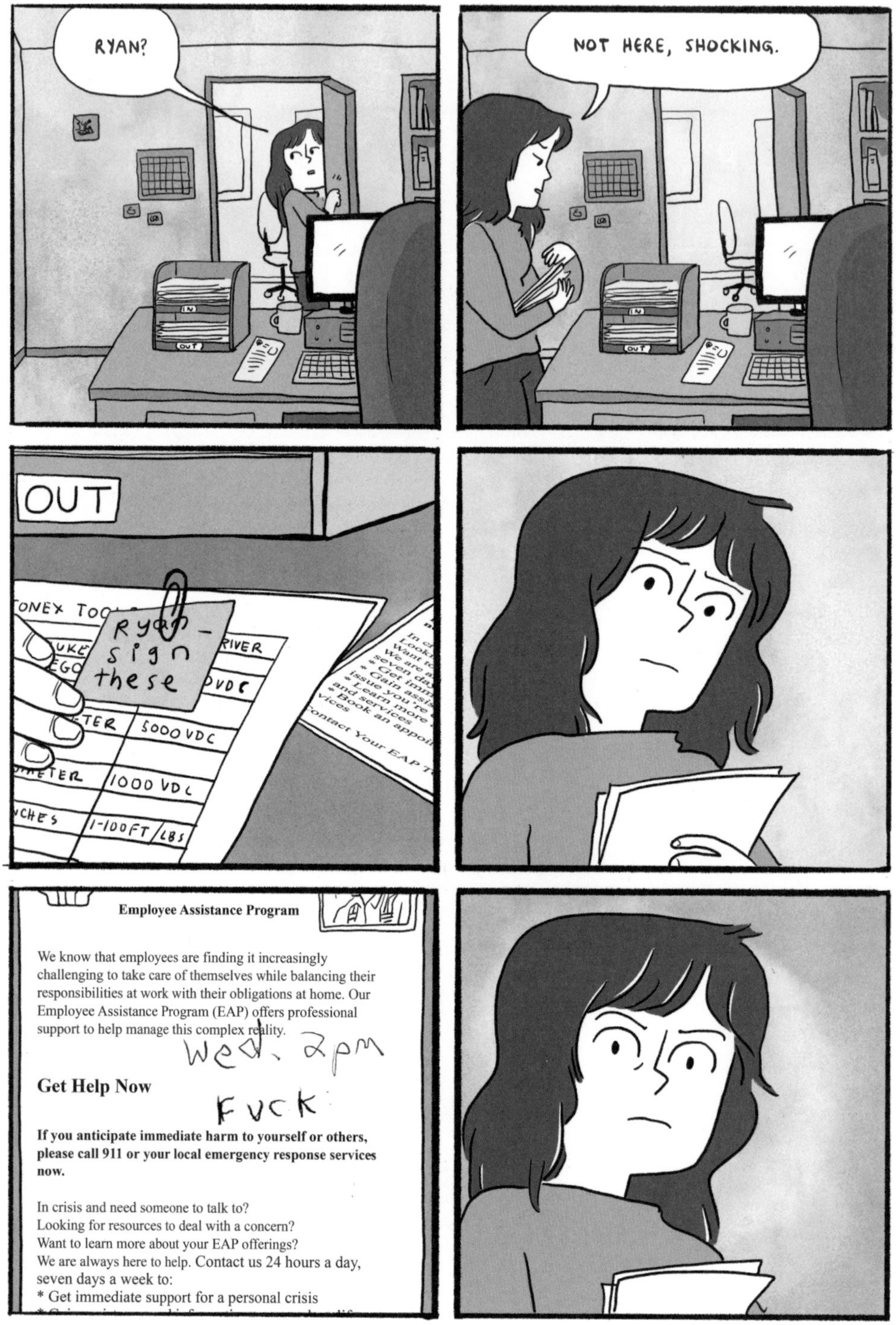
RYAN?
NOT HERE, SHOCKING.
OUT
IN
Ryan - sign these
5000 VDC
1000 VDC
1-100FT/LBS
Employee Assistance Program
We know that employees are finding it increasingly challenging to take care of themselves while balancing their responsibilities at work with their obligations at home. Our Employee Assistance Program (EAP) offers professional support to help manage this complex reality.
Wed. 2pm
Get Help Now
FUCK
If you anticipate immediate harm to yourself or others, please call 911 or your local emergency response services now.
In crisis and need someone to talk to?
Looking for resources to deal with a concern?
Want to learn more about your EAP offerings?
We are always here to help. Contact us 24 hours a day, seven days a week to:
* Get immediate support for a personal crisis

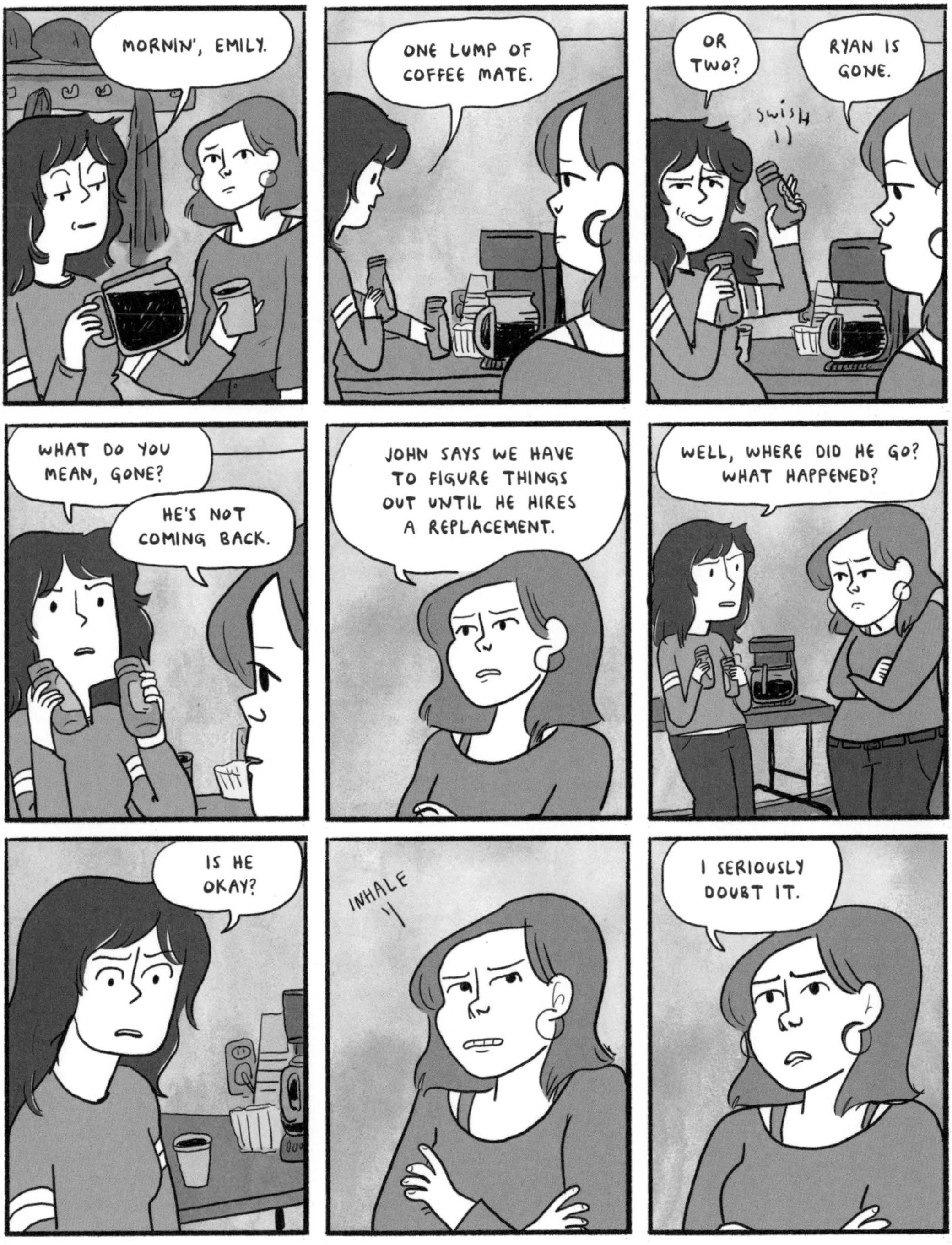
MORNIN', EMILY.
ONE LUMP OF COFFEE MATE.
OR TWO?
SWISH
RYAN IS GONE.
WHAT DO YOU MEAN, GONE?
HE'S NOT COMING BACK.
JOHN SAYS WE HAVE TO FIGURE THINGS OUT UNTIL HE HIRES A REPLACEMENT.
WELL, WHERE DID HE GO? WHAT HAPPENED?
IS HE OKAY?
INHALE
I SERIOUSLY DOUBT IT.

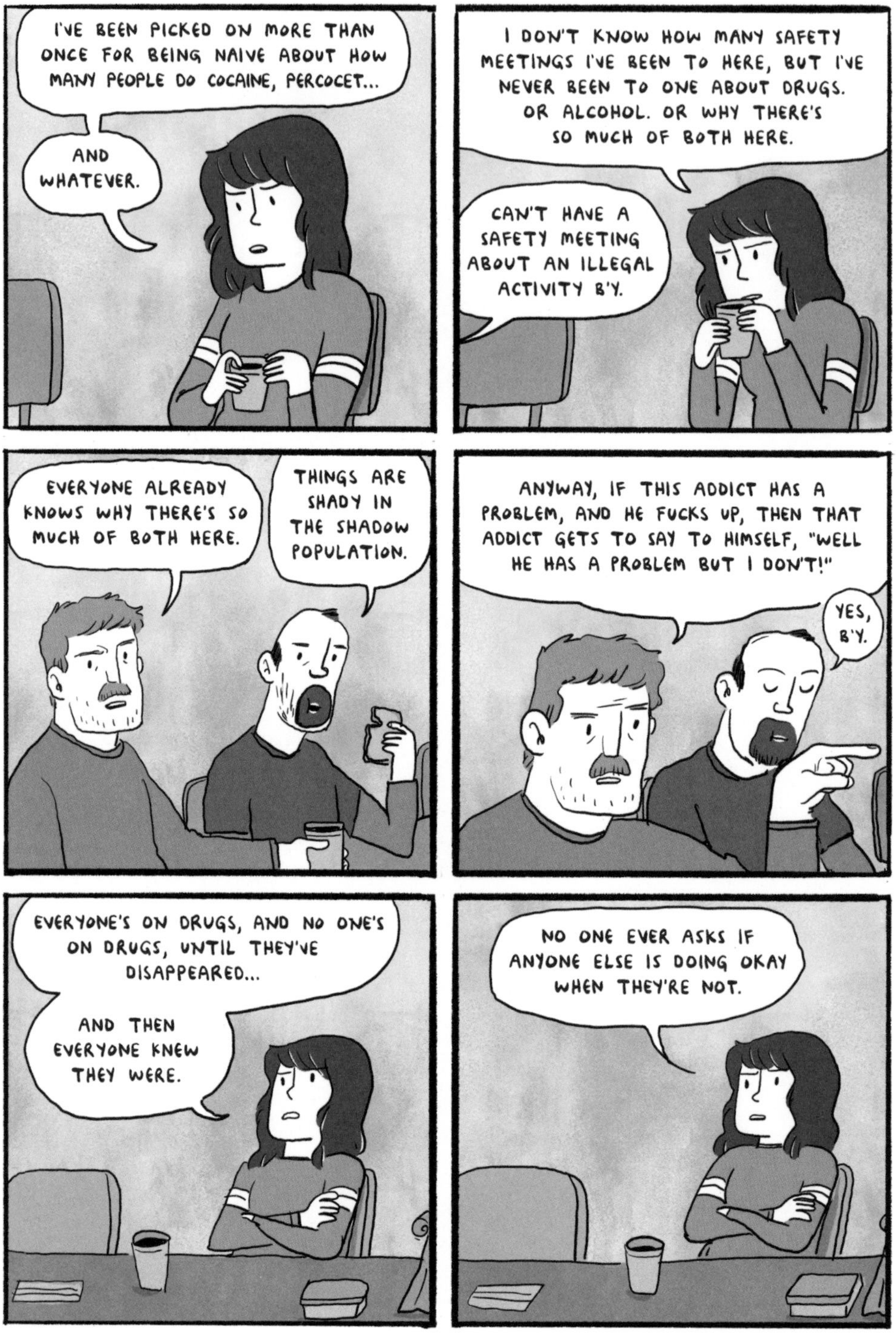
I'VE BEEN PICKED ON MORE THAN ONCE FOR BEING NAIVE ABOUT HOW MANY PEOPLE DO COCAINE, PERCOCET...
AND WHATEVER.
I DON'T KNOW HOW MANY SAFETY MEETINGS I'VE BEEN TO HERE, BUT I'VE NEVER BEEN TO ONE ABOUT DRUGS. OR ALCOHOL. OR WHY THERE'S SO MUCH OF BOTH HERE.
CAN'T HAVE A SAFETY MEETING ABOUT AN ILLEGAL ACTIVITY B'Y.
EVERYONE ALREADY KNOWS WHY THERE'S SO MUCH OF BOTH HERE.
THINGS ARE SHADY IN THE SHADOW POPULATION.
ANYWAY, IF THIS ADDICT HAS A PROBLEM, AND HE FUCKS UP, THEN THAT ADDICT GETS TO SAY TO HIMSELF, "WELL HE HAS A PROBLEM BUT I DON'T!"
YES, B'Y.
EVERYONE'S ON DRUGS, AND NO ONE'S ON DRUGS, UNTIL THEY'VE DISAPPEARED...
AND THEN EVERYONE KNEW THEY WERE.
NO ONE EVER ASKS IF ANYONE ELSE IS DOING OKAY WHEN THEY'RE NOT.

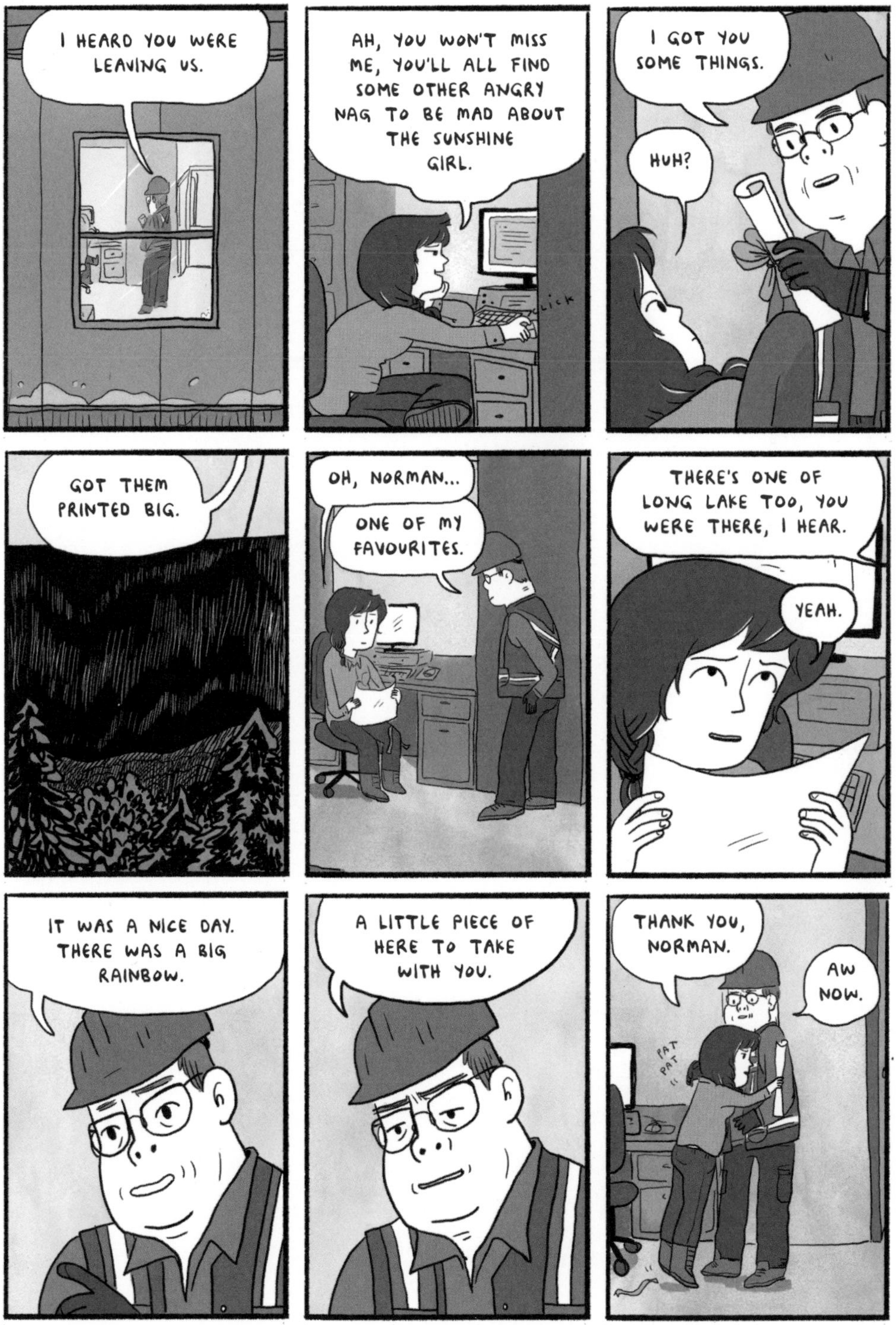
I HEARD YOU WERE LEAVING US.
AH, YOU WON'T MISS ME, YOU'LL ALL FIND SOME OTHER ANGRY NAG TO BE MAD ABOUT THE SUNSHINE GIRL.
CLICK
I GOT YOU SOME THINGS.
HUH?
GOT THEM PRINTED BIG.
OH, NORMAN...
ONE OF MY FAVOURITES.
THERE'S ONE OF LONG LAKE TOO, YOU WERE THERE, I HEAR.
YEAH.
IT WAS A NICE DAY. THERE WAS A BIG RAINBOW.
A LITTLE PIECE OF HERE TO TAKE WITH YOU.
THANK YOU, NORMAN.
AW NOW.
PAT PAT

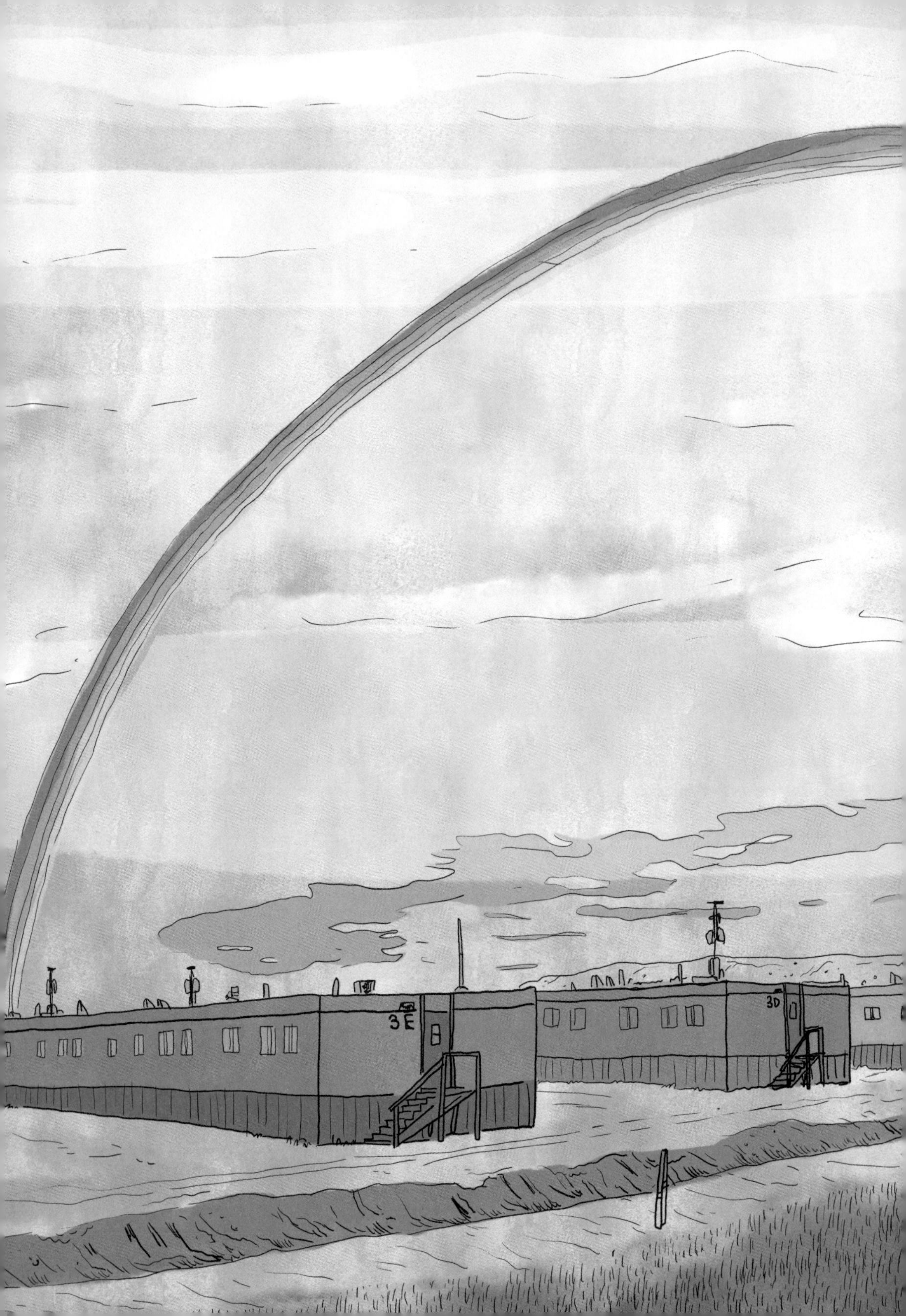
3E
3D

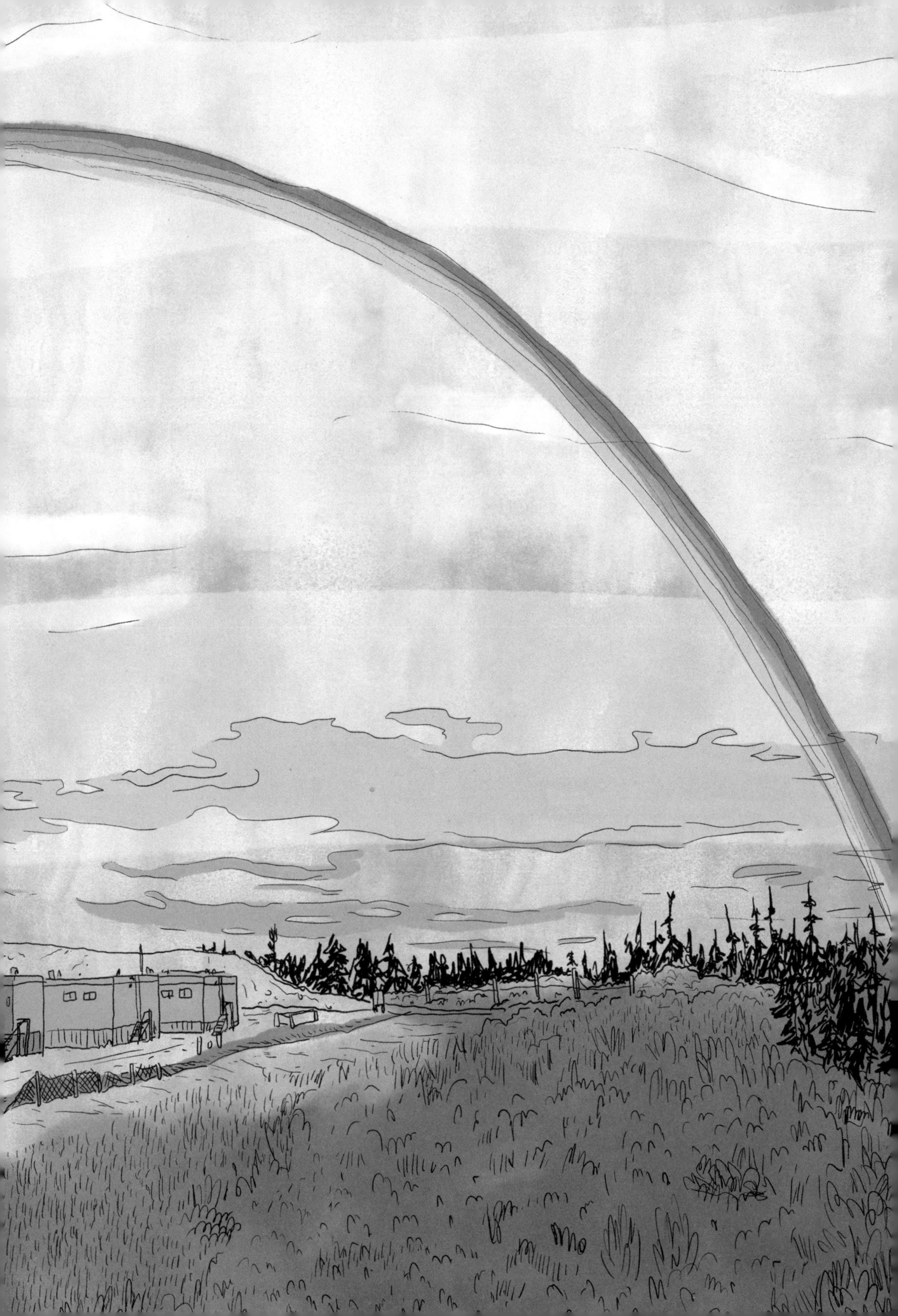

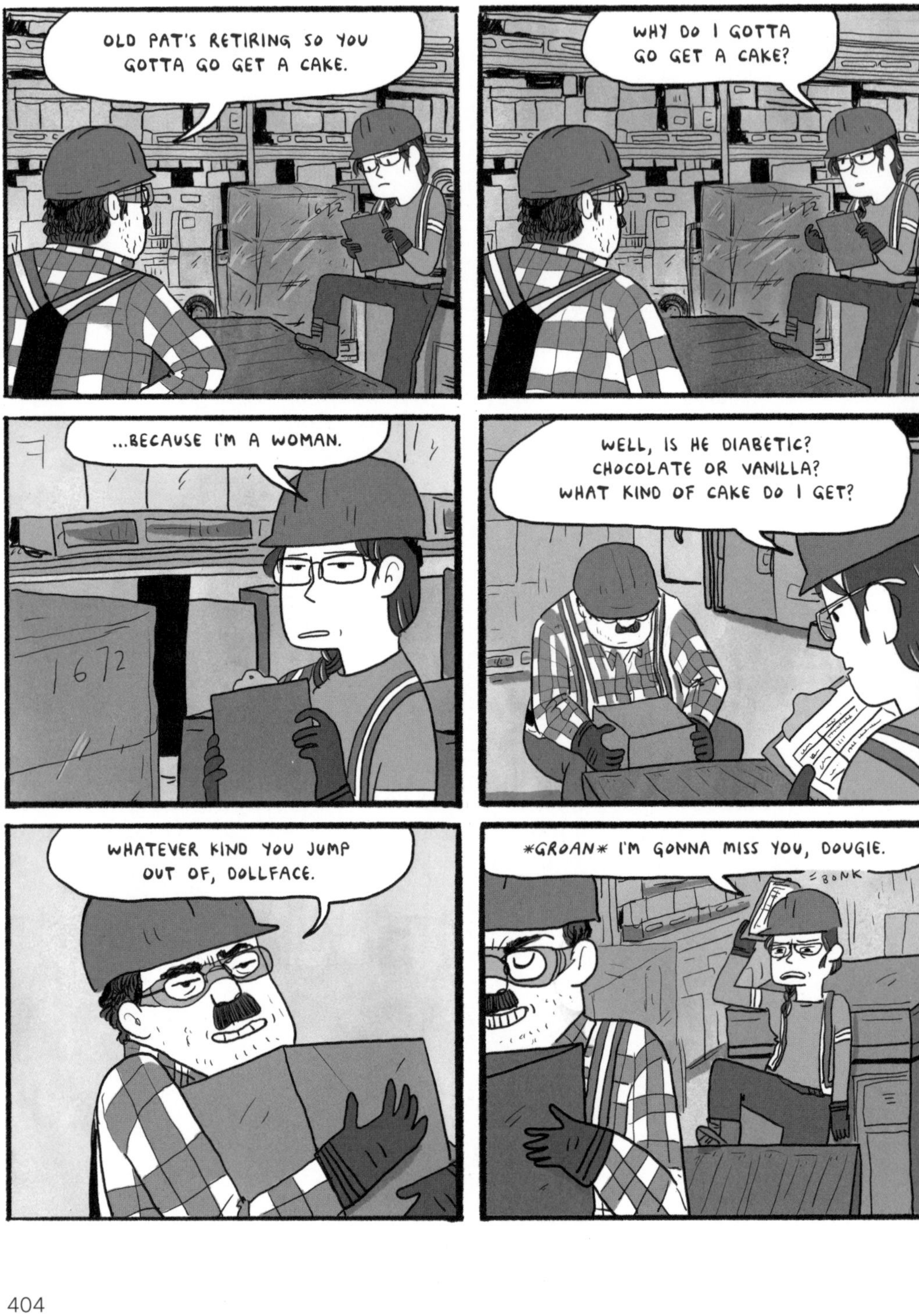
OLD PAT'S RETIRING SO YOU GOTTA GO GET A CAKE.
WHY DO I GOTTA GO GET A CAKE?
...BECAUSE I'M A WOMAN.
WELL, IS HE DIABETIC? CHOCOLATE OR VANILLA? WHAT KIND OF CAKE DO I GET?
WHATEVER KIND YOU JUMP OUT OF, DOLLFACE.
GROAN I'M GONNA MISS YOU, DOUGIE.
BONK

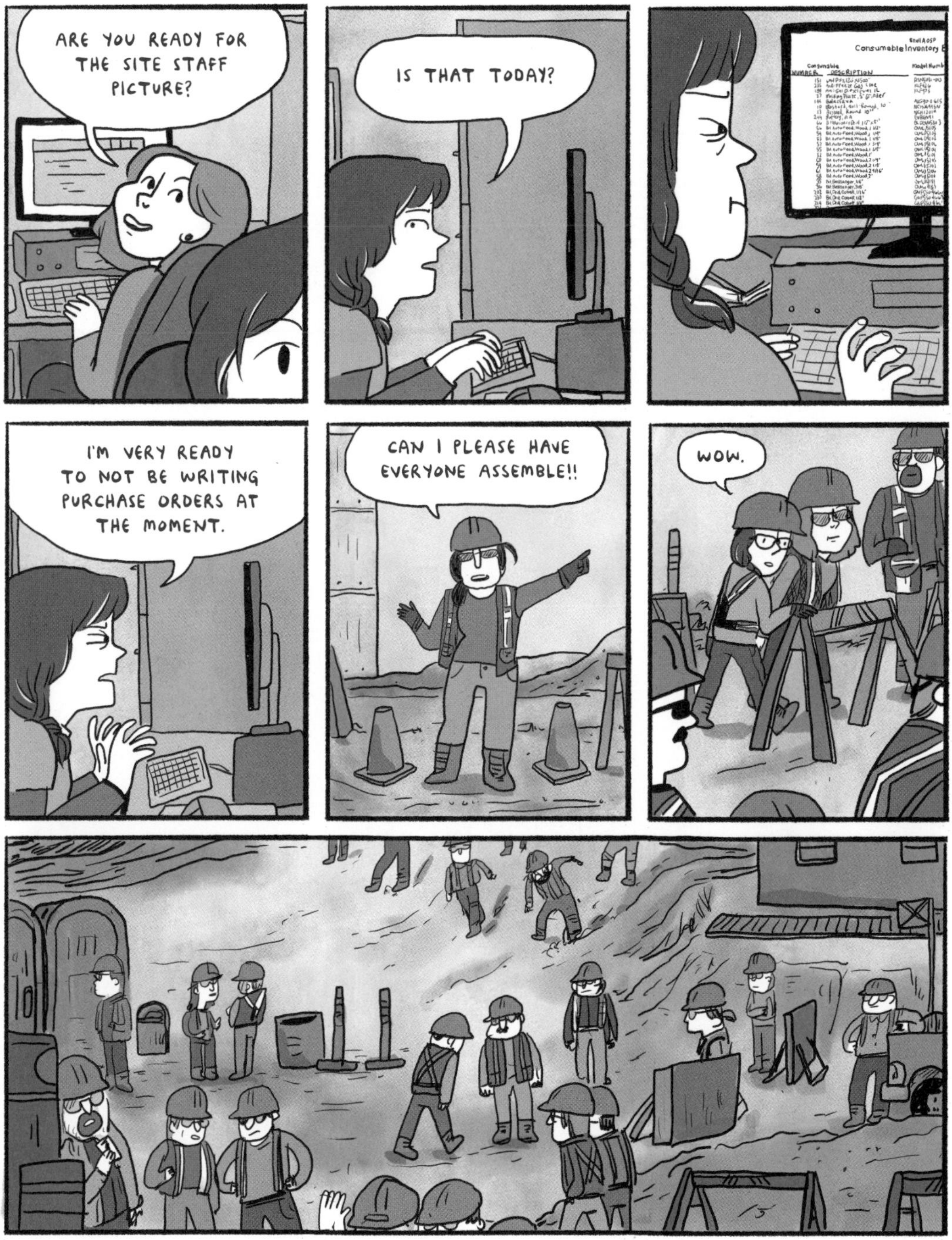
ARE YOU READY FOR THE SITE STAFF PICTURE?
IS THAT TODAY?
I'M VERY READY TO NOT BE WRITING PURCHASE ORDERS AT THE MOMENT.
CAN I PLEASE HAVE EVERYONE ASSEMBLE!!
WOW.

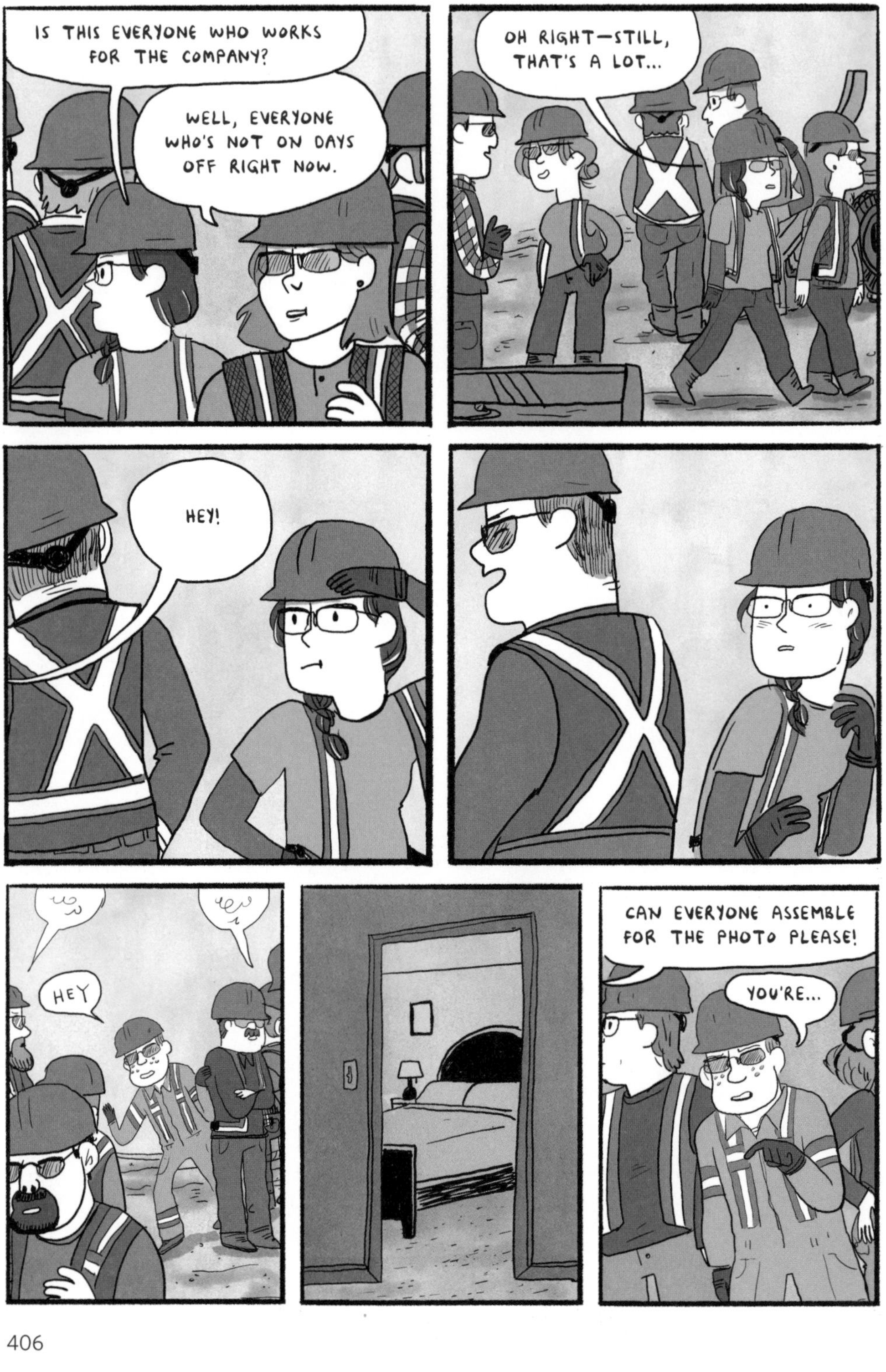
IS THIS EVERYONE WHO WORKS FOR THE COMPANY?
WELL, EVERYONE WHO'S NOT ON DAYS OFF RIGHT NOW.
OH RIGHT—STILL, THAT'S A LOT...
HEY!
HEY
CAN EVERYONE ASSEMBLE FOR THE PHOTO PLEASE!
YOU'RE...

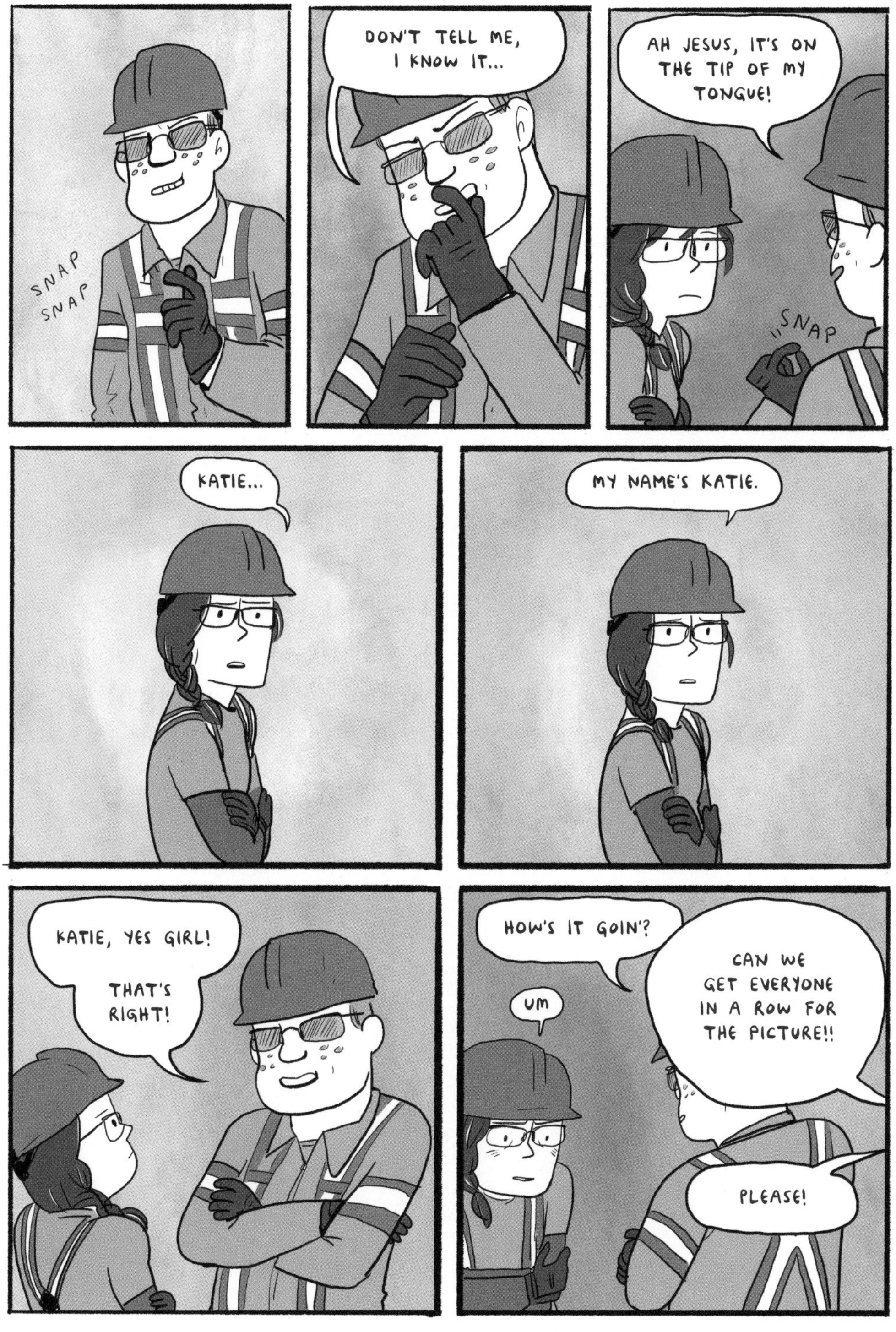
SNAP SNAP
DON'T TELL ME, I KNOW IT...
AH JESUS, IT'S ON THE TIP OF MY TONGUE!
SNAP
KATIE...
MY NAME'S KATIE.
KATIE, YES GIRL!
THAT'S RIGHT!
HOW'S IT GOIN'?
UM
CAN WE GET EVERYONE IN A ROW FOR THE PICTURE!!
PLEASE!

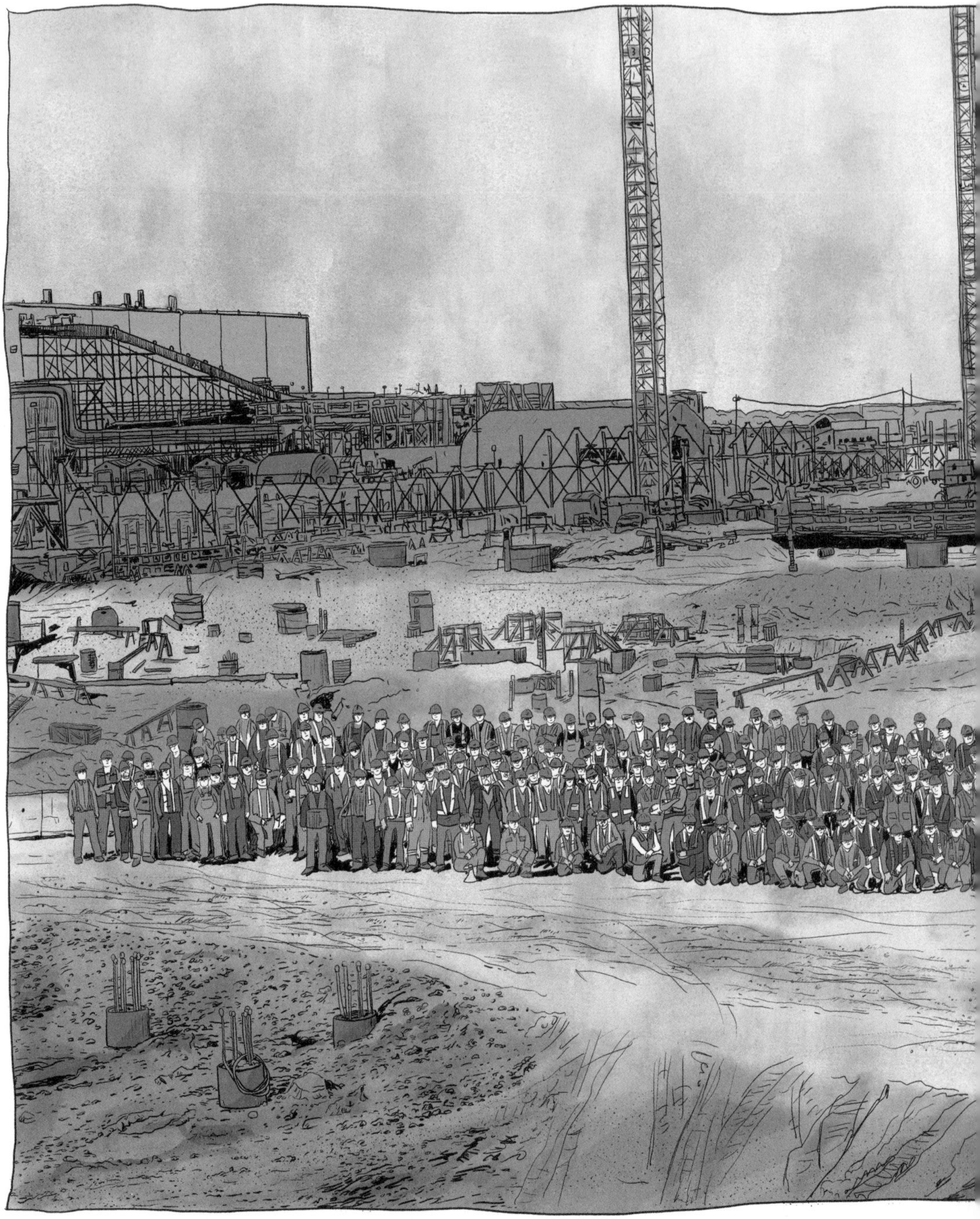

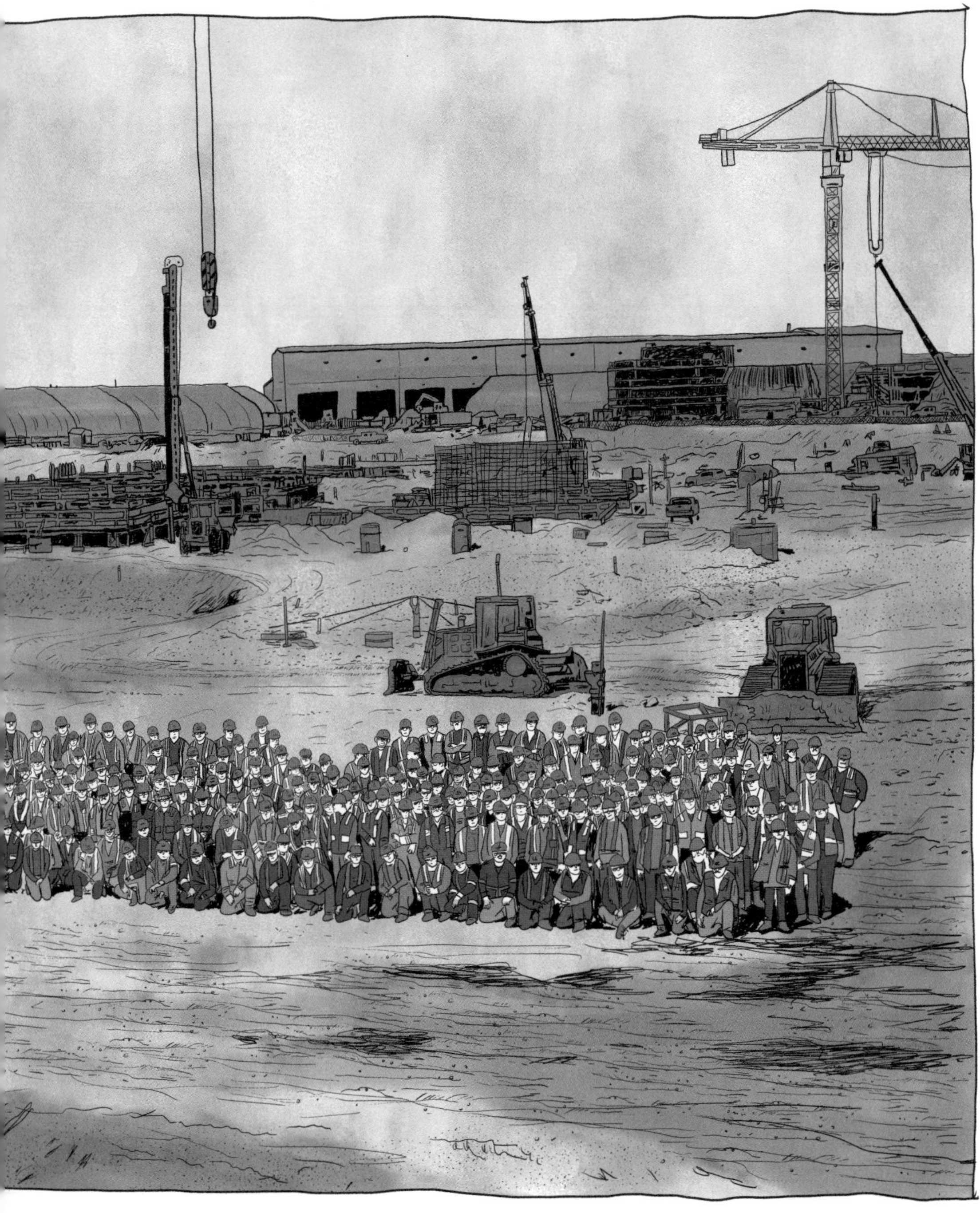

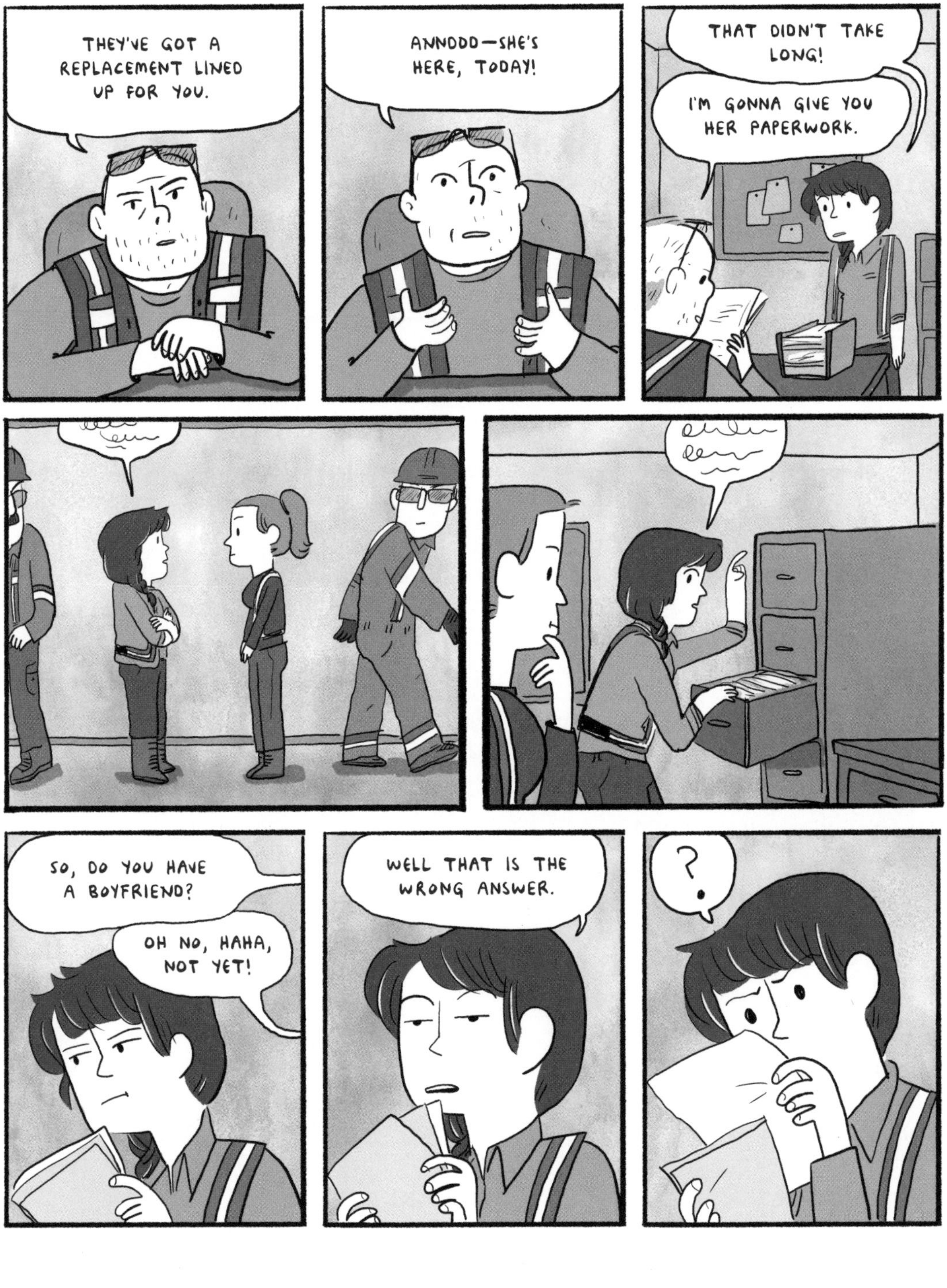
THEY'VE GOT A REPLACEMENT LINED UP FOR YOU.
ANNODD—SHE'S HERE, TODAY!
THAT DIDN'T TAKE LONG!
I'M GONNA GIVE YOU HER PAPERWORK.
SO, DO YOU HAVE A BOYFRIEND?
OH NO, HAHA, NOT YET!
WELL THAT IS THE WRONG ANSWER.
?

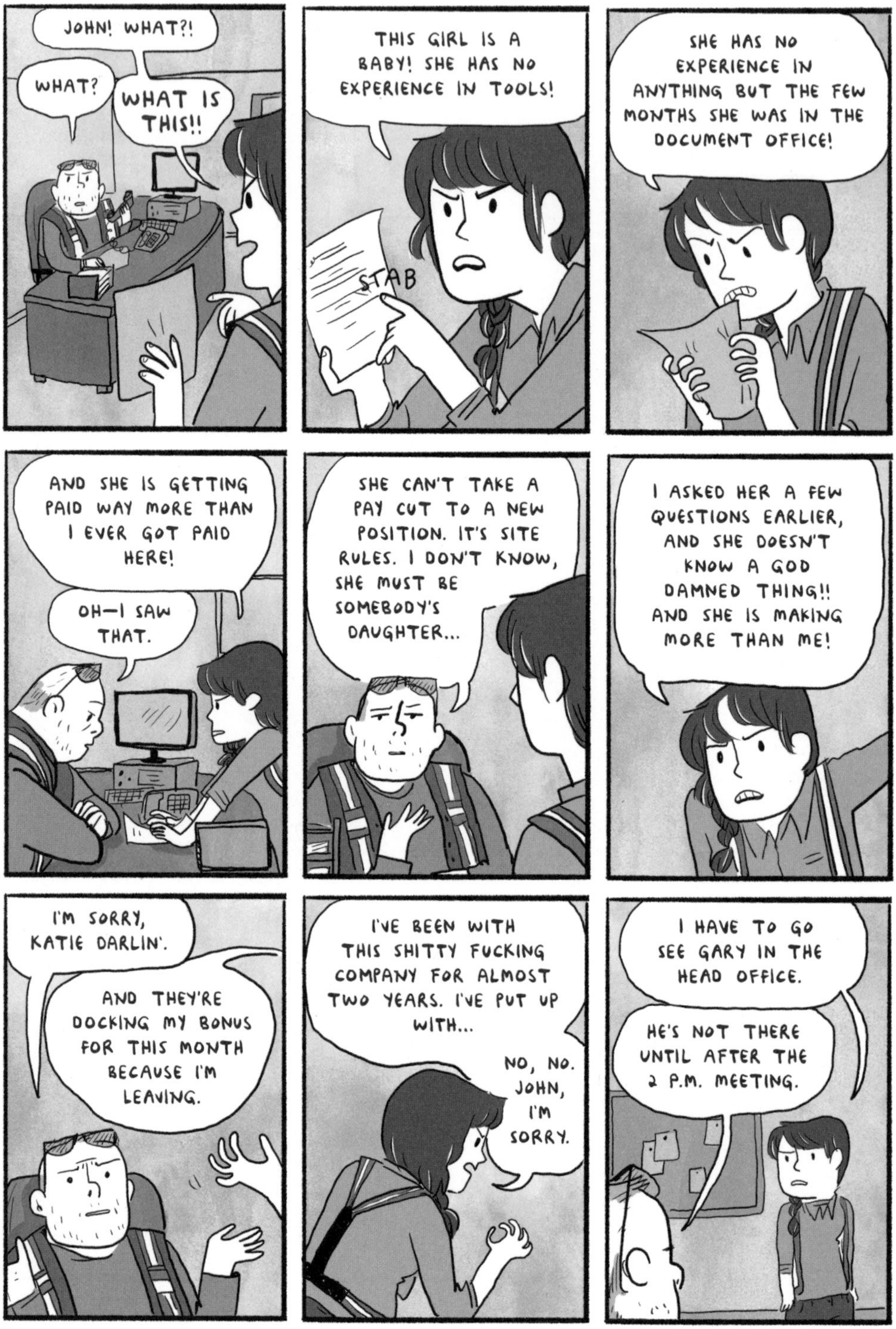
JOHN! WHAT?!
WHAT?
WHAT IS THIS!!
THIS GIRL IS A BABY! SHE HAS NO EXPERIENCE IN TOOLS!
STAB
SHE HAS NO EXPERIENCE IN ANYTHING BUT THE FEW MONTHS SHE WAS IN THE DOCUMENT OFFICE!
AND SHE IS GETTING PAID WAY MORE THAN I EVER GOT PAID HERE!
OH—I SAW THAT.
SHE CAN'T TAKE A PAY CUT TO A NEW POSITION. IT'S SITE RULES. I DON'T KNOW, SHE MUST BE SOMEBODY'S DAUGHTER...
I ASKED HER A FEW QUESTIONS EARLIER, AND SHE DOESN'T KNOW A GOD DAMNED THING!! AND SHE IS MAKING MORE THAN ME!
I'M SORRY, KATIE DARLIN'.
AND THEY'RE DOCKING MY BONUS FOR THIS MONTH BECAUSE I'M LEAVING.
I'VE BEEN WITH THIS SHITTY FUCKING COMPANY FOR ALMOST TWO YEARS. I'VE PUT UP WITH...
NO, NO. JOHN, I'M SORRY.
I HAVE TO GO SEE GARY IN THE HEAD OFFICE.
HE'S NOT THERE UNTIL AFTER THE 2 P.M. MEETING.

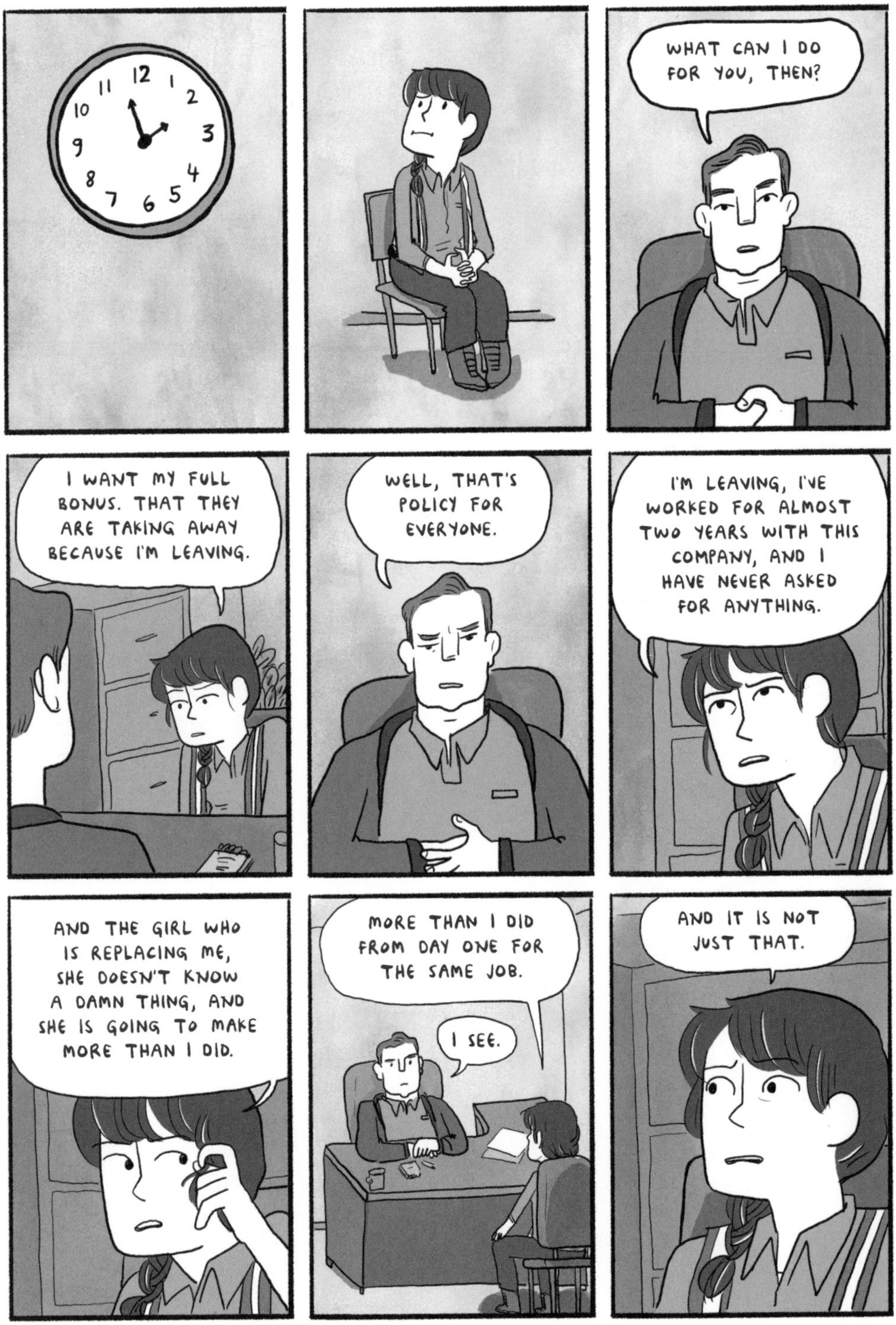
WHAT CAN I DO FOR YOU, THEN?
I WANT MY FULL BONUS. THAT THEY ARE TAKING AWAY BECAUSE I'M LEAVING.
WELL, THAT'S POLICY FOR EVERYONE.
I'M LEAVING, I'VE WORKED FOR ALMOST TWO YEARS WITH THIS COMPANY, AND I HAVE NEVER ASKED FOR ANYTHING.
AND THE GIRL WHO IS REPLACING ME, SHE DOESN'T KNOW A DAMN THING, AND SHE IS GOING TO MAKE MORE THAN I DID.
MORE THAN I DID FROM DAY ONE FOR THE SAME JOB.
I SEE.
AND IT IS NOT JUST THAT.

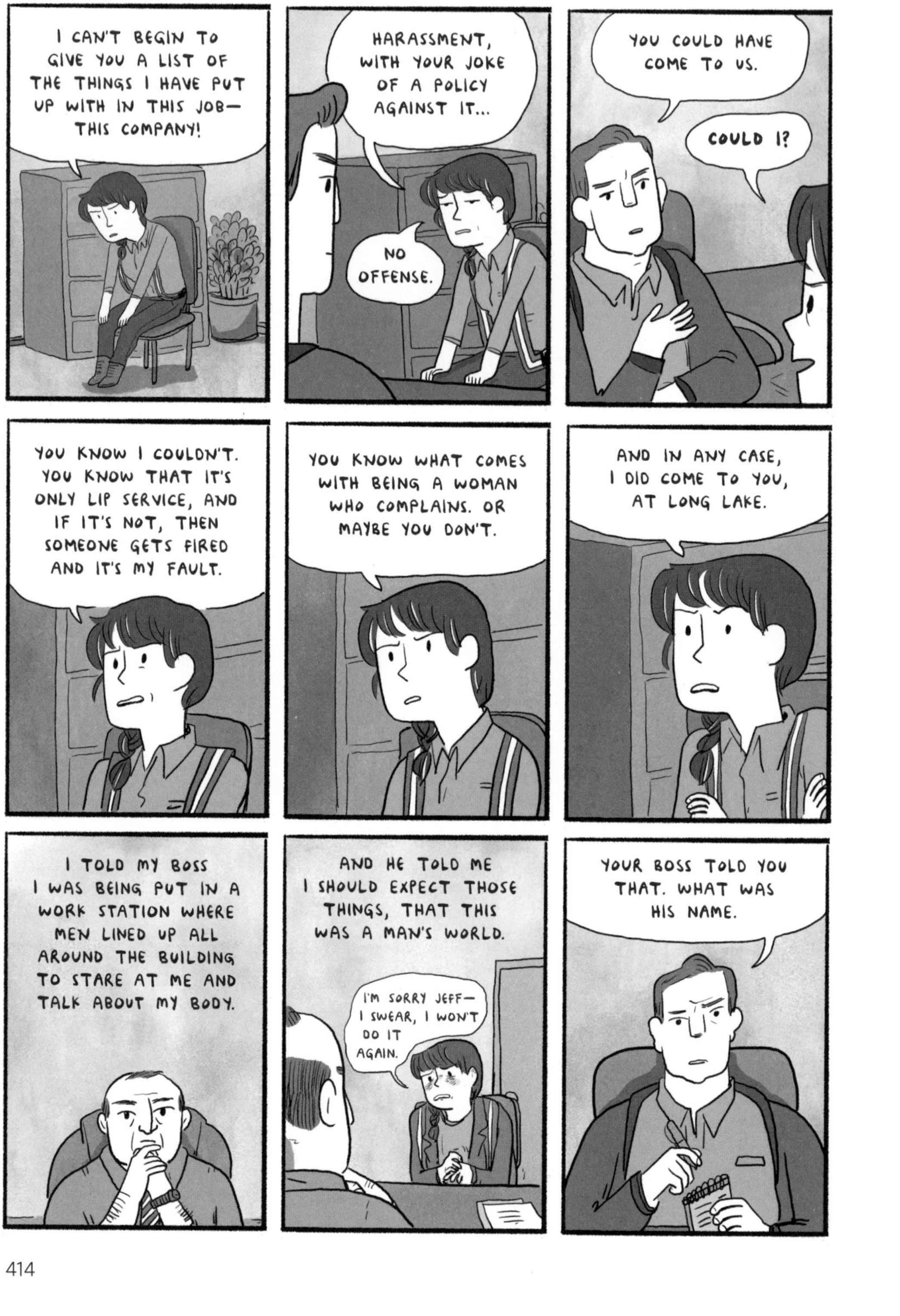
I CAN'T BEGIN TO GIVE YOU A LIST OF THE THINGS I HAVE PUT UP WITH IN THIS JOB— THIS COMPANY!
HARASSMENT, WITH YOUR JOKE OF A POLICY AGAINST IT...
NO OFFENSE.
YOU COULD HAVE COME TO US.
COULD I?
YOU KNOW I COULDN'T. YOU KNOW THAT IT'S ONLY LIP SERVICE, AND IF IT'S NOT, THEN SOMEONE GETS FIRED AND IT'S MY FAULT.
YOU KNOW WHAT COMES WITH BEING A WOMAN WHO COMPLAINS. OR MAYBE YOU DON'T.
AND IN ANY CASE, I DID COME TO YOU, AT LONG LAKE.
I TOLD MY BOSS I WAS BEING PUT IN A WORK STATION WHERE MEN LINED UP ALL AROUND THE BUILDING TO STARE AT ME AND TALK ABOUT MY BODY.
AND HE TOLD ME I SHOULD EXPECT THOSE THINGS, THAT THIS WAS A MAN'S WORLD.
I'M SORRY JEFF— I SWEAR, I WON'T DO IT AGAIN.
YOUR BOSS TOLD YOU THAT. WHAT WAS HIS NAME.

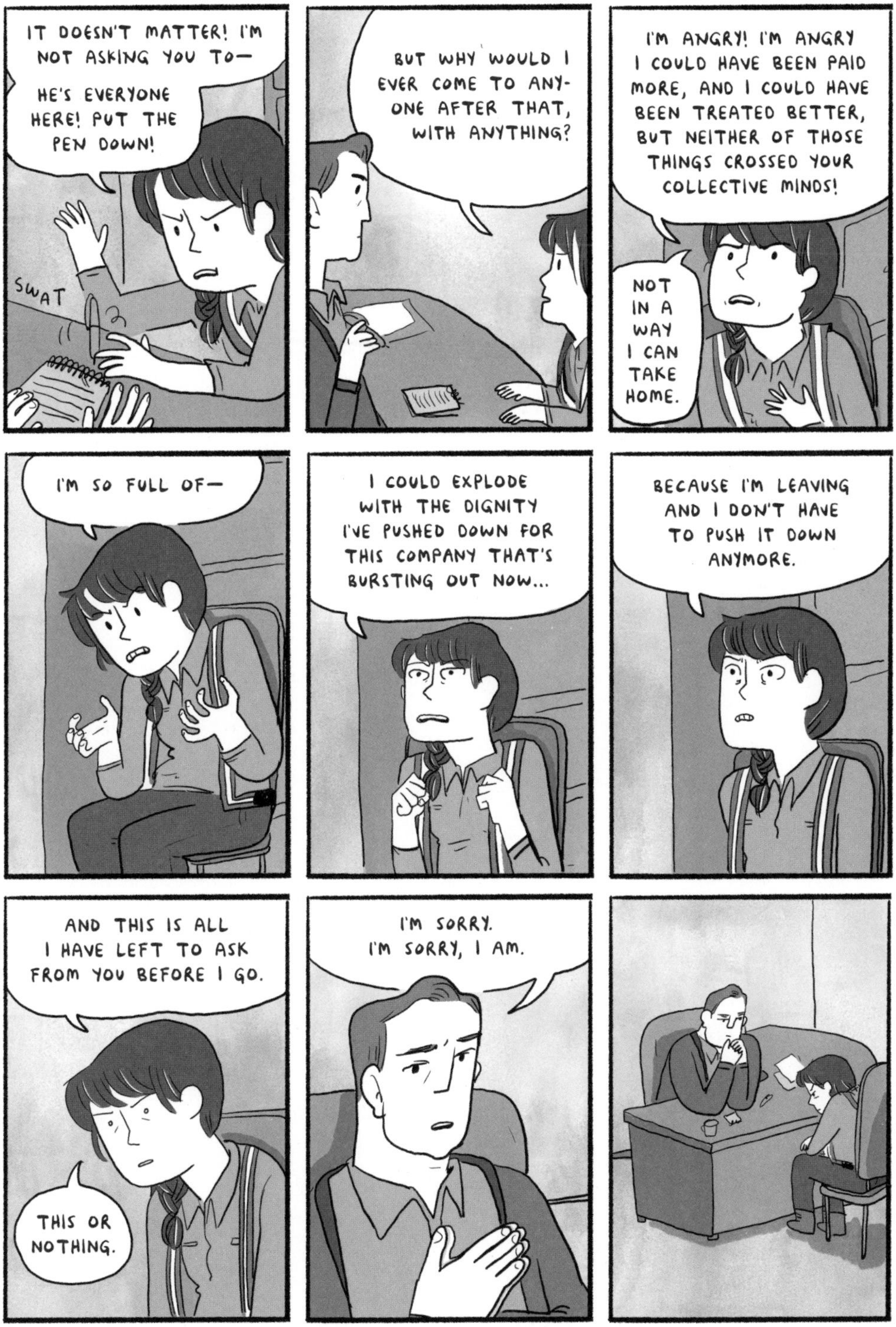
IT DOESN'T MATTER! I'M NOT ASKING YOU TO—
HE'S EVERYONE HERE! PUT THE PEN DOWN!
SWAT
BUT WHY WOULD I EVER COME TO ANY-ONE AFTER THAT, WITH ANYTHING?
I'M ANGRY! I'M ANGRY I COULD HAVE BEEN PAID MORE, AND I COULD HAVE BEEN TREATED BETTER, BUT NEITHER OF THOSE THINGS CROSSED YOUR COLLECTIVE MINDS!
NOT IN A WAY I CAN TAKE HOME.
I'M SO FULL OF—
I COULD EXPLODE WITH THE DIGNITY I'VE PUSHED DOWN FOR THIS COMPANY THAT'S BURSTING OUT NOW...
BECAUSE I'M LEAVING AND I DON'T HAVE TO PUSH IT DOWN ANYMORE.
AND THIS IS ALL I HAVE LEFT TO ASK FROM YOU BEFORE I GO.
THIS OR NOTHING.
I'M SORRY. I'M SORRY, I AM.

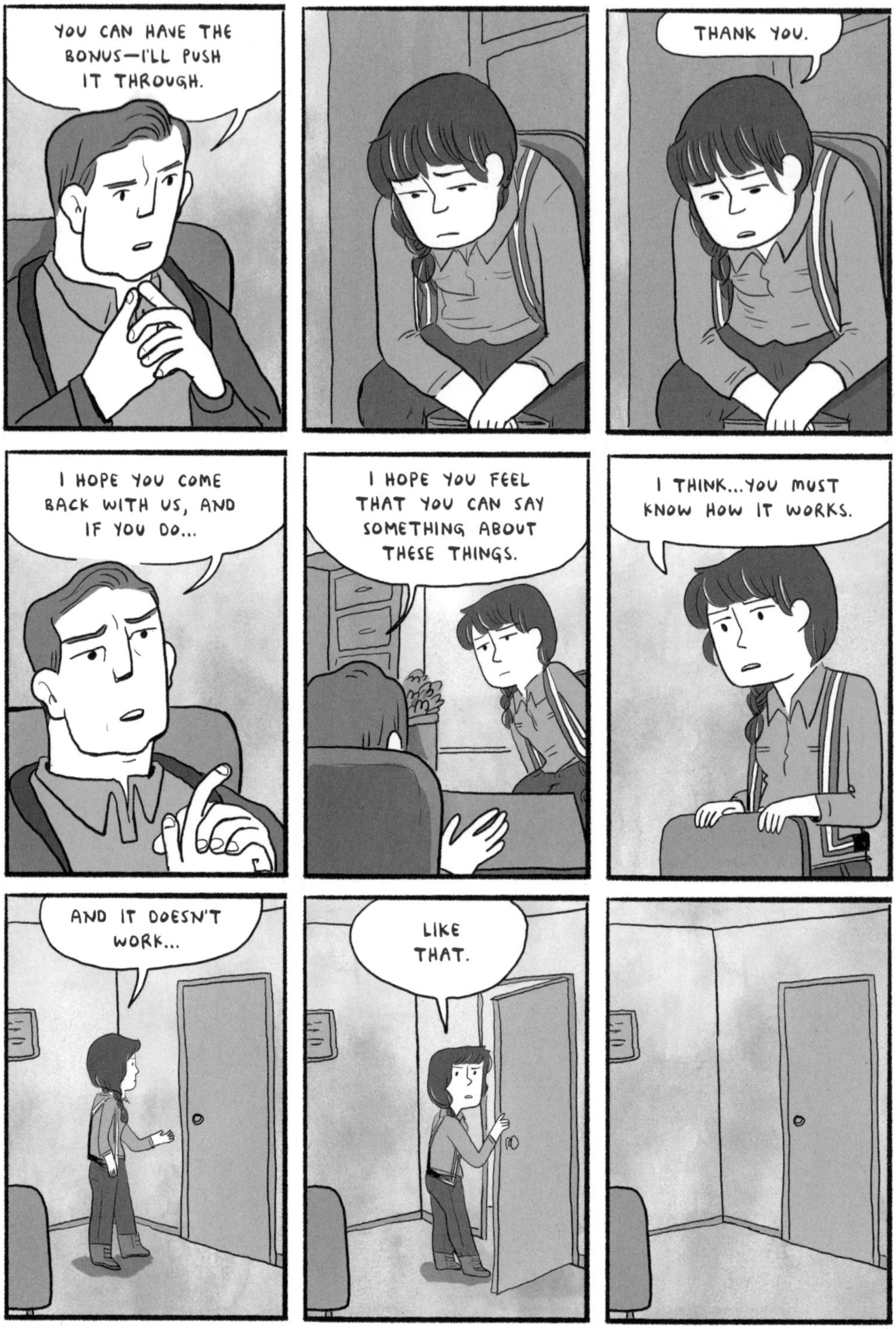
YOU CAN HAVE THE BONUS—I'LL PUSH IT THROUGH.
THANK YOU.
I HOPE YOU COME BACK WITH US, AND IF YOU DO...
I HOPE YOU FEEL THAT YOU CAN SAY SOMETHING ABOUT THESE THINGS.
I THINK...YOU MUST KNOW HOW IT WORKS.
AND IT DOESN'T WORK...
LIKE THAT.

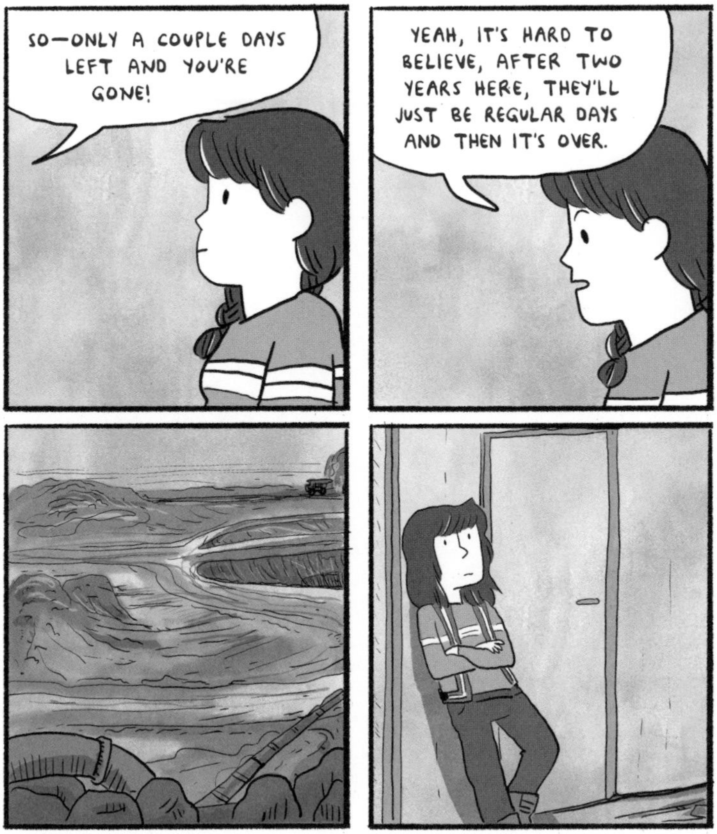
SO—ONLY A COUPLE DAYS LEFT AND YOU'RE GONE!
YEAH, IT'S HARD TO BELIEVE, AFTER TWO YEARS HERE, THEY'LL JUST BE REGULAR DAYS AND THEN IT'S OVER.

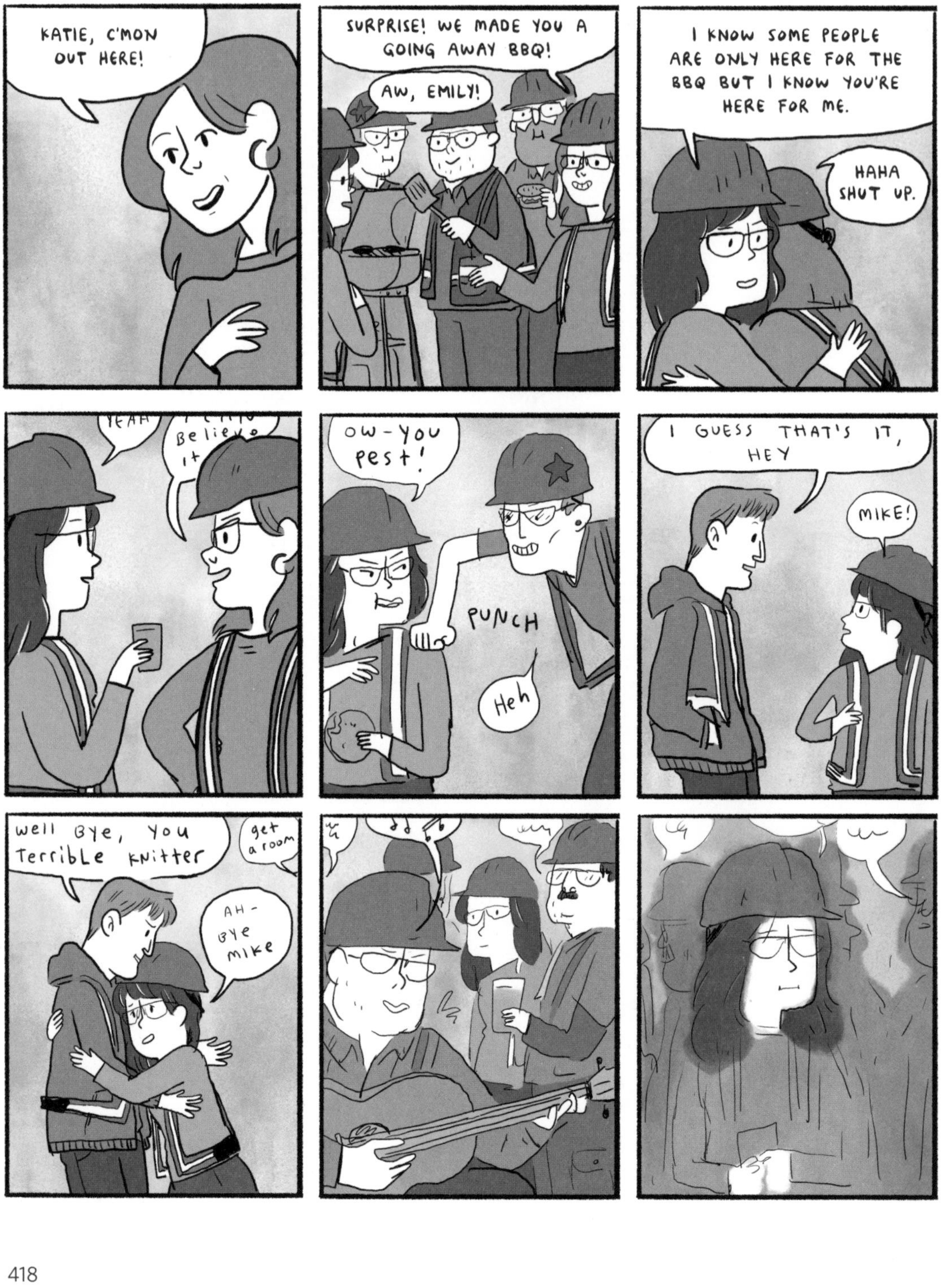
KATIE, C'MON OUT HERE!
SURPRISE! WE MADE YOU A GOING AWAY BBQ!
AW, EMILY!
I KNOW SOME PEOPLE ARE ONLY HERE FOR THE BBQ BUT I KNOW YOU'RE HERE FOR ME.
HAHA SHUT UP.
OW-YOU pest!
PUNCH
Heh
I GUESS THAT'S IT, HEY
MIKE!
well Bye, you Terrible knitter
get a room
AH- Bye mike

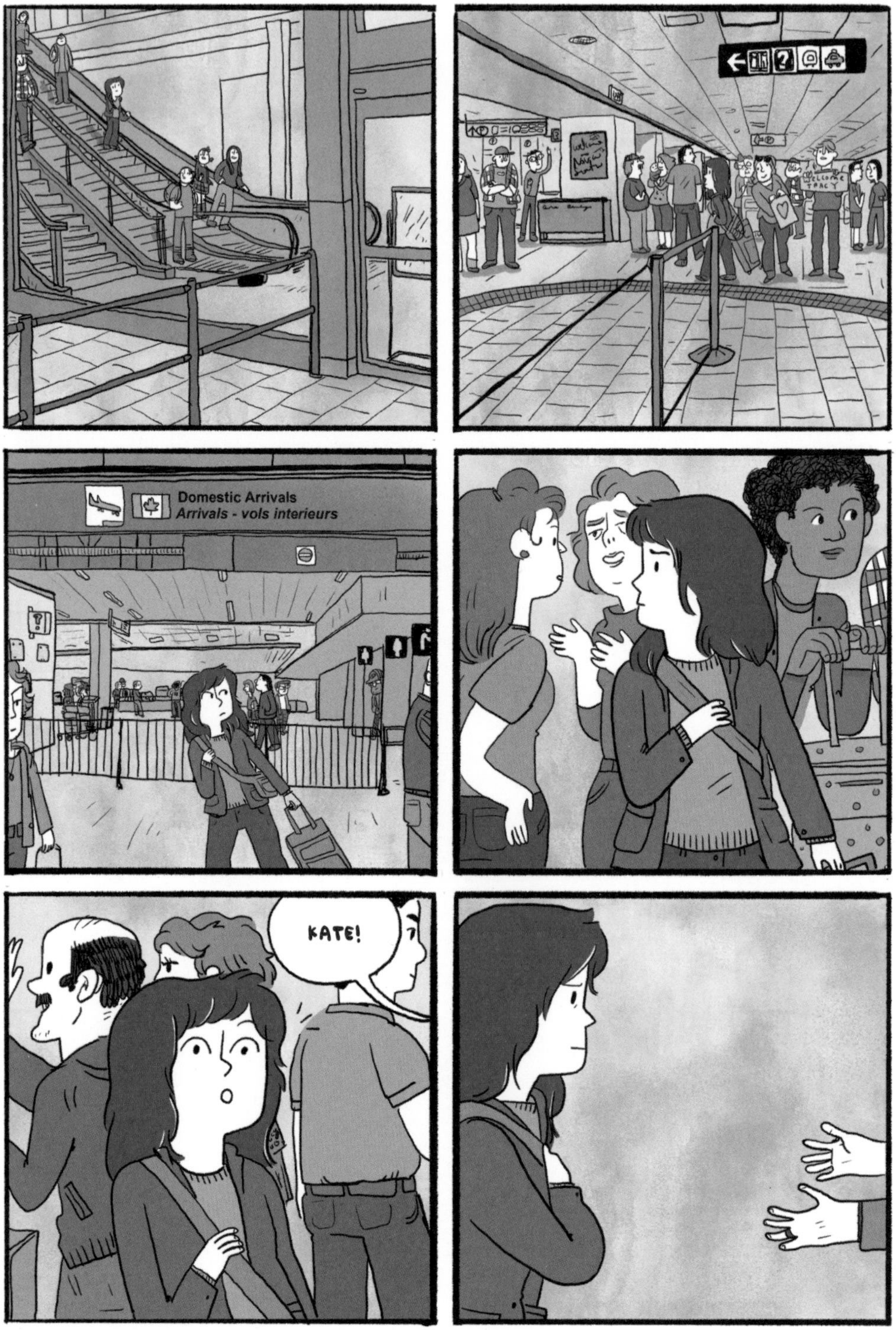
WELCOME TRACY
Domestic Arrivals
Arrivals - vols interieurs
KATE!

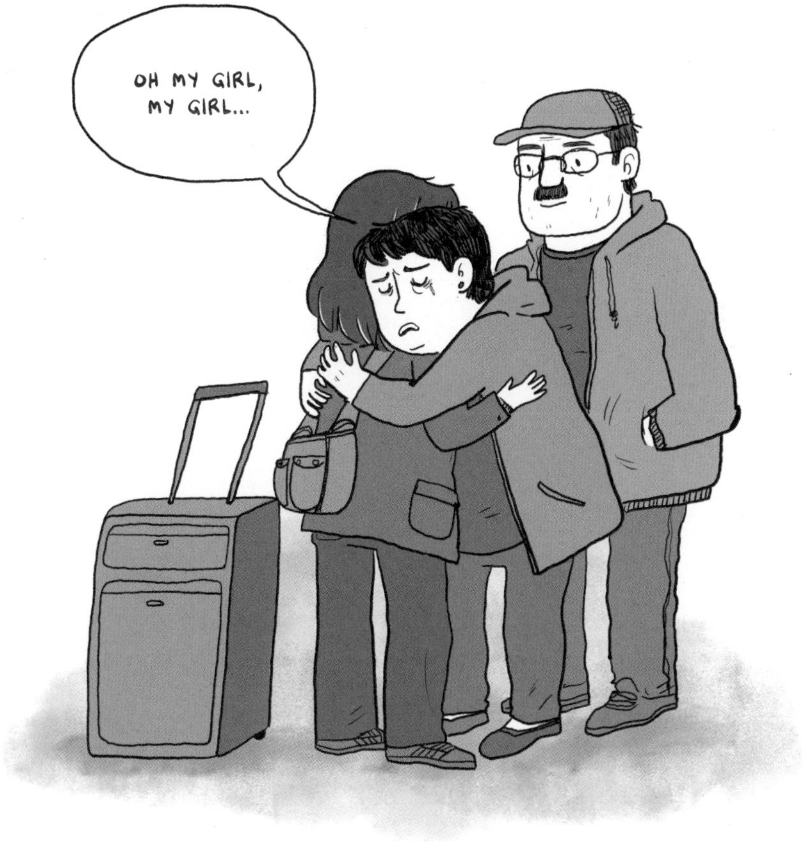
OH MY GIRL,
MY GIRL...

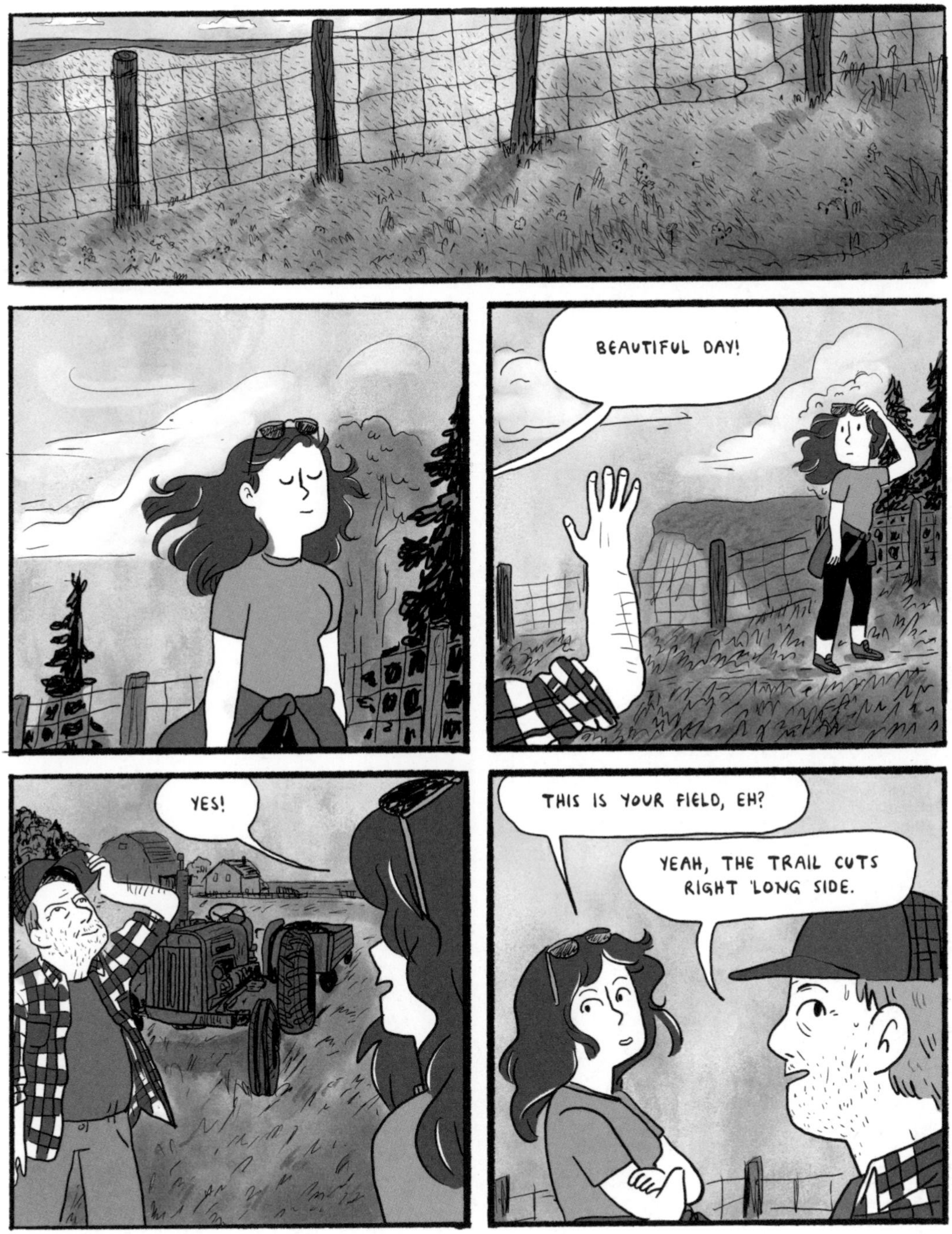
BEAUTIFUL DAY!
YES!
THIS IS YOUR FIELD, EH?
YEAH, THE TRAIL CUTS RIGHT 'LONG SIDE.

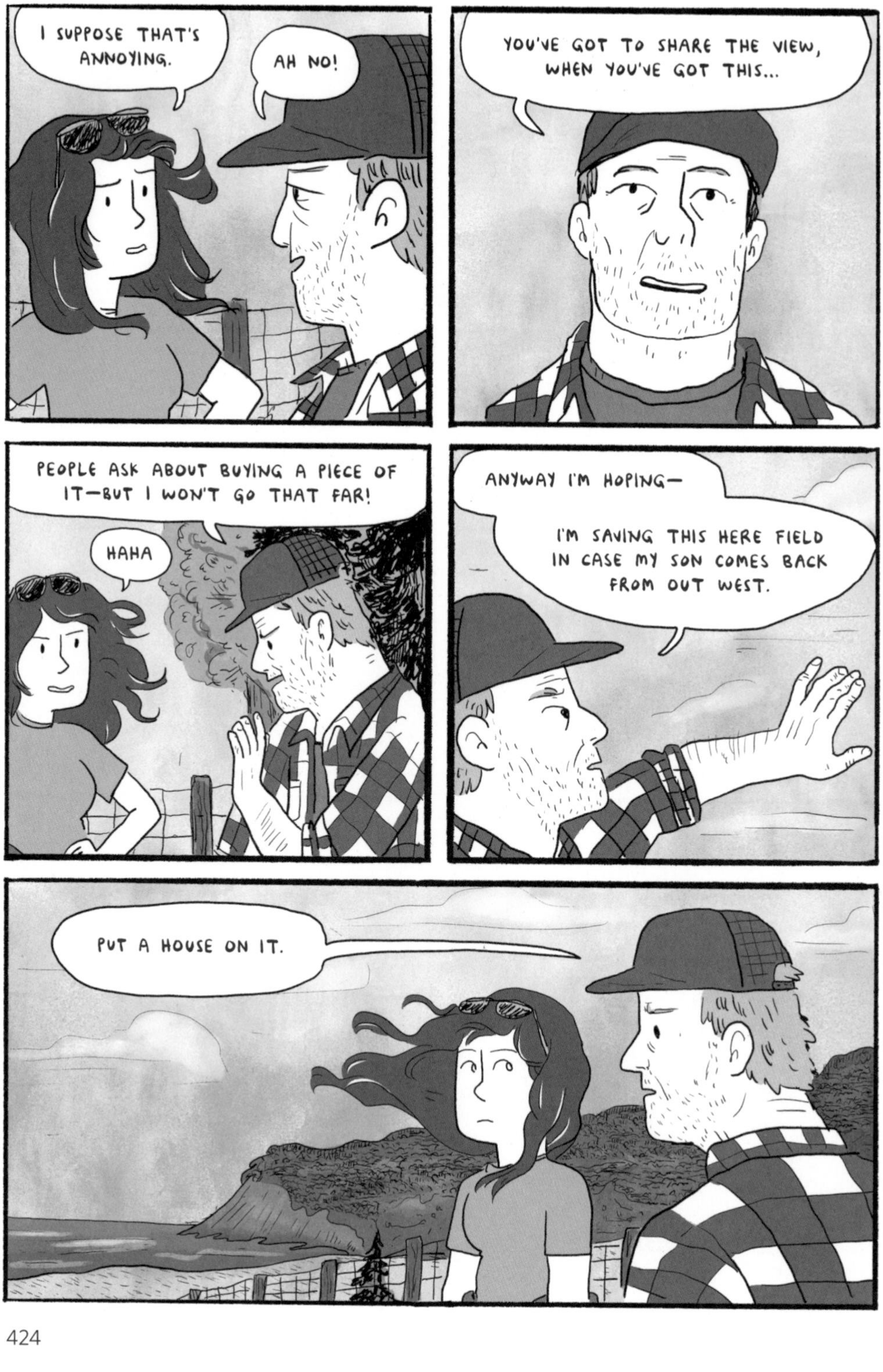
I SUPPOSE THAT'S ANNOYING.
AH NO!
YOU'VE GOT TO SHARE THE VIEW, WHEN YOU'VE GOT THIS...
PEOPLE ASK ABOUT BUYING A PIECE OF IT—BUT I WON'T GO THAT FAR!
HAHA
ANYWAY I'M HOPING—
I'M SAVING THIS HERE FIELD IN CASE MY SON COMES BACK FROM OUT WEST.
PUT A HOUSE ON IT.

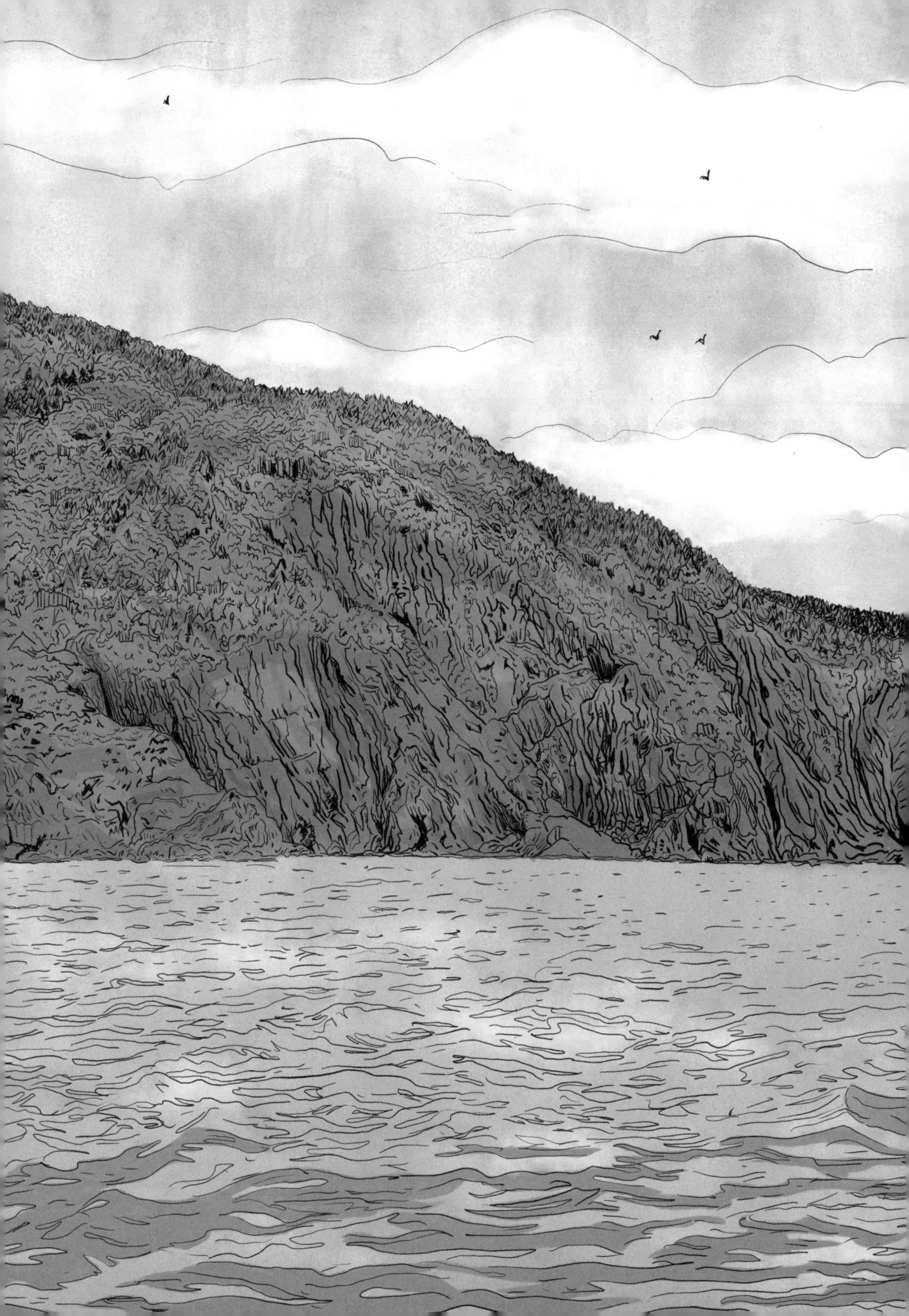

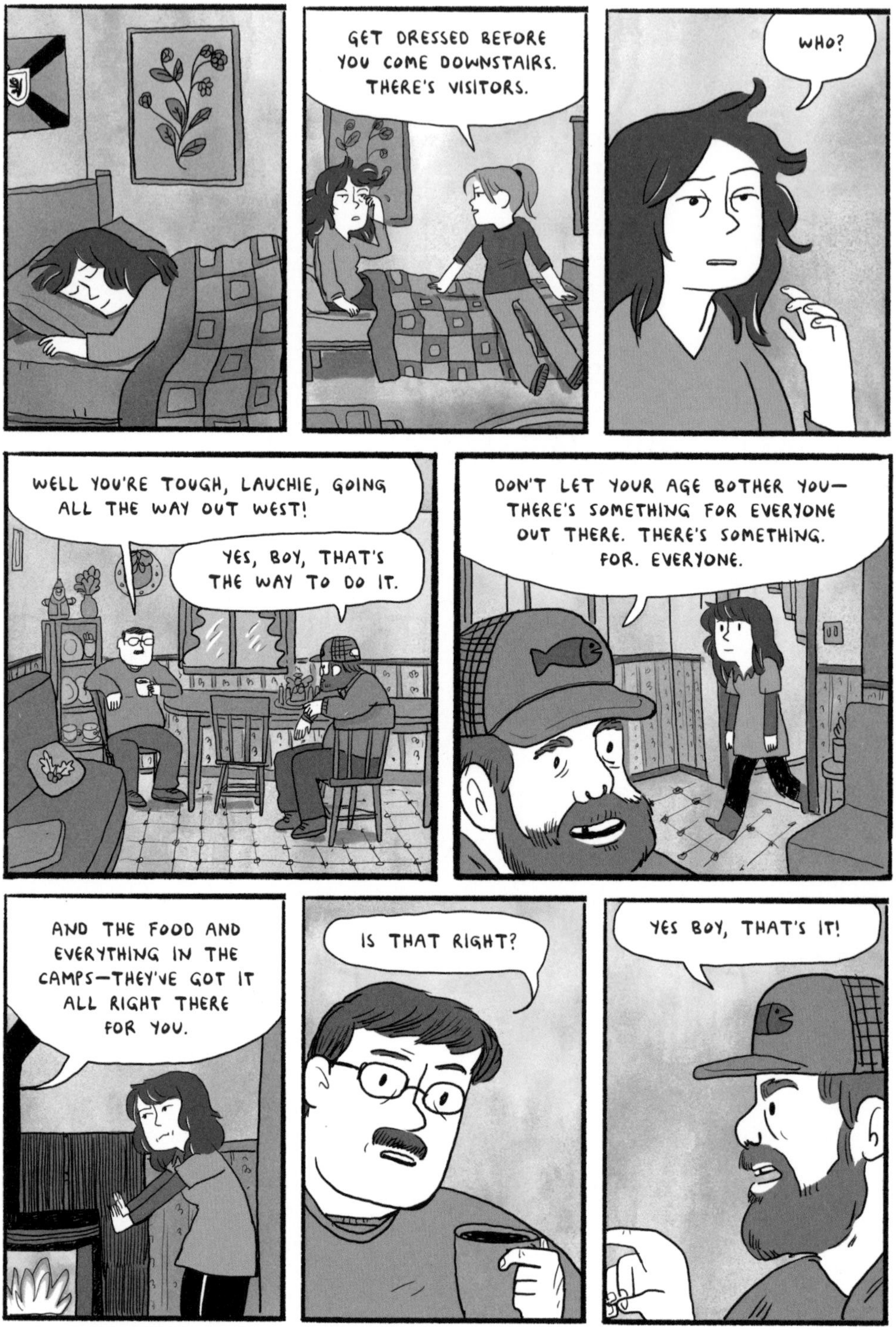

GET DRESSED BEFORE YOU COME DOWNSTAIRS. THERE'S VISITORS.
WHO?
WELL YOU'RE TOUGH, LAUCHIE, GOING ALL THE WAY OUT WEST!
YES, BOY, THAT'S THE WAY TO DO IT.
DON'T LET YOUR AGE BOTHER YOU— THERE'S SOMETHING FOR EVERYONE OUT THERE. THERE'S SOMETHING. FOR. EVERYONE.
AND THE FOOD AND EVERYTHING IN THE CAMPS—THEY'VE GOT IT ALL RIGHT THERE FOR YOU.
IS THAT RIGHT?
YES BOY, THAT'S IT!

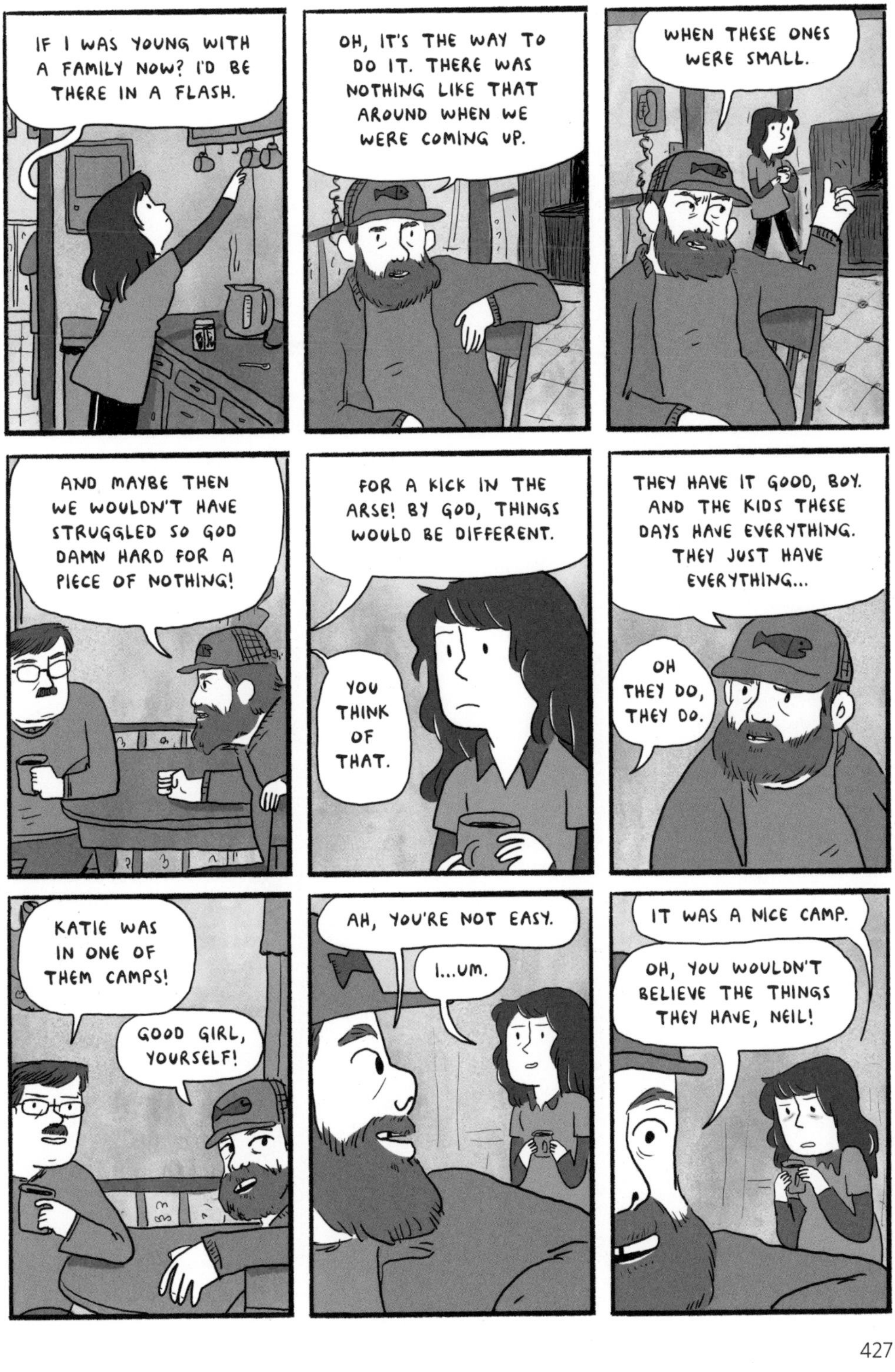

IF I WAS YOUNG WITH A FAMILY NOW? I'D BE THERE IN A FLASH.
OH, IT'S THE WAY TO DO IT. THERE WAS NOTHING LIKE THAT AROUND WHEN WE WERE COMING UP.
WHEN THESE ONES WERE SMALL.
AND MAYBE THEN WE WOULDN'T HAVE STRUGGLED SO GOD DAMN HARD FOR A PIECE OF NOTHING!
FOR A KICK IN THE ARSE! BY GOD, THINGS WOULD BE DIFFERENT.
YOU THINK OF THAT.
THEY HAVE IT GOOD, BOY. AND THE KIDS THESE DAYS HAVE EVERYTHING. THEY JUST HAVE EVERYTHING...
OH THEY DO, THEY DO.
KATIE WAS IN ONE OF THEM CAMPS!
GOOD GIRL, YOURSELF!
AH, YOU'RE NOT EASY.
I...UM.
IT WAS A NICE CAMP.
OH, YOU WOULDN'T BELIEVE THE THINGS THEY HAVE, NEIL!

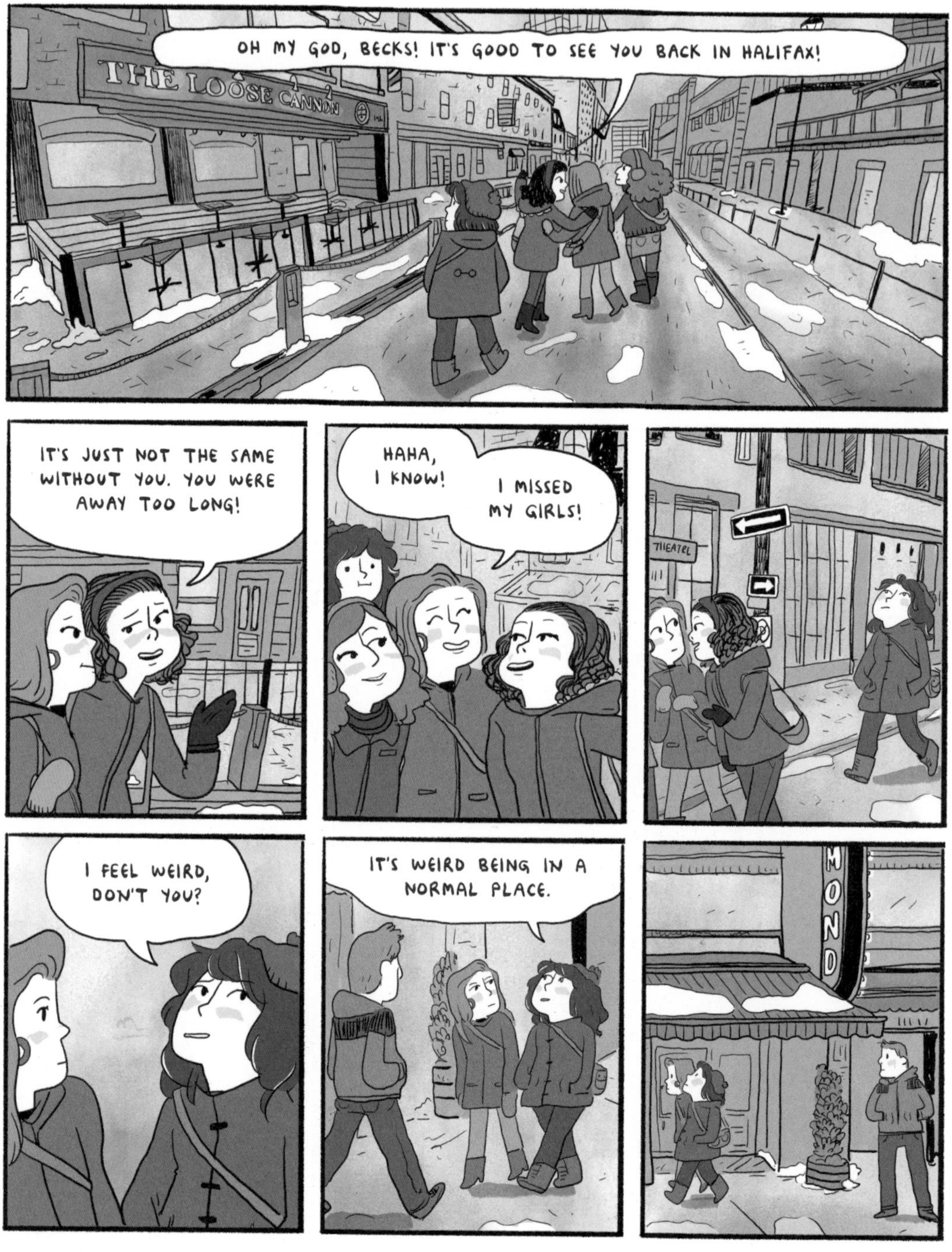
OH MY GOD, BECKS! IT'S GOOD TO SEE YOU BACK IN HALIFAX!
THE LOOSE CANNON
IT'S JUST NOT THE SAME WITHOUT YOU. YOU WERE AWAY TOO LONG!
HAHA, I KNOW!
I MISSED MY GIRLS!
THEATRE
I FEEL WEIRD, DON'T YOU?
IT'S WEIRD BEING IN A NORMAL PLACE.
MOND

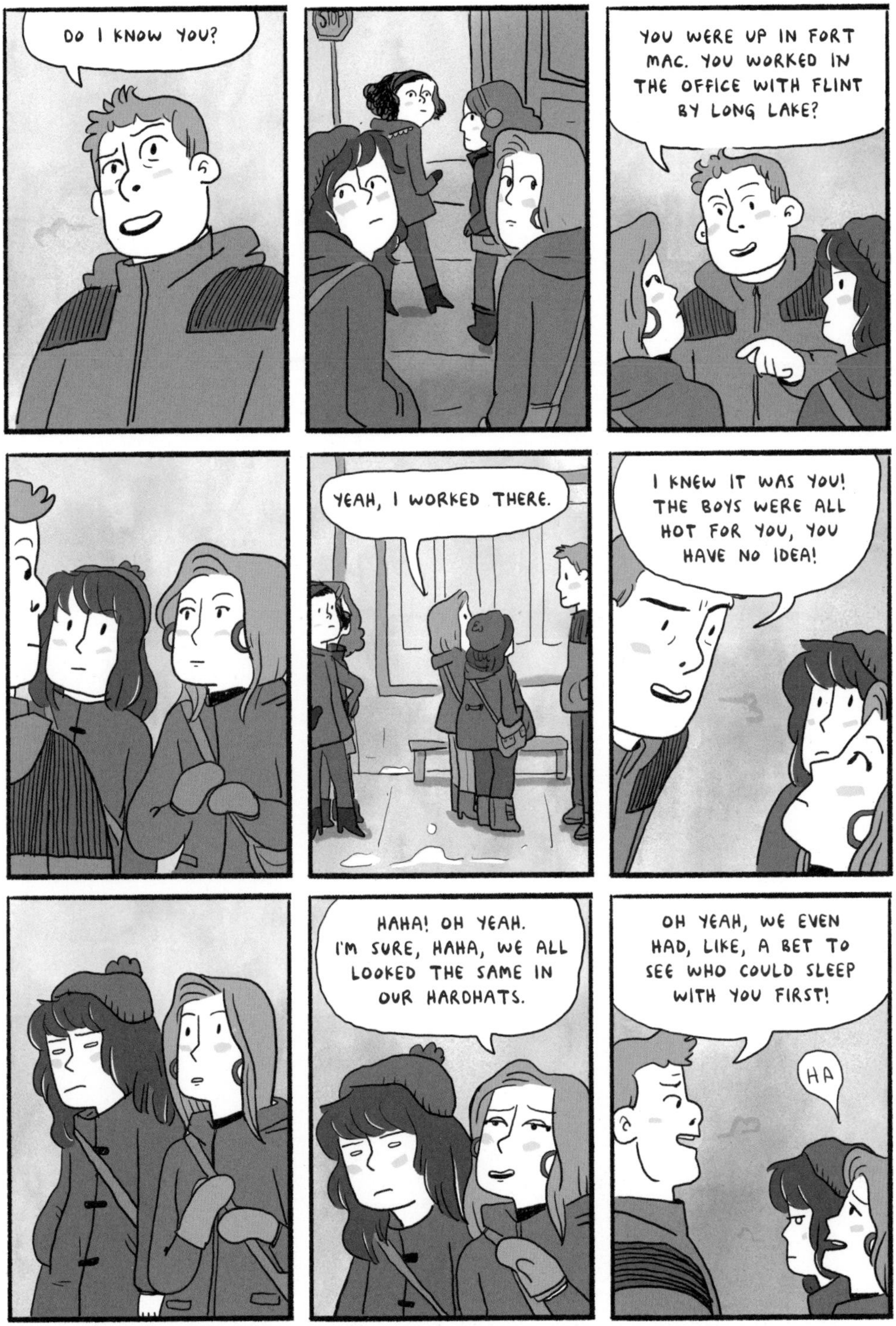
DO I KNOW YOU?
STOP
YOU WERE UP IN FORT MAC. YOU WORKED IN THE OFFICE WITH FLINT BY LONG LAKE?
YEAH, I WORKED THERE.
I KNEW IT WAS YOU! THE BOYS WERE ALL HOT FOR YOU, YOU HAVE NO IDEA!
HAHA! OH YEAH. I'M SURE, HAHA, WE ALL LOOKED THE SAME IN OUR HARDHATS.
OH YEAH, WE EVEN HAD, LIKE, A BET TO SEE WHO COULD SLEEP WITH YOU FIRST!
HA

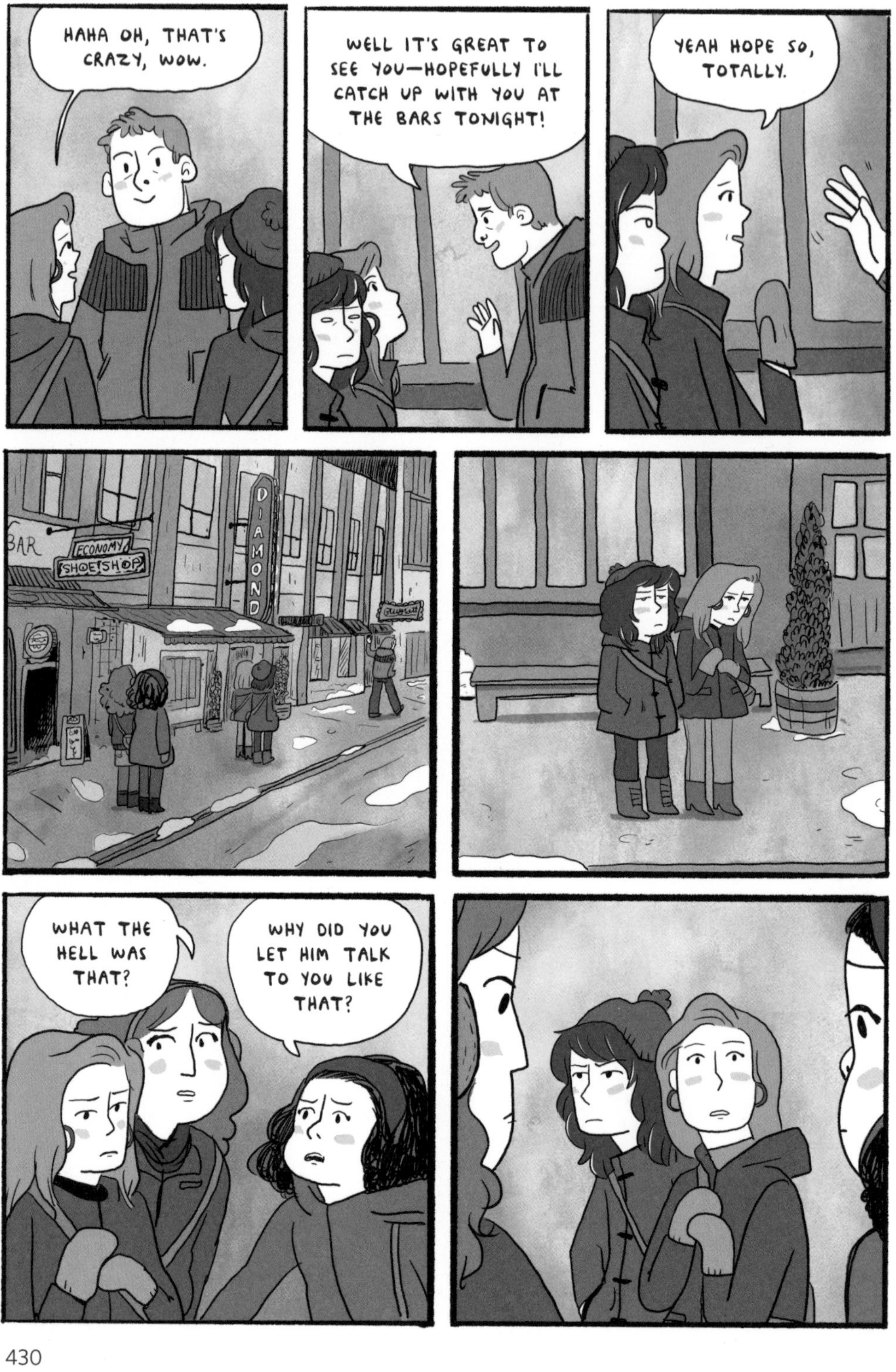
HAHA OH, THAT'S CRAZY, WOW.
WELL IT'S GREAT TO SEE YOU—HOPEFULLY I'LL CATCH UP WITH YOU AT THE BARS TONIGHT!
YEAH HOPE SO, TOTALLY.
BAR
ECONOMY
SHOE SHOP
DIAMOND
WHAT THE HELL WAS THAT?
WHY DID YOU LET HIM TALK TO YOU LIKE THAT?

AFTERWORD

Everyone's oil sands are different, and these were mine.

I was there for two years between 2005 and 2008, working for a number of different companies, at a number of different sites, and living in both sprawling temporary work camps and in the city of Fort McMurray. There is often a tendency to want to characterize the Northern Alberta oil sands as either entirely good or entirely bad—the jobs and profits vs. the climate rattling destruction. But, over my time there, I learned you can have both good and bad at the same time in the same place, and the oil sands defy any easy characterization.

My experiences were very much coloured by their place in time—a time just on the doorstep of ubiquitous smartphones and social media, but not there yet. We were still largely unconnected compared to now. It was also a time of unprecedented population growth, relative radio silence on climate change, and record high oil prices, accompanied by an optimistic belief that the well on oil and money would never run dry. And of course, my experiences are heavily marked by my being a woman in a workforce that was so overwhelmingly male.

This was also a time when discussion surrounding the mental health of workers—especially itinerant male workers in a hypermasculine environment like the oil sands work camps—barely existed. Camp life fosters a certain unique set of mental health challenges in an environment that is probably the least suited to contend with them. The boredom, isolation, loneliness, and depression add up for many—and for some, are too much to bear. Few resources existed on site, and in reality, they were nothing more than lip service. Instead, the industry prized itself on having millions of hours without lost time incidents while hiding away the human wreckage. Anecdotally, in researching for this book, I rarely found this topic researched or reported on, and for an industry as large and far reaching as the oil sands, I found that very alarming. The humanity of camp workers is often lost in the popular image we have constructed about who goes there and why. I hope this book pokes another needed hole in that image.

I am wary of the sensationalization of my narrative because it contains sexual violence. The sad fact is, however, that sexual assault of every kind is far too common everywhere to be sensational. This doesn't mean I am not deeply and negatively affected by it. I will always be affected by it. But I guarantee you that neither of the men who raped me consider what they did to be rape, if they consider it at all. I know the name of one of them; he is a father now with a woman who was his girlfriend when he raped me. I was nothing in his life but a short release from the boredom and loneliness endemic in camp life, but he was a major trauma in mine.

I have seen many people quick to become defensive against the suggestion that gendered violence exists in places like the oil sands. They may either work there and are proud of the work they do and the livelihoods they support with it, or they know and love men there, and are insulted by the insinuation of being lumped in with anything to do with something as abhorrent as sexual assault. Fort McMurray, a city of young families looking to the future, has little patience for outsiders with accusations of old Wild West stereotypes.

But work camps are a uniquely capsuled-off society, a liminal space, and analogue for so many other male-dominated spaces. Gendered violence does happen when men outnumber women by as much as fifty to one, as they can in the camps or work sites. Of course it does. Of course this happens when men are in isolation for long stretches of time, away from their families and relationships and communities, and completely resocialized in a camp and work environment like that of the oil sands. It does not matter how many decent people are there. I knew plenty of those.

This is all particularly and profoundly true for Indigenous women and girls in Canada, who are far more likely to be the victims of sexual violence around places like remote work camps.

In 2005, despite all my education, I knew very little about this. Indigenous rights and the legacy of colonial violence were not in the news, not in any textbooks, not given a voice or the time of day. Thankfully, this is beginning to change. But, that doesn't change my past self's relative ignorance of these things. And because this is my memoir, I can only tell you about my oil sands, where my world was very small and very white.

So I'm extremely grateful to Celina Harpe, an elder from the Cree community of Fort McKay, for giving me permission to use her words and her likeness in this book. Listening to her speak on a YouTube video in 2008 was a sword that cut through my ignorance and my coddled perception of myself and my participation in an industry that towered over her existence.

The oil sands operate on stolen lands. Their pollution, work camps, and ever-growing settler populations continue to have serious social, economic, cultural, environmental, and health consequences for the Indigenous communities in the region. I urge everyone to work to further listen and understand the history and ongoing issues facing the Athabasca Chipewyan First Nation, Chipewyan Prairie First Nation, Fort McKay First Nation, Fort McMurray No. 468 First Nation, Mikisew Cree First Nation, as well as the Métis communities in Northern Alberta.

Thank you to everyone I contacted, some whom I have not spoken to since I left Fort Mac, some I had never spoken to at all, for your time and thoughtful consideration of the time we spent together so long ago. Most names have been changed for privacy, except in special cases.

Thank you to everyone who supported me in making this book. I am sorry I couldn't fit everyone in, I wish I could have. Thank you especially to Lindsay Bird, who helped me reconstruct shared memories, and allowed me to tell her story as well. Thank you Morgan, my husband; my parents, Marion and Neil; my sisters, Becky, Maura, and Laureen. Thank you to Becky's former coworkers in the oil sands, who were the first ones to pool some money together and send it when she got cancer. I will never forget that. I started this book before Becky died, and I wish she was here to see it, because she was always going to be a big part of it. She was the first person I told about making it. Thank you to my publisher and editors who worked diligently with me and were very patient. Thank you to the whole team at Drawn & Quarterly: Peggy, Tracy, Julia, Shirley, Megan, Lucia, Tom, Alison, Rebecca, Kaiya, Trynne, and Francine. It was a group effort to get this book finished, and I could not have done it without you. Thank you Seth, my agent, and thank you to the many friends who supported and encouraged me in the many years it took to make this book. I love you all.

Kate
January 24, 2022
Mabou, Cape Breton

KATE BEATON was born and raised in Cape Breton, Nova Scotia, Canada. After graduating from Mount Allison University with a double degree in History and Anthropology, she moved to Alberta in search of work that would allow her to pay down her student loans. During the years she spent out West, Beaton began creating webcomics under the name *Hark! A Vagrant*, quickly drawing a substantial following around the world.

The collections of her landmark strip *Hark! A Vagrant* and *Step Aside, Pops* each spent several months on the *New York Times* graphic novel bestseller list, as well as appearing on best of the year lists from *Time*, *The Washington Post*, *Vulture*, *NPR Books*, and winning the Eisner, Ignatz, Harvey, and Doug Wright Awards. She has also published the picture books *King Baby* and *The Princess and the Pony*.

Beaton lives in Cape Breton with her family.

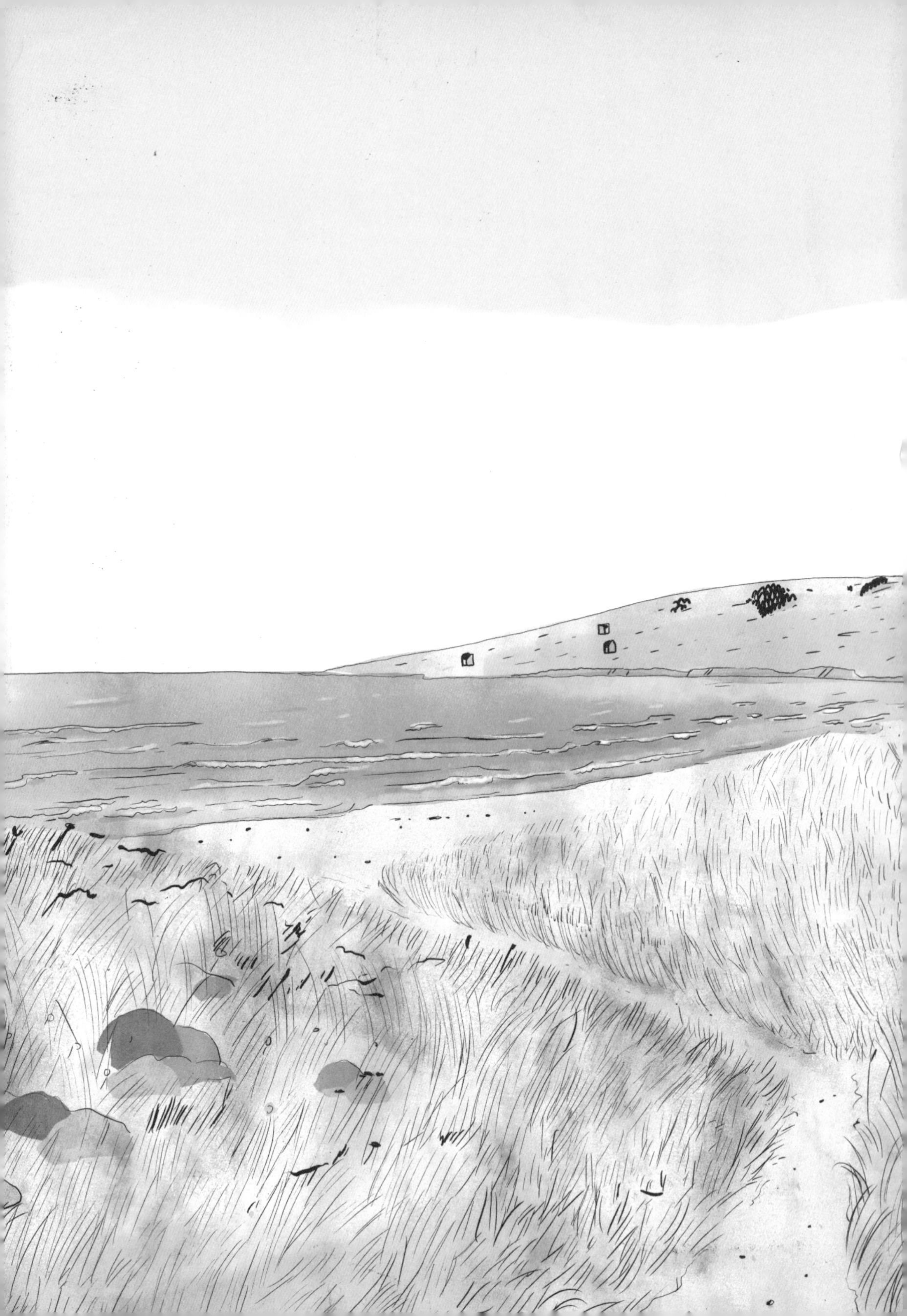